# PROGRAMMING ESSENTIALS USING JAVA

# PROGRAMMING ESSENTIALS USING JAVA

## A Game Application Approach

**William McAllister and S. Jane Fritz**

*St Joseph's College, New York*

**MERCURY LEARNING AND INFORMATION**
Dulles, Virginia
Boston, Massachusetts
New Delhi

Publisher: David Pallai

MERCURY LEARNING AND INFORMATION
22841 Quicksilver Drive
Dulles, VA 20166
info@merclearning.com
www.merclearning.com
(800) 232-0223

W. McAllister and S. Jane Fritz.
*Programming Essentials Using Java: A Game Application Approach.*
ISBN: 978-1-683920-37-3

Library of Congress Control Number: 2017900331

171819321   Printed in the USA on acid-free paper

Our titles are available for adoption, license, or bulk purchase by institutions, corporations, etc.
For additional information, please contact the Customer Service Dept. at (800) 232-0223 (toll free).

All of our titles are available in digital format at authorcloudware.com and other digital vendors. *Companion disc files for this title are available by contacting info@merclearning.com.*

*To the memory of my mother Alma, who cherished in me something she was not afforded - a formal education.*

—Bill McAllister

*To all those who have taught me by example that "if you can dream it, you can do it," with gratitude.*

—S. Jane Fritz

*To our students, whose enthusiasm for learning has always inspired us to pursue improved teaching techniques.*

—Bill McAllister
—S. Jane Fritz

# Contents

# *Preface*

This is a Java textbook for beginning programmers that uses game programming as a central pedagogical tool to improve student engagement, learning outcomes, and retention. Game programming is incorporated into the text in a way that does not compromise the amount of material traditionally covered in a basic or advanced programming course and permits instructors who are not familiar with game programming and computer graphics concepts to realize the verified pedagogical advantages of game programming.

The book's DVD includes a game environment that is easily integrated into projects created with the popular Java Development Environments, including Eclipse, NetBeans, and JCreator in a student-friendly way and also includes a set of executable student games to peak their interest by giving them a glimpse into their future capabilities. The material presented in the book is in full compliance with the 2013 ACM/IEEE computer science curriculum guidelines. It has been used to teach programming to students whose majors are within and outside of the computing fields.

## Features

We use an objects-early approach to learning Java in that the defining and implementation of classes is introduced in the middle of Chapter 3. In preparation for this material, the terms object and class are introduced in Chapter 1 in the context of game piece objects and reinforced in Chapter 2 by continually referring to strings as string objects and differentiating between the primitive types and the `String` class. In addition, the concept of a reference variable is introduced within the concept of string objects in Chapter 2, and students become familiar with the idea that classes contain data members and methods via the chapter's discussion of the `Math` class, dialog boxes, and the formatting of numeric values. All of this facilitates the discussion in Chapter 3 of the definition and implementation of methods and classes and the declaration of objects.

The pedagogical tool, game programming, makes the concepts of object-oriented programming more tangible and more interesting to the student. For example, objects are output by drawing them at their current location rather than outputting their (x, y) coordinates to the system console. The functionality of `set` and `get` methods and the counting algorithm is illustrated by using them to relocate and animate game piece objects and keep a game's score. Decision statements are used to reflect animated game pieces, detect collisions between them, and to decide when a game is over, and loops are used to draw checkerboard squares and checkers. Because of this new pedagogical approach, student smiles have replaced frowns, enthusiasm has replaced complacency, and "teach us this" has replaced "do we have to know that?" Our classrooms have been transformed from a lecture-based venue to a highly engaged interactive learning environment.

Throughout the book, after a concept is introduced and discussed, its use is illustrated in a succinctly composed working program, and the parts of the program that utilize the new concepts are fully discussed.

## Use of the Book

The material in this book can be covered within a one semester college level introductory Java programming course or as a year-long high school AP Computer Science course. All of the necessary (tested) AP topics are integrated throughout the book, as well as many of the non-tested topics that are considered useful. For easy reference, Appendix H is a tabulation of these topics and the section numbers that cover the topics. The text and its associated resources can also be used as a tutorial in Java programming as well as for game development in a self-instructional mode.

## Chapter Overviews

Chapter 1: Introduction

This chapter includes a brief history of computer science and topics that are fundamental to an understanding of the concepts presented in the remainder of the textbook. These topics include an overview of the computer system and the representation of data in memory, the programming process and the role of an IDE in that process, platform independence and how Java achieves it, as well as an overview of object-oriented programming and the Application Programming Interface (API). Readers are asked to execute several student-written games contained on the book's DVD, which usually peaks their interest, as does the brief description of the game environment included in this chapter.

Chapter 2: Variables, Input/Output, and Calculations

Primitive variables, dialog box input, performing calculations, and performing output to dialog boxes, the system console, and to the game-board window are discussed in this chapter. The declaration of objects and the topic of reference variables are introduced within the context of the declaration of `String` objects, as are the topics of classes and methods within the chapter's discussion of the `Math` class, the formatting of text and numeric output, and graphical text output.

Chapter 3: Methods, Classes, and Objects: A First Look

The foundational object-oriented programming concepts used in the next three chapters are discussed in this chapter. It begins with the techniques used to write methods and pass information via value parameters and statements, and the API Graphics class' 2-D shape-drawing methods are used in the discussion of parameter passing. The techniques used to specify and write classes are then discussed via a progressively developed game piece class's UML diagram and the progressive implementation of its data members, constructors, and methods. The motivation for `set` and `get` methods, and the `toString`, `input`, and `show` methods are discussed and these methods are implemented. The `Javadoc` documentation utility is introduced and illustrated. Throughout the chapter, sketches are used to illustrate the reference variable and data-member memory model, and the chapter concludes with a graphical application that utilizes the learned concepts.

Chapter 4: Boolean Expressions, Making Decisions, and Disk Input and Output

This chapter begins a two-chapter sequence on control of flow. After a discussion of Boolean expressions and relational and logic operators, the students are introduced to Java's `if`, `if-else`, and `switch` statements. Their use is illustrated within a graphical context to reflect animated objects, detect when they collide, and to decide which direction to move them in response to a keystroke input. Disk text file I/O is also introduced in this chapter, which is preceded by a discussion of input using the scanner class and followed by an introduction to the concept and processing of thrown exceptions. The chapter concludes with a graphical application that utilizes the learned concepts.

Chapter 5: Repeating Statements: Loops

The `for`, `while`, and `do-while` loops are presented in this chapter, as are the concepts of counting loops, sentinel loops, and nested loops. The role that the `break` and `continue` statements play in repetition constructs is discussed, and Chapter 2's discussion of the formatting of numeric information and the generation of pseudorandom numbers is extended via a discussion of currency formatting and the API `DecimalFormat` and `Random` classes. The chapter includes with a discussion of which loop construct to use for a particular application, and uses a graphical guessing game application and an application that draws a checker board to illustrate these learned concepts.

Chapter 6: Arrays

We placed this chapter after the loops chapter in an effort to immediately reinforce the student's understanding of loops via a discussion of the role loops play in the processing of arrays and the implementation of that processing. The chapter begins with a discussion of the concept of an array and arrays of primitive variables, and it illustrates the primitive array memory model. It then extends these concepts to arrays of reference variables and the objects they reference, and it discusses the passing of arrays to and from methods and illustrates the memory model used to accomplish this. The enhanced for loop, which can be used to fetch all of the elements of an array sequentially, is explained. The concept of parallel arrays is discussed as well as the array copying, sorting, minimum, and maximum algorithms and the API implementations of these algorithms. The sequential search and binary search algorithms are presented and compared in terms of their speed and efficiency. The selection sort, merge sort and insertion sort are all explained and evaluated in terms of their complexity.

The chapter also discusses multidimensional arrays and the role arrays play in the addition, and deletion of information contained in disk files. The learned concepts are illustrated within graphical applications that use arrays of game piece objects to display an animated parade and to sort and locate particular game piece objects.

Chapter 7: Methods, Classes, and Objects: A Second Look

This chapter extends the object oriented programming concepts discussed in Chapter 3 and serves as the OOP foundation on which the remaining chapters of the text are built. It begins with a discussion of static data members, shallow and deep copying and comparisons, and the cloning of objects. The concept of aggregation is presented and is shown to have a HAS-A relationship with an object integrated into a class, e.g., a Snowman object has a Hat. The implementation of aggregation is then discussed, as are inner classes and their methods and the autoboxing feature of the wrapper classes.

The processing of large numeric values is also covered in this chapter, as well as enumerated types and the methods of the `String` class. The learned concepts are illustrated within graphical applications that clone objects, use aggregated game piece objects, parse words from sentences, and perform calculations on large numbers.

Chapter 8: Inheritance

In this chapter, the terminology and concept of inheritance are discussed, as is the way this concept is used in the design and implementation phases of a software project to reduce the time and effort required to complete the project. The topics of extended classes, the child IS-A parent relationship, overriding methods, sub and super classes invoking each other's methods, and the role of abstract and final classes and methods in the design process are also discussed.

All of these topics lead into a discussion of polymorphism and polymorphic arrays and the role of polymorphism in the design process. The chapter concludes with a discussion of interface and adapter classes and the serialization of objects. These learned concepts are illustrated in an evolving series of graphical applications that begin with the inheritance of a boat's hull and ends with a polymorphic display of all of the types of boats in a boat dealer's inventory.

Chapter 9 Recursion

This chapter begins by explaining the concept of recursion and recursive methods and a methodology for formulating and implementing recursive algorithms correctly. It then illustrates the use of the methodology in the discovery and implementations of several recursive algorithms, including the Towers of Hanoi. As students progress through the discovery and implementation of these algorithms, they develop the ability to think recursively and to extend the methodology to the discovery and implementation of other recursive algorithms. The chapter concludes with a discussion of the runtime problems associated with recursive algorithms, the role of dynamic programming in the implementation process, and when it is appropriate or efficient to use recursion in the programs we write. The learned concepts are illustrated in applications that compute the terms of the Fibonacci sequence, draw a Sierpinski fractal, and solve the Towers of Hanoi problem.

Chapter 10: The API Collections Framework

The chapter begins by introducing the programming concept of generics and its role in extending the reusability of classes and methods, and then discusses a subset of the generic interfaces and classes defined within the API Collections Framework. Included in this discussion is the difference between the two generic interface inheritance chains rooted in the interfaces `Map` and `Collection`, and the methods defined in the child interface `List`. The meaning and syntax of type-safe declarations of instances of generic collection classes is discussed and illustrated using the Framework's `ArrayList` class, as are the `ArrayList`'s implementation of the `List` interface and its use in the creation of a generic class. Also discussed is the polymorphic use of the `List` interface, the syntax and use of generic parameter lists, and the passing of information to generic methods. The chapter concludes with a discussion of the use of the methods contained in the generic `Collections` class.

## Appendices Included in the Textbook

The ten appendices contain:

- A description of the game programming environment (Appendix A)
- Directions on how to incorporate the game environment into a programming project (Appendix B)
- *Note*: The book's DVD contains the game environment and predefined Eclipse, NetBeans, and JCreator project templates that have the game environment incorporated into them.
- An ASCII table that contains the decimal, octal, hexadecimal, and binary representation of each the characters defined in the table (Appendix C)
- A list of Java keywords (Appendix D)
- A list of all of the Java operators and their precedence (Appendix E)
- A glossary of programming terms (Appendix F)
- A brief description of using the online API documentation (Appendix G);
- A table of the correlation of the College Board AP Computer Science Topics with the textbook sections that cover the topics (Appendix H)
- A table of the ACM/IEEE curriculum guideline topics included in the text and the minimum recommended instruction time (Appendix I)
- Solutions to selected odd-numbered Knowledge Exercises (Appendix J)

## Companion Files *(also available from the publisher by writing to info@merclearning.com)*

The disc in the back of the book contains a table of contents and the following materials, arranged in separate folders:

- Samples of student-written games in an executable format with instruction on how to run them
- The game environment

- o Eclipse, NetBeans, and JCreator template projects with the environment incorporated into them and instructions on how to use them to begin a new project without altering the system's CLASSPATH variable
- o A description of the environment and its call back methods used to draw and animate objects and respond to mouse, keyboard, and timer events
- o The environment's classes and methods in the form of class files, a jar file, and an importable package
- The source files for all of the applications presented in the text
- All of the book's figures
- All of the book's appendices

## The Instructor's Disc *(available upon adoption to instructors)*

The disc contains a table of contents and the following materials, arranged in separate folders:
- Solutions to the programming exercises
- Answers to all of the knowledge exercises that appear at the end of each chapter
- Microsoft PowerPoint lecture slides for each chapter
- The source files for all of the applications presented in the text
- Sample syllabi
- Sample chapter quizzes and final exams
- Final game project assignment
- All of the book's figures
- Samples of student-written games in an executable format with instruction on how to run them

## Digital Versions

Digital versions of this text and its resources are available on the publisher's electronic delivery site, *www.authorcloudware.com,* as well as other popular e-vendor sites.

W. McAllister
S. Jane Fritz
Patchogue, NY
January, 2017

# Acknowledgments

We would like to thank three of our students who graciously granted us permission to include their game projects on the DVD that accompanies this book: Arielle Gulino, Andrew Zaech, and Ryan McAllister. We also thank all of our students whose enthusiasm for the incorporation of game programming into our pedagogy was the inspiration for the preparation of this book.

We would also like to thank the administration of St. Joseph's College and the members of the Promotions and Awards Committee for granting Bill a sabbatical, which was dedicated to the preparation of this manuscript, as well as our colleagues, and the entire St. Joseph's College Community who offered encouragement and support during its preparation.

We also thank David Pallai, the publisher and founder of Mercury Learning and Information for establishing and managing a publishing company that produces a high-quality product at an affordable cost, and his production team for guiding us through the development and production process, specifically Jennifer Blaney.

Finally, we would like to thank our families and friends for their endless patience when we were too busy to be ourselves.

# To the Students

It It is our hope that the approach to the material in this book will challenge you, engage you, and inspire you to continue your study of computer science and to enjoy a rewarding career by immersing yourself in this area of national need.

# *Credits*

## Chapter 1

Computer © Robert Lucian Crusitu/Shutterstock.com, Image ID: 156076811

Figure 1.5 Abacus, by Gisling (Own work) [CC-BY-3.0 (http://creativecommons.org/licenses/by/3.0)], via Wikimedia Commons), (http://upload.wikimedia.org/wikipedia/commons/d/d4/Positional_decimal_system_on_abacus.JPG )

Figure 1.6 Slide rule, by Ricce (Own work) [Public domain], via Wikimedia Common,

(http://upload.wikimedia.org/wikipedia/commons/9/98/Regolo_calcolatore.jpg)

Figure 1.7 Blaise Pascal, by Mahlum (Own work) [Public domain], via Wikimedia Commons, (http://upload.wikimedia.org/wikipedia/commons/4/4d/Pascal_Blaise.jpeg)

Figure 1.8 Jacquard's Loom,

(http://upload.wikimedia.org/wikipedia/commons/6/65/Jacquard_loom.jpg)

Figure 1.9 Charles Babbage, (http://upload.wikimedia.org/wikipedia/commons/1/1d/Charles_Babbage_Difference_Engine_No1.jpg)

Figure 1.10 Ada, Margaret Sarah Carpenter [Public domain], via Wikimedia Commons (http://commons.wikimedia.org/wiki/Ada_Lovelace#mediaviewer/File:Carpenter_portrait_of_Ada_Lovelace_-_detail.png)

Figure 1.11 Hollerith (https://www.census.gov/history/img/HollerithMachine.jpg)

Figure 1.12 Turing Statue © Guy Erwood/Shutterstock.com

Figure 1.13a. Troubleshooting the ENIAC (http://ftp.arl.army.mil/ftp/historic- computers/jpeg/eniac3.jpg)

Figure 1.13b. Troubleshooting the ENIAC (http://ftp.arl.army.mil/ftp/historic- computers/jpeg/eniac1.jpg)

Figure 1.14a. Programming the ENIAC (http://ftp.arl.army.mil/ftp/historic-computers/jpeg/first_four.jpg)

Figure 1.14 b. Programming the ENIAC (http://ftp.arl.army.mil/ftp/historic-computers/gif/eniac4.gif)

Figure 1.15 John von Neumann, (Public domain), (http://commons.wikimedia.org/wiki/File:JohnvonNeumann-LosAlamos.gif )

Figure 1.16 Grace Hopper (http://www.history.navy.mil/photos/pers-us/uspers-h/g-hoppr.htm)

Figure 1.17 Grace Hopper's Bug (http://www.history.navy.mil/photos/pers-us/uspers-h/g-hoppr.htm)

Figure 17.18 Steve Jobs, by Kees de Vos from The Hague, The Netherlands [CC-BY-SA-2.0 (http://creativecommons.org/licenses/by-sa/2.0)], via Wikimedia Commons, (http://upload.wikimedia.org/wikipedia/commons/5/54/Steve_Jobs.jpg)

Figure 1.19 Bill Gates, by Matthew YoheAido2002 at en.wikipedia [CC-BY-3.0 (http://creative-commons.org/licenses/by/3.0)], from Wikimedia Com, (http://upload.wikimedia.org/wikipedia/commons/7/7f/Bill_Gates_2004_cr.jpg)

Figure 1.20 Vinton Cerf and Robert Kahn (http://georgewbush-whitehouse.archives.gov/ask/20051109-2.html)

Figure 1.21 Donald Knuth (Case Alumni Association and Foundation 2010, Flicker and (http://www.casealum.org/view.image?Id=1818)

Figure 1.22 Tim Berners-Lee, Courtesy of World Wide Web Consortium, Massachusetts Institute of Technology (www.w3.org/People/Berners-Lee)

# Chapter 3

Green tea cup on windowsill © GoodMood Photo/Shutterstock.com, Image ID: 158310728

# Chapter 4

Two Game Figurines © Melanie Kintz, Mellimage/Shutterstock.com, Image ID: 70027117

# Chapter 5

Loops of a scaring roller coaster © Marcio Jose Bastos Silva /Shutterstock.com, Image ID: 97819241

# Chapter 8

Boats on phewa-lake-nepal © Worapan Kong /ShutterStock.com, Image ID: 132349601

# Chapter 9

Nested Traditional Matryoschka Dolls © PiXXart/Shutterstock.com, Image ID: 112054022

# Chapter 10

Collection of spaceship planets and stars © Motuwe/Shutterstock.com, ImageID 140336917

# INTRODUCTION

### In this chapter

This chapter presents topics that are fundamental to computing and the programming process and discusses tools that programmers use to write programs. Because the focus of this text is on learning to program, an understanding of these concepts and tools is essential. The topics include a brief history of computing, which will highlight some of the important contributions to the field and facilitate an understanding of the modern computer system as well as how data is stored. The tools discussed in the chapter are used to develop an unambiguous description of a program and to minimize the effort required to transform this description into a functional program that can run on any computer system or mobile device.

After successfully completing this chapter, you should:

- Understand the hardware and software components of a computer system
- Gain an appreciation for the history and evolution of computing
- Be able to specify simple programs and games
- Have used some examples of student-written game programs
- Understand why Java programs can be run on any computer system
- Be familiar with the concept of objects, classes, and the object-oriented programming paradigm
- Understand the programming process and the role of Integrated Development Environment programs in this process
- Be familiar with the features of the game-development tool on the DVD that accompanies this textbook
- Understand how data is represented inside computer systems

## 1.1  THE COMPUTER SYSTEM

Over the last twenty years, computers and the use of the Internet have become part of our everyday lives. Daily communication that was performed using postal systems and telephone conversations are now performed more efficiently using computer-based e-mails and text messaging. Much of the information gathering we performed in libraries is now done from the comfort of our homes using a computer attached to the Internet, as is much of the shopping we do. As a result, the number of computers available in the world continues to grow (Figure 1.1).

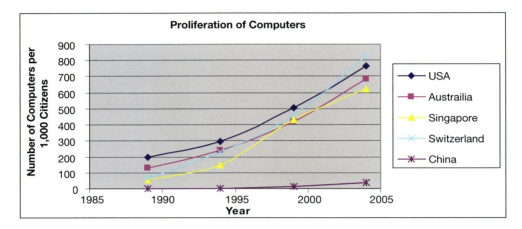

**Figure 1.1**
Growth in the number of computers per capita over a fifteen-year period.

In many of the developed countries of the world there is now one computer, or more accurately, one computer system for every citizen in the country. Although many of these people would say that they use a computer every day, they really should say that they use a computer system every day.

As shown in Figure 1.2, a computer system is comprised of two major components: software and hardware. As its name implies, hardware is the hard, or tangible, part of the computer system. It is the collection of electronic circuits, mechanical devices, and enclosures manufactured in a factory. When we purchase a computer system and look into the box it comes in, what we see is the hardware.

However, the box also contains software, but, as its name implies, it is the soft, or less-tangible portion of the computer system, and so it is not as easy to detect. Software, or programs, consists

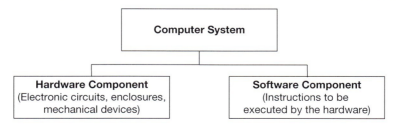

**Figure 1.2**
The two major components of a computer system.

of sequences of instructions written by programmers to perform specific tasks. These instructions are executed by the computer system's hardware, and both components are essential to a computer system. A computer system that contained only hardware would have no instructions to execute, so it would do nothing but consume electrical power. A computer system that contained only software would not be able to execute the program's instructions.

The software of a computer system is comprised of two major subcomponents: operating system software and application software (Figure 1.3). Microsoft Windows, Apple OS, and Linux are all examples of operating system programs. This set of programs contains instructions to manage the hardware resources of the computer system and provides an interface, usually a point-and-click interface, through which the user interacts with the computer system. In addition, most application software interacts with the hardware through various groups of operating system instructions.

Although nonoperating system software can be categorized in several groupings, we will consider all nonoperating system software to be collected into one group, application software, as shown in Figure 1.3. In this textbook, we will learn how to write application software using the programming language Java.

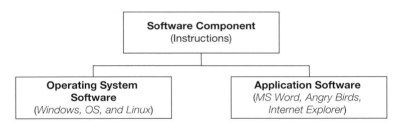

**Figure 1.3**
Computer software subcomponents.

The hardware of the computer system can be divided into three main categories, or subcomponents, based on the function they perform. Hardware that communicates with humans and other computer systems is grouped into the category input/output (I/O) devices. Hardware used to store information inside the computer system is grouped into the category storage devices. Finally, all other functions performed by the hardware are part of a category named the central processing unit (CPU).

Figure 1.4 shows the standard conceptual arrangement of the three hardware categories with the CPU at the center of the arrangement. The storage devices are shown on the right and bottom of the figure and are divided into two types of devices: backing storage, often referred to as secondary storage, and random access memory (RAM), also called main memory. With the exception of backing storage, each of the hardware components has been assigned an acronym, which is shown parenthetically below the name of the component in Figure 1.4. For brevity, the components are most often referred to using their acronyms: I/O devices, CPU, and RAM (pronounced as "ram").

The arrows into and out of the I/O devices at the top left of Figure 1.4 indicate the flow of information entering (input) and leaving (output) the computer system. The other arrows in the

**Figure 1.4**
Arrangement of the hardware subcomponents of a computer system.

figure represent the flow of information among the computer-system components. The central processing unit can receive information from (arrows labeled "input") and send information to (arrows labeled "output") the other system components. The flow of information is always relative to the CPU. Information sent to the CPU is considered input, and information sent from the CPU is considered output.

Hardware that communicates with humans and other computer systems is grouped into the component I/O devices. These devices are the interface between the computer system and the rest of the world. Input devices send information into the system. Examples of input devices include a keyboard, a touch screen, a mouse, a microphone, a digitizer, and a modem. Output devices send information out from the system. Examples of output devices include a monitor, a printer, a speaker, and a modem. A modem is both an input and output device and is normally used to transfer information between computer systems.

Hardware devices that have the ability to store and recall information are grouped into the component storage services. All but one of these devices fall into the subcomponent backing storage, shown on the top right side of Figure 1.4. Examples of storage devices include hard drives, flash drives, subscriber identification module (SIM ) cards, CD drives, and magnetic tape drives. One storage device, random access memory (RAM) is depicted separately at the bottom of Figure 1.4. One difference between this storage device and all of the other storage devices is its speed. It can access information, meaning store and recall information, faster than any other storage device. Its information-access speed approaches the speed at which the CPU can transfer information.

Programs run faster when their instructions are stored in RAM, so it is an advantage to have a high-capacity RAM in a computer system. Unfortunately, the materials and manufacturing process used to achieve RAM's speed make it the most expensive type of storage. To make computer systems affordable, backing-storage devices are added to the system. When a program is in execution, the operating system software attempts to transfer the program's instructions and the data the instruction processes from backing storage to RAM before this information is needed by the CPU.

Another reason for adding backing storage, or secondary storage, to a computer system is the fact that RAM is volatile, which means that it only retains its memory when it is attached to an electrical power source: no electricity, no memory. All backing-storage devices are nonvolatile, which means that the information they store is not lost when they are detached from a power source. As a result, these devices can be used to archive program instructions and data within the computer system when it is powered down (e.g., hard drives), and can be used to manually transport information between computer systems (e.g., flash drives).

The I/O and storage components of the computer system give us the ability to transfer information into and out of the computer system and the ability to store and recall that information. The CPU depicted in the center of Figure 1.4 gives us the ability to process the information, and so it is aptly named the central processing unit. If we were inclined to designate one of the computer-system components as the brain of the system, we would probably bestow that title on the CPU. However, despite the remarkable tasks that computers perform, the CPU's electronic circuits only perform five very basic processing operations:

1. Transfer information (i.e., instructions and data) to and from the other components of the computer system and interpret instructions
2. Store a very small amount of information, e.g., one instruction and sixteen pieces of data
3. Perform arithmetic operations such as addition, subtraction, multiplication, and division
4. Perform logic operations involving relational operators (such as $10 < 6$, and $a >= 12$) and logical operators (such as A AND B, and A OR B)
5. Execute instructions in the order in which they are written or skip some instructions based on the truth value of a logic operation

The magic here is that all of the remarkable tasks that computers do have been expressed as a sequence of these five basic processing operations. A step-by-step sequence of these operations to perform a particular task is called an **algorithm**. The most difficult part of a programmer's job is to develop, or discover, algorithms. Once an algorithm is discovered, it is written into a programming language and verified via a testing process.

---

**Definition**

An **algorithm** is a step-by-step sequence of the five processing operations a computer system can execute to solve a problem or perform a particular task.

A **computer program** is an algorithm written in a programming language.

---

## ■1.2■ A BRIEF HISTORY OF COMPUTING

Long before our modern computers existed, people had the need to count or compute. As a matter of fact, the early meaning of the term computer referred not to a machine but to a person who performed calculations. In this section, we will see the amazing development of the revolutionary machines that have changed the way we learn, teach, shop, do research, and are entertained.

### 1.2.1 Early Computing Devices[1]

If computers are really such an important part of our lives today, you might wonder and ask the question: Who invented the computer?

Although this is a simple question, it does not have a simple answer such as Thomas Edison invented the light bulb or Alexander Graham Bell invented the telephone. One reason for this complexity is that computers evolved over thousands of years, and many people from different cultures and diverse fields such as mathematics, physics, engineering, business, and even textile design were involved in laying the foundation for the modern electronic computer.

**Figure 1.5**
The abacus.

The roots of computing dates from about 50,000 to 30,000 BC when people counted their sheep and other possessions using their fingers, stones, or notches on sticks. The first computing device, the abacus, was introduced in China around 2,600 BC and used pebbles or stones. A later version of the abacus (shown in Figure 1.5) used beads that could be moved on a wire frame to perform basic counting and arithmetic functions. These were widely used in Europe and Asia, and some of these devices are still in use today.[2]

It was not until the seventeenth century that there were other notable attempts at building computing devices. Napier's bones and the slide rule (Figure 1.6) were two of these devices.

**Figure 1.6**
A typical modern slide rule.

Blaise Pascal (Figure 1.7), at the age of 18, built a mechanical calculator called the Pascaline to perform basic addition and multiplication.

Because manufacturing technology was not yet well developed, these devices had to be carved or forged by hand, which required tedious work. Although it would seem likely that the development of computing devices would continue at a more rapid pace, very little progress was made from the seventeenth century until the 1800s, and we might ask why. Perhaps it was because this was a time of war, colonization, and the struggle for survival in much of the world. (If you think about the United States, for example, from 1776 through the 1800s, building a calculator was not considered a priority at that time.)

**Figure 1.7**
Blaise Pascal: philosopher, mathematician, inventor.

In 1801, Joseph Marie Jacquard, a textile designer, discovered that he could program his weaving loom (Figure 1.8) to create intricate patterns in the fabric, by storing the instructions on punched cards or paper tape. These binary instructions directed the loom to raise or lower certain threads depending upon whether or not a hole was punched on the tape. Later on, this concept would develop into the idea of creating a stored program computer based on binary instructions; it would be implemented in the twentieth century using punched cards for computer input.

**Figure 1.8**
A Jacquard Loom.

## 1.2.2 Computers Become a Reality

Charles Babbage, a mathematician working in England around 1822, designed the prototype of a machine, known as the Difference Engine, to compile mathematical tables. It was a large hand-cranked machine built of metal wheels and gears and although he continued to add refinements to it, he never fully completed it. By 1837, Babbage took his ideas one step further and designed a more complex Analytical Engine Figure 1.9), which he envisioned to be a general purpose computational machine and which had many characteristics in common with modern computers. He designed it to be steam powered, which would not make it portable, but would automate mathematical calculations. Due to the limitations of available technology, it was not completed in his lifetime, but it has recently been completed and works as he described it. Charles Babbage has been called the father of the computer for his innovative work on the first mechanical computer.

Lady Ada Augusta Byron Lovelace (Figure 1.10), the daughter of the poet Lord Byron, became intrigued with Babbage's work and began to write instructions, or what we now call programs, for his machine. She is known today as the first programmer, and the programming language used for U.S. government applications is named Ada in her honor. Ada was unique in being a well-educated woman, skilled in mathematics, at a time when women had little formal or advanced schooling. She was able to perform the advanced mathematical and engineering design functions required for programming a theoretical computer that was not yet completely operational.

In the 1890s, in the United States, Herman Hollerith was working on a mechanical calculator and was asked by the government to design a machine that could record and store census data. The population was growing so fast that hand calculation could not keep pace with the growing volume of data: by the time the data was tabulated it was outdated and the next census had begun. Hollerith used punched cards to input the data to his new machine (Figure 1.11), which successfully compiled and tabulated even greater amounts of data in record time. Following this success, he founded a company with Thomas Watson, which later became known for computing, the International Business Machine Corporation (IBM).

**Figure 1.9**
Charles Babbage's Analytical Engine.

**Figure 1.10**
Lady Ada Augusta Byron Lovelace, the first programmer.

**Figure 1.11**
Hollerith's electric tabulating machine.

**Figure 1.12**
Alan Turing, father of
theoretical computer
science.

In the 1900s, the demand for recording and processing large amounts of data continued to increase, and there were numerous attempts to design more advanced computing machines. The need came from businesses as well as the military. Large universities and mathematicians throughout the world began to design and build these early computing machines. Around 1939–1942, the Atanasoff-Berry computer (ABC) was built by Dr. John V. Atanasoff and Clifford Berry at Iowa State University. It was the first electronic digital computer. At about the same time, Konrad Zuse, working in Germany, built the first fully programmable computer, the Z3.

Also in the early 1940s, the Colossus was built with the assistance of the brilliant British mathematician Alan Turing (Figure 1.12). It was designed as a code-breaking machine that could decipher the German codes created with the Enigma encoding machine. Turing's contribution to breaking the German codes helped to defeat Hitler in World War II. Turing also explored Artificial Intelligence (Google "Turing Test" for specific details), and he is highly regarded as the father of theoretical computer science, laying a foundation upon which to build advanced computing machines.

In 1944, the Harvard Mark I was designed and built through the efforts of Howard Aiken working with Grace Hopper. Built at Harvard University by IBM, the Mark I was the first electromechanical computer, and it was used to produce mathematical tables. It could be programmed using paper tape.

The first electronic general purpose digital computer, the Electronic Numerical Integrator and Computer (ENIAC) was built at the University of Pennsylvania in 1946 by John Mauchly and J. Presper Eckert. This computer weighed 30 tons and had over 18,000 vacuum tubes and thousands of electronic relays (Figure 1.13). It filled a large room that was required to be air conditioned because of the heat this machine generated. It could add or subtract 5,000 times a second, a thousand times faster than any other machine at that time. It also had modules to multiply, divide, and calculate square roots.

(a) Replacing vacuum tubes.                                                    (b) Programming the ENIAC.
                                   U.S. Army photos.

**Figure 1.13**
Troubleshooting the ENIAC.

U.S. Army photo

U.S Army photo

**Figure 1.14**
First programmers of the ENIAC.

Most of the ENIAC's programming was done by six women, including those shown in Figure 1.14.

**Figure 1.15**
John von Neumann, father of the modern computer and game theory.

John von Neumann (Figure 1.15) proposed modifications to the ENIAC, which included using binary instead of decimal numbers. His design for a stored program binary computer where both the program and the data could be stored in the computer's memory became known as the von Neumann architecture, which is still in use today. In 1945, he proposed the design for the Electronic Discrete Variable Automatic Computer (EDVAC) and later worked on the Institute for Advanced Study (IAS) computer in Princeton. He is often called the father of the modern computer and game theory.

### 1.2.3 Computer Generations[3]

The computers that followed are usually grouped into generations, each characterized by a specific component or technology. The dates are approximate.

### First-Generation (1937–1946): *Vacuum Tubes*

These very large computers used thousands of vacuum tubes, generated a lot of heat, and were fairly unreliable. Memory storage was on magnetic drums, input was performed using punched cards or paper tape, and output was displayed on paper printouts. Computers of this generation could only perform a single task, lacked an operating system, and were programmed using a sequence of ones and zeros known as machine language. First-generation machines include the ENIAC, Electronic Delay Storage Automatic Calculator (EDSAC), and EDVAC computers.

### Second-Generation (1947–1963): *Transistors*

This generation of computers used transistors, which were much more reliable than the vacuum tubes they replaced. Transistors were also smaller, cheaper, and consumed less electrical power. Machine language was replaced with assembly language, which was a more English-like language, and higher-level languages such as Common Business Oriented Language (COBOL) and Formula Translation (FORTRAN) were developed for this generation of computers. In 1951, the universal automatic computer (UNIVAC 1) was introduced as the first commercial computer. In 1953, the IBM 650 and 700 series computers were introduced. Operating systems were designed for these machines, and over 100 computer-programming languages were developed during this generation. Storage media such as magnetic tape and disks were in use, and printers were available for output.

### Third-Generation (1964–1971): *Integrated Circuits (IC) or "chips"*

Transistors were miniaturized and placed on chips and integrated circuits (IC), developed by Jack Kilby and Robert Noyce. This invention resulted in smaller, more powerful, more reliable, and cheaper computers. Users could now interact with computers through keyboards and monitors instead of punched cards and printouts. Operating systems monitored memory usage and controlled the scheduling of multiple applications that could share the system resources.

### Fourth-Generation (1971-present): *Microprocessors and Very Large Scale Integration (VLSI)*

Very-large-scale integration (VLSI) resulted in thousands of computer circuits being reduced to fit on a chip, reducing the room-size computers of the first generation to something that could fit in your hand. Components of the computer, from the central processing unit and memory to input/output controls, could now be located on a single microprocessor chip. In addition to their small size, computers became affordable for individuals, and in 1977, the personal computer (PC) became available from three companies: Apple, Tandy/Radio Shack, and Commodore. In 1980, Microsoft released its disk operating system (MS-DOS), and in 1981, IBM introduced the PC for home and office use. Three years later, Apple introduced the Macintosh computer with its icon-driven interface. In 1985, Microsoft released the Windows operating system. Fourth-generation computers also used graphical user interfaces (GUI, pronounced "gooey") and provided a mouse for ease of use. Object-oriented languages, such as Java, were developed for more efficient software development. These smaller, more reliable and powerful computers could now be linked together, resulting in the growth of networks and the Internet.

### Fifth-Generation (Present and Beyond): *Artificial Intelligence, Parallel Processing, Quantum Computing*

Fifth-generation computing devices are characterized by artificial intelligence and the advancement of devices that will respond to natural language and be capable of learning. Although these features are still in the early stages of development, some applications such as voice recognition are currently available. The use of parallel processing, quantum computing, and nanotechnology will help to achieve these advances and will change computing in the future.

### 1.2.4 More Notable Contributions

In addition to the achievements already mentioned, there were many others who made notable contributions to the computing field. The names and contributions of a few of these innovators follow, and you are invited to continue to add to the list.

Admiral Grace Murray Hopper (Figure 1.16) was a pioneer in the field of computing. She was one of the first programmers of the Harvard Mark I computer and is known for the development of the first compiler and assembly language. Her work in programming led to the development of the language COBOL, and she later worked on Ada.

**Figure 1.16**
Admiral Grace Hopper.

She coined the term "debugging" when she removed a bug (or moth) from a computer's circuitry that was interrupting the flow of electricity, and taped it into her notebook (Figure 1.17).

Steve Jobs (Figure 1.18) and Steve Wozniak were the cofounders of Apple Computers. The Apple I was one of the three personal computers introduced in 1977 for home use. Together they developed the point-and-click approach to computing. In 1984, they introduced the MAC OS that developed into the modern graphical user interface, which today is standard on modern computers. Steve Jobs is also a cofounder of Pixar Animation and has been described as the father of the digital revolution.

Bill Gates (Figure 1.19) and Paul Allen cofounded Microsoft, one of the largest U.S. corporations, and supplied the disk operating system (DOS) to IBM to run on its PCs. In 1985, Microsoft developed a graphical operating system known as Windows, which is the operating system used on over 80% of today's computers.

James Gosling is credited with the development of the object-oriented programming language known as Java. He is called the father of Java programming.

Bob Metcalfe and David Boggs invented the Ethernet, the technology upon which local computer area networks are based.

Vinton Cerf (Figure 1.20a) and Robert Kahn (Figure 1.20b) are considered to be the fathers of the Internet and the Transmission Control Protocol/Internet Protocol (TCP/IP) upon which the

**Figure 1.17**
Grace Hopper's first recorded computer "bug."

**Figure 1.18**
Steve Jobs, cofounder of Apple Computer.

**Figure 1.19**
Bill Gates, cofounder of Microsoft Corporation.

(a)                    (b)

**Figure 1.20**
Vinton Cerf and Robert Kahn, inventors of the Internet.

**Figure 1.21**
Donald Knuth, father of the analysis of algorithms.

**Figure 1.22**
Tim Berners-Lee, inventor of the World Wide Web.

Internet is based. Vinton Cerf created the first commercial Internet e-mail system and is now Vice President and Chief Internet Evangelist for Google.

Donald Knuth (Figure 1.21), a computer scientist, mathematician, and Professor Emeritus at Stanford University, has been called the father of the analysis of algorithms. His multivolume set of books entitled *The Art of Computer Programming* is the classical reference for all programmers. He is also the developer of the text document (TEX) typesetting system for creating high-quality digital publications.

Tim Berners-Lee (Figure 1.22) is known as the inventor of the World Wide Web and continues to direct the Web's development as the director of The World Wide Web Consortium (W3C). He is also a director of the World Wide Web Foundation, which furthers the potential of the Web to benefit humanity.

### 1.2.5 Smaller, Faster, Cheaper Computers[4]

Computing has made more progress in 15 years than transportation has made in 2,000 years, having gotten smaller, faster, and cheaper during that time. Your cell phone today is about a million times cheaper, a thousand times more powerful, and a hundred thousand times smaller than the one computer that was used at MIT in 1965.

According to Ed Lazowska, chairman of the University of Washington's Computer Science and Engineering Department, if Detroit car makers could have paralleled the innovations that hardware and software manufacturers have realized for computers, today's cars would be tiny, powerful, and inexpensive. They would be as small as toasters, cost $200, travel 100,000 miles per hour, and would run 150,000 miles on a gallon of fuel. "In Roman times, people traveled along on horses or in carts at about 20 miles per day," he said. "In the early part of this century, the automobile allowed people to travel at 20 miles per hour. Today, supersonic military aircraft travel at about 20 miles per minute. That progress is about a factor of 1,000 in about 2,000 years," Lazowska wrote in an e-mail message.

Another analogy by Rick Decker and Stuart Hirshfield in *The Analytical Engine* states, "If automotive technology had progressed as fast as computer technology between 1960 and today, the car today would have an engine less than a tenth of an inch across, would get 120,000 miles per gallon, have a top speed of 240,000 miles per hour, and would cost $4.00."[5] Also, at a recent Computer Dealers Exhibition (COMDEX) meeting, Bill Gates is reported to have said that if GM had kept up with technology like the computer industry has, we would all be driving $25 cars that get 1,000 miles per gallon.

Computers and the programs that provide their instructions will continue to increase in speed, reliability, and functionality, limited only by human creativity.

## 1.3 SPECIFYING A PROGRAM

As discussed in Section 1.1, an increasingly large number of people own and use a computer as part of their everyday lives, yet a very low percentage of these computer users actually know how to write a computer program. In fact, if you understand the material in the first two sections of this textbook, you already know more about computer programming than most of the world's population. As a result, most programs are not written by the program users. Rather, they are written by a group of computer processionals most people would refer to as programmers, but more accurately, they should be called **software engineers**. A new program that does not meet the needs of the end user is not going to be well received, so it is important that there be a way to describe the requirements of a new program in a way that is understandable to the end users.

| Definition |
| --- |
| A **software engineer** is a computer professional who produces programs that are on time, within budget, are fault free, and satisfy the end users' needs. |

The more formal techniques for describing the requirements of a new program are part of the discipline of systems analysis, which is a subset of software engineering. These formal techniques are all based on one specification of the arrangement of the components of the computer system shown Figure 1.4. They assume that the users' interaction with the program is via the input and output devices, so the simplest way for end users to define what task the program is to perform is to enter into conversation with a systems analyst aimed at defining the inputs to, and the outputs from, the program.

For example, suppose your friend Annie recently purchased a computer and is having trouble managing her money. Knowing you completed a course in computer programming, she comes to you for help. You and Annie enter into the following conversation, which typically involves the probative words who, what, why, where, when, and how:

Annie: I want to know *where* my money goes.

You: OK Annie, *what* bills do you pay each month?

Annie: Well, there's food, rent, electric, telephone, and clothing.

You: *How* much is each bill?

Annie: That's part of the problem; they change each month, and so does my income because I work on commission.

You: Well, do you know roughly *what* percent of your income is spent on each?

Annie: No, but I sure would like to know that. I have a feeling some months I'm spending too much of my income on food and clothing, which leaves me with no mad money.

You: *What* is mad money?

Annie: You know, money I can spend on anything I like other than these bills. I want to know *how* much that is each month. I am sure someone is taking my money.

You: Gee, Annie, you sound a little paranoid.

Annie: You'd be paranoid too if everyone was out to get you!

You (whispered): Why do I bother?

Based on this conversation, you know the two things Annie would like her computer system to determine and output are the amount of "mad money" (discretionary funds) she will have at the end of a month and the percent of her monthly income she spent on each of her five monthly bills. To determine this, she will have to input the amount of each of her five monthly bills and her income for that month. You have decided to include the month and year as two additional inputs to the program, so she will be able to save and distinguish one month's results from another. A simple description, or specification, for this program is shown below. It is a tabulation of the program inputs and outputs preceded by the name of the program and a brief statement that describes the overall task the program performs.

## Program Specification

### Program Name: *Annie's Money Manager*

Task:        To determine Annie's monthly discretionary funds and the distribution of her monthly expenses

Inputs (8):    Month and Year

              Income for the month

              Amount spent during the month on each of the following five items: food, rent, electric, telephone, and clothing

Outputs (6):  Percent of monthly income spent on each of these five items: food, rent, electric, telephone and clothing

              Amount of discretionary funds

Typically, the program specification is refined through an iterative process that involves its review by the end user and a subsequent conversation. This process could introduce more functionality into the specification of Annie's program. For example, it could also include the ability to output an annual report showing the values of the six outputs for any given year, or perhaps for a range of months. Obviously, this would expand the specification given above.

Given the specification of the program, the programmers' goal is to write a program that accepts the specified inputs and produces the desired outputs. The programmers may have to consult with other experts if it is unclear to them how to determine the outputs from the given inputs. For example, if the programmers assigned to write Annie's program did not know how to compute percentages, they would have to consult a mathematician.

### 1.3.1 Specifying a Game Program

The technique discussed to specify Annie's program is similar to that of specifying any program: conduct a brief conversation with the user and then tabulate the program's name, the task it performs, the inputs, and the outputs. This approach can also be used to specify a program that is used to play a game. In addition, the realization that all game programs share a common set of features can facilitate the specification process if the systems analysts include questions about these features in the conversations they have with the game's inventor.

For example, most games involve game objects (e.g., trucks, cars, and a frog). In addition, all games have an objective or a way to win the game (e.g., moving a frog object to the other side of a road without having it run over by a truck or a car). Most games also have other features in common. A list of common features to include in a game's specification conversation is given in Figure 1.23.

---

- Name of the game
- Objects (starships, trucks, sling shots, etc.) that will be part of the game
- Objective of the game
- Way to calculate the score of the game
- Time limits imposed on the game
- Game pieces (objects) that will be animated
- Game pieces controlled by the game player (the program's user)
- Input devices used to control the game objects
- Particular colors to include in the game
- Determining when the game ends
- Events that take place when the game ends
- Keeping track of the highest game score achieved and the name of the game player who achieved it

---

**Figure 1.23**
Common game features.

Armed with this checklist of common game features, a typical conversation with your friend Ryan (an aspiring game inventor who has not taken a programming course) could be:

You: Hi Ryan, what's up?

Ryan: I've got a great idea for a video game called Deep Space Delivery.

You: *What* is the objective of the game?

Ryan: To deliver as many supply packets as possible (picked up from a supply depot) to five different planets before time runs out.

You: *How* is a player's score calculated?

Ryan: The player gets one point for each packet delivered, and if the player delivers all of the packets at the depot before the time runs out, the player receives one point for each second of time remaining.

You: *What* is the time limit on the game, and *how many* packets will be in the depot?

Ryan: One minute and 30 packets.

You: Looks like the game pieces (objects) are the planets, the supply packets, and the supply ship. Is that correct?

Ryan: Yes, but don't forget to include the supply depot.

You: *How* will the player move the supply ship and pick up and drop off the packets?

Ryan: Using keys on the keyboard.

You: Will any of the other game pieces be moving?

Ryan: Yes, the planets will be moving and bouncing off the edges of the game board. Also, make one of the planets white and another red.

You: Would you want to keep track of the highest game score achieved and the name of the game player that achieved it?

Ryan: Yes, that's a good idea.

You: Sounds good Ryan. I'll write up a specification for the game for you to look over. Then, I'll write the program, and we'll split the profits. How's that sound?

Ryan: How about a 40% share for you?

Ryan (whispered): It's all my idea.

You: OK.

You (whispered): But I'm doing all the work.

Based on this conversation, the specification of Ryan's game is given below.

## Program Specification

### Program Name: *Deep Space Delivery*

Task:     A starship is to pick up supply packets at a supply depot and deliver as many supply packets as possible to five moving planets before time runs out. The player will receive one point per packet delivered and one point per second remaining on the game time after all packets are delivered.

Inputs (7):     The four cursor control keys (up, down, right, and left) used to control the position of the starship

The 'A' key, which is used to pick up a supply packet when the ship is at the supply depot

The 'Z' key, which is used to drop off a packet when the starship is at a planet

The game player's name input when the game is launched

Outputs (5): The time remaining in the game, in seconds, beginning from 60 seconds

The player's score

The message "Game Over" when the game time reaches zero, or when all packets are delivered

The highest score achieved and the name of the person who achieved it to be output to the game board and a disk file when the game time reaches zero

The details for more functionality could be added to the specification of Ryan's program. For example, the delivery of a packet to a faster moving planet could be awarded multiple points, multiple levels of difficulty could be added to the game, and the highest game score achieved with the name of the game player who achieved it could be announced at the beginning of the game.

## 1.4 ■ SAMPLE STUDENT GAMES

We will soon be able to write a program that implements the specification of the Deep Space Delivery game presented in the preceding section. The game programs on the DVD that accompanies this textbook were specified and written by students enrolled in an introductory programming course. To run these programs, simply double click the "Sample Student Games" folder on the DVD and copy the subfolders onto your hard drive. Double click one of the subfolders and then double click the file with the .jar extension. Running these programs will give you a sense of what you will be able to accomplish after gaining an understanding of the material in the first five chapters of this textbook.

## 1.5 ■ JAVA AND PLATFORM INDEPENDENCE

A computer system's platform is the CPU model and the operating system software it is running. For example, many PCs run on an Intel CPU/Windows platform, and Apple computers manufactured after the midpoint of 2011 run on an Intel CPU/OS X platform. As a result of the evolution of CPUs and operating system software that has taken place over the last 30 years, there are many different platforms in use today.

The variety of platforms has always been a problem for software developers because each platform has a language of its own, meaning that a platform can only execute a program that is written in its language. To produce a program that could run on two different platforms, the programmer either had to write the program twice, first in the language of one platform and then in the language of the other, or write the program in a more generic language (for example, C++) and then use two other programs to translate that program into the language of the individual platforms. In this case, the C++ program is referred to as source code, and the resulting translations of this source code are called executable modules or executables.

**Figure 1.24**
The C++ multiple-platform translation process.

When we consider the number of platforms that exist and the fact that writing in the language of a particular platform is a very tedious and time-consuming process, writing programs in a generic language is the most efficient and cost-effective approach. Figure 1.24 illustrates the use of this process to produce executable modules for three different platforms. The programmer would have to translate the program using three different translators to generate the three different executable modules.

During the early 1990s, the Internet was made commercially available to private individuals, which made it possible for them to share information between their computer systems. The idea that this information could be a program resident on one computer system (perhaps a program to display a Website) presented a fundamental problem. If the two computers were not running the same platform, the executable module downloaded from one platform (the host platform) would not run on the other (the client platform), and the Website would not be displayed on the client machine. Using the process illustrated in Figure 1.24 to produce a downloadable executable module for all platforms was an impractical solution because, for one thing, a program that was written today should be able to be run on the platforms of tomorrow. Fortunately, a team of computer scientists at Sun Microsystems lead by James Gosling had already come up with a more practical solution.

The team's idea was to change the process used to produce an executable module. Instead of the host machine producing the executable module, the client machine would produce it. The host machine would simply translate the program, written in a new programming language named Java, into a set of bytecodes. Bytecodes should be thought of as a pseudo-executable module for a virtual machine, named the Java Virtual Machine (JVM), which are not in the language of any platform in existence. Once generated, the bytecodes could then be downloaded to any client machine, and the client machine would use a bytecode translator program to translate the downloaded bytecodes into the language of its platform. Figure 1.25 illustrates the Gosling team's new process.

**Figure 1.25**

The Java multiple-platform translation process.

**NOTE** *The grammatical rules for writing a program in the Java language were described by the Gosling team in the Java Language Specification (JLS), available online.*

To make this process work, Gosling's team assumed that the manufacturer of the client computer system would install a translator that translated Java bytecodes into the language of their system's platform. Realizing that all future customers would want to attach their new computer to the Internet, computer manufacturers complied and proudly advertised their system as "Internet ready."

The fact that the same set of bytecodes could be downloaded and used to produce an executable module on any platform that had a bytecode translation program on it made Java programs platform independent. Programs written in Java (or more accurately, the program's bytecodes) could be downloaded, translated, and then executed on any platform that contained a platform-specific bytecode translator.

The Java programs that we will write in this book are called *applications*. They are launched and run from your desktop. Another type of Java program is called an *applet*. Applet programs are run from within another program such as a Java-enabled Web browser or an applet viewer, and are usually smaller programs.

### 1.5.1 The Java Application Programming Interface

In addition to providing a translator that translates Java programs into bytecodes, the creators of Java also identified a group of data (e.g., the mathematical constant pi) and tasks (e.g., computing the square root of a given number) that were likely to be used in Java programs. A description of these data and tasks was then published as the Java Application Programming Interface (API) specification. If a Java programmer wanted to create a new window for a program, which normally most programmers want to do, it could be easily done by incorporating the API task that contained all of the Java bytecodes necessary to display a window into that program.

For ease of use, the data and tasks that are similar were grouped together. These grouping are called packages, and within the packages there are subgroupings called **classes**. There are approximately 200 packages and 4,000 classes in the Java API. Most of these classes contain both data and the Java instructions to perform common tasks. A set of instructions to perform a task is called a method. The data and methods that are in the same class are said to be **members** of the class.

| Definition |
| --- |
| A **class** is made up of a group of related data members and member methods. |
| A **method** is a set of instructions used to perform a task. |
| **Data members** are the instance variables that contain the data values for the class. |

Java also provides packages for drawing graphics and creating graphical user interfaces (GUI). The Abstract Windowing Toolkit (AWT) and Swing packages contain classes that are part of the Java API. You will notice that these are used in creating and interacting with game window objects. The AWT classes are often used to draw graphical objects in a window by importing them using a statement such as:

```
import java.awt.*;
```

Most applications use the newer Swing classes, which extend the range of GUI components available in the AWT package. The Swing components provide additional features such as dialog boxes and the ability to interact with objects in a drag-and-drop mode. These API Swing classes can be imported using a similar statement such as the following:

```
import javax.swing.*;   // notice the "x" in javax
```

**Figure 1.26**
System-specific components of the Java Virtual Machine.

Just as Java's creators assumed that the manufacturers of computer systems would install a translator that translated bytecodes into the language of their system's platform, they also assumed that the manufacturers would install an implementation of the data and methods defined in the API specification. Once again, to advertise that their system was Internet ready, the manufacturers complied. Technically speaking, the bytecode translator and the API implementation on the client machine (along with a memory manager) are called the Java Runtime Environment (JRE), and the JRE and the client system's operating system are considered an implementation of the Java Virtual Machine. Figure 1.26 gives the components of the Java Virtual Machine specific to a system running an Intel CPU/Windows platform.

Based on Gosling's team's idea, any programming language can achieve platform independence if the language designers provide a translator that translates the language into Java bytecodes. The resulting translation will run on any computer system or mobile device that implements the Java Virtual Machine.

## ■1.6■ OBJECT-ORIENTED PROGRAMMING LANGUAGES

Just as related methods and data are grouped into classes in the API specification, they can also be grouped into classes that are defined within programs written using object-oriented programming (OOP) languages. Java, by design, is an OOP language. Grouping related methods and data inside a class that is defined in a Java program is more than a convenient way of arranging related data and methods. The real motivation for permitting this class grouping in object-oriented programming languages is that it is a good way of modeling the objects that the program will deal with.

As an example, consider a video game program that involves starship objects. Each starship object will have a name and a (x, y) location. In addition, as the game is played a new starship can be created, starships can be drawn on the monitor, and a starship's location can be changed. A good model for these starship objects would be to define a class named Starship (depicted as the blue rectangle in Figure 1.27). As shown in the figure, the class would have three data members (name, x, and y), and three member methods (create, draw, and move).

It is important to understand that a class is not itself an object, but rather it is a description of an object. From one class we can create an unlimited number of **objects** or instances of the class. A useful analogy is to consider classes we encounter in everyday life: a blueprint, a cookie cutter, a stencil, a pottery mold, a dress pattern, and the human genome pattern. From one blueprint we can create lots of houses, from one cookie cutter lots of cookies, from one stencil lots of pictures, from one pottery mold lots of vases, from one pattern lots of dresses, and from one human genome pattern lots of people.

| Definition |
| --- |
| In an object-oriented programming language, a **class** is a template for an object, and an **object** is a particular instance of a class. |

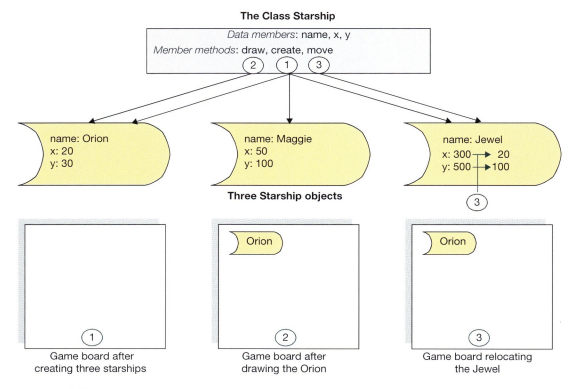

**Figure 1.27**
The Starship class, three Starship objects, and the use of the class's methods.

The Starship class would be a template for a starship object. Each time a starship enters the game, a new starship would be created from this template with a given name and initial (x, y) location using the class's create method. A starship's name and (x, y) location would be stored in its three data members, which each object created from the class Starship would contain. In addition, the tasks of drawing and relocating a starship would be performed by the Java instructions that make up the class's draw and move methods.

The center and bottom sections of Figure 1.27 depict the use of the Starship class's three member methods used in the following order:

1. The create method (indicated by the number 1 in the figure) was used to create or construct the three starship objects shown in the center of the figure: the Orion at (20, 30), the Maggie at (50, 100), and the Jewel at (300, 500). Notice that after they are created, each starship contains three data members to store the ship's name and its (x, y) location. Although these three starships have been created, they are not displayed on the game board shown at the lower left portion of the figure because the draw method has not been used.

2. The draw method (shown as number 2 in the figure) was used to display the starship Orion at its current location (20, 30), as depicted in the bottom center of the figure. The draw method has not operated on the other two starships, so, even though they exist, they do not appear on the game board. (Note: The origin is located at the upper left corner of the game board and positive y is downward.)

3. The move method (represented by the number 3 in the figure) was used to change the current location of the starship Jewel from (300, 500) to (20, 100) as depicted on the center right portion of the figure. As shown at the bottom right portion of the figure, it is not displayed because the draw method was not performed on it. After relocating the starship, if the draw task were performed on the Jewel, it would have been displayed directly below the Orion at (20, 100).

**NOTE**    *Each object contains the data members of its class and can be operated on by the class's methods.*

## 1.7 INTEGRATED DEVELOPMENT ENVIRONMENTS AND THE PROGRAM DEVELOPMENT PROCESS

An Integrated Development Environment (IDE) is a program to help programmers write programs. Usually they are language specific in that a particular IDE can be used to develop programs in one, and only one, programming language. For example, NetBeans and Eclipse are two popular IDEs used to develop programs written in Java, and the IDE Microsoft Visual C++ can be used to develop programs written in the language C++. Many popular IDEs can be downloaded for free from the IDE's Website.

What these programs have in common is that they integrate a set of program development tools into one program. Examples of these tools are a text editor used to type, edit, save, and re-open the program's instructions, and a translator used to translate the program instructions into the language of the platform it is to run on. In the case of a Java IDE, this would be a translation from Java into Java bytecodes. In addition, most IDEs have an autocomplete feature to facilitate the typing of the program and a grammar checker to help locate and correct grammatical errors in the program's instructions.

Armed with a good specification of a program and a good IDE, we are almost ready to begin the program development process, which is illustrated in Figure 1.28. Before we begin, we must read the

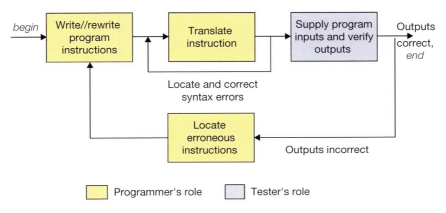

**Figure 1.28**
An overview of the program development process.

program's task contained in its specification and discover a set of algorithms that perform the tasks. For example, how will we determine when a starship delivers a supply packet to a planet in Ryan's Deep Space Delivery program? As mentioned at the end of Section 1.1, this can be the most difficult part of writing a program, and most software engineers take an advanced course in algorithm discovery. We will illustrate the discovery process via the programming examples presented throughout this textbook.

After discovering the program's algorithms, we are ready to begin the program development process (Figure 1.28). Generally, the process begins with representing the algorithms as a set of program instructions (called code), translating the code, and then correcting the grammatical errors (called syntax errors in computer science). Once all of the syntax errors have been eliminated, the IDE's translator will produce an executable module that it then runs. In the case of Java, the IDE generates and then executes the Java bytecodes on the Java Virtual Machine installed on the programmer's computer.

The programmer then changes roles from programmer to program user to test the program for correctness. To do this, the user (or tester) supplies the inputs to the program and examines the outputs it produces. If the program produces the correct outputs for several well-chosen sets of inputs, the program is complete. If it does not, the tester changes back to the role of a programmer, locates the erroneous instruction(s), and the process is repeated beginning with rewriting those instructions.

One refinement to the process is necessary for anything other than a very, very small program because of the fact that we cannot effectively solve large problems. When we consider that we humans have visited the moon and that many of the more common operating systems consist of over a million lines of instructions, this statement leads us to a paradox: If we can't solve large problems, how did we do these things?

The answer lies in the 4,000 BC writings on a Chinese cave wall that explain that big things can be divided into little things, little things can be divided into nothing. Today's version of this is: divide and conquer. Just as the task of going to the moon was divided into hundreds of small problems whose solutions were integrated into the lunar mission, a large program is divided into many small parts, which can be combined to become the large program.

Object-oriented programming languages present several obvious dividing lines. Because the specification identifies the types of objects the program will deal with, the program is first divided into classes, one for each type of object. Then, within each class, the tasks to be performed on the class's objects are defined. Simple tasks become member methods, complex tasks are divided into several simple tasks (each of which also becomes a member method). Each method within a class is written and tested separately. Basically, each method is considered to be a small program, and it is developed using the process illustrated in Figure 1.28. Once all of the methods in a class are operating correctly, the methods in another class are developed using this divide-and-conquer concept. When all the classes are complete, they are integrated into the large program. Object-oriented programming languages make it easy to integrate the classes into the large program.

As an example, consider the development of the Starship class shown in Figure 1.27, which is part of a game program. Three methods (create, draw, and move) have to be developed using the process illustrated in Figure 1.28. Because we cannot draw or move a Starship that has not yet been created, the create method would be developed first. After the method is written and the syntax errors are found and corrected, we would write a few more lines of Java to test the method. This code is often referred to as **driver** code because it takes the method for a "test drive." It would use the method to construct a Starship object, perhaps Maggie in the center of Figure 1.27, and output its data members. If the name Maggie and position (50, 100) were output, we would conclude the create method was working. If not, we would examine the instructions that make up the create method, locate and correct the errors, and repeat the translation and test portion of the process.

| **NOTE** | *Driver code is disposable Java instructions use to test a method. It normally does not become part of the final program's instructions.* |
|---|---|

The next logical step would be to develop the draw method because, as we will see, it can be used in the testing of the move method. After the syntax errors are found and corrected, we would write a few more lines of Java driver code to test the method. The code would use the create method to construct a Starship object, perhaps Orion shown on the left side of Figure 1.27, and then use the draw method to display it on the game board. If it were displayed in its proper location with the name Orion on the side of the ship, we would conclude the draw method was working. If not, we would examine the instructions that make up the draw method, locate and correct the errors, and then repeat the translation and test portion of the process.

Next, we would develop the move method, write its code, translate the code and correct the syntax errors, and then write a few more lines of Java driver code to test it. The code would create a Starship object, perhaps Jewel at (300, 500), as shown on the right side of Figure 1.27, then use the move method to change its position to (20, 100) and the draw method to display it on the game board (monitor). If it were displayed in its new location (20, 100) with the name Jewel on the side of the ship, we would conclude the move method was working. If not, we would examine the instructions that make up the move method, locate and correct the errors, and repeat the translation and test portion of the process.

After completing the development of our Starship class in three manageable steps, we would eliminate the driver code and replace it with the instructions to use the Starship class and its methods in our game program.

## 1.7.1 Mobile-Device Application Development Environments

The level of miniaturization of the basic components of a computing system that has taken place in the last ten years has brought to the marketplace a variety of hand-held computing devices. These devices, often referred to as mobile devices, include smart phones, personal digital assistants (PDAs), and tablet devices.

The development of a program for a mobile device follows the same process as that used to develop a program for a non-mobile computing device discussed in this chapter. After a specification is written and the program's algorithms are discovered, an IDE is used to develop the specification into a functional program using the process shown in Figure 1.28. However, two problems arise when applying the development process to mobile-device applications. Because these devices have limited computing power, it is impractical to conduct the development process on them, so the process is conducted on a more powerful non-mobile computing system. In addition, the concept of platform independence has not been extended to mobile devices, so an executable module must be produced for each mobile-device platform.

Because a majority of mobile applications run on smartphones, and a great majority of smartphones run an Android-based platform, this section will conclude with an overview of the tools available for developing applications for any Android-based smartphone or tablet device. Although the details presented are specific to those devices, the concepts presented are typical of the tools employed to develop applications on most mobile devices.

Android device applications can be written in Java on a personal computer. The preferred IDE is Eclipse, which is a free download. Eclipse is preferred because two sets of tools that facilitate the development of an Android-device application are easily integrated into it. Both of these tools can be freely downloaded. The first of these, the Android Software Development Kit (SDK), can be downloaded from the Android developers' Website. The second set of tools, the Android Development Tools (ADT) Eclipse plug-in can be downloaded from the Eclipse Website. If your personal computer is running a Windows operating system, you can download the Eclipse IDE, the SDK, and the ADT as one bundle from the Android Developers Website, found at *http://developer.android.com/sdk/index.html*.

Some of the features the two sets of tools provide include:

- The latest version of the Android operating system
- Platform-dependent translators
- A set of emulators that run the translated code on a simulation of any Android-based mobile device including displaying its screen and emulating all of its I/O functionality
- The ability to upload developed applications to the Android Market (a Web-based store for free and purchased applications)

Using these tools and knowledge of Java, you will be able to develop and market applications for any Android device from the comfort of your own personal-computer system.

## 1.8 OUR GAME DEVELOPMENT ENVIRONMENT: A FIRST LOOK

In Section 1.4, you were asked to run several of the sample game programs contained on the DVD that accompanies this textbook. The DVD also contains a folder named Package that contains a Java package named `edu.sjcny.gpv1`. This package can be thought of as a game development addition to the API because it contains methods that perform tasks that are common to most game programs. Appendix A contains descriptions of the methods contained in this package.

The incorporation of this package, or game development environment, into a game program facilitates its development. The students who created all the sample game programs contained on

**Figure 1.29**
The game environment's window.

the book's DVD incorporated it into their programs. In this section, we will describe how to easily create and display a game window using the methods in this package, how to incorporate the package into a game program, and how to change some of the game window's properties.

### 1.8.1 The Game Window

When incorporated into a Java program, two of the game environment's methods can be used to create and display the game window shown in Figure 1.29. The Pause and Start buttons on the right side of the game window can be used by the game player to pause the game and to start/restart the game. The directional buttons below them, or the keyboard keys, can be used to control the position of the game objects during the game.

The coral-colored area on left side of the game window, called the game board, is where the game objects appear. Like most windows, it can be dragged around by its title bar, minimized to the status bar, and redisplayed by clicking its icon on the status bar. It cannot be maximized, however, the programmer can change its size to accommodate the needs of a particular game. The default size of the game window is 622x535 pixels, which are closely spaced dots of color that make up the surface of a computer monitor.

### 1.8.2 The Game Board Coordinate System

Figure 1.30 shows the game board coordinate system. Game objects are positioned on the game board by specifying their x and y game board coordinates. The system is a two-dimensional Cartesian system with its origin at the upper left corner of the game window. The positive x direction is to the right, and positive y direction is down. The units of the axis system are pixels.

**Figure 1.30**
The game board coordinate system.

As shown on the upper right and lower left sides of Figure 1.30, the title bar of the window is 30 pixels high, and the left boundary of the window is 5 pixels wide. The coordinates of the lower right corner of the game board for the default window size are (500, 500). If the programmer decides that a larger or smaller game board is appropriate for the game being developed, the x and y coordinates of the lower right corner of the game board can be changed, which will be described in Section 1.8.5.

### 1.8.3 Installing and Incorporating the Game Package into a Program

Appendix B contains detailed instructions on how to incorporate the game package, which contains the game development environment, into a Java program. The simplest approach is to use one of the projects contained in the "IDE Specific Tools" subfolder on the DVD that accompanies this book. This subfolder contains an Eclipse, a NetBeans, and a JCreator project that has the game package already incorporated into them as well as the code described in the next section, which creates and displays the game window. When the projects are run, they display the game window shown in Figure 1.29. Game program specific code and classes can be added to them.

The JCreator and NetBeans projects on the DVD can be copied from the DVD and pasted into a folder, and then the project can be opened, modified, and run from within the IDEs. The Eclipse project must be imported into an Eclipse workspace folder using the Import feature available on the Eclipse File drop-down menu. After the Eclipse project is imported from the DVD, it can be opened, modified, and run from within Eclipse. Detailed instructions on the use of the DVD's three preexisting game projects are given in Appendix B.

As an alternative, the game package edu.sjcny.gpv1 in the "Game Environment" folder on the DVD can be added to any newly created Java project by following the procedures given in Appendix B, most of which do not include having to change the system's CLASSPATH variable. When these alternative approaches are used, the code described in the next section, which creates and displays the game window, must be added to the project's code.

### 1.8.4 Creating and Displaying a Game Window and Its Title

After you have incorporated (imported) the game package into your program, you can use the methods in the package to create and display the graphical window in which your game will run. The Java program shown in Figure 1.31 is a template, or starting point, for all of our graphical game application programs. When this program is run, the game window shown in Figure 1.29 is created and displayed.

As we will learn in Chapter 2, lines 2, 3, 7, 8, 10, and 11 are the minimum set of instructions that make up a Java application program. For that reason, many IDEs generate these instructions when a new programming application is created. The one exception is the phrase **extends** DrawableAdapter, which must be added to the end of line 2 if the game package is to be used in the program. Lines 1, 4, 5, and 9 complete the game program template.

The import statement on line 1 of Figure 1.31 makes the methods in the game package available to the program. Lines 4, 5, and 9 use these methods to create and display the game window shown in Figure 1.29. Each Java program is given a name, which is part of its specification. This program is named GameWindowDemo, which is typed on line 2 after the word class and typed two more times on line 4.

```
1    import edu.sjcny.gpv1.*;
2    public class GameWindowDemo extends DrawableAdapter
3    {
4        static GameWindowDemo ga = new GameWindowDemo( );
5        static GameBoard gb = new GameBoard(ga, "The Game Window");
6
7        public static void main(String[] args)
8        {
9            showGameBoard(gb);
10       }
11   }
```

**Figure 1.31**
The Java instructions to create and display the game window.

As previously mentioned, Figure 1.31 will be the template for all of our graphical game application programs. To adapt it to a particular game program, the new program's name would appear on lines 2 and 4, and the game's title and perhaps the name of its creator would appear at the end of line 5. For example, if a new game program's name was Project1, and the game was Frogger created by Bob, the changes to lines 2, 4, and 5 would be as highlighted below:

```
1    import edu.sjcny.gpv1.*;
2    public class Project1 extends DrawableAdapter
```

```
 3  {
 4      static Project1 ga = new Project1 ( );
 5      static GameBoard gb = new GameBoard(ga, "Frogger, by Bob");
 6
 7      public static void main(String[] args)
 8      {
 9          showGameBoard(gb);
10      }
11  }
```

### 1.8.5 Changing the Game Board's Size

As mentioned in Section 1.8.1, the default size of the game window is 622x535 pixels. This was chosen to make the coordinates of the game board's lower right corner (500, 500). To change the game board's size, and thus the window size, we add the new coordinates of the game board's lower right corner to the end of line 5 of Figure 1.31. This is the line that constructs the window. For example, to obtain a game board whose lower right corner is located at (700, 650), we would change line 5 to:

```
static GameBoard gb = new GameBoard(ga, "The Game Window",700, 650);
```

The title bar of the window would still be 30 pixels high, and the left border of the window would still be 5 pixels wide, as shown in Figure 1.29, but the window's height and width would be increased to accommodate the larger game board.

## 1.9 REPRESENTING INFORMATION IN MEMORY

As discussed in Section 1.1, the memory component of the computer system has the ability to store and recall information, and that information could be the data that the program processes or the instructions that make up the program. The scheme used to store or represent the information in memory is dependent on the type of information being stored. Data is stored using a different scheme than translated program instructions. In addition, character data, which is data typed into a word processor or IDE, is stored differently than numeric data, which is data that will be used in arithmetic expressions.

There are three memory storage schemes used to represent three different types of information: (1) character data, (2) translated instructions, and (3) numeric data. All three of these schemes were designed around the basic hardware memory unit: a bit, which stands for *b*inary dig*it*. Conceptually, a bit should be thought of as a single switch that can be turned on or off. All of memory uses this storage concept, and storage devices such as RAM, disks, flash drives, and tape drives may contain billions (giga) and even trillions (tera) of these bits.

For brevity, when a bit is turned on we say it is in state 1 (one), and when it is off we say it is in state 0 (zero). These should only be thought of as the numerics one and zero when the information stored is numeric data. Figure 1.32 depicts eight adjacent bits in on-off states and their briefer binary (1-0) depiction.

| off on off off off off on off | 01000010 |
|---|---|
| on-off Depiction | 1-0 Depiction |

**Figure 1.32**
The state of eight adjacent on-off bits and their 1-0 depiction.

### 1.9.1 Representing Character Data

The scheme used to represent character data in memory is rather straightforward. A table[7] was composed in which each character to be represented was assigned a unique eight-bit pattern. For example, the character B was assigned the pattern 01000010, the lower-case version of this character, b, was assigned the pattern 01100010, and the character 1 was assigned the pattern 00110001.

The table is named the Extended American Standard Code for Information Interchange because it was an expansion of a table named the American Standard Code for Information Interchange, which represented characters using patterns of seven bits. The seven-bit table was assigned the acronym ASCII (pronounced "ask ee"), and the extended table is referred to as the Extended ASCII table. Both tables include all of the upper- and lower-case letters of the Modern Latin (English) alphabet, the digits 0 to 9, a set of special characters (e.g., !, @, #, $, %, ^, etc.), and some control characters such as horizontal tab and line feed. Because there are 128 ($2^7$) unique ways to arrange 7 bits and 256 ($2^8$) unique ways to arrange 8 bits, adding the eighth bit to the Extended ASCII table doubled the size of the ASCII table.

The first 128 characters in the Extended ASCII table are given in Appendix C. The bit patterns in this table are used to represent character information on all computer systems when the alphabetic characters the system is processing are limited to the Modern Latin (English) alphabet. When this is the case, and we want to represent the letter B in storage, eight adjacent (or contiguous) bits of storage (called a **byte** of storage) are set to the Extended ASCII pattern for B: 01000010. If we fetched a byte of storage from an area of memory in which we knew that characters were stored, and that byte contained the pattern 01000010, we would know that the character B was stored there. We say that a keyboard is an ASCII keyboard if it generates this bit pattern when a capital B is struck, and a printer is an ASCII printer if it prints the character B when it receives this bit pattern.

| **Definition** |
|---|
| Eight adjacent or contiguous bits are called a **byte** of storage |

To accommodate the international exchange of information over the Internet, the Extended ASCII table was expanded to include unique bit patterns for the symbols used in the other alphabets of the world. To provide a unique bit pattern for each entry in this expanded table, named the UNICODE table, the number of bits assigned to each character was increased from 8 to 16 bits (2 bytes) per character. The first 256 entries in the UNICODE table are the characters in the Extended ASCII table, with the leftmost 8 bits of their 16-bit pattern set to 0 and the rightmost 8 bits set to their Extended ASCII table patterns. For example, because the Extended ASCII representation of

B is 01000010, its UNICODE representation is 00000000 01000010. Characters processed by Java programs are stored in memory using their UNICODE table representations.

> **NOTE** *Character data is represented in memory using either the Extended ASCII or UNICODE table.*

### 1.9.2 Representing Translated Instructions

The technique used to represent translated instructions in memory is the same technique used to represent characters in memory. A table is composed containing all of the possible translated instructions, and a unique bit pattern is assigned to each of them. For example, the bit pattern for the translated instruction to subtract two integers could be 01000000, and the bit pattern to divide two integers could be 01000010.

Unlike the Extended ASCII and UNICODE tables that are used by all computer systems to store characters, these translated instruction tables vary from one CPU to another. Not only do the bit patterns vary, but the number of bits used to represent a translated instruction also varies. The tables are platform dependent, which is the reason Java came into being. To determine the translated memory representation of a divide instruction on a particular platform, we have to look up the bit pattern for the divide instruction in the instruction table of the CPU of that platform.

For the Java Virtual Machine, each translated instruction is assigned an eight-bit pattern. Because the patterns consist of eight bits, or one byte, the patterns are called bytecodes. Table 1.1 gives the Java bytecodes for the translated integer arithmetic instructions: add, subtract, multiply, and divide. As indicated in this table, when the Java Virtual Machine receives a bytecode of 01101100, it performs a divide operation.

**Table 1.1**
Java Bytecodes for Integer Arithmetic Instructions

| Instruction | Java Bytecode |
|-------------|---------------|
| add | 01100000 |
| subtract | 01100100 |
| multiply | 01101000 |
| divide | 01101100 |

> **! TIP** Translated Java instructions are represented in memory using patterns of eight bits called bytecodes.

### 1.9.3 Representing Numeric Data

Unlike the two previously described schemes, the scheme used to represent numeric data does not use a table because, for one thing, the table would be infinitely long. Rather, the scheme is based on the theory of numbers. All number systems have a base. Our number system's base is 10, which anthropologists speculate is due to the fact that we have ten fingers and ten toes. In number theory, the base of a number system determines the number of digits in the system. Because our number system is base 10, it has 10 digits (0 through 9). Conversely, the theory of numbers tells us that if a number system has 10 digits, its base is 10.

Armed with this knowledge of number systems, it was decided that numeric data would be represented in memory using a number system whose base is 2 because one bit can represent the system's two digits: 0 and 1[*]. Anthropologists would tell us that a base-2 number system would probably be our number system if we had two fingers. Because we do not have two fingers, we need to understand how to convert from base 2 to base 10 to interpret what base-10 number a bit pattern represents and how to convert numbers from base 10 to base 2 so we can store numbers in memory.

 Numeric data (data that will be used in a mathematical expression) is represented in memory using a binary number system.

Fundamental to these conversions is the realization that digit position values in a base-2 number system are not the same as in our base-10 system. Starting from the right, the digit position values in our number system are the 1s position, the 10s position, the 100s position, etc. These represent $10^0$, $10^1$, $10^2$, etc. Extrapolating this to a base-2 system, the digit position values starting from the right are $2^0$, $2^1$, $2^2$, etc. Figure 1.33 gives the first eight digit position values of the base-2 number system with their decimal (base 10) equivalent below them. Knowing the digit position values of the binary number system, we can now convert from base 2 to base 10, and base 10 to base 2.

| $2^7$ | $2^6$ | $2^5$ | $2^4$ | $2^3$ | $2^2$ | $2^1$ | $2^0$ | |
|-----|-----|-----|-----|-----|-----|-----|-----|-----|
| 128 | 64 | 32 | 16 | 8 | 4 | 2 | 1 | base-2 position values |

**Figure 1.33**
First eight digit position values of the binary number system.

To convert a base-2 representation (e.g., 01000010) of an integer numeric value stored in memory to base 10, we simply write the bit pattern below the base-10 digit position values that are shown in Figure 1.33 and add the values that have a 1 under them. For example, for the bit pattern 01000010, the process would be:

| 128 | 64 | 32 | 16 | 8 | 4 | 2 | 1 | base-2 position values |
|-----|-----|-----|-----|-----|-----|-----|-----|-----|
| 0 | 1 | 0 | 0 | 0 | 0 | 1 | 0 | internal representation |
| | 64 | | | | | 2 | | |

Therefore, 01000010 represents the base-10 number 66 (64 + 2).

This conversion process implies that the bit pattern 11111111 represents the largest integer that can be represented using 8 bits, which is the base-10 number 255 (255 = 128 + 64 + 32 + 16 + 8 + 4 + 2 + 1). To represent integers larger than 255, more bytes of storage would be dedicated to each integer numeric value.

---

[*]John von Neumann, often called the father of the modern computer, originally proposed this scheme.

To convert a base-10 integer to its binary bit pattern to store the numeric value in memory, we begin by writing out the base-10 digit position values that are shown in Figure 1.33. Then starting on the left, we place a 1 under all of the position values that when added together give the base-10 number. The remaining position values are filled in with zeros.

To quickly determine which positions that should have a 1 placed under them, use the following algorithm until the right most position value is reached:

1. Let n (e.g., 66) be the base-10 integer value to be represented in memory
2. Start at the left most bit, b
3. Set v to b's position value (e.g., v = 128)
4. If (n − v) is positive or equal to zero then:
   a. Place a 1 under b's position
   b. Set n = (n − v)
   Else place a 0 under b's position
5. Move b to the next bit to the right
6. Go to step 3

Table 1.2 illustrates the use of this algorithm to convert 66 to its 8-bit binary representation. Each row in the table represents an execution of steps 3 and 4 of the algorithm.

**Table 1.2**
Conversion of the Integer 66 to its 8-Bit Binary Representation

| n | b | v | n − v | Binary Representation of n |
|---|---|---|---|---|
| 66 | 7 | 128 | −62 | 0 |
| 66 | 6 | 64 | 2 | 01 |
| 2 | 5 | 32 | −30 | 010 |
| 2 | 4 | 16 | −14 | 0100 |
| 2 | 3 | 8 | −6 | 01000 |
| 2 | 2 | 4 | −2 | 010000 |
| 2 | 1 | 2 | 0 | 0100001 |
| 0 | 0 | 1 | −1 | 01000010 |

Before we conclude our discussion on how numeric data is stored in memory, we should comment on how negative integers and numbers with fractional parts, which are called real numbers in mathematics, are represented in memory. The short answer is that negative integers are represented using a scheme named twos complement form, and numbers with fractional parts are represented in a standardized[6] form analogous to scientific notation (as when 235.2374 is expressed as $2.352374 \times 10^2$). The details of these schemes are beyond the scope of this text, however, an understanding of the representation of positive integers as binary numbers discussed in this section is fundamental to an understanding these two representation schemes.

Finally, consider a byte of storage that contained the bit pattern 01000010. When we attempt to determine what is stored in this byte, a dilemma arises. If we look into the Extended ASCII table we would conclude the character B is stored there. We have also learned that this could also be the base-10 integer 66. It is also the bytecode instruction to store an integer in RAM memory. To resolve these kinds of dilemmas, the language translator keeps track of the types of information that is stored in various parts of RAM. If we knew that the bit pattern 01000010 was in the area of RAM where characters are stored, then it represents character B.

## 1.10 CHAPTER SUMMARY

In this chapter, you learned about the hardware and software components of a computer system, how they are arranged, and how they interact with the user. The hardware components consist of the central processing unit, memory, and input/output devices. Main or RAM memory interacts with the CPU and stores the data and instructions that are about to be processed by the CPU. The backing store or secondary memory, such as a hard drive, stores data and instructions more permanently.

The modern computer was developed over centuries through the efforts of many people. It has become smaller, faster, cheaper, and more reliable as it evolved from a room-sized device to the small hand-held mobile and wearable devices common today.

Java is an object-oriented programming language that allows a programmer to represent and process real-world objects within application programs and computer games. Classes are the templates for creating objects, which contain both data and methods to operate on the data. All information contained in a computer is represented in binary as translated instructions, numeric data, and character data. Java programs are translated into bytecodes, which can be executed by the Java Virtual Machine, making them platform independent and portable.

New programs are defined in a written specification, then the program's algorithms are discovered and an IDE is used to compose and test the program. Game programs are more easily composed by importing a game environment into the program, such as the one contained on the DVD that accompanies this textbook. Game environments supplement the Java API by providing methods that perform tasks common to most games, such creating an interactive game board on which the game objects can be drawn and moved.

The discovery of a program's algorithms is usually the most difficult part of producing a new program. Throughout this text, we will use game programming to illustrate the use of programming concepts and use game algorithms to introduce the reader to the algorithm discovery process.

### Knowledge Exercises

1. Between 1989 and 2004, the number of computers per 1,000 U.S. citizens increased by a factor of approximately:

   **a)** 2          **b)** 4

   **c)** 8          **d)** 12

2. What is the difference between hardware and software?

3. Explain the difference between operating systems and application programs.

**4.** Which of the following characteristics are associated with RAM (main) memory?
   **a)** Nonvolatile                 **b)** Very fast
   **c)** Very large capacity        **d)** Expensive

**5.** Which of the following characteristics are associated with backing (secondary) storage?
   **a)** Nonvolatile                 **b)** Very fast
   **c)** Very large capacity        **d)** Expensive

**6.** Give three examples of:
   **a)** Input devices              **b)** Output devices
   **c)** Backing (secondary) storage devices

**7.** Some computer devices have a single use while others have multiple uses.
   **a)** Name a device that is only used for output.
   **b)** Name a device that is only used for input.
   **c)** What device can be used for both input and output?

**8.** Name and explain the function of each of the three major hardware components of a computer system.

**9.** How would you respond to a friend who asked you who invented the computer?

**10.** Examples of operating system programs include all of the following except:
   **a)** MAC OS               **b)** Windows
   **c)** Java                    **d)** Linux

**11.** Volatile memory refers to memory that:
   **a)** Permanently stores data
   **b)** Loses its contents if power is interrupted
   **c)** Is added to the computer externally

**12.** Word processing, e-mailing, and searching the Web are all examples of using:
   **a)** Application software       **b)** Systems software
   **c)** Programming            **d)** None of the above

**13.** Which of these replaced vacuum tubes in second-generation computers?
   **a)** Paper tape            **b)** The mouse
   **c)** Chips                  **d)** Transistors

**14.** Who developed assembly language, the first compiler, and the language COBOL?
   **a)** Alan Turing           **b)** Ada Lovelace
   **c)** Grace Hopper         **d)** John von Neumann

**15.** Name the person referred to by each of these titles or descriptions:
   **a)** First programmer        **b)** Inventor of the Java programming language

**16.** Give the four features of a program that are identified in its specification.

**17.** What is meant by platform independence?

18. True or False: To achieve platform independence, Java bytecodes are translated on the end user's computer system.

19. What is the difference between a class and an object?

20. In a video game, a paddle will be used to reflect a ball into a pile of 200 bricks.
    a) How many objects will be involved in the game? What are they?
    b) How many classes will be defined in the program? Name them.

21. Give the terms that are represented by the following acronyms:
    a) CPU                         b) RAM
    c) I/O                         d) IDE
    e) JVM                         f) API
    g) GUI

22. Which of these refers to the process of breaking a problem into smaller parts in order to solve or program it?
    a) Divide and conquer          b) Platform independence
    c) Portability                 d) Translation

23. The upper left corner of the game environment's game board is located at the (x, y) pixel coordinates:
    a) (0, 0)                      b) (500,500)
    c) (622,535)                   d) (5, 30)

24. Which of these is not a component of a typical game program?
    a) Score                       b) Time limits
    c) Napier's bones              d) Game piece objects

25. Name the three types of information represented in memory.

26. Write the 8-bit binary equivalent for each of these base-10 numeric values:
    a) 51                          b) 77
    c) 115                         d) 131
    e) 227                         f) 254

27. Write the base-10 (decimal) equivalent number for each of these binary values:
    a) 01010011                    b) 00101111
    c) 00000000

28. Give the 8-bit memory representation of the characters C and c.

## Preprogramming Exercises

1. Think of a video game and conduct a conversation with yourself that includes the features common to most games that are tabulated in Figure 1.1.23. Based on that conversation, write a specification for the game that gives the game's name, the task or objective of the game, and a description of the inputs and outputs. The game must include at least two different types of

game objects and one of the objects has to be controlled by the user via the cursor control keys and the game board directional buttons.

2. Logan is a teacher with 25 students in his class. Write a specification for a program that will show Logan the lowest, highest, and average class grades on an examination.

3. Using the template given in Figure 1.31 and the directions given in Section 1.8.5, write the line of code necessary to change the game window's size to 800x600 with the new title "My Great Game Window."

## Enrichment

In the same way that computers and programming languages have evolved over time, game programs also have developed from very simple games to the present multiuser, interactive games. Search the Internet to discover some of the historical developments of computer games. Some of the questions you might research are:

- When and where the first games were developed
- What companies were created for developing games
- Who are the leaders today in the field of games
- How do today's games differ from the earliest computer games

(Be sure to record the sources of your information.)

## References

Fullerton, Tracy, *Game Design Workshop*, 2nd ed. Burlington, MA: Morgan Kaufman Publishers, 2008.

Iverson, Jakob, and Michael Eierman. *Learning Mobile App Development*. Upper Saddle River, NJ: Addison-Wesley, 2013.

Lucci, Stephen, and Danny Kopec. *Artificial Intelligence in the 21st Century.* Dulles, VA: Mercury Learning and Information, 2013.

Swade, Doron. *Charles Babbage and his Calculating Machines*. London: Science Museum, 1998.

## Endnotes

[1] http://en.wikipedia.org/wiki/History_of_computing

[2] http://www.computersciencelab.com/ComputerHistory/History.htm

[3] http://www.webopedia.com/DidYouKnow/Hardware_Software/2002/FiveGenerations.asp

[4] http://community.seattletimes.nwsource.com/archive/?date=19961124&slug=2361376

[5] Decker, Rick and Stuart Hirschfield. *The Analytical Engine. Belmont, CA. Wadsworth Publishing Company, 1992, p.17* ( Now online: http://www.course.com/downloads/computerscience/aeonline/)

[6] The standard is named IEEE 754-2008

[7] http://docs.oracle.com/javase/specs/jvms/se7/html/jvms-7.html

# VARIABLES, INPUT/OUTPUT, AND CALCULATIONS

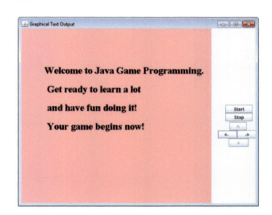

## In this chapter

In this chapter, you will learn how to use the basic Java program template to develop a program that performs input, mathematical calculations, and output. Various methods to facilitate meaningful input and understandable output will be introduced, as will techniques for storing data in RAM memory and performing mathematical calculations that go beyond basic arithmetic operations. All these techniques are used in most programming applications.

After successfully completing this chapter you should:

- Understand the basic components of a Java program
- Recognize the difference between primitive and reference variables and how they store data
- Be able to declare and use variables in a program
- Perform input from a dialog box
- Perform output to a dialog box, as well as output to the system console  and a graphical window
- Use arithmetic calculations and mathematical functions and constants in the Java Math class
- Perform basic formatting of numeric output
- Understand and be able to use the counting algorithm
- Apply these concepts to begin producing a computer game

## 2.1 THE JAVA APPLICATION PROGRAM TEMPLATE

If you were writing a letter to you friend Sally, it would probably begin with an opening salutation, for example, "Dear Sally," and end with a closing salutation, for example, "Sincerely," followed by your signature. Opening and closing salutations are usually considered to be a minimum template for any letter we compose. In between these salutations, we would put the text specific to the letter we are writing.

Similarly, most programming languages have templates for composing a program in that language. These templates begin and end with text specific to the language, and we write, or *code*, the instructions specific to the program we are composing inside the template. The minimum template for a Java program is depicted in the top half of Figure 2.1.

```
1 public class ProgramName
2 {
3     public static void main(String[] args)
4     {
5
6     }
7 }
```
**Java Program Template**

```
1 public class ProgramName
2 {
3     public static void main(String[] args)
4     {
5         System.out.println("Hello");
6     }
7 }
```
**Java Program to Output the Word "Hello"**

**Figure 2.1**
Template of a Java program and a program that outputs the word "Hello."

The phrase `ProgramName` on line 1 of this template is replaced with the name of the program being composed, and the instructions specific to the program are placed within the program's *code block,* within the braces that appear on lines 4 and 6. For example, in the bottom half of Figure 2.1 an instruction, or *executable* statement, has been added to line 5 of the template to produce a program that outputs the word "Hello."

**NOTE**   *All Java **executable** statements end with a semicolon.*

When a Java program is run, the first instruction to execute is always the first executable instruction coded after the open brace on line 4. In programming jargon this statement is said to be the program entry point, and all programming languages designate a location in the program template to be the program's entry (starting) point. By default, the program statements that follow the program entry point usually execute sequentially in the order they appear in the program.

If an Integrated Development Environment (IDE) is being used to compose a program, it will normally ask for the name of the program (or project). Then the IDE generates the code template with the phrase `ProgramName` on line 1 replaced with the program's name. In addition to the seven lines shown in the top of Figure 2.1, some IDEs add several other lines to the template, the most common of which is a statement on line 5 to output the phrase "Hello World." However, for the template to be grammatically correct, all IDEs will include the seven lines shown in the top portion of Figure 2.1.

## 2.2 VARIABLES

Most programs process data that is input to the program. For example, a program may compute the sum of two input bank deposits. To be processed, data must be stored in the memory of the computer system. All programming languages contain statements for defining *variables,* which are memory cells that can store one piece of data. Before a variable can be used in a Java program, it must first be declared. When a variable is defined, or declared in a program, the programmer assigns it a name and designates the type of information to be stored in the cell. For example, a variable named `deposit` could be used to store the amount of a deposit, in which case its type would be a number with a fractional part.

| Definition |
|---|
| A **variable** is a named memory cell that can store a specific type of data. |
| Variables must be declared before they can be used. |

In Java, valid variable names must begin with a letter and cannot contain spaces. After the first letter, the remaining characters can be letters, digits, or an underscore. They cannot be Java keywords. (See Appendix D.) Variable names that do not follow these rules are invalid and are identified by the Java translator as syntax (grammatical) errors. Good coding style dictates that variables begin with a lowercase letter, and new words in the variable name begin with an uppercase letter. In addition, the name of the variable should be representative of the data item being stored in the memory cell yet be as brief as possible. For example, a variable used to store the balance of my savings account could be named `myBalance`.

Good choices for variable names make our programs more readable. The variables on the left side of Figure 2.2 are well composed: they are syntactically correct, use good naming conventions, and imply what they store. The variable names on the right side of the figure are not well composed, concise, or meaningful.

| Well Composed | Poorly Composed |
|---|---|
| firstName | Fst |
| deposit1 | theFirstOftheBankDeposits |
| myBalance | mb |
| **Valid** | **Invalid** |
| zipCode | zip  Code |
| phoneNum | phone# |
| grade1 | 1stGrade |

**Figure 2.2**
Variable names.

The information stored in a memory cell can change or vary during the execution of the program (which is why these storage cells are call variables). However, once designated, the *type* of the information stored in the memory cell (e.g., a number with a fractional part) cannot be changed.

In Java, there are two kinds of variables: **primitive** variables and **reference** variables. The type of data stored in primitive variables can be a single numeric data value, one character, or one Boolean truth value. Reference variables store RAM memory addresses. The grammar, or syntax, used to declare a primitive variable is the same grammar used to declare a reference variable. In the next section, we will discuss this syntax and the use of primitive variables in our programs. The use of reference variables will be discussed in Section 2.5.

> ### Definition
>
> **Primitive variables** store one numeric value, one character, or one truth value.
>
> **Reference variables** store memory addresses.

## 2.3 PRIMITIVE VARIABLES

The Java statement used to declare a variable begins with the type of the information stored in the variable, said to be the variable's *type*, followed by the name of the variable. Like all Java statements, variable declaration statements end with a semicolon. Optionally, the declaration statement can also include the value to be initially stored in the variable. If the initial value is not specified within the variable declaration statement, the variable is set to a default value. Default values are dependent on the type of information stored in the variable. For example, the statements

```
double deposit;
double price = 5.21;
```

declare the variables named `deposit` and `price`, with `deposit` initialized to the default value 0.0 and `price` initialized to the value 5.21. The word **double** is a *keyword* in Java.

In programming languages, keywords are words that have special meaning to the translator that translates program statements into the language of the computer system. The keyword **double** means that the memory cell being defined will store a number with a fractional part and the size of the storage cell will be 8 bytes (64 bits). Table 2.1 gives the keywords used to specify the type of a primitive variable. The size of the storage cell implied by the use of the keywords is also given. As noted in the table, the keywords used to declare integer and real numeric types are different, and the size of the storage cell limits the numeric range and precision of the stored numeric value.

When storage is not at a premium, it is best to use the type `int` for integer variables because most programs deal with integers within the range -2,147,483,648 to +2,147,483,647. This range of values can be fetched with the following lines of code:

```
int min = Integer.MIN_VALUE;
int max = Integer.MAX_VALUE;
```

If a data item were beyond this range, it would not be properly represented in an `int` variable. For integer values beyond this range, the type `long` should be used. Integer data beyond the range

**Table 2.1**

Primitive Data Types

| Data Type | Keyword | Cell Size (bytes) | Range and Precision |
|---|---|---|---|
| | `byte` | 1 | -128 to +127 |
| | `short` | 2 | -32,768 to +32,767 |
| Integer Numeric | `int` | 4 | -2,147,483,648 to +2,147,483,647 |
| | `long` | 8 | -9,223, 372,036,854,775,808 to +9,223, 372,036,854,775,807 |
| Real Numeric | `float` | 4 | ±1.40129846432481707 E-45  to ±3.4028234663852886 E+38  *(7 digits of precision)* |
| | `double` | 8 | ±4.94065645841246544 E-324  to ±1.797693134862157 E+308  *(15 digits of precision)* |
| Truth Value | `boolean` | 1 | `true` or `false` |
| One Character | `char` | 2 | Upper and lowercase keyboard characters and other entities  (see Appendix C) |

of the type long (see the 4th row right column of Table 2.1, or code `Long.MIN_VALUE` and/or `Long.MAX_VALUE`) cannot be stored in a primitive variable. The Java API class `BigInteger` provides a remedy for this situation and will be discussed in Chapter 7, "Methods and Objects: A Second Look."

When storage is not at a premium, it is best to use the type **double** for variables that will store real numbers (numbers with fractional or decimal parts) because the range of the real numbers processed by a program is usually within the range of the type **double**. As is the case for large integers, Java provides an API class (`BigDouble`) for storing real numbers whose range exceeds that of a double. In addition, because numeric literals, (e.g., 1.5) are represented as type `double`, an `f` (for `float`) must be added to the end of an initial value in a float variable declaration to inform the translator that the loss of precision is acceptable:

```
float change = 1.5f;
```

When the initial value of a character variable is specified, it is enclosed in single quotation marks, and the initial values of Boolean variables begin with a lowercase letter:

```
char myFirstIntial = 'W';
boolean isRaining = false;
```

Multiple variables of the same type can be declared in a single Java statement. The variables are separated by commas, and the statement cannot include initial values:

```
short n1, n2, n3;
```

```
boolean isRaining, isSnowing;
char letter1, letter2, digit1, digit2;
```

When initial values are not specified in a variable declaration statement, the variables are set to default values. The default value for the integer types (**byte**, **short**, **int**, and **long**) is zero, and the default value for the real types (**float** and **double**) is 0.0. For the Boolean type (**boolean**), the default value is **false**, and for the character type (**char**), it is `''`. The values **true** and **false** are Java keywords.

When the keyword **final** is included in the declaration of a variable, the value it stores cannot be changed during the execution of the program. It is considered to be good programming to use this keyword when we declare constants for use in our programs. For example:

```
final int DEGREES_PER_CIRCLE = 360;
final double DENSITY_OF_WATER = 62.4; //pounds per cubic foot
```

It is also considered to be good programming practice to use all upper case letters in the names of final variables with an underscore separating words.

## 2.4 SYSTEM CONSOLE OUTPUT

The system console is a window that a program can use to communicate with the user of the program. When information flows from the program to the system-console window, we say that the program is performing output. Conversely, when the information flow is from the system-console window to the program, we say the program is performing input. For brevity, these information transfers are referred to as console input and console output, respectively, or more simply console I/O. In this section, we will discuss console output, and console input will be discussed in Chapter 4 "Boolean Expressions, Making Decisions, and Disk I/O."

The two Java statements used to perform output to the system console are:

```
System.out.print( );
System.out.println( );
```

Like all Java executable statements, they both end with a semicolon. The output item, which is referred to as an argument, is coded inside the statement's open and close parentheses. The only difference between these two statements is that the first one leaves the console's cursor at the end of the output item, and the second one positions it at the beginning of the next line.

### 2.4.1 String Output

Technically speaking, the item to be output must be a sequence of characters, which in programming languages is called a *string* (e.g., This is Console Output). In Java, strings can either be *string literals* or `String` objects. String objects will be discussed in Section 2.5.

String literals are strings enclosed in double quotes. To output "*This is Console Output*" we would code the string literal `"This is Console Output"` inside the parentheses of a console output statement. The following code fragment would display two lines of output:

```
System.out.println("This is Console Output");
```

```
System.out.print   ("from the program");
```

The first line would contain *This is Console Output*, and the second line would contain *from the program*. Because the second line is a `print` statement, the console's cursor would appear on the second line just after the word program.

### 2.4.2 The Concatenation Operator and Annotated Numeric Output

The concatenation operator, which is coded as a plus (+) sign, can be used to combine two strings into one. The statement

```
System.out.println("Hello" + "World");
```

produces the output *Hello World* to the system console. Before the output is performed, the first string literal, containing the word `"Hello"`, is combined with the second string literal `"World"`. The resulting string, `"Hello  World"`, is then output to the console. There is no limit to the number of string literals that can be combined using concatenation operators to produce the string argument output by the `print` and `println` methods. The statement

```
System.out.println("Hello" + "World," + " I'm Bill.");
```

produces the console output *Hello World, I'm Bill.*

To make the output of numeric data more meaningful and user-friendly, the output should always be identified or annotated. For example, the output *The price is $5.21* is much more informative than the output *5.21* The annotation *The price is $* can be included in the output using the concatenation operator.

```
System.out.println("The price is $" + price);
```

The Java translator interprets the plus sign used in this context as the concatenation operator because the item to its left is a string literal. It will fetch the contents of the variable `price`, convert it to a string, and then concatenate that string with the previous string literal. The resulting console output is "The price is $5.21."

In Section 3.5.4 we will see that if `price` were the name of an object, the concatenation operator would perform a similar conversion of the object to a string using a method named `toString`.

Because there is no limit to the number of string literals that can be combined to produce the string argument of the `println` and `print` methods, the annotated contents of several variables can be output to the console using one console output statement. The console output *The price of the 10 items is $5.21.* is produced by the code fragment:

```
int quantity = 10;
double price = 5.21;
System.out.println( "The price of the " + quantity +
                    " items is $" + price + ".");
```

The indentation in the above `System.out.println` statement has been used to improve its readability. It prevents the statement from going beyond the eightieth column and is considered good programming practice.

### 2.4.3 Escape Sequences

It is often necessary to output strings containing characters that have special meaning to the Java translator. For example, a double quotation mark (") is meant either to begin or end a string literal, and a single quote (') is meant to begin or end a character literal. Suppose we wanted to output *Joe said, "Hello"* followed by a period. To be grammatically correct in English, the word Hello has quotes around it because it is something Joe said. However, the output statement

```
System.out.println("Joe said, "Hello".");
```

would result in a syntax error because a double quotation mark in Java is meant to be either the beginning or end of a string literal. Therefore, the translator would assume the quotation mark preceding the word `Hello` was meant to terminate the string literal, which began with the quotation mark preceding the word `Joe`. Under this assumption, the translator expects the next character to be a close parenthesis followed by a semicolon, or a concatenation operator. Instead, it finds the character `H`, which produces a syntax error.

To solve this problem, Java provides escape sequences, which are a sequence of two characters coded inside a string literal. The first character in the sequence is always the backslash (\) character. When the translator encounters a backslash inside a string literal, it always considers this to be the beginning of an escape sequence and effectively looks up the meaning of the escape sequence, given in Table 2.2. In other words, the backslash tells the translator to **escape** from its normal way of interpreting this backslash and the next character, and instead look into the table of escape sequences for the meaning of these two characters.

For example the escape sequence \" (coded inside a string literal) means don't interpret the quotation mark as the beginning or end of a string literal but output a quotation mark. Therefore, the syntactically correct way to output the sentence *Joe said, "Hello".* is:

```
System.out.printlin("Joe said, \"Hello\".");
```

Now the quotation mark preceding the `H` in `Hello` is part of the escape sequence to output a quotation mark. It is not interpreted as the close of the string literal, which began with the quotation mark preceding the word `Joe`. Another escape sequence is coded after the `o` in `Hello` for the same reason. Proceeding to the right in the string literal, the translator encounters the quotation mark that follows the period, which it correctly interprets as the close of the string literal.

Because a backslash inside a string literal is interpreted as the beginning of an escape sequence, one obvious question is "how would we output a backslash?" The answer is that there is an escape sequence for outputting a backslash, which is a double backslash. The statement

```
System.out.println("Down \\/    Up /\\");
produces the output:   Down ∨    Up ∧
```

The escape sequence \' is used to output a single quotation mark, and the escape sequence \n causes the cursor to move to a new line before completing the output. The escape sequence \t tabs the cursor to the right; this is useful when you want output to appear in columns. A list of the escape sequences is shown in Table 2.2.

**Table 2.2**

Escape Sequences

| Escape Sequence | Sequence Name | Meaning |
|---|---|---|
| \" | Double quote | Output the double quotation mark (") character |
| \\ | Backslash | Output the backslash (\) character |
| \' | Single quote | Output the single quotation mark (') character |
| \b | Backspace | Move the cursor back one character position |
| \t | Horizontal tab | Move the cursor to the next horizontal tab position |
| \n | New line | Move the cursor to beginning of the next line |
| \r | Carriage return | Move the cursor to beginning of the current line |
| \f | New page (form feed) | Move the cursor to the top left of the next page |

The application shown in Figure 2.3 illustrates the declaration and initialization of primitive variables and the use of string literals and escape sequences to output the data stored in these variables. The program's outputs are included in the figure after the program's code.

```java
1    public class ConsoleOutput
2    {
3      public static void main(String[] args)
4      {
5        // Primitive variable declarations
6        int age = 21;
7        double weight = 185.25;
8        boolean isRaining = false;
9        char letter1 = 'A';
10
11       System.out.println("The Program's Output Appears Below");
12       System.out.println("\t\t\"Hello World!\"");
13       System.out.print("\nJohn is " + age + " years old");
14       System.out.println(" and weighs " + weight + " pounds");
15       System.out.println("Today it is " + isRaining +
16                          " that it is raining\n");
17       System.out.println("The first letter of the alphabet is " +
18                          letter1);
19
20       System.out.println("1/2 + 1/4 = 3/4");//blank lines are ignored
21     }
22  }
```

**Program Output**

The Program's Output Appears Below
        "Hello World!"

> John is 21 years old and weighs 185.25 pounds
> Today it is false that it is raining
>
> The first letter of the alphabet is A
> 1/2 + 1/4 = 3/4

**Figure 2.3**
The application **ConsoleOutput** and the output it produces.

 **TIP** It is good coding style to declare all variables at the beginning of a program.

Lines 6-9 declare and initialize four different types of primitive variables. Lines 11 and 12 produce the first two lines of the program's output. Each statement contains one string literal. The string literal on line 12 begins with two tab escape sequences, which are used to center the second line of output under the first. In addition, `Hello World!` coded on line 12, is surrounded by two double-quote escape sequences, which produces the quotation marks on the second output line.

Lines 13–18 output the variables declared and initialized on lines 6-9. A new-line escape sequence begins the first string literal on line 13, which produces the blank line that precedes the third line of text output. Two concatenation operators are used on line 13 to combine the two string literals and the contents of the variable `age` after it is converted to a string. Line 14 uses similar operations to annotate the output of John's age and weight. The output displayed by lines 13 and 14 appear on the same line because line 13 uses a `print` rather than a `println` statement. As a result, the cursor is not advanced to the beginning of the next line after line 13 completes execution, which causes the output produced by line 14 to begin immediately after the word old. One subtlety on line 14 of the program is that its string literal begins with a space. This space becomes the space that separates the word *old* from the word and in the output produced by lines 13 and 14.

Lines 15-16 produce the next line of output, which contains the string version of the contents of the Boolean variable `isRaining`. They also produce the next blank line of output because the last string literal ends in a new-line escape sequence. The final two lines of output are produced by lines 17-18, which output the contents of the character variable `letter1`, and line 20, which outputs a single string literal.

### Comments and Blank Lines

Line 5 of the program contains a single-line comment. A single-line comment begins with two forward slashes (//) and is terminated by a new line (`Enter`) keystroke. Comments are added to a program to improve the program's readability; they are ignored by the translator.

 **TIP** It is good practice to include comments in your program to describe the portions that are not obvious to the reader.

A second comment appears at the end of line 20, stating blank lines (e.g., lines 10 and 19) in a program are ignored by the translator. It is good programming practice to separate major portions of a program with a blank line. This technique, like comments, improves the readability of a program. We will see more examples of the use of blank lines in a program later in this chapter.

## 2.5  STRING OBJECTS AND REFERENCE VARIABLES

As previously mentioned, in Java there are two kinds of variables: primitive variables and reference variables. Primitive variables store numeric, character, or Boolean data values. Reference variables store memory addresses. These addresses are the addresses of memory resident programming constructs called objects, and the contents of a reference variable is used to locate a particular object. We say they refer to an object, which is how they get their name, reference variables.

Suppose that we were writing a program and we wanted store the string `John` in memory. Based on what we have learned about primitive variables, we should declare a string variable, perhaps named `firstName`, and then initialize it to the string `"John"`. Unfortunately, Java does not contain string type variables, so the statement

```
string firstName = "John";   // error
```

is grammatically incorrect. However, there are `String` objects in Java. A `String` object can store a sequence of characters, and the address of the object can be stored in a reference variable. We begin by declaring a `String` reference variable that will store the address of our String object. Then we store the address of a newly created `String` object, containing the string `"John"` in the reference variable:

```
String firstName;
firstName = new String("John");
```

As we will learn in Chapter 3 "Methods, Classes and Objects: A First Look," this two-line grammar can be used to create objects in any class. For example, `Starship` objects, `Snowman` objects, or `Paddle` objects can be created simply by replacing the word `String` on both lines with the class names `Starship`, `Snowman`, or `Paddle`, and replacing the string "John" with something more relevant to these objects. The first line creates an uninitialized reference variable that, like uninitialized primitive variables, is set to a default value. The default value for reference variables is **null**. When the variable is a `String` reference variable, we say that the reference variable stores the **null** string.

 "String s contains the null string," means that s stores a **null** value.

Because strings are so commonly used in programs, Java provides a simplified one-line grammar for creating and initializing `String` objects:

```
String firstName = "John";
```

 *The abbreviated grammar to declare a string* `String` *object is:*
*String referenceVariableName = intialStringLiteralValue;*

This one-line grammar can only be used to create `String` objects and is modeled on the grammar used to declare and initialize primitive variables. Although the grammar is very similar, we must keep in mind that unlike the primitive variable `age`, initialized to store the value `21` on line 6 of Figure 2.3, the reference variable `firstName` is not initialized to the string `"John"`. Rather, the reference variable `firstName` stores the address of and refers to the `String` object that is initialized to the string `"John"`. Figure 2.4 shows the statements used to allocate memory to primitive variables and objects/reference variables. The arrow in the figure indicates that the reference variable `firstName` refers, or points, to the object.

**Figure 2.4**
Memory allocated to primitive variables and objects/reference variables.

In addition to providing a simplified grammar for creating `String` objects, Java also provides a simplified grammar for outputting the strings contained inside these objects. Once again, it is modeled after the grammar used to output primitive variables. To output the string contained in a `String` object, we simply code the name of the variable that refers to the object. For example, the following code fragment produces the output *My name is John Smith, my age is 21* on the system console:

```
int age = 21;
String firstName = "John";
String lastName = "Smith";
System.out.print ("My name is " + firstName  + " " + lastName);
System.out.println (", my age is "  +  age);
```

The differences between the way Java stores primitive data items and string data items can be ignored when writing variable declaration statements and output statements. As we will see in Chapter 3, these differences cannot be ignored for any other kind of object.

## 2.6 CALCULATIONS AND THE MATH CLASS

The first operational computers were used by mathematicians to compute the values of equations, which is how they obtained their name *computers*, and a significant portion of the processing that modern computers perform is still calculations. Java, like most programming languages, provides the ability to perform basic arithmetic calculations and provides additional features to perform more complex calculations. This section begins with a discussion of how to incorporate basic arithmetic calculations into a Java program and then discusses how to incorporate commonly used mathematical constants and functions into these calculations.

### 2.6.1 Arithmetic Calculations and the Rules of Precedence

Arithmetic calculations are performed in Java using arithmetic expressions. Arithmetic expressions consist of a series of operands separated by operators. In the simplest case, the operands are numeric constants, and the operators are the four arithmetic operators: add subtract, multiply, and divide. For example, $10 + 21 - 5$ is a simple arithmetic expression that evaluates to 26. Generally, simple arithmetic expressions are evaluated from left to right. The addition would therefore be performed before the subtraction.

The symbols used for the four arithmetic operators are given in Table 2.3. The third entry in the table, the modulo (or mod) operator, is used to find the remainder in division. For example, $14 \% 3$ evaluates to 2. All of the operators can be used with integer or real operands.

**Table 2.3**
The Java Symbols for the Arithmetic Operators (In Order of Precedence)

| Arithmetic Operation | Java Symbol |
|---|---|
| multiply | * |
| divide | / |
| Modulo or mod | % |
| add | + |
| subtract | - |

In addition to numeric constants, called numeric literals, operands can be the names of variables that store numeric values. When a memory cell name is used in an arithmetic expression, the value stored in the memory cell is fetched, substituted for the memory cell name, and the arithmetic expression is evaluated. For example, given the variable declarations:

```java
int x = 10;
int y = 29;
int z = 5;
```

the arithmetic expression $x + y - z$ evaluates to 34. A mix of numeric literals and memory cell names can be used as the operands in any arithmetic expression, so the expression $x + 29 - z$ is a valid arithmetic expression that also evaluates to 34.

An arithmetic operation performed on two integers always results in an integer value, and an arithmetic operation performed on two real values always results in a real value. When one operand is an integer and the other is a real value, the result is always a real value, and the arithmetic is referred to as *mixed mode* arithmetic. Before mixed mode arithmetic is performed, the integer value is converted to a real value (e.g., 10 becomes 10.0).

If an arithmetic expression coded in a program contains division ($/$), the divisor cannot be zero when the expression is evaluated by the Java Virtual Machine. That is it cannot be the name of a memory cell that stores the value zero, or a math expression that evaluates to zero, or the numeric literals 0 or 0.0. If it is, the program's execution will be terminated by the Java Runtime Environment, which will output the following error message when the operands are integers:

```
Exception in thread "main" java.lang.ArithmeticException: / by zero
```

The attempt during the program's execution to divide by zero is said to have caused the Java Runtime Environment to produce, or "throw", an `ArithmeticException` error. A more in depth discussion of exceptions is given in Section 4.9.

### Integer Division

When the two operands are integers and division is performed, the results are sometimes surprising. That is because the division of two integers always produces an integer result that is truncated and not rounded. For example, given the variable declarations

```java
int x = 10;
int y = 29;
int z = 5;
```

the following arithmetic expressions would evaluate to the values on the far right side of each expression:

x / z = 10 / 5 = 2
y / x = 29 / 10 = 2  (0.9 lost, due to truncation)
z / x = 5 / 10 = 0  (the most surprising result, 0.5 is truncated to zero)

### Precedence Rules

Consider the arithmetic expression 10 + 6 − 2. The expression evaluates to 14 whether we perform the addition first (16-2) or the subtraction first (10+4). Similarly, the expression 10 * 6/2 evaluates to 30 whether we perform the multiplication first (60/2) or the division first (10*3). In both cases, the value of the expressions is independent of the order in which we apply the arithmetic operators. In general, if an expression contains just addition and subtraction operators, or contains just multiplication and division operators, then the evaluation of the expression is independent of the order in which we apply the arithmetic operators. Java considers these expressions to be simple arithmetic expressions and, as previously stated, they are evaluated from left to right.

This is not the case for arithmetic expressions that mix addition and/or subtraction operators with multiplication and/or division operators. Consider the expression 10 + 6 * 2, which performs addition and multiplication. If we perform the addition first, the expression evaluates to 32 (16 * 2), but if the multiplication is done first it evaluates to 22 (10 + 12). The arithmetic expression appears to be ambiguous. Fortunately, mathematicians have stipulated a way of resolving the ambiguity called the *rules of precedence*. These rules state that multiplication and division are performed before, or take precedence over, addition and subtraction. Using this rule, the expression 10 + 6 * 2 evaluates to 22.

Operators that are performed first, such as multiplication and division, are said to have higher precedence. Table 2.3 lists the arithmetic operators in high-to-low precedence order, with multiplication and division being the highest precedence operators in the table, and addition and subtraction the lowest. The expression 5 * 7 % 2 would evaluate to 1 because multiplication is of higher precedence than the mod operator. Java contains other operators, for example logic operators, and each Java operator has been assigned a precedence level. A complete list of Java operators and their assigned precedence level is given in Appendix E.

> **NOTE** *Java evaluates arithmetic expressions using this mathematical rule of precedence: multiplication and division are performed before modulo (mod) operations, which are performed before addition and subtraction operations.*

If we wanted the addition or subtraction in an arithmetic expression to be performed before multiplication or division, we would use a set of parentheses to override the precedence rules. The expression (10 + 6) * 2 would evaluate to 32. To average the numbers 2, 4, and 6, we would write (2 + 4 + 6) / 3, which would evaluate to the correct average 4 = 12 / 3. (Without the parentheses, only the 6 would be divided by the 3 because the division operation would be performed first.)

> **NOTE** *Parentheses override the rules of precedence.*

In summary, the parts of an arithmetic expression inside parentheses are evaluated first using the rules of precedence to determine the order of the operations. If the operators are of equal precedence, they are evaluated from left to right. The following example, which contains a set of nested parentheses and evaluates to 36, illustrates this process.

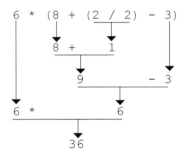

## 2.6.2 The Assignment Operator and Assignment Statements

In Section 2.3, we learned that a variable named `price` could be declared and initialized to the value 5.21 by coding:

```
double price = 5.21;
```

The equals (=) symbol used in this declaration is called the *assignment operator* because it assigns values to memory cells. In this case, the memory cell named `price` is assigned the value 5.21. Although the statement should be read as "double price *is assigned* 5.21," most programmers would read it as "double price *equals* 5.21," which is unfortunate because (as we will see) the operator does not represent the mathematical concept of equality. Rather, it represents the flow of the data value on its right side (in the above statement, 5.21) into the memory cell named on its left side, (in the above statement, `price`).

### Assignment Statements

In addition to being used to initialize variables in a declaration statement, the assignment operator is also used in statements that reassign (actually overwrite) the contents of memory cells previously declared in a program. These statements are called assignment statements. For example, after the following two statements execute, the variable `price` stores the value `6.25`.

```
double price = 5.21;
price = 6.25;
```

In addition to being a numeric literal, the entity on the right side of the assignment operator can be an arithmetic expression. For example:

```
answer = x + 21 - z;
```

When this is the case, we should realize that the execution of the statement is performed in three steps:

1. *Fetch* the contents of the variables coded on the right side of the assignment operator from memory and substitute these values into the arithmetic expression
2. *Evaluate* the arithmetic expression considering parentheses and the rules of precedence
3. *Store* the value of the arithmetic expression in the memory cell coded on the left side of the assignment operator

In an assignment statement, the item on the left side of the assignment operator must be the name of a variable. The statement cannot be reversed by placing the name of the variable on the right side of the assignment operator. That is,

```
answer = x + 21 - z;
```

is *not* the same as

```
answer = x + 21 - z;
```

The second expression will produce a syntax error. Armed with this understanding, the assignment statement (which is probably executed on a person's birthday)

```
age = age + 1;
```

will increase the value stored in the memory cell `age` by one. In addition, a mathematician would now understand that the assignment operator does not represent equality and would not run from this statement in horror proclaiming that nothing (in this case age) could be equal to itself plus one. Surveys of programs conducted in the 1970s indicate that 47% of the statements contained in programs are assignment statements, so this is an important concept to understand.

## Additional Assignment Operators

There are five additional operators each of which combines the assignment operator (=) with one of the five math operators show in Table 2.3. As shown in the lower right portion of Appendix E, they are coded as: +=, -=, *=, /=, and %=. These operators can be used to write assignment statements that perform addition, subtraction, multiplication, division, or modulo arithmetic more succinctly. For example, the following statements are equivalent:

```
count += 1;       is equivalent to   count = count + 1;
total -= 6.0;     is equivalent to   total = total - 6.0;
price *= 1.2;     is equivalent to   price = price * 1.2;
price /= 1.2;     is equivalent to   price = price / 1.2;
```

```
index %= 6607;          is equivalent to     index = index % 6607;
```

As implied in the above examples, these operators should only be used when the variable being assigned (i.e. the variable on the left side of the operator) is intended to be the first operand in the arithmetic expression on the right side of the operator. To illustrate this point, consider the below statements in which the variable being assigned is intended to be the second operand in the arithmetic expression.

```
double total = 24.0;
total = 6.0 - total;
```

After the two statements execute, the variable total would store the value minus 18. If the second statement was coded using the -= operator as shown below, the variable total would store a different value after they execute: *plus* 18.

```
double total = 24.0;
total -= 6.0; // which is equivalent to: total = total - 6.0;
```

As with any assignment statement, the arithmetic expression on the right side of the operator can contain more than one term. When this is the case, the variable on the left side of the operator still becomes the first operand in the arithmetic expression on the right side of the assignment operator. For example, the third statement in the below sequence of statements is equivalent to total = total + 6.0 / two; which, when we consider the rules of precedence, evaluates to 27.

```
double two = 2.0;
double total = 24.0;
total += 6.0 / two ;
```

### 2.6.3 Promotion and Casting

Generally speaking, the type of the value being assigned to a variable should match the type of the variable. When this is not the case, the Java translator checks this to make sure that there is no chance that part of the value being assigned to the variable could be lost when the value is stored in the variable. For example, if a real number (e.g., 2.7) was assigned to an integer-type variable, the fractional part of the value (0.7) would be lost. As a result, the statement below produces the translation error "possible loss of precision," because it assigns a double value (2.7) to an integer memory cell.

```
int newValue = 2.7;
```

 Avoid assigning a numeric with a fractional part (e.g., types float and double) to an integer type variable because it will generate a translation error.

This statement does not produce a syntax error because performing an arithmetic operation on two integers (21 / 10) always results in an integer (in this case, 21 / 10 = 2).

```
int newValue = 21/10;
```

The Java translator also checks assignment statements to determine if the value being assigned to the variable, coded on the left side of the assignment operator, is within the variable's range. As shown in the right column of Table 2.1, the range of the numeric values that can be stored in a numeric variable depends on its type. Within the four integer types, the type `long` has the largest numeric range, and within the real types, the type `double` has the largest range.

The progression shown in Figure 2.5 summarizes the valid assignments between types (those that will not result in a loss of precision and guarantees that the range of the variable being assigned is large enough to store the value assigned to it). A valid assignment is when the type of the variable being assigned is to the left of the type of the value being assigned to it (e.g., a `double` variable can be assigned `int` values). When this is the case, we say that the value has been promoted to the type of the variable.

| | | | | | | | | | | | |
|---|---|---|---|---|---|---|---|---|---|---|---|
| double | ← | float | ← | long | ← | int | ← | short | ← | byte ← char |

Note: a valid promotion is from right to left (←)

**Figure 2.5**
Valid promotions of numeric types.

Although the types of the variables used in the code fragment in the assignment statements below are not the same, they are valid because they follow the promotion order given in Figure 2.5.

```java
byte aByte = 20;
char a = 'a';
int anInt;
double aDouble;
anInt = aByte;
anInt = a;
aDouble = aByte;
aDouble = anInt;
```

## Mixed Mode Arithmetic Expressions

Mixed mode arithmetic expressions are expressions in which the operands are not of the same type. To evaluate the terms of these expressions, the operand whose type is further to the right in Figure 2.5 is promoted to the type of the other operand, the term is evaluated, and the resulting value is in the promoted type. For example, the following code fragment contains a mixed mode arithmetic expression:

```java
double salary = 523.56;
float raise = 1.1f;
salary = 10 + salary * raise;
```

The arithmetic expression in the assignment statement contains an integer literal, a **double** variable, and a **float** variable. During the evaluation of this expression, the value stored in `raise` would be converted to a double, and then the multiplication operation would be performed. The result would be a double value. That value would then be added to the integer literal 10 after it was converted to double. The resulting double value would be assigned to the variable `salary`.

## Casting

One use of the word casting is the process of turning an entity into something it is not. For example, a frail mild-mannered actor could be *cast* into the role of a professional wrestler. In computer science, the term is used to describe the process of changing the type of a value to another type.

Changing the type of a variable or numeric literal in mixed mode arithmetic expressions previously discussed is an example of automatic casting. Even when an arithmetic expression is not a mixed-mode expression, there are times when it is desirable to cast operands into other types before the expression is evaluated. For example, a value that is an integer variable could be cast into a real value before it is used in an arithmetic expression. This is a very common use of casting.

Consider the calculation of the ratio of two integer variables n1 and n2.

```
int n1 = 111;
int n2 = 10;
double ratio = n1 / n2;
```

The arithmetic expression will evaluate to an integer because both operands are integers. As a result, we will lose the factional part of the ratio, and the variable ratio will be assigned 11.0.

A situation that is more confusing is illustrated in the code fragment below. The integer denominator (100) is larger than the integer numerator (90). In this case, the variable ratio is always assigned 0.0.

```
int numberOfStudents = 100;
int numberPassing = 90;
double ratio = numberPassing / numberOfStudents;
```

To retain the factional part of a value calculated by dividing to integers, we change, or cast, the type of one of the operands into one of the real types (double or float). The syntax of this nonautomatic casting is to enclose the numeric type into which the operand is being cast inside of parentheses. The following fragment uses casting to change the fetched contents of the variable n1 into a double before the arithmetic operation is performed. The outer set of parentheses in the third statement is necessary because arithmetic operators take precedence over casting.

```
int n1 = 111;
int n2 = 10;
double ratio = ((double) n1) / n2;
```

After casting is performed, the arithmetic expression involves a double value (111.0) and an integer variable (n2): a mixed mode expression. Automatic casting then converts n2 to a double, and then the division is performed that produces a double (11.1). The value 11.1 is assigned to ratio. In this code fragment, ratio would be assigned the value 0.9.

```
int numberOfStudents = 100;
int numberPassing = 90;
double ratio = ((double) numberPassing) / numberOfStudents;
```

**NOTE**  *Arithmetic operators take precedence over nonautomatic casting.*

Another common use of casting is to inform the translator that you want to violate the promotion-only rules it imposes on assignment statements, shown in Figure 2.5. If we wanted the integer part of a double value to be assigned to an integer variable, we would use casting. The following statements assign the value 1 to the integer variable age:

```java
double daysSinceBirth = 401.5;
int age = (int) daysSinceBirth / 365;
```

The mixed mode arithmetic in the second statement produces the value 1.1, which the casting converts to an integer (1) before it is assigned to the variable age. If the casting were left out of the second statement, it would not translate because it would be a violation of the promotion rules given in Figure 2.5. This use of casting informs the translator that we are intentionally violating these rules.

Casting can also be used to round a floating-point number to the nearest integer. If the variable x stores a positive floating-point number, this can be accomplished with the following line of code:

```java
int age = (int) (x + 0.5);    // truncates for fractional parts
                              // less than 0.5
```

The analogous line of code for negative floating point numbers is:

```java
int age = (int) (x - 0.5);    // truncates for fractional
                              // parts less than 0.5
```

### 2.6.4 The Math Class

If we were to examine the code of applications written by several different programmers, we would quickly come to the realization that mathematical calculations, such as raising a number to a power or calculating the square root of a number, are performed in many programs. For example, a program that computes the radius of a circle given its area would divide the area by the constant PI, and then take the square root of the result. Obviously, the accuracy of the calculation is dependent on a precise value of PI. In addition, because the square root is not one of the mathematical operators available in most programming languages, the programmer would have to know the algorithm for computing the square root of a number using the math operators available in the programming language.

To facilitate the coding of programs that use common mathematical constants and calculations, Java, like most programming languages, provides precoded libraries containing these constants and mathematical functions. The constants are coded as initialized variables, and the mathematical functions are coded into subprograms. In Java, subprograms are called *methods*, and related methods and variables are collected into **classes**. As discussed in Section 1.5.1, the collection of the precoded classes available in Java is called the Java Application Programming Interface, or Java API. A complete description of the classes contained in the API, is available online. To locate this documentation, simply type "Java API Specification" into the search window of your browser.

The API class that contains mathematical constants and methods is called the Math class. Table 2.4 lists a mathematical constant and some of the most commonly used methods that are included in this class. The third column of the table gives a series of assignment statements that illustrate the use of the class's constants and methods. Notice that the name of the Math class followed by a dot precedes the name of the constant or method used in the statement. The angles used in the trigonometric functions that appear in the last three rows must be expressed in radians. The methods compute and return a value, which the coding examples in the rightmost column of the table assign to a variable.

**Table 2.4**
Commonly Used Math Class Constants and Methods

| Constant or Method | Description | Coding Example |
|---|---|---|
| `PI` | The ratio of the circumference of a circle to its diameter (a `double`) | area = Math.PI * r * r; |
| `abs` | Computes and returns the absolute value of a number, n (returns the type it is sent) | nAbsolute = Math.abs(n); |
| `pow` | Computes and returns a number, n, raised to the power p (returns a `double`) | nToTheP = Math.pow(n, p); |
| `sqrt` | Computes and returns the square root of a number, n (returns a `double`) | rootN = Math.sqrt(n); |
| `toRadians` | Converts an angle, a, in degrees to radians (returns a `double`) | aRads = Math.toRadians(a); |
| `sin` | Computes and returns the sine of an angle, aRads, specified in *radians* | sinA = Math.sin(aRads); |
| `cos` | Computes and returns the cosine of an angle, aRads, specified in *radians* | cosA = Math.cos(aRads); |
| `tan` | Computes and returns the tangent of an angle, aRads, specified in *radians* | tanA = Math.tan(aRads); |

The following code fragment calculates and outputs the sine of 45 degrees and 2 raised to the third power:

```
double angle = 45.0;
double angleInRadians = Math.toRadians(angle); //returns a double
double sineOfAngle = Math.sin(angleInRadians); //returns a double

System.out.println("The sine of " + angle + " is " + sineOfAngle);
System.out.println("2 cubed = " + Math.pow(2, 3));
```

## Random Numbers

"A random number is a number generated by a process whose outcome is unpredictable and which cannot be subsequently reliably reproduced."[2] Random numbers are used in many computer applications such as game programs, encryption programs, and simulation programs. For example, flight simulator programs used to train pilots to react to air turbulence introduce turbulence into the flight at random times during the simulation.

The Math class contains a method named `random` that can be used to generate pseudorandom numbers. The numbers are not truly random because the sequence of numbers the method generates is based on the computer's real-time clock (i.e., the time of day) resolved to one millisecond, and therefore can be reliably reproduced.

The method returns a double in the range: $0.0 \leq$ randomNumber $< 1.0$. (The highest number generated by the method is always less than 1.0.) The following code fragment outputs two random numbers in that range. The specific numbers output would depend on the time of day the code fragment was executed.

```
double randomNumber;
randomNumber = Math.random();
System.out.println(randomNumber);
randomNumber = Math.random();
System.out.println(randomNumber);
```

The method can be used to generate numbers in the range: $min \leq randomNumber < max$ using the assignment statements:

```
double randomNumber1 = min + Math.random() * (max - min);
int randomNumber2 = int(min + Math.random() * (max - min));
```

The second assignment statement uses casting to change the computed real number into an integer.

## 2.7 DIALOG BOX OUTPUT AND INPUT

Dialog boxes are a graphical way to communicate with the user of a Java program and offer an alternative to the console-based output produced by the `println` method in the System class. The *message dialog box* (Figure 2.6) is used to convey output to the user, and the **input dialog box** (Figure 2.7) is used to obtain input from the user. They are predefined graphical objects that automatically resize themselves to display the string argument sent to them. The string sent to a message dialog box is the text to be output to the user. In the case of an input dialog box, the string is an input prompt to be displayed to the user.

After a dialog box is displayed, the program execution is halted until the user clicks a button displayed in the box or strikes the return key. In the case of a graphics application, dialog boxes are normally used for all communication between the program and its user. Two methods in the class `JOptionPane`, `showMessageDialog`, and `showInputDialog` are used to display message (output) and input dialog boxes, respectively.

### 2.7.1 Message Dialog Boxes

The method `showMessageDialog` is a *static* method, as are the `Math` class's methods presented in Table 2.4 and its `random` method. As we will learn in Chapter 3, not all methods are static methods. When static methods are invoked, we must precede the name of the method with the name of its class followed by a dot. The `showMessageDialog` method and the `Math` class's `pow` method have another thing in common: they are both sent two arguments that are coded inside the parenthesis that follows the name of the method. For the `pow` method, we learned that these are the numbers to be raised to a power followed by the power to which to raise it.

In the case of the `showMessageDialog`, its two arguments describe the window to which the message box will be output followed by a string that contains the text of the output message. To output the message "Frogger, by George Smith," we would code

```
JOptionPane.showMessageDialog(null, "Frogger, by George Smith");
```

This would produce the message box shown in Figure 2.6(a). Coding **null** as the first argument causes the message dialog box to be displayed in the center of the monitor.

(a)            (b)

**Figure 2.6**
Two message dialog boxes.

The second argument, the string, can contain all of the elements and features of the string sent to the `println` method used to perform output to the console. As we have learned, the string can be a concatenation of a mix of string literals and numeric variables. Just as with console output, the string will be output on one line unless new-line escape sequences (\n) are included in the string. The width and height of the message box will expand to accommodate the string. For example, the statement

```
JOptionPane.showMessageDialog(null, "Frogger," + "\nby George Smith," +
                              "\nAKA Game Boy Georgie." + "\nOK?");
```

produces the output in Figure 2.6(b).

These features are especially useful in a very common use of a message box: to display a game's splash screen. A game splash screen is used to describe a game, its objective, and the manner in which the game pieces are controlled by the player. Usually, the name of the game and its creator (e.g., "Created by Game Boy Georgie") are also included.

## 2.7.2 Input Dialog Boxes

Input dialog boxes, which are displayed by the static method `showInputDialog`, are used to obtain input from the program's user (Figure 2.7). It is sent one argument, which the method displays as a prompt to the user. A text box is displayed below the prompt into which the user types the input. The box contains two buttons labeled "OK" and "Cancel." The string sent to the method can be a concatenation of a mix of string literals and variables, and the width and height of the input box is adjusted to accommodate the string and its embedded new-line escape sequences. Figure 2.7 shows the input dialog box produced by the statement

```
String s = JOptionPane.showInputDialog("Frogger has five " +
                                       "difficulty levels:" +
                                       "\n1 is the easiest," +
                                       "\n5 the most difficult," +
                                       "\nEnter your level");
```

**Figure 2.7**
An input dialog box before the user enters input.

If, in response to the displayed prompt, the user types into the text box and then clicks "OK" (or strikes the Enter key), the location of a String object that stores the user input text would be placed in the reference variable s. (For brevity, we would say that the InputDialogBox method "returns a string," when in fact it actually creates and returns the address of a String object.) If the user clicked "OK" or struck the Enter key without making an entry in the text box, the returned String object would contain the empty string (""). Finally, if the user clicked "Cancel," s would store the null string. (It would be set to **null**.)

### 2.7.3 Parsing Strings into Numerics

Most of us would agree that there is a fundamental difference between the string "one hundred seventy-six" and the number 176. For one thing, we would not try to add the string "one hundred seventy six" to the string "ten" to obtain "one hundred eighty six". Rather, if we read the question, "what is the sum of one hundred seventy-six and ten?" we would first convert the numbers to their numeric representations, 176 and 10, and then perform the addition. In computer science, the difference between strings and numerics goes deeper than that because even if we were told to add "176" and "10", we would still have to convert these two strings to their numeric representations before performing the addition.

Operands in arithmetic expressions cannot be strings.

As discussed in Chapter 1, characters are stored using their Extended ASCII representation, and numerics are represented using their binary representation. Inside of String objects, the Extended ASCII representation is used. The difference between these two representations is shown below.

| **Extended ASCII Representation of 176** | **Binary Representation of 176** |
|---|---|
| 00110001  00110111  00110110 | 10110000 |
| '1'          '7'          '6' | 176 |

Because an input dialog box returns a string, when 176 is typed into its text box it returns the string "176", which must be converted to a numeric if it is to be used in an arithmetic expression. This conversion process is referred to as *parsing* strings into numerics. There is a set of classes in the API, called wrapper classes, which contain static methods to perform this conversion. The string to be converted to a numeric is sent to the method as an argument coded inside the open and close parentheses that follow the name of the method. The decision as to which class and method to use is based on the primitive numeric type the string is being converted to, as shown in Table 2.5.

**Table 2.5**
Numeric Wrapper Classes and Their Parsing Methods

| To Convert a String to the Numeric Type | Use the Static Method | In the Wrapper Class |
|---|---|---|
| byte | parseByte | Byte |
| short | parseShort | Short |
| int | parseInt | Integer |
| long | parseLong | Long |
| float | parseFloat | Float |
| double | parseDouble | Double |

To change the string literal "176" to its integer numeric representation, we would code:

```
int numericValue = Integer.parseInt("176");
```

To convert the string s to a numeric double, we would code:

```
double numericValue = Double.parseDouble(s);
```

Most often, the statements to accept a user input via an input dialog box, and the conversion of the returned string to a numeric, are coded one after the other.

```
String s =  JOPtionPane.showInputDiaog("Enter your age");
int age = Integer.parseInt(s);
s =  JOPtionPane.showInputDiaog("Enter your weight");
double weight = Double.parseDouble(s);
```

If the string sent to the wrapper class methods contains anything other than digits (i.e., the characters '0', '1', ..., '9'), a *runtime error* NumberFormatException occurs, and the program terminates. If the empty string is passed to the methods (the user clicked "OK" in an input dialog box without typing an input) or the null string is passed to methods (the user clicked "Cancel" without making an entry), the same runtime error occurs. We will learn how to deal with these errors at runtime to bring the program to a more informative conclusion in Chapter 4 and how to permit the user to correct the erroneous input in Chapter 5 "Repeating Statements: Loops."

**NOTE**    *A runtime error is an error that occurs while the program is in execution.*

The application shown in Figure 2.8 calculates the area of a circle given its radius, and it also calculates the radius of a circle given its area. The inputs to the program (a radius of 10 and an area of 200) and the corresponding outputs are show in Figure 2.9. The program demonstrates the use of assignment statements, parsing a string into a numeric, performing calculations, the use of the Math class, and dialog box I/O.

```
1   import javax.swing.JOptionPane;
2
3   public class AssignmentMathAndDialogIO
4   {
5      public static void main(String[] args)
6      {
7         String s;
8         double area, radius;
9
10        JOptionPane.showMessageDialog(null, "Circle area and radius" +
11                                            "\n calculation program");
12        s = JOptionPane.showInputDialog("To calculate an area," +
13                                        "\n     enter a radius");
14        radius = Double.parseDouble(s);
15        area = Math.PI * Math.pow(radius, 2);
16        JOptionPane.showMessageDialog(null, "The area of a circle" +
17                                            " whose radius = " +
18                                            radius + "\n is " + area);
19
20        s =JOptionPane.showInputDialog("To calculate a radius" +
21                                       "\n     enter an area");
22        area = Double.parseDouble(s);
23        radius = Math.sqrt(area / Math.PI);
24        JOptionPane.showMessageDialog(null, "The radius of a circle" +
25                                            " whose area = " +
26                                            area + "\nis " + radius);
27     }
28  }
```

**Figure 2.8**
The application `AssignmentMathAndDialogIO`.

Line 1 of Figure 2.8 is an `import` statement. Import statements make API classes, and the constants and methods they contain, available to our programs. In this case, the class `JOption-Pane`, which contains the methods to perform dialog box input and output, is imported into the program. These methods are used to output the program's splash screen (lines 10–11) and to input the radius of a circle (lines 12–13). The new-line escape sequences (\n) in the strings sent to these methods produce a two-line message on the splash screen and a two-line input prompt, as shown at the top of Figure 2.9.

Line 14 parses the string representation of the input radius returned from the input dialog box into a double and assigns that double to the variable `radius`. Line 15 calculates the area of the circle. It uses the Math class's method `pow` to square the input radius and then multiplies that by the constant pi (`Math.PI`). Lines 16–18 output the radius and the computed area to a message dialog box (Figure 2.9c). The input radius and the calculated area are added to the output string with the use of the concatenation operator on line 18.

In a similar way, lines 20–26 accept an input area and compute the circle's radius. This calculation uses the Math class's `sqrt` method on line 23 to perform the calculation. The method accepts

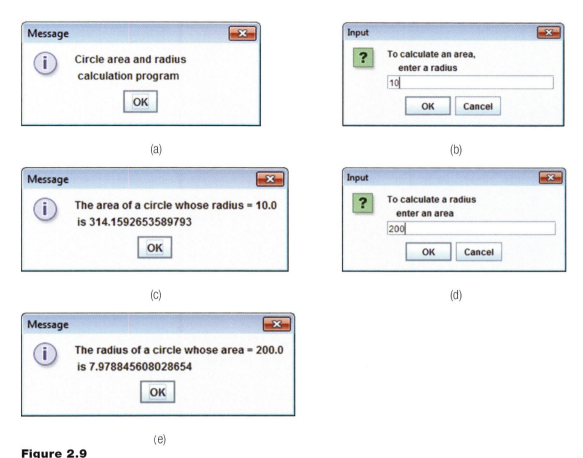

**Figure 2.9**
Input and resulting output from the application **AssignmentMathAndDialogIO**.

one argument, which in this case is the result of dividing the area by pi. The input to and output from this portion of the program is shown in Figure 2.9e.

## 2.8 GRAPHICAL TEXT OUTPUT

In Section 2.4, we invoked (or some would say "used" or "called") the `println` and `print` methods of the `PrintStream` class to perform text output to the system console. In this section, we will learn how to use the method `drawString` in the API `Graphics` class to perform text output to a graphics window. This type of output is called graphical text output. Unlike console output, we can specify the font type, size, and style (e.g., bold style) of graphical text output. In addition, we can output the text to any location in a graphics window. In game programming, text output is typically used to display the game's level of difficulty, the remaining time, the score, or other information on the game's status.

With this added capability come added responsibilities. For example, every time a graphics window that has been minimized is restored, the graphical text must be output again, or it will not be visible in the window. In fact, anything that appears in the window before it was minimized must be redrawn when the window is restored. One mechanism for doing this in graphics programs is to place the graphical output in a *call back* method. Our game environment contains several call back methods. In this section, we will learn how to use the call back method `draw`, the `Graphic` class's `drawString` method, and how to set the font type, size, and style of graphical text output.

### 2.8.1 The `drawString` Method

The `drawString` method is a part (member) of the API Graphics class and is used to output text to a graphical object (perhaps a window). When the method is invoked three arguments are passed to it. The first argument is the text to be output. The second and third arguments are the x and y coordinates where the text will be output. These coordinates locate the lower left position of the first character of text. Their origin is the upper left corner of the graphical object in which the text is to be displayed (e.g., our game board), with x positive to the right and y positive down.

To output the text "Hello World" to our game environment's game board, positioned with the lower left corner of the "H" at (200, 300), we would code:

```
g.drawString("Hello World", 200, 300);
```

Notice that the two characters `g.` precede the name of the method. This is because the method must draw its text on a `Graphics` object. In our case, the object g would have to be a `Graphics` object attached to our game board because we want the text to be drawn on the game board. As we will see in the next section, the attachment of the object g to our game board is performed for us by the game environment.

A method that operates on an object is called a nonstatic method. The syntax used to invoke these methods is the name of the object it is operating on, followed by a dot, followed by the name of the method and its argument list. We have used this syntax in Section 2.4 to invoke the `print` and `println` methods. They were invoked by proceeding their names with the Java pre-defined `PrintStream` object `System.out` followed by a dot. (As previously discussed, when we invoke static methods, we precede the method's name with the name of the method's class followed by a dot. For example, `Math.sqrt(9);`)

The simplest way to determine if a method is static or nonstatic is to click on its class name in the lower left window of the online Java API Specification then scroll down through the API documentation to the method's name. If the method is static, the word "static" will appear in the column to the left of the method's name. For example:

| static double | sqrt(double a) |
|---|---|
| | Returns the correctly rounded positive square root of a `double` value |

If the method is a nonstatic method, the word "static" will not appear in the column to the left of the methods name.

The remaining issue is determining where in our game application program we place the invocation to `drawString`. The short answer is in the `draw` call back method, which we will discuss next.

## 2.8.2 The `draw` Call Back Method

Figure 2.10 presents the Java application class `GraphicalTextOutput` that creates a game window object on line 7, which is displayed by line 11 when the `main` method executes. Lines 2–12 are identical to that of the game code template in Figure 1.31 except for the change in the application's class name (lines 4 and 6) and the title of the window (line 7). When the program is run, the window shown in Figure 2.11 appears on the monitor.

Lines 14–18 is a coding of the game environment's `draw` call back method. The first line of the `draw` method, called the method's signature, must always be identical to the code on line 14, and it requires that the game environment be added (imported) to the program (line 1). The invocation to the `drawString` method has been coded on line 16, which, when executed, outputs the graphical text "Hello World" to our game board beginning at pixel location (250, 220). To use the `drawString` method the Graphics class must be imported into the program (line 2). But, when does it execute?

We have learned that the `main` method is invoked by the Java runtime environment causing its statements to execute, beginning with its first executable statement (the program entry point) and ending when the execution reaches the end of its code block, in this case, line 12. Thus, it would appear that line 11 would display the application's window, and then the program would end. But the `draw` method must have executed because the characters *Hello World* appear in the program's window (Figure 2.11). So again, we ask the question, "when does it execute?"

The answer is fundamental to why the method `draw` is referred to as a call back method. Line 11 in the main method invokes the method `showGameBoard`, which requests that the

```
1    import edu.sjcny.gpv1.*;
2    import java.awt.Graphics;
3
4    public class GraphicalTextOutput extends DrawableAdapter
5    {
6      static GraphicalTextOutput ga = new GraphicalTextOutput( );
7      static GameBoard gb = new GameBoard(ga, "Graphical Text Output");
8
9      public static void main(String[] args)
10     {
11       showGameBoard(gb);
12     }
13
14     public void draw(Graphics g) //the drawing call back method
15     {
16       g.drawString("Hello World", 250, 220);
17
18     }
19   }
```

**Figure 2.10**
The application **GraphicalTextOutput.**

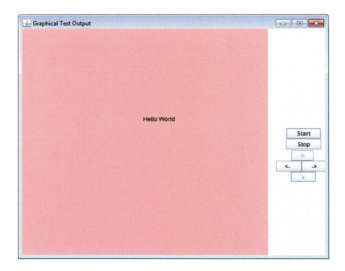

**Figure 2.11**
The output produced by the application **GraphicalTextOutput**.

game environment display the game board window. Before the game environment displays the game's window, it invokes, or calls back, the draw method coded in the application, causing it to execute. When the draw method ends, the game environment completes the display of the game's window requested by the showGameBoard method. Thus, the application calls the game environment to display the game board window (line 11), and the game environment calls back the application's draw method to perform its drawings on the game board before the window is displayed. Specifically, the execution sequence is line 11 in the method main, the code of the showGameBoard method, the code at the beginning of a method in the game environment, the draw call back  method lines 14-18), and finally, the remainder of the code in the game-environment method.

In fact, every time the program's window has to be redrawn (e.g., the window was minimized and then the window's icon on the status bar is clicked), the game environment's code invokes the draw method to redo its drawings on the game board. This can easily be verified by adding the statement

```
System.out.println("the draw method was invoked");
```

to the draw call back method. Then, every time the draw method is invoked, we will see an output on the system console.

 **NOTE**   *Even though the main method containing the program's entry point ends its ex-ecution, a graphical program continues to execute until the program's graphical window (e.g., the gameboard window) is closed.*

### 2.8.3 The setFont Method: A First Look

Like the drawString method, the setFont method is a part (member) of the API Graphics class. It is used to change font type, style, and size. The output in Figure 2.11 used the default font values. Once changed, all subsequent graphical text output will use the new (or current) font type, style, and size until it is changed again. The method is passed one argument. The following code, when added to the `draw` method, changes the font type to Arial, the style to bold italic, and the font size to 16 points, and then outputs the text *The Font was Changed*. The syntax of the argument sent to the `setFont` method will be explained in Chapter 3.

```
g.setFont(new Font("Arial", Font.BOLD + Font.ITALIC, 16));
g.drawString("The Font was Changed", 150, 300);
```

## 2.9 THE COUNTING ALGORITHM

Counting is something that is done in most programs and is considered to be a fundamental algorithm in computer science. For example, in game programs it is used to count the number of seconds remaining in a game or the number of seconds since the game began. In the first case, the time starts at a designated amount of time and counts down to zero; in the second case, the time starts at zero and counts up. In both cases, the game's time is usually displayed on the game board. In this section, we will discuss the counting algorithm, and we will learn how to use it inside the game environment's call back method `timer1` to count seconds.

Most of us began to learn how to count by memorizing the integers beginning with 1. Our parents may have said to us, "say this: one, two, three, four." Most of us, on the first try, perhaps said "three, four," or "one, two, four," or some other erroneous sequence. Through repetition, eventually we memorized the sequence and extended it by recognizing that each new element is "one more."

Somewhere along our cognitive development path, we discovered the counting algorithm. In support of that is the realization that most people never memorized the integers from 1,242,518 to 1,243,589. However, most of us could recite that sequence of integers if asked to do so because we use the counting algorithm to determine the sequence. Below is the generalized counting algorithm that can be used to count forward or backward by any increment:

```
int count = aBeginningValue;
// repeat the next statement until count reaches the ending value
count = count + aCountingIncrement
```

For example, to count upward from 1 to 10 by 1s, we code:

```
int count = 1;
// repeat the next statement until count reaches 10
count = count + 1; // 1 becomes 2, 2 becomes 3, 3 becomes 4, …
```

To count backward by 5s, from 1,165 to 875, we code:

```
int count = 1165;
// repeat the next statement until count reaches 875
count = count  + -5; // 1165 becomes 1160, 1160 becomes 1155, …
```

Repeating statements is the topic of Chapter 5, so we will revisit the counting algorithm in that chapter. However, if we want to count seconds within a game program, the second line of the counting algorithm can be repeated by placing it inside a call back method named `timer1`.

This method is invoked by the game environment once every second causing the statement to be repeated once a second.

### 2.9.1 A Counting Application: Displaying a Game's Time

The game environment has three timer call back methods named timer1, timer2, and timer3. Their signatures (first lines) are:

```
public void timer1( )
public void timer2( )
public void timer3( )
```

If you code these methods into your game program, they will be invoked every time their respective timers "tick." For example, the method timer2 will be invoked every time timer2 ticks. Because counting seconds is so common in games, by default timer1 ticks every second. It begins ticking when the game window's Start button is clicked, pauses when the Stop button is clicked, and resumes ticking when the Start button is clicked. After a timer call back method ends its execution, the game environment invokes the draw call back method. The details of the other two timers, which are normally used to animate game objects, will be discussed in Chapter 6.

```
1    import edu.sjcny.gpv1.*;
2    import java.awt.Graphics;
3    import java.awt.Font;
4    public class CountingSeconds extends DrawableAdapter
5    {
6      static CountingSeconds ga = new CountingSeconds( );
7      static GameBoard gb = new GameBoard(ga, "The Counting Algorithm");
8      static int count = 0;    // a class level variable
9
10     public static void main(String[] args)
11     {
12       showGameBoard(gb);
13     }
14
15     public void draw(Graphics g) // the drawing call back method
16     {
17       g.setFont(new Font("Arial", Font.BOLD, 18));
18       g.drawString("Your game time is: " + count, 10, 50);
19     }
20
21     public void timer1()
22     {
23       count = count + 1;
24     }
25   }
```

**Figure 2.12**
The application **CountingSeconds**.

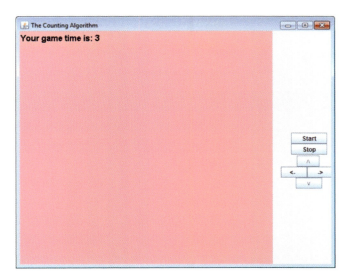

**Figure 2.13**
The output produced by the application **CountingSeconds** three seconds after the Start button is clicked.

Figure 2.12 presents the graphical application `CountingSeconds` that illustrates the use of the counting algorithm to count upwards by one, starting from zero. The output produced by the program three seconds after the user clicks the `Start` button is shown in Figure 2.13.

The declaration of the counter variable `count` and its initialization to zero seconds is coded on line 8. (Note that the keyword **static** is coded at the beginning of this line. The need for it will be explained in Chapter 3.) Declaring this variable on line 8 places it outside of the code blocks (the open and close braces) of all of the class's methods, which makes it makes available to *all* of the class's methods. Variables declared in this way are said to be *class level* variables.

The second line of the counting algorithm is coded on line 23 inside the `timer1` call back method (lines 21–24). Because timer1 ticks once a second (by default), line 23 is repeated every second, causing the counter variable `count` to count seconds. Each time the `timer1` method ends, the game environment invokes the `draw` method, which displays the new time on the game board by outputting the contents of the class-level variable `count` (line 18). The output appears in bold Arial 18 point font because line 17 invokes the *Graphic* class's `setFont` method to change the current font values. The import statement on line 3 makes the constants and methods of the *Font* class available for use by that statement.

Counting up and down by 1 is so common in computer science, that Java provides two additional operators, `++` and `--` to perform the algorithm. Coding `c++;` is equivalent to coding `c = c + 1;`, and coding `c--;` is equivalent to coding `c = c - 1;`.

## 2.10 FORMATTING NUMERIC OUTPUT: A FIRST PASS

In this chapter, we have discussed how to perform numeric output, but we have not discussed how to format numeric output to improve its readability, such as adding a comma every three

```
1    import java.text.DecimalFormat;
2
3    public class BasicNumericFormatting
4    {
5      public static void main(String[] args)
6      {
7        double speedOfLight = 299792458.7153;
8        int population = 1097603176;
9
10       DecimalFormat df = new DecimalFormat("#,###.##");
11
12       System.out.println(df.format(speedOfLight));
13       System.out.println(df.format(population));
14     }
15   }
```

**Figure 2.14**
The application **BasicNumericFormatting**.

digits to the left of the decimal point, or adjusting the precision of the fractional part of a number output to the right of the decimal point. The `format` method in the `DecimalFormat` class can be used to accomplish both of these commonly used types of output formatting. We will conclude this chapter with an introduction to the techniques used to format numeric output; we will present more details on these techniques in Chapter 5.

The application presented in Figure 2.14 uses the `DecimalFormat` class's `format` method to format the output of a real number (line 12) and an integer (line 13). The method returns a string containing the formatted numeric value and is sent one argument. The argument is the numeric variable to be formatted: `speedOfLight` and `population` on lines 12 and 13 respectively.

This nonstatic method is invoked (on lines 12 and 13) using the `DecimalFormat` object `df` declared on line 10. The formatting to be performed is associated with the decimal format object and is specified as a string literal coded inside the parentheses at the end of line 10. The string literal `#,###.##` coded on this line indicates that commas will appear every three digits to the left of the decimal point, and *real* numbers (nonintegers) will be output with two digits of precision. The level of precision used in the formatting can be changed by adding or removing pound signs to the right of the decimal point on line 10.

The output produced by the program is given in Figure 2.15. As this output shows, real numbers are always rounded up (299792458.7153 was output as 299792458.72), and integer output does not contain a decimal point.

```
299,792,458.72
1,097,603,176
```

**Figure 2.15**
The output produced by the **BasicNumericFormatting** application.

## 2.11 CHAPTER SUMMARY

This chapter introduced the basic components of a Java program and the Java template for developing a program that performs input, mathematical calculations, and output. Variables are declared to store data during the program's execution. Primitive variables store one data value, and reference variables store a memory address where the object that contains the data is located. The type of the data (for example, character or integer), must also be declared. Good coding style dictates that variable names be meaningful as well as syntactically correct. Meaningful variable names indicate what the data represents. They begin with a letter and cannot contain spaces.

The `print` and `println` methods are used to output a string to the console window to which the object `System.out` is attached. Escape sequences permit characters with special meaning to be used in output statements. The concatenation operator joins data values and strings into a single output string.

`String` objects, which are reference variables store the memory address that refers to, or references, the actual string. Strings can be created and initialized using either a one-line or two-line grammar. The default value for an uninitialized string is `null`. Strings have to be converted into numeric values to perform mathematical operations, and there is a set of classes in the API, called wrapper classes, which contain static methods to perform this conversion.

Java, like most programming languages, provides the ability to perform basic arithmetic calculations and provides additional features, including the API `Math` class, to perform more complex calculations. Arithmetic calculations are performed in Java using arithmetic expressions. Arithmetic expressions consist of a series of operands separated by operators. The parts of an arithmetic expression inside the parentheses are evaluated first using the rules of precedence to determine the order of the operations. If the operators are of equal precedence, they are evaluated from left to right. Higher precedence operators are evaluated first. The division of two integers always results in a truncated integer value, and the mod operator is used to determine the remainder of integer division.

Values are assigned to variables using the assignment operator. Generally, the type of the value being assigned to a variable should match the type of the variable. Type casting and promotion are provided and are used with mixed-mode expressions to ensure that the variable types are compatible and there is no loss of precision.

Dialog boxes are a graphical way to communicate with the user of a Java program and offer an alternative to console-based input and output. The method `drawString` in the API `Graphics` class can be used to perform text output to a graphics window, and the setFont method can be used to change the default font, style, and size. The counting algorithm is used to keep track of elapsed seconds in a game program. Chapter 3 will extend the concepts of objects, classes, and methods and their application to creating game programs.

Finally, the `DecimalFormat` class is introduced to provide ways to format numeric output to improve its readability.

## Knowledge Exercises

1. True or False:
   a) The type of the data stored in a variable can change as the program executes.
   b) Variables must be declared in a program before they are used.
   c) Variables must be initialized when they are declared.
   d) It is grammatically incorrect to begin a variable name with an upper-case letter.
   e) Spaces can be used in variable names for better readability.

2. Which statement in a Java application program is executed first?

3. What are variables? Name two types of variables and the information each one stores.

4. Which of the following is not a primitive data type?
   a) boolean          b) char          c) String          d) int

5. Give the default initial values for variables declared to be of the following types:
   a) boolean          b) char          c) double          d) int

6. Write a well-composed declaration statement to declare variables that can store:
   a) Maggie's age initialized to 32
   b) The first initial of Ryan's name initialized to the letter 'R'
   c) The cost of a taco
   d) The number 21,234,096,464
   e) The fact that it is snowing

7. Is a numeric literal, coded in a program, represented as a float or a double? Explain.

8. Determine if each of the following variables is well composed and valid. For those that are not, explain why not.
   a) 2ndplace          b) middleInitial          c) winningTeam
   d) fgp3              e) test1 grade            f) myScore
   g) SalePrice

9. Give the code to output two lines to the system console. The first line will contain your name, and the second line will contain the town in which you live, using:
   a) Two statements                     b) One statement

10. Write a well-composed variable declaration statement to declare a string String object initialized to Skyler's address, which is 21 First Avenue, using the:
    a) One-line object-declaration grammar     b) Two-line object-declaration grammar

11. Draw a picture of the memory allocated by the statements:
    a) `int distance = 675;`               b) `String myName = new String("Jane");`

12. Give one statement to:
    a) Output the annotated contents of the memory cell `priceOfCorn`

**b)** Output the sentence: Martin said: "I had a dream."

**c)** Change the contents of the variable `myBalance` to 234.54.

13. Evaluate each of these expressions:

    **a)** 17 - 5 * 2 + 12                 **b)** 31 - 7 * 2 + 14

    **c)** (48 + 12) / 12 + 18 * 2       **d)** 21 - 9 + 18 + 4 * 3.7

14. Give the code to:

    **a)** Declare the variable `quizAverage` and store the average of the variables `quiz1`, `quiz2`, `quiz3`, and `quiz4` in it

    **b)** Calculate the sine of 45 degrees and store the value in the variable `sineOf45`

    **c)** Calculate and output the square root of 45.67

    **d)** Calculate and output 34.7 to the 5th power

15. Write the variable declaration to declare the variable `average` and the assignment statement to store the average of three speed limits: 55, 57, and 60 miles per hour.

16. Give an assignment statement to store the integer part of the value stored in the double variable `bankBalance` in the variable `dollars`.

17. True or False:

    **a)** You must include an import statement in a program to perform I/O using dialog boxes.

    **b)** A message dialog box can be used to obtain input from the program user.

    **c)** A string is always returned from an input dialog box.

    **d)** When the user clicks "OK" without making an input into an input dialog box, null is returned.

    **e)** Dialog boxes will size themselves to accommodate the string argument sent to them.

18. Write the code to output two lines to a message dialog box. The first line will contain your first and last name, and the second line will contain your date of birth in the format "My birthday is: dd\mm\yyyy" (yes, those are backslashes).

19. Give the code to allow the program user to enter a checking account balance using an input dialog box. Include a well-composed user prompt.

20. Think of a game. Write the code to output the name of the game and its creator, the task (objective) of the game, and how the game pieces are controlled to a message dialog box of reasonable size.

21. Give the code to declare a double variable named `deposit` and to parse the input contained in the string `sDeposit` into it.

22. Write the code to declare an integer variable named `speedLimit` and to parse the input contained in the string `sSpeedLimit` into it.

23. Write a declaration of a constant that stores the number of days in a week.

24. Use the combined division assignment operator to set the memory cell `sum` to half its current contents.

## Programming Exercises

1. Write a Java application that outputs your name on one line followed by the town in which you live to the system console.

2. Write a program to calculate the average of five quiz grades: 100, 97, 67, 85, and 79. Output the quiz grades and the average to the system console. The output should be well annotated with the quiz grades on one line and the average on another.

3. Write a program to accept an angle (input in degrees) and a real number. Then, output the angle and its sine, cosine, and tangent. Follow that output with the output of the input real number, its cube, and the square root of the number. The outputs should occupy several lines and be sent to both the system console and to a message dialog box. The input prompts should be well composed, and the outputs should be well annotated.

4. Repeat Programming Exercise 3, but output the information to the system console and to the middle of the game board. Use 20-point italic Arial font for the game-board output.

5. Write a program to ask the user to enter the product of a pair of real numbers (of your choosing), with the input rounded to one digit of precision. After the product is entered, output the user's input and the correct product, rounded to one digit of precision. The outputs should occupy several lines, and be sent to the system console and to a message dialog box. The input prompts should be well composed, and the outputs should be well annotated.

6. Write a program to ask the user to enter the product of a pair of real numbers of your choosing. After the product is entered, output the correct answer and the number of seconds it took the user to enter the product to the center of the game board and to the system console. Use 20-point italic Arial font for the game-board output. The output should be on two lines and well annotated.

7. Repeat Programming Exercise 6, but output the numbers with commas every three digits on the left side of the decimal point, and use one digit of precision.

## Endnotes

[1] The URL of the Edition 7 API documentation is: *http://docs.oracle.com/javase/7/docs/api/* It is named: Java Platform, Standard Edition 7 API Specification.

[2] http://www.randomnumbers.info/content/Random.htm

# METHODS, CLASSES, AND OBJECTS: A FIRST LOOK

### In this chapter

This chapter extends the concepts of methods, classes, and objects discussed in the previous chapter to enable us to design and implement our own classes and the methods that they contain. These concepts facilitate the development of our programs by allowing us to divide a large program into several smaller classes, separately develop these classes, and then integrate them into the larger program. Once written, these classes can also be used in other programs, just as the API classes are. Several design tools will be introduced in the chapter to methodize the specification of a class and the object it defines. The understanding of material presented in this chapter is the foundation of the advanced OOP topics discussed in Chapters 7 and 8.

After successfully completing this chapter, you should:

- Be able to write void and nonvoid methods
- Understand how to share primitive information and objects between methods
- Understand the concept of value parameters
- Be able to read a Unified Modeling Language (UML) diagram and use it to specify a class
- Understand how to design and specify graphical and nongraphical objects
- Be able to identify, write, and use a set of methods that most classes contain
- Understand the concept and use of public and private data members and methods
- Be able to design, construct, modify, and access an object using its class's methods
- Use methods of the Graphics class to draw lines, rectangles, ovals, and circles
- Have acquired the foundational skills required for a study of Chapters 7 and 8

## 3.1 ■ METHODS WE WRITE

In Chapter 2, we became familiar with several methods available in the Java Application Programming Interface. For example, the methods `println` and `print` perform output to the system console, `pow` and `sqrt` perform calculations, and `drawString` and `setFont` perform text output to the program window. Being resident in the API, these methods are available to all Java programmers, and their use expedites the program development process because only one programmer, the API programmer, had to discover their algorithms and then write, test, and debug their code. The rest of us simply use the methods by importing them into our program and writing a one-line invocation statement. Because most of the cost of software development is the salaries paid to the programmers, the use of prewritten methods also makes software more affordable.

In this section, we will learn how to write our own methods. Not only will this allow us to reuse the code that we write in other programs, but it also facilitates the development of our programs by dividing a large program into several smaller subprograms called methods. By dividing a large program into subprograms, these methods can be developed by several programmers working in parallel, which greatly reduces the calendar time required to produce a program.

**The Motivation for Writing Methods**

*Extends our problem solving capabilities: Humans are good at solving small problems but not large problems*

**NOTE**

*Reduces development time: Methods can be developed in parallel by several members of a programming team*

*Reduces cost: Methods can be written in such a way that they can be used in any program using a one-line invocation statement*

### 3.1.1 Syntax of a Method

In Java, all the methods we write must be part of a class. They must be coded within the class's code block, the open and close braces that begin and end a class statement. The class statement can be the one that contains the program entry point, the method `main`, or some other class that we will learn how to create later in this chapter. When methods are coded inside the class that contains the method `main`, good coding style dictates that they be coded after it.

The minimum code required to create a method is:

```
returnType methodName( )
{
    //the code of the method is placed here
}
```

The first line of the method is called the method's *signature*. The signature is followed by a set of open and close braces that define the bounds of the method's *code block*. The statements to be executed when the method is invoked are coded inside this code block.

The method's signature, the first line of the method's code, must include the type of the information returned from the method, followed by the method's name, followed by an open and close set of parentheses. If the method does not return a value to the invoker, for example, simply output a string value, the keyword **void** is used as the return type. In this case, the method is said to be a void method.

A method that simply outputs the name of the student newspaper to the system console every time it is invoked would be an example of a void method.

```
void outputNewspaperName()
{
    System.out.println("The Student Voice");
}
```

The syntax and coding style used for naming methods are the same as those used to name variables:

- they cannot contain spaces
- they should begin with a lower-case letter
- new words should begin with an upper-case letter

Normally, they are only comprised of letters. Digits, the dollar sign, and the underscore are not normally used in their names. For example, a method that adds two integers together and returns the result could be named addTwoInts rather than add _ 2 _ Ints.

Figure 3.1 presents the application AVoidMethod that contains the implementation and two different invocation forms of the void method outputNewspaperName. The output it produces is shown in Figure 3.2.

```
1    public class AVoidMethod
2    {
3        public static void main(String[] args)
4        {
5            AVoidMethod.outputNewspaperName(); //1st method invocation
6            System.out.println("Page 1\n");
7            outputNewspaperName();              //2nd method invocation
8            System.out.println("Page 2\n");
9        }
10
11       static void outputNewspaperName()       //method signature
12       {
13           System.out.println("The Student Voice");
14       }
15   }
```

**Figure 3.1**
The console application **AVoidMethod**.

```
The Student Voice
Page 1

The Student Voice
Page 2
```

**Figure 3.2**
The output produced by the console application **AVoidMethod**.

The program consists of two methods: the method `main` (lines 3–9) and the method `output-NewspaperName` (lines 11–14). Both of these methods are coded within the program class's code block that begins on line 2 and ends on line 15.

> **NOTE** *A method cannot be coded inside of another method's code block.*

The signature of the method `outputNewspaperName`, coded on line 11, begins with the keyword **static**. Not all method signatures begin with this keyword. As we have learned, methods fall into two categories: those that operate on objects (non-static methods) and those that do not operate on objects (static methods). An example of a method that operates on an object is the method `println`. It operates on, or sends its output string to, the console object whose name is `System.out`. Methods that do not operate on an object must include the keyword **static** in their signature. The method `outputNewspaperName` does not operate on an object, so its signature begins with the keyword static. In Section 3.5, we will discuss methods that we write that do operate on objects, and we will gain more insight into what it means to say a method operates on an object.

> **NOTE** *Methods that do not operate on an object must include the keyword **static** in their signature.*

The method `outputNewspaperName` is invoked in lines 5 and 7 of the application's main method. Line 7 just mentions the name of the method followed by open and close parentheses. This invocation syntax is valid because the static method is coded within the same class, `AVoid-Method`, as the invocation statement (line 7). The more generalized syntax for invoking a static method is used on line 5. Here, the invocation statement begins with the name of the class in which the method is coded followed by a dot:

```
AVoidMethodApp.outputNewspaperName();
```

We used this syntax to invoke the static methods `pow` and `sqrt` that are coded in the Math class.

```
double ans = Math.pow(3.0, 2.0);
double root = Math.srt(9.0);
```

Because these two methods are not coded in the same class in which they are normally invoked, the name of the class must be included in the invocation statement. The only exception to this is the use of a static import statement. When either syntax is valid, the shorter syntax makes our programs more readable and is therefore preferred.

The execution sequence of the application begins on line 5 of the main method. This invocation statement causes the code in the code block of the `outputNewspaperName` method to execute (lines 12–14), which produces the first line of output (Figure 3.2). Then line 6 of the main method executes, producing the second line of output. Line 7 causes the `outputNewspaperName` method to execute a second time, which produces the third line of output. Finally, line 8 executes, which produces the last output line.

> **NOTE** *After a method executes, the next statement to execute is the statement immediately after the statement that invoked it.*

## 3.2 ■ INFORMATION PASSING

For a method to function properly, information must often be passed to it when it is invoked, and some methods must return one piece of information to the invoking statement. Consider the Math class's nonvoid static method pow. When it is invoked, a number (n) and a power (p) are passed to it, and the method returns the result of its calculation: $n^p$. The left side of Figure 3.3 depicts this sharing of information between the invoker (top left) of the method pow and the method (bottom left). The right side of the figure generalizes this concept of shared information between the invoker, often called the client, and the method that performs some "work" for the client, often referred to as the worker method. For example pow's work is to compute a given number (n) raised to a given power (p).

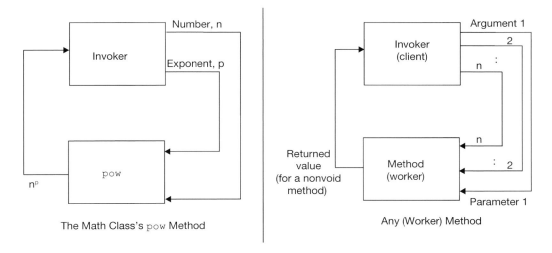

The Math Class's pow Method                 Any (Worker) Method

**Figure 3.3**
The sharing of information between a method and its invoker.

As depicted in the right side of Figure 3.3, an unlimited number of pieces of information can be sent from the invoking client to a worker method, however, only one piece of information can be sent back to the client from the worker method. We say that the client sends the method an *argument list* containing the shared information, and the worker method receives the shared information in its *parameter list* (either or both of which could be empty).

**NOTE**  *No more than one piece of information can be returned from a method.*

### 3.2.1 Parameters and Arguments

If a method is to receive information passed to it from the client, then its signature must contain a parameter list. The parameter list is coded inside the open and close parenthesis of the method's signature. The parameters in the list are separated by commas, and each parameter consists of a variable name preceded by its type. For example, the signature of a method whose work is to output a person's age and weight would have an int and a double parameter in its parameter list.

```
static void outputAgeAndWeight(int age, double weight)
{
    System.out.println(age: "  + age + " weight: " + weight);
}
```

Each parameter receives *one* piece of information sent to it by the client code's invocation statement, and the *type* of the parameter must match the type of the information sent to it. The client's statement used to invoke the method `outputAgeAndWeight` would contain two arguments in its argument list, within parentheses.

```
outputAgeAndWeight(myAge, myWeight);
```

This statement passes the contents of the variables `myAge` and `myWeight` to the method.

Arguments, information that is to be shared with the worker method, can be variables (e.g., `myAge, myWeight`) that have been previously declared in the client code, or string or primitive literals.

If the order, number, and type of the arguments and parameters don't match, most IDE's will identify the mismatch as a translation error. If the error is not identified by the translator, when the method is invoked the Java Runtime Environment will throw an `IllegalArgumentException` error and terminate the program's execution.

> **NOTE** *The order, number, and type of the arguments in a method invocation statement must match the order, number, and type of the parameters in the method's signature.*

Each time a method is invoked, the variables in the method's parameter list are allocated and paired up with the arguments in the invocation's argument list (the first parameter paired with the first argument, the second parameter paired with the second argument, etc.), and the value stored in each of the arguments is copied into the paired parameters. For the invocation statement

```
outputAgeAndWeight(myAge, myWeight);
```

the value in the argument `myAge` is copied into the parameter `age` of the method `outputAgeAnd-Weight`, and the value contained in the argument `myWeight` is copied into the parameter `weight`. This type of information passing is called *passing by value*, and the parameters are called *value parameters* because the values contained in the arguments are copied into the parameters. Once the parameters have been allocated and this transfer of information is complete, the code in the worker method's code block begins execution.

Consider the sequence of code that contains a main method and the method `outputAgeAndWeight`:

```
public static void main(String[] args)
{   int myAge = 23;
    double myWeight = 185.4;

    outputAgeAndWeight(myAge, myWeight);
}
```

```
static void outputAgeAndWeight(int age, double weight)
{
    System.out.println("age: "  + age + " weight: " + weight);
}
```

Figure 3.4 depicts a sequence of seven events that occur when this code executes and illustrates the process of passing information using value parameters. The left side of figure shows the main method's (client) code and its execution sequence (events 1, 2, 3), which includes the RAM memory allocated to its two arguments (event 2 is depicted in the bottom left portion of the figure).

The right side of the figure shows the code of the method and its execution sequence (events 4, 5, 6, and 7), which includes the RAM memory allocated to its two parameters (event 5 is depicted in the bottom right portion of the figure). The passing of the values stored in the client's arguments into the paired worker parameters is depicted as event 6 in the bottom center of the figure. After the information is passed, the code block of the method executes (event 7).

The dotted line in the figure is a line that the code in the client and worker methods cannot cross. The client code on the left of the figure cannot access the contents of the member cells `age` and `weight`, and the worker method code cannot access the memory cells `myAge` and `myWeight`. Inserting the statement

```
myAge = myAge + 1;
```

into the code of the method `outputAgeAndWeight` would result in a translation error because `myAge` is only known to the client code.

When the method completes its execution, the variables named in its parameter list are de-allocated, and their storage is returned to the memory manager. The result is that the values stored in these memory cells are lost, in that they are no longer available to the program. An understand-

**Figure 3.4**
The transfer of information to a method via value parameters.

ing of this is fundamental to the notion of value parameters. It is also important to realize that the four memory cells created during events 2 and 5 are separate and distinct. To emphasize this, the names of the parameters (`age` and `weight`), coded in the worker method's signature, were intentionally chosen to be different than the names of the arguments passed to method (`myAge` and `myWeight`). Even if the argument and parameter names were the same (e.g., both coded as `age` and `weight`), event 5 would still create two distinct memory cells on the right side of Figure 3.4 named `age` and `weight`. A coding of the symbols `age` and `weight` in the worker method would refer the contents of these to memory cells, which would be de-allocated when the method ends its execution.

**NOTE** *Every time a method is invoked, the variables in its parameter list are allocated, and they are de-allocated when the method ends its execution.*

### 3.2.2 Scope and Side Effects of Value Parameters

The only way to pass information between arguments and parameters (i.e., between client code and worker method code) in Java is via value parameters, so it is important that we understand the limitations of the value parameter memory model presented in Figure 3.4 and its implications. As depicted in the figure, the client code has two variables it can access, `myAge` and `myWeight`, and the method has two variables it can access, `age` and `weight`. The client code cannot access the variables `age` and `weight`, and the worker method cannot access the variables `myAge` and `myWeight`.

In programming language jargon, we say that the worker method's variables `age` and `weight` are defined within the **scope** of its code, and the variables `myAge` and `myWeight` are out of its scope. A Java statement can only access variables that are within its scope.

> **Definition**
>
> The **scope** of a variable is the portion of a program in which it is defined and can therefore be accessed.

It is syntactically correct to make the argument names in a method invocation the same as the parameter names coded in the method's signature. For example, the names of the variables declared in the main method and the worker method's parameter list could both be named `myAge` and `myWeight`.

```java
public static void main(String[] args)
{   int myAge = 23;
    double MyWeight = 185.4;

    outputAgeAndWeight(myAge, myWeight);
}

static void outputAgeAndWeight(int myAge, double myWeight)
{
    System.out.println("age: "  + myAge + " weight: " + myWeight);
}
```

As previously mentioned, this coding of the method would still create two memory cells assigned to the method's parameters on the lower right side of Figure 3.4, but their names would now be `myAge` and `myWeight`. Now, the statement

```
myAge = myAge + 1;
```

written into the worker method's code would not result in a translation error because there is now a variable named `myAge` that is within its scope. The method's code would access the contents of its memory cell `myAge`, and the contents of that variable would be changed to 24. When the method ends and execution returns to the client code, the contents of the client code's memory cell `myAge` would be unchanged. It would still contain the value 23.

Normally, this is a good thing because it prevents an unwanted *side effect* of the method's code changing the client's data. Preventing this side effect assures that the values stored in the client code variables before the method was invoked will be the same values stored in those variables after the method completes it execution. In some cases, however, this is not what we want.

Consider the case of a method, named `swap`, that the client invokes to swap the contents of two of its variables, a and b, via the statements

```
int a = 10;
int b = 20;
swap(a, b);
System.out.println("a is: " + a + " and b: is " + b);
```

If the method is successful, the output produced after `swap` completes its execution should be a is 20 and b is 10.

The method `swap` would have two integer parameters to receive the values to be swapped, and its code would implement the swapping algorithm. The code of the method, preceded by a main method that invokes it, is given below:

```
public static void main(String[] args)
{
    int a = 10;
    int b = 20;

    swap(a, b);
    System.out.println("a is:" + a + " and b: " + b);
}

static void swap(int a, int b)
{
    int temp = a;
    a = b;
    b = temp;
}
```

Unfortunately, because Java uses value parameters, this coding of the method does not swap the client's variables, and the output produced by the last statement in the main method is a is 10 and b is 20.

Consistent with the memory model of value parameters, the client and the method each have their own memory cells named a and b. The method swaps the values contained in its two memory cells a and b, which has no side effects on the contents of the memory cells a and b allocated in the client code. These two cells remain unchanged (they still contain 10 and 20, respectively), which makes it appear that the swap algorithm was improperly coded in the worker method.

It turns out that it is impossible to write a method that swaps the contents of two client variables using primitive-type parameters because, by design, value parameters prevent a method from changing the values in the client's argument list. Some programming languages (e.g., C and C++) solve this problem by allowing another type of parameter called a reference parameter. Java does not support this type of parameter because it can lead to some undesirable side effects

### 3.2.3 Returned Values

A worker method can return one, and only one value to the method that invokes it. A method that returns a value is called a value returning or nonvoid method, and the keyword **void** is not used in its signature. It is replaced with the type of the information the method returns. For example, the method showInputDialog in the API class JOptionPane is a nonvoid method that returns a reference to a String, so its signature contains the type String rather than the keyword **void**.

Methods can return the contents of reference variables, as the method showInputDialog does, or they can return the contents of primitive variables. In both cases, the returned value should be thought of as replacing the invocation of the method in the statement that invoked the method after the method executes. If the value is to be used later in the program, the invocation should be coded as the right part of an assignment statement that assigns the returned value to a variable.

For example, the two statements below prompt the user to enter a person's age and return the characters that are entered, but only the second one retains the location of the String object that is returned.

```
JOptionPane.showInputDialog("enter a person's age");
String sAge = JOptionPane.showInputDialog("enter a person's age");
```

A nonvoid method must contain a return statement or the method will not translate. The statement begins with the keyword **return**, which is followed by the value that is to be returned. The value to be returned can be a literal, a variable, the value of an arithmetic expression, or a value returned from a method invocation. The following code segment contains a nonvoid method multiply preceded by the code of the main method that invokes it. The method multiply calculates and returns the product of two numbers passed to it.

```
public static void main(String[] args)
{
   double a = 10.0;
   double b = 20.0;

   double product = multiply(a, b);
```

```
    System.out.println(a + " x " +  b + " = " product);
}

static double multiply(double a, double b)
{
    double c;
    c = a * b;
    return c;
}
```

Because, as previously mentioned, an arithmetic expression can be coded in a **return** statement, the method could have been coded more succinctly as:

```
static double multiply(double a, double b)
{
    return a * b;
}
```

There can be more than one return statement in a nonvoid method, but we will not have a use for that feature of the language until we gain an understanding of the material presented in the next chapter.

### 3.2.4 Class Level Variables

Class level variables are another way of sharing information among methods. However, the manner in which the information is shared and the syntax used to code class level variables are both very different than when arguments, parameters and return statements are used to share information.

To begin with, unlike using arguments and parameters to pass information to a worker method, in order for methods to share information using class variables, the methods must be coded in the same class. The information sharing is accomplished by coding the variable outside of the code blocks of the methods in the class. Good coding style dictates that they be coded at the top of the class before the code of any of the methods. When this done, the variable is within the scope of all of the methods in the class. The methods actually share the same variable, which permits any method in the class to fetch and overwrite the variable's contents. Unlike arguments and parameters, class variables provide a two-way path for methods to share information. One method can write a value into the variable, and another method can read the value from it.

Although we did not explain class variables in this much detail in Chapter 2, the program presented in Figure 2.12 used a class variable named count (line 8) to share the game's time between the method timer that was incrementing it (line 23), and the method draw that was outputting it to the game board (line18). As shown on line 8 when a class variable is used in the program's class, its declaration must begin with the keyword **static:**

```
static int count = 0;
```

Aside from that, its declaration syntax is the same as that used to declare a variable inside of a method's code block.

A variable can be declared inside a method's code block that has the same name as a class level variable. When this is done, a memory cell is created with the same name as the class variable and is called a *local variable*. All uses of the variable's name inside the method's code block refer to the local variable, and the local variable can only be accessed by the method's code. To access the class variable from inside the method, the name of the variable would be preceded by the name of the class followed by a dot (just as when we invoke static methods).

Wherever possible, it is good programming practice not to use the names of class variables for naming variables declared inside of methods. For one thing, it reduces the program's readability because, if we fail to realize that the local variable is declared, we would erroneously believe that the class variable is being used inside the method. In addition, if we neglect to declare the local variable when coding the method, the translator will assume we want to use the class variable, and it will not remind us that we neglected to declare the local variable.

It is good programming practice not to use the names of class variables for naming local variables declared inside of methods.

Figure 3.5 presents a program that contains four worker methods and demonstrates information sharing via value parameters, return statements, and class variables, the use of local variables, and the features of methods that make them reusable. The inputs to the program and the outputs the program produces are shown Figure 3.6.

Lines 30–36 contain the code of the method `inputInteger`. Its signature (line 30) indicates that it is a nonvoid method that returns an integer and has a `String` parameter named `prompt`. The method passes the string sent to it to an input dialog box (line 33) to be displayed as a `prompt` to the program user. The returned user input is parsed into the integer variable a (line 34), and then the parsed value is returned to the invoker (line 35). The inclusion of a string parameter in its signature allows the invoker to specify the prompt sent to the input dialog box. In addition, the method parses the input integer, freeing the invoker from that responsibility. Both of these features make this a highly reusable method. It is invoked five times within the program (on lines 11, 17, 18, 23, and 24), and each time it is sent a different prompt.

Two class variables, a and b, are declared on lines 4 and 5 with a initialized to 10. The value in the class variable a is included in the string passed to the invocation of `inputInteger` on line 11, which is displayed as the prompt in the input dialog box (Figure 3.6a) produced by line 33. The method `inputInteger` declares its own local variable a on line 32, so the assignment of the parsed value of the user input into the variable a (line 34) changes the contents of the local variable, leaving the class variable unchanged. This is verified by the first output (Figure 3.6b) produced by the program (lines 14–15), which indicates that a 10-year-old child will be 13 in 3 more years.

The method `dif` is invoked on line 13 to calculate the first output: the years to reach the desired age. It is passed the desired age, input on lines 11-12, as the first argument on line 13. Because the method main does not declare a local variable named a, the second argument on line 13, a, is the class variable. The method then calculates the difference between the two values passed to its two parameters (line 40), the desired age and the value stored in the class variable. Because the desired age was input as 13, and the output indicates that it will be reached in 3 more years, the class variable passed to the method's second parameter must have contained the value 10 at the time dif was invoked. The previous assignment into the local variable a on line 34 had no effect on it.

It should be noted that even if the parameter a was reassigned inside the method dif, the class variable would still retain the value 10 because Java uses value parameters. All references in the method dif to the variable a refer to the parameter, which can be thought of as a local variable.

Two swap methods, swapParameters and swapClassLevels, are coded on lines 43–55. The first of these methods is invoked on line 19. It contains two parameters, a and b (line 43), to receive the values to be swapped, which are input on lines 17 and 18 (Figures 3.6 c and d). Although the names of the parameters are the same as the names of the class-level variables, they are not the same memory cells as the class variables. When the values stored in the parameters are swapped (lines 45–47), the output produced by lines 20–21 of the main method confirms a feature of value parameters: changes to parameters have no effect on the arguments sent to the method. The numbers output by the main method are output in the same order in which they were input: 1111 followed by 2222 (Figure 3.6 e).

Because the main method does not declare local variables named a and b, lines 23 and 24 store the values returned from inputInteger in the program's class variables (Figures 3.6 f and g). The second swap method, swapClassLevels, is invoked on line 25. It has an empty parameter list (line 50) and only one local variable, temp. Therefore, the variables a and b used in this method default to the class-level variables. Because these are shared with the main method, the swapping of the values in these variables performed on lines 52–55 does have an effect on the output produced

```
1    import javax.swing.JOptionPane;
2
3    public class MethodsAndParms
4    {   static int a = 10; // Two classlevel variables
5        static int b;
6
7        public static void main(String[] args)
8        {
9            int desiredAge, first, second, difference; // local Variables
10
11           desiredAge = inputInteger("You are " + a + " years old" +
12                                     "\nHow old do you wish you were?");
13           difference = dif(desiredAge, a);
14           JOptionPane.showMessageDialog(null, + "Only " + difference +
15                                         " Years to go");
16
17           first = inputInteger("Enter the first number to swap");
18           second = inputInteger("Enter the second number to swap");
19           swapParameters(first, second);
20           JOptionPane.showMessageDialog(null, "Swapped using parameters: " +
21                                         first + " " + second);
```

```
22
23          a = inputInteger("Enter the first number to swap");
24          b = inputInteger("Enter the second number to swap");
25          swapClassLevels();
26          JOptionPane.showMessageDialog(null, "Swapped using class " +
27                                          "levels: " + a + " " + b);
28      }
29
30      static int inputInteger(String prompt)
31      {
32          int a; // a local variable
33          String sInput = JOptionPane.showInputDialog(prompt);
34          a = Integer.parseInt(sInput);
35          return a;
36      }
37
38      static int dif(int desiredAge, int a)
39      {
40          return desiredAge - a;
41      }
42
43      static void swapParameters(int a, int b)
44      {
45          int temp = a;
46          a = b;
47          b = temp;
48      }
49
50      static void swapClassLevels()
51      {
52          int temp = a;
53          a = b;
54          b = temp;
55      }
56 }
```

**Figure 3.5**

The application **MethodsAndParameters**.

(a)

(b)

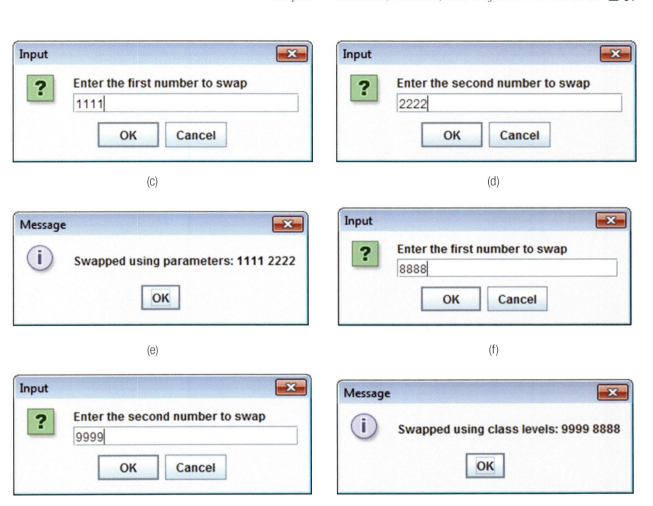

(c)

(d)

(e)

(f)

(g)

(h)

**Figure 3.6**
Inputs and resulting outputs produced by the application **MethodsAndParameters.**

by the main method (lines 26–27). As a result, the numbers input on lines 23 and 24 (8888 and 9999) are output in reverse order (9999 followed by 8888) by lines 26 and 27 (Figure 3.6 h).

### 3.2.5 Javadoc Documentation

The JDK contains a utility program named Javadoc that automates the generation of web based documentation of Java source code. The format of the webpage it produces is the format used in the online documentation of the classes, methods, and other constructs that make up the Java Application Programming Interface (see Appendix G). For example, Javadoc was used to generate the online documentation of the API Math class discussed in Section 2.6.4.

The program can be launched via a few clicks from within most IDEs, including Netbeans and Eclipse. When launched, it scans the source code file to be documented for entities to be added to various parts of the webpage template. Among these entities are *public* class headings, method signatures, and class level variables. Information contained in multi-line comments added to the source code *immediately* before an entity (e.g., just before the signature of a *public* class) is also added to the webpage.

Multi-line `Javadoc` comments begin with /** and end with */. Within these comments, the programmer types descriptive documentation that becomes part of the entity's `Javadoc` generated documentation. When used with a class, the import statements precede the Javadoc description as shown:

```
// import statements

/**
 *   Description of the purpose of the class
 * @author   Author's Name
 */
public class ClassName
{
    // code of the class

}
```

The multi-line comments immediately preceding a method's signature usually consist of a description of the method's functionality followed by a description of its parameters and returned value. Preceding the description of a method's parameter with the `Javadoc` *tag* `@parm` and the description of its returned value with the `Javadoc` tag `@return` within the multi-line comment, places their descriptions into the portion of the webpage dedicated to parameter and return type descriptions. In addition, HTML formatting tags, such as <p> to begin a new paragraph, can be inserted into the text of a multi-line comment.

For example, to document the `inputInteger` method that begins on line 30 of the class `MethodsAndParms` shown in Figure 3.5, the multi-line comment shown below could be added to the class just before the method's signature.

```
/**
 * Acquires and parses an input integer using an input dialog box
 * @param prompt  the prompt to be displayed in the dialog box
 * @return the parsed input integer
 */
public static int inputInteger(String prompt)
{
    int a;
    String sInput = JOptionPane.showInputDialog(prompt);
    a = Integer.parseInt(sInput);
    return a;
}
```

When this expanded source code of the class `MethodsAndParms` is processed by `Javadoc`, the two portions of the class's webpage that describes the inputInteger method would appear as shown below.

| Method Summary | |
|---|---|
| **Methods** | |
| Modifier and Type | Method and Description |
| static int | inputInteger(java.lang.String prompt) |
| | Acquires and parses an input integer using an input dialog box |

**inputInteger**

```
public static int inputInteger(java.lang.String prompt)
```

Acquires and parses an input integer using an input dialog box

Parameters:

    prompt - the prompt to be displayed in the dialog box

Returns:

    the parsed input integer

Aside from their influence on the automated generation of web based documentation, multi-line comments also provide more information to anyone reading the source code of a class. Other commonly used Javadoc tags are @author, @version, @throws, and @exception. The set of Javadoc tags, and the standard webpage documentation template, were defined by Oracle.

## 3.3 THE API GRAPHICS CLASS

Having gained a deeper understanding of methods and the techniques for sharing information between methods and the program code that invokes them, we will reinforce those concepts in this section by examining several worker methods in the API Graphics class. As discussed in Chapter 2, this class contains methods for drawing text on Graphics objects. It also contains methods used to change the drawing color and for drawing lines, rectangles, ovals, and circles on Graphics objects.

### 3.3.1 Changing the Drawing Color

All drawing performed on a Graphics object is performed in the current color. The default current color is black. The setColor method in the Graphics class can be used to change the current drawing color. One argument, used to specify the new value of the current drawing color, is passed to the method. Table 3.1 gives the names of the thirteen predefined color variables in the class Color. Because these variables are static variables, they are referred to by their name preceded by Color followed by a dot. For example, to set the color of all subsequent drawings on the Graphics object g to red, we would code:

```
g.setColor(Color.RED);
```

As previously discussed, the Graphics object attached to our game board is passed into the draw method's parameter g when the game environment invokes the draw method. Therefore, if this statement were coded in the draw call back method, the current drawing color of the game board would be changed to red.

**Table 3.1**

Thirteen of the Predefined Colors in the Color Class

| Color | Variable Name |
|---|---|
| black | BLACK |
| blue | BLUE |
| cyan | CYAN |
| dark gray | DARK_GRAY |
| gray | GRAY |
| green | GREEN |
| light gray | LIGHT_GRAY |
| magenta | MAGENTA |
| orange | ORANGE |
| pink | PINK |
| red | RED |
| white | WHITE |
| yellow | YELLOW |

### 3.3.2 Drawing Lines, Rectangles, Ovals, and Circles

Figure 3.7 presents five of the methods in the `Graphics` class. These methods are nonstatic void methods. As their names imply, the first method is used to a draw line, and the remaining four methods are used to draw rectangles and ovals. To specify the location of the item to be drawn, all of the methods are passed (x, y) coordinates whose units are pixels.

The line drawing method, `drawLine`, is passed two sets of (x, y) coordinates, which are the endpoints of the line to be drawn. For example, to draw a line from (30, 50) to (60, 80) on the `Graphics` object g, we would code:

```
g.drawLine(30, 50, 60, 80);
```

The rectangle drawing methods `drawRect` and `fillRect` are used to draw the outline of a rectangle and to draw a filled (solid) rectangle, respectively. Their first two arguments specify the coordinates of the upper left corner of the rectangle, and the third and forth coordinates specify the width and height of the rectangle in pixels. For example, to draw the outline of a rectangle whose upper left corner is at (100, 200) and is 50 pixels wide and 75 pixel high on the `Graphics` object g, we would code:

```
g.drawRect(100, 200, 50, 75);
```

To draw this rectangle as a solid rectangle, filled with the current drawing color, we code:

```
g.fillRect(100, 200, 50, 75);
```

The method `drawOval` is used to draw the outline of an oval, and the method `fillOval` is used to draw a solid oval filled with the current color. These ovals are drawn within a specified rectangle (which is not drawn). The method's four parameters are identical to those of the rectangle methods previously discussed and are used to specify the rectangle's (x, y) location and its width and height. For example, to draw the outline of an oval 50 pixels wide and 70 pixels high inscribed inside a rectangle whose upper left corner is at (100, 200), we would code:

```
g.drawOval(100, 200, 50, 75);
```

To draw this oval as a solid oval filled with the current drawing color, we code:

```
g.fillOval(100, 200, 50, 75);
```

| drawLine(int x1, int y1, int x2, int y2) |
| --- |
| Draws a line, using the current color, between the points (x1, y1) and (x2, y2) |
| drawRect(int x, int y, int width, int height) |
| Draws the outline of a rectangle whose upper left corner is at (x, y) and whose width and height are width and height, using the current color |
| drawOval(int x, int y, int width, int height) |
| Draws the outline of an oval bounded by the rectangle whose upper left corner is at (x, y) and whose width and height are width and height, using the current color |
| fillRect(int x, int y, int width, int height) |
| Draws a rectangle whose upper left corner is at (x, y) and whose width and height are width and height, filled with the current color |
| fillOval(int x, int y, int width, int height) |
| Draws an oval bounded by the rectangle whose upper left corner is at (x, y) and whose width and height are width and height, filled using the current color |

**Figure 3.7**
Primitive-shape drawing methods in the **Graphics** class.

The oval drawing methods can be used to draw circles by making the third and fourth arguments, the height and width of the rectangle that encloses the oval, the same number of pixels. For example, to draw a solid circle 50 pixels in diameter inscribed inside a rectangle whose upper left corner is at (100, 200) we would code:

```
g.fillOval(100, 200, 50, 50);
```

When the statements presented in this section are coded in the game environment's draw call back method, the lines and shapes they draw appear on the game board because, as mentioned at the end of Section 3.3.1, the Graphics object passed into the draw call back method's parameter g is attached to our game board.

Figure 3.8 presents the application LinesAndShapes that draws two lines in the default color (black), two dark-gray rectangles, a red oval, and a blue circle on the game-board object. The graphical output of the program is shown in Figure 3.9. Lines 16–26 coded inside the draw method perform the drawing. Consistent with the variable names given in Table 3.1, the argument sent to the setColor method on line 19 has an underscore separating the words DARK and GRAY.

```
1      import edu.sjcny.gpv1.*;
2      import java.awt.*;
3
4      public class LinesAndShapes extends DrawableAdapter
5      {
6        static LinesAndShapes ga = new LinesAndShapes( );
7        static GameBoard gb = new GameBoard(ga, "Lines and Shapes");
8
9        public static void main(String[] args)
10       {
11         showGameBoard(gb);
12       }
13
14       public void draw(Graphics g) // the drawing call back method
15       {
16         g.drawLine(100, 75, 260, 75);      //Lines
17         g.drawLine(300, 50, 400, 100);
18
19         g.setColor(Color.DARK_GRAY);
20         g.drawRect(100, 170, 100, 60);     //Rectangles
21         g.fillRect(280, 170, 150, 40);
22
23         g.setColor(Color.RED);
24         g.drawOval(55, 300, 180, 80);      //Ovals
25         g.setColor(Color.BLUE);
26         g.fillOval(280, 300, 100, 100);
27
28       }
29    }
```

**Figure 3.8**
The application **LinesAndShapes**.

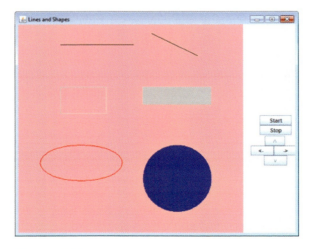

**Figure 3.9**
The output produced by the application **LinesAndShapes**.

## 3.4 OBJECT ORIENTED PROGRAMMING

Early programming languages were designed in the procedural paradigm. In this paradigm, a program is decomposed into smaller parts called subprograms, and the language provides a mechanism for combining the subprograms into the larger program. During the design process, the programmer focuses on the definition of the subprograms and how the program's data will be stored. In this paradigm, the subprograms and the program's data are separated and coded into two distinct entities.

Object oriented programming is a more recent programming paradigm. The paradigm is an attempt to facilitate the development of programs that deal with objects, such as starships, or people, or Web pages. In this paradigm, the program is decomposed into the various classes to which the objects belong. During the design process, the programmer focuses on determining the objects the program will deal with, the attributes of each object (e.g., a starship's name), and the operations that can be performed on each object (e.g., changing a starship's location). In this paradigm, the operations (subprograms) and attributes (data) are collected and coded into one entity called a class.

Both paradigms are in use today. Some programming solutions are better designed and more easily implemented using the procedural paradigm, and others are more easily designed and implemented using the object paradigm. C is a procedural language, C++ is a language that can be used in both the procedural and object paradigm, and Java is an object oriented language. If the program deals with objects, then the object paradigm should be strongly considered.

### 3.4.1 What Are Classes and Objects?

A **class** is a blueprint of how to construct an item, and an **object** is a particular item or instance of a class. For example, we all belong to the class human. That class contains a genetic blueprint of how to construct a human object, which we call a person. As per the human blueprint, all people have common attributes. For example, all people have colored-eyes, colored-hair, and eventually grow to an adult height. But clearly, all people (except identical twins) are also different. For example, people grow to different heights, have different-colored eyes, and different hair colors, what makes objects different is that each object contains its own value of the attributes contained in the blueprint.

> **Definition**
>
> A **class** is a blueprint of how to construct an item, and an **object** is a particular item or instance of a class.

The value of Mary's three attributes could be 63 inches for height, blue for eye color, and red for hair color. The value of her sister Kate's attributes could be 68 inches for height, brown for eye color, and black for hair color. No wonder these two objects look different. Now suppose Kate, who always admired her sister's red hair and blue eyes, dyed her hair to a red color and inserted a set of blue contact lenses into her eyes. These hair coloring and lens insertion operations would change the values of two of Kate's attributes, and she would then look like a taller version of Mary.

In object oriented languages, a class is the mechanism for defining the blueprint of an entity. As such, it contains the attributes that each object in the class will have (e.g., height, hair color, and eye color). To store the different values of these attributes for each object constructed from the blueprint, the attributes are represented within the class as variables. In addition, because the values of the attributes of an object can change, the class contains methods (e.g., `setEyeColor` and `setHairColor`) that can operate on the variables to change, or set, the values they store to new values.

## 3.5 DEFINING CLASSES AND CREATING OBJECTS

During the design process of an object oriented program, the programmer focuses on determining the objects the program will deal with, the attributes of each object, and the operations that can be performed on them. The blueprint for each type of object will be coded into a programming construct called a class that will represent the attributes as variables and the operations as methods. In the remainder of Section 3.5, we will discuss a graphical tool used to specify a class and the Java syntax used to code that specification into a Java program.

**NOTE** *The programming construct* **class** *is comprised of variable definitions and method definitions.*

### 3.5.1 Specifying a class: Unified Modeling Language Diagrams

A unified modeling language (UML) diagram is a graphical representation of a class. The diagram consists of three rectangles stacked on top of each other. From top to bottom, as shown in Figure 3.10, these rectangles are used to specify the class name, the variables that will be part of the class, and the class's methods. The variables are called data members (of the class), and the methods are called member methods because they are both part of (members of) the class being specified.

As an example, consider a program that is going deal with people objects where each person has three attributes: eye color, hair color, and height. The UML diagram used to specify the class, whose name was chosen to be `Person`, is shown in Figure 3.11. The name of the class appears at the top of the diagram, and the class's three data members are tabulated in the second box of the diagram.

To succinctly convey information about a class's data members and methods, UML diagrams employ a standardized notation, some of which is included in Figure 3.11. For example, the type of each data member is specified by following its variable name with a colon and the type of the variable. As shown in the figure, the class `Person` has two String data members and one integer data member.

The three data members of the class `Person` are preceded with a plus (+) sign. The plus sign is used to denote the *access* property of a data member of a class. When the UML specification of a class is coded into a Java class construct, the + sign is coded as the keyword **public**. Another alternative is to precede the names of the data members with a minus (–) sign, which is coded as the keyword **private**. We will learn more about the implications of the use of access modifiers in the next section.

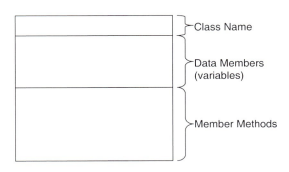

**Figure 3.10**
The template of a UML diagram.

| Person |
| --- |
| + eyeColor: String |
| + hairColor: String |
| + height: int |
|  |

**Figure 3.11**
The specification of the class Person, Version 1.

### 3.5.2 The Class Code Template

Like the data members of a class, a class itself can be public or private, although most classes are public. We will discuss private classes in Chapter 7. The code template for a public Java class is given below:

```java
public class ClassName
{
    //data members are coded here
    //member methods are coded here
}
```

The name of the class, given at the top of the UML diagram, is substituted for `ClassName` on the first line of the template. The declaration of the class's data members and the code of its member methods are coded inside of a pair of braces that make up the class's code block. The variables that represent a class's data members are coded before the code of the class's member methods. While this is not a Java syntax rule, it is considered good coding practice. The code of the class specified by the UML diagram presented in Figure 3.11 is given in Figure 3.12 with the data members set to initial values.

```java
public class Person
{
    //data members
    public String eyeColor = "blue";
    public String hairColor = "red";
    public int height = 65;

    //member methods

}
```

**Figure 3.12**
The code of the class Person specified in Figure 3.11.

Normally, the initial values are chosen to be the most common value of the data members. In this case, the assumption is that most people have blue eyes, red hair, and are 65 inches tall.

### 3.5.3 Creating Objects

In Section 2.5, we examined a two-line syntax for declaring objects in the class `String`. For example:

```
String firstName;
firstName = new String("John");
```

The first line creates the reference variable `firstName` that can store the address of a `String` object, which is initialized to the default value **null**. The second line creates a new `String` object, stores the string "John" inside of it, and then overwrites the **null** value stored in the variable `firstName` with the address of the object. Alternately, the two lines of code can be consolidated into one line:

```
String firstName = new String("John");
```

When talking about the object created with either the two- or one-line syntax, in the interest of brevity we say that "we created a string object named `firstName`," or we might be asked to "output the object `firstName`." However, experienced programmers know that it is more accurate to say, "we created a string object referenced by the variable `firstName`," or "output the object referenced by `firstName`." With that understanding, we will use the brief version in the remainder of this text.

By changing the name of the class coded in the one- or two-line syntax and usually the code inside the parentheses, both versions of the syntax can be used to declare an object in any class. The code fragment below uses the one-line grammar to create two `Person` objects, one named `mary` and the other named `kate`:

```
Person mary = new Person();
Person kate = new Person();
```

The memory allocated by these two statements is shown in Figure 3.13. As defined in the `Person` class (Figure 3.12), each object contains the same three variables set to initial values. The variables `hairColor` and `eyeColor` store the address of string objects that contain the initial values. At this point, Mary and Kate are identical twins and will remain so until we add methods to the class that can change the values of the data members.

### Constructor methods

Let us assume that the two lines of code that created the objects `mary` and `kate`

```
Person mary = new Person();
Person kate = new Person();
```

were coded in the main method of a program that dealt with people, or more precisely, `Person` objects. These two lines of code should be thought of as the main method's request to the class to create

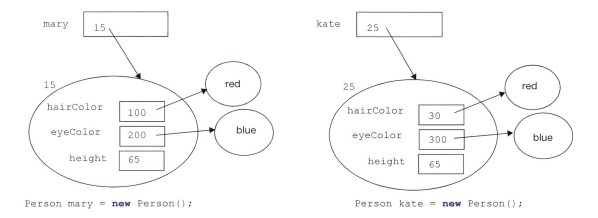

**Figure 3.13**
Two Person objects and the statements that constructed them.

two `Person` objects. If I call a carpenter and request that he create, or construct, a shed for me, I become his client. The two terms, *construct* and *client*, used in this analogy are used in the programming jargon of classes and objects. We would say that the class `Person` has constructed two objects for the client code main. Any section of code that declares an object in a class is considered to be client code (of that class), and the class is said to have constructed the objects for the client code.

Every class has at least one member method that constructs new objects. These non-void methods are called *constructors*, and they execute every time the object declaration syntax is used to declare an object. During the execution of a constructor method, the storage is allocated for the class's data members, the initial values are stored in the data members, the collection of data members is assigned a memory location (considered to be the location of the object), and that location is returned to the client code. The assignment operator included in the object-declaration grammar then stores the returned location of the object in the object's reference variable (e.g., `mary`).

The name of a constructor method is always the name of its class, so the code to the right of the keyword **new** in the declaration of `mary`'s object

```
Person mary = new Person();
```

is actually an invocation to the constructor method named `Person` that has no parameters and returns the address of a newly created `Person` object.

The class `Person` shown in Figure 3.12 does not contain a constructor method, which in this case would be a method named `Person`. When a class does not contain a constructor, a Java-provided constructor method is used to construct objects. This constructor, referred to as the default constructor, has no parameters, and it performs the functions previously mentioned:

1. Allocates the storage for the data members of the class
2. Stores the initial values in the data members
3. Assigns the collection of data members a memory location
4. Returns the location to the client code

Because the class `Person` does not contain any methods, the two `Person` objects `mary` and `kate` declared as

```
Person mary = new Person();
Person kate = new Person();
```

would be created by the default constructor, which would perform the four functions listed above. Each object's data members would be set to the initial values specified in the data-member portion of their class (Figure 3.12) during function 2. In Section 3.6.2, we will learn how to add constructor methods that we write to a class. These methods can contain parameters and code to extend the four functions performed by the default constructor.

### 3.5.4 Displaying an Object

Objects can be displayed to the system console and to a graphical game board in one of two ways. We can simply mention the name of the object or invoke the `toString` method on the object inside a method invocation used to display strings, or we can add a method to the object's class that, when invoked, outputs the object. The following statements use the first approach to display the `Person` object `mary` to the system console object, `System.out` and then to a `GameBoard` object named `g` at location (210, 100).

```
System.out.println(mary); //implicit toString method invocation
g.drawString(mary.toString(), 210, 100);
```

This approach is usually not too interesting. The class Person shown in Figure 3.12 does not contain a method named `toString`, and so the `toString` method in the API class `Object` is invoked. It returns a string containing the location of the object that is stored in the reference variable mary preceded by an ampersand (@) and the name of the object's class. Referring to Figure 3.13, Mary's object is located at address 15, so the output to system console and the game board would be `Person@f` (f is 15 in hexadecimal). The second alternative, adding a method, such as a `show` method, to the object's class that when invoked outputs the object, produces a more interesting and useful output. This technique will be discussed in Section 3.6.1.

Figure 3.14 presents an application that creates two `Person` objects, whose class is defined in Figure 3.12, and outputs their locations to the system console and the game board. The output is shown in Figure 3.15, except that the program does not produce the more interesting output of the actual object `Mary` shown in the middle of the game board. As previously mentioned, the techniques for producing that output will be discussed Section 3.6, and the code to produce the output will be left as an exercise for the student.

Lines 7, 10, and 11 create two `Person` objects using the two-line syntax. The reference variables `mary` and `kate` are declared as class variables on line 7, so they can be accessed from the main method and the `draw` call back method. Lines 13–14 and lines 21–22 output the object's locations to the system console and the game board, respectively. These locations can be thought of as the locations assigned to the two objects by Java's memory manager when lines 10–11 execute.

```
1   import edu.sjcny.gpv1.*;
2   import java.awt.*;
3   public class ClassAndObjectBasics extends DrawableAdapter
4   {
5       static ClassAndObjectBasics ge = new ClassAndObjectBasics();
6       static GameBoard gb = new GameBoard(ge, "Class & Object Basics");
7       static Person mary, kate;
8
9       public static void main(String[] args)
10      {   mary = new Person();
11          kate = new Person();
12
13          System.out.println(mary);
14          System.out.println(kate);
15
16          showGameBoard(gb);
17      }
18
19      public void draw(Graphics g)
20      {
21          g.drawString(mary.toString(), 210, 100);
22          g.drawString(kate.toString(), 210, 120);
23      }
24  }
```

**Figure 3.14**
The application **ClassAndObjectBasics.**

*System console output:*
Person@3a6727
Person@4a65e0
*Game board output:*

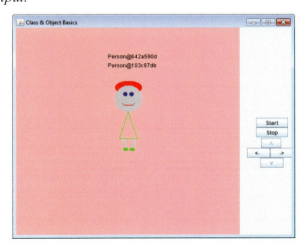

**Figure 3.15**
The object locations output by the application **ClassAndObjectBasics.**

### 3.5.5 Designing a Graphical Object

During the specification and design of a program we identify the types of objects that the program will deal with and the operations to be performed on them. Then during the program development process, a class is developed for each of the object types, and the operations performed on the objects become the methods of the class. A common operation performed on objects is to display them, and in the previous section we were able to display a `Person` object's location without adding a method to the `Person` class. To produce the more interesting display of an object, such as the drawing of the object `mary` with her red hair and blue eyes shown in the middle of Figure 3.15, we add a method to the object's class that uses the shape and line drawing methods of the `Graphics` class to produce the output.

In Section 3.6, we will learn how to add this method, whose name usually begins with the prefix `show`, and other methods that perform common operations on objects to an object's class. In preparation for the coding of this method, the programmer has to design each type of graphical object using the basic drawing shapes available in the `Graphics` class. In this section, we will become familiar with techniques used to design these objects so that the drawing can be easily coded into a `show` method, and the object can be easily manipulated by other class methods that perhaps relocate the object, erase the object, or animate the object.

### Drawing an Object

To begin, we draw a picture of the object using the graphical shapes available in the API `Graphics` class discussed in Section 3.3. The object should be inscribed in a rectangle, and if ovals are used, they should be inscribed in their own rectangle. Figure 3.16 shows a sketch of a snowman-type object comprised of two rectangles and two circles. The rectangles that inscribe the ovals and the entire object are shown in red.

The dimensions, in pixels, of each of the basic shapes that make up the game piece should be given in the drawing. For example, the snowman's hat is specified on the upper right side of the figure to be 10 pixels wide and 15 pixels high. Ovals that are circles, such as a snowman's head and body, can be specified with one dimension (e.g., the diameter of the snowman's head is 20 pixels). After the dimensions of all of the shapes that make up the object have been noted on the drawing, the overall width and height of the inscribing rectangle is added to the drawing. This is shown in Figure 3.16 on the bottom and left side of the inscribing rectangle. The width is simply the width of the snow-

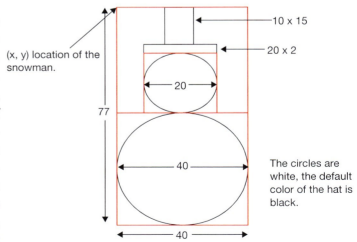

**Figure 3.16**
The design of a snowman game piece.

man's body, 40, and the height is the sum of the heights of the shapes that make up the snowman, 77 (15 + 2 + 20 + 40).

The color of each shape that makes up the object should also be given, as shown in the lower right portion of the figure. The word default used in the object's color specification implies that snowmen objects could be constructed with hats that are not black. Finally, a point that will be used to locate the object on the game board is noted on the drawing. As shown in the upper left side of the figure, this point is typically the upper left corner of the inscribing rectangle.

The next step in this design process is to determine the locations of each of the shapes' upper-left corner relative to the (x, y) location of the game piece, which for our snowman is the upper left corner of the inscribing rectangle. These locations, along with the width and height of each of the shapes, are entered into in a table that will be used in the `show` method to draw each of the shapes. The table is a digital representation of the object, and the process of determining the data is referred to as digitizing the object.

The digital representation of our snowman object is given in Table 3.2. As previously mentioned, each location in the table is relative to the (x, y) location of the upper corner of the rectangle that inscribes the snowman object. Therefore, each location given in the table begins with an x or y followed by the x or y distance to the corner of the shape. When reading the locations in the table, it should be remembered that the positive x direction is to the right, and the positive y direction is down.

To determine these distances, we either consider the dimensions of each of the shapes given in Figure 3.16, or we draw the object on a piece of graph paper whose origin is the upper left corner of the object's inscribing rectangle. Then, the x and y distances to the upper-left corner of each shape are simply the x and y coordinates of the shape's inscribing rectangle's upper left corner. The following two examples illustrate the technique of determining the x and y coordinates of each shape by considering the dimensions given in Figure 3.16.

1. To determine the x location of the upper left corner of the snowman's hat, which is x + (20-5) as indicated in the first row and third column of the table, half the width of the snowman's inscribing rectangle (20) is added to x because the center of the hat is at the center of the inscribing rectangle. Half the width of the hat (5) is subtracted from x because the left side of the hat is half the width of the hat closer to the left side of the snowman's inscribing rectangle than is the center of the hat.

**Table 3.2**
Digital Representation of the Snowman Object Shown in Figure 3.16

| Component | Shape | Shape's X or Line's $X_1$ Coordinate | Shape's Y or Line's $Y_1$ Coordinate | Width or Line's $X_2$ Coordinate | Height or Line's $Y_2$ Coordinate |
|---|---|---|---|---|---|
| Hat | Rectangle | x + (20 − 5) | y | 10 | 15 |
| Hat Brim | Rectangle | x + (20 − 10) | y + (15) | 20 | 2 |
| Head | Circle | x + (20 − 10) | y + (15 + 2) | 20 | 20 |
| Body | Circle | x | y + (15 + 2 + 20) | 40 | 40 |

2. To determine the y location of the upper left corner of snowman's head, which is y + (15+2) as indicated in the third row and fourth column of the table, the height of the hat (15) and the height of the hat brim (2) are added to y.

It should be noted that when lines are used in the object's drawing, each line is entered on a separate row of the table and, as indicated in the column headings of Table 3.2, the coordinates of the endpoints of the lines are entered into the rightmost four columns of the table. During the design phase of the program, a table is produced for each type of object in the program.

## 3.6 ADDING METHODS TO CLASSES

Many of the methods added to a class perform operations on the objects in the class. Some of these operations are so commonly performed, such as a method to display an object or a method to change the value of a data member, that they are included in most classes. To improve program readability, the names of these methods usually begin with a designated prefix. For example, the names of methods that display objects usually begin with the prefix show, and a method that begins with the prefix set usually changes the value of one of an object's data members.

In this section, we will study the techniques for adding methods to classes and how to use them to perform operations on objects. These methods will be added to a class named SnowmanV1 that defines the object depicted in Figure 3.16 and digitized in Table 3.2. Its UML diagram will be progressively developed, by adding methods to it, as we move through the next few sections of this chapter.

Our starting point will be the UML diagram shown in Figure 3.17, which is implemented in Figure 3.18. The class has three data members, two integers, and a reference variable used to specify the location of a SnowmanV1 object and its hat color. As shown in the UML diagram, the data member hatColor will refer to a color constant in the class Color. The code of the class SnowmanV1 is presented in Figure 3.18. The three data members are coded on lines 4–6. The default location of the snowman is (5, 30), which is the upper left corner of the game board. The hat color has been initialized to the color constant BLACK.

| SnowmanV1 |
| --- |
| + x: int <br> + y: int <br> + hatColor: Color |
|  |

**Figure 3.17**
The UML diagram of the class
**SnowmanV1**

```
1    public class SnowmanV1
2    {
3        //data members
4        public int x = 5;
5        public int y = 30;
6        public Color hatColor = Color.BLACK;
7    }
```

**Figure 3.18**
The Class **SnowmanV1**

The use of a graphical snowman in this chapter will make the concept of operating on an object less abstract, and therefore more easily understood. For example, rather than the class' show method simply displaying an object's (x, y) location, its show method will display the object in a more tangible way: by drawing it on the game board at its (x, y) location. Rather than simply outputting the increased value of an object's x location, we will see the object move to the right.

## 3.6.1 The show Method

A method that begins with the prefix show is used to display an object and is a nonstatic method. Because the drawing methods of the Graphics class cannot be used to draw on the system console, we have to define what it means to show an object on the system console. The commonly accepted meaning is that the output would consist of the annotated values of the object's data members. This version of a show method, named showXYToSC (SC for system console) would invoke the println method and pass it a string that concatenates the annotation and the class's x and y data members. For example:

```java
public void showXYToSC()
{
    System.out.println("x is: " + x +
                        "\ny is: " + y);
}
```

After this code is added to the class then snowman sm1 could be output to the system console using the statement:

```java
sm1.showXYToSC();
```

which would produce the output:

x is: 5

y is: 30

The statement sm1.showXYToSC(); can be read in three different ways:

1. The object sm1 is invoking the showXYToSC method.
2. The method showXYToSC is invoked on the object sm1.
3. The showXYToSC method is operating on the object sm1.

All three of these are synonymous; that is, they mean the same thing. In general, to cause a method to operate on an object, we precede the name of the method with the name of the object followed by a dot.

An important point to remember is that if we just focused on the code of the showXYToSC method and asked the question, when it mentions the data members x and y, which object's data members is it talking about, the answer is the data members of the object that invoked it. The true meaning of the statement "a method operates on an object" is that all occurrences of the names of the data members coded inside the method refer to the data members of the object that invoked it.

Figure 3.19 presents the expanded UML diagram that reflects the addition of two show methods, showXYToSC and show. The method show will use the digitized version of a snowman, presented in

Table 3.2, to display a SnowmanV2 object on the game board. Because the shape drawing methods in the Graphics class will need access to the game board object, the show method will have one parameter: a reference to a Graphics object. The characters g: Graphics that appear inside the parentheses of this method in the UML diagram is UML notation to indicate that this method has one parameter named g that is a reference to a Graphics object.

| SnowmanV2 |
|---|
| + x : int<br>+ y : int<br>+ hatColor: Color |
| + showXYToSC()<br>+ show(g: Graphics) |

**Figure 3.19**
The UML diagram of the class
**SnowmanV2.**

The code of this expanded class is given in Figure 3.20. A client application that declares a SnowmanV2 object and outputs the object's address to the system console and the object to both the system console and the game board is shown in Figure 3.21. The application's output is shown in Figure 3.22.

The client code (Figure 3.21) invokes the default constructor on line 7 to declare a SnowmanV2 object named sm1. The declaration uses the one-line object declaration syntax and is at the class

```java
1    import java.awt.Color;;
2    import java.awt.Graphics;; //needed for drawing shapes
3
4    public class SnowmanV2
5    {
6      //data members
7      public int x = 5;
8      public int y = 30;
9      public Color hatColor = Color.BLACK;
10
11     //member methods
12     public void showXYToSC()
13     {
14       System.out.println("x is: " + x +
15                          "\ny is: " + y);
16     }
17
18     public void show(Graphics g) //g is passed to the method
19     {
20       g.setColor(hatColor);
21       g.fillRect(x + 15, y, 10, 15);   //hat
22       g.fillRect(x + 10, y + 15, 20, 2); //brim
23       g.setColor(Color.WHITE);
24       g.fillOval(x + 10, y + 17, 20, 20); //head
25       g.fillOval(x, y + 37, 40, 40);     //body
26     }
27   }
```

**Figure 3.20**
The class **SnowmanV2.**

```
1     import edu.sjcny.gpv1.*;
2     import java.awt.Graphics;
3     public class ShowMethods extends DrawableAdapter
4     {
5       static ShowMethods ga = new ShowMethods( );
6       static GameBoard gb = new GameBoard(ga, "Show Methods");
7       static SnowmanV2 sm1 = new SnowmanV2();
8
9       public static void main(String[] args)
10      {
11        System.out.println(sm1);
12        sm1.showXYToSC();
13
14        showGameBoard(gb);
15      }
16
17      public void draw(Graphics g) //the drawing call back method
18      {
19        sm1.show(g);
20
21      }
22    }
```

**Figure 3.21**
The application **ShowMethods**.

*System Console Output*
SnowmanV2@3a6727

x is: 5

y is: 30

*Graphical Output*

**Figure 3.22**
The console and graphical output produced by the application **ShowMethods**.

level, so the object can be accessed by the `main` method and the `draw` call back method. Line 11 outputs the object's location to the system console, and line 12 invokes the `showXYToSC` method of the `Snowman`'s class to display snowman `sm1` to the system console. This method is coded on lines 12–16 of the `Snowman` class (Figure 3.20).

Line 19 of the application invokes the `SnowmanV2` class's `show` method to display snowman `sm1` on the game board. This invocation is coded in the `draw` call back method for two reasons. First, the `show` method must be passed a `Graphics` object on which to perform its drawing, and the `draw` method is the only call back method that is passed a `Graphics` object when it is invoked. It passes the Graphics object to the `show` method as an argument on line 19. Secondly, when the game board needs to be redrawn, the game environment invokes `draw`, which will then invokes `show` to redraw the snowman.

Lines 18–26 of Figure 3.20 are the code of the `show` method. The method's signature (line 18) includes the parameter `g` specified in the class's UML diagram (Figure 3.19). It uses this parameter to invoke methods in the `Graphics` class used to change the current drawing color (`setColor` lines 20 and 23) and to draw the rectangles and circles specified in Table 3.2. All of the shape locations sent to the `Graphics` class methods as arguments on lines 21–25 are those contained in the table. They contain the variables x and y because they are relative to the upper left corner of the rectangle that inscribes the snowman. Because the method does not declare local variables named x and y, the class-level data members x and y are used in these arguments. As a result, the snowman is drawn as shown in Figure 3.21 with the upper left corner of its inscribing rectangle at (5, 30).

## 3.6.2 Constructors and the Keyword `this`

In Section 3.5.3, we learned that constructors are methods that construct objects, and the names of these methods must be the same as the class of the objects they construct. If a constructor method is not included in the specification and code of a class, a Java provided default constructor creates the object by performing the following four functions:

1. Allocate the storage for the data members of the class
2. Set the initial values into the data members
3. Assign the collection of data members a memory location
4. Return the location to the client code

Because the class `SnowmanV2` does not contain a constructor method, the default constructor is used to create all instances of this class (objects declared in this class). As a result, function 2 would locate them all at (5, 30), and they would all have black hats. When displayed, they would be displayed on top of each other giving the appearance that only one of them was displayed.

To allow the client code to specify the values of the data members of a newly constructed object, we add a constructor method to its class. Its code template is the same as the template used to code any other method, except its name must be the same as the class's name, and its signature cannot contain a return type. Its signature can contain a parameter list, and it can contain Java statements in its code block. When a constructor method is included in the code of a class, the default constructor is no longer available to construct objects in the class.

Figure 3.23 presents the UML diagram of the class SnowmanV3 that contains a two-parameter constructor, which is a constructor with a parameter list that contains two parameters. When the client code uses this constructor method to create an object, just before the fourth function normally performed by the default constructor is performed, the constructor method executes. Storage is allocated for the constructor's parameters, the values of the client's arguments are copied into them, and then the code of the constructor executes.

| SnowmanV3 |
| --- |
| + x : int<br>+ y : int<br>+ hatColor: Color |
| + SnowmanV3(xLoc: int, yLoc: int)<br>+ showXYToSC()<br>+ show(g: Graphics) |

**Figure 3.23**
The UML diagram of the class **SnowmanV3**.

As with any method, the values copied into the parameters of the constructor could be used anywhere in the constructor's code block by coding the names of the parameters. It is often the case that these parameters are used by the client code to specify the initial values of the data members. When this is the case, the constructor's code block simply assigns the parameters to the data members:

```
public SnowmanV3(int xLoc, int yLoc)
{   x = xloc;
    y = yLoc;
}
```

After this two-parameter constructor's code is included in the code of the class SnowmanV3, the client could use the following code to declare two snowmen located at the upper right and lower left corners of the game board:

```
SnowmanV3 sm1 = new SnowmanV3(5, 30);
SnowmanV3 sm1 = new SnowmanV3(460, 423);
```

## The Keyword this

A method in a class can contain a parameter whose name is the same as the name of one of the class's data members. When this occurs, we say that the parameters *shadow* the data members. For example, the signature of the SnowmanV3 class's two-parameter constructor could have been coded as:

```
public SnowmanV3(int x, int y)
```

When the parameter names shadow data member names, the use of the name within the constructor refers to the parameter, not to the data member. As previously stated, parameters should be considered to be local variables. An assignment into the variable x within the constructor's code body changes the value stored in the parameter, not the value stored in the class-level data member x. We can refer to the data member within the code of constructor (or any other member method whose parameter list employs shadowing), by preceding the data member's name with the keyword **this** followed by a dot, e.g., **this**.x. This syntax could be thought of as the variable x that is a data member of *this* class. Using this syntax, the SnownanV3 class's two-parameter constructor could be coded as:

```
public SnowmanV3(int x, int y)
{   this.x = x;
    this.y = y;
}
```

```
              SnowmanV3

+ x: int
+ y: int
+ hatColor: Color


+ SnowmanV3(x: int, y: int)
+ showXYToSC()
+ show(g: Graphics)
```

**Figure 3.24**
The modified UML diagram of the class
**SnowmanV3**.

This coding of the two-parameter constructor, which uses shadowing, is actually preferred when the parameter list is being used to reset the initial values of the data members. When shadowing is used, the name and type of the parameters and the class's data members in the UML diagram (Figure 3.24) are the same, which is a cue to anyone looking at the UML diagram that the constructor will reset the initial values of the data members.

Figure 3.25 is the implementation of the SnowmanV3 class specified in Figure 3.24. A client application that declares and displays two instances of the class is

```java
1    import java.awt.Color;
2    import java.awt.Graphics; //needed for drawing shapes
3
4    public class SnowmanV3
5    {
6      //data members
7      public int x = 5;
8      public int y = 30;
9      public Color hatColor = Color.BLACK;
10
11     // member methods
12     public SnowmanV3(int x, int y)
13     {
14       this.x = x;
15       this.y = y;
16     }
17
18     public void showXYToSC()
19     {
20       System.out.println("x is: " + x +
21                          "\ny is: " + y);
22     }
23
24     public void show(Graphics g) // g is passed to the method
25     {
26       g.setColor(hatColor);
27       g.fillRect(x + 15, y, 10, 15); //hat
28       g.fillRect(x + 10, y + 15, 20, 2); //brim
29       g.setColor(Color.WHITE);
30       g.fillOval(x + 10, y + 17, 20, 20); //head
31       g.fillOval(x, y + 37, 40, 40); //body
32     }
33   }
```

**Figure 3.25**
The class **SnowmanV3**.

shown in Figure 3.26, and the output to the game board produced by the application is shown in Figure 3.27.

The two-parameter constructor is coded on lines 12–16 of Figure 3.25. It is good programming style to code the constructor as the first method after the data member declarations. Because the

```
1     import edu.sjcny.gpv1.*;
2     import java.awt.Graphics;
3
4     public class ConstructorAndThis extends DrawableAdapter
5     {
6        static ConstructorAndThis ga = new ConstructorAndThis();
7        static GameBoard gb = new GameBoard(ga,"Constructors and " +
8                                            "Keyword:this");
9        static SnowmanV3 sm1 = new SnowmanV3( 5, 30);
10       static SnowmanV3 sm2 = new SnowmanV3(460, 423);
11
12    public static void main(String[] args)
13    {
14       showGameBoard(gb);
15    }
16
17    public void draw(Graphics g) //the drawing call back method
18    {
19       sm1.show(g);
20       sm2.show(g);
21    }
22    }
```

**Figure 3.26**
The application **ConstructorAndThis**.

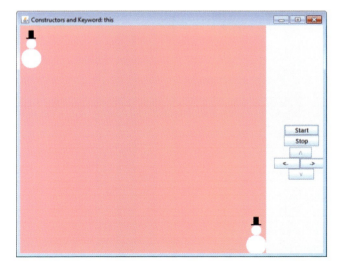

**Figure 3.27**
The output from the application **ConstructorAndThis**.

names of the constructor's parameters are the same as the class's data members, the keyword **this** is used on lines 14 and 15 to access the class's data members and assign the initial values passed into the parameters to them.

The client code (Figure 3.26) invokes the constructor twice, once on line 9 and again on line 10, to create two snowmen named `sm1` and `sm2`. The arguments sent to the constructor specify the initial (x, y) locations of the snowmen, which the constructor stores in the two data members of the objects. Lines 19 and 20 of the client code invoke the `show` method. During the first execution of the method, the variables x and y on lines 27–31 of Figure 3.25 refer to the x and y data members of snowman `sm1`. Because these variables contain the coordinates (5, 30), this snowman is drawn in the upper left corner of the game board. Similarly, during the second invocation of the `show` method of the `SnowmanV3` class, the variables x and y on lines 26–31 refer to the x and y data members of snowman `sm2`, and it is drawn at the lower right corner of the game board (460, 423).

### 3.6.3 Private Access and the set/get Methods

In the interest of simplicity, the data members and the member methods of the classes we have discussed all had public assess as indicated by the plus (+) sign that precedes them in their UML diagrams. Another type of access available in Java is private access, which is denoted in a UML diagram by a minus (-) sign. In this section, we will examine the difference between public and private access and learn which access modifier is normally used for the data members and member methods of a class. This will lead us to a discussion of methods that begin with the prefixes `set` and `get` that are commonly coded in most classes.

### Public and Private Access

In the case of a member method, *access* is the act of invoking the method. In the case of a data member, access is the act of fetching or assigning the contents of the data member. Designating *private* access to the data members or methods of a class places no restrictions on the code of the methods contained in the class. Any line of code in a method of a class can invoke any private or public method in the class and can fetch and assign the value stored in any of its data members.

Private access places restrictions on client code. Client code cannot invoke methods of a class that are assigned private access, nor can it access the data members of a class that are assigned private access. If an application declared an object named `mary`, and the object's class contained a method named `show`, then the client code statement

```
mary.show();
```

would result in a translation error if the method was assigned private access.

> **NOTE** *Public access allows client code to access a class's data member or method, but private access does not.*

The syntax we have used in client code to access (invoke) a public method can also be used in client code to access an object's public data. The syntax is the member (method or data) name proceeded by the object name followed by a dot. This syntax was used on line 12 of the application shown in Figure 3.21

```
sm1.showXYToSC()
```

to invoke the public method `showXYToSC` coded on lines 12–16 of Figure 3.20. This method outputs two data members, `x` and `y`, to the system console. Because the access modifier used in the declaration of these two data members is public, their contents could have been fetched and then output by the client code by replacing line 12 of the client code (Figure 3.21) with the statement:

```
System.out.println("x is: " + sm1.x + "\ny is: " + sm1.y);
```

In addition, the client code could set the x location of snowman `sm1` to 10 by coding:

```
sm1.x = 10;
```

Normally, methods in a class are assigned public access. Exceptions to this will be given in subsequent chapters. Assigning them public access allows the client code to invoke them.

Good programming practice dictates that all data members in a class be assigned private access because allowing the client public access to an object's data members can lead to some insidious and difficult to find programming errors.

That being said, it is often the case that client code has a need to obtain (get) the value stored in an object's private data member, or set the value to a new value. Because any method in a class can access both private and public data members that are part of its class, public methods that begin with the prefixes `get` and `set` are added to the class. The client then invokes these methods to fetch and change the values stored in an object's private data members.

**NOTE** *Normally, methods in a class are assigned public access, and data members are assigned private access. Client code invokes the* set *and* get *methods of the class to access an object's private data.*

## set **Methods**

A `set` method is a `void` method used to change, or set, the value stored in an object's private data member to a new value. The new value is passed into it as an argument. Because most classes have more than one data member, `set` is not a method name, but a prefix used in naming methods. Normally, we code a `set` method for every private data member in the class. The method names begin with the `set` prefix, which is followed by the name of the data member they operate on. For example, `setX` would be the name of the method the client code would invoke to change the contents of an object's private data member named `x`.

The signature of a `set` method contains one parameter and its code block contains one line of code. The method's parameter receives the new value of the data member, and the line of code simply assigns the new value to the data member. Because the value passed into the method is to be the new value of the data member, the parameter's type always matches the type of the data member. Below is the code of the `setX` method that sets the value of a private integer data member named `x` to the value of the argument passed to it.

```java
public void setX(int x)
{
    this.x = x;
}
```

Because the method is public, the client code could invoke it to change the data member x of the object sm1 to 100:

```java
sm1.setX(100);
```

## String Immutability

The String class does not contain set methods to change the value of the characters stored in a String object. This is because Java strings are *immutable*. Once a value has been stored in a String object, the value cannot be changed. Although the following code fragment appears to change the value "Robert" stored in the string object created on the first line to "Bob", in fact it does not. Rather, it creates a new string object, stores "Bob" in it, and assigns the address of the newly created object to the variable name.

```java
String name = "Robert";
name = "Bob";
```

Although this gives the appearance that the value stored in the object has changed, in reality, the new string value "Bob" is stored in a different object. The process is illustrated in Figure 3.28.

**Figure 3.28**
The immutability of **String** objects.

## get Methods

A get method is a nonvoid method used to fetch, or get, the value stored in an object's private data member. The value is returned via a return statement. Like set, get is a prefix used in naming methods that fetch and return private data, and normally, a get method is coded for every private data member in a class.

Good programming practice dictates that the names of these methods begin with the prefix get, which is followed by the name of the data member on which they operate. For example, getX would be the name of the method the client code would invoke to fetch the contents of an object's private data member named x.

The signature of a `get` method contains a return type, and its parameter list is empty. The return type is always the same as the type of the data member it fetches. Its code block contains one line of code that simply returns the value of the data member. Below is the code of the `getX` method that returns the integer value of an object's private data member named `x`:

```java
public int getX()
{
    return x;
}
```

Assuming a client application had declared an object named `sm1`, the following client code increases the object's private data member `x` by one:

```java
int currentX = sm1.getX();
sm1.setX(currentX + 1);
```

Figure 3.29 shows the code of the class `SnowmanV4`. It is the same code as the class `SnowmanV3` shown in Figure 3.25, except its three data members have been assigned private access (lines 6–8) and the console output method has been removed. In addition, `set` and `get` methods for its private data members `x` and `y` have been added to the class. The code of these four methods, `getX`, `setX`, `getY`, and `setY` begin on lines 27, 32, 37, and 42, respectively.

```java
1    import java.awt.*;
2
3    public class SnowmanV4
4    {
5       //data members
6       private int x = 7;
7       private int y = 30;
8       private Color hatColor = Color.BLACK;
9
10      // member methods
11      public SnowmanV4(int x, int y)
12      {
13         this.x = x;
14         this.y = y;
15      }
16
17      public void show(Graphics g) // g, is passed to the method
18      {
19         g.setColor(hatColor);
20         g.fillRect(x + 15, y, 10, 15); //hat
21         g.fillRect(x + 10, y + 15, 20, 2); //brim
22         g.setColor(Color.WHITE);
23         g.fillOval(x + 10, y + 17, 20, 20); //head
24         g.fillOval(x, y + 37, 40, 40); //body
25      }
26
27      public int getX()
28      {
```

```
29      return x;
30    }
31
32    public void setX(int newX)
33    {
34      x = newX;
35    }
36
37    public int getY()
38    {
39      return y;
40    }
41
42    public void setY(int newY)
43    {
44      y = newY;
45    }
46  }
```

**Figure 3.29**
The class **SnowmanV4.**

The application class SetGetButtonClick shown in Figure 3.30 illustrates the use of set and get methods to access private data members.

```
1    import edu.sjcny.gpv1.*;
2    import javax.swing.*;
3    import java.awt.Graphics;
4
5    public class SetGetButtonClick extends DrawableAdapter
6    {
7      static SetGetButtonClick ga = new SetGetButtonClick ( );
8      static GameBoard gb = new GameBoard(ga,"Get Set and Button Click");
9      static SnowmanV4 sm1 = new SnowmanV4(5,30); //top-left corner
10     static SnowmanV4 sm2 = new SnowmanV4(460,423); //bottom-right corner
11
12     public static void main(String[] args)
13     {
14       String s = JOptionPane.showInputDialog("sm2's new x location?");
15       int newX = Integer.parseInt(s);
16       sm2.setX(newX);
17       showGameBoard(gb);
18     }
19
20     public void draw(Graphics g) //the drawing call back method
21     {
22       sm1.show(g);
23       sm2.show(g);
24     }
25
```

```
26      public void rightButton() //moves sm1 one pixel right per click
27      {
28        int currentX = sm1.getX( );
29        sm1.setX(currentX + 1);
30      }
31   }
```

**Figure 3.30**
The application **SetGetButtonClick**.

The program is identical to the ConstructorAndThis application shown in Figure 3.26, except that lines 14–16 and 26–30 have been added. Lines 16 and 29 illustrate the use of the setX method to change the x value of Snowman sm2 and thus reposition it horizontally. Lines 26–30 illustrate the use of the getX method and the rightButton call back method to move snowman sm1 to the right one pixel every time the right button is clicked.

When the program begins, two snowmen, sm1 and sm2, declared on lines 9 and 10, are displayed on the game board by lines 22 and 23 of the draw call back method (Figure 3.30) at the upper-left and lower-right corners of the game board. Then, line 14 displays an input dialog box asking the user to enter the new value of snowman sm2's x coordinate. Line 16 invokes the setX method to operate on snowman sm2, passing it the new x coordinate parsed on line 15. The method stores the new value in sm2's x data member (line 34 of Figure 3.29). The result is that when the game board is redrawn after the dialog box closes, the snowman is drawn at its new x position. Figure 3.31 shows snowman sm2 in its new location, at the middle of the game board, after the user enters 250 in the input dialog box.

Lines 26–30 is an implementation of the game environment's rightButton call back method. As its name implies, this method is invoked every time the button on the game window with the

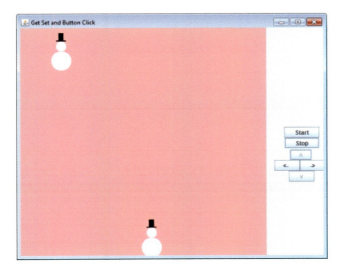

**Figure 3.31**
The output of the application **SetGetButtonClick** after the snowmen are relocated.

right arrow head (→) is clicked. It uses the `getX` method on line 28 to fetch the current x coordinate of `sm1`. Then it invokes the `setX` method to set the x data member of snowman `sm1` to one more than its current value. Because the `rightButton` call back method executes every time the right button is clicked, and the `draw` method is invoked when it completes its execution, `sm1` moves one pixel to the right very time the button is clicked. The upper portion of Figure 3.31 shows `sm1`'s new location after 60 clicks of the game board's right (→) button.

## 3.6.4 The `toString` and `input` Methods

The methods we have developed in Section 3.6 perform work for a client application. They construct objects, display objects, and access the values of an object's private data members. The methods `toString` and `input` are two other methods we can add to a class to perform work for the client applications. These methods expand the client's ability to access private data members, and both of the methods normally permit access to all of an object's data members in one invocation.

> **NOTE** *If a class does not contain a* `toString` *method, and the method is invoked on an instance of the class, the API class Object's* `toString` *method will be executed (see section 3.5.4).*

### The `toString` Method

The `toString` method is a nonvoid method that returns a string containing all the annotated values of an object's data members to the client application. The method's parameter list is empty. Its code progressively concatenates identifying annotation with the value of each of an object's data members, and the resulting string is the method's returned value. For example, the `SnowmanV4` class shown in Figure 3.29 contains three data members: x, y, and `hatColor`. A typical coding of this class's `toString` method would be:

```
1    public String toString()
2    {
3        String s;
4        s = "x is: " + x +
5            "\ny is: " + y +
6            "\nhatColor is: " + hatColor;
7        return s;
8    }
```

Because a class can have an unlimited number of data members, it is good coding practice to code the concatenation of each data member's annotation and variable name on a separate line, as coded on lines 4, 5, and 6. Because the client code often sends the returned string to an output device, the inclusion of a new-line escape sequence in all but the first data member's annotation improves the readability of the output.

The variable `hatColor`, coded at the end of line 6, is declared as a reference variable in the `SnowmanV4` class. When a reference variable is coded where a string is expected (as is expected here because the variable is preceded by the concatenation operator), the translator considers it to be an implicit invocation of another `toString` method. In Section 3.5.4, the location stored in the reference variable `mary` was output with an explicit invocation of a Java-provided default `toString` method, which is part of the API class `Object`. Because the class `Color` contains its own `toString` method, that method is implicitly invoked on line 6, and the string it returns is then concatenated into the string s. Rather than returning contents of the variable `hatColor` (an address), `Color`'s `toString` method places a description of the color stored in the `Color` object `hatColor` into the returned string.

### The `input` Method

The input method is a `void` method that allows the program user to enter new values for all of the data members of an object. The method's parameter list is empty. Its code prompts the user to enter new values for each of an object's data members, parses numeric inputs, and assigns the new values to the object's data members. For example, the `SnowmanV4` class shown in Figure 3.29 contains three data members: x, y, and `hatColor`. A typical coding of this class's input method would be:

```
1    public void input()
2    {
3       String s;
4       int red, green, blue;
5
6       s = JOptionPane.showInputDialog("enter the value of x");
7       x = Integer.parseInt(s);
8       s = JOptionPane.showInputDialog("enter the value of y");
9       y = Integer.parseInt(s);
10      s = JOptionPane.showInputDialog("enter hat's red intensity");
11      red = Integer.parseInt(s);
12      s = JOptionPane.showInputDialog("enter hat's green intensity");
13      green = Integer.parseInt(s);
14      s = JOptionPane.showInputDialog("enter hat's blue intensity");
15      blue = Integer.parseInt(s);
16      hatColor = new Color(red, green, blue);
17   }
```

Because the variables x,y, and `hatColor` are not declared within the method, assignments into them (on lines 7, 9, and 16) change the values stored in the `SnowmanV4` object's data members.

Line 16 creates a new color object using the `Color` class's three-parameter constructor and stores its address in the data member `hatColor`. The arguments sent to the constructor are the shade intensities of the colors red, green, and blue that combine to produce the desired new color. The range of a color's intensity is 0 (lowest intensity) to 255 (highest intensity). High intensities produce bright colors. The program user would have to have knowledge of how to mix shade intensities of these three colors to produce a desired color. These intensities are input and parsed on lines 10–15. In the simplest case, if the desired color were to be either red, green, or blue, the intensity of the other two colors would be input as zero. White is an equal mix of the three colors, and black is the absence (zero intensity) of the three colors.

Figure 3.32 presents the class `SnowmanV5` that includes the code of the `toString` (lines 29–36) and `input` methods (lines 38–54) discussed in this section, and Figure 3.33 presents the application `ToStringAndInput` that demonstrates the use of these methods. The console and graphical outputs produced by the program are presented in Figure 3.34.

```java
1    import java.awt.*;
2    import javax.swing.*; // needed for dialog box input
3
4    public class SnowmanV5
5    {
6      //data members
7      private int x = 7;
8      private int y = 30;
9      private Color hatColor = Color.BLACK;
10
11     //member methods
12     public SnowmanV5(int x, int y)
13     {
14       this.x = x;
15       this.y = y;
16     }
17
18     public void show(Graphics g) //g is passed to the method
19     {
20       g.setColor(hatColor);
21       g.fillRect(x + 15, y, 10, 15); //hat
22       g.fillRect(x + 10, y + 15, 20, 2); //brim
23       g.setColor(Color.WHITE);
24       g.fillOval(x + 10, y + 17, 20, 20); //head
25       g.fillOval(x, y + 37, 40, 40); //body
26
27     }
28
29     public String toString()
30     {
31       String s;
32       s = "x is: " + x +
33           "\ny is: " + y +
34           "\nhatColor is: " + hatColor;
35       return s;
36     }
37
38     public void input()
39     {
40       String s;
41       int red, green, blue;
42
43       s = JOptionPane.showInputDialog("enter the value of x");
44       x = Integer.parseInt(s);
45       s = JOptionPane.showInputDialog("enter the value of y");
46       y = Integer.parseInt(s);
```

```
47        s = JOptionPane.showInputDialog("enter hat's red intensity");
48        red = Integer.parseInt(s);
49        s =JOptionPane.showInputDialog("enter hat's green intensity");
50        green = Integer.parseInt(s);
51        s = JOptionPane.showInputDialog("enter hat's blue intensity");
52        blue = Integer.parseInt(s);
53        hatColor = new Color(red, green, blue);
54     }
55  }
```

**Figure 3.32**
The class **SnowmanV5**.

```
1    import edu.sjcny.gpv1.*;
2    import java.awt.*;
3
4    public class ToStringAndInput extends DrawableAdapter
5    {
6       static ToStringAndInput ge = new ToStringAndInput();
7       static GameBoard gb = new GameBoard(ge,"toString And input
                                                   Methods");
8       static SnowmanV5 sm1 = new SnowmanV5(7, 30);
9       static SnowmanV5 sm2 = new SnowmanV5(460, 420);
10
11      public static void main(String[] args)
12      {
13         System.out.println("sm1's\n" + sm1.toString());
14         System.out.println("sm2's\n" + sm2.toString());
15         showGameBoard(gb);
16         sm1.input();
17         sm2.input();
18         showGameBoard(gb);
19      }
20
21      public void draw(Graphics g)
22      {
23         sm1.show(g);
24         sm2.show(g);
25      }
26   }
```

**Figure 3.33**
The application **ToStringAndInput**.

**Console Output:**
sm1's
x is: 7
y is: 30
hatColor is: java.awt.Color[r=0,g=0,b=0]
sm2's

x is: 460
y is: 420
hatColor is: java.awt.Color[r=0,g=0,b=0]

**Game Board Output:**

(a)                                        (b)

**Figure 3.34**
The console and game board output from the application **ToStringAndInput.**

Lines 8 and 9 of the application (Figure 3.33) declares two snowmen, sm1 and sm2, located at (7, 30) and (460, 420), respectively. The SnowmanV5 class's toString method is invoked inside of the println method's argument list on lines 13 and 14 to obtain annotated versions of the current values of each snowman's data members. The returned string is concatenated with the names of the snowman and output to the system console (top of Figure 3.34).

The output contains a description of each the snowman's current hat color: *java.awt. Color[r=0,g=0,b=0].* This is the string returned from the SnowmanV5 class's toString method's implicit invocation of the Color class' toString method (line 34 of Figure 3.32). The *r=0, g=0, b=0* portion of the output indicates that the red (r), green (g), and blue (b) intensities of the color are all zero: the default hat color black.

Line 15 of the application displays the game board, with the two snowmen drawn on it at their initial locations wearing their black hats (Figure 3.34a). The SnowmanV5 class's input method is invoked on lines 20 and 21 of the application (Figure 3.33), which allows the user to input new values of the two snowmen's data members. Finally, line 18 redisplays the game board, and the two snowmen are drawn at their new locations with their new colored hats as shown on in Figure 3.34b. This output reflects user inputs of:

(200, 200) for sm1's location and (0, 255, 0) for its (red, green, blue) color intensities;
(250, 200) for sm2's location and (0, 0, 255) for its (red, green, blue) color intensities.

## 3.7 OVERLOADING CONSTRUCTORS

Overloading constructors is an object oriented programming term used to describe a class that contains more than one constructor method. The code of each constructor is different, which is the motivation for coding more than one constructor. There is no limit on the number of constructors a class can contain. The name of a constructor method must be the name of the class, so all of the constructor methods in a class have the same name. For example, if the class's name is SnowmanV4, then the name of all of the constructors would be SnowmanV4.

Any of a class's constructors can be used by a client application to allocate an object in the constructor's class. Because the names of the methods are the same, the only way the Java translator knows which constructor is being used is to examine the type and number of arguments in the client's invocation statement.

Consider the code of the class SnowmanV6 presented in Figure 3.35. It contains three constructors, which begin on lines 12, 15, and 20. The signature (line 12) of the first of these constructors contains no parameters and is therefore referred to as the no-parameter constructor. To use the no-parameter constructor, the client's declaration statement would not contain any arguments:

```java
SnowmanV6 s1 = new SnowmanV6();
```

```java
1    import java.awt.Color;
2    import java.awt.Graphics; // needed for drawing shapes
3
4    public class SnowmanV6
5    {
6      //data members
7      private int x = 7;
8      private int y = 30;
9      private Color hatColor = Color.BLACK;
10
11     // member methods
12     public SnowmanV6( )
13     {
14     }
15     public SnowmanV6(int x, int y)
16     {
17       this.x = x;
18       this.y = y;
19     }
20     public SnowmanV6(int x, int y, Color hatColor)
21     {
22       this.x = x;
23       this.y = y;
24       this.hatColor = hatColor;
25     }
26     public void show(Graphics g)    // g is passed to the method
27     {
```

```
28        g.setColor(hatColor);
29        g.fillRect(x + 15, y, 10, 15);      // hat
30        g.fillRect(x + 10, y + 15, 20, 2);  // brim
31        g.setColor(Color.WHITE);
32        g.fillOval(x + 10, y + 17, 20, 20); // head
33        g.fillOval(x, y + 37, 40, 40);      // body
34      }
35    public int getX()
36    {
37      return x;
38    }
39    public void setX(int newX)
40    {
41      x = newX;
42    }
43    public int getY()
44    {
45      return y;
46    }
47
48    public void setY(int newY)
49    {
50
51      y = newY;
52    }
   }
```

**Figure 3.35**
The class **SnowmanV6**.

Because the constructor's code block is empty, the snowman's x, y, and hatColor data members would retain their default values set on lines 7–9, and when the snowman was drawn it would appear at (7, 30) with a black hat.

To use the two-parameter constructor on line 15, the client's declaration statement would have to contain two integer arguments:

```
SnowmanV6 s1 = new SnowmanV6(250, 250);
```

This constructor allows the client to specify the initial location of the newly created snowman. Lines 17–18 would execute and set the value copied into the method's parameters (250) into the object's x and y data members. When the snowman was drawn, it would appear at (250, 250) wearing a black hat.

To use the three-parameter constructor on line 20, the client's declaration statement would have to contain two integer arguments and a reference to a Color object:

```
SnowmanV6 s1 = new SnowmanV6(350, 250, Color.BLUE);
```

This constructor allows the client not only to specify the initial location of the snowman, but also its hat color. Lines 22–24 would execute and set the values 350 and 250 into the object's x and y data members, and it would set the object's data member `hatColor` to blue. In this case, when the snowman was drawn, it would appear at (350, 250), and because line 28 of Figure 3.35 uses the object's `hatColor` data member to set the current color before drawing the hat, it would be wearing a blue hat.

An attempt to create a snowman with an argument list that does not match one of the parameter lists on lines 12, 15, or 20 would result in a translation error. For example, the client statement

```
SnowmanV6 s1 = new SnowmanV6(350.34, 200, Color.BLUE);
```

would result in a translation error indicating that the translator cannot find a constructor whose parameters are a double, followed by an integer, followed by a `Color` object.

> **NOTE**  *Each constructor in a class must have a unique parameter list, and the type and number of the arguments in the client's object declaration statement must match one of these lists.*

It should be noted that once a constructor is coded in a class, the Java-provided default constructor discussed in Section 3.5.3 can no longer be used to create an instance of the class. As a result, to default to the values in data member's declaration statements, a no-parameter constructor (e.g., lines 12–14 of Figure 3.35) must be added to the class.

Figure 3.36 presents the application `OverloadingConstructors` that uses the three constructors shown in Figure 3.35 to construct three snowmen on lines 8, 9, and 10: one at the default location (7, 30), one at the center of the game board (250, 250), and one to its right at (350, 250) with a blue hat. Before each snowman's hat is drawn, line 28 of the snowman's class's show method (Figure 3.35) sets the current drawing color to the snowman's hat color. As a result, when the three snowmen are drawn on the game board (lines 19–21 of Figure 3.36) at their initial locations, one is wearing a blue hat (Figure 3.37).

```
1    import edu.sjcny.gpv1.*;
2    import java.awt.*;
3
4    public class OverloadingConstructors extends DrawableAdapter
5    {
6       static OverloadingConstructors ga= new OverloadingConstructors();
7       static GameBoard gb = new GameBoard(ga, "Overloading
                                            Constructors");
8       static SnowmanV6 sm1 = new SnowmanV6( 7, 30);
9       static SnowmanV6 sm2 = new SnowmanV6 (250, 250);
10      static SnowmanV6 sm3 = new SnowmanV6(350, 250, Color.BLUE);
11
12      public static void main(String[] args)
13      {
14         showGameBoard(gb);
15      }
16
```

```
17    public void draw(Graphics g) //the drawing call back method
18    {
19      sm1.show(g);
20      sm2.show(g);
21      sm3.show(g);
22    }
23  }
```

**Figure 3.36**
The application **OverloadingConstructors**.

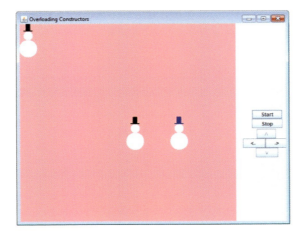

**Figure 3.37**
The output from the application **OverloadingConstructors.**

## 3.8 PASSING OBJECTS TO AND FROM WORKER METHODS

The techniques and syntax used to pass primitive information (i.e., values stored in primitive variables) between client and worker methods were discussed in Section 3.2. The same techniques and syntax presented in that section can be used to pass objects between client and worker methods. In the case of objects, the information passed is actually the addresses of the objects stored in the reference variables that refer to the objects. An unlimited number of object addresses can be passed to a worker method via its parameter list, and the address of one object can be returned from a worker method via its return statement.

### Passing Objects to Worker Methods

The first row of Table 3.3 gives the syntax used to invoke the Game class's *static* method add-1ToX passing it the address of the SnowmanV6 object sm1. The right-most column gives the syntax of the method's signature. For comparative purposes, the second row of the table gives the syntax used to pass the integer age to static method add1toAge and the syntax of the method's signature. As shown in the table, the syntax used to pass objects to worker methods is the syntax used to pass primitive values to worker methods. The primitive type coded in the method's parameter list is replaced with the type of the reference variable (i.e., the object's class name), as shown in the rightmost column of the table.

The following code segment is a `static` worker method named `moveRight` that increases the x data member of the `SnowmanV6` object passed to it by one pixel:

```
public static void moveRight(SnowmanV6 aSnowman)
{
  int currentX = aSnowman.getX( );
  aSnowman.setX(currentX + 1);
}
```

**Table 3.3**
Syntax Used To Pass Objects and Primitives to Worker Methods

| Information Passed | Client Method's Invocation Statement | Worker Method's Signature Coded in the Class Game |
|---|---|---|
| An Object's address | `Game.add1ToX(sm1)` | `static void add1ToX(SnowmanV6 sm)` |
| An Integer value | `Game.add1ToAge(age1)` | `static void add1ToAge(int age)` |

Figure 3.38 is modified version of the program presented in Figure 3.30 that moves a snowman one pixel to the right every time the game board's right arrow button is clicked. The method `moveRight` has been added to the program (lines 32–37), and it is used to move two snowmen to the

```
1    import edu.sjcny.gpv1.*;
2    import javax.swing.*;
3    import java.awt.*;
4
5    public class ObjectsAsParameters extends DrawableAdapter
6    {
7      static ObjectsAsParameters ga = new ObjectsAsParameters();
8      static GameBoard gb = new GameBoard(ga, "Objects As Parameters");
9      static SnowmanV6 sm1 = new SnowmanV6(5, 40, Color.RED);
10     static SnowmanV6 sm2 = new SnowmanV6(460, 423, Color.BLUE);
11
12     public static void main(String[] args)
13     {
14       String s = JOptionPane.showInputDialog("sm2's new x location?");
15       int newX = Integer.parseInt(s);
16       sm2.setX(newX);
17       showGameBoard(gb);
18     }
19
20     public static void draw(Graphics g) // the drawing call back method
21     {
22       sm1.show(g);
23       sm2.show(g);
24     }
25
```

```
26      public void rightButton() //moves sm1 & sm2 one pixel right per
                                                     click
27      {
28        moveRight(sm1);
29        moveRight(sm2);
30      }
31
32      public void moveRight(SnowmanV6 aSnowman)
33      {
34        int currentX = aSnowman.getX( );
35        currentX++;
36        aSnowman.setX(currentX);
37      }
38    }
```

**Figure 3.38**
The application **ObjectsAsParameters**.

right every time the right arrow button is clicked. This method is invoked on lines 28 and 29 to move the two SnowmanV6 objects, sm1 and sm2, to the right one pixel. The objects are created on lines 9 and 10 using the class's three-parameter constructor. The first invocation of moveRight (line 28) passes the location of sm1 to the method, and the second invocation (line 29) passes sm2's location to the method. Because the static method moveRight is coded in the same class as the invocation statements on lines 28 and 29, the name of the class need not be included in the invocations.

Figure 3.39 illustrates the passing of the location from the reference variable sm1 into the method's moveRight parameter aSnowman, and the change in the x data member of the object

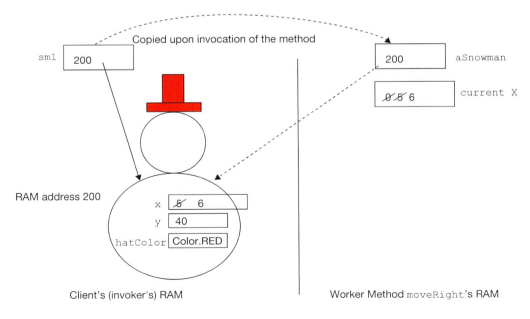

**Figure 3.39**
The passing of the object sm1 to the worker method moveRight.

after the method executes. The client code's RAM memory is shown on the left side of the figure, and the worker method's RAM memory is shown on the right side of the figure. Each time the method is invoked, the value stored in the invocation's argument is copied into the parameter `aSnowman`. The dashed arrow at the top of the figure illustrates this process for the first invocation of the method (line 28) when the location of snowman `sm1` is passed to the parameter `aSnowman`.

After the snowman's location, 200, is copied into the worker method's parameter `aSnowman`, the use of this variable on lines 34 and 36 of Figure 3.38 refers to the client's snowman object `sm1`. Line 34 fetches `sm1`'s `x` data member, and line 36 changes the value stored in this data member. While the method is in execution, the snowman object is shared between the client code and the worker method it invoked. Although we normally say we are "passing an object to a method," we really should say we are "passing the address of the object to a method."

**NOTE** *Technically speaking, objects are not passed to and from methods. Rather, the addresses of the objects are passed between the methods.*

Because the `sm1`'s address is shared, when the worker method ends the initial value of its `x` data member (5) stored inside the object has been overwritten with the value 6 to be consistent with Figure 3.39. This is not a contradiction of the idea that value parameters prevent worker methods from changing the client's information passed to it as parameters because the information passed to the method `moveRight` is the contents of the variable `sm1`, not the object's data member `x`. This is a subtle but important point to understand. While it is true that the worker method can change the contents of the data members of the object `sm1` because `aSnowman` stores the object's address, it cannot change the address stored in the variable `sm1` (which was passed to it).

### Returning an Object from a Worker Method

An object's address can be returned from a method using the same syntax used to return a primitive value from a method. The keyword **void** in the method's signature is replaced with the type of the information being returned. To return the location of an object from a method, the name of the returned object's class replaces the keyword **void**. As is the case when primitive values are returned from a method, if the returned address is to be used by the client code that invoked the method, the client code must assign the returned address to a variable.

The static method shown in Figure 3.40 creates a snowman object located half way between the two snowmen whose addresses are passed into its parameters, and returns the address of the newly created snowman. Assuming the method is added to the class `SnowmanV6`, the following code fragment invokes the method and stores the returned address of the newly created snowman in the reference variable `aSnowman`:

```
SnowmanV6 aSnowman;
aSnowman = SnowmanV6.halfWayBetween(snowman1, snowman2);
```

The signature of the method on line 1 of Figure 3.40 states that the address of a `SnowmanV6` object will be returned from the method. A `SnowmanV6` object is created on line 4, and its address is returned on line 9.

```
1    public static SnowmanV6 halfWayBetween(SnowmanV6 sm1,SnowmanV6 sm2)
2    {
3      int x, y;
4      SnowmanV6 aSnowman = new SnowmanV6();
5      x = (sm1.getX() + sm2.getX()) / 2);
6      y = (sm1.getX() + sm2.getX()) / 2);
7      aSnowman.setX(x);
8      aSnowman.setY(y);
9      return aSnowman;
10   }
```

**Figure 3.40**
A method that returns an object.

### Implicit Arguments

In Section 3.6.2 we saw that the keyword **this** followed by a dot can be used within a constructor method to refer to a data member of its class that has the same name as one of its parameters. In this context the keyword **this** represents the object being created. More generally it represents the object that invoked the method.

That being said, any method in a class can pass the object that invoked it to another method it invokes by coding the keyword **this** as an argument in the invocation statement. The argument is said to be an implicit argument, because it implies the name of the object being passed.

For example, Line 7 of Figure 3.40 invokes the setX method of the SnowmanV6 class (Figure 3.35) to operate on the object aSnowman declared on Line 4. Therefore, during this invocation any coding of the keyword **this** within the setX method would refer to the object aSnowman. To pass this object to the *static* method named meltSnowman whose signature is:

```
public static void meltSnowman(SnowmanV6 s1)
```

the invocation inside of the getX method would be:

```
meltSnowman(this); //implicit argument used here
```

 **NOTE**   *An implicit argument is used to pass the object that invoked a method to a method it invokes, by coding the keyword **this** as an argument in the invocation.*

The method invoked using the implicit argument can be a non-static method, and can be passed more than one parameter. For example:

```
snowman1.meltThreeSnowmen(snowman2, this);
```

### 3.9 CHAPTER SUMMARY

This chapter began our study of the concepts used to design and implement classes, which will be expanded in Chapters 7 and 8. We learned that a class is similar to a blueprint enabling us to define and construct an item, and that an object is a particular item or instance of the class. In the same manner that we use the classes and methods available in the Java API to facilitate the design and development of a program, we can also use and reuse the classes we create.

Methods are subprograms, which are key components of classes. They perform the work of the class by creating, displaying, and manipulating the class's objects. Several versions of a class's constructor methods are normally available in a class to create an object and initialize various subsets of its data members. The names of methods that perform tasks common to most classes have been standardized, and they are included in most classes. The methods named `toString` and `show` are used to display an object on the console or on the game board, and the `input` method and methods that whose names begin with the prefixes `set` and `get` are used to change the values of an object's data members.

The first line of a method is called the method's signature. Java uses value parameters to pass information to a method and a return statement to transfer one value from a method. The list of information passed to a method is called an argument list, which is a sequence of variables and literal values separated by commas. This information is copied into the list of variables declared in the method's signature, which is called a parameter list. Before the method begins execution, the value stored in the $i^{th}$ argument of the invocation statement is copied into the ith parameter of the method. An argument's type must match the type of its corresponding parameter. Value parameters prevent a method from changing the value stored in thevariables coded in the argument list.

Several methods in a class can have the same name if their parameter lists are different. When this feature is used in the coding of a class's methods, we say that the methods with the same name are overloaded. Constructor methods are often overloaded because their names must be the same as the class's name. Normally, methods have public access to permit methods defined outside of the class to invoke them, and data members have private access to prevent methods defined outside of the class from inadvertently changing their values.

A class's data members are declared as class level variables. Class level variables are variables declared outside of the code block of a method and inside the code block of the class. It is good programming practice to declare these class-level variables at the beginning of the class's code block before the implementation of the class's methods.

All class variables declared in a class, whether they are declared public or private, can be directly accessed within the class's methods by simply coding the name of the variable. The only exceptions to this are if the method declares a parameter, or variable, within its code block with the same name. When this is the case, the class variable is accessed within the method by preceding its name with the keyword **this** followed by a period. The context in which direct access syntax can be used to access a variable is called the scope of the variable.

A UML diagram is a graphical depiction of a class developed during the design of the class. This tool not only facilitates the design of the class, but it also documents the data members and methods that make up the class. It is used as the starting point for the implementation of the class. Other class design tools discussed in this chapter are the techniques used to depict and digitize a graphical object, which serve as the basis for the implementation of their `show` methods.

The methods in the API `Graphics` class can be used to implement a graphical object's `show` method. This class provides methods for drawing lines and basic shapes on a previously declared `Graphics` object. The units of the (x, y) location of the lines, shapes, and the size of the shapes passed to these methods is pixels or picture elements. These methods provide the foundation for the rest of the graphical topics in this text.

## Knowledge Exercises

1. Indicate whether the following statements are true or false:
   a) Methods must be coded inside the code block (i.e., the open and close brackets) of a class.
   b) The first line of a method is called its title.
   c) The first line of a method always ends with a semicolon.
   d) All methods must contain a code block.
   e) The method `pow` in the `Math` class is an example of a void method.
   f) We can invoke methods we did not write.

2. Indicate whether the following statements are true or false.
   a) It is good programming practice to begin a method name with an uppercase letter.
   b) It is good programming practice to make the names of methods representative of the work they perform.
   c) A method's name should not contain capital letters.

3. Fill in the blank:
   a) The signature of a method that does not operate on an object must contain the keyword _____.
   b) The signature of a method that does not return a value must contain the keyword _____.
   c) When we invoke a static method, we begin the invocation statement with the name of _____ followed by a dot.
   d) When we invoke a nonstatic method, we begin the invocation statement with the name of _____followed by a dot.

4. Give the invocation statement to invoke the class `Boat`'s `moveBoat` method whose signature is: **public static void** moveBoat().

5. Indicate whether the following statements are true or false:
   a) Client code is code that invokes a method.
   b) A method can invoke the same method more than once.
   c) Parameters are used to pass information to a method, and the information is passed into the method's arguments.
   d) One or more pieces of information can be passed to a method.
   e) One or more pieces of information can be returned from a method.
   f) The type of a parameter must match the type of the information it receives.

**g)** Parameters and arguments share the same variable.

**h)** Java passes information to methods using the concept of reference parameters.

**i)** When a method changes the value of an integer passed to it, the original value is no longer available to the client code.

6. Give the signature of a public method named `add` that adds two integers sent to it and returns the result.

7. After an invoked method completes its execution, which statement executes next?

8. Indicate whether the following statements are true or false:

   **a)** A class-level variable must be coded inside a method in the class.

   **b)** Class-level variables are used to share information among all of the methods defined in the class.

   **c)** A method cannot declare a variable with the same name as a class-level variable.

   **d)** When a method changes the value stored in a class-level variable, the original value is no longer available to the other method in the class.

   **e)** More than one class-level variable can be coded in a class.

9. Give the declaration of a class-level variable named `checkAmount` that is coded in the program's class.

10. Fill in the blank:

    **a)** The method _____ in the `Graphics` class is used to change the current drawing color.

    **b)** The constant_____in the `Color` class stores the color red.

    **c)** The import statement _____ is used to access the methods defined in the `Graphics` class.

    **d)** The import statement _____ is used to access the color constants defined in the `Color` class.

11. Give the name of the method in the `Graphics` class used to:

    **a)** Draw the outline of a rectangle

    **b)** Draw a filled rectangle

    **c)** Draw the outline of an ellipse

    **d)** Draw the outline of a circle

    **e)** Draw a filled circle

    **f)** Draw a line

12. Give the Java statement (or statements) to draw the following shapes and lines on the `Graphics` object `g`:

    **a)** A line from (200, 30) to (100, 75) drawn in the current color

    **b)** The outline of a 100-pixel wide by 50-pixel high rectangle located at (20, 200) drawn usingthe current color

    **c)** A blue filled circle whose diameter is 30 pixels located at (250, 300)

    **d)** A blue filled ellipse 100-pixel wide by 50-pixel high located at (300, 100)

**13.** Fill in the blank:

    **a)** Using the words object and class in: House is to _____ as blueprint to_____.

    **b)** Classes are comprised of member _____ and _____.

    **c)** The name of the graphic used to specify a class is a _____ diagram.

    **d)** Data members of a class are usually designated to have _____ access.

    **e)** Member methods of a class are usually designated to have _____ access.

**14.** Give the Java code to declare an object named `joe` in the class `Person` using the class's no-parameter constructor, and:

    **a)** the one-line declaration syntax.

    **b)** the two-line declaration syntax.

**15.** Referring to Exercise 14:

    **a)** What is actually stored in the variable `joe`?

    **b)** Is `joe` a primitive-type variable? If not, what is the its type?

    **c)** Draw a picture (similar to Figure 3.13) of the memory allocated by Exercise 14a, assuming the class `Person` has two integer data members named `age` and `idNumber`.

**16.** Give the Java code to declare a class whose object will be coffee cups. Each coffee cup will have a size (ounces) and a price. The class will not contain any methods.

**17.** Referring to Exercise 16:

    **a)** Give the code of the two-parameter constructor of the class defined in Exercise 16.

    **b)** Give the client code used to declare a $3.85 coffee cup whose size is 8 ounces.

    **c)** Give the code to output the coffee cup declared in part B to the system console using an implicit invocation of the `toString` method.

    **d)** Repeat part C of this question using an explicit invocation of the `toString` method.

    **e)** What is output to the console by the invocation in part C and B?

    **f)** Give the code to produce the same output generated by part D to the graphic object `g`.

**18.** Give the code of a method named `toString` that, when added to the class defined in Exercise 16, returns the values of its two data members fully annotated.

**19.** Give the code of a method named `show` that, when added to the class defined in Exercise 16, outputs the values of its two data members to the center of a 500 wide by 500 high `Graphics` object named `g`.

**20.** Using a sketch similar to Figure 3.16, show the design of a recreational vehicle (RV) that has two side windows, tires a large entrance door.

**21.** Give a table similar to Table 3.2 that contains the digitized version of the RV design specified in Exercise 20.

**22.** When must the keyword **this** be used in a method to access one of the data members of its class?

**23.** A class contains one integer data member named `total` whose access is private.

    **a)** Use the keyword **this** in a statement coded inside one of the class's method that doubles the value stored in the data member `total`.

**b)** Give a statement coded inside one of the class's method that doubles the value stored in the data member `total` without using the keyword **this**.

**c)** Give the code of a `set` method that client code could use to change the value of the data member `total`.

**d)** Give the code of a `get` method that client code could use to fetch the value of the data member `total`.

**e)** Assuming the appropriate `set` and `get` methods exist, give the client code to double the value of the total of the object named `myAccount` that uses the `set` and `get` methods.

**f)** Assuming the data member `total` was declared to have public access, give the client code to double the value of the total of the object named `myAccount` without using `set` and `get` methods.

**g)** Give the code of the class's `toString` method.

**h)** Give the code of the class's `input` method.

**i)** Which access modifier keyword, **public** or **private**, results in more restricted access?

**24.** Indicate whether the following statements are true or false:

**a)** A class need not contain an explicitly coded constructor.

**b)** A class can contain several constructors.

**c)** A class can contain several constructors with different names.

**d)** A class can contain several constructors with the same signature.

**e)** When a constructor invocation is proceed by the keyword **new**, an object is created, and its address is returned.

**f)** The Java provided default constructor has no parameters.

**25.** A client application has declared three objects named `ship1`, `ship2`, and `ship3` that are instances of the existing class `Starship`. Each starship contains a data member that stores the color used to draw the starship.

**a)** Give the signature of a static method in the `Starship` class named `largest` that is passed two `Starship` objects and returns the address of one of them.

**b)** Give the client code statement used to invoke the static method described in part A of this exercise and place the returned address in `ship1`.

**c)** If the method changed the value of the color data member of one of the starships passed to it, would it be drawn in the new or old color after the method completes its execution?

**d)** Give the signature of a nonstatic method in the `Starship` class named `sameModel` that compares two `Starship` objects and returns a Boolean value.

**e)** Give the client code statement used to invoke the nonstatic method described in part D of this exercise and store the returned Boolean value in the variable `isSame`.

**26.** Using a sketch similar to Figure 3.16, show the design of the user-controlled game piece that is part of the game you specified in Preprogramming Exercise 1 of Chapter 1.

**27.** Give a table similar to Table 3.2 that contains the digitized version of the game piece design specified in Exercise 26.

## Programming Exercises

1. Write a nongraphical application that contains a static method with an empty parameter list that outputs your name and your age on one line to the system console. The main method of the application should invoke it three times. The output it produces should be annotated as shown below (assuming your name is Tommy and you are 18 years old):

    The author of this program is Tommy who is 18 years old.

2. Write a graphical application that contains a static method that is invoked by the `draw` call back method. It should have one parameter to receive the `Graphics` object `g` passed to it. When invoked, the method should output your name and your age to the center of the game board as shown below (assuming your name is Tommy and you are 18 years old):

    The author of this program is Tommy who is 18 years old.

3. Write a nongraphical application that contains a static method to compute and return the square root of the product of three real numbers passed to it. The `main` method of the application should invoke it and then output the three numbers and the returned value clearly annotated.

4. Write a graphical application that contains a static method to compute and return the square root of the product of three real numbers passed to it. The `draw` method should invoke it and then output the three numbers and the returned value clearly annotated.

5. Write a nongraphical application that contains a static method to compute and return the square root of the product of three real numbers that are declared and initialized as class-level variables. The `main` method of the application should invoke it and then output the three numbers and the returned value clearly annotated.

6. Write a graphical application whose `draw` method displays an old television on a table with an antenna on it.

7. The statistics kept for each player on a ladies softball team include each player's name, number of homeruns, and batting average as a real number.

    a) Give the UML diagram for a class named `TeamMember` whose objects can store the three private pieces of data for a player. The class should include a three-parameter constructor, a `toString` method, a method to input the statistics for a player, and a `showSC` method to output a player's statistics to the system console.

    b) Progressively implement and test the `TeamMember` class by adding one method and verifying it before adding the next method. A good order to add the methods is the `toString` method, followed by the constructor, the `showSC` method, and finally the `input` method. (The client code can create a `TeamMember` object using the Java supplied default constructor to test the `toString` method.)

    c) After all of the methods are verified, comment out the test code in the client application and add two `TeamMember` instances to the program whose statistics are passed to the three-parameter constructor. Output these players to the system console and then output them again after the user inputs new names, homerun counts, and batting averages for each player.

8. Write a graphical application that contains a class named `RV` whose objects are the recreational

vehicle designed and digitized as described in Knowledge Exercises 20 and 21. The class's private data members should be the vehicle's body color and (x, y) location.

a) Give the UML diagram for the class. It should include a three-parameter constructor, a `toString` method, a method to input the values of all of an object's data members, and a `show` method to draw the RV at its current (x, y) location.

b) Progressively implement and test the `RV` class by adding a method and verifying it before adding the next method. A good order to add the methods to the class is the three-parameter constructor, followed by the `toString` method, the `show` method, and finally the `input` method. The client code should create an `RV` object using the three-parameter constructor to test all of the methods as they are progressively added to the class.

c) After all of the methods are verified, comment out the test code in the client application and add two `RV` instances to the program whose location and color are passed to the three-parameter constructor. Output these vehicles to the system console and the game board and then output them again after the user inputs a new color and a new (x, y) location for each vehicle.

9. After implementing and testing the class described in Programming Exercise 7, progressively add a `set` and a `get` method to the class for each of the class's data members. After the `set` and a `get` methods have been verified, create two instances of the class using the three-parameter constructor and display them to the system console. Then, ask the user how many home runs and batting average points should be added to each player's statistics. Use the `set` and a `get` methods to change the statistics and then output the two players to the system console.

10. After implementing and testing the class described in Programming Exercise 8, progressively add a `set` and a `get` method to the class for each of the class's data members. After the `set` and a `get` methods have been verified, create an instance of the class using the three-parameter constructor and display it on the system console and the game board. Every time one of the game board's directional buttons is clicked, the RV's location should be changed by two pixels in the appropriate direction.

11. Using the skills developed in this chapter, begin to implement the game you specified in Preprogramming Exercise 1 of Chapter 1. Begin by completing Knowledge Exercises 26 and 27 to design and digitize the user-controlled game piece. Then, implement the class of the digitized game object, beginning with a UML diagram of the game piece that includes a constructor with the appropriate number of parameters, a `show` method to draw the object on the game board at its current (x, y) location, a `toString` method, and a `set` and a `get` method for each of the class's data members. After progressively implementing and testing all of the class's methods, write a graphical application that displays the game piece on the game board and then moves the game piece by two pixels in the appropriate direction every time one of the game board's directional buttons is clicked.

## Endnotes and References

[1] Lanzinger, Franz. *Classic Game Design: From Pong to Pac-Man with Unity*. Dulles, Virginia: Mercury Learning and Information, 2014.

[2] Schell, Jesse. *The Art of Game Design*. Burlington, MA: Morgan Kaufmann Publishers, 2010.

# BOOLEAN EXPRESSIONS, MAKING DECISIONS, AND DISK INPUT AND OUTPUT

## In this chapter

To control the sequence of operations, Java provides three decision-making statements, and in this chapter, we will learn how to write the Boolean condition on which these decisions are based. By default, Java statements execute in the order in which they are coded, although at some point in most algorithms, a decision has to be made as to which of its steps should be executed next. When depicted in a flow chart, this part of the algorithm begins with a diamond shape. To implement these algorithms, programming languages include decision statements that use Boolean expressions as conditions to determine whether to execute or skip statements. Java also provides two statements that always skip a predetermined set of statements, one of which will be discussed in this chapter.

In addition, this chapter extends the input and output techniques of the previous chapters to include input from the system console as well as disk I/O, and it introduces a technique used to alter the sequential execution path of a program when an unexpected error occurs.

After successfully completing this chapter, you should:

- Be familiar with the logical and relational operators and their order of precedence
- Be able to write and evaluate simple and complex Boolean expressions
- Understand how to compare strings and determine their alphabetic order
- Be able to write if, if-else, and switch statements to implement the decision-making part of an algorithm

- Understand the use of the `break` statement
- Be able to perform console input using the `Scanner` class and its methods
- Be able to create, open, read, and write sequential text files to and from a disk
- Begin to understand how to use `try` and `catch` blocks to handle an error exception
- Use decision-making statements to control a timer, a graphical object's visibility and motion, and detect collisions between two objects

## 4.1 ALTERNATIVES TO SEQUENTIAL EXECUTION

When a Java application begins, the first statement to execute is the first executable statement in the method main. The order in which the remainder of the instructions execute is referred to as the *execution path* of the program, or the *flow* of the program. The default execution path of a Java statement block is sequential. It can be thought of as the statements executing in line number order. After the first statement in the block executes, the remaining statements execute in the order in which they are written unless one of the statements specifically alters the execution path.

Many algorithms cannot be formulated in a way that all of its steps are executed sequentially. Therefore, programming languages provide statements to change the default sequential execution path. Programmers use these statements, or constructs, to alter the sequential flow of the program, so they are referred to as *control-of-flow* or *control* statements. We have already used one of these constructs: the invocation of a method. Assuming a method was invoked on line 10 of a program, the next statement to execute would not be line 11, but rather, the first executable statement in the method's code block. Line 11 would execute after the method completed its execution.

Aside from method invocation statements, programming languages provide additional control-of-flow statements to alter the default execution path. Some of these statements are used to skip a group of statements, and others are used to repeat a group of statements. Most often, these control-of-flow statements include a logical expression, called a Boolean expression, to decide when to skip statements or to decide how many times to repeat statements. In this chapter, we will discuss the Java statements used to skip a group of statements. The Java statements that are used to repeat a group of statements will be discussed in Chapter 5.

## 4.2 BOOLEAN EXPRESSIONS

Boolean (logical) expressions are named after George Boole, an English mathematician who conceived of a symbolic algebra for logic. Like mathematical algebraic expressions, Boolean expressions consist of operators and operands. Unlike mathematical expressions, Boolean expressions evaluate to one of two values: `true` or `false`. Boolean expressions used in control-of-flow statements can either be a *simple* Boolean expression, or a combination of two or more simple Boolean expressions called compound Boolean expressions.

### 4.2.1 Simple Boolean Expressions

A simple Boolean expression evaluates to either `true` or `false`. In Java, these expressions consist of a relational or an equality operator surrounded by two operands. Java's four relational operators are given at the top of the Table 4.1, and its two equality operators are at the bottom of the table. The first column in the table gives the name (which implies the meaning) of each operator, and the second column gives the Java symbols (keystrokes) that represent them. The symbols for the last four operators in the table are typed as two keystrokes without spaces. The third column of the table gives examples of simple Boolean expressions involving each of the six operators, all of which evaluate to `true`.

**Table 4.1**
Java's Relational and Equality Operators

| Operator | Java Symbol | Examples that Evaluate to true |
|---|---|---|
| Less than | < | 5 < 7 |
| Greater than | > | 6.31 > 3.14 |
| Less than or equal to | <= | 5 <= 5 |
| Greater than or equal to | >= | 'c' >= 'a' |
| Equal to | == | 6 == 3 * 2 |
| Not equal to | != | 23 != 54 |

**! TIP** A common mistake made when coding simple Boolean expressions is to code the equal to operator as a single equal (=) keystroke, which is interpreted by the translator as the assignment operator. Think of this operator as "is equal" to (==).

When one of the four relational operators is used, the two operands can be anything that can be converted to (interpreted as) a numeric. This includes numeric literals, numeric variables, and arithmetic expressions, as well as character literals and character variables. When a character literal or character variable is used, the character (e.g., `'A'`) is interpreted as an integer (e.g., 65), and the numeric value is used to evaluate the relational expression. The following code fragments are syntactically correct, and the third one evaluates to `true` because `'A'` and `'C'` are interpreted as 65 and 67 (see Appendix C), then the expression is evaluated.

```java
int age = 13;
5 < 2 * 21
100 >= age
'A' < 'C'
25 <= 2 * (age + 1)
```

The interpretation of characters in simple Boolean expressions as numeric imposes an ordering on them called *lexicographical* or dictionary order, which is the order in which they appear in the Extended ASCII table (Appendix C).

When the types of the operands used with one of the four relational operators do not match (e.g., one is a float and one is a double, or one is an integer and the other is a character), one of the operands is promoted before the expression is evaluated. For example, the following simple Boolean expressions are syntactically correct and evaluate to `true`:

```
4.521 < 10       // 10 is promoted to the double 10.0
Math.PI >= -2    // -2 is promoted to double -2.0
2 < 'A'          // 'A' is promoted to 65
```

When one of the two equality operators is used in a simple Boolean expression, the choices for the operands are expanded. Not only can the two operands be anything that can be converted to a numeric, but they can also be two Boolean operands (literals or variables) or two reference variables (including the value `null`). For example:

```
4.535 != 21
65 == 'A'
true != false
myName != yourName
name == null
```

Like the arithmetic operators, the operators in Table 4.1 have an order of precedence associated with them. The four relational operators have equal precedence, and the two equality operators have equal precedence. The precedence value of the relational operators is higher than the precedence value of the equality operators. The expression

```
true == 'C' >= 'A'
```

is syntactically correct and evaluates to `true` because first `'C' >= 'A'` evaluates to `true`, and then `true == true` evaluates to `true`. As shown in Appendix E, the arithmetic operators have higher precedence than the relational and equality operators.

**NOTE** *Arithmetic expressions in simple Boolean expressions are evaluated first. In more complex expressions, the relational operators are evaluated next, followed by the equality operators, and then the logical operators. The assignment operator is evaluated last.*

### 4.2.2 Compound Boolean Expressions

Like simple Boolean expressions, compound Boolean expressions also evaluate to either `true` or `false`. When used in a control-of-flow statement, compound Boolean expressions use the Java conditional binary logical operators AND and OR to combine the truth values of two or more operands. Alternately, compound Boolean expressions can use the unary logic operator NOT to reverse the truth value of a single operand, just as the negation operator reverses the sign of an operand in a mathematical expression. The operands in compound Boolean expressions must evaluate to Boolean values (`true` or `false`). Most often, these operands are simple Boolean expressions but could be a Boolean literal or a non-void method invocation that returns a Boolean value.

Table 4.2 gives the three Java logical operators normally used in control-of-flow statements and the symbols used to represent them. The three operators are shown in decreasing precedence order: the NOT operator has the highest precedence, followed by the AND operator, and the OR operator has the lowest precedence. As shown in Appendix E, the arithmetic operators and the relational and equality operators have higher precedence than the logic operators. The Java symbols for the AND (`&&`) and OR (`||`) operators given in the second column of the table are each two keystrokes. The keystrokes `||` used in the symbol for the OR operator is located above the Enter key on the keyboard.

**Table 4.2**

Java's Logical Operators

| Logical Operator | Java Symbol | Examples that Evaluate to true |
|:---:|:---:|:---:|
| Not | ! | ! ('p' > 'x') |
| And | && | 8 < 10 && 6 == 2 * 3 |
| Or | \|\| | 7 < 4 \|\| 8 >= 5 |

All of the compound logical expressions shown in the rightmost column of Table 4.2 evaluate to `true`. To evaluate the truth value of a complex Boolean expression, we must know the meaning of the conditional logic operators. As previously stated, the meaning of the unary NOT(!) operator is simply to reverse the truth value of its operand. For example, because `'p'` comes before `'x'` in the extended ASCII table, `('p' > 'x')` evaluates to `false` and `!('p' > 'x')` evaluates to `true`. Similarly, `!(6 > 10)` evaluates to `true`.

The meaning of the two binary logical operators, AND and OR, is usually conveyed in truth tables such as the one shown in Table 4.3. The four possible combinations of the truth values of their two Boolean operands, A and B, are given in the two columns on the left side of the table. The corresponding values of the AND and OR operators for each of the four possible values of their operands is given in the two columns on the right side of the table. Summarizing the resulting values, `A && B` evaluates to `true` only when `A` and `B` are both `true`, and `A || B` evaluates to `false` only when `A` and `B` are both `false`. The compound Boolean expression in the third row of Table 4.2 evaluates to `true` because one of the operands, 8 >= 5, is `true`.

**Table 4.3**

Meaning of Java's Binary Logical Operators

| Operand Truth Values | | Meaning of Operators | |
|:---:|:---:|:---:|:---:|
| A | B | A && B | A \|\| B |
| true | true | true | true |
| true | false | false | true |
| false | true | false | true |
| false | false | false | false |

Figure 4.1 presents an application that evaluates simple Boolean expressions whose operands are literals, primitive and reference variables, and a compound Boolean expression. The output produced by the program is given at the bottom of the figure.

When a compound expression is evaluated, it follows the order of precedence from left to right. Parentheses can also be used to make the ordering clear or to enforce a certain ordering in the evaluation. For example, the expression on line 23 might be written as

```
((i1 == 5 || c1 < 'A') && (d1 != 21.8 ))
```

to specify the order of evaluation. Evaluating the sub-expressions in a different order might give a different result.

```
1   public class BooleanExpressions
2   {
3       public static void main(String[] args)
4       {
5       int i1 = 5;
6       double d1 = 3.53;    double d2 = 54.88;
7       char c1 = 'A';    char c2 ='C';
8       boolean b1 = true;    boolean b2 = false;
9       String s1 = new String("Bob");
10      String s2 = new String("Bob");
11
12      System.out.println(i1 < 5);
13      System.out.println(d1 > d2);
14
15      System.out.println(i1 >= d1); // integer i1 promoted
16      System.out.println(d1 <= 3); // integer 3 is promoted
17
18      System.out.println(c1 < c2); // lexicographical order used
19      System.out.println(10 > c2); // c2 promoted to numeric 67
20
21      System.out.println(b1 == b2) ;
22
23      System.out.println( i1 == 5 || c1 < 'A' && d1 != 21.8 );
24
25      System.out.println(s1 == s2); // compares contents of s1 and s2
26      }
27  }

Output
false
false
true
false
true
false
false
true
false
```

**Figure 4.1**
The application **BooleanExpressions** and the output it produces.

Lines 5–8 declare and initialize integer, double, character, and Boolean variables. These variables are used in simple Boolean expressions that are evaluated and output on lines (12–21). The types of the operands in the expressions on lines 15, 16, and 19 do not match, so promotion is used before these expressions are evaluated. The contents of the character variables on line 18 are interpreted as numerics before the Boolean expression is evaluated. Because 65 ('A') is less than 67 ('C'), the fifth output is true.

Line 23 contains an example of a compound Boolean expression containing two conditional logical operators OR and AND. Although the order of the operations in this expression is not important, the AND operation, having higher precedence, is evaluated first. This reduces the expression to

```
i1 == 5 || false
```

which evaluates to `true` (the next to the last output in Figure 4.1).

The operands in the Boolean expression output on line 25 are the two string variables declared on lines 9 and 10. Both strings are initialized to "Bob" by the `String` class's one-parameter constructor, yet the comparison for equality on line 25 produces an output of `false` (the last output). This is because the equality operators always compare the contents of the reference variables rather than the contents of the objects they refer to. Because the objects s1 and s2 are stored in different locations, the contents of s1 and s2 are not equal, and the Boolean expression on line 25 evaluates to `false`. Most often, to compare the contents of two objects, we have to add a method to the object's class that performs the comparison and then returns a Boolean value.

## Short Circuit Evaluation

Java employs short circuit evaluation of compound Boolean expressions. Under this form of evaluation the truth value of the operand on the left side of the logical operator (i.e., && or || operator) is evaluated first. If the resulting truth value uniquely determines the truth value of the compound Boolean expression, it is adopted for the value of the expression and the operand to the right of the operator is not evaluated.

This is the case when the first operand is true and the logical operator is || (OR), which can be verified by examining the first two rows of Table 4.3. It is also the case when the first operand is false and the operator is && (AND), which can be verified by examining the last two rows of Table 4.3. The truth value of both of the following compound Boolean expressions is independent of the truth value of their second operand: a > 23.

```
int n = 50;
(n == 50 || a > 23) // evaluated to true, without evaluating a > 23
(n != 50 && a > 23) // evaluated to false, without evaluating a > 23
```

### 4.2.3 Comparing String Objects

In Chapter 7, we will discuss techniques for comparing the contents of any two objects. Strings are used so often in programs that the `String` class provides several methods for comparing them. One of these is the `equals` method. It is a non-static method that returns a Boolean value. The returned value is `true` when the contents of the string object sent to it is the same as the contents of the string object that invoked it. The comparison of the two strings is case sensitive. The following code fragment demonstrates the use of the method. The first three invocations to the method return `true`, and the last two return `false`.

```java
String name1 = new String("Bob");
String name2 = new String("Bob");
String name3 = "BOB";
String name4 = "Mary";
System.out.println(name1.equals(name2));
System.out.println(name1.equals("Bob"));
System.out.println(name1.equals("Bob") || name1.equals("Mary");
System.out.println(name1.equals(name3)); // false, case mismatch
System.out.println(name1.equals(name4)); // false, different names
```

The third invocation demonstrates that a method that returns a Boolean value can be used as an operand in a compound Boolean expression.

The `String` class contains three other non-static methods for comparing strings. Their names are: `equalsIgnoreCase`, `compareTo`, and the `compareToIgnoreCase`. Like the `equals` method, the `equalsIgnoreCase` method returns a Boolean value, which is `true` when the contents of the string object sent to it is the same as the contents of the string object that invoked it. Unlike the `equals` method, case sensitivity is ignored when making the comparison.

The `String` class's `compareTo` and `compareToIgnoreCase` methods determine the relative lexicographical order of two `String` objects. These non-static methods return an integer whose value reflects the lexicographical order of the string that invoked it relative to the string sent to it as an argument. The `compareTo` method considers case sensitivity, and the `compareToIgnore-Case` ignores case sensitivity. The code fragment below compares the lexicographical order two strings `s1` and `s2`:

```java
int order1 = s1.compareTo(s2);
int order2 = s2.compareToIgnoreCase(s2);
```

The values returned to the variables `order1` and `order2` would be:

- negative when `s1` comes before `s2` in lexicographical order
- positive when `s1` comes after `s2` in lexicographical order
- zero when `s1` and `s2` are equal in lexicographical order

Although the `compareTo` and the `CompareToIgnoreCase` methods can be used to determine when two strings are equal, it is good coding practice to use the `equals` and `equalsIgnoreCase` methods when testing two strings for equality because it makes our code more readable.

## 4.3 THE `if` STATEMENT

The `if` statement is one of two Java control-of-flow statements that can be used to alter the default sequential execution of a program based on the truth value of a Boolean expression. The other statement is the `if-else` statement, which will be discussed in Section 4.4.

The syntax of the `if` statement begins with the keyword **if**, followed by a Boolean expression inside parentheses, followed by a statement or group of statements to be skipped or executed. When there is a group of statements, they must be coded as a statement block; that is, they must be enclosed in braces. The group of statements will be executed when the Boolean condition is `true`, and skipped when the Boolean expression is `false`. Thus, the syntax of the statement is:

|  One Statement Syntax  |  Multiple Statement Syntax  |

```
if(a Boolean expression)
a Statement to be skipped
or executed
```

```
if(a Boolean expression)
{ Statement1 to be skipped or executed
          :
   Statementn to be skipped or executed
}
```

Even when there is just one statement, it is better coding practice to enclose the one statement in braces, which makes the statement more readable and less prone to errors. For example, if during the development of the program we were to decide to add a second statement and neglected to add the open and close braces around the two statements, the second statement would not be considered part of the `if` statement. It would always execute. The two coding examples given below are not equivalent:

```
if(a false Boolean expression)        if(a false Boolean expression)
    statement1                        {    statement1
    statement2                             statement2
                                      }
```

The code on the left always executes `statement2`, even though the indentation seems to imply that its execution is dependent on the truth value of the Boolean expression. A good habit to acquire when writing an `if` statement is to write this code fragment first:

```
if( )
{

}
```

and then fill in the Boolean condition and the statements to be skipped when the condition is `false`. Most often, we see the `if` statement coded as:

```
if(a Boolean expression)
{
   //One or more statements possibly to be skipped
}
```

The meaning, or *semantics*, and the execution path of the `if` statement is illustrated in Figure 4.2.

We conclude this section with a discussion of a use of the `if` statement, making game objects disappear, and then present a game programming application that demonstrates several uses of the `if` statement.

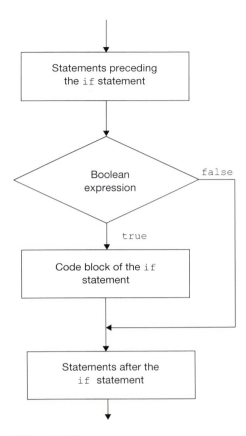

**Figure 4.2**
The meaning and execution path of the **if** statement.

### Using the **if** Statement

In many games, the game's objects disappear based on events that occur as the game progresses. When Pac-Man collides with a food pellet, the pellet disappears, or when Frogger is hit by a car, she disappears. Often, after the event occurs the object not only becomes invisible, but it is eliminated from the game. Graphic objects can be made to disappear by either drawing them in the color of the program's window (or in our case the game board), or by not drawing them at all.

To convey the visibility status of a game piece object, e.g., a food pellet, a Boolean data member is added to the object's class. When an event occurs that changes the status (for example, when food pellet p1 is eaten by Pac-Man), the truth value of the data member is reversed by the code that detected the event. The draw call back method can use the truth value of this data member in an if statement's Boolean condition to decide whether or not to draw the object. If a Boolean data member named eaten, initialized to false, was added to the class of Pac-Man's pellets, and the data member was set to true when the pellet was eaten, then adding the following code fragment to the draw call back method would make pellet p1 disappear after the pellet is eaten.

```java
if( p1.getEaten( ) == false )
{
   p1.show(g);
}
```

If the variable count was being used to keep track of the game's time, and pellet p1 was only to appear after the game had been played for 20 seconds, then a compound Boolean expression would be used in the above code fragment.

```java
if( p1.getEaten( ) == false && count >= 20)
{
  p1.show(g);
}
```

In this case the pellet, p1, would appear 20 seconds into the game, and it would disappear when an event changes that pellet's data member eaten to true.

In Section 2.9.1 (Figure 2.12), the counting algorithm was used to keep track of a game's time. Figure 4.3 presents the code discussed in that section with three if statements added to it: two to the draw call back method (lines 17–31) and one to the timer1 method (lines 33–40). In addition, a BoxedSnowman object s1, whose class is given Figure 4.4, has been added to the application (line 10). The graphical output produced by the program is given in Figure 4.5.

```java
1    import edu.sjcny.gpv1.*;
2    import java.awt.Graphics;
3    import java.awt.Font;
4
5    public class IfStatement extends DrawableAdapter
6    {
7       static IfStatement ga = new IfStatement();
8       static GameBoard gb = new GameBoard(ga, "The if Statement");
9       static int count = 0;
10      static BoxedSnowman s1 = new BoxedSnowman(250, 215, Color.BLACK);
11
12      public static void main(String[] args)
13      {
14         showGameBoard(gb);
15      }
16
17      public void draw(Graphics g) // the draw call back method
18      {
19         g.setFont(new Font("Arial", Font.BOLD, 18));
20         g.drawString("Your game time is: " + count, 10, 50);
21         if(s1.getVisible() == true && count >= 5)
22         {
23            s1.show(g);
24         }
25
26         if(count == 10)
27         {
28            g.drawString("Game Over", 10, 70);
29            g.drawString("Have a Good Day", 10, 90);
30         }
31      }
```

```
32
33     public void timer1()
34     {
35        count = count + 1;
36        if(count == 10)
37        {
38           gb.stopTimer(1);
39           s1.setVisible(false);
40        }
41     }
42  }
```

**Figure 4.3**
The application **IfStatement**.

```
1    import java.awtGraphics;
2    import java.awt.Color;
3
4    public class BoxedSnowman
5    {
6      private int x = 8;
7      private int y = 30;
8      private Color hatColor = Color.BLACK;
9      private boolean visible = true;
10
11     public BoxedSnowman(int intialX, int intialY, Color hatColor)
12     { x = intialX;
13       y = intialY;
14       this.hatColor = hatColor;
15     }
16
17     public void show(Graphics g) //g is the game board object
18     {
19       g.setColor(hatColor);
20       g.fillRect(x + 15, y, 10, 15); //hat
21       g.fillRect(x + 10, y + 15, 20, 2); //brim
22       g.setColor(Color.WHITE);
23       g.fillOval(x + 10, y + 17, 20, 20); // head
24       g.fillOval(x, y + 37, 40, 40); //body
25       g.setColor(Color.RED);
26       g.fillOval(x + 19, y + 53, 4, 4); //button
27       g.setColor(Color.BLACK);
28       g.drawRect(x, y, 40, 77); //inscribing rectangle
29     }
30
31     public int getX()
32     {
33       return x;
```

```
34      }
35
36      public void setX(int newX)
37      {
38        x = newX;
39      }
40
41      public int getY()
42      {
43        return y;
44      }
45
46      public void setY(int newY)
47      {
48        y = newY;
49      }
50
51      public boolean getVisible()
52      {
53        return visible;
54      }
55
56      public void setVisible(boolean newVisible)
57      {
58        visible = newVisible;
59      }
60    }
```

**Figure 4.4**
The **BoxedSnowman** class.

When the application shown in Figure 4.3 is launched, the number of elapsed seconds is displayed on the game board starting from zero (top left side of Figure 4.5). To begin the game the start button is clicked, which causes the elapsed time to be updated every second. Five seconds into the game, the snowman s1 appears at the center of the game board (top right side of Figure 4.5). After ten seconds, the game ends. The elapsed time remains at ten seconds, a message appears on the game board indicating that the game is over, and the snowman disappears from the game board (bottom portion of Figure 4.5).

Line 20 of the application displays the number of elapsed seconds, which is stored in the class variable count. This variable is incremented on line 35 of the timer1 call back method, which (by default) executes once a second. Ten seconds into the game, the Boolean condition of the if statement that begins on line 36 becomes true, and line 38 invokes the game environment's stopTimer method to stop timer 1 from ticking. As described in Appendix B, this method is passed one argument, which specifies the timer number (1, 2, or 3) that is to be stopped. It is a nonstatic method, invoked on the program's GameBoard object gb, which was declared on line 8.

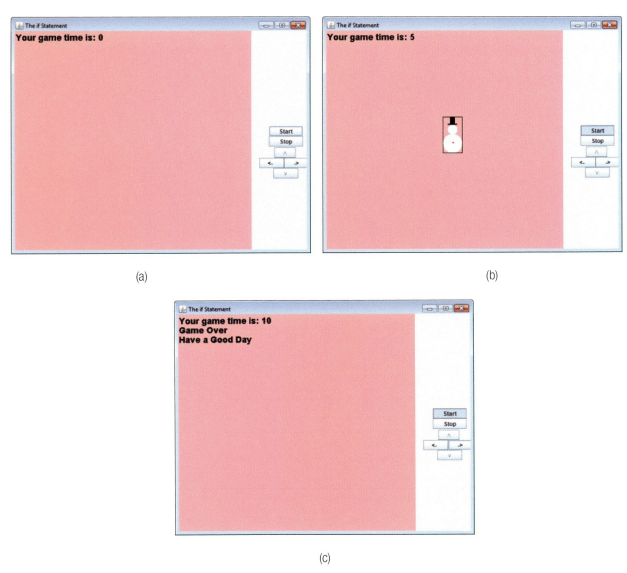

**Figure 4.5**
The output produced by the application **IfStatement**.

The Boolean data member `visible` has been declared on line 9 of the `BoxedSnowman` class (Figure 4.4) to store the visibility status of a snowman, and the class contains a `set` and `get` method (lines 51–59) to allow client code to access this private data member. To make the snowman appear after five seconds has elapsed, snowman `s1`'s visibility status is fetched by a call to the `getVisible` method on line 21 of the application, and the returned value is used in the compound Boolean expression to decide when to show the snowman on the game board. The snowman will be shown when its `visible` data member is `true` *and* the game's time is five seconds or greater. Since `visible` is initialized to on line 9 of the `BoxedSnowman` class to `true`, the snowman is displayed on the game board five seconds into the game.

To make the snowman disappear after ten seconds, the `if` statement inside the `timer1` call back method (lines 33–41) sets snowman `s1`'s visible property to `false` (line 36) when `count` equals ten. This causes the first term in the Boolean expression on line 21 to become `false`, and line 23, which displays the snowman on the game board, does not execute.

The `if` statement that begins on line 26 displays the game ending messages when the game time reaches ten seconds.

## 4.4 THE `if-else` STATEMENT

Like the `if` statement, the `if-else` statement is a Java control-of-flow statement that can be used to alter the default sequential execution path of a program by skipping statements based on the truth value of a Boolean expression. This statement can be thought of as having two clauses: an `if` clause and an `else` clause. Each clause has a statement block associated with it. One, and only one, of these blocks will execute. When the Boolean condition is `true`, the statement block associated with the `if` clause executes. When it is `false`, the statement block associated with the `else` clause executes. The syntax of the `if-else` statement is:

```
if(a Boolean expression)
{
    // One or more if clause statements
}
else
{
    // One or more else clause statements
}
```

and its meaning and execution path is given in Figure 4.6.

Because the statements in the code block that follow the `else` clause are executed when the `if` statement's Boolean expression is `false`, the `else` clause does not contain its own Boolean expression. The following code fragment determines what weight jacket to wear based on the temperature stored in the memory cell `temperature`:

```
if(temperature <= 45)
{
    System.out.println("It is a frigid " + temperature + " degrees,");
    System.out.println("Wear your heavy jacket.");
}
else
{
    System.out.println("It is rather mild " + temperature + " degrees,");
    System.out.println("Wear your light weight jacket");
}
```

The `if-else` statement is used to choose one of two statement blocks to execute: the first when the `if` statement's Boolean condition is `true` and the second when it is `false`. By coding just one statement into the `else` clause's statement block that is another `if-else` statement, we

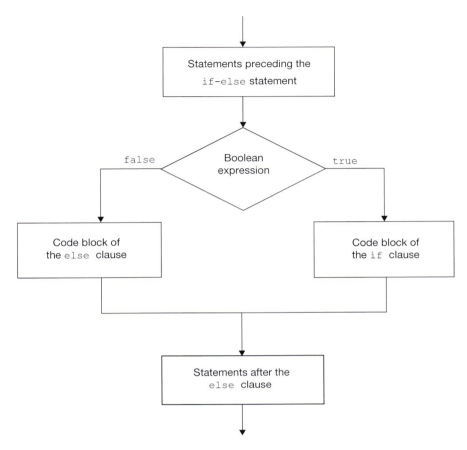

**Figure 4.6**
The meaning and execution path of the **if-else** statement.

can choose between one of three mutually exclusive alternatives, as illustrated in the following coding template:

```java
if(Boolean expression 1)
{
  // One or more if clause statements in code block 1
}
  else if(Boolean expression 2)
{
  // One or more if clause statements in code block 2
}
  else
{
  // One or more else clause statements in code block 3
}
```

As indicated by the second comment in the template, the second set of open and close parentheses defines the code block of the second `if` statement. Because the second `if` statement is the

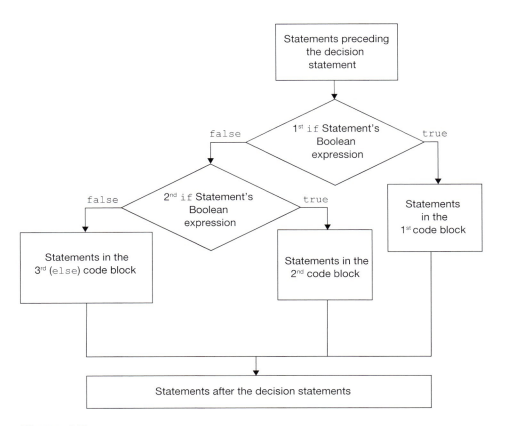

**Figure 4.7**
The meaning and execution path of an **if-else** statement whose **else** clause statement is an **if-else** statement.

only statement in the first else clause's code block, not coding it inside a set of brackets improves readability. Figure 4.7 illustrates the meaning and execution path of the code template.

This coding process can be progressively repeated when there are more than three mutually exclusive alternatives. The following code template illustrates the use of this concept to choose one of four mutually exclusive code blocks to execute:

```
if(Boolean expression 1)
{
    // One or more if clause statements in code block 1
}
else if(Boolean expression 2)
{
    // One or more if clause statements in code block 2
}
else if(Boolean expression 3)
{
    // One or more if clause statements in code block 3
}
else
{
```

```java
    // One or more else clause statements in code block 4
}
```

To improve the readability, it is good programming practice to indent as shown above and to keep the first line of the `if` statements on the same line as the `else` clauses that proceeded them.

As an example, the following code fragment determines which one of four colors, red, green, blue, or white, was contained in the `String` object `carColor`.

```java
if(carColor.equals("Red"))
{
  System.out.println("the car color is Red");
}
else if(carColor.equals("Green"))
{
  System.out.println("the car color is Green");
}
else if( carColor.equals("Blue") )
{
  System.out.println("the car color is Blue");
}
else
{
  System.out.println("the car color is White");
}
```

These decision statements are executed in the sequence shown in Figure 4.8. The Boolean expressions are evaluated in the order in which they are coded. Only one of the statement blocks will execute, which will be the statement block associated with the first `true` Boolean condition. When none of the Boolean conditions are `true`, the statement block associated with the last `else` clause executes. The last `else` clause and its associated statement block are optional. When it is included, one and only one statement block in the construct always executes.

We conclude this section with a discussion of a common use of the `if-else` statement (detecting collisions between game pieces) and then present a game-programming application that utilizes this common game event.

### Detecting Collisions: Use of the `if` and `else-if` Statements

Most games involve some sort of interaction between the game-piece objects. For example, the ball in a Pong game rebounds off a paddle, the frog in a Frogger game is hit by a truck, or a meteorite collides with a space craft. All of these interactions are referred to as collisions, and usually the score or the length of the game is influenced by these collisions. The Boolean conditions in an `if-else` construct are used to detect the occurrence of collisions, and the code blocks inside the construct are used to take the appropriate action (e.g., change the score or end the game) when a collision occurs.

There are several algorithms used to detect collisions, all of which involve the use of decisions statements. In one of the simplest algorithms, we imagine a rectangle enclosing each game piece.

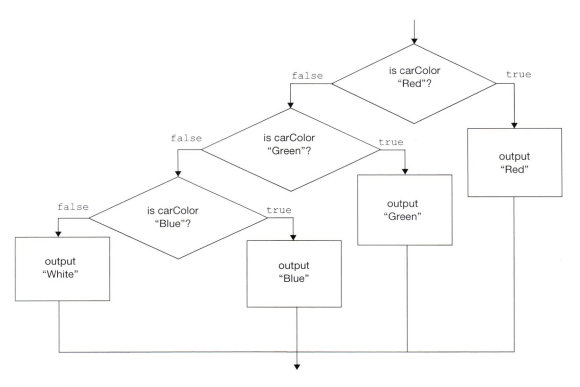

**Figure 4.8**
Determining the color contain in the **String** object **carColor**.

That is, the entire game piece is inscribed inside a rectangle, as shown in Figure 4.9, and the location of the upper-left corner of the rectangle is the game piece's (x, y) location. Then, we consider two objects to be in a collided state when their rectangles touch or overlap.

For example, consider the two snowmen s1 and s2 depicted in Figure 4.9a that are 40 pixels wide and 77 pixels high. If snowman s2 were moving to the left, a collision with snowman s1 would occur when the left side of s2's rectangle was at the same x location as the right side of s1's rectangle. This situation is depicted in Figure 4.9b. The following Boolean expression, which is true when this event occurs, can be used to detect this collision state.

```
s2.getX( ) == s1.getX + 40; // The snowmen are 40 pixels wide
```

Although this collision detection scheme is simple, it is not always accurate. When the rectangles of the two snowmen depicted in Figure 4.9b are at the same x location, the bodies of the two snowmen are touching each other. This is not the case for the two snowmen, s3 and s4, shown in Figure 4.9c. If snowman s4 were moving to the left when the left side of its rectangle is at the same x location as the right side of s3's rectangle, as shown in Figure 4.9d, the two snowmen would not be in a collided state. There would still be a small amount of separation between the left side of s4's body and the right side of s3's head.

Fortunately, in most cases, the game's player would not notice the separation and would visually confirm this pseudo-collision as an actual collision. If we are willing to accept this limitation

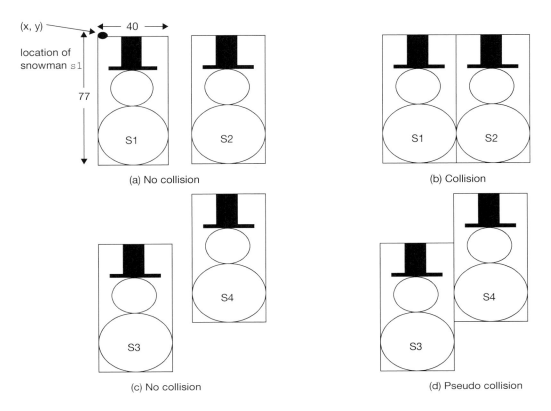

**Figure 4.9**
Noncollided and collided game pieces.

of our collision-detection scheme, we can extend this simple scheme to detect a collision between the two snowmen as they approach each other from any direction.

Figure 4.10 depicts snowman s2 in the following four positions relative to snowman s1:

- Position 1: s2 is to the right of s1
- Position 2: s2 is to the left of s1
- Position 3: s2 is below s1
- Position 4: s2 is above s1

When snowman s2 is in any of these positions relative to snowman s1, then the two snowmen cannot be in a collided state. In fact, s2 could be in two of these positions simultaneously, e.g., to the right and above of snowman s1, which would also be a non-collided state.

Each of the four positions depicted in Figure 4.10 can be easily detected with a simple Boolean expression. Assuming the snowman is inscribed inside a rectangle that is w pixels wide and h pixels high, the right column of Table 4.4 gives the Boolean conditions that evaluate to true when the snowmen are in each of the four positions.

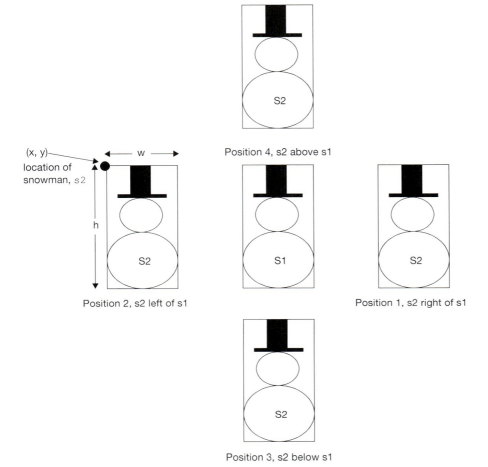

**Figure 4.10**
The non-collided positions of snowman **s2** relative to snowman **s1**.

**Table 4.4**
Boolean Expressions to Detect the Four Non-collided Positions in Figure 4.8

| Position of Snowman s2 Relative to s1 | Boolean Expression to Detect the Position |
|---|---|
| 1. s2 is to the right of s1 | s2.getX( ) > s1.getX( ) + w |
| 2. s2 is to the left of s1 | s2.getX( ) + w < s1.getX( ) |
| 3. s2 is below s1 | s2.getY( ) > s1.getY( ) + h |
| 4. s2 is above s1 | s2.getY( ) + h < s1.getY( ) |

These four Boolean expressions can be used in `if-else` statements to determine when the two snowmen have not collided; otherwise they have collided.

```
if(s2.getX() > s1.getX() + w) // s2 right of s1
{
   System.out.println("no collision");
}
```

```java
else if(s2.getX() + w < s1.getX()) // s2 left of s1
{
  System.out.println("no collision");
}
else if(s2.getY() > s1.getY() + h) // s2 below s1
{
  System.out.println("no collision");
}
else if(s2.getY( ) + h < s1.getY( )) // s2 above s1
{
  System.out.println("no collision");
}
else // collision
{
    System.out.println("collision");
}
```

Alternately, the Boolean conditions could be combined to form a compound Boolean condition that would evaluate to `true` for a non-collision.

```java
(s2.getX( ) > s1.getX() + w || s2.getX() + w < s1.getX() ||
 s2.getY( ) > s1.getY() + h || s2.getY() + h < s1.getY())
```

Using this compound Boolean expression, the series of `if-else` statements to detect a collision would become

```java
if(s2.getX( ) > s1.getX() + w || s2.getX() + w < s1.getX() ||
   s2.getY( ) > s1.getY() + h || s2.getY() + h < s1.getY())
{
  System.out.println("no collision");
}
   else //collision
{
  System.out.println("collision");
}
```

The truth value of the Boolean condition could also be reversed, using Java's `not` (!) logical operator, and the `if` clause of the `if-else` statement would detect a collision between the two snowmen.

```java
if( !(s2.getX( ) > s1.getX() + w || s2.getX() + w < s1.getX() ||
   s2.getY( ) > s1.getY() + h || s2.getY() + h < s1.getY()) )
{
  System.out.println("collision");
}
else // no collision
{
  System.out.println("no collision");
}
```

The following code fragment uses an expanded version this `if-else` statement's Boolean expression to detect when a collision occurs and snowman `s2` is in a visible state. When this occurs, the game's score (the variable `score`) is increased by 1, and snowman s1's visible property is set to `false`.

```java
if( !(s2.getX( ) > s1.getX() + w || s2.getX() + w < s1.getX()||
      s2.getY( ) > s1.getY() + h || s2.getY() + h < s1.getY()) &&
      s1.getVisible == true) // collision and s1 is visible
{
    score = score + 1;
    s1.setVisible(false);
}
```

An additional term has been added at the end of the Boolean expression. Because it is preceded by the `&&` (AND) operator, the expanded expression is only `true` when the two snowmen collide *and* snowman s1 is visible. This prevents the score from increasing when a game object (i.e., s2) collides with an invisible game object that is no longer part of the game (i.e., s1).

## 4.5 NESTED `if` STATEMENTS

Just as the `else` clause of an `if-else` statement can contain an `if` statement, the statement block of an `if` statement can also contain other `if` statements. This method of coding is referred to as nested `if` statements, because the second `if` statement can be thought of as an egg inside the nest formed by the first `if` statement's code block.

The following code fragment contains a Boolean variable `raining` and an integer variable `temperature`, and uses a nested `if` statement to determine if a sweater and a raincoat should be carried on a cold day when it is raining.

```java
if(raining == true)
{
  System.out.println("Take your umbrella, ");
  if(temperature <= 50) // begins a nested if-else statement
  {
      System.out.println("take a sweater, ");"
      System.out.println("and your raincoat.");
  }
}
```

An `if-else` statement can also be nested inside an `if` statement as demonstrated in the below code fragment:

```java
if(raining == true)
{
  System.out.println("Take your umbrella, ");
  if(temperature <= 50) // begins a nested if statement
  {
      System.out.println("take a sweater, ");"
      System.out.println("and your raincoat.");
  }
  else // temperature is > 50 degrees
```

```java
    {
        System.out.println("and your raincoat");
    }
}
```

The `else` clause in an `if` statement is always paired with the `if` statement whose code block ends just before the `else` clause. The indentation used in the code fragment above is considered good programming practice because it implies this pairing: the `else` clause is part of the `if` statement that checks the temperature. This code fragment is equivalent to the code fragment below, which is considered to be poor programming style because its indentation erroneously implies that the `else` clause is part of the `if` statement that determines if it is raining.

```java
if(raining == true)
{
  System.out.println("Take your umbrella, ");
  if(temperature < 50) // begins a nested if statement
  {
      System.out.println("and carry your raincoat too");
  } // end of the inner if statement
else
{
      System.out.println("but not your raincoat");
}
{ // end of the outer if statement
```

The following code segment is another example of the use of a nested `if` statement. It is an alternate way of determining when snowmen `s1` and `s2` have collided *and* `s1` is visible.

```java
if( !(s2.getX( ) > s1.getX() + w || s2.getX() + w < s1.getX()||
     s2.getY( ) > s1.getY() + h || s2.getY() + h < s1.getY()))//collision
{
      if(s1.getVisible == true) // and s1 is visible
      {
        score = score + 1;
        s1.setVisible(false);
      }
}
```

## 4.6 THE `switch` STATEMENT

The `switch` statement is another control-of-flow statement available in Java. It is not as versatile as the `if` and `if-else` statements in that the decisions these statements make cannot be based on an explicitly written simple or compound Boolean expression. The syntax of the `switch` statement limits the operator used in its decision making to equality. In addition, the equality must be between:

- two `String` objects
- two `byte`, `short`, `char`, or `int` primitive-data types (or classes that "wrap" these data types), or

- two instances of a previously defined enumerated type (which will be discussed in Chapter 7)

All uses of the `switch` statement can be coded using an `if-else` statement, but not vice-versa. That being said, there are times when the use of the `switch` statement makes our programs more readable and therefore easier to understand, modify, and maintain. It can only be used when the decision as to which statements to execute and which statements to skip is based on a choice selected from a group, or menu, of *finite* choices. When this is the case, the use of the `switch` statement is considered to be good programming practice.

The syntax of the `switch` statement is depicted in Figure 4.11. The indentation used in the figure also reflects good programming practice.

```
switch (choiceExpression)
{
  case choiceValue1:
  {
        // statement block for choiceValue1
        break;
  }
  case choiceValue2:
  {
        // statement block for choiceValue2
        break;
  }

          :
          :
  case choiceValueN:
  {
        // statement block for choiceValueN
        break;
  }
  default:
  {
        // default statements
  }
}
```

**Figure 4.11**
The syntax of the **switch** statement.

As shown in the figure, the first line of the statement begins with the keyword **switch**, and the remaining lines of the statement consist of `case` clauses and a `default` clause enclosed in a set of brackets. When typing the statement, it is best to begin by typing the following required syntax and then filling in the remainder of the statement's first line and the `case` and `default` clauses that are appropriate to the particular use of the statement.

```
switch( )
{

}
```

Referring to Figure 4.11, the three most common (and difficult to discover) syntax errors made when coding a `switch` statement are:

1. neglecting to code the open and close parentheses after the keyword **switch**
2. coding a semicolon after the close parenthesis on the first line of the statement
3. neglecting to code the colon (not semicolon) after the choiceValue1, or choiceValue2... or after the keyword **default**

The entity enclosed in the parentheses after the keyword **switch** is referred to as the *choice expression*. The choice expression must be a variable whose type is one of the allowable types previously mentioned (e.g., a `String` object, an integer variable, etc.) or it can be an expression that evaluates to one of these types.

```
switch(choice)
{
    case choiceValue1:
    {
      // statements for choiceValue1
      break;
    }
    case choiceValue2:
    {
      // statements for choiceValue2
      break;
    }
       :
       :
    case choiceValueN:
    {
      // statements for choiceValueN
      break;
    }
    default
    {
      // default statements
    }
}
              (a)
```

```
if (choice == choiceValue1)
{
    // statements for choiceValue1
}
else if(choice == choiceValue2)
{
    // statements for choiceValue2
}
    :
    :
else if(choice == choiceValueN)
{
    // statements for choiceValueN
}
else
{
    // default statements
}
              (b)
```

**Figure 4.12**
Semantically equivalent **switch** and **if-else** statements.

When a `switch` statement begins execution, the value of the choice expression is determined and then the statement block of the *first* `case` clause whose choice value is equal to that value is executed. If the choice expression is not equal to one of the choice values, the default clause's statement block executes. Figure 4.12 illustrates the meaning and execution path of a `switch` statement (Figure 4.12a) by comparing it with an equivalent `if-else` statement (Figure 4.12b).

As an example, the following code fragment determines which one of four colors, red, green, blue, or white, is contained in the String object carColor:

```java
switch (carColor)
{
  case "red":
  {
    System.out.println("the car color is red");
    break;
  }
  case "green":
  {
    System.out.println("the car color is green");
    break;
  }
  case "blue":
  {
    System.out.println("the car color is blue");
    break;
  }
  default:
  {
    System.out.println("the car color is white");
  }
}
```

The following code fragment illustrates the use of an arithmetic expression as the choice expression in a switch statement:

```java
int i;
String s = JOptionPane.showInputDialog("enter an integer");
i = Integer.parseInt(i);

switch (i * 2)
{
  case 10:
  {
    System.out.println("two times the number is 10");
    break;
  }
  case 20:
  {
    System.out.println("two times the number is 20");
    break;
  }
  default:
  {
    System.out.println("two times the number is not 10 or 20");
  }
}
```

There is no limit to the number of case clauses that can be used in a `switch` statement. The `default` clause is optional and, if used, must be coded as the last clause in the statement. The brackets surrounding the statements in the `case` and `default` clauses are not necessary and are only used to improve readability.

Several cases can be assigned to the same statement block using the syntax

```java
case 2: case 5: case 7:
{
  // statement block for all three cases
   break;
}
```

The previous statement block would execute when the choice expression evaluates to 2, 5, or 7.

The `break` statement at the end of the code block of each `case` is also optional. However, unlike the optional bracket pairs, its presence has a major impact on the execution path of the construct. A `break` statement is a control-of-flow statement that does not use a logical expression to decide when to execute or skip statements. Rather, when a `break` statement is executed inside a `switch` statement, it always ends the execution of the `switch` statement in which it is coded. Basically, it means: break out of this statement. It can also be used inside `if` or `if-else` statements to end their execution.

When a `break` statement inside a control-of-flow statement is executed, the next statement to execute is the one that immediately follows the control-of-flow statement. When executed inside a `switch` statement, the statement blocks in all of the subsequent `case` clauses and the statement block in the `default` clause are skipped, and the next statement to execute is the one that follows the close brace at the end of the `switch` statement. (That is, the close brace that is paired with the open brace after the keyword `switch`.)

When the `break` statement is not coded at the end of a `case` clause, after the statements in that clause execute, the statements in all subsequent case clauses execute until a `break` statement is encountered. If a `break` statement is not encountered, the `default` clause also executes. Because most times the choices coded into the `switch` construct are mutually exclusive, a `break` statement is usually coded as the last statement in each `case` clause.

Figure 4.13 shows a game application that uses the `switch` and `break` statements to change the position of a snowman on a game board, uses the `if` and `if-else` statements to determine the game's score, make a second snowman disappear and then reappear at a new location, and to determine when the game is over.

When the application is launched, two snowmen, one wearing a black hat and the other wearing a green hat, appear on the game board below the game's score and remaining time (Figure 4.14a). The game begins when the player clicks the Start button on the game board. The objective of the game is to make the two snowmen collide as many times as possible before time runs out, using the keyboard cursor control keys to move the black-hat snowman. Each time they collide, a point is awarded and the green-hat snowman disappears. It reappears at a new location after the black-hat snowman has been moved to a location such that the two snowmen are no longer in a collision state.

The game's snowmen, s1 and s2, are instances of the BoxedSnowman class (Figure 4.4). They are created on lines 9 and 10 of the application shown in Figure 4.13 using a three parameter constructor to specify the snowmen's position and hat color: s1 green, s2 black. Line 29 of the draw call back method outputs the remaining time, and line 60 outputs the player's score just before the draw method ends.

Lines 54–58 invokes the BoxedSnowman class's show method to draw the snowmen on the game board at their current (x, y) locations. The if statement that begins on line 55 checks the visibility status of snowman s1 to decide if it should be drawn (line 57). The initial value of a BoxedSnowman's visible property is true (Figure 4.4, line 9), so when the game is launched, it appears on the game board.

```
1    import edu.sjcny.gpv1.*;
2    import java.awt.*;
3    //Use of decision statements
4
5    public class DecisionsControlOfFlow extends DrawableAdapter
6    {
7       static DecisionsControlOfFlow ge = new DecisionsControlOfFlow();
8       static GameBoard gb = new GameBoard(ge, "Control Of Flow");
9       static BoxedSnowman s1 = new BoxedSnowman(300, 200, Color.GREEN);
10      static BoxedSnowman s2 = new BoxedSnowman(30, 100, Color.BLACK);
11      static int score = 0;
12      static int count = 10;
13
14      public static void main(String[] args)
15      {
16         showGameBoard(gb);
17      }
18
19      public void draw(Graphics g) //call back method
20      {
21         int w = 40;
22         int h = 77;
23         int s1X, s1Y, s2X, s2Y, temp;
24
25         s1X = s1.getX(); s1Y = s1.getY();
26         s2X = s2.getX(); s2Y = s2.getY();
27         g.setColor(Color.BLACK);
28         g.setFont(new Font("Arial", Font.BOLD, 18));
29         g.drawString("Time remaining: " + count, 260, 50);
30
31         if(count == 0) //game over
32         {
33            g.setColor(Color.BLACK);
34            g.drawString("Game Over", 205, 70);
35            g.drawString("Have a Good Day", 175, 90);
```

```
36              }
37          else if( !(s2X > s1X + w || s2X + w < s1X || s2Y > s1Y + h ||
38                 s2Y + h < s1Y) && s1.getVisible() == true) // collision
39          {
40              score = score + 1;
41              s1.setVisible(false);
42          }
43          else if( s2X > s1X + w || s2X + w < s1X || s2Y > s1Y + h ||
44                 s2Y + h < s1Y) // no collision
45          {
46              if(s1.getVisible() == false) // not visible
47              {   temp = s1.getX();
48                  s1.setX(s1.getY());
49                  s1.setY(temp);
50                  s1.setVisible(true);
51              }
52          }
53
54          s2.show(g);
55          if(s1.getVisible() == true)
56          {
57              s1.show(g);
58          }
59          g.setColor(Color.BLACK);
60          g.drawString("Score: " + score, 150, 50);
61      }
62
63      public void keyStruck(char key) // call back method
64      {
65          int newX, newY;
66
67          switch (key)
68          {
69              case 'L':
70              {
71                  newX = s2.getX() - 2;
72                  s2.setX(newX);
73                  break;
74              }
75              case 'R':
76              {
77                  newX = s2.getX() + 2;
78                  s2.setX(newX);
79                  break;
80              }
81              case 'U':
82              {
83                  newY = s2.getY() - 2;
84                  s2.setY(newY);
```

```
85                   break;
86                }
87                case 'D':
88                {
89                    newY = s2.getY() + 2;
90                    s2.setY(newY);
91                }
92          } // end of switch statement
93      }
94      public void timer1() // call back method
95      {
96          count = count - 1;
97          if(count == 0)
98          {
99              gb.stopTimer(1);
100         }
101     }
102 }
```

**Figure 4.13**
The **DecisionsControlOfFlow** application: A decision statement case study.

The use of a `switch` statement is illustrated on lines 67–92. In this case, the `switch` statement is used to determine which of the four cursor-control keyboard keys was struck to move the snowman `s2` two pixels from its current location. The statement is coded inside the game environment's call back method `keyStruck` (line 63), which is invoked by the game environment every time a keyboard key is struck. The method has one parameter named `key` whose type is `char`, and the game environment passes a character, the key that was struck, into it. After `keyStruck` completes its execution, the game environment invokes the `draw` call back method.

The parameter `key` on line 63 is used as the `switch` statement's choice expression on line 67. When the keyboard left, right, up, or down cursor-control keys are struck, they generate the characters 'L', 'R', 'U', or 'D', respectively. These characters are used as the `switch` statement's cases on lines 69, 75, 81, and 87 to decide in which direction to move snowman `s2`.

 When a key on the keyboard is held down, it transmits characters 20 times a second just as if the key was being pressed and released 20 times a second. For this reason, to control the motion of game pieces, key strokes are preferred over button clicks.

Figure 4.14b shows the game board three seconds after the Start button was clicked and the right and down cursor keys were used to move snowman `s2` adjacent to snowman `s1`. One more right cursor keystroke will cause a collision.

Line 31 begins an `if-else` statement that contains a nested `if-else` statement (line 37) and two nested `if` statements (lines 43 and 46). The keyword `else` that appears on lines 37 and 43 are part of the `if-else` statements that begin on lines 31 and 37, respectively. Line 31 decides if the game is over, and when it is, it announces it to the game's player.

The if-else statement that begins on line 37 decides if the two snowmen have collided when snowman s2 is visible. Its Boolean expression, as discussed at the end of Section 4.4, is true when it is not the case that snowman s2 is to the right, to the left, or below or above snowman s1, and s1 is visible. When this is the case, the if clause's code block increases the player's score by one point using the counting algorithm (line 40) and sets the visible property of snowman s1 to false (line 41). Setting s1's visible property to false causes it to disappear from the game board (Figure 4.14c) because the Boolean condition in the if statement that draws s1 (line 55) is now false. The setting of s1's visible property to false also prevents the awarding of points until s1 is again visible which occurs when the two snowmen are no longer in a collision state. The determination that the two snowmen are no longer in a collision state is performed by the if statement on line 43. Its Boolean condition is the same as the condition on lines 37 and 38, except that the

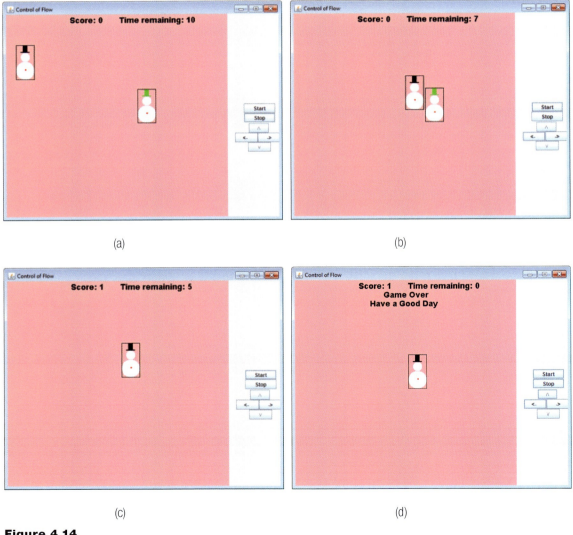

(a)

(b)

(c)

(d)

**Figure 4.14**
The output of the **DecisionsControlOfFlow** application.

NOT (!) operator and the test for visible have been removed. This Boolean condition is `true` when the snowmen are not in a collision state. Then the nested `if` statement that begins on line 46 executes and decides if snowman `s1` is invisible. When it is invisible, the nested `if` statement's code block executes relocating snowman `s1` by swapping its x and y coordinates. This code block also sets `s1`'s `visible` property to `true` (line 50), which causes the `if` statement that begins on line 55 to draw snowman `s1` on the game board at its new location (Figure 4.14d).

## 4.7  CONSOLE INPUT AND THE Scanner CLASS

We have already learned how to perform input and output using message dialog boxes and how to send output to the system console using the `println` method. The system console can also be used to perform keyboard input using methods in the `Scanner` class. These nonstatic methods can also be used to perform input from a disk file, which will be discussed in the next section.

Just as there is a predefined output object attached to the system console, `System.out`, there is a predefined input object attached to the console, `System.in`. However, before we use the input methods in the `Scanner` class we have to declare a `Scanner` object and pass the console object to the `Scanner` class's one-parameter constructor. The following code fragment declares the `Scanner` object `consoleIn`:

```
Scanner consoleIn = new Scanner(System.in);
```

The `Scanner` object, `consoleIn`, can then be used to invoke non-void methods in the `Scanner` class, which accept input from the system console. As the user types the input, the keystrokes are output to the console. The names of the three most frequently used methods in this class all begin with the word next. Their full names and the type of data they return are given in Table 4.5. To use the methods, include the following import statement in your program:

```
import java.util.Scanner;
```

**Table 4.5**
Commonly Used Input Methods in the **Scanner** Class

| Method Name | Returned Type |
| --- | --- |
| nextInt | int |
| nextDouble | double |
| nextLine | String |

As their names imply, `nextInt` and `nextDouble` are both used to accept numeric input. When the input is an integer, `nextInt` is used, and `nextDouble` is used when the input is a real number. Both methods parse the input characters into a numeric value, and so there is no need to use the parsing methods in the wrapper classes `Integer` and `Double`. The method `nextLine` is used to accept `String` input.

When these methods are invoked, the program's execution is suspended until the user completes the keyboard input by striking the Enter key. Then, the methods return the input value. Until that point, the user can edit the input using the Backspace and Delete keys. It is good programming practice to precede the method invocations with a well-composed prompt output to the system console. The following code fragment accepts a person's name, age, and weight entered into the system console:

```java
Scanner consoleIn = new Scanner(System.in);
String name;
int age;
double weight;

System.out.print("Enter your name: ");
name = consoleIn.nextLine();

System.out.print("\nEnter your age: ");
age = consoleIn.nextInt();

System.out.print("\nEnter your weight: ");
weight = consoleIn.nextDouble();
```

Several numeric inputs can be entered on one line as long as they are separated (delimited) by at least one space. Spaces that precede a numeric input are ignored. The following code segment accepts a person's age and weight input on one line to the system console.

```java
int age;
double weight;
Scanner consoleIn = new Scanner(System.in);

System.out.print ("Enter your age and weight on one line " +
  "separated by at least one space: ");
age = consoleIn.nextInt();
weight = consoleIn.nextDouble();
```

 Several numeric inputs, separated by at least one space, can be input on the same line.

Spaces that precede a string input are not ignored. They are considered, and become, part of the input string. Spaces typed after a numeric input will become part of a string input subsequently read from the same line. For this reason, strings should not be input on the same line as numeric inputs.

 Numeric and string inputs should not be input on the same line.

When a numeric input and a string are read from two separate input lines, and the numeric input precedes the string, two invocations of nextLine are required to capture the string. This is because numeric inputs leave the character generated by the Enter key "behind," and the nextLine method considers this a valid input string (the empty string ""). The following statements accept a person's age, followed by the person's name and address. The first string input is properly preceded by an additional invocation of the `nextLine` method.

```
Scanner consoleIn = new Scanner(System.in);
int age;
String name;
String address;

System.out.print("\nEnter your age: ");
age = consoleIn.nextInt();

consoleIn.nextLine(); // clears the enter keystroke left behind
System.out.print("Enter your name: ");
name = consoleIn.nextLine();

System.out.print("Enter your address: ");
address = consoleIn.nextLine();
```

To fully understand `Scanner` class input, we must recognize that the characters the user types are transferred to a memory resident storage area called an input *buffer*. When a `Scanner` method is invoked and the buffer is empty, the method pauses until an Enter key is struck. If the buffer is not empty, the method accepts an input from the buffer, and then the input is deleted from the buffer. The `nextLine` method also deletes the Enter keystroke from the buffer; however, `Scanner` methods that return numeric values do not remove this character from the buffer.

When reading numeric inputs, this is not a problem because the numeric input methods not only skip leading spaces in the buffer, they also skip the Enter keystroke. This whitespace is ignored until the buffer is empty or they find an input to process. However, the `newline` method does not skip the Enter keystroke. As a result, when an invocation to `nextLine` follows a numeric input it encounters a nonempty buffer containing an Enter keystroke. The `nextLine` method reads and removes the Enter keystroke from the buffer and returns the empty string ("").

<hr>

**NOTE**

*When reading a string from the console after a numeric input, two invocations of the* `newLine` *method are required to read the string. The first invocation flushes the new line (empty string) from the buffer.*

Figure 4.15 presents an application that demonstrates the use of the `Scanner` class's methods to accept input from the system console. The console inputs and corresponding outputs are given at the bottom of the figure.

Line 1 imports the `Scanner` class's methods into the application, and line 6 uses the `Scanner` class's one-parameter constructor to create the object `consoleIn` passing it the predefined console input object `System.in`. Lines 11–16 accept a string, integer, and a double from the system console, each input on a separate line. These values are output on lines 17–18.

Lines 20-25 change the order of the inputs beginning with two numeric inputs on the same console line (lines 20–22). Then, a string is input (lines 23–25). Line 24 clears the Enter keystroke left in the buffer after the second numeric is read (line 22). Lines 26–27 outputs the second set of inputs. Referring to the bottom of Figure 4.15, the user entered several spaces between the input age, 5, and the input weight, 35. These spaces were ignored by the nextDouble method invoked on line 22. The weight output (35.4) on the last line of the figure confirms this.

```java
1    import java.util.Scanner;
2    public class ScannerConsoleInput
3    {
4       public static void main(String[] args)
5       {
6          Scanner consoleIn = new Scanner(System.in);
7          String name;
8          int age;
9          double weight;
10
11         System.out.print("Enter your name: ");
12         name = consoleIn.nextLine();
13         System.out.print("Enter your age: ");
14         age = consoleIn.nextInt();
15         System.out.print("Enter your weight: ");
16         weight = consoleIn.nextDouble();
17         System.out.println("Age: " + age + " Weight: " + weight +
18                            " Name: " + name);
19
20         System.out.print("\nEnter your age and weight on one line: ");
21         age = consoleIn.nextInt();
22         weight = consoleIn.nextDouble();
23         System.out.print("Enter your name: ");
24         consoleIn.nextLine(); // clears the enter keystroke from buffer
25         name = consoleIn.nextLine();
26         System.out.println("Age: " + age + " Weight: " + weight +
27                            " Name: " + name);
28      }
29   }
```

Console inputs and outputs:
Enter your name: Breanne
Enter your age: 18
Enter your weight: 125.7
Age: 18 Weight: 125.7 Name: Breanne

Enter your age and weight on one line: 5        35.4
Enter your name: Nora
Age: 5 Weight: 35.4 Name: Nora

**Figure 4.15**
The application **ScannerConsoleInput** followed by sample inputs and the corresponding outputs.

## 4.8 DISK INPUT AND OUTPUT: A FIRST LOOK

Unlike RAM memory, disk storage is nonvolatile, which means it retains the information stored on it when the computer system is powered down. As a result, it is used to archive data and program instructions. There are two types of disk files: text files and binary files. Information stored in binary files normally occupies less storage on the disk, and the information transfer is faster. That being said, text files are in wide use because all of the information in the file is stored as ASCII characters, which means it can be opened, read, modified, and restored using any text editor.

In this section, we will limit our discussion of disk file I/O to text files and the techniques for accessing the file's data items in the order in which they appear in the file. This type of access is called sequential access. The alternate form of access, called random *access*, allows the data items to be accessed in any order. We will extend our discussion of disk I/O in subsequent chapters.

### 4.8.1 Sequential Text File Input

Information stored in a text file can be sequentially read into a program using the `Scanner` class's methods presented in Table 4.5. In fact, all of the concepts discussed in Section 4.7 used to read or input data from the system console apply to sequential text file input. The one exception is the creation of the `Scanner` object.

To accept input from the system console, the object was created by passing the predefined object `System.in` to the `Scanner` class's one-parameter constructor. To accept input from a sequential text file, a `File` object is passed to the `Scanner` class's one-parameter constructor. This `File` object is created using the `File` class's one-parameter constructor that accepts a string argument containing the file's path and name. Case sensitivity in this string is ignored. The import statement `import java.io.*;` is used to access the `File` class.

The code fragment presented in Figure 4.16 reads an integer from the beginning of the file named `data.txt` resident on the root of the C drive.

```
1    File fileObject = new File("c:/data.txt");
2    Scanner fileIn = new Scanner(fileObject);
3    int score;
4
5    score = fileIn.nextInt();
```

**Figure 4.16**
Code fragment to read an integer from the disk file **data.txt** resident on the root of the C drive.

The string argument sent to the `File` class's constructor (on line 1 of Figure 4.16) contains a forward slash, which is preferred over the backslash for two reasons. First, all operating systems accept a forward slash in a path definition. Second, to use a backslash the escape sequence for a backslash (\\) would have to be used inside the string argument. Most Windows-friendly programmers often forget to code the escape sequence and code the string argument as `"c:\data.txt"`. This would result in a translation error: illegal escape character, because \d is not a valid escape sequence.

A more insidious error occurs when a single backslash is erroneously coded, and the character that comes after it is a valid escape character. For example, if the file name was `newData.txt`, and it was located on the root of the C drive, the following line of code would not result in a translation error on a Windows system because \n is a valid escape sequence.

```
File fileObject = new File("c:\newData.txt");
```

However, it would result in a runtime error indicating that the file does not exist because the \n would be replaced at compile time with a new line or line feed (LF) character, and the name of the file passed to the constructor would be the LF character followed by ewData.txt.

 **TIP**    Always use forward slashes ( / ) when specifying a file path.

Even when the forward slash is used to specify the path to the file, the file must exist or a run-time error indicating that the file does not exist will occur. If the path is not specified (i.e., just the file name and its extension is coded), the file is assumed to be inside the project folder created by the IDE or a subfolder of that folder. The exact location may be IDE-specific.

Except for lines 1 and 2 of Figure 4.16, the code used to read data from a text file is the same as the code used to read data from the system console, except that no prompts are output. We simply imagine that instead of the user typing the data into the system console in response to input prompts, the same data (character for character, line for line) was typed into a text editor and then saved to the disk file.

For example, if a person's age, weight, and name were typed into the C-drive resident text file data.txt whose contents are shown in Figure 4.17, then the code fragment presented in Figure 4.18 would read these values from the disk file. With the exception of lines 1 and 2, Figure 4.18 contains the same code used to read an age, weight, and name from the system console (lines 7–9 and 20–25 of Figure 4.15) with the two user prompts (lines 20 and 23) removed and the name of the Scanner object changed.

```
5      35.4

Nora
```

**Figure 4.17**
The data contained in the disk file **data.txt** resident on the root of the C drive.

```
1    File fileObject = new File("c:/data.txt");
2    Scanner fileIn = new Scanner(fileObject);
3    String name;
4    int age;
5    double weight;
6
7    age = fileIn.nextInt();
8    weight = fileIn.nextDouble();
9    fileIn.nextLine();
10   name = fileIn.nextLine();
```

**Figure 4.18**
The code fragment to read the data contained in the file shown in Figure 4.17.

To process a sequential file, Java maintains a read position pointer that is initially positioned at the first character in the file. Each time a data item is read from the file, this pointer is moved to the next item in the file. After the last item in the file has been read, the pointer is positioned at a special character called an end of file (EOF), which is automatically placed at the end of all disk files. In Chapter 5, we will discuss the importance of the addition of the EOF character to the file and how to detect when we have reached it.

There are some additional issues to consider when reading data from a text file that do not arise when performing console input. These include the need to know:

- the name and the path to the file to declare the `File` object (line 1 of Figure 4.18)
- the order of the information in the file, so the statements on lines 7, 8, 9, and 10 of Figure 4.18 are coded in the proper sequence
- the type of each piece of information in the file, so the proper `Scanner` class method can be invoked to read each piece of information

This information is described in a file specification given to the programmer by the software engineer who designed the file.

### 4.8.2 Determining the Existence of a File

Another issue to consider when reading data from a text file that does not arise when performing console input is how to prevent a runtime error if the data file does not exist. The `File` class contains a non-void method named `exists` that can be used to detect the existence of a file, and the `System` class contains a static method named `exit` that can be used to end a program.

The `exists` method in the `File` class returns `true` when the file exists, and the `exit` method in the `System` class has one integer parameter, which is usually passed a zero. The following code segment demonstrates the use of these two methods to bring a program to a more informative user-friendly ending when it tries to use a disk file that does not exist:

```java
File fileObject = new File("c:/data.txt");


if(!fileObject.exists()) // file does not exist
{
  System.out.println("the file does not exist, the program is terminating")
  System.exit(0);
}
```

 It is good programming practice to check for a disk file's existence to avoid a runtime error that is normally difficult for the user to understand.

### 4.8.3 Sequential Text File Output

Information can be sequentially output (written) to a text file using the `print` and `println` methods that are used to write information to the system console. In addition, the Java syntax used to format console output data, such as the spacing of the output information, moving to a new line, and specifying the precision of numeric outputs, is the same syntax used to format disk-file output. The one exception to this is the output annotation.

Output annotation is normally not included in the string sent to the methods and `print` and `println` when writing to a disk file because most disk files are read by programs, not people. When the file's data will not be processed or read by a program (perhaps the file's contents will be examined after it is printed), output annotation is included. Alternately, the reader could refer to the file's specification to identify unannotated file information.

To write to the system console, the `print` and `println` methods operate on a predefined object `System.out` attached to the system console. To write to a sequential text file, these methods operate on a programmer-defined object in the `PrintWriter` class. This object is created using two lines of code that are analogous to the two lines used to create the `Scanner` object used to perform disk input.

The `PrintWriter` object is created using the class's two-parameter constructor, which is passed to an object in the `FileWriter` class. The file's path and name is passed to the `FileWriter` object when it is created. Case sensitivity in this string is ignored. The import statement `import java.io.*;` is used to access the `PrintWriter` and the `FileWriter` classes.

The code fragment presented in Figure 4.19 creates a sequential text file named `data.txt` on the root of the C drive and then outputs the contents of the variable `score` followed by a new-line character to the beginning of the file.

```
1    FileWriter fileWriterObject = new FileWriter("c:/data.txt");
2    PrintWriter fileOut = new PrintWriter(fileWriterObject, false);
3    int score = 20;
4
5    fileOut.println(score);
```

**Figure 4.19**
Code fragment to write an integer to the beginning of the disk file **data.txt** resident on the root of the C drive.

Lines 1 and 2 of Figure 4.19 create the disk file and the object `fileOut` that is used to invoke the `println` method on line 5. A generic term used to describe the functionality of these two lines is that they create and open the file. If the file had already existed, it would have been deleted and then recreated. All the information previously written to a deleted file is lost.

Data written to a text file using the `print` and `println` methods should be thought of as being placed in the file exactly as the data would have appeared on the system console (line for line, character for character) had the methods operated on `System.out`. The only exception is that a new-line character does not appear on the system console. Rather, it causes the cursor to move to the beginning of the next line. The characters of the first data item are followed in the file by the characters of the second item, which are followed by the third, etc.

Figure 4.20 presents an application that writes a person's age, weight, and name to a sequential text file named `data.txt` and then reads the data from the file and outputs the information to the system console. The system console output produced by the program is shown at the end of the figure, and the characters written to the disk file are shown in Figure 4.21.

Lines 1 and 2 of Figure 4.20 make the Scanner, File, FileWriter, and PrintWriter classes available to the program. Their constructors are used on lines 8–12 to create objects fileIn and fileOut, which are used on lines 18–19 and lines 23–26, respectively, to write to and read from the file.

```java
1    import java.util.Scanner;
2    import java.io.*;
3
4    public class DiskIO
5    {
6      public static void main(String[] args) throws IOException
7      {
8        File fileObject = new File("data.txt"); // input
9        Scanner fileIn = new Scanner(fileObject);
10       FileWriter fileWriterObject = new FileWriter("data.txt"); // output
11       PrintWriter fileOut = new PrintWriter(fileWriterObject, false);
12
13       String name = "Nora Smith";
14       int age = 5;
15       double weight = 35.4;
16
17       // write three data items to the disk file
18       fileOut.println(age + " " + weight);
19       fileOut.println(name);
20       fileOut.close();
21
22       //read the data from the disk file
23       age = fileIn.nextInt();
24       weight = fileIn.nextDouble();
25       fileIn.nextLine(); // clears New Line after a numeric from the buffer
26       name = fileIn.nextLine();
27       fileIn.close();
28
29       System.out.println("Age: " + age + " Weight: " + weight +
30                          " Name: " + name);
31     }
32  }
```

**System console output**
Age: 5 Weight: 35.4 Name: Nora Smith

**Figure 4.20**
The application **DiskIO** and the console output it produces.

> 5 35.4**n**$^l$Nora Smithn$^l$**e**$^{of}$
> **n**$^l$ represents a new-line character
> **e**$^{of}$ represents an end of file (EOF) character

**Figure 4.21**
The characters output to the file data.txt by the application **DiskIO**.

A `throws` clause has been added to the end of the signature of the main method (line 6). This tells the translator that the programmer is aware that some serious runtime problems (e.g., an attempt was made to read past the EOF character) could develop during the execution of the program. However, the programmer has chosen not to include code to deal with those problems. Without the throws clause, this program will not translate. We will discuss the code to deal with these problems in the next section of this chapter.

The string containing the name of the file on lines 8 and 10 does not contain a path. Therefore, the file is created inside the project folder created by the IDE. This is not always desirable but is often used in game programs because the file contains information about the game, such as the highest score achieved to date.

Line 18 writes two numbers to the file separated by a space as shown in Figure 4.21. The space is a very important part of the output. Without it, Nora's age (5) and her weight (35.4) would be adjacent to each other and would therefore be considered one number (534.4) by anyone reading the file including line 23 of the program. The result would be one of the serious runtime errors the programmer chose to ignore because a double, 534.4, cannot be parsed into the integer variable age.

Lines 20 and 27 invoke the `close` method in the `FileWriter` and `Scanner` classes. These statements release the system resources required to perform disk I/O. If they are not included in a program that performs disk input and/or output, the Java Runtime Environment releases the resources when the program ends. It is not only good programming practice to code them immediately after the last disk I/O statements, but in this program it is essential that line 20 be part of the program.

Here's why: During the execution of a program that writes to a disk file, the data is actually written to a RAM resident buffer. The characters stored in the buffer are written to the disk file when the buffer is full or the `FileWriter`'s `close` method is executed. This method flushes a partially full buffer to the disk file during the program's execution. Because the number of characters written by this program does not fill the buffer, eliminating line 20 from the program presents line 23 with an empty disk file from which to read. This situation causes the program to terminate in a runtime error.

When the `FileWriter` class's `close` method executes an end of file (EOF) character is added to the end of the file.

**NOTE**

*Always invoke the* `FileWriter` *class's* `close` *method after the last file output statement.*
*Always invoke the* `Scanner`'s *class's* `close` *method after the last file input statement.*

### 4.8.4 Appending Data to an Existing Text File

Data can be appended (added to the end) of a disk file by changing the second argument sent to the `PrintWriter`'s two-parameter constructor from `false` to `true`. For example, line 11 of Figure 4.20 to would be changed to:

```
PrintWriter fileOut = new PrintWriter(fileWriterObject, true);
```

When the program is run, if the file does exist it would not be deleted. (If it does not exist, it would be created.) Each execution of the program would add data to the end of the file followed by an EOF character. Figure 4.22 shows the contents of the file after three executions of the program, assuming the file did not exist before the program's first execution and the value `true` was passed to the `PrintWriter` constructor.

---

5 35.4**n**ʹNora Smith**n**ʹ5 35.4**n**ʹNora Smith**n**ʹ5 35.4**n**ʹNora Smith**n**ʹ**e**ᵒᶠ

**n**ʹ represents a new-line character

**e**ᵒᶠ represents an EOF character

---

**Figure 4.22**
The output by 3 executions of **DiskIO** with the file open for append.

### 4.8.5 Deleting, Modifying, and Adding File Data Items

Java, like most programming languages, does not contain a method to delete or modify a file data item or add a data item anywhere in the file except at its end. These operations can be accomplished by including the disk I/O methods discussed in this chapter in algorithms that perform these tasks. For example, the delete algorithm would be:

1.  Read all of the file's information into RAM memory
2.  Close the file
3.  Delete the file
4.  Recreate the file
5.  Write all of the information except the item to be deleted back into to the file
6.  Close the file

Because the coding of these algorithms requires knowledge of the material covered in Chapters 5 and 6, we will return to this topic in Chapter 6.

## 4.9 CATCHING THROWN EXCEPTIONS

An exception is a Java feature that a method can use to communicate to its invoker that an unexpected event has occurred during the method's execution when the method does not contain code to deal with it. In Chapters 2 and 3 we discussed two events, dividing by zero and argument-parameter mismatch, which Java does not consider to be serious events. When the event is one that Java deems serious, a `throws` clause must be added to the signature of the method in which the invocation is coded, or instructions to deal with the event must be added to the code block that contains the invocation statement.

The former approach was taken in the program that appears in Figure 4.20 on line 6. The `Scanner` and `FileWriter` class constructors invoked on lines 9 and 10 are methods that can encounter serious unexpected events during their execution. Therefore, a `throws` clause was added to the signature of the main method (line 6) because the main method contains these two invocations. In this section, we will cover a brief introduction to the alternative to the `throws` clause: adding instructions to deal with the event in the code block that contains the invocation statements.

As the word "throws" implies, a baseball analogy was used in the selection of the Java keywords associated with exceptions, and the analogy is helpful in gaining an understanding of exceptions. Imagine that when the serious event occurs during a method's execution the method says, "I take *exception* to that event, and I am not going to continue executing. My last action will be to let my invoker know of this problem by *throwing* an exception object back to it."

If the invoker wants to deal with the problem, its code block *catches* the exception object and deals with the problem. Otherwise it *throws* the exception object on to the Java Runtime Environment. The term `throws` is a Java keyword we have already used (line 6 of Figure 4.20) when we did not want to deal with an unexpected problem. Two other keywords, **try** and **catch**, are used when we want to deal with the problem.

Each of these keywords begins a code block, and the `try` code block is always coded immediately before the `catch` code block. The following code fragment is a template for a `try` statement that will catch a thrown `IOException` object. As shown in the template, the type of exception object caught is coded in a parameter list after the keyword `catch`.

```java
try
{
   // the code containing the method invocations and other statements
}
catch(IOException e)
{
   // the statements to deal with the unexpected events
}
```

The statements that invoked the methods that could throw the exception object must be coded inside the `try` block. Other statements can be included in the `try` block. Effectively, you are trying these invocation statements to see if the methods they invoke throw an exception object.

When an exception object is thrown by a method invoked inside the `try` block, the remainder of the statements in the `try` block does not execute, and execution passes to the first statement in the `catch` block. If an exception is not thrown, the statements in the `try` block complete their execution, and the `catch` block statements are not executed. In either case, the statements following the `catch` code block executes after the `try` block or the `catch` block completes execution.

The use of the template is illustrated in the following code fragment. It attempts to read the value stored in a disk file into the variable `score` and catches the `IOException` object thrown by the `Scanner` class's constructor when this constructor encounters a problem.

```
int score;
try
{
  File fileObject = new File("data.txt"); // input
  Scanner fileIn = new Scanner(fileObject);

  score = fileIn.nextInt();
  fileIn.close();
}
catch(IOException e)
{
  System.out.print ("The score could not be read from the disk file,");
  System.out.println(" but the game will continue.");
}
//rest of the game's statements
```

If the reading of the score was essential to the continuation of the program, the second statement in the catch block would be replaced with the following two statements to terminate the program's execution:

```
System.out.println(" the program is terminating.");
System.exit(0);
```

The program in Figure 4.23 illustrates the use of disk input and output in a game program and the use of exceptions to deal with unexpected disk I/O problems. It is the same program presented in Figure 4.13, modified to keep track of the highest game score ever achieved. When the game is over, this score is read from a disk file. If a new high score was not achieved, the game player is informed and encouraged to keep practicing. Otherwise, the new high score is written to the disk file and the game player is congratulated.

```
1    import edu.sjcny.gpv1.*;
2    import java.awt.*;
3    import java.util.Scanner;
4    import java.io.*;
5    //illstrates basic exceptions
6
7    public class ExceptionBasics extends DrawableAdapter
8    {
9      static ExceptionBasics ge = new ExceptionBasics ();
10     static GameBoard gb = new GameBoard(ge, "Exception Basics");
11     static BoxedSnowman s1 = new BoxedSnowman(300, 200, Color.GREEN);
12     static BoxedSnowman s2 = new BoxedSnowman(30, 100, Color.BLACK);
13     static int score = 0;
14     static int count = 10;
15
16     public static void main(String[] args)
17     {
18       showGameBoard(gb);
19     }
```

```
20
21    public void draw(Graphics g) // a call back method
22    {
23      int w = 40;
24      int h = 77;
25      int s1X, s1Y, s2X, s2Y, temp;
26
27      s1X = s1.getX(); s1Y = s1.getY();
28      s2X = s2.getX(); s2Y = s2.getY();
29      g.setColor(Color.BLACK);
30      g.setFont(new Font("Arial", Font.BOLD, 18));
31      g.drawString("Time remaining: " + count, 260, 50);
32
33      if(count == 0) // the game is over
34      {
35        g.setColor(Color.BLACK);
36        g.drawString("Game Over", 205, 70);
37        g.drawString("Have a Good Day", 175, 90);
38
39        try
40        {
41          int highScore;
42          File fileObj = new File("HiScore.txt");
43          Scanner fileIn = new Scanner(fileObj);
44          highScore = fileIn.nextInt();
45          fileIn.close();
46
47          if(score >= highScore) // a new high score
48          {
49            g.drawString("Great, Your Score is the Highest Ever.," +
50                         "It Will Be Saved", 10, 110);
51            FileWriter fileWriterObj = new FileWriter("HiScore.txt");
52            PrintWriter fileOut = new PrintWriter(fileWriterObj, false);
53
54            fileOut.println(score);
55            fileOut.close();
56          }
57          else // not a new high score
58          {
59            g.drawString("Best Score is: " + highScore +
60                         ", Keep Practicing", 110, 110);
61          }
62        }
63        catch(IOException e)
64        {
65          g.drawString("Problems With High Score File", 120, 110);
66        }
67      }
```

```
68      else if( !(s2X > s1X + w || s2X + w < s1X || s2Y > s1Y + h ||
69                s2Y + h < s1Y) && s1.getVisible() == true)
70      {
71        score = score + 1;
72        s1.setVisible(false);
73      }
74      else if( s2X > s1X + w || s2X + w < s1X || s2Y > s1Y + h ||
75             s2Y + h < s1Y) // no collision
76      {
77        if(s1.getVisible() == false) // not visible
78        {  temp = s1.getX();
79           s1.setX(s1.getY());
80           s1.setY(temp);
81           s1.setVisible(true);
82        }
83      }
84
85      s2.show(g);
86      if(s1.getVisible() == true)
87      {
88        s1.show(g);
89      }
90        g.setColor(Color.BLACK);
91        g.drawString("Score: " + score, 150, 50);
92    }
93
94    public void keyStruck(char key) // a call back method
95    {
96      int newX, newY;
97
98      switch (key)
99      {
100       case 'L':
101       {
102         newX = s2.getX() - 2;
103         s2.setX(newX);
104         break;
105       }
106       case 'R':
107       {
108         newX = s2.getX() + 2;
109         s2.setX(newX);
110         break;
111       }
112       case 'U':
113       {
114         newY = s2.getY() - 2;
115         s2.setY(newY);
116         break;
```

```
117          }
118        case 'D':
119        {
120           newY = s2.getY() + 2;
121           s2.setY(newY);
122        }
123      }
124    }
125    public void timer1() // a call back method
126    {
127      count = count - 1;
128      if(count == 0)
129      {
130         gb.stopTimer(1);
131      }
132    }
133 }
```

**Figure 4.23**
The **ExceptionBasics** Application: A decision and exceptions case study.

When the application is launched, two snowmen, one wearing a black hat and the other wearing a green hat, appear on the game board below the game's score and remaining time (Figure 4.24a). The game begins when the player clicks the Start button on the game board. The objective of the game is to make the two snowmen collide as many times as possible before time runs out using the keyboard cursor-control keys to move the black-hat snowman. Each time they collide, a point is awarded, and the green-hat snowman disappears. It reappears at a new location after the black-hat snowman has been moved to a location such that the two snowmen are no longer in a collision state.

The changes to the program are the additions of the lines 3–4 that make the Scanner, File, FileWriter, and PrintWriter classes needed to perform disk I/O available to the program, the elimination of the throws clause in the main method's signature and the addition of lines 40–67 that perform the disk I/O. Figure 4.24 presents several outputs produced by the program under various game conditions.

The signature of the main method (line 16) does not contain a throws clause because the disk I/O is performed inside the code block of a try statement (line 39). Line 44 reads the highest score ever achieved from the disk file HiScore.txt using the Scanner object inFile created by lines 42–43. Then, the file is closed (line 45). Normally, the programmer would use a text editor to create the file and store a score of zero in it as part of the program's development. Because the file's path is not specified on line 42, the file must be stored inside the project folder created by the IDE.

When a new high score is achieved, as determined by line 47, line 49–50 informs the game player of this achievement (Figure 4.24b). The new high score is written to the disk file (line 54) using the PrintWriter object fileOut created on lines 51–52, and the file is closed (line 55). Because the second argument sent to the PrintWriter constructor on line 52 is false, the file containing the old high score is deleted and recreated before the new high score is written to it. (The new high score is not appended to the file.)

When a new high score is not achieved, lines 59–60 of the if-else statement that begins in line 47 produces the output shown in Figure 4.24c. If a problem occurs during the disk I/O performed inside of the try block, execution of the try block is terminated, and the catch block (lines 63–66) executes producing the error message at the end of the text output shown in Figure 4.24d.

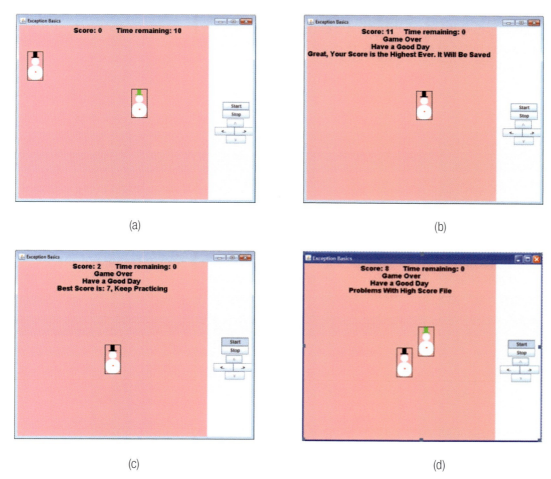

**Figure 4.24**
Outputs produced by the application **ExceptionBasics**.

## 4.10 CHAPTER SUMMARY

Ordinarily, a Java program executes its statements sequentially. The if, if-else, and switch statements are used to alter this sequential path of execution by selecting which statement, or group of statements, to execute next. When the resulting decision of an if or if-else construct effect more than one statement, these statements must be coded inside a code block.

Both the if and if-else statements evaluate Boolean expressions to determine whether to execute or skip the statements included in their code blocks. Boolean expressions use the logical and relational operators (all of which have a precedence order associated with them) and evaluate to `true` or `false`. These statements may be nested, which allows them to test for several conditions, or several conditions can be tested by one statement using compound Boolean conditions. The `if` statement is used to decide to skip or execute one group of statements, and the `if-else` statement is used to decide which of two mutually exclusive groups of statements to execute.

Although all uses of the `switch` statement can be coded using an equivalent set of nested `if-else` statements, the use of the `switch` statement makes our programs more readable when the decision to be made is based on one or more discrete values. The values can be references to a strings or primitive values whose type is `byte`, `short`, `char` or `int`, or the values of an enumerated type.

Most often, a `break` statement is used to prevent the cases coded below the one that is equivalent to the current value of the switch variable from executing. A `default` clause can be included at the end of the statement that will execute when the value of the switch variable does not match any of the statement's cases. Decision statements have many applications to game programming, such as controlling the value of a timer, increasing a score when an event occurs, testing to see when there is a collision between objects, and determining which keystroke has been entered and responding to it.

The `String` class provides methods for comparing `String` objects because they cannot be compared using the relational operators. The equality operator compares the contents of variables, but `String` reference variables contain the address of the strings they refer to, not the strings themselves. Therefore, to compare strings, the `String` class provides methods such as `equals` and `compareTo`, which make case sensitive comparisons, and `equalsIgnoreCase` and `compareToIgnoreCase`, which ignore case sensitivity.

Disk I/O is useful for storing game data, such as the highest score achieved, and any other type of data that must be retained after a program ends. When data is stored in RAM buffers, it is volatile and is not preserved from one game to the next. In contrast, when data is stored in a text file, it can be read and compared each time the game is played. The constructors in the `File` and `Scanner` classes, and the constructors in the `FileWriter` and `PrintWriter` classes, can be used to "attach" `Scanner` and `PrintWriter` I/O objects to a file. Text output can then be sent to the file using the methods in the `PrintWriter` class, and information can be read from the file using the `Scanner` class's methods. Methods in the scanner class can also be used to accept input from the system console. The `File` class method, `exists`, can determine if a file exists before attempting to use it, and it is always good programming style to close a file after using it.

Disk I/O often causes errors such as when code attempts to access a file that does not exist or whose pathname is incorrect. This causes an exception error to be generated, which disrupts the normal flow of a program. Java provides two exception-related constructs, called `try` and `catch` blocks. When an exception occurs within the code of a `try` block, the program's execution path is transferred into the code of the `catch` block, which is designed to process (handle) and recover from runtime exceptions. A `System` class method, `exit`, can be used inside a `catch` block to terminate a program gracefully.

## Knowledge Exercises

1. The variables i, j, k and m have been declared as: **int** i = 10; **int** j = 20; **int** k = 30; **int** m = 40. Evaluate the following as true or false:

   **a)** i <= j

   **b)** k == 30

   **c)** i != j && j >= k

   **d)** i != j || j >= k

   **e)** (i <= k && k >= m) || (j * 2 == m && k > j)

   **f)** m <= k || i + j + k >= m

2. What is the normal default execution sequence (path) of all Java programs?

3. What are the two types of statements available in Java to alter the default execution path?

4. Write the Java code to output the contents of the variable myBalance when it stores the value 10.0 to the system console.

5. Modify the Java code in Question 4 by adding a statement to output *my balance is not 10.0* when the memory cell myBalance does not store 10.0.

6. Write an if or if-else statement to perform each of these tasks:

   **a)** Add 5 to a grade if the grade is greater than 75

   **b)** Produce the output *buy tickets* if the cost is less than $150.00, otherwise output *too expensive.*

   **c)** Output the value stored in the variable GPA to the system console if the String object name contains the string Anna

   **d)** For the strings referenced by s1 and s2, if s1 comes before s2 in alphabetical order, output *in alphabetical order* otherwise output the message *not in order.*

7. True or false:

   **a)** An if statement must contain one Boolean expression.

   **b)** An if-else statement must contain two Boolean expressions.

   **c)** An if statement must contain a statement block.

   **d)** The code block of an if statement executes when its Boolean condition is true.

   **e)** The code block of an if statement can contain another if statement.

   **f)** The code block of an else clause cannot contain another if statement.

   **g)** An if or if-else statement may be nested within another if statement's code block.

   **h)** Java contains an if-else-if statement.

8. The string s1 just received input from an input dialog box. Give the statement to output *OK* to the system console when the user enters *Stop Sign* (case sensitive).

9. True or false:

   **a)** A switch statement must contain a default clause.

   **b)** A switch statement can have multiple cases.

**c)** The choice values of a `switch` statement can be strings.

**d)** A `switch` statement must contain at least one `break` statement.

**e)** A `switch` statement is normally used to determine a choice between several alternatives.

**f)** Every `switch` statement can be written as equivalent `if-else` statements.

**g)** A sequence of `if-else` statements can always be written as an equivalent `switch` statement.

10. Write the `switch` statement to output the menu selection stored in the string variable `item`, assuming the choices are *Hamburger*, *Taco*, or *BLT* (use system-console output).

11. Write the equivalent `if-else` statements to output the menu selections given in Question 10.

12. What API class must be imported into your program to accept input from the system console?

13. Give all of the statements, excluding import statements, to:
    **a)** accept the year of a person's birth input from the system console (include a prompt)
    **b)** accept a person's name input from the system console (include a prompt)

14. What is the advantage of saving information in disk files versus saving the information in main memory?

15. True or false:
    **a)** Text files can be viewed using the program Notepad.
    **b)** Text files cannot be printed on a printer.
    **c)** By convention, text files end with the extension .txt
    **d)** It is best to use two forward slashes to specify the path name where the file is located.

16. Write all of the import statement(s) necessary to perform disk I/O.

17. Give all of the statements, excluding import statements, to:
    **a)** read the year of a person's birth from the disk file `Dates.txt` stored on the root of the E drive
    **b)** read a person's age and name from the disk file `Names.txt` stored on the root of the E drive
    **c)** read the year of a person's birth from the disk file `bDays.txt` stored on the root of the E drive

18. Give all the statements necessary to append the contents of the variables `myBalance` and `yourBalance` to the disk file `Balances.txt` stored on the root of the C drive.

19. Give all the statements necessary to output the contents of the variables `myBalance` and `yourBalance` to the disk file `Balances.txt` stored on the root of the C drive. If the file already exists, delete it before performing the output.

20. Give all the statements necessary to determine if the file `Data.txt` exists on the root of the C drive, and output *The File Exists* to the system console if it does.

21. Write the statement needed to close the file attached to the scanner object `inputFile`.

22. Briefly discuss how the `try` and `catch` block can be used to handle exceptions detected by methods invoked within a program.

## Programming Exercises

1. Write a program to ask a user to input two strings from the system console. If the strings are identical output *Strings Identical* to the system console. Otherwise output them in alphabetical order.

2. Write a program for a travel agency, which presents the user with the following menu as a console input prompt:

    Where do you want to vacation?

    Enter: 1 for Disney World, 2 for Las Vegas, 3 for Paris or 4 for Alaska

    After accepting the customer's numeric response from the system console, use either an `if-else` or a `switch` statement to output two destination-appropriate messages to the text file `vacation.txt` (for example, if the user chose 4 for Alaska, you might want to output the messages *Bring a warm jacket and enjoy Alaska* and *Say "Hello" to Frosty for me*). Feel free to add bells and whistles such as adding a welcome message or adding additional destinations.

3. Write a program to ask a user to enter a student name, major, and GPA from the system console. If the GPA is greater than 3.5, set a Boolean variable, `honors`, to `true`, otherwise set it to `false`. Create a text file called `StudentInfo.txt` and output the name, major, GPA, and the student's honors status to four separate lines of the file.

4. Extend the program described in Programming Exercise 4 to ask the user the name of the file in which to store the data. After writing the data to a text file with that name, add the phrase *End of Student Record* as the last line of the file. Then, read five lines store in the file and output them on five separate lines to a message box with the appropriate annotation. Before reading the data, ask the user the name of the file from which to read. Use a `try` and a `catch` block to output the message *problems opening or reading the file* when an `IOException` is thrown.

5. Write a graphical game application that contains a class named `RV` whose objects are the recreational vehicle designed and digitized as described in Knowledge Exercises 20 and 21 of Chapter 3. When the application is launched, the RVs appear on the screen. The game player is given 10 seconds to move any part of the RV beyond the top, bottom, right side, and left side of the game board using the keyboard cursor control keys. The game begins when the game player clicks the Start button and ends when the time expires or some part of the RV has moved beyond all four boundaries of the game board. During the game, a countdown of the time remaining should be displayed at the top of the game board, and the countdown should stop at the end of the game.

6. Write a graphical game application that contains a class named `RV` whose objects are the recreational vehicles designed and digitized as described in Knowledge Exercises 20 and 21 of Chapter 3. The application should also contain a class named `Mouse` whose objects are designed and digitized in a similar manner. When the application is launched, one RV

and one mouse appear on the screen at different random locations. The user is given 10 seconds to move the mouse to the RV using the keyboard's cursor control keys. The game begins when the game player clicks the Start button and ends when the time expires or the mouse has collided with the RV. During the game, a countdown of the time remaining should be displayed at the top of the game board, and the countdown should stop at the end of the game.

7. Write the game application described in Programming Exercise 6 modified to include three RVs at different locations. In this version of the game, the game player has to make the mouse collide into all three RVs and the RVs disappear when the mouse collides with them. The player's score will be the time remaining after all the RVs have disappeared. A record of the lowest score ever achieved will be kept in the disk file LowScore.txt.

8. Using the skills developed in this chapter, continue the implementation of the parts of your game (specified in Preprogramming Exercise 1 of Chapter 1) that require cursor-key motion control, disk I/O, collision detection, and stopping a time countdown. To test the collision detection, you will have to add a class to your application that implements your second type of game piece.

# REPEATING STATEMENTS: LOOPS

## In this chapter

In this chapter, we will learn the techniques used to repeat the execution of a designated group of statements an unlimited number of times, which gives us the ability to perform a significant amount of processing with just a few repeated statements. Not only does this reduce the time and effort required to produce a program, but it also allows us to utilize algorithms whose implementation require the use of these repetition, or loop, statements. We will discuss the syntax and execution path of Java's three repetition statements, consider which one is best suited for particular applications, and learn how to nest these statements. Our knowledge of these statements will be expanded in Chapter 6, which covers the concept of arrays, because loops are used to unlock the power of arrays.

We will learn why repetition statements are an integral part of repetition statements, consider which one is best suited for particular applications, and learn of two fundamental algorithms, summing and averaging, and how to generate a repeatable sequence of pseudorandom numbers using loops and the methods in the class Random. In addition, we will extend our knowledge of numeric formatting introduced in Chapter 2 and learn to produce output consistent with any of the world's currency systems.

After successfully completing this chapter you should:

- Understand the syntax and execution path of Java's for, while, and do-while statements
- Know which statement to use for a particular application
- Understand why a for loop is an automatic counting loop
- Understand the role of sentinels and their use in while and do-while loops

- Be able to explain the totaling and counting algorithms and the role loops play in their implementation
- Know how to generate a set of random numbers using the `Random` class methods
- Be able to use the `NumberFormat` class's methods to format currency output in a local specific format
- Be able to use the `DecimalFormat` class's methods to format numeric output with leading/trailing zeros and comma separators and display a numeric value as a percentage or using scientific notation

## 5.1 A SECOND ALTERNATIVE TO SEQUENTIAL EXECUTION

Often, the proper execution path of a program's statements requires that a sequence of instructions be executed several times. For example, a program accepts three input deposits and adds them to a bank balance after each input. In this case, the input statement and the arithmetic statement to add the input deposit to the bank balance would be repeated three times.

One alternative would be to code one input and one arithmetic statement, copy and paste them into the program two more times, and then execute the three groups of statements sequentially. Another alternative would be to enclose one input and one arithmetic statement in a repetition statement's code block, which is repeated three times. Although both approaches would produce the same result, the second alternative is most often preferred, especially when the statements are to be repeated a large number of times. Not only does this approach save coding time, but it also improves the readability of our programs by significantly reducing the length of the program, and, more importantly, making it obvious to the reader that the statements are being repeated.

A repetition statement is most often referred to as a *loop* statement. The term loop comes from an aircraft "loop" maneuver often performed at air shows during which the aircraft repeatedly travels in a vertical circle. Figure 5.1 illustrates the maneuver and programming analogy.

Like many programming languages, Java provides three repetition or loop statements: the `for`, the `while`, and the `do-while` statements. While there is the possibility for significant overlap in

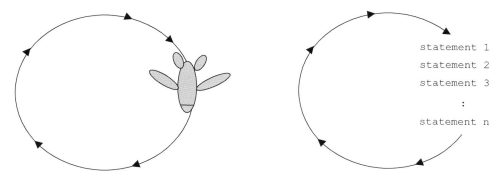

**Figure 5.1**
Airplane and programming loops.

the use of these three statements in our programs, good coding practice and ease of use greatly narrow the choice of which statement to use in a particular context. One of the objectives of this chapter is to specify clear criteria for when each of these three statements is best used in our programs. We will begin our study of repetition statements with the `for` statement.

## 5.2 THE `for` STATEMENT

The `for` statement is often called an automatic counting loop. It is most often used when we know how many times to repeat the loop's statements. In some cases, this is known at the time the program is written; for example, a program that always processes three deposits. In other cases, the number of times the loop is to execute is specified, or determined, during the program's execution. For example, before entering deposits the program users are asked to enter the number of deposits they will be making into their bank account during this execution of the program. The criterion common to both of these alternatives is that *before* the loop executes the number of repetitions is known. When this is the case, the `for` loop is the best repetition statement to use.

### 5.2.1 Syntax of the `for` Statement

The left side of Figure 5.2 shows an example of a `for` statement containing a group of statements that will execute its statement block three times. The meaning of the statement and its execution path are illustrated on the right side of Figure 5.2. The integer variable `i` is called the loop or

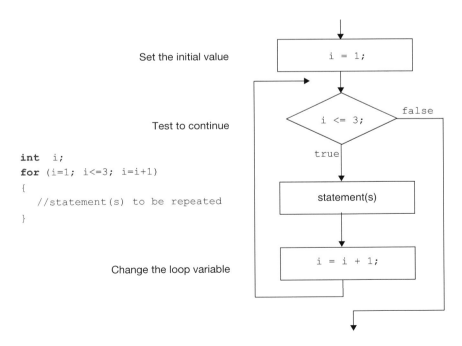

**Figure 5.2**
A **for** loop that executes three times and its execution path.

*loop control variable*. The statement(s) enclosed inside the braces are called the loop's code block, or the *body of the loop*. They are said to be inside the loop. These are the statements to be repeated.

When a loop is correctly written, the loop variable is initialized, tested, and changed. In a `for` loop, all three of these actions are coded within the `for` statement's parentheses. Referring to the left side of Figure 5.2, the statement `i=1;` sets the initial value, `i<=3;` tests to see if `i` has reached its terminating value or if the loop should continue, and `i=i+1;` changes or increments the value of the loop's control variable.

Referring to the items enclosed inside the parentheses after the keyword **for**, the code:

- `i=1;` is called the initialization expression
- `i<=3;` is called the condition to continue expression or continuation condition
- `i=i+1;` is called the increment

The initialization expression is an assignment statement. As shown on the top-right side of Figure 5.2, this assignment statement always executes once to initialize the loop variable just before the loop begins. The condition to continue expression is a Boolean expression involving the loop variable, which executes at least once. The loop body is repeatedly executed while this Boolean expression is `true`. If the Boolean condition is `false` when the loop begins, the statements in the loop body are not executed. The increment is an assignment statement. The statement is used to change the loop variable after the statements in the loop body are executed. When the increment is one, the equivalent coding `i++;` is commonly used.

The loop shown in Figure 5.2 executes its statement body three times. When the `for` statement begins, the loop variable `i` is initialized to 1. The condition to continue (`i <= 3`) evaluates to `true` (`1 <= 3`), and the statements in the loop body execute for the first time. The loop variable is then incremented to 2, the condition is tested and is still `true` (`2 <= 3`), and the statements execute a second time. The loop variable is then incremented to 3, the condition is still `true` (`3 <= 3`), and the statements execute a third time. Finally, the loop variable becomes 4, the condition (`4 <= 3`) is `false`, and the loop ends. After the loop ends, the statement immediately following its close brace executes.

The following code fragment contains a `for` statement that executes its loop body 500 times:

```java
int i;
for(i=1; i<=500; i=i+1)
{
    //statement(s) to be repeated
}
```

The most common errors made when coding the `for` statement are:

- placing a semicolon after the close parenthesis
- neglecting to code the semicolon after the initial condition or after the condition to continue, both of which result in a translation error
- neglecting to code the open and close braces around the statements when more than one statement is to be repeated

- modifying the loop variable within the body of the loop which alters the automatic counting

When a semicolon is coded after the close parenthesis, the statement is syntactically correct, however, none of the statements that would have normally formed the loop body are considered to be part of (inside) the loop. They default to sequential execution and each statement executes once. When braces are not coded, the statement is also syntactically correct, however, the first statement after the `for` statement is the only statement considered to be part of the loop. Regardless of the indentation used, it is the only statement repeated.

The generalized syntax of the `for` statement and its execution path are shown at the top and bottom of Figure 5.3, respectively.

```
for(initialization expression; condition to continue; increment)
{
    //statement(s) to be repeated
}
```

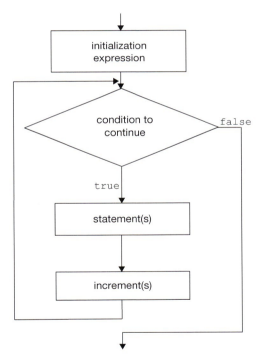

**Figure 5.3**
The generalized syntax of the **for** statement and its execution path.

In addition to the loop variable, the initialization expression, test to continue, and the increment can all contain other variables that can be used to adjust the flow of the statement at runtime. For example, the following code fragment outputs the values in the five times table from 10 to 50 on one line:

```
int i;
int beginValue = 10;
```

```
int endValue = 50;
int tableValue = 5;

for(i=beginValue; i<=endValue, i=i+tableValue)
{
    System.out.print(i + " ");
}
```

Figure 5.4 presents a console application named ForLoopCounting that utilizes this feature of the statement to count from a user input starting value to a specified ending value, by a specified increment. The bottom part of the figure gives the user prompts and inputs and the corresponding outputs generated by the program.

The input starting and ending values, and the increment to count by, are parsed into the variables start, end, and increment on lines 10, 12, and 14 of Figure 5.4. These variables are used in the initialization expression, condition to continue, and increment of the for statement that begins on line 18. As indicated by the input and output at the bottom of Figure 5.5, the program user inputs 3 as a starting value, 27 as an ending value, and an increment of 5. After the value 23 is output, the loop variable i becomes 28 (= 23 + 5). Because 28 is not less than or equal to the ending value 27, the loop ends and 28 is not output.

```
1    import javax.swing.*;
2
3    public class ForLoopCounting
4    {
5      public static void main(String[] args)
6      { int start, end, increment;
7        String input;
8
9        input = JOptionPane.showInputDialog("Enter the starting value:");
10       start = Integer.parseInt(input);
11       input = JOptionPane.showInputDialog("Enter the ending value: ");
12       end = Integer.parseInt(input);
13       input = JOptionPane.showInputDialog("Count by?: ");
14       increment = Integer.parseInt(input);
15
16       System.out.println("Counting from " + start + " to " + end +
17                          " by " + increment + "s:");
18       for(int i=start; i<=end; i=i+increment)
19       {
20         System.out.println(i);
21       }
22     }
23   }
```

**Input prompts and user inputs:**
Enter the starting value: 3
Enter the ending value: 27
Count by?: 5

```
Outputs:
Counting from 3 to 23 by 5s:
3
8
13
18
23
```

**Figure 5.4**
The application **ForLoopCounting** and typical inputs and outputs.

Line 18 presents a feature of the for statement we have not previously discussed. It declares the loop variable i as part of the initialization expression by proceeding its assignment statement with the keyword **int**. When this is done, the scope of the loop variable is limited to the for statement and its statement body. The loop variable cannot be used by statements that follow the loop or by statements that precede the loop. After the loop ends, the Java memory manager reclaims the storage assigned to the loop variable, and the variable's lifetime is said to be over. If another variable named i had been declared in the program before or after the loop statement, all references to the variable i inside the for statement (lines 18-21) would refer to the loop variable, not the variable declared outside the loop. This feature ensures that the loop will count correctly.

A for loop can also be used to count down to an ending value. In this case, the loop variable is initialized to the starting countdown value, and it is decremented each pass through the loop. The statement's Boolean condition checks to see if the ending value is reached. The following code fragment counts down from ten to zero:

```
for(int i= 10; i>= 0; i--)
{
   System.out.println(i);
}
```

In general, the initialization expression and the increment can contain more than one assignment statement. When this is the case, they are separated with commas as shown in code fragment below. The loop's execution path is shown in Figure 5.5.

```
int i, j, k;
for(i=1, j=10, k=4; i<= 3; i=i+1, j=j+3, k=k-1)
{
   //statement(s) to be repeated
}
```

### 5.2.2 A for Loop Application

Figure 5.6 shows a graphical application that draws the first row of a checkerboard on a light-gray-colored game board as shown in Figure 5.7. The program uses a for loop to draw the eight checkerboard squares and then uses another for loop to draw a red checker on the row's black squares.

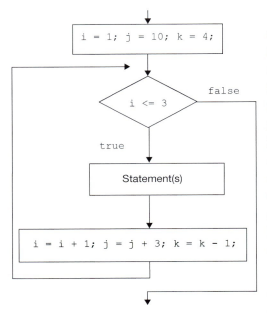

**Figure 5.5**
Execution path of a **for** loop containing multiple initialization-expression and increment-assignment statements.

Inside the `draw` method, line 26 of Figure 5.6 uses the game environment's `setBackground` method to change the game board's background color to light gray. Then line 29 begins a `for` loop that executes eight times. During each iteration of the loop, a black or red checkerboard box is drawn (line 36) using the current drawing color. The first statement in the loop body (line 31) sets the current color to `firstColor` (black), then line 32 uses the modulus operator to determine if the loop variable, `col`, is even (`col % 2 == 0`). If it is, the current color is changed to `secondColor` (red), which causes the even checkerboard boxes (2, 4, 6, and 8) to be drawn in red. The counting algorithm, whose increment is the width of the checkerboard boxes, is used on line 37 to calculate the x location of the next checkerboard box to be drawn.

Line 42 begins a second `for` loop that draws a red checker (line 45) on the black checkerboard boxes. Before the loop begins, the current drawing color is set to red (line 41). Because the `for` statement's increment adds 2 to the loop variable `col`, this variable stores the column numbers 1 (`firstChecker-Col`), then 3, 5, and 7. These are the column numbers of the black boxes, which are used on line 44 to calculate the x location of each column's checker. In this calculation, one is subtracted from the column number `col` before it is multiplied by the box width because column 1's checker should be drawn at an x value of 20.

```
1    import java.awt.*;
2    import edu.sjcny.gpv1.*;
3
4    public class CheckerBoardRow extends DrawableAdapter
5    {
6        static CheckerBoardRow ge = new CheckerBoardRow();
7        static GameBoard gb = new GameBoard(ge, "Checker Board Row");
8
9        public static void main(String[] args)
10       {
11           showGameBoard(gb);
12       }
13
14       public void draw(Graphics g)
15       {
16           int boxX = 12;
17           int boxY = 50;
18           int boxWidth = 60;
19           int boxHeight = 53;
20           int checkerX = 20;
```

```
21        int checkerY = 55;
22        int firstCheckerCol = 1;
23        Color firstColor = Color.BLACK;
24        Color secondColor = Color.RED;
25
26        gb.setBackground(Color.LIGHT_GRAY);
27
28        //Draw the Checker board boxes
29        for(int col = 1; col <= 8; col++)
30        {
31          g. setColor(firstColor); //black
32          if(col % 2 == 0)
33          {
34            g. setColor(secondColor); //red
35          } //end if
36          g.fillRect(boxX, boxY, boxWidth, boxHeight);
37          boxX = boxX + boxWidth;
38        } //end for loop
39
40        //Draw the Red checkers
41        g.setColor(Color.RED);
42        for(int col = firstCheckerCol; col <=8; col= col + 2)
43        {
44          checkerX = 20 + (col - 1) * boxWidth;
45          g.fillOval(checkerX, checkerY, 40, 40);
46        }
47      }
48  }
```

**Figure 5.6**
The application **CheckerBoardRow**.

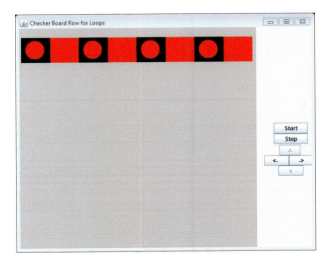

**Figure 5.7**
The output from the application **CheckerBoardRow**.

### 5.2.3 The Totaling and Averaging Algorithms

The totaling or summation algorithm, like the counting algorithm, is a fundamental algorithm of computer science. Both of these algorithms are used in most programs. As the totaling algorithm's name implies, it is used to calculate a total, or sum, of a group of values. For example, it could be used to calculate the total of a group of deposits input to a program, and once the total is known, the average deposit can be easily determined by dividing the total by the number of deposits.

The totaling algorithm is very similar to the counting algorithm, except that the counting algorithm adds (or subtracts) a *constant* increment to the current value of the counter every time it is executed, and the totaling algorithm adds the *next item* to be totaled to the current value of the total every time it is executed:

counting algorithm: `count = count ± constantIncrement;`
totaling algorithm: `total = total + newItem;`

If we were adding a group of deposits, the variable `newItem` would contain the next deposit. As was the case with the counting algorithm, the name of the variable on the left side of the assignment operator can be any valid variable name. Similarly, the same variable name must be used on the right side of the assignment operator, and the name should be representative of what it stores. For example, when calculating a new bank balance:

`balance = balance + deposit;`

The chosen variable is generically referred to as the totaling or summation variable. Before the algorithm is used, the variable is set to an initial value, which is the current (beginning) value of the sum. For example, it could be the bank balance before the new deposits are made. Often, this value is zero. As is the case with the counting algorithm, once the initial value is set, the summation algorithm is repeatedly executed.

The following code fragments add up the integers from one to four:

```
int sum = 0;                        int sum = 0;
sum = sum + 1;                      for(int i = 1; i <= 4; i = i + 1)
sum = sum + 2;          OR         {
sum = sum + 3;                         sum = sum + i;
sum = sum + 4;                     }
```

The contents of the memory cell `sum` would progress from 0, to 1, to 3, to 6, and finally to 10. In most cases, as shown on the right, a loop is used to repeat the summation algorithm.

Figure 5.8 presents a Java console application named `TotalingLoop` that demonstrates the use of the totaling algorithm and the calculation of an average. A set of sample inputs and the program's corresponding outputs is given at the bottom of the figure. The monetary outputs produced by lines 15–16 and lines 30–34 are formatted as U.S. currency using an object in the `NumberFormat` class declared on line 13. This class and its methods used to produce this currency formatting will be discussed in the next section.

The program accepts a given number of input deposits and uses the totaling algorithm (line 25) to calculate their total. The number of deposits to be processed is input on line 17, then the parsed value is used in the Boolean condition of the for statement that begins on line 21 to process that number of deposits.

Before the loop begins, the totaling variable, total, is initialized to zero (line 20). During each iteration of the loop that begins on line 21, a new deposit is input and parsed. Then, the total algorithm is used on line 25 to add the new deposit to the total of the previously input deposits. After all the deposits are processed, the new balance (line 27) and the average deposit (line 28) are calculated. Lines 15–16 output the beginning balance, and lines 30–34 output the total of the deposits, the average deposit, and the new balance to the system console.

```
1    import javax.swing.JOptionPane;
2    import java.text.NumberFormat;
3    import java.util.Locale;
4
5    public class TotalingLoop
6    {
7      public static void main(String[] args)
8      {
9        double balance = 1000.24;
10       int numOfDeposits;
11       double deposit, total, newBalance, averageDeposit;
12       String input;
13       NumberFormat us = NumberFormat.getCurrencyInstance(Locale.US);
14
15       System.out.println("Your beginning balance is: " +
16                           us.format(balance));
17       input = JOptionPane.showInputDialog("How Many Deposits?");
18       numOfDeposits = Integer.parseInt(input);
19
20       total = 0.0;
21       for(int i = 1; i <= numOfDeposits;  i++)
22       {
23         input = JOptionPane.showInputDialog("Enter a deposit");
24         deposit = Double.parseDouble(input);
25         total = total + deposit;
26       }
27       balance = balance + total;
28       averageDeposit = total / numOfDeposits;
29
30       System.out.println("The total of the " + numOfDeposits +
31                           " deposits is " + us.format(total));
32       System.out.println("The average deposit was: " +
33                           us.format(averageDeposit));
34       System.out.println("Your new balance is: " + us.format(balance));
35     }
36  }
```

```
Inputs
3
20.10
30.20
40.30

Outputs
Your beginning balance is: $1,000.24
The total of the 3 deposits is $90.60
The average deposit was: $30.20
Your new balance is: $1,090.84
```

**Figure 5.8**
The application **TotalingLoops** and typical inputs and outputs.

### 5.3 FORMATTING NUMERIC OUTPUT: A SECOND PASS

The use of the `DecimalFormat` class to improve the readability of numeric outputs was briefly discussed in Chapter 2 (Section 2.10). In this section, we will expand that discussion and also discuss the use of the `NumberFormat` and `Locale` classes that were used to format the currency outputs produced by the program shown in Figure 5.8. We will begin with an introduction to the techniques used to format numeric output as currency.

**NOTE**
*All numeric formatting rounds up the fractional part of a numeric value, and all of the digits in the integer portion of the numeric value are always included in the formatted version of the number.*

#### 5.3.1 Currency Formatting

The monetary outputs produced by the program shown in Figure 5.8 are formatted as United States currency. There is a leading dollar sign and a decimal point separating the dollar amount from the cents, which are displayed as two rounded digits to the right of the decimal point. In addition, a comma is used as a thousands separator in the dollar amount. Had the output been negative, it would have been enclosed in parentheses. All of this formatting conforms to the way U.S. currency is displayed within the world of finance and makes the units of the output recognizable as dollars and cents.

Two methods in the `NumberFormat` class, `getCurrencyInstance` and `format`, and constants defined in the class `Locale` can be used to format numeric values as currency. The constants in the class `Locale` are used to specify which of the world's currencies to use in the formatting.

The `NumberFormat` class's method `getCurrencyInstance` is used on line 12 of Figure 5.8 to create a currency formatting object named `us`. The method accepts one argument, which is normally one of the predefined static constants in the `Locale` class. As the name of the class implies, this argument specifies the locale of the format that will be associated with the formatting object. Line 13 uses the constant `Locale.US`, to specify that the currency formatting associated with the object `us` will be United States currency: dollars and cents.

The object `us` is then used on lines 15-16 and lines 30-33 to invoke the `NumberFormat` class's `format` method. This method converts the numeric value passed to it to a string using the formatting associated with the object that invoked it. As a result, the four numeric outputs produced by the program are formatted as U.S. currency.

By changing the argument passed to the method `getCurrencyInstance` on line 13, the numeric output produced by the program could be made to conform to other currency formats used in the financial world. For example, the following code fragment produces the two outputs, which are formatted as pounds (the United Kingdom's currency) and euros (the European Union currency), respectively. The output of the code fragment is given below the code.

```java
double price = 1234567.889;
NumberFormat uk = NumberFormat.getCurrencyInstance(Locale.UK);
NumberFormat france = NumberFormat.getCurrencyInstance(Locale.FRANCE);

    System.out.println(uk.format(price));
    System.out.println(france.format(price));
```

***Output:***

```
£1,234,567.89
1 234 567,89 €
```

**NOTE** *The formatting performed does not take into account monetary exchange rates.*

## The Default Locale

The `getCurrencyInstance` method invoked on line 13 of Figure 5.8 is overloaded. There are two version of it: a one-parameter version that was invoked on line 13 and a no-parameter version. The no-parameter version of the method can be used to format numeric currency in the default locale of the computer's operating system. Assuming the default locale of the operating system was Italy, the following code fragment would produce two identical lines of output formatted as euros (Italy's currency).

```java
double price = 1435.2;
NumberFormat italy = NumberFormat.getCurrencyInstance(Locale.ITALY);
NumberFormat osDefault = NumberFormat.getCurrencyInstance();

System.out.println(italy.format(price));
System.out.println(osDefault.format(price));
```

## 5.3.2 The DecimalFormat Class: A Second Look

The methods in the DecimalFormat class, which were briefly discussed in Section 2.10 of Chapter 2, can also be used to format numeric output. Normally, these methods are used when the numeric value is not currency.

Like the NumberFormat class, the DecimalFormat class contains a nonstatic method named format that returns a string containing the formatted version of the numeric value sent to it as an argument. This method is invoked with a DecimalFormat object that can be declared using the class's one-parameter constructor. The constructor is passed a string argument, called the *formatting string*, which contains the formatting information. In Section 2.10, we used the formatting string argument "#,###.##" to produce an output that contained a comma every three digits to the left of the decimal point and to format real numbers (nonintegers) with a maximum of two digits of precision.

Other characters can be used in the formatting string to produce other forms of numeric output formatting. The pound signs (#) to left and right of the decimal point can be replaced with zeros, which are used to format the numeric value with leading and trailing zeros. In addition, a percent sign (%) can be added to the end of the formatting string. The percent sign is used to format the numeric value as a percentage. For example, the value 0.237 would be formatted as 23.7%, assuming one digit of precision was specified in the formatting string. Numeric values can also be formatted in scientific notation.

Regardless of the characters used in the formatting string, the fractional part of a numeric value is always rounded up and all of the digits in the integer portion of the numeric value or a leading zero are always included in the formatted value unless scientific notation is being used.

### Leading and Trailing Zeros

Inserting zeros into the formatting string adjacent to the decimal point will add leading or trailing zeros to the formatted value. For example, when the numeric value being formatted does not have an integer part (e.g., .254), inserting a zero to the left of the decimal point in the formatting string will format the value as 0.254. Adding a zero the right of the decimal point will format the value 167 as 167.0. If the number does have a fractional or integer part, then the digit adjacent to the decimal point in the numeric value always appears in the formatted value.

The code fragment below formats numeric values with one leading zero and two trailing zeros and produces the output shown below the code. The third output value is rounded to the specified two digits of precision.

```java
double n1 = .2;
double n2 = 167.0
double n3 = 1.4672
DecimalFormat ltz = new DecimalFormat("#,##0.00");
System.out.print(ltz.format(n1) + " " + ltz.format(n2) + " " +
                 ltz.format(n3));
```

**Output:**
```
0.20 167.00 1.47
```

## Percentages

A formatting string that ends with a percent sign is used to format a numeric value as a percentage. The value will be multiplied by 100, and a percent sign will be added to the right side of the string from the `format` method. For example, the value 0.254 would be formatted as 25.4%. The code fragment below formats numeric values as percentages with one leading zero and one trailing zero. The output it produces is shown below the code.

```java
double n1 = 0.002;
double n2 = 0.16 DecimalFormat pct = new DecimalFormat("#,##0.0%");
System.out.println(pct.format(n1) + " " + pct.format(n2));
```

*Output*:

```
0.2% 16.0%
```

## Scientific Notation

Scientific notation is a formatting of a numeric value into a mantissa followed by an exponent. Usually, the mantissa and the exponent are separated by the letter E. The mantissa contains the digits of the numeric value with its decimal point shifted left or right. To determine the numeric value, the mantissa is multiplied by 10 raised to the value of the exponent. For example, `23.971E2` represents the numeric value `2,397.1`.

A formatting string that ends with the character E followed by the number of leading zeros to be displayed in the exponent is used to format a numeric value in scientific notation. At least one zero must be included after the letter E in the formatting string. The formatted value will contain the mantissa and the exponent separated by the letter E. The mantissa is formatted using the portion of the formatting string to the left of the letter E, which should contain only zeroes and a decimal point.

The code fragment below formats numeric values in scientific notation with the mantissa shown with one digit to the left of the decimal. The output it produces is shown below the code.

```java
double n1 = 0.00000215;
double n2 = 16123067533.1
DecimalFormat sn = new DecimalFormat("0.0000E0");
System.out.println( sn.format(n1) + " " + sn.format(n2));
```

Output:

```
2.1500E-6 1.6123E10
```

---

**NOTE** *All digits of the exponent will always be included in the scientific formatted version of a numeric value.*

Table 5.1 summarizes the characters used in the `DecimalFormat` class's format string and the formatting they produce. All digits in the integer portion of numeric value will always be included in the formatted version of the numeric unless scientific notation is being used. All digits of the exponent are always displayed when using scientific notation.

**Table 5.1**

The **DecimalFormat** Class's Formatting Characters and Their Meaning

| Character | Formatting Produced | Formatting String Example |
|---|---|---|
| . | Output a decimal point in this position | |
| # | Output a digit in this position if it exists | `"#.#"` |
| 0 | Output a digit in this position if it exists, else a zero | `"0.00"` <br> One leading zero, two digits of precision |
| , | Output a comma separator in this position, as necessary | `"#,##0.00"` <br> Comma separator every three digits (with one leading zero and two digits of precision) |
| % | Output a numeric value as a percentage <br> (Multiply the numeric by 100 and add a percent sign to its right) | `"0.000%"` <br> Convert numeric to a percentage followed by a percent sign (with one leading zero, three digits of precision) |
| E | Output the numeric value in scientific notation | `"0.0000E0"` <br> Mantissa formatted with 5 digits <br> x.xxxxEx <br> All digits of the exponent are displayed |

Figure 5.9 illustrates the use of the methods in the `DecimalFormat` class to format numeric outputs. The program produces four groupings of outputs, which are shown in Figure 5.10. Each grouping outputs the same three numbers: n1, n2, and n3 (lines 15–33) using different formatting strings, which are defined on lines 7–10.

The first three output groupings use comma separators every three digits. The second and third groupings also use leading and trailing zeros, with the outputs in the third grouping displayed as percentages. The fourth output grouping uses scientific notation.

The first numeric output in the first grouping (0.006) has been truncated because its formatting string (line 7) only contains three digits of precision. It contains a leading zero because all numeric values contain a leading zero unless scientific notation is being used. The last two outputs in the first grouping do not contain trailing zeros because the pound sign (#) was used on line 7 to specify their precision.

The outputs in the second grouping contain trailing zeros because a zero was used in their formatting string to specify their precision (line 8). Finally, the exponent (11) in the second numeric output of the last grouping contains two digits even though its formatting string specifies one digit of precision. All the digits of an exponent are always displayed, regardless of the number of zeros used to specify the leading zeros of the exponent.

```java
1 import java.text.DecimalFormat;
2
3 public class DecimalFormatClass
4 {
5    public static void main(String[] args)
6    {
7       DecimalFormat cs = new DecimalFormat("#,###.###"); //commas
8       DecimalFormat ltz = new DecimalFormat("#,##0.000"); //zeros
9       DecimalFormat pct = new DecimalFormat("#,##0.00%"); //percentages
10      DecimalFormat sn = new DecimalFormat("0.0000E0"); //scientific
11      double n1 = 0.0062;
12      double n2 = 161234563468.5;
13      double n3 = 1.530;
14
15      System.out.println("Comma-separators");
16      System.out.println(cs.format(n1));
17      System.out.println(cs.format(n2));
18      System.out.println(cs.format(n3));
19
20      System.out.println("\nLeading & Trailing Zeros, & Commas");
21      System.out.println(ltz.format(n1));
22      System.out.println(ltz.format(n2));
23      System.out.println(ltz.format(n3));
24
25      System.out.println("\nPercentages");
26      System.out.println(pct.format(n1));
27      System.out.println(pct.format(n2));
28      System.out.println(pct.format(n3));
29
30      System.out.println("\nScientific Notation");
31      System.out.println(sn.format(n1));
32      System.out.println(sn.format(n2));
33      System.out.println(sn.format(n3));
34   }
35 }
```

**Figure 5.9**
The application **DecimalFormatClass**.

```
Comma separators
0.006
161,234,563,468.5
1.53

Leading & Trailing Zeros &Commas
0.006
161,234,563,468.500
1.530

Percentages
0.62%
16,123,456,346,850.00%
153.00%

Scientific Notation
6.2000E-3
1.6123E11
1.5300E0
```

**Figure 5.10**
The output produced by the application **DecimalFormatClass.**

## 5.4 NESTING for LOOPS

As we have learned, loops can be used to repeat a statement or a group of statements contained inside a statement block. When the statement block contains a loop, we say that the loop that is inside the statement block is *nested* inside the other loop. The loop in the statement block is called the *inner* loop because it is inside the other loop, which is referred to as the *outer* loop. The loop in the statement block can be thought of as an egg inside the nest formed by the outer loop. Consider the following code fragment that computes the average of a runner's ten qualifying race times:

```java
total = 0;
for(int i = 1; i<=10;  i++)
{
  input = JOptionPane.showInputDialog("Enter a race time");
  aRaceTime = Double.parseDouble(input);
  total = total + aRaceTime;
}
System.out.println(" Your average time is " + total / 10);
```

This code could be used to process 100 runners by nesting it inside an outer loop that executes 100 times.

```java
for(int j = 1; j<=100; j++) //each runner (the outer loop)
{
```

```
   total = 0;
   for(int i = 1; i<=10;  i++) //each race (the inner loop)
   {
      input = JOptionPane.showInputDialog("Enter a race time");
      aRaceTime = Double.parseDouble(input);
      total = total + aRaceTime;
   }
   System.out.println(" Your average time is + total / 10);
}
```

As is the case with nested decision statements, there is no limit on how many loops can be nested inside of other loops. The following code fragment processes the 10 qualifying times for 100 racers in 5 states using two levels of nesting.

```
for(int k = 1; k<=5; k++) //each state
{
   for(int j = 1; j<=100; j++) //each runner
   {
      total = 0;
      for(int i = 1; i<=10;  i++) //each race
      {
         input = JOptionPane.showInputDialog("Enter a race time");
         aRaceTime = Double.parseDouble(input);
         total = total + aRaceTime;
      }
      System.out.println("Your average time is + total /10);
   }
}
```

The indentation used in the above code fragment is considered good programming practice because it makes the use of nested loops, and the nesting levels, obvious to anyone reading the code. It can be quickly determined that the three statements in the innermost loop will execute 5,000 times (= 5 * 100 * 10). When using nested loops, it is also good programming practice to progressively develop the code from the inside of the nest outward. The innermost loop (e.g., one that processes 10 races) is coded first, tested, and corrected.  Then, this loop is enclosed in a loop (e.g., one that processes 100 runners), and this nested structure is again tested. The process continues until the outermost loop (e.g., one that processes 5 states) is complete.

Figure 5.11 contains a graphics application that illustrates the use of nested `for` loops to draw the checkerboard shown in Figure 5.12, and a second set of nested `for` loops to draw three rows of red checkers on the board. A significant portion of the code is the same as the code shown in Figure 5.6 that drew *one* row of a checkerboard containing red checkers.

Lines 31 to 49 contain the first set of nested `for` loops used to draw the eight rows of the checkerboard. The inner loop, that begins on Lines 33 and ends on Line 42, is same code used on Lines 29 to 38 of Figure 5.6 to draw one row of a checkerboard. This loop is now nested inside an outer loop that begins on line 31, which executes eight times. With each pass through the outer loop, the inner loop draws another row of the board. To prevent the rows from being drawn on top of each other, line 43 increases the y location of the next row of boxes to be draw in the inner loop by the

```
1    import edu.sjcny.gpv1.*;
2    import java.awt.Color;
3    import java.awt.Graphics;
4
5    public class CheckerBoard extends DrawableAdapter
6    {
7      static CheckerBoard ge = new CheckerBoard();
8      static GameBoard gb = new GameBoard(ge, "Nested For loops");
9
10     public static void main(String[] args)
11     {
12       showGameBoard(gb);
13     }
14
15     public void draw(Graphics g)
16     {
17       int xBox = 12;
18       int yBox = 50;
19       int boxWidth = 60;
20       int boxHeight = 53;
21       int firstCheckerCol = 1;
22       int checkerX = 20;
23       int checkerY = 55;
24       Color firstColor = Color.BLACK;
25       Color secondColor = Color.RED;
26       Color temp;
27
28       gb.setBackground(Color.LIGHT_GRAY);
29
30       //Draw the checker board boxes
31       for(int row = 1; row <= 8; row++) //each row
32       {
33         for(int col = 1; col <=8; col++) //each column
34         {
35           g. setColor(firstColor);
36           if(col % 2 == 0)
37           {
38             g. setColor(secondColor);
39           }
40           g.fillRect(xBox, yBox, boxWidth, boxHeight);
41           xBox = xBox + boxWidth;
42         }
43         yBox = yBox + boxHeight;
44         xBox = 12;
45
46         temp = firstColor; //swap the box colors
47         firstColor = secondColor;
48         secondColor = temp;
49       }
```

```
50
51      //Draw the red checkers
52      for(int row = 1; row <= 3; row++) //first three rows
53      {
54        if(row % 2 == 0) //an even numbered row
55        {
56          checkerX = checkerX + boxWidth;
57          firstCheckerCol = 2;
58        }
59        g.setColor(Color.RED);
60        for(int col = firstCheckerCol; col <=8; col= col + 2)
61        { //red checker locations
62          checkerX = 20 + (col -1) * boxWidth;
63          g.fillOval( checkerX, checkerY, 40, 40);
64        }
65        checkerY = checkerY + boxHeight;
66        checkerX = 20;
67        firstCheckerCol = 1;
68      }
69    }
70 }
```

**Figure 5.11**
The graphical application **CheckerBoard**.

height of the boxes, and line 44 resets the x location of the each row's first box to 12. Before the outer loop ends, lines 46–48 swap the colors of the odd and even column boxes. This will make the colors of the boxes to be drawn in each column of the next row different from the color of the boxes in the row above them.

**Figure 5.12**
The output produced by the application **CheckerBoard**.

The inner loop that begins on lines 60 and ends on line 64 is the same code used on lines 42–46 of Figure 5.6 to draw one row of red checkers. This loop is now nested inside an outer loop that begins on line 31, which executes three times. With each pass through the outer loop, the inner loop draws the next row of checkers. After a row is drawn, the y location of the next row of checkers is calculated and assigned to the variable checkerY on line 65. The value stored in this variable is increased by the height of the boxes then used during the next iteration of the inner loop (line 63) to draw a row of checkers.

Line 66 reinitializes the x location of the first checker in a row to 20. The if statement on line 54 decides when the row number is even. Because only the odd-numbered rows (rows 1 and 3) should have a checker in the first column of the board (at x = 20), checkerX is increased by the width of a checkerboard box (line 56) when the row number is even. Then, line 57 sets the variable firstCheckerCol, used on line 60 as the column number of a row's first checker, to 2 (line 57)

## 5.5 THE while STATEMENT

Many applications require that a sequence of statements be repeated until a Boolean condition becomes `false`, rather than repeating until the statements have been executed a given or known number of times. For example, a program might continue to ask for a password until the correct password is entered. When this is the case, the `while` or the `do-while` statements are normally used to code the loop that repeats the statements. If the statements should be executed at least once, the `do-while` statement is used. Otherwise, the `while` statement is used. In this section, the `while` statement will be discussed, and the `do-while` statement will be discussed in Section 5.6.

### 5.5.1 Syntax of the while Statement

The generalized syntax of the `while` statement and its execution path are shown on the left and right sides of Figure 5.13, respectively:

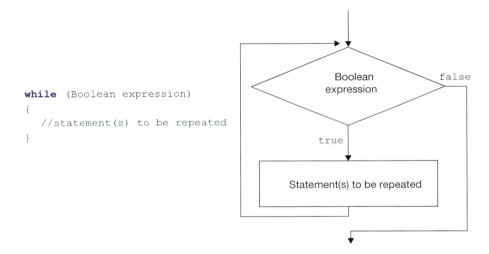

```
while (Boolean expression)
{
    //statement(s) to be repeated
}
```

**Figure 5.13**
The syntax and execution path of the **while** statement.

The statement begins with the keyword **while** followed by a Boolean expression enclosed in parentheses, which is followed by a code block containing the statements to be repeated. While it is the case that a single statement to be repeated need not be coded inside a statement block, as discussed in Section 5.2.1, it is good programming practice to do so.

As shown on the right side of Figure 5.13, the statements in the block will be repeated as long as the Boolean condition is `true`. If, when the statement begins execution, the Boolean condition is `false`, the statement block will not be executed.

The following code fragment outputs the square root of 1.2, 2.3, 3.4, and 4.5:

```
double n = 1.2;
while(n != 5.6)
{
```

```
   System.out.println(Math.sqrt(n));
   n = n + 1.1;
}
```

The most common errors made when coding the `while` statement are:

- placing a semicolon after the close parenthesis
- neglecting to code the open and close brace around the statements when more than one statement is to be repeated

When a semicolon is coded after the close parentheses, the statement is syntactically correct, however, none of the statements that would have normally formed the loop body are considered to be part of (inside) the loop. They default to sequential execution, and each statement executes once. When braces are not coded, the statement is also syntactically correct, however, the first statement after the `while` statement is the only statement considered to be part of the loop. Regardless of the indentation used, it is the only statement repeated. When coding a `while` loop, it is good programming practice to code the following fragment and then add the Boolean condition and the statements to be repeated:

```
while()
{

}
```

A common logic error made when coding the `while` statement is that the statements inside the statement block, during some repetition of the loop, do not change the Boolean expression to `false`. The statement, or statements, intended to do that were either incorrectly coded or were not included in the loop's statement block. In either case, once the loop begins, it never ends, and the loop is said to be an *infinite* loop. The following code fragment is an infinite loop because the statement that increments n is not part of the loop's statement block. On each iteration through the loop, n's value remains 1.2, and the Boolean condition never becomes `false`.

```
double n = 1.2;
while(n != 5.6)
{
   System.out.println(Math.sqrt(n));
}
n = n + 1.1;
```

Infinite loops can also occur when the loop's Boolean expression is improperly coded, as is the case in the following code fragment. The variable n assumes the values 1.2, 2.3, 3.4, 4.5, 5.6 …, but never the value 5.5.

```
double n = 1.2;
while(n != 5.5) //n never becomes 5.5
{
   System.out.println(Math.sqrt(n));
   n = n + 1.1;
}
```

## 5.5.2 Sentinel Loops

Many applications require that a sequence of instructions be repeated until a signal to stop is detected. The signal is referred to as a sentinel value, and a loop that ends when it detects a sentinel value is called a *sentinel* loop.

Sentinel loops are commonly used to process a set of input data, and the sentinel value is chosen to be a specific value of the input data. The value selected must be a value that would never occur in that data set (for example, a student grade of -1). As another example, you might want to continue to process bank deposits until a negative deposit is entered, or when data is being read from a disk file to continue to process data until an End of File (EOF) marker is encountered. Although `for` loops that contain `break` statements could be used to code sentinel loops, they are more easily coded using the `while` and `do-while` statements.

Often, the use of sentinel loops in our programs makes them easier to use. Imagine you are a data-entry person using the program shown in Figure 5.8 to process a group of input deposits. When the program is launched, you are asked for the number of deposits. If the first item on the list of deposits you were given to enter was the number of deposits, the automatic counting performed by the `for` loop used in the program would be perfect for the application.

However, if the number of deposits was not included in the list of deposits, then before you used the application, you would have to count the number of deposits. Not only would this be time consuming when the list of deposits was long, but if you miscounted the number of deposits, the program would either terminate before all the deposits were entered (because your count was too low) or ask you to enter a deposit that did not exist (because your count was too high). Generally speaking, when the number of data items to be processed is not easily determined, sentinel loops make our programs much easier to use.

The following code fragment is a template for a sentinel loop that uses a `while` statement to process a set of inputs. Each input is read into a variable called the sentinel variable.

```
//obtain the first input into the sentinel variable
while( //the input is not the sentinel value )
{
    //statement(s) to perform the loop's processing
    //obtain the next input into the sentinel variable
}
```

The template begins with a statement to accept the first input and the same statement, which accepts all subsequent inputs, is also coded as the last statement in the `while` statement's code block. The other statements in the statement block perform the processing of each input. This placement of the input statements in a sentinel loop prevents the processing of the sentinel value, even if it is the first input (i.e., the data set is empty).

The three most common errors made when coding a sentinel loop are:

- neglecting to code the statement to accept the first sentinel variable input before the `while` statement

- neglecting to code the statements to accept all subsequent inputs of the sentinel variable at the end of the loop's code block

- coding the statements to accept all subsequent inputs of the sentinel variable inside the loop's code block before the processing statements

The first error results in the loop processing the default value of the sentinel variable, or if the default value is the sentinel value, the loop does not execute at all. The second error results in an infinite loop because once the loop is entered, the sentinel variable is not changed. When the third error is made, the first input is not processed.

The application `SentinelWhileLoop` presented in Figure 5.14 demonstrates the use of the code template. It is a sentinel loop version of the program shown in Figure 5.8 that totals and averages a set of input deposits. Typical inputs and outputs are shown at the bottom of Figure 5.14. As previously discussed, this version would be preferred if the number of deposits was not the first data item.

Following the format of the `while` loop sentinel template, line 18 accepts the initial value of the sentinel variable `input`. The Boolean expression (on line 19) of the `while` statement uses this variable to decide if the statement's code block should be executed. If anything other than the sentinel value (-1) has been input, an execution of the loop's statement block is performed.

Because an average is to be calculated and the user is no longer required to enter the number of deposits, the counting algorithm is used on line 23 to count the number of deposits processed. The counting variable, `numOfDeposits`, is initialized to zero on line 15. Consistent with the `while` sentinel loop template, the last line of the loop's code block (line 24) accepts the next input value and stores it in the sentinel variable `input`.

```
1    import javax.swing.JOptionPane;
2    import java.text.NumberFormat;
3
4    public class SentinelWhileLoop
5    {
6      public static void main(String[] args)
7      {
8        double balance = 1000.24;
9        int numOfDeposits;
10       double deposit, total, newBalance, averageDeposit;
11       String input;
12       NumberFormat us = NumberFormat.getCurrencyInstance();
13
14       System.out.println("Your beginning balance was:
                           "+ us.format(balance));
15       numOfDeposits = 0;
16       total = 0.0;
17
18       input = JOptionPane.showInputDialog("Enter a deposit, -1 to end");
19       while( !input.equals("-1") ) //input is not "-1"
```

```
20        {
21          deposit = Double.parseDouble(input);
22          total = total + deposit;
23          numOfDeposits++;
24          input = JOptionPane.showInputDialog("Enter a deposit, -1 to end");
25        }
26
27      balance = balance + total;
28      averageDeposit = total / numOfDeposits;
29
30      System.out.println("The total of the " + numOfDeposits +
31                         " deposits is "+ us.format(total));
32      System.out.println("The average deposit was: " +
33                         us.format(averageDeposit));
34      System.out.println("Your new balance is: " + us.format(balance));
35    }
36  }
```

**Inputs**
20.10
30.20
40.30
-1

**Outputs**
Your beginning balance was: $1,000.24
The total of the 3 deposits is $90.60
The average deposit was: $30.20
Your new balance is: $1,090.84

**Figure 5.14**
The console application **SentinelWhileLoop** and the output it produces.

Another commonly used form of a `while` sentinel loop parses the input after each input is accepted. This adaptation of the `while` loop sentinel template in the program shown in Figure 5.14 would be coded as:

```
input = JOptionPane.showInputDialog("Enter a deposit, -1 to end");
deposit = Double.parseDouble(input);
while (!deposit == -1.0)
{
  //statement(s) to perform the loop's processing, less the parsing
  input = JOptionPane.showInputDialog("Enter a deposit, -1 to end");
  deposit = Double.parseDouble(input);
}
```

### 5.5.3 Detecting an End Of File

Often, large data sets are stored in disk files, and the programs that process them read the data from the disk file until a sentinel value is detected. Because the sentinel value is chosen to be a value outside the range of the data set's values, most sentinel values vary from one application to another. In the case of a disk-based data file, there is one sentinel value that works for all data sets: the End of File (EOF) marker that is placed at the end of each file.

In Section 4.8.1 of Chapter 4, we used the methods in the Scanner class to read data from a disk text file. The Scanner class also contains a method named hasNext that can be used to detect the EOF marker in a file. The method has no parameters and returns false when the EOF marker is encountered. The following code fragment uses a sentinel loop to read all the integer data values from the disk text file data.txt stored on the root of the C drive and outputs the values to the system console. The value returned from the method hasNext is stored in the sentinel-variable notEOF.

```java
int dataItem;
File fileObject = new File("c:/data.txt");
Scanner fileIn = new Scanner(fileObject);
boolean notEOF; //the sentinel variable

notEOF = fileIn.hasNext(); //fetch the 1st sentinel variable value
while(notEOF) //more data to process
{
  dataItem = fileIn.nextInt();
  System.out.println(dataItem);
  notEOF = fileIn.hasNext(); //fetch next sentinel value
}
fileIn.close();
```

The following code fragment is a more succinct and more commonly used version of an EOF sentinel loop:

```java
int dataItem;
File fileObject = new File("c:/data.txt");
Scanner fileIn = new Scanner(fileObject);

while(fileIn.hasNext()) //more data to process
{
    dataItem = fileIn.nextInt();
    System.out.println(dataItem);
}
fileIn.close();
```

Figure 5.15 presents a modified version of the program shown in Figure 5.14 that processed a group of deposits entered from the keyboard. The new version of the program reads the deposits from a disk file using the file's EOF marker as a sentinel value. A set of file inputs and the corresponding program outputs are given at the bottom of Figure 5.15.

The instructions in Figure 5.14 that accept input from the keyboard have been removed from the program. Lines 1 and 2 of Figure 5.15 have been added to access the `Scanner` and `File` classes. In the interest of brevity, exceptions that could be generated during the disk file input performed by the program are not processed by the modified program. Rather, a `throws` clause has been added to the end of line 7.

Line 21 begins a sentinel `while` loop that ends when an EOF marker is detected. Inside the loop, line 23 reads and parses the next deposit using the `Scanner` object created by lines 13 and 14. Line 35 closes the disk file after the console output is performed.

```java
1    import java.util.Scanner;
2    import java.io.*;
3    import java.text.NumberFormat;
4
5    public class EndOfFile
6    {
7      public static void main(String[] args) throws IOException
8      {
9        double balance = 1000.24;
10       int numOfDeposits;
11       double deposit, total, newBalance, averageDeposit;
12       NumberFormat us = NumberFormat.getCurrencyInstance();
13       File fileObject = new File("c:/data.txt");
14       Scanner fileIn = new Scanner(fileObject);
15
16       numOfDeposits = 0;
17       total = 0.0;
18
19       System.out.println("Your beginning balance is: " +
20                           us.format(balance));
21       while(fileIn.hasNext()) //more data to process
22       {
23         deposit = fileIn.nextDouble();
24         total = total + deposit;
25         numOfDeposits++;
26       }
27       balance = balance + total;
28       averageDeposit = total / numOfDeposits;
29
30       System.out.println("The total of the " + numOfDeposits +
31                           " deposits is " + us.format(total));
32       System.out.println("The average deposit was: " +
33                           us.format(averageDeposit));
34       System.out.println("Your new balance is: " + us.format(balance));
35       fileIn.close();
36     }
37   }
```

Disk File Inputs
20.10
30.20
40.30

**Outputs**
Your beginning balance was: $1,000.24
The total of the 3 deposits is $90.60
The average deposit was: $30.20
Your new balance is: $1,090.84

**Figure 5.15**
The application **EndOfFile**, a set of file inputs, and corresponding outputs.

An alternate approach to using the `Scanner` class's `hasNext` method to detect the end of a file is to write the number of data items into the file as the file's first value. If the data file processed by the program shown in Figure 5.15 had been written this way, lines 21-26 would be coded as shown below:

```
21      numOfDeposits = fileIn.nextInt();  //read the number of data items
22      for(int i = 1; i <= numOfDeposits; i++) //each data item
23      {
24        deposit = fileIn.nextDouble();
25        total = total + deposit;
26      }
```

Most often, the use of the `hasNext` method to detect the end of the file is the better approach because if new data were added to end of the file, updating the number of data items at the beginning of the file would require reading, deleting, and rewriting the entire file. This is a time-consuming process.

## 5.6 ■ THE do-while STATEMENT

As previously discussed, when a loop in an application is to execute a known number of times, the `for` statement is best suited for the application. When the number of times to execute the loop is not known, either the `while` or the `do-while` statements are preferred. Of these two statements, the `do-while` statement is the better alternative when the loop's statements should be executed *at least once*. For example, the code to check a password is normally coded inside a `do-while` loop because the password has to be entered at least once.

### 5.6.1 ■ Syntax of the do-while Statement

The generalized syntax of the `do-while` statement and its execution path are shown on the left and right sides of Figure 5.16, respectively.

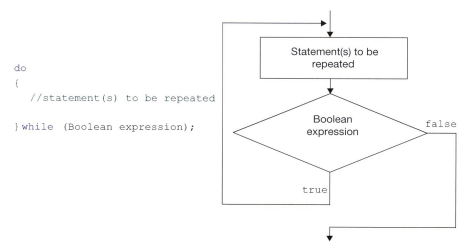

```
do
{
    //statement(s) to be repeated

} while (Boolean expression);
```

**Figure 5.16**
The generalized syntax of the **do-while** statement.

The statement begins with the keyword **do** followed by the loop's statement block. The keyword **while** and the statement's Boolean expression enclosed in parentheses are coded after the statement block's close brace. It is good programing style to code the keyword **while** and the Boolean expression on the same line as the close brace because it improves the readability of the statement. The do-while statement ends with a semicolon coded after the close parentheses that terminates the Boolean expression.

As shown on the right side of Figure 5.16, the loop's statement(s) will be executed at least once because they are executed before the Boolean condition is tested. After they execute, the Boolean expression is tested, and the statements are repeated until the Boolean condition becomes false. The do-while loop is called a *post-test* loop because the test to terminate the loop is performed after the loop's statement block has executed at least once.

The most common syntactical errors made when coding the do-while statement are:

- placing a semicolon after the keyword **do**
- neglecting to include a semicolon after the Boolean expression
- neglecting to code the open and close braces around the statements when more than one statement is to be repeated

All of these coding errors are syntax errors and are detected and reported by the Java translator. When coding a do-while loop, it is good programming practice to code the following code fragment and then add the statements to be repeated and the Boolean condition, even if only one statement is to be repeated.

```
do
{

} while( );
```

The most common logic error made when coding this statement is that the statements inside the statement block, during some repetition of the loop, do *not* change the Boolean expression to `false`. In this case, once the loop begins, it never ends and is said to be an infinite loop. For example, the following code sequence is an infinite loop because the loop's statement does not change the string variable `password`, which is used in the Boolean condition. The user-entered password is mistakenly stored in the string object `pw` leaving the string `password` unchanged each time through the loop.

```
String password = "";
String pw;
do
{
    pw = JOptionPane.showInputDialog("Enter The Password");
}while(!password.equals("Mercury"));
```

The following code fragment is the correct coding of a `do-while` statement that verifies the entry of the correct password, *Mercury*.

```
String password = "";
do
{
    password = JOptionPane.showInputDialog("Enter The Password");
}while(!password.equals("Mercury"));
```

Infinite loops can also occur when the loop's Boolean expression is improperly coded. In the code fragment below, the logical operator NOT( `!`) has been left out of the Boolean expression, and any password other than the correct password, *Mercury*, is accepted.

```
String password = "";
do
{
    password = JOptionPane.showInputDialog("Enter The Password");
}while(password.equals("Mercury"));
```

## 5.7 THE break AND continue STATEMENTS

The `break` and `continue` statements are used inside a `for`, `while`, or `do-while` loop's code block to alter the loop's execution path. Just as a `break` statement terminates the execution of a `switch` statement, a `break` statement may also be used to terminate a loop. Execution continues with the statement that follows the loop.

NOTE *When a `break` statement is executed inside a loop, the execution of the loop terminates.*

When a `continue` statement is executed in a loop, the *current* iteration of the loop is terminated, and statements that come after it in the loop's body are not executed during that iteration of the loop. Execution continues with the testing of the loop statement's Boolean condition. When a `continue` statement is executed inside a `for` loop, the loop variable is incremented before the Boolean condition is tested.

NOTE

*When a* `continue` *statement is executed inside a loop, the current iteration of the loop terminates.*

To illustrate the use of these two statements, the code fragment below gives a game player three chances to enter the password "*Mars*" to access a game. The `break` statement is used to exit the loop after the message *Look up your password* is output. The `continue` statement is used to skip the message box output and the `break` statement until three incorrect passwords are entered.

```java
int count = 1;
String password = "";
do
{
   if(count <= 3)
   {
     password = JOptionPane.showInputDialog("Enter your password");
     count++;
     continue;
   }
   JOptionPane.showMessageDialog(null, "Look up your password");
   break;
}while(!password.equals("Mars"));
```

## 5.8 WHICH LOOP STATEMENT TO USE

When the number of times to repeat the loop's statements is known, the `for` statement should be used to code the loop. The number of times to repeat the loop could be known at the time the program is written (e.g., the program will always process 100 race times), or it is determined during the program's execution before the loop statement is executed. For example, before entering a group of deposits, the program users are asked to enter the number of deposits they will be making into their bank account. In both of these cases the `for` loop is the preferred loop statement.

When the number of times to execute the loop is not known, either a `while` or a `do-while` loop is preferred to a `for` loop. The `while` statement is the better alternative when there are times (cases) when the loop body should not execute even once. The `do-while` statement is the better alternative when the loop's statements should always be executed at least once. Table 5.2 summarizes the criteria for selecting the best loop statement for a particular application.

**Table 5.2**
Criteria for Selecting the Best Loop Statement

| Is the Number of Times the Loop Will Execute Known? | Loop Statement |
| --- | --- |
| Yes | `for` |
| No, and there are cases when the loop body should *not* execute even once | `while` |
| No, and the loop body should always execute *at least once* | `do-while` |

The boundaries between the use of the three loop statements become somewhat blurred with the use of the counting algorithm inside a `while` loop and the use of a `break` statement inside a `for` loop. For example, to average 100 items, most programmers would use a `for` loop. However, a `while` loop that contains the counting algorithm can also be used, as illustrated in the following code fragment:

```java
int count = 1;
double total = 0;
double average;
String sItem;
while (count <= 100)
{
    sitem = JOptionPane.showInputDialog("Enter an item");
    total = total + Double.parseDouble(sItem);
    count++;
}
average = total / 100;
System.out.println("The average of the 100 items is: " + average);
```

The `for` loop is preferred for this application because when a `while` loop is used and we neglect to increment the counter (`count++;`) in the loop's body, the loop becomes an infinite loop. If we use a `for` loop and neglect to increment the counter in the first line of the `for` statement, the translator would alert us to the oversight.

Consider a program that totals input items until a -1 is entered or 100 items have been entered. Most programmers would use a `while` loop for this application. However, it can be coded using a `for` loop that contains a `break` statement.

```java
double total = 0;
String sItem;

for(int i = 1; i <= 100; i++)
{
    sItem = JOptionPane.showInputDialog("enter an item");
    if(sItem.equals("-1"))
    {
        break;
    }
    total = total + Double.parseDouble(sItem);
}
System.out.println("The total of the items is: " + total);
```

When this `for` loop is used it would appear that the loop will always execute 100 times. However, the loop terminates before 100 iterations when the `break` statement executes. From a code readability point of view, the following `while` loop is the preferred loop statement for this application because the first line of the `while` loop clearly states the two conditions that will end the input loop.

```java
int count = 1;
double total = 0;
String sItem;
```

```
sItem = JOptionPane.showInputDialog("enter an item, or -1");
while (!sItem.equals("-1") && count <= 100) //tests both conditions
{
    total = total + Double.parseDouble(sItem);
    count = count++;
    sItem = JOptionPane.showInputDialog("enter an item, or -1");
}
System.out.println("The total of the items is: " + total);
```

## 5.9 THE Random CLASS

Pseudorandom numbers, their use in computer programs, and the ability to generate them with the Math class's random method were discussed in Section 2.6.4 of Chapter 2. The methods in the class Random can also be used to generate pseudorandom numbers. In fact, these methods do the work of the Math class's random method in that the method random invokes the Random class's methods to generate the numbers it returns.

Table 5.3 lists the Random class's constructors and some of its methods used to generate pseudorandom numbers. Each time these methods are invoked, they return the next number in a sequence of random numbers. An object in the class Random is used to invoke them, which is created using one of the class's constructors.

```
Random randomObject1 = new Random();
Random randomObject2 = new Random(123456);
```

**Table 5.3**
**Random** Class Methods

| Method | Description | Coding Example |
|---|---|---|
| Random() | Creates a Random object based on the seed value time of day | Random ro = new Random(); |
| Random(long seed) | Creates a Random object based on the seed argument sent to it | Random ro = new Random(675); |
| nextDouble() | Returns the next pseudo-random real number in the range: 0.0<=randomNumber<1.0 | double rn = ro.nextDouble(); |
| nextInt() | Returns the next pseudorandom integer in the range of the int primitive type | int rn = ro.nextInt(); |
| nextInt(int max) | Returns the next pseudo-random integer in the range zero to one less than max | int rn = ro.nextInt(20); |

When the one-parameter constructor is used to create the object, the sequence of numbers the methods generate is based on the integer argument sent to the constructor, which is called a *seed* value. When the no-parameter constructor is used to create the object, the sequence of numbers the methods generate is based on the time of day because the seed value defaults to the real-time clock's value expressed in milliseconds. Sequences of numbers generated with objects created using the same seed value will be identical.

The one-parameter constructor is used when it is desirable to generate the same sequence of pseudorandom numbers every time the program is run. Conversely, the no-parameter constructor is used when it is desirable to generate a sequence of pseudorandom numbers that rarely repeats because the program would have to be run at exactly the same time of day to generate the same sequence of numbers.

Like the `Math` class's `random` method, the method `nextDouble` generates and returns a pseudorandom real number (a `double`) in the range: 0.0 <= randomNumber < 1.0. The method can be used to generate a real number in the range: min ≤ randomNumber < max using the following assignment statement (and sample object declaration):

```
Random randomObject2 = new Random(98765);
randomNumber = min + randomObject2.nextDouble() * (max - min);
```

The following code sequence outputs a sequence of ten pseudorandom real numbers in the range 20.0 ≤ randomNumber < 50.0. It would be very unusual for this code to generate the same sequence of numbers during two executions of the program because the sequence's seed value is the time of day in milliseconds. (The `Random` object is created with the no-parameter constructor.) Alternately, the one-parameter constructor could be used to generate a repeatable sequence of numbers.

```
double randomNumber;
double min = 20.0;
double max = 50.0;
Random randomObject2 = new Random(); // time of day seed value

for(int i = 1; i<=10; i++)
{
    randomNumber = min + randomObject2.nextDouble() * (max - min);
    System.out.println(randomNumber);
}
```

As shown in the Table 5.3, there are two versions of the `nextInt` method, which is used to generate and return a random integer (of type `int`). The no-parameter version returns a pseudorandom number over the full range of an `int` type variable (see Table 2.1).

The one-parameter version of the `nextInt` method is used to generate a sequence of integers, each of which are within a specified range. The numbers returned from the method are in the range zero to one less than the argument sent to it. The following code sequence generates a pseudorandom number between zero and nine, inclusive:

```
Random randomObject2 = new Random();
randomNumber = randomObject2.nextInt(10)
```

The use of this method can be generalized. The following code sequence outputs ten random integers in the range three to six, *inclusive*. The initial values of the variables max and min specify the lowest and highest numbers generated in the sequence. Every time this code is run, the same sequence of numbers is generated (5, 5, 5, 4, 3, 5, 5, 3, 6, 4) because the one-parameter constructor was used to create the Random object.

```
int randomNumber;
int min = 3;
int max = 6;
Random randomObject1 = new Random(98765); //repeatable random set

for(int i = 1; i<=10; i++)
{
   randomNumber = min + randomObject1.nextInt(max - min + 1);
   System.out.println(randomNumber); //in the range min to max inclusive
}
```

Figure 5.17 shows a number-guessing game program in which the player is asked to guess a number between 32 and 38, inclusive. The inputs and outputs for a correct answer on the second guess are shown in Figure 5.18.

Line 1 imports the Random class into the program. Line 8 declares an instance of this class, randomObject, which is used to invoke the nextInt method on line 15. The use of the no-parameter constructor on line 8 ensures that each time the program is run, there is the possibility that a different pseudorandom number will be generated by line 15. The maximum and minimum values of the pseudorandom numbers used on line 15 are specified on lines 9 and 10.

```
1    import java.util.Random;
2    import javax.swing.*;
3
4    public class RandomClass
5    {
6      public static void main(String[] args)
7      {
8        Random randomObject = new Random(); //time of day seed value
9        int min = 32;
10       int max = 38;
11       int secretNumber;
12       String sGuess;
13       int count = 1;
14
15       secretNumber = min + randomObject.nextInt(max - min + 1);
16       JOptionPane.showMessageDialog(null, "Secret Number Guessing Game" +
17                                     "\nguess a number between " +
18                                     max + " and " + min);
19       do
20       {
```

```
21          sGuess = JOptionPane.showInputDialog("Enter guess" + count +
22                                      "\nOr click Cancel to quit");
23          count++;
24          if(sGuess == null) //Cancel was clicked
25          {
26             break;
27          }
28       }while(secretNumber != Integer.parseInt(sGuess));
29
30       if(sGuess == null) //Cancel was clicked
31       {
32          JOptionPane.showMessageDialog(null, "Secret Number was " +
33                                      secretNumber);
34       }
35       else
36       {
37          JOptionPane.showMessageDialog(null, "Great, you guessed it.");
38       }
39    }
40 }
```

**Figure 5.17**
The application **RandomClass.**

(a)                         (b)

(c)                         (d)

**Figure 5.18**
The inputs and corresponding outputs produced by the application **RandomClass.**

## 5.10 CHAPTER SUMMARY

Many applications require that the statements in a statement block be repeated, and in this chapter we discussed three ways to perform this repetition: a `for` loop, a `while` loop, and a `do-while` loop. The `for` loop is an automatic counting loop used when the number of times to repeat the statements is known. The `do-while` and `while` loops end when their Boolean condition becomes `false` and they are usually used to detect a sentinel value of the data they are processing. The `do-while` loop is used whenever the loop's block should be executed at least once, and the `while` loop is a more general-purpose loop that can be used in most applications.

The loop control variable of a `for` loop is used to control the number of iterations of the loop. The statement's initialization expression sets its initial value. At the end of each loop iteration, the increment expression executes, which normally changes the value of the loop variable. The `for` and `while` loops are called pretest loops: they test their Boolean condition to continue at the beginning of the loop; the `do-while` loop is a posttest loop, testing its condition to continue at the end of an iteration.

The totaling or summation algorithm is a loop-based algorithm because it sums a set of items by repeatedly adding the value of a new item to an existing subtotal and making the result the new subtotal. Its template is: `total = total + newItem`. Each time through the loop, the value of the variable `newItem` assumes the next value to be totaled, which is often input by the user or from a disk file. The variable total is initialized to zero before the totaling loop begins. The counting algorithm can use used inside a loop's statement block to count the number of times the loop executes and can then be divided into the total the loop calculates to determine the average of the totaled values.

Often, a sentinel value is used to terminate a loop when the number of input values to be processed is unknown. Two Java statements, `break` and `continue`, also enable us to control the number of times all or some of the statements within the body of the loop will be executed. When a `break` is executed within a loop, the loop terminates. The `continue` statement can be used to end the current iteration of the loop and is useful when conditions dictate that the remaining statements in the loop's block should be skipped during the current iteration. When a loop is used to obtain and process an unknown number of inputs from a file, Java's End of File (EOF) character or the `Scanner` class's `hasnext` method can be used as a sentinel to terminate the loop.

Nested loops are used to repeat loop-based algorithms. Examples include averaging 10 grades and repeating this for 20 students or processing a set of race times for 100 runners. Nested loops are particularly useful in creating two-dimensional graphics that are composed of many instances of the same repetitive shape, such as the eight rows of eight squares of a checkerboard.

The `Random` class's `nextInt` and `nextDouble` methods can be used to generate a random integer or real number and, when used inside of a loop, to generate a set of random numbers. The `nextInt` method is easier to use than the `Math` class's `random` method because it returns an integer in the positive range of the `int` type or within a specified range. This makes it ideal for generating random game board pixel locations. In addition, when the methods are invoked using a `Random` object created with the class's one-parameter constructor, they generate a repeatable sequence of pseudorandom numbers. This is particularly useful in applications that require the same starting point every time they are launched and is always used when the random numbers are generated within a graphics call back method.

The methods in the `DecimalFormat` class can be used to insert leading/training zeros and comma separators into numeric output, specify the output's precision, and convert the output to a percentage or display it using scientific notation. The methods in the `NumberFormat` and `Locale` classes are used to produce local dependent currency formatting for use in financial and international applications.

Our knowledge of these statements will be expanded in Chapter 6, which covers the concept of arrays because loops are used to unlock the power of arrays. Also, in the next chapter, we will see how loops can be used with arrays to enable us to input, output, and process large data sets.

## Knowledge Exercises

1. True or false:
   a) The body of a `while` loop will always execute at least once.
   b) The `for` loop is an automatic counting loop and should be used where the number of repetitions is known.
   c) A sentinel is a data value that can be used to terminate a loop.
   d) The `do-while` loop will continue until the Boolean expression in the `while` statement becomes `true`.
   e) A `while` loop is a posttest loop.
   f) Checking for the EOF condition can be used to control a loop.
   g) A nested loop is a loop within a loop.
   h) Every `while` loop can be written as a `for` loop without using a break statement.
   i) Every `for` loop can be written as a `while` loop.
   j) The `break` statement ends the current iteration of a loop.
   k) A `for` loop ends when Boolean condition becomes `true`.
   l) The `continue` statement can be coded inside any loop.
   m) Placing a semicolon after the parenthesis in a `while` loop can cause an infinite loop.
   n) The statement block of a do-while loop may not be executed.
   o) A `for` loop may be designed to count down by decrementing the control variable.
   p) Loops may be used to validate user input or to give the user another chance to enter a value, such as a password, that was typed incorrectly.

2. Write a loop that outputs the integers from 20 to 100 to the system console and the appropriate term, odd or even, next to each output value.

3. Write a loop that outputs the sum of the even integers from 1 to n, where n is a value input by the user, to a message box.

**4.** Consider the following code fragment:

```
int i = 10;
int  sum = 0;
while (i <= 100)
{
    sum = sum + i;
    i++;
}
System.out.println("The sum of the integers from 10 to 100 is: " +
                    sum);
```

**a)** How many times does this loop execute?

**b)** Write an equivalent `for` loop.

**c)** Write an equivalent `do-while` loop.

**5.** Consider the following code fragment:

```
int i = 1;
while (i != 20)
{
    i = i + 2;
}
System.out.println("The value of i is " + i);
```

**a)** Will this loop terminate? If not, why not?

**b)** What numbers does it output?

**6.** Consider the following code fragment:

```
int num = 4;
for (int i = 2; i <= 7; i++)
{ System.out.println( "Number is " + num);
    num = num + i;
}
```

**a)** What is the value of `num` after the loop has executed twice?

**b)** How many times will the body of the loop be executed?

**c)** What value will be output on the fourth time through the loop?

**d)** What is the value of `num` when the loop ends?

**e)** What causes this loop to terminate?

**7.** Consider the following code fragment:

```
int x = 11;
while (x > 0)
{   x = x - 3;
    System.out.println(x);
}
```

**a)** Give its output

**b)** Write an equivalent `for` loop

**8.** Write the code fragment for an input validation loop that asks a user to enter an integer in the range of zero to five, displays an error if the input is out of range, and gives the user an *unlimited* number of chances to enter it correctly.

9. Write the code fragment for an input validation loop that asks a user to enter an integer in the range of zero to five, displays an error if the input is out of range, and gives the user at most three chances to enter it correctly.

10. Explain the difference in the execution paths of a `while` loop and a `do-while` loop.

11. Give a code fragment to produce the following output to the system console every time it is executed:

   **a)** A different set of 20 random integers in the range 0 to 500

   **b)** The same set of 20 random integers in the range 0 to 500

   **c)** The same set of 20 random integers in the range 7 to 500

   **d)** The same set of 20 random integers in the range `min` to `max`

12. Give the declarations and output statements required to display the value stored in the double variable `balance`, formatted as specified below. Also give the resulting formatted output.

   **a)** US currency

   **b)** One leading and one trailing zero, with comma separators every three digits to the left of the decimal point

   **c)** Scientific notation with four digits of precision

   **d)** Two trailing zeros, comma separators every three digits to the left of the decimal point, and a leading zero only when the balance contains a value that only has a fractional part

   **e)** Spanish currency

## Programming Exercises

1. Write a program that uses a `for` loop to calculate and output the product of the integers from n to 1 (n factorial) to a message box. For example, when n = 4, the output would be 24 = 4 * 3 * 2 * 1. The value of n will be input by the user via an input dialog box, and the output should be properly annotated.

2. You have just been hired by the TravelStars agency, and your first assignment is to produce a histogram to graphically represent the ratings that travelers have given to various hotels. Your program will begin by asking the user to enter the number of hotels to be including in the histogram. Then, ask a user to input each hotel's name, the hotel's star rating, an integer between 1 and 10 stars inclusive. The histogram should be output to the system console and formatted as shown below.

| Hotel Name | Rating |
|------------|--------|
| Hotel 1 | ********* |
| Hotel 2 | ****** |
| Hotel 3 | ******** |
| Hotel 4 | ** |
| Hotel 5 | **** |

3. Write a program that uses nested loops to output one or more of these patterns (or create some of your own):

```
a)  * * * * * * * * * *      b)  *                  c)              *
    * * * * * * * * * *          * * *                          *   *
    * * * * * * * * * *          * * * * *                   *   *   *
    * * * * * * * * * *          * * * * * * *            *   *   *   *
    * * * * * * * * * *          * * * * * * * *       *   *   *   *   *
```

4. Write a program that asks the program users for the country in which they were born and their salary for the each of the last 12 months. Output each month's salary, as well as the total pay for that year in the format of their local currency, to the system console, properly annotated.

5. Write a program that outputs 25 random integers to the system console that are within a range (minimum value and maximum value) specified by the user.

6. Write a program to simulate the toss of two dice. Every time the user clicks the OK button on a message generate two random outputs between 1–6, as well as the sum of the two dice. If the total is 7 or 11, output *You win*, otherwise output *Better luck next time*.

7. Write a graphical application that displays 650 of the 2,500 stars that can be seen in the night time sky. The stars will be drawn on the game board as filled ovals whose diameter is a random number between one and three pixels. There will be 400 white, 200 yellow, and 50 red stars, positioned at random (x, y) locations on a black-colored game board. You can change the color of the game board by invoking the `Component` class's `setBackground` method in the `main` method and passing it the color black.

8. Write the application described in Programming Exercise 7 using three nested loops to draw the stars.

9. Write a graphical application to simulate a journey to the sun by Captain Burk. Before the game board is displayed, the captain will be required to enter the noncase sensitive password "SS" (short for Starship). Then, he will be asked to enter the tonnage of each item in his cargo. When a -1 is entered, output the total weight of the cargo to a message box and display the game board described in Programming Exercise 7 or 8 with a 50-pixel-diameter sun positioned at the center of the game board. The sun will be a yellow instance of a `HeavenlyBodies` class you will add to the application that contains:
   - The four data members of a heavenly body: its (x, y) location coordinates, its diameter, and its color
   - A four-parameter constructor
   - A `show` method, and `set` and `get` methods for all the data members

   Use an input dialog box for all input.

10. Write the graphical application described in Programming Exercise 9 expanded to include these features:
   - Before the game board is displayed, the captain will be asked how many (of a maximum of three) planets to add to the night sky and then asked to enter the location and diameter of each planet. The color of the three planets will be red, green, and blue, respectively, and they will be instances of `HeavenlyBodies` displayed on the game board.

- When the Start button is clicked, the diameter of the sun should increase by 2 pixels every 20 milliseconds to simulate the Captain Burk's journey to the sun.
- When the Start button is clicked a white comet (a `HeavenlyBodies` object) will travel from the upper-left to the lower-right corner of the gameboard with its diameter increasing from 3 to 50 pixels.

11. Using the skills developed in this chapter, continue the implementation of the parts of your game requiring knowledge of loops. Be sure to add this feature:
    - Do not permit the game to be played until the case-sensitive password "gp" (game player) is entered. After three unsuccessful password entries, output the statement *passwords are case sensitive* and terminate the program by invoking the `System` class's `exit` method.

# ARRAYS

## In this chapter

In this chapter, we will introduce the concept of an array and the powerful features of the construct that make it a part of most programs. These features include the ability to store and retrieve large data sets, and, when combined with the concept of a loop, these data sets can be processed with only a few instructions. Array processing algorithms such as sorting, searching, and copying will be discussed and implemented, as will algorithms introduced in Chapter 4 for inserting and deleting items stored in a disk text file. We will also explore the API methods that implement many of the classical array processing algorithms.

One-dimensional arrays, which can be used to store a list of items, will be discussed as well as multi-dimensional arrays, and we will use two-dimensional arrays to organize data in tables as rows and columns.

After successfully completing this chapter you should:

- Understand the advantages and importance of using arrays
- Be familiar with the Java memory model used to store arrays
- Be able to construct and use arrays of primitives and objects
- Understand and be able to implement the algorithms used to search an array, sort it, and find the minimum and maximum values stored in it
- Be familiar with and be able to use the array-processing methods in the API
- Understand the concept of parallel arrays and use them to process data sets
- Know how to use arrays to insert, delete, or update data items stored in a disk file
- Be able to apply array techniques to game programs

## 6.1 THE ORIGIN OF ARRAYS

The machines we call computers received their name because the first operational versions of these machines were primarily used by mathematicians to perform rapid computations on large data sets. They were machines whose task was to compute; they were computers. However, long before computers were operational, mathematicians were using subscripted variables, such as $x_2$ or $x_4$, to represent the data used in their formulas and calculations, so it was natural for them to want to use these subscripted variables in the formulas evaluated by these early computing machines.

To facilitate the writing of these subscripted variables into a program, the designers of FORTRAN (which stands for *For*mula *Tran*slation), the first high level programming language used by mathematicians, included a construct that modeled subscripted variables. The construct was named *array*. Thus, the computer concept of an array has its roots in the mathematical model of subscripted variables.

## 6.2 THE CONCEPT OF ARRAYS

Consider a program that processes five people's ages stored in the integer memory cells age0, age1, age2, age3, and age4. The declaration of these variables would be rather straightforward:

```
int age0, age1, age2, age3, age4;
```

But suppose that instead of processing five people's ages, the program processed five million people's ages. Although the declaration syntax for the five million memory cells would still be straight forward, it would be quite lengthy and very time consuming to write. In fact, a good typist would take more than a month to type just the variable declarations for this program, assuming the typist typed continuously for eight hours each day without stopping to eat. (This, by the way, is a violation of the federal labor laws.) Using the construct array, the same typist could type the declaration of the five million memory cells in seconds.

That's all an **array** is: a technique used to declare memory cells, which is rooted in the mathematical concept of subscripted variables.

| Definition |
| --- |
| An **array** is a programming concept used to declare groups of related memory cells in which each member of the group has the same data type, the same first name, the array's name, and a unique last name called an **index**. |

The memory cells are related in the same way that our integer memory cells age0 through age4 were related: each one stores a person's age, or perhaps a person's weight, or perhaps an address of a snowman game piece. In Java the unique last names, the indexes (or indices), are always sequential integers beginning with zero (i.e., 0, 1, 2, 3, 4, …). In addition, Java syntax requires that the unique last name is enclosed in open and close brackets, for example, [2].

Figure 6.1 shows ten memory cells used to store people's ages. The five memory cells on the left were declared to be five separate integer variables with the statement

```
int age0, age1, age2, age3, age4;
```

The five memory cells on the right were declared to be part of a five-member or element array named age.

| Non-array | | | Array | |
|---|---|---|---|---|
| age0 | 0 | | 0 | age[0] |
| age1 | 0 | | 0 | age[1] |
| age2 | 0 | | 0 | age[2] |
| age3 | 0 | | 0 | age[3] |
| age4 | 0 | | 0 | age[4] |

**Figure 6.1**
Storage allocated to five integer variables and to a five-element array named age.

As shown in Figure 6.1, the amount of storage allocated to the integer variables on the left side of the figure is the same as the amount of storage allocated to array elements shown on the right side of the figure: five distinct integer memory cells. From a memory-allocation viewpoint, the only difference in the way memory is allocated to the memory cells that make up the elements of an array is that the array elements are always allocated as contiguous memory; that is, if each memory cell occupied four bytes of storage, and age[0] was stored in bytes 100–103, the memory allocated to the subsequent four elements of the array would begin at byte addresses 104, 108, 112, and 116. (In contrast, the five integer variables might be stored in different locations scattered around memory.)

Array elements can be used in our programs anywhere it is syntactically correct to code the name of a memory cell: in input and output statements, in arithmetic and logic expressions, on the left side of an assignment operator, and as arguments and parameters. To use them, we simply code their complete names. For example, the statements on the left and right sides of Figure 6.2 are equivalent, although they are syntactically different because the statements on the right side of the figure use the array construct.

```
age3=new Scanner(System.in).nextInt();        age[3]=new Scanner(System.in).nextInt();
age3 = age3 + 1;                               age[3] = age[3] + 1;
System.out.println("Your age is"  +           System.out.println("Your age is"  +
                  age3);                                         age[3]);
if(age3 >= 18)                                 if(age[3] >= 18)
{                                              {
    System.out.println("You can " +               System.out.println("You can " +
                "Drive now");                                 "Drive now");
}                                              }

double avgAge = averageTwo(age0,               double avgAge = averageTwo(age[0],
                  age1);                                         age[1]);
```

| Without arrays | With arrays |
|---|---|

**Figure 6.2**
Equivalent statements with and without the use of arrays.

Although the syntax involved in using arrays is a bit more cumbersome because of the coding of the open and close brackets, as previously mentioned, they do give us the ability to rapidly declare large numbers of variables. In addition, as we will see later in this chapter, when arrays are used inside of loops they also give us the ability to process large data sets with just a few lines of code. For these two reasons, most programs use arrays.

## 6.3 DECLARING ARRAYS

In Java, all arrays are stored inside of an object. Although we most often state that we are "declaring an array," it is more accurate to state that we are "declaring an object that contains an array." In fact, as we shall see, the object contains not only the array but an also an integer data member named `length`.

The syntax used to declare an array object is similar to the syntax used to declare non-array objects in that a reference variable is declared that will refer to the array object, and the keyword **new** is used to construct the object. Where they differ is that the array-object declaration syntax also includes a set of brackets to indicate that the reference variable will refer to an array object, and the number of elements the array will contain (called the size of the array) is enclosed in another set of brackets. The generalized syntax is:

```
aType[] arrayName = new aType[arraySize];
```

where:

aType is the type of the elements of the array

arrayName is the name of a reference variable that will store the address of the array object, also considered to be the name of the array

arraySize is the number of elements in the array

To declare an array object that could store five integer ages we would write:

```
int[] ages = new int[5];
```

This statement allocates the memory shown in Figure 6.3. Not only is the storage for the array's elements allocated inside the object, but an integer named `length` is allocated and initialized to the size of the array. The index of the first element of an array is always zero, and the indexes of the remaining elements of an array are assigned sequential integer values in ascending order. This implies that the index of the last element of an array is always one less than the size of the array. In a five-element array, `ages[5]` does not exist, which is somewhat counterintuitive, and attempting to access it results in a runtime error.

**NOTE** *The indices of an array containing n elements are 0 through n-1, and the size of the array is n. An attempt to use an array index outside of the range 0 to n-1 results in an* `ArrayIndexOutOfBoundsException` *runtime error.*

Conceptually, the array object declaration would be drawn as shown on the right side of Figure 6.1, which is the way we most often visualize an array. Figure 6.3 gives a more accurate depiction of the storage allocated to the array object created by the declaration given in the figure's caption and the reference variable, `ages`, that refers to the array object.

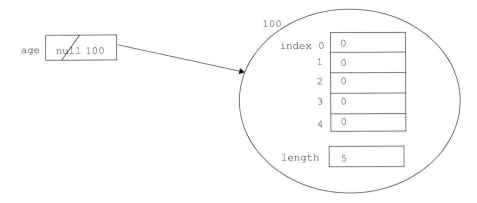

**Figure 6.3**
The array object created by the statement **int**[] ages = **new int**[5];.

When an array object is created, the elements of the array are initialized to their default values (e.g., zero for an array of integers), and the array object is assigned an address (address 100 in Figure 6.3). The data member length is initialized to the size of the array. For example in Figure 6.3, length stores the value 5 inside the array object ages.

The data member length is a public final data member, so rather than using a get method to access it, it can be accessed by coding the name of the array object followed by length, preceded by a dot. The following code fragment outputs a 5, the size of the array ages:

```
int[] ages = new int[5];
System.out.println(ages.length);
```

The data member length is a final variable and cannot be assigned a value. The following code fragment results in a translation error:

```
int[] ages = new int[5];
ages.length = 23; //syntax error: can't re-assign a final constant
```

### 6.3.1 Dynamic Allocation of Arrays

An array object, like any other object, can be allocated dynamically during the execution of the program. As we have learned, to do this we most often use the two-line object declaration syntax. The first line is used to declare the reference variable that will refer to the object, and good programming practice dictates that this line is coded at the top of the method or class in which the array will be used. The second line of the syntax is used to allocate the object and set the reference variable pointing to it. This line is normally coded further down in a method.

The splitting of the array object declaration syntax permits the size of the array to be determined by the processing the program performs. For example, the size of the array could be read from the first line of a disk file that also contains the data that will be stored in the array, or the size of the array could be input by the user. For example:

```
int[] ages;
String sSize = JOPtionPane.showInputDialiog("How many ages" +
                                            "will be entered?");
```

```
int size = Integer.parseInt(sSize);
ages = new int[size];
```

Many applications, in which the number of data items to be processed is determined at run time, would be very difficult to code without the use of arrays. For example, consider an application that outputs a set of input data in reverse order. This requires declaring a variable for every data item because they must all be saved until the last data item is input and then output. Because the number of inputs is not known until runtime, without the use of arrays, we would have to guess the maximum number of inputs, allocate that number of variables, and keep our fingers crossed that we did not guess too low.

The fact that the `length` data member of an array object cannot be changed is consistent with the fact that, in Java, the size of an array cannot be changed. As is the case with all objects, the reference variable that refers to the object can be assigned to another object. In the case of an array, we can make use of this fact to effectively resize the array at runtime by assigning the reference variable to the address of a smaller, or a larger, array object.

For example, an array initially sized to five elements could be made to refer to a new array object whose size is based on a user input.

```
int[] data = new int[5];
        :
        :
String sSize = JOPtionPane.showInputDialiog("How many ages" +
                                            "will be entered?");
int size = Integer.parseInt(sSize);
data = new int[size];
```

Assuming the user entered a "3" in response to the above prompt, Figure 6.4 shows the changes in the contents of the reference variable `data` and the array object that `data` refers to, resulting from the execution of the above code. It should be noted that if the original five-element array contained five people's ages, these ages would be lost after the dynamic allocation.

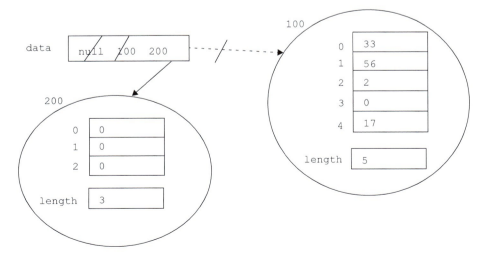

**Figure 6.4**
The effect of the statement data = **new int[3];**.

As shown in Figure 6.4, the five-element array object's address is overwritten with the address of the new three-element array object, causing the storage allocated to the five-element array to be reclaimed by the Java runtime memory manager. In Java, the storage allocated to objects that are not referred to by a reference variable is reclaimed for use by other programs. In Section 6.9, we will discuss techniques for transferring the values into a resized array when it is created.

## 6.4 ARRAYS AND LOOPS

Using arrays inside loops gives us the ability to process large data sets with just a few lines of code. This is because the index used to specify which element of the array is being processed can not only be a numeric literal (e.g., a = age[2];), but it can also be an integer variable. The only restriction on the integer variable is that the value stored in it must be a valid element number of the array. The following code segment outputs the third element of the array price twice. When the last statement executes, the current contents of the variable index is fetched, substituted for the variable index, and the output is performed.

```java
double[] price = new double[100];
int index = 2;

System.out.println(price[2]);
System.out.println(price[index]);
```

This array feature is commonly used with the loop variable of a for statement as the array index. Using this approach, the code to decrease the price of each of the 10,000 items a department store sells by 10% in preparation for its annual Labor Day sale can be coded in just two lines of code:

```java
for(int i = 0; i < 10000; i++)
{
    salePrice[i] = price[i] * 0.9;
}
```

The first time through the loop the variable i stores the value 0, and salePrice[0] is computed. The second time through the loop i stores the value 1, and salePrice[1] is computed. This process continues until finally salePrice[9999] is computed.

Two common mistakes are made when processing arrays inside of loops, both of which are syntactically correct:

- the loop variable is initialized to 1 instead of to 0
- the Boolean condition is incorrectly coded using the <= operator instead of <

The first mistake stems from the fact that most of us begin with 1 when we count: 1, 2, 3, etc., so our natural tendency is to initialize the loop variable to 1 instead of 0. When this mistake is made, the first element of the array (element zero) is not processed.

Coding the Boolean condition incorrectly is the most common mistake. When all the elements of the array are to be processed, our code is much more understandable if we use the size of the array, `price.length`, in the Boolean condition. However, when we do this, we must use the less than (<) operator in the condition (e.g., `i < price.length`). Unfortunately, most novice programmers, intent on processing the last element of the array, use the <= operator, and the last iteration of the loop generates an index that is one greater that of the last element of the array (e.g., 5 for a five-element array). The result is a runtime error indicating that the program generated an `Array-IndexOutOfBoundsException`. This error occurs whenever a program uses an array index that is not in the range 0 to one less than the array's size.

Figure 6.5 presents the application `ArraysAndLoops` that uses many of the array concepts discussed thus far in this chapter to compute, and output, the sale price of a group of input items. It accepts the prices of a set of items to be placed on sale, then computes and outputs the sale price of the items. A sample set of inputs and the corresponding outputs produced by the program are given at the bottom of the figure.

```java
1    import javax.swing.*;
2    import java.text.NumberFormat;
3
4    public class ArraysAndLoops
5    {
6      public static void main(String[] args)
7      {
8        double[] price, salePrice;
9        String s;
10       int size;
11       NumberFormat fm = NumberFormat.getCurrencyInstance();
12       s = JOptionPane.showInputDialog("How many sale items?");
13       size = Integer.parseInt(s);
14       price = new double[size];
15       salePrice = new double[size];
16
17       for(int i = 0; i < size; i++)
18       {
19         s = JOptionPane.showInputDialog("Enter item " + (i + 1) +
20                                       " 's price");
21         price[i] = Double.parseDouble(s);
22       }
23
24       for(int i = 0; i < price.length; i++)
25       {
26         salePrice[i] = price[i] * 0.9;
27         System.out.println("The sale price of item " + (i + 1)  +
28                             " is " + fm.format(salePrice[i]));
29       }
30     }
31   }
```

```
Inputs:
5
10.00
20.00
30.00
40.00
50.00
Outputs:
The sale price of item 1 is $9.00
The sale price of item 2 is $18.00
The sale price of item 3 is $27.00
The sale price of item 4 is $36.00
The sale price of item 5 is $45.00
```

**Figure 6.5**
The application **ArraysAndLoops** and a set of inputs and corresponding outputs.

After the user enters the number of items to be placed on sale (line 12), two array objects are dynamically allocated on lines 14 and 15, and their addresses are assigned to the reference variables `price` and `salePrice`. These variables were declared on line 8.

The program uses two `for` loops that begin on lines 17 and 24. The first loop accepts the input of the non-sale prices, and the second loop computes and outputs the sale prices. The loop variable, `i`, of the `for` loop that begins on line 17 is used to change the element of the array `price` (line 21) that stores the parsed input. The second `for` loop, which begins on line 24, uses its loop variable to index its way through the array `price` and the array `salePrice` (line 26) as it computes the new values of the `salePrice` array.

The first loop uses the variable `size`, which was used to size both arrays on lines 14 and 15, in its Boolean condition. The second loop uses the `length` data member of the array object `price` in its Boolean condition. Either approach can be used. However, the latter approach is preferred because it more clearly indicates that the entire array is being processed within the loop, and eliminates the chance that an incorrect variable (other than size) would be coded in the Boolean condition. The second approach is also preferred when the array is passed into a method that will process the array's contents for reasons that we will discuss in Section 6.6. Both `for` statements correctly use the less than operator (<) in their Boolean conditions.

### 6.4.1 The Enhanced `for` Statement

The enhanced `for` statement, sometimes referred to as the for-each statement, is an alternate syntax of a `for` loop that is used to fetch *all* of the elements of an array sequentially. During the execution of the loop, the elements of the array cannot be modified, so its use is limited. It can be used to output or total the elements of an array.

The syntax of the statement is given below, in which `anElement` is a variable whose type, `aType`, is always the type of the elements of the array `arrayName`:

```java
for( aType anElement: arrayName )
{
  //statement(s) that use the variable anElement
}
```

For example, if the array is an array of references to `String` objects, the statement would be coded as shown below:

```java
for( String anElement: arrayName )
{
  //statement(s) that use the variable anElement
}
```

A colon is always coded after the variable `anElement`. If there is only one statement to be executed within the loop, the open and close braces need not be coded, but it is good programming practice to include them.

The number of times the loop executes is always equivalent to the length of the array, in the above case `arrayName.length`, unless the loop contains a `break` statement. During the execution of the loop, the variable `anElement` assumes the value of each element of the array in ascending order, beginning with the first element (during the first iteration of the loop) and ending with the last element (during the last iteration of the loop). The two loops shown below are equivalent, and both produce the system console output `Nora Ryan Logan`.

```java
String anArray = {"Nora", "Ryan", "Logan"};

for(String anElement: anArray)
{
  System.out.print (anElement + " ");
}

System.out.println( );

for(int i = 0; i < 3; i++)
{
  System.out.print (anArray[i] + " ");
}
```

Within the loop's body, the variable used in the enhanced `for` statement (e.g., `anElement`), can be used anywhere it is syntactically correct to use a variable of its type. An advantage of the enhanced `for` loop is that it cannot produce an `ArrayIndexOutOfBounds` error because it does not use a loop variable to access the elements of the array. A disadvantage is that the elements of the array cannot be changed inside the loop.

## 6.5 ARRAYS OF OBJECTS

Technically speaking, there is no way to declare an array of objects. The elements of an array cannot be objects; they can only be primitive or reference variables. However, when the array elements are reference variables, each element of the array can contain the address of an object. When this is the case, we often say that we have "an array of objects" because it is easier to say than "an array of reference variables that refer to objects" (which is what we actually have).

Leaving aside the technical jargon, when we set each element of an array of reference variables to point to an object, we can rapidly process all of the objects by indexing through the array of reference variables. In addition, just as it was easy to declare a large number of variables using arrays, we can easily declare a large number of objects using arrays of reference variables.

The first step in applying the power of arrays to programs that process objects is to declare (an array object that contains) an array of reference variables. The second step is to declare the objects and set their addresses into the elements of the array. The syntax used to declare the array of reference variables is the same syntax used to declare an array of primitive variables. The following declaration creates an array of reference variables that could refer to five Snowman objects:

```
Snowman[] sm = new Snowman[5];
```

The storage allocated by this declaration is shown in Figure 6.6. Because the array contains reference variables, they are initialized to the default value of a newly created reference variable: null. Otherwise, the figure is identical to Figure 6.3, which shows the storage allocated when an array of five integers is declared.

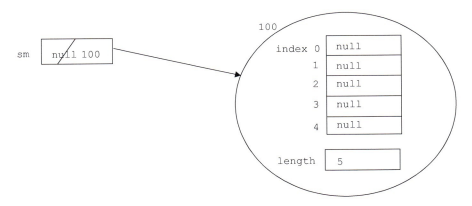

**Figure 6.6**
The storage created by the declaration **Snowman[] sm = new Snowman[5];**.

As shown in Figure 6.6, the declaration of the array object does not allocate any Snowman objects. To do this, we have to invoke a constructor in the Snowman class and set the returned address of the newly constructed Snowman into an element of the array. Assuming the class has a two-parameter constructor, one way to do this is to write five declaration statements:

```
sm[0] = new Snowman(50, 100);
sm[1] = new Snowman(100, 100);
sm[2] = new Snowman(150, 100);
sm[3] = new Snowman(200, 100);
sm[4] = new Snowman(250, 100);
```

Assuming the constructor's parameters are the (x, y) location of a `Snowman` object, our five newly created snowmen will be standing shoulder to shoulder (at x = 50, 100, 150, 200, and 250) when they are drawn on the game board. An equivalent but more efficient way to construct the five snowmen would be to place the invocation of the constructor inside a loop. The use of a loop is the preferred coding technique, which we would quickly realize if we had to declare a group of 5,000 snowmen.

```java
for(int i = 0; i < 5; i++)
{
    sm[i] = new Snowman(50 +  i * 50, 100);
}
```

Because the loop variable is used as the index into the array `sm`, `sm[0]` receives the address of the first `Snowman` created inside the loop. During each additional pass through the loop, the next sequential element of the array receives the address of a newly created `Snowman`. In addition, the loop variable is used to change the x coordinate of the snowmen, using the expression (50 + i * 50), each time through the loop. The storage created after the loop completes its execution is shown in Figure 6.7.

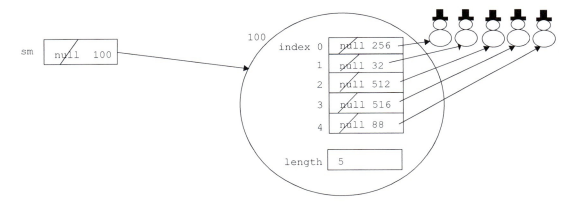

**Figure 6.7**
An array of five reference variables pointing to five **Snowman** objects.

### 6.5.1 Processing an Array's Objects

In Section 6.4, we learned that large primitive data sets could be processed with just a few lines of code using the concepts of arrays and loops. To accomplish this, the data set was stored in an array of primitive variables, and the processing instructions were coded inside a loop. The loop variable was used as the index into the array, which caused the processing instruction(s) to operate on a different element of the array during each pass through the loop.

Similarly, we can process large sets of objects with just a few lines of code by storing the objects' addresses inside an array of reference variables and then perform the processing on each object inside a loop. The only difference is that instead of performing the processing on the array elements themselves, the array elements are used to invoke the class's processing methods on the objects they reference.

For example, the code to add one to each of five people's ages stored in an array of integers named `ages` is very similar to the code that moves each of five snowmen stored in an array of objects named `sm` one pixel to the right. The following code fragment illustrates the similarities:

```
int x;
for(int i = 0; i < 5; i++)
{
   ages[i] = ages[i] + 1; //increment the ages

   x = sm[i].getX(); //move the snowmen
   sm[i].setX(x + 1);
}
```

Each time through this loop, the loop variable is used to change the element of the two arrays involved in loop's processing instructions. In the case of the integer array, the value stored in one of the elements of the array, `ages`, is incremented by one; that is, the contents of the array `ages` is changed. However, the loop processing does not change the contents of the array `sm`. Rather, it uses the contents of the array `sm` to specify which `Snowman` object will be changed (operated on) by the `getX` and `setX` methods during each pass through the loop. In this case, the `x` data member of each `Snowman` object is increased by one.

That is not to say that the contents of an array of reference variables cannot be changed inside a loop. As we have already seen, this is done when objects are constructed and the default `null` values stored in the elements of the array are overwritten with the location of the newly constructed (`Snowman`) objects. Conversely, all five snowmen could be eliminated from a game by overwriting their addresses stored in the array with the value `null`:

```
for(int i = 0; i < 5; i++)
{
   sm[i] = null;
}
```

This would cause the Java memory manager to recycle the storage allocated to the five `Snowman` objects and make it available to other programs running on the system.

The game application in Figure 6.8 uses the concepts discussed in this section to conduct a parade of eight snowmen whose class is shown in Figure 6.9. The output produced by the program when it is launched and the output produced several seconds after the start button is clicked are shown on the left and right sides of Figure 6.10, respectively.

An array of reference variables named `parade` that will be used to store the addresses of eight `Snowman` objects, is created on line 7 of Figure 6.8. When the game is launched, the snowmen are displayed along a left-to-right downward-sloping diagonal (as shown in Figure 6.10a), until the Start button is clicked. Then they parade around the game board reflecting off its boundaries, eventually coming to the positions shown in Figure 6.10b.

The creation, display, animation, and reflection of the snowmen are performed inside four loops. Within each iteration of these loops, a different snowman is processed because the loop variable is used as an index into the `parade` array. The first of these loops (lines 11–14 of Figure 6.8) is used to create the snowmen and place the addresses of these eight objects in the reference variable array `parade`. On line 13, the loop variable, `i`, is used inside the argument list sent to the `SnowmanV7` class's two-parameter constructor to calculate each snowman's initial (x, y) location along a downward-sloping diagonal. During each iteration of the loop that begins on line 21, a different snowman is displayed on the game board at its current (x, y) location.

The remaining two loops, which begin on lines 31 and 41, move the snowmen around the game board and bounce (reflect) them off the vertical and horizontal boundaries of the game board. The loops are coded inside the `timer3` call back method (lines 27–56), whose interval is set to 20 milliseconds on line 15. As a result, every 20 milliseconds (1/50th of a second), the game environment invokes this method, and the loops are executed. After the `timer3` method completes its execution, the game environment invokes the application's `draw` method (line 19), which displays the snowmen at their new (x, y) position.

The `for` loop coded on lines 31–39 of the application performs the animation of the snowmen. By using the loop variable, `i`, as an index into the parade array, each snowman's x and y position is fetched (lines 33 and 36), incremented by their corresponding speed data members (lines 34 and 37), and set to their new values (lines 35 and 38). Being coded inside the `timer3` method, this code changes each snowman's (x, y) position every 20 milliseconds. The rapid repositioning and redrawing of the snowmen (every 1/50th of a second) gives the appearance of continuous motion.

The `for` loop coded on lines 41–55 of Figure 6.8 performs the reflection of the snowmen off the boundaries of the game board. The two data members, `xSpeed` and `ySpeed` were added to the class `SnowmanV7` (Figure 6.9, lines 7 and 8) along with their corresponding `set` and `get` methods (lines 41, 45, 49, and 53) to perform this reflection. The loop variable, `i`, is used inside two `if` statements (that begin on lines 43 and 49 of Figure 6.8) to index into the `parade` array. Their Boolean conditions determine when a snowman's current (x, y) position is at or beyond the vertical (line 43) and horizontal (line 49) boundaries of the game board.

When this is the case, the snowman's speed is fetched (lines 45 and 51), its sign is reversed (lines 46 and 50), and the new value is set into the snowman's speed data member (lines 47 and 53). Then, during the next execution of the `timer3` method, when each snowman's speed is used to reposition it on the game board, those that reached a game board edge appear to bounce off the edge because the sign of their speed has been reversed.

```
1     import java.awt.Graphics;
2     import edu.sjcny.gpv1.*;
3
4     public class SnowmanParade  extends DrawableAdapter
5     { static SnowmanParade ge = new SnowmanParade();
6       static GameBoard gb = new GameBoard(ge, "Snowman Parade");
7       static SnowmanV7[] parade = new SnowmanV7[8];
8
9       public static void main(String[] args)
10      {
```

```
11      for(int i=0; i < parade.length; i++) //create each snowman
12        {
13          parade[i] = new SnowmanV7(10 + i * 50 , 100 + i * 30);
14        }
15      gb.setTimerInterval(3, 20);
16      showGameBoard(gb);
17    }
18
19    public void draw(Graphics g) //draw each snowman
20    {
21      for(int i = 0; i < parade.length; i++)
22      {
23        parade[i].show(g);
24      }
25    }
26
27    public void timer3()
28    {
29      int x, speed, y;
30
31      for(int i = 0; i  <parade.length; i++) //move each snowman
32        {
33          x = parade[i].getX();
34          x = x + parade[i].getXSpeed();
35          parade[i].setX(x);
36          y = parade[i].getY();
37          y = y + parade[i].getYSpeed();
38          parade[i].setY(y);
39        }
40
41      for(int i = 0; i < parade.length; i++) //reflect each snowman
42        {
43          if(parade[i].getX() >= 460 || parade[i].getX() <= 6)//x
44          {
45            speed = parade[i].getXSpeed();
46            speed = -speed;
47            parade[i].setXSpeed(speed);
48          }
49          if(parade[i].getY() >= 420 || parade[i].getY() <= 30)//
50          {
51            speed = parade[i].getYSpeed();
52            speed = -speed;
53            parade[i].setYSpeed(speed);
54          }
55        }
56    }
57 }
```

**Figure 6.8**
The application **SnowmanParade**.

```
1    import java.awt.*;
2
3    public class SnowmanV7
4    {
5      int x;
6      int y;
7      int xSpeed = 2;
8      int ySpeed = 2;
9
10     public SnowmanV7(int x, int y)
11     { this.x = x;
12       this.y = y;
13     }
14
15     public void show(Graphics g) // g is the game board object
16     { g.setColor(Color.BLACK);
17       g.fillRect(x + 15, y, 10, 15); // hat
18       g.fillRect(x + 10, y + 15, 20, 2); // brim
19       g.setColor(Color.WHITE);
20       g.fillOval(x + 10, y + 17, 20, 20); // head
21       g.fillOval(x, y + 37, 40, 40); // body
22       g.setColor(Color.RED);
23     }
24
25     public int getX()
26     { return x;
27     }
28
29     public void setX(int newX)
30     { x = newX;
31     }
32
33     public int getY()
34     { return y;
35     }
36
37     public void setY(int newY)
38     { y = newY;
39     }
40
41     public int getXSpeed()
42     { return xSpeed;
43     }
44
45     public void setXSpeed(int newXSpeed)
```

```
46      { xSpeed = newXSpeed;
47      }
48
49      public int getYSpeed()
50      { return ySpeed;
51      }
52
53      public void setYSpeed(int newYSpeed)
54      { ySpeed = newYSpeed;
55      }
56    }
```

**Figure 6.9**
The class **SnowmanV7**.

(a) Initial output

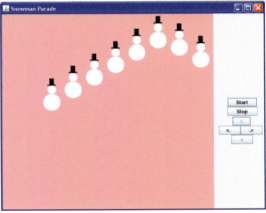

(b) Output several seconds after Start is clicked

**Figure 6.10**
The output of the application **SnowmanParade**.

## 6.6 PASSING ARRAYS BETWEEN METHODS

As discussed in Section 3.8, reference variables can be part of a worker method's parameter list. This gives us the ability to pass the location of objects declared in a method into a worker method it invokes. Knowing the object's location enables the worker method to perform some processing on the object by referring to it using the parameter name that received the object's location. In addition, when the returned type of a non-void worker method is the name of a class, the worker method can return the location of *one* object in that class to the method that invoked it.

Because arrays are stored in objects, the ability to pass reference variables to and from worker methods also gives us the ability to pass arrays to and from worker methods. To do this, we simply pass the array object's reference variable to and from the worker method. While there are no conceptual differences to consider when passing array and non-array objects to and from worker methods, there are some minor syntactical differences in the signature of the worker method.

In the remainder of this section, we will discuss these differences and present examples of passing arrays to and from worker methods. We will begin with a discussion of passing arrays to a worker method and conclude with a discussion of returning an array from a worker method.

### 6.6.1 Passing Arrays of Primitives to a Worker Method

Consider the array `age`, shown on the left side of Figure 6.11, which stores the ages of five people that have the same birthday. The following code fragment defines and initializes this array and passes it to the static worker method `birthday` coded in the class `Party`.

```java
int[] age = new int[5];
for(int i=0; i < age.length; i++)
{
   age [i] = 21 + i;
}
Party.birthday(age); //method invocation statement
```

**Figure 6.11**
Passing an array of primitives to a method.

Looking at the method invocation statement, there is no way to tell if the argument `age` sent to the method `birthday` is a primitive variable or an array. This is because the syntax of an invocation statement used to pass an array reference to a worker method is the same syntax used to pass a primitive variable to a worker method, which is also the same syntax used to pass any reference variable to a worker method. From an invocation statement's viewpoint, there is nothing new to learn about passing arrays to worker methods.

As previously discussed, it is the syntax of the signature of the worker method that is different. When a parameter listed in a method's signature is an array, a pair of braces `[]` is coded in between the parameter's name and its type. The following is the code of the static worker method `birthday` that is passed an integer array. The work of the method is to add one to each element of the array.

```java
static void birthday(int[] theAges)
{
  for(int i=0; i < theAges.length; i++)
  {
    theAges[i] = theAges[i] + 1;
  }
}
```

_____
**NOTE**
*When a parameter in a worker method's signature is an array, code a pair of braces `[]` in between the parameter's name and its type. For example:*
```java
        static void birthday(int[] theAges)
```

As indicated by the dashed arrows at the top of Figure 6.11, when the method is invoked and passed the argument `ages`, Java's use of value parameters copies the value stored in the argument (100) into the method's parameter `theAges`. Then the method's code is able to access the elements of the array object because its parameter, `theAges`, now stores the array's address. Effectively, while the method is executing, the array object is *shared* between the client code and the worker method it invokes. Although we normally say we are "passing an array to a method," we really should say we are "passing the *address* of an array object to a method."

_____
**NOTE**
*When passing an array to a worker method, the address of the array is passed to the method, and the array object is shared between the client and worker methods.*

Because the array's address is shared, if the worker method changes the contents of the array, the client code no longer has access to the original contents of the array. This is not a contradiction of the idea that value parameters prevent worker methods from changing the client's information passed to it because the information passed to the worker method is the array's *address*, not the array's *elements*. This is a subtle but important point to understand. Referring to Figure 6.11, while it is true that the worker method can change the contents of the elements of the array because `theAges` stores the object's address, it cannot change the address of the array stored in the variable `age` (which was the information passed to it).

If the worker method contained the statement below, it would lose access to the client's array object, but the client code would not. The address of the client's array object would still be stored in the variable `age`.

```java
        theAges = new int[20];
```

### 6.6.2 Passing Arrays of Objects to a Worker Method

As mentioned in Section 6.5, technically speaking, Java does not support arrays of objects. However, an array's elements can be reference variables that each store the address of an object. When this is the case, we often say that the array is "an array of objects" because it is simpler than saying the array is "an array of reference variables that point to objects." When passing an array of objects to a method, the invocation statement and the method's signature use the same syntax used to pass an array of primitive variables to a method. As discussed in the previous section, the only indication that arrays are being passed is the inclusion of a pair of braces `[]` in between the parameter's name and its type in the signature of the worker method.

The left side of Figure 6.12 shows the array, `parade`, containing five reference variables that store the addresses of five `SnowmanV7` objects whose class is shown in Figure 6.9. To pass this array to a worker method, we take advantage of Java's value parameter implementation and pass the address of the array to the method using the same syntax we used to pass the address of an array of primitives to a method.

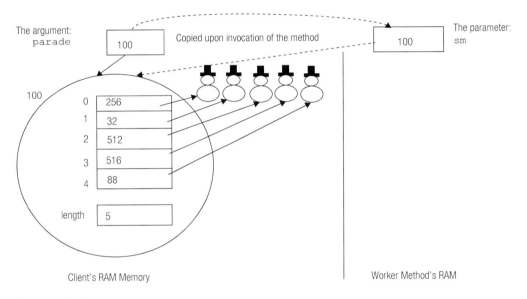

**Figure 6.12**
Passing the location of an array of objects to a method.

For example, suppose we wanted to use the static worker methods `move` and `bounce` coded in the class `PassingArrays` to reposition the `SnowmanV7` objects on the game board and reflect them off the edges of the board. Assuming these methods each had one parameter used to pass the array of snowmen named `parade` to the methods, the client code statements to invoke the worker methods would be:

```
PassingArrays.move(parade);
PassingArrays.bounce(parade);
```

If the parameter name in the worker methods was `sm`, the signature of the methods would be:

```
static void move(SnowmanV7[] sm);
static void bounce(SnowmanV7[] sm);
```

The dashed arrows at the top of Figure 6.12 illustrate the passing of the array's location into the method's parameter, sm, which permits the methods to reference the array of snowmen during their execution. The result is that while the methods are executing, the client code and the worker methods share the array of reference variables *and* the objects they refer to. If the worker methods' code writes new values into the data members of the snowmen objects, then these new values would be available to the client code after the worker methods completed their execution.

The application PassingArrays, shown in Figure 6.13, illustrates the sharing of the information contained in integer and object arrays with invoked methods and the methods' ability to change the contents of the array's elements and the objects they reference. Figure 6.14 shows the console output produced by the program, and Figure 6.15 shows the graphical output it produces (which is the same as that produced by the application SnowmanParade). The class SnowmanV7 referred to in Figure 6.13 is the same class (shown in Figure 6.9) used in the SnowmanParade application.

To verify the concept that the client and worker methods share primitive arrays, we have also included the array object ages and the method birthday within the PassingArrays application. Referring to Figure 6.13, the application's main method declares an array of five integers named ages on line 11. These variables are initialized to the values 21 through 25 inside the for loop that begins on line 13. On line 17, this array is passed to the method birthday (lines 45–51), and the address of the array is stored in the method's parameter theAges (line 45). The code of the method increases each element of the array by 1 inside its for loop (line 49). When the method ends, the for loop in the method main (lines 18–20) outputs the contents of the array, producing the console output shown in Figure 6.14. The fact that all of the ages output by the method main have been increased by 1 verifies that the methods main and birthday shared the same array of integers.

The code of the graphical portion of the applications PassingArrays is the same as the code of the application SnowmanParade (Figure 6.8) except that the code that moves and reflects the snowmen (coded on lines 29–55 of Figure 6.8) have been placed inside the static methods move and bounce (lines 53–87 of Figure 6.13). In addition, invocations of these methods have been placed inside the game environment's timer3 method, lines 41 and 42. Thus, the graphical output of the two programs is the same. When the game is launched, the snowmen are displayed along the left-to-right downward-sloping diagonal, as shown Figure 6.15a. When the Start button is clicked, they parade around the game board bouncing off its edges. Figure 6.15b shows the program's graphical output several seconds after the Start button is clicked.

The timer3 method now consists of two statements: the invocations of the move and reflect methods (lines 41 and 42 of Figure 6.13). The address of the array parade (declared on line 7) is passed into the parameter sm of these methods, whose signatures are given on lines 53 and 68. Inside their for loops, the methods change the (x, y) location (lines 61 and 64) and speed data members (lines 78 and 84) of the snowmen referenced by sm's elements. Because the array is shared between these methods and the timer3 method, the new locations and speed of the snowmen have been placed into the `Snowman` array reference by `parade`. This fact is verified during the next invocation of the game environments `draw` method when the snowmen are drawn at their new locations and reflected off the edges of the game board.

```java
1    import edu.sjcny.gpv1.*;
2    import java.awt.*;
3
4    public class PassingArrays   extends DrawableAdapter
5    { static PassingArrays ge = new PassingArrays();
6      static GameBoard gb = new GameBoard(ge, "Snowman Parade");
7      static SnowmanV7[] parade = new SnowmanV7[8];
8
9      public static void main(String[] args)
10     {
11       int[] ages = new int[5];
12
13       for(int i = 0; i < 5; i++)
14       {
15         ages[i] = 21 + i;
16       }
17       birthday(ages);
18       for(int i = 0; i < 5; i++)
19       { System.out.print(ages[i] + " ");
20       }
21
22       for(int i = 0; i < 8; i++)
23       {
24          parade[i] = new SnowmanV7(10 + i * 50, 100 + i * 30);
25       }
26
27       gb.setTimerInterval(3, 20);
28       showGameBoard(gb);
29     }
30
31     public void draw(Graphics g)
32     {
33       for(int i = 0; i < 8; i++)
34       {
35         parade[i].show(g); // show the parade at its current location
36       }
37     }
38
39     public void timer3()
40     {
41       move(parade);
42       bounce(parade);
43     }
44
45     static   void birthday(int[] theAges)
```

```
46     {
47         for(int i = 0; i < theAges.length; i++)
48         {
49             theAges[i] = theAges[i] + 1;
50         }
51     }
52
53     static void move(SnowmanV7[] sm)
54     {
55         int x, y;
56
57         for(int i = 0; i < 8;  i++)
58         {
59             x = sm[i].getX();
60             x = x + sm[i].getXSpeed();
61             sm[i].setX(x);
62             y = sm[i].getY();
63             y = y + sm[i].getYSpeed();
64             sm[i].setY(y);
65         }
66     }
67
68     static void bounce(SnowmanV7[] sm)
69     {
70         int speed;
71
72         for(int i = 0; i < 8; i++)
73         {
74             if(sm[i].getX() >= 460 || sm[i].getX() <= 6)
75             {
76                 speed = sm[i].getXSpeed();
77                 speed = -speed;
78                 sm[i].setXSpeed(speed);
79             }
80             if(sm[i].getY() >= 420 || sm[i].getY() <= 30)
81             {
82                 speed = sm[i].getYSpeed();
83                 speed = -speed;
84                 sm[i].setYSpeed(speed);
85             }
86         }
87     }
88 }
```

**Figure 6.13**

The application **PassingArrays**.

```
22 23 24 25 26
```

**Figure 6.14**

The console output produced by the application **PassingArrays.**

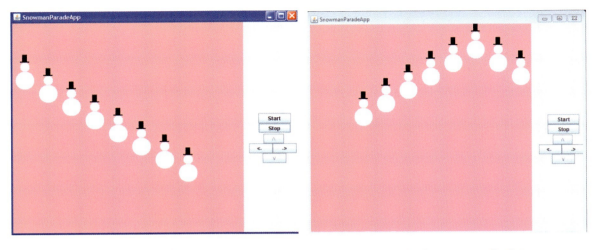

(a) Initial output    (b) Output after several reflections

**Figure 6.15**
The graphical output of the application **PassingArrays**.

### 6.6.3 Returning an Array from a Worker Method

As discussed in Section 3.8, an object's address can be returned from a method via a `return` statement. Because arrays are stored in objects, this also gives us the ability to return the address of an array from a worker method. The only syntactical difference to consider when returning the address of an array object is in the signature of the worker method. When a method returns an array, a pair of braces `[]` is coded in between the method's name and its returned type. As is the case when any value or address is returned from a method, if the returned address is to be used by the client code that invoked the method, the client code must assign the returned address to a variable.

The following is the code of the static worker method `birthdayV2` that is passed an integer array and returns a copy of the array with all of its elements increased by one. The contents of the array `theAges` passed into the method are unchanged.

```
static int[] birthdayV2(int[] theAges)
{
  int[] newAges = new int[length.theAges]; //declares the returned array
  for(int i = 0; i < theAges.length; i++)
  {
    newAges[i] = theAges[i] + 1;
  }

  return newAges; //returns the address of the new array
}
```

The syntax of the signature of a method that returns an array of objects is the same as the syntax used in the above method's signature, except the primitive type is replaced with the name of the object's class (e.g., `SnowmanV7[]` would replace `int[]`). In Chapter 7, we discuss and present a very important example of returning an array of objects from a method.

> When a method returns an array, a pair of braces [] is coded in between the method's name and its returned type in the method's signature. For example:

─────
**NOTE**
─────

```
static int[] birthday(int[] theAges)
```

> The return statement only contains the name of the array without the braces. For example:

```
return newAges;
```

## 6.7 PARALLEL ARRAYS

Suppose you were writing a program to maintain a database of student information for a school that had 1,000 students. Specifically, three pieces of information would be stored for each student: the student's identification number, age, and grade point average (GPA). If you were an object oriented programmer, you would begin by creating a class, probably named Student, which contained three data members, one for each piece of information. In addition, the class would contain a constructor to construct student objects and an input method to input information into a student object. Your application could then create the database as shown below:

```
Student[] studentInfo = new Student[1000]; //1,000 Student object array

for(int i = 0; i < 1000, i++)
{
    studentInfo[i] = new Student(); //create a new Student object
    student[i].input; //input a student's information
}
```

Now suppose that your program was going to be maintained by Anna, a programmer who was not trained in object oriented programming. She is not familiar with the concept of classes, the construction of objects, data members, and the idea that a class's non-static methods (e.g., the input method) can operate on an object's data members.

Anna's programming training was in the alternate programming paradigm, the *procedural* paradigm, in which objects do not play a central role in the language's constructs. She is not "object friendly". Because both the procedural and object oriented paradigms include the concept of arrays, you have decided to eliminate the use of the Student class from your program and simply use three arrays. One array will store all the student identification numbers, another will store all the student ages, and the third array will store all the student grade point averages (GPAs). Your application would then create the database as shown below:

```
1  int[] id = new int[1000];
2  int[] age = new int[1000];
3  double[] gpa = new double[1000];
4  String sInput;
```

```
 5
 6  for(int i = 0; i < 1000, i++)
 7  {
 8    sInput = JOptionPane.showInputDialog("Enter a student's ID number);
 9    id[i] = Integer.parseInt(sInput);
10    sInput = JOptionPane.showInputDialog("Enter THAT student's age);
11    age[i] = Integer.parseInt(sInput);
12    sInput = JOptionPane.showInputDialog("Enter THAT student's GPA);
13    gpa[i] = Double.parseDouble(sInput);
14  }
```

The code that is used to input the student information is an example of the use of parallel arrays. This is easily recognized when we examine the input prompts on lines 8, 10, and 12. On line 8, the user is instructed to *input a student's ID number*, implying that any of the 1,000 student IDs could be entered. Perhaps ID number 15647. However, on lines 10 and 12, the user is instructed to enter *THAT student's age* and *THAT student's GPA*. This implies that the next two entries must be the age and GPA of the student whose ID number was just entered.

Because the loop variable is used as the index into the three arrays, a student's information is stored in the *same* element of all three arrays. This is the concept of parallel arrays. Each piece of data that is associated with a particular student is stored in the same element of each of the three arrays that comprise the data set. We would not be using the concept of parallel arrays if a particular student's ID number was stored in element 3 of the `id` array, and that student's age and GPA were stored in element 24 of the `age` array and element 6 of the `GPA` array, respectively.

The name *parallel arrays* comes from the idea that if we were to draw the three arrays side by side and then draw parallel horizontal lines below and above each element of the array, as depicted in Figure 6.16, all of a student's information would be contained between two of the lines. For example, the age of the student whose ID is 76892 would be 19, and the student's GPA would be 4.0. All of Al's information, including his GPA of 1.7, would have been entered during the first iteration of the input loop. (Please study more, Al.)

| | id | | age | | gpa | |
|---|---|---|---|---|---|---|
| 0 | 15647 | | 18 | | 1.7 | Al's info |
| 1 | 3452 | | 21 | | 2.55 | Flo's info. |
| 2 | 76892 | | 19 | | 4.0 | Bob's info. |
| 3 | 34376 | | 22 | | 3.85 | Jo's info. |
| 4 | 77834 | | 19 | | 3.3 | Ed's info. |
| ⋮ | ⋮ | | ⋮ | | ⋮ | ⋮ |
| 999 | 45823 | | 20 | | 2.3 | Jen's info. |

**Figure 6.16**
Three parallel arrays.

It is important to remember that parallel arrays are a concept or a model, not a programming language construct. The concept is used when the programmer stores all the data for a particular entity in the same elements of two or more arrays.

Parallel arrays are used less frequently in programs coded in object oriented programming languages like Java because all of the data for a particular entity can be stored inside an object as its data members, rather than in the elements of several arrays. However, if we wanted to group several different objects together, e.g., a snowman and its child, then a set of parallel arrays of objects is a perfect way to do this.

For example, suppose that five snowmen had one snow child each. Then, if the arrays `parent` and `child` were used to store the addresses of the snowmen and the snow children, respectively, by considering the two arrays to be parallel, we could quickly locate a child's parent or locate a parent's child. The address of a parent and the address of its child would be stored in the same two elements of the arrays: `parent[2]`'s child's address would be stored in `child[2]`.

Figure 6.17 shows the graphical application `ParallelArrays` that uses three parallel arrays to associate a parent snowman with its snow child and their family name. The parent snowman's class, `ParentSnowman`, is shown in Figure 6.18, and the snow child's class, `SnowChild`, is shown in Figure 6.19.

When the program is launched, the graphical output shown in Figure 6.20a is produced. The parent snowmen are lined up vertically on the left of the game board, and the snow children are located at random locations to their right. Every child and parent has their family name (last name) displayed on their bellies. When a key is struck, the children are repositioned next to their parents as shown Figure 6.20b. Parallel arrays are used to make the association between a parent, its child, and the family name.

Three array objects are created on lines 14–16, with the first of these (the array `names`) initialized to the names of the five families (B, D, A, E, and C). Then the other two array objects are filled with references to `ParentSnowman` and `SnowChild` objects inside the `for` loop that begins on line 20. The constructors used to create the objects on lines 24 and 25 accept three arguments. The first two are the x and y location of the object, which for the children are random numbers generated on lines 22 and 23. The third parameter is the family name that will appear on the object's belly. The constructors store this name in the parent and child classes' data member `name` on line 17 of Figures 6.18 and 6.19, respectively.

The loop that begins on line 20 of Figure 6.17 establishes the arrays as parallel arrays. With each pass through the loop, the loop variable `i` is used on lines 24 and 25 as an index into the array `names` to select the family name of a parent (line 24) and its child (line 25). This name is passed to the `ParentSnowman` and `SnowChild` constructors, and the returned addresses are stored in the element `i` of the `parent` and `child` arrays. Because the same index number is used in all three arrays, a parent, its child, and their family name are all stored in the same element number of their respective arrays.

The parallel construction of the arrays makes it easy to reposition the children next to their parents, which is done in the `for` loop that begins on line 42 of the `keyStruck` call back method. Lines 44 and 45 fetch the (x, y) location of the ith child's parent, and these values are used on lines 46 and 47 to reposition the ith child to the right of its parent. Fifty pixels are added to the parent's x coordinate to move the child to the right of its parent, and 35 pixels are added to the y coordinate of the parent to account for the difference in height of the parent and child objects.

Parallel arrays are also used in the API `Graphics` class's method `fillPolygon`. This method is used on lines 31 and 28 of Figures 6.18 and 6.19, respectively, to draw the triangular noses of the parent snowmen and their children. The method has three parameters, two of which are arrays of integers:

```java
public void fillPolygon(int[] xPoints, int[] yPoints , int nPoints)
```

The parameters are used to specify the x coordinates of the vertices of a polygon (`xPoints`), the y coordinates of the vertices of a polygon (`yPoints`), and the number of vertices (`nPoints`). Within the method, the two arrays are used as parallel arrays. The coordinate of the ith vertex of the polygon is assumed to be (`xPoints[i]`, `yPoints[i]`). That is, the x and y coordinates of a vertex are assumed to be at the same element number in the `xPoints` and `yPoints` arrays. Knowing this, the two arrays `xPoly` and `yPoly` passed to the method on line 31 of Figure 6.18 have been set up as parallel arrays on lines 20 and 21. Because the desired coordinates of the three vertices of a parent's nose are (x + 20, y + 25), (x + 15, y + 30), and (x + 25, y + 30), these x and y parings are coded in the same elements of both arrays. A similar set of parings defines a child's nose on lines 21 and 22 of Figure 6.19, which are used to draw the child's nose on line 28 of that figure.

```java
1    import edu.sjcny.gpv1.*;
2    import java.awt.*;
3    import java.util.Random;
4
5    public class ParallelArrays extends DrawableAdapter
6    {
7      static ParallelArrays ge = new ParallelArrays();
8      static GameBoard gb = new GameBoard(ge, "Parallel Object ArraysApp");
9      static ParentSnowman[] parent;
10     static SnowChild[] child;
11
12     public static void main(String[] args)
13     {
14       String[] names = { "B", "D", "A", "E", "C"};
15       parent = new ParentSnowman[5];
16       child = new SnowChild[5];
17       Random rn = new Random(500);
18       int x, y;
19
20       for(int i = 0;  i < 5;  i++)
21       {
22         x = 100 + rn.nextInt(500 - 100 - 30);
23         y = 30 + rn.nextInt(500 - 30 - 30);
24         parent[i] = new ParentSnowman(50, 50 + 90*i, names[i]);
25         child[i] = new SnowChild(x, y, names[i]);
26       }
```

```
27        showGameBoard(gb);
28     }
29
30     public void draw(Graphics g)
31     {
32        for(int i = 0; i<5; i++)
33        {
34           parent[i].show(g);
35           child[i].show(g);
36        }
37     }
38
39     public void keyStruck(char key)
40     {
41        int x, y;
42        for(int i = 0; i< 5; i++)
43        {
44           x = parent[i].getX();
45           y = parent[i].getY();
46           child[i].setX(x + 50);
47           child[i].setY(y + 35);
48        }
49     }
50   }
```

**Figure 6.17**
The application **ParallelArrays**.

```
1     import java.awt.*;
2
3     public class ParentSnowman
4     {
5        private int x = 8;
6        private int y = 30;
7        private boolean visible = true;
8        private String name;
9
10       public ParentSnowman()
11       {
12       }
13
14       public ParentSnowman(int intialX, int intialY, String name)
15       { x = intialX;
16          y = intialY;
17          this.name = name;
18       }
19
20       public void show(Graphics g) //g is the game board object
21       { int[] xPoly = {x + 20, x + 15, x + 25};
```

```
22        int[] yPoly = {y + 25, y + 30, y + 30};
23
24        g.setColor(Color.BLACK);
25        g.fillRect(x + 15, y, 10, 15); //hat
26        g.fillRect(x + 10, y + 15, 20, 2); //brim
27        g.setColor(Color.WHITE);
28        g.fillOval(x + 10, y + 17, 20, 20); //head
29        g.fillOval(x, y + 37, 40, 40); //body
30        g.setColor(Color.RED);
31        g.fillPolygon(xPoly, yPoly, 3); //nose
32        g.setColor(Color.BLACK);
33        g.setFont(new Font("Arial", Font.BOLD, 16));
34        g.drawString(name, x + 16, y + 62); //name
35      }
36
37     public int getX()
38     { return x;
39     }
40
41     public void setX(int newX)
42     { x = newX;
43     }
44
45     public int getY()
46     { return y;
47     }
48
49     public void setY(int newY)
50     { y = newY;
51     }
52
53     public boolean getVisible()
54     { return visible;
55     }
56
57     public void setVisible (boolean newVisible)
58     { visible  = newVisible;
59     }
60
61     public String getName()
62     { return name;
63     }
64   }
```

**Figure 6.18**
The class **ParentSnowman**.

```
1    import java.awt.*;
2
3    public class SnowChild
4    {
5      private int x = 8;
6      private int y = 30;
7      private boolean visible = true;
8      private String name;
9
10     public SnowChild()
11     {
12     }
13
14     public SnowChild(int intialX, int intialY, String name)
15     { x = intialX;
16       y = intialY;
17       this.name = name;
18       }
19
20     public void show(Graphics g)  //g is the game board object
21     { int[] xPoly = {x + 15, x + 12, x + 18};
22       int[] yPoly = {y + 5, y + 8, y + 8};
23
24       g.setColor(Color.WHITE);
25       g.fillOval(x + 8, y, 14, 14); //head
26       g.fillOval(x, y + 14, 28, 28); //body
27       g.setColor(Color.RED);
28       g.fillPolygon(xPoly, yPoly, 3); //nose
29       g.setColor(Color.BLACK);
30       g.setFont(new Font("Arial", Font.BOLD, 16));
31       g.drawString(name, x + 10, y + 33);   //name
32     }
33
34     public int getX()
35     { return x;
36     }
37
38     public void setX(int newX)
39     { x = newX;
40     }
41
42     public int getY()
43     { return y;
44     }
45
46     public void setY(int newY)
47     { y = newY;
48     }
49
```

```
50      public boolean getVisible()
51      { return visible;
52      }
53
54      public void setVisible (boolean newVisible)
55      { visible  = newVisible;
56      }
57
58      public void setName(String newName)
59      { name = newName;
60      }
61
62      public String getName()
63      { return name;
64      }
65  }
```

**Figure 6.19**
The class **SnowChild**.

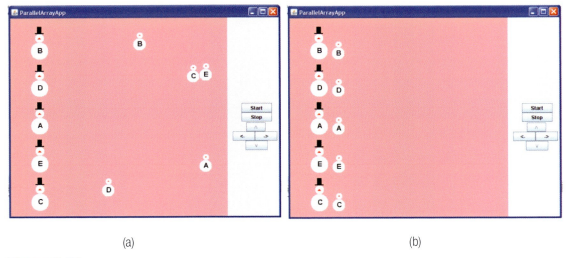

(a)                                                                    (b)

**Figure 6.20**
The graphical output of the application **ParallelArrays**.

## 6.8 COMMON ARRAY ALGORITHMS

As we have seen, arrays can be used to easily declare and process large data sets. Often, the processing performed on these data sets involves searching for a particular piece of data (e.g., the snowman family whose name is C), finding the name of the snowman family that is first or last in alphabetical order, or displaying the snowman families in sorted order based on their names. Searching, finding minimums and maximums, and sorting are all array-processing algorithms that are very commonly used in programs. We will begin our study of these algorithms with the array searching algorithm.

### 6.8.1 The Sequential Search Algorithm

As its name implies, this algorithm is used to search an array to determine the element number of the array that contains a given value. For example, it could be used to search an array containing a group of people's ages to find the element number whose value is 32. If a parallel array contained the names of the people, then the element number could be used as an index into the name array to output the name of a person who is 32 years old. In an object oriented context, it could be used to search an array of parent snowmen to find the element number of the snowman whose `name` data member contains the string "C" and then use this element number to display its family name on the game board.

An algorithm to search for, or locate, a particular value contained in an array is shown in Figure 6.21. Named the Sequential Search, beginning at element zero it sequentially examines the elements of the array from the beginning until it finds the value it is searching for. The implementation on the left side of the figure searches the *integer* array `ages` for the value 32, and the code on the right searches the *object* array `parent` for an object whose `age` data member is 32. These *target* values are specified on line 1. Lines 2–12 constitute the searching algorithm. Except for the names of the arrays and the Boolean conditions on line 6, the algorithms are identical. Line 6 of the array of objects version of the algorithm (the right side of the figure) assumes that the class of the objects contains a `getAge` method to fetch an object's `age` data member.

```
1  int target = 32;                          1  int target = 32;
2  int elementNumber = -1;                    2  int elementNumber = -1;
3  boolean found = false;                     3  boolean found = false;
4  for(int i = 0; i < ages.length; i++)       4  for(int i = 0; i< parent.length; i++)
5  {                                          5  {
6    if(ages[i] == target)                    6    if(parent[i].getAge() == target))
7    {                                        7    {
8      found = true;                          8      found = true;
9      elementNumber = i;                     9      elementNumber = i;
10     break;                                 10     break;
11   }                                        11   }
12 }                                          12 }
```

|  **Searching an Array of Primitives**  |  **Searching an Array of Objects**  |

**Figure 6.21**
The Sequential Search algorithm.

The initializing value on line 1 of Figure 6.21 is the target value to be found. Line 2 initializes the Boolean variable `found` to `false`. This variable will be set to `true` if the target being searched for is found. The loop that begins on line 4 indexes its way through the array. Inside that loop, the `if` statement on line 6 determines if element `i` of the array contains the target value. If it does, `found` is set to `true` (line 8), `elementNumber` is set on line 9 to the element number that contains the target value, and the code breaks out of the loop (line 10). Subsequent code would have to examine the variable `found` before using the index stored in the variable `elementNumber` because, if the target value is not found, the value stored in the variable `elementNumber` would be out of bounds (i.e., equal to its initial value, -1).

The algorithm on the right side of Figure 6.21 can be used to locate a value stored in any primitive-type data member contained in the array's objects, as long as the class of the objects contains a `get` method to fetch the data member (which would be invoked on line 6). If the data member is not a primitive-type variable, but rather a reference variable, then the class of the object it references also must contain an `equals` method to be used in the Boolean condition on line 6. Typically, this method returns `true` when the object that invoked it is equal to the argument sent to it (the variable `target`). The `String` class contains an implementation of this method.

Assuming the data member's name was `lastName` that referenced a string, and we were searching for the name Jones, lines 1 and 6 of the algorithm would become:

```
Line 1: String target = "Jones";
Line 6: if(parent[i].getLastName().equals(target))
```

It should be noted that if several elements of the array contained the target value, the variable `elementNumber` would be set to the index of the lowest of these elements. If the highest element number of the array that contains the minimum value is desired, then the `break` statement on line 10 of Figure 2.21 would be eliminated from the algorithm. In addition, when the algorithms are implemented as a method that returns the element number of the target value, the method returns the variable `elementNumber`. The signature of the method would be:

**public static int** findValue(ArrayType[] arrayOfvalues, TargetType target)

where `ArrayType` and `TargetType` are the types of the array and the value being searched for, respectively. The method below is an implementation of the sequential search algorithm. It searches the array of `SnowChild` objects passed to its first parameter and returns the index of the first child whose name is the string passed to its second parameter. Otherwise, it returns a -1. Another popular searching algorithm, the Binary Search Algorithm, will be discussed in Section 6.11.1.

```java
public static int findValue(SnowChild[] anArray, String target)
{
  int elementNumber = -1;

  for(int i = 0; i < anArray.length; i++)
  {
    if(anArray[i].getName().equals(target))
    {
      elementNumber = i;
      break;
    }
  }
  return elementNumber;
}
```

## 6.8.2 Minimums and Maximums

The algorithms to locate the minimum or maximum value contained in an array are very similar to the searching algorithm discussed in the previous section. They also use a `for` loop to search the entire array, but when the loop terminates, the variable `elementNumber` contains the element number of the minimum or maximum value in the array. When the array is an array of objects, this value is the minimum or maximum value stored in a particular data member of the objects.

The code shown on the left side of Figure 6.22 is an implementation of the algorithm to locate the *minimum* value contained in an array of primitive values (in this case, an array of people's ages). The code on the right searches the object array `parent` for the minimum value stored in one of the object's data members (in this case, the integer data member `age`). Except for lines 1, 6, and the different array names the algorithms are identical.

Lines 1 and 6 of the array of objects version of the algorithm (right side of the figure) assume that the class of the objects contains a `getAge` method to fetch the object's data member (`age`).

Both algorithms begin with the assumption that the minimum value is stored in, or is referenced by, the first element of the array. Therefore, line 1 sets the variable `min` to that value, and line 2 stores its index (zero) in the variable `elementNumber`. The `for` loop that begins on line 4 compares the value stored in the variable `min` to all of the other members of the array. If it finds a value smaller than the value stored in `min` (line 6), it saves that value in `min` (line 8) and its element number in the variable `elementNumber` (line 9). When the loop ends, `elementNumber` contains the index of the minimum value in the array.

| | |
|---|---|
| ```
1 int min = ages[0];
2 int elementNumber = 0;
3
4 for(int i = 1; i < ages.length; i++)
5 {
6    if(ages[i] < min)
7    {
8       min = ages[i];
9       elementNumber = i
10   }
11}
``` | ```
1 int min = parent[0].getAge();
2 int elementNumber = 0;
3
4 for(int i = 1; i< parent.length; i++)
5 {
6    if(parent[i].getAge() < min)
7    {
8       min = parent[i].getAge();
9       elementNumber = i
10   }
11}
``` |
| **Minimum Primitive Array Value Algorithm** | **Minimum Object Array Value Algorithm** |

**Figure 6.22**
The minimum value algorithm.

Using an approach similar to the search algorithm, the algorithm on the right side of Figure 6.22 can be used to locate the minimum value of any primitive type data member contained in the array's objects, as long as the objects' class contains a `get` method to fetch the data member (invoked on lines 1, 6, and 8). If the data member is not a primitive type variable, but rather a reference variable, then the class of the object it references also must contain a `compareTo` method to be used in the Boolean condition on line 6. Typically, this method returns a negative number when the object that invoked it is less than the argument sent to it (the variable `min`). The `String` class contains an implementation of this method.

Assuming the data member referenced a `String` object, and the data member's name was `lastName`, lines 1 and 6 of the algorithm would become:

```
Line 1: String min = parent[0].getLastName();
Line 6: if(parent[i].getLastName().compareTo(min) <  0)
```

Finally, when the array is an array of `String` objects, lines 1 and 6 of the algorithm would become:

```
Line 1: String min = parent[0];
Line 6: if(parent[i].compareTo(min) <  0)
```

It should be noted that if several elements of the array contained the minimum value, the variable `elementNumber` would be set to the index of the lowest value of these elements. If the highest index of the array that contains the minimum value is desired, then the less than operator (<) used in the Boolean expression on line 6 would be changed to the less than or equal to operator (<=). When the algorithms are coded as a method that returns the element number of the minimum value, the method returns the variable `elementNumber`. The signature of the method would be:

```
public int findMin(ArrayType[] arrayOfvalues)
```

where `ArrayType` is the types of the array elements (e.g., `double`, `String`, `SnowChild`, etc.). The following method searches the array of `SnowChild` objects passed to it and returns the index of the snow child that contains the minimum value of the primitive data member x.

```
public int findMin(SnowChild[] arrayOfvalues)
{
  int min = arrayOfValues[0].getX();
  int elementNumber = 0;

  for(int i = 1; i  <  arrayOfValues.length; i++)
  {
    if(arrayOfValues[i].getAge() < min)
    {
    min = arrayOfValues[i].getAge();
    elementNumber = i;
    }
    return elementNumber;
}
```

## Locating Maximums

The algorithm to locate the maximum value contained in an array is the same as that used to locate the minimum value, except that the less than operator (<) used on line 6 of Figure 6.22 is replaced with the greater than operator (>), and good coding style dictates that the variable `min` be renamed `max`.

### 6.8.3 The Selection Sort Algorithm

As we will see in Section 6.11, there are many alternative algorithms for sorting the elements of an n element array. One of the simplest is the Selection Sort algorithm. It begins by locating the minimum value contained in elements 1 to n-1, and if it is smaller than element zero (j = 0), it is swapped into element zero. Then it locates the next smallest value, and if it is smaller than element one (j = 1), swaps it into element one. This process is repeated for j = 2, 3, ... n-2. When the algorithm ends, the array is sorted in ascending order.

For example, suppose we wanted to sort an array of five integers, 12, 9, 3, 4, and 11, shown in the left column of Table 6.1 in ascending order. First, we locate the smallest value among 9, 3, 4, and 11 which is 3. Because it is less than 12 (the value in element j = 0), it is swapped with 12, which produces the ordering shown in the second column of the table. Then the smallest value among 12, 4, and 11 is located, which is 4. Because it is less than 9 (the value in element j = 1), it is swapped with 9, producing the ordering shown in the third column of the table. The remaining two steps for j = 2 and j = 3 and the final sorted array are shown in the three right-most columns. When the array is an array of objects, the algorithm sorts the objects based on the value of one of the class's data members.

**Table 6.1**
The Progression of the Selection Sort Algorithm

|  | j = 0 | j = 1 | j = 2 | j = 3 |  |
|---|---|---|---|---|---|
| index 0 | 12 | 3 | 3 | 3 | 3 |
| 1 | 9 | 9 | 4 | 4 | 4 |
| 2 | 3 | 12 | 12 | 9 | 9 |
| 3 | 4 | 4 | 9 | 12 | 11 |
| 4 | 11 | 11 | 11 | 11 | 12 |
|  | Original Array | After 12 and 3 were swapped | After 9 and 4 were swapped | After 12 and 9 were swapped | After 12 and 11 were swapped |

The code shown on the left side of Figure 6.23 is an implementation of the Selection Sort algorithm for sorting an array of primitive values (in this case an array of people's ages). It uses nested loops: the inner loop searches for a minimum value, and the outer loop places it into its correct position in the array. The right side of the figure is an implementation of the algorithm used to sort an array of ParentClass objects based on the value of one of their primitive type data members (in this case, the integer data member age). Except for the names of the arrays, the type of the variable declared on line 2, and the use of the getAge method on lines 6, 10, and 12 on the right side of the figure, the implementations are identical.

The code that begins on line 6 and ends on line 15 is essentially the algorithm to locate the minimum value of an array's elements, which was discussed in Section 6.8.2 and implemented in Figure 6.22. The differences are that line 6 initializes the minimum value, min, to the jth element of the array rather than the first element, and line 7 initializes the minimum element number, iMin, to j rather than zero. In addition, the loop that begins on line 8 initializes its loop variable to j + 1 rather than one. The variable j is the loop variable of an outer loop that begins on line 4 and ends on line 23. Because it is initialized to zero on line 4 the first time lines 6–15 execute, this code is in fact identical to the minimum value algorithm.

After the search for the minimum value ends (line 15), if j is not the index of the minimum value of the remaining unsorted portion of the array (as determined by the if statement on line 17), then lines 19–21 place the minimum value in element j by swapping element j with element iMin. Lines 17, 18, and 22 could be removed from the code, in which case element j would be swapped with itself when it is smaller than the remaining unsorted portion of the array. This can be unnecessarily time consuming when the array to be sorted is already sorted, or the array being sorted is a member of a set of parallel arrays (see lines 125–136 of Figure 6.24).

The first time through the outer loop, element zero stores the minimum value contained in the array. After the second iteration of the outer loop, the next lowest element is stored in element 1. This process continues and, when the algorithm ends, the array is sorted in ascending order. To sort the elements of an array in *descending* order, the less than (<) operator in the Boolean condition on line 10 is changed to the greater than (>) operator, the variable names iMin and min would be changed to iMax and max to make the code more readable.

It should be noted that when sorting an array of objects (right side of Figure 6,23), lines 19–21 swaps the references to the objects contained in the array parents. For example, on the first iteration of the outer loop, the location of the object whose age data member is the minimum value is placed in the first element of the array parents. The alternative is to swap the contents of the data

| Sorting an Array of Primitives | The selection sort algorithm. |
|---|---|

```
1    int iMin, min;
2    int temp;
3
4    for (int j = 0; j < ages.length; j++)
5    {
6        min = ages[j];
7        iMin = j;
8        for (int i = j+1; i < ages.length; i++)
9        {
10            if (ages[i] < min)
11            {
12                min = ages[i];
13                iMin = i;
14            }
15        }
16
17        if ( iMin != j )
18        {
19            temp = ages[j];
20            ages[j] = ages[iMin];
21            ages[iMin] = temp;
22        }
23    }
```

```
1    int iMin, min;
2    ParentClass temp;
3
4    for (int j = 0; j < parent.length; j++)
5    {
6        min = parent[j].getAge();
7        iMin = j;
8        for (int i = j+1; i < parent.length; i++)
9        {
10            if (parent[i].getAge() <   min)
11            {
12                min = parent[i].getAge();
13                iMin = i;
14            }
15        }
16
17        if ( iMin != j )
18        {
19            temp = parent[j];
20            parent[j] = parent[iMin];
21            parent[iMin] = temp;
22        }
23    }
```

**Figure 6.23**
The minimum value algorithm.

members of the objects, which is more time consuming. In either case, if the sorted objects were output from the first element of the array to the last, they would appear in sorted order based on the contents of the `age` data member.

The algorithm on the right side of Figure 6.23 can be used to sort an array of objects based on any primitive type data member contained in the array's objects, as long as the class of the objects contains a `get` method to fetch the data member (which would be invoked on lines 6, 10, and 12).

If the data member is *not* a primitive type variable, but rather a reference variable, then the class of the object it references also must contain a `compareTo` method to be used in the Boolean condition on line 10. Typically, this method returns a negative number when the object that invoked it is less than the argument sent to it (the variable `min`). The `String` class contains an implementation of this method. Assuming the data member referenced a `String` object and the data member's name was `lastName`, line 10 of the algorithm would become:

Line 10: **if**(parent[i].getLastName().compareTo(min) < 0)

When the array is an array of `String` objects, line 10 of the algorithm would become:

Line 10: **if**(parent[i].compareTo(min) < 0)

### An Array Algorithm Case Study

Figure 6.24 presents the graphical application `ArrayAlgorithms` that illustrates the use of the array processing algorithms discussed in this chapter to process parallel arrays of snow families. When the application begins, the user is asked to enter the names of five snow families (e.g., "I", "B", "N", "E", and "G"). Then the five families, each consisting of a `ParentSnowman` and a `SnowChild` object, whose classes are shown in Figures 6.18 and 6.19, respectively, are displayed (Figure 6.25a).

After the program is launched, when the user types the name of a snow family (e.g., "I"), the family is searched for and alternately disappears (Figure 6.25b) and reappears (Figure 6.25a). When the up-arrow cursor key is struck, the family whose name is the minimum in sorted order (e.g., "B"), alternately disappears (Figure 6.25c) and reappears (Figure 6.25a). Finally, when the "S" key is struck, the visible snow families are displayed in sorted order by family name (Figure 6.25d).

```
1    import edu.sjcny.gpv1.*;
2    import java.awt.*;
3    import javax.swing.*;
4
5    public class ArrayAlgorithms extends DrawableAdapter
6    {
7       static ArrayAlgorithms ge = new ArrayAlgorithms();
8       static GameBoard gb = new GameBoard(ge, "ArrayAlgorithmsApp");
9       static ParentSnowman[] parent;
10      static SnowChild[] child;
```

```java
11
12    public static void main(String[] args)
13    {
14      String name;
15      parent = new ParentSnowman[5];
16      child = new SnowChild[5];
17
18      for(int i = 0; i < 5; i++)
19      {
20        name = JOptionPane.showInputDialog("enter a family name");
21        name = name.toUpperCase();
22        child[i] = new SnowChild(50 + 60, 80 + 90 * i, name);
23        parent[i] = new ParentSnowman(50, 50 + 90 * i, name);
24      }
25      showGameBoard(gb);
26    }
27
28    public void draw(Graphics g)
29    {
30      for(int i = 0; i<5; i++)
31      {
32        if(parent[i].getVisible() == true)
33        { parent[i].show(g);
34          child[i].show(g);
35        }
36      }
37    }
38
39    public void keyStruck(char key)
40    {
41      int index;
42
43      String sKey = Character.toString(key);
44      index = findValue(parent, sKey);
45      if(index != -1) //name is valid, reverse family's visibility
46      {
47        if(parent[index].getVisible() == true)
48        {
49          parent[index].setVisible(false);
50        }
51        else
52        {
53          parent[index].setVisible(true);
54        }
55      }
56
57      if (key == 'U') //up arrow struck, reverse visibility of min name
58      {
59        index = findMin(parent); //index of first family in alphabetic order
```

```java
60        if(parent[index].getVisible() == true)
61        {
62          parent[index].setVisible(false);
63        }
64        else
65        {
66          parent[index].setVisible(true);
67        }
68      }
69      if(key == 'S') //sort the families
70      {
71        selectionSort(parent);
72      }
73    }
74
75    public static int findValue(ParentSnowman[] parent, String targetValue)
76    {
77      int elementNumber = -1;
78      for(int i = 0; i< parent.length; i++)
79      {
80        if(parent[i].getName().equalsIgnoreCase(targetValue))
81        {
82          elementNumber = i;
83          break;
84        }
85      }
86      return elementNumber;
87    }
88
89    public static int findMin(ParentSnowman[] parent)
90    {
91      String min = parent[0].getName();
92      int elementNumber = 0;
93      for(int i = 1; i <  parent.length; i++)
94      {
95        if(parent[i].getName().compareToIgnoreCase(min) < 0)
96        {
97          min = parent[i].getName();
98          elementNumber = i;
99        }
100     }
101     return elementNumber;
102   }
103
104   public static void selectionSort(ParentSnowman[] parent)
105   {
106     int iMin, tempInt;
107     ParentSnowman tempParent;
108     SnowChild tempChild;
```

```
109      String min;
110
111      for (int j = 0; j < parent.length; j++)
112      {
113        min = parent[j].getName();
114        iMin = j;
115        for (int i = j+1; i < parent.length; i++)
116        {
117          if (parent[i].getName().compareToIgnoreCase(min) <  0)
118          {
119            min = parent[i].getName();
120            iMin = i;
121          }
122        }
123        if(iMin != j) //swap element j with minimum element
124        {
125          tempParent = parent[j]; //swap array references
126          parent[j] = parent[iMin];
127          parent[iMin] = tempParent;
128          tempChild = child[j];
129          child[j] = child[iMin];
130          child[iMin] = tempChild;
131
132          tempInt = parent[j].getY();  //swap Y positions
133          parent[j].setY(parent[iMin].getY());
134          parent[iMin].setY(tempInt);
135          child[j].setY(parent[j].getY() + 30);
136          child[iMin].setY(parent[iMin].getY() + 30);
137        }
138      }
139    }
140 }
```

**Figure 6.24**
The application **ArrayAlgorithms**.

The loop that begins on line 18 of the main method accepts the five family names (line 20) and allocates the five child and parent objects (lines 22 and 23). With each pass though the loop, a child and a parent object is created, assigned positions next to each other on the game board, and given their family name. Then, the loop variable is used to write the addresses of these two newly created family members into the same (ith) element of the child and parent arrays, making these two arrays parallel.

The loop that begins on line 30 of the draw method displays the five snow families on the game board, if they are visible as determined by the if statement's Boolean condition on line 32. When the Boolean condition is true, the ith parent and the ith child are drawn. Because the arrays were set up to be parallel, a parent and its child are drawn (lines 31–34).

## Use of the Search Algorithm

The code, to make a family alternately disappear and reappear when their one-character family name is typed, is on lines 43–55 of the `keyStruck` method. This method is invoked by the game environment whenever a key is typed, and the typed character is passed into the method's parameter, `key` (line 43). To locate a `ParentSnowman` object with that family name, line 44 invokes the `findValue` method (lines 75–87) passing it the parent array (`parent`) and the string version of the family name (`sKey`). The method `findValue` is an implementation of the object version of the search algorithm discussed at the end of Section 6.8.1. If an object is found with that family name (the returned array index is not -1 on line 45), then the index is used on lines 47–54 to reverse the visibility of the parent object. Assuming an "I" was struck twice, the game board would change from the board displayed in Figure 6.25a to that shown in Figure 6.25b and then back again.

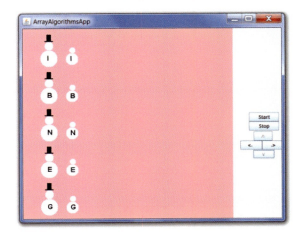

(a) After the program is launched

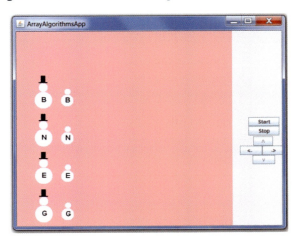

(b) After the "I" key is struck the first time

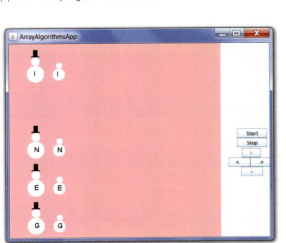

(c) Second strike of "I" key followed by a strike of the up cursor key

(d) After the "S" key is struck

**Figure 6.25**
The graphical output of the application **ArrayAlgorithms**.

Because in this application the search is for a particular value of a `String` object (the case-insensitive family name), this implementation of the search algorithm uses the `String` class's `equalsIgnoreCase` method on line 80 to compare the name passed to it (contained in the parameter `targetValue`) to the name returned by the `ParentSnowman` class's `getName` method.

## Use of the Minimum Value Algorithm

The code to make a family whose name is first in alphabetical order alternately disappear and reappear when the up-arrow curser key is struck is coded on lines 57–68 of the `keyStruck` method. To locate a `ParentSnowman` object whose family name is first in alphabetic order, line 59 invokes the `findMin` method (lines 89–102), passing it the parent array. The method `findMin` is an implementation of the algorithm discussed in Section 6.8.2 that searches an array for a minimum value. In this coding of the algorithm, the method returns the array element number (line 101) that references the object whose `name` data member is first in alphabetic order (line 95). The returned element number is used on lines 60–67 to reverse the visibility of the parent object. Because the `draw` method (lines 28–37) only draws the snowman parent and its child when the parent's `visible` data member is `true` (line 32), both the parent and child disappear and reappear when the up-arrow key is typed.

In this application, the search is for a minimum value of a `String` object (the case-insensitive family name), `findMin` uses the `String` class's `compareToIgnoreCase` method on line 95 to determine if the name returned by the `ParentSnowman` class's `getName` method is less than the string referenced by `min`.

## Use of the Selection Sort Algorithm

The code to sort the parent and child arrays in ascending order based on family names when the S key is struck is coded on lines 69–72 of the `keyStruck` method. To sort the parent and child arrays, line 71 invokes the `selectionSort` method (lines 104–139) passing it the parent array. The method `selectionSort` is an implementation of the sorting algorithm discussed in Section 6.8.3. In this coding of the algorithm, the method not only swaps the elements of the array passed to it (lines 125–127) but also the elements of its parallel array `child` (lines 128–130). (Because the address of the child array is declared as a class-level variable, the `selectionSort` method has access to it.) In addition, the method swaps the `y` data members of the parent objects (lines 132–134) and then positions the children next to their parents (lines 135–137), so the families will appear in sorted order from the top to the bottom of the game board.

Because in this application, the sorting is based on a `String` object (the case-insensitive family name), the method `selectionSort` uses the `String` class's `compareToIgnoreCase` method on line 117 to determine if the name returned by the `ParentSnowman` class's `getName` method is less than the string referenced by `min`.

## 6.9 APPLICATION PROGRAMMING INTERFACE ARRAY SUPPORT

The `System` and `Arrays` classes in the Java Application Programming Interface contain methods for processing arrays, and the API class `ArrayList` provides a means of storing data in an "array-like" object that can expand beyond its original size. The `ArrayList` class is one of the API's generic collection classes, which will be discussed in Chapter 10. In the remainder of this section, we will discuss the array processing support in the API `System` and `Arrays` classes.

### 6.9.1 The `arraycopy` Method

As its name implies, the `arraycopy` method in the `System` class is used to copy the contents of one array (called the *source* array) into another array (called the *destination* array). The method is a `static` method and is therefore invoked by first coding the name of its class, `System`, rather than the name of an object. Its signature contains five parameters, and a typical invocation would be:

```
System.arraycopy(sourceArray, sourceIndex, destinationArray,
                 destinationIndex, numElements);
```

where:

`sourceArray` is the name of the array that is being copied (an array object reference variable)
`sourceIndex` is the index of the first element copied from `sourceArray` (an int)
`destinationArray` is the name of the array being copied to (an array object reference variable)
`destinationIndex` is the index of the first element copied into `destinationArray` (an int)
`numElements` is the number of sequential elements to be copied (an int)

Both the source array and destination arrays must exist (have been previously declared) before the method is invoked. Figure 6.26 shows the result of executing the invocation:

```
System.arraycopy(age, 0, sum, 1, 2);
```

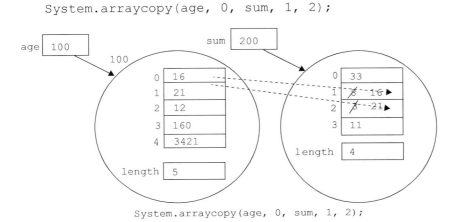

System.arraycopy(age, 0, sum, 1, 2);

**Figure 6.26**
The use of the System class's **arraycopy** method.

If the `sourceIndex`, `destinationIndex`, and `numElementsvalues` passed to the method are such that the copying causes element numbers to be generated that do not exist, a runtime error (`ArrayIndexOutOfBoundsException`) will occur. This error is a more specific error than an `IndexOutOfBoundsException` error, because as we will see in Chapter 7, the characters of a String object are also assigned an index value and an attempt to use a character index that does not exist results in an exception specific to this error, `StringIndexOutOfBoundsException`.

### 6.9.2 The Arrays Class

The API `Arrays` class contains two methods that can be used to copy one array into another and contains several other useful methods for processing arrays of primitives and strings. These include a method to facilitate the output of all of the elements of an array by converting them to a single string, a sorting method, a search method, a method to determine if the corresponding elements of two arrays are equal, and a method that sets the elements of an array to a specified value. The searching and sorting method algorithms execute faster than the algorithms discussed in Sections 6.8.1 and 6.8.3. Some of the methods in the class `Arrays` are summarized in Table 6.2.

**Table 6.2**
Methods in the API Arrays Class

| Function | Method Name | Typical Invocation |
|---|---|---|
| **Copies** all or a portion of an array beginning with the *first* element | copyOf | `int[] a = Arrays.copyOf(sourceArray, 10);` Returns an array containing the first *ten* elements of the array `sourceArray` |
| **Copies** an array beginning with *any* element | copyOfRange | `int[] a = Arrays.copyOfRange(sourceArray, 2, 10);` Returns an array containing the *third* (index 2) through the *ninth* elements of array `sourceArray` |
| **Converts** an array's contents to a string | toString | `String arrayContents = Arrays.toString(anArray);` Returns a string enclosed in braces containing the contents of the array's elements, each separated by a comma and a space |
| **Sorts** the elements of an array in ascending order | sort | `Arrays.sort(anArray);` Sorts all of the elements of the array `anArray` `Arrays.sort(anArray, 1, 5);` Sorts the values at index 1 through index 4 of the array `anArray` |
| **Searches** for (locates) a target value in a *sorted* array | binarySearch | `int i = Arrays.binarySearch(anArrray, targetValue)` Returns the index of an occurrence of `targetValue` in the sorted array anArray or returns a negative value if an occurrence is not found |
| **Sets** the elements of an array to a given value | fill | `Arrays.fill(intArray, 4);` Sets all of the elements of the array `intArray` to the value 4 `Arrays.fill(stringArray, 1, 4, "FillValue");` Sets the second (index 1) to the fourth (index 3) elements of the array `stringArray` to "FillValue" |

All of these methods are static methods, and the program presented in Figure 6.27 illustrates their use. The output generated by this program appears in Figure 6.28.

Lines 15 and 16 of Figure 6.27 output all of the elements of the string and integer arrays `stringArray` and `intArray` created on lines 6 and 8. The parameter sent to the `println` method on lines 15 and 16 is the string returned from the `Arrays` class's `toString` method. The returned string is a concatenation of all of the elements of the array sent to the method separated by a comma and a space (lines 2 and 3 of Figure 6.28). It begins with an open bracket [ and ends with a close bracket ].

Lines 21 and 23 of Figure 6.27 use the `Arrays` class's static `copyOf` method to create a copy of the arrays `stringArray` and `intArray` and assign the newly created array addresses to the variables `copyStringArray` and `copyIntArray`, respectively. The second parameter sent to this method specifies the number of elements to be copied, and the copy always begins at element 0. If the number of elements to be copied exceeds the size of the source array (as it does on line 21), the elements are filled in with default values consistent with their type (`null` for string references) as shown on line 6 of Figure 6.28.

The `Arrays` class's `equals` method is used on lines 29 and 31 of Figure 6.27 to compare two integer arrays for equality. The method returns `true` if all of the corresponding elements of the two arrays passed to it are equal, as they are on line 29; otherwise, it returns `false` (line 31). The returned Boolean values are output and shown on lines 10 and 11 of Figure 6.28.

Line 36 of Figure 6.27 uses the one-parameter version of the `Arrays` class's static method `sort` to sort all of the elements of the array `stringArray`, and line 38 uses the three-parameter version of the method to sort the values at indices 1 through 4 of the array `intArray`. The third argument sent the three-parameter version of the method is always one larger than the index of the highest element to be sorted. This can be verified by comparing the output of the unsorted values (line 7 of Figure 6.28) to the output of the sorted values (line 15 of Figure 6.28). The sort is always performed inside the arrays passed to the method.

After the array `stringArray` is sorted (line 36), the `Arrays` class's method `binarySearch` can be used to determine the index of a given value in the array. Line 44 invokes this method to search the array for the index of the element containing the string "`Fred`." This string's position in sorted order is index 2 (line 14 of Figure 6.28), so the method returns the value 2 (line 18 of Figure 6.28). If there were several occurrences of the item being searched for in the array, it is uncertain as to which occurrence's index would be returned. Line 45 searches for the name "Doris," which is not contained in the array. When the item searched for is not in the array, a negative index is returned, in this case the value -3 (line 19 of Figure 6.28). When the search value is not found, the absolute value of the returned index is one greater than the index where the item would be if it were in its sorted position in the array. Line 14 of Figure 6.28 shows the sorted version of the array.

The `Arrays` class's methods `copyOf` and `copyOfRange` can be used to copy all or part of the elements of an array. As previously stated, the `copyOf` method always begins its copy at index 0 of the array, and the second argument passed to it indicates the number of elements to copy. The method is used on line 50 of Figure 6.27 to copy the first four elements of the array intArray into a newly created array whose address is assigned to the variable copyIntArray. The contents of the returned array is shown on line 22 of Figure 6.28, which can be compared to the contents of the array intArray shown on line 15 of the figure.

When the copyOfRange method is used, the copying can begin and end anywhere in the source array. As shown on line 52 of Figure 6.27, the source array is specified as the first argument sent to the method, the starting index is the second argument, and the third argument is always one more that the last index to be copied. Therefore, line 52 specifies that the elements at index 2–9 should be copied into a newly created array. If the value of the last argument specifies an index that is beyond the bounds of the source array (as it is on line 52), default values (e.g., zero for numeric types, null for char and String types) are entered into the out-of-bounds elements of the returned array. Thus, the last four elements in the integer array returned from the invocation on line 52 contain zeros (line 22 of Figure 6.28).

Lines 58 and 60 of Figure 6.27 use the Arrays class's fill method to set sequential elements of the arrays intArray and stringArray (specified as the first argument sent to this method) to a value specified by the last argument sent to the method. The two-parameter version of this method (invoked on line 58) fills all of the elements of the array sent to it. The four-parameter version of this method, invoked on line 60, fills a specified sequential range of elements of the array sent to it. The index at which to start the fill is the second argument sent to the four-parameter version of the method, and the third argument is always one more than the last index to be filled. The contents of the filled arrays are shown on lines 25 and 26 of Figure 6.28.

```
1    import java.util.Arrays;
2    public class ArraysClass
3    {
4      public static void main(String[] args)
5      {
6        String[] stringArray = {"Tom","Mary","Bob","Alice","Joe","Fred"};
7        String[] copyStringArray;
8        int[] intArray = { 3, 5, 2, 8, 6, 4};
9        int[] copyIntArray;
10       int[] filledIntArray;
11
12       //outputting the elements of an arrays
13       System.out.println("Outputing arrays using the " +
14                          "Arrays.toString method");
15       System.out.println(Arrays.toString(stringArray));
16       System.out.println(Arrays.toString(intArray));
17
18       //copying the elements of an array;
```

```java
19          System.out.println("\nCopying arrays using the " +
20                          "Arrays.copyOf method");
21          copyStringArray = Arrays.copyOf(stringArray, 10);
22          System.out.println(Arrays.toString(copyStringArray));
23          copyIntArray = Arrays.copyOf(intArray, intArray.length);
24          System.out.println(Arrays.toString(copyIntArray));
25
26          //determining if all the elements of two arrays are equal
27          System.out.println("\nTesting two arrays for equality " +
28                          "using the Arrays.equals method");
29          System.out.println(Arrays.equals(intArray, copyIntArray));
30          copyIntArray[0] = 1;
31          System.out.println(Arrays.equals(intArray, copyIntArray));
32
33          //sorting arrays
34          System.out.println("\nSorting all or part of an array: " +
35                          "the Arrays.sort method");
36          Arrays.sort(stringArray);
37          System.out.println(Arrays.toString(stringArray));
38          Arrays.sort(intArray, 1, 5);
39          System.out.println(Arrays.toString(intArray));
40
41          //searching for an element of a sorted array
42          System.out.println("\nSearching for a value: the " +
43                          "Arrays.binarySearch method");
44          System.out.println(Arrays.binarySearch(stringArray, "Fred"));
45          System.out.println(Arrays.binarySearch(stringArray, "Doris"));
46
47          //copying a part of an array
48          System.out.println("\nPartial copies: the " +
49                          "Arrays.copy and copyRange methods");
50          copyIntArray = Arrays.copyOf(intArray, 4);
51          System.out.println(Arrays.toString(copyIntArray));
52          copyIntArray = Arrays.copyOfRange(intArray, 2, 10);
53          System.out.println(Arrays.toString(copyIntArray));
54
55          //setting all elements of a array to one value
56          System.out.println("\nFilling all or part of an array: " +
57                          "the Arrays.fill method");
58          Arrays.fill(intArray, 4);
59          System.out.println(Arrays.toString(intArray));
60          Arrays.fill(stringArray, 1, 4, "FillValue");
61          System.out.println(Arrays.toString(stringArray));
62      }
63  }
```

**Figure 6.27**
The application **ArraysClass**.

```
1    Outputting arrays using the Arrays.toString method
2    [Tom, Mary, Bob, Alice, Joe, Fred]
3    [3, 5, 2, 8, 6, 4]
4
5    Copying arrays using the Arrays.copyOf method
6    [Tom, Mary, Bob, Alice, Joe, Fred, null, null, null, null]
7    [3, 5, 2, 8, 6, 4]
8
9    Testing two arrays for equality: the Arrays.equals method
10   true
11   false
12
13   Sorting all or part of an array: the Arrays.sort method
14   [Alice, Bob, Fred, Joe, Mary, Tom]
15   [3, 2, 5, 6, 8, 4]
16
17   Searching for a value: the Arrays.binarySearch method
18   2
19   -3
20   Partial copies: the Arrays.copy and copyRange methods
21   [3, 2, 5, 6]
22   [5, 6, 8, 4, 0, 0, 0, 0]
23
24   Filling all or part of an array: the Arrays.fill method
25   [4, 4, 4, 4, 4, 4]
26   [Alice, FillValue, FillValue, FillValue, Mary, Tom]
27
```

**Figure 6.28**
The output produced by the application **ArraysClass**.

## 6.10 MULTI-DIMENSIONAL ARRAYS

Java, like most programming languages, supports multidimensional arrays. Like one-dimensional arrays, each memory cell in a multidimensional array shares the same "first name," the name of the array, and all of the array's element must be the same type. To close out this analogy, unlike one-dimensional arrays, each element of multi-dimensional arrays have *two or more* unique last names.

The simplest multi-dimensional array is a two-dimensional array, which conceptually is a group of memory cells arranged in rows and columns (left side of Figure 6.29). In Java, there is no limit to the number of dimensions an array can have. Three-dimensional arrays can be visualized as multiple two-dimensional arrays each in a different plane (right side of Figure 6.30). In effect, we have added a depth dimension to the two-dimensional array. Because we live in a three-dimensional world, multi-dimensional arrays with more than three dimensions are not often used in programs, although there are times when they are useful.

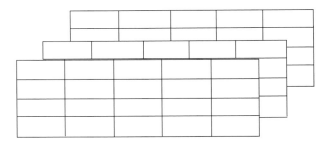

A Two-Dimensional Array

A Three-Dimensional Array

**Figure 6.29**
Visualization of a two- and three-dimensional array.

### 6.10.1 Two-Dimensional Arrays

A two-dimensional array is similar to a two-dimensional table with rows and columns. Two-dimensional arrays are typically used to store a group of data items for several entities. For example, a group of 5 examination grades for each of 4 students, or the 10 qualifying times for each of the 100 cyclists in the Tour de France. (A three-dimensional array with five planes could store the last five years' Tour de France qualifying time results, one year per plane.)

The names of the cells, called elements, that make up a two-dimensional array begin with the name of the array followed by the element's row and column number. Figure 6.30 shows the names of all of the twenty elements of a four-row by five-column two-dimensional array named grades.

The name of an array element can be used anywhere the name of a non-array variable can be used, e.g., in arithmetic expressions, in output and input statements, in argument lists, and on the right side of the assignment operator. When they are used, the element's row number is always written *before* its column number. Thus, we would code grades[2][4] to access the contents of the third row and fifth column of the grades array shown in Figure 6.30.

**NOTE**  *The indices of both the row and column numbers start from zero.*

The syntax used to declare a two-dimensional array is a simple extension of the one-dimensional array declaration syntax discussed in Section 6.3. The only difference is that an additional set of empty brackets is added before the name of the array, and the number of columns is specified

|  | column 0 | column 1 | column 2 | column 3 | column 4 |
|---|---|---|---|---|---|
| row 0 | grades[0][0] | grades[0][1] | grades[0][2] | grades[0][3] | grades[0][4] |
| row 1 | grades[1][0] | grades[1][1] | grades[1][2] | grades[1][3] | grades[1][4] |
| row 2 | grades[2][0] | grades[2][1] | grades[2][2] | grades[2][3] | grades[2][4] |
| row 3 | grades[3][0] | grades[3][1] | grades[3][2] | grades[3][3] | grades[3][4] |

**Figure 6.30**
The element names of a four-by-five two-dimensional array named grades.

after the number of rows. (In a similar way, a third set of empty brackets and the number of planes is added to declare a three-dimensional array.) The Java statement to declare the two-dimensional *integer* array `grades`, shown in Figure 6.30, would be:

```
int[][] grades = new int[4][5]; //four rows and five columns
```

The equivalent two-line syntax is:

```
int[][] grades;
grades = new int[4][5];
```

The numeric literals in the second line of the two-line grammar can be replaced with integer variables to specify or change the size of the array at run time.

The memory model of a two dimensional array is different than the one dimensional array memory models shown in Figures 6.3 and 6.7, and will be discussed in Section 6.10.2. It provides additional constants that store the number of elements in each row of the array. For example, for the array depicted in Figure 6.30, there would be four additional constants:

```
grades[0].length, grades[1].length, grades[2].length, and grades[3].length
```

These variables would store the number of elements in row 0, 1, 2, and 3 respectively; in this case integer value 5. The public final constant `grades.length` would still store the number of rows in the array.

### Initializing Two-Dimensional Arrays

The elements of a two-dimensional array can be initialized when the array is declared. As with one-dimensional arrays, when this is done the number of rows and columns in the array is not specifically stated but is implied from the number of initial values, and an initial value must be specified for each element of the array. The initialization syntax is most easily understood if we consider a two-dimensional array to be a one-dimensional array with each of its elements being a row of the two-dimensional array. In addition, it is most easily read if we write each row's initial values on a separate line. The array declaration below uses this coding style to declare the two-dimensional array `ages` depicted in Figure 6.31, initializing all of its values to those shown in the figure.

```
int[][] ages = { {10, 11, 12, 13, 14},
                 {20, 21, 22, 23, 24},
                 {30, 31, 32, 33, 34},
                 {40, 41, 42, 43, 44} };
```

**NOTE**    *If one element of an array is to be initialized, all of the elements must be initialized.*

The number of initial values specified in each row of a two-dimensional array need not be the same. The following declaration produces the array `ages`, shown in Figure 6.32, which has a different number of elements in each of its three rows:

```
int[][] ages  = { {10, 11, 12},
                  {20, 21, 22, 23, 24},
                  {30, 31} };
```

| | column 0 | column 1 | column 2 | column 3 | column 4 |
|---|---|---|---|---|---|
| row 0 | 10 | 11 | 12 | 13 | 14 |
| row 1 | 20 | 21 | 22 | 23 | 24 |
| row 2 | 30 | 31 | 32 | 33 | 34 |
| row 4 | 40 | 41 | 42 | 43 | 44 |

**Figure 6.31**
The elements of the array grades after its initialization.

Inside the array object ages, the public variables named ages[0].length, ages[1].length, and ages[2].length would store the integer values 3, 5, and 2, respectively. These variables are used in the code fragment below to output all of the elements of the array ages shown in Figure 6.32 and are often used by methods that are passed two-dimensional arrays to determine the number of columns in each row of the array.

```java
for(int row = 0; row < ages.length; row++) //each row
{
    for(int col = 0, col < ages[row].length; col++) //each column in a row
    {
        System.out.print(ages[row][col] + " ");
    }
    System.out.println();
}
```

| | column 0 | column 1 | column 2 | column 3 | column 4 |
|---|---|---|---|---|---|
| row 0 | 10 | 11 | 12 | | |
| row 1 | 20 | 21 | 22 | 23 | 24 |
| row 2 | 30 | 31 | | | |

**Figure 6.32**
The elements of the array ages after its initialization.

## 6.10.2 The Multi-Dimensional Array Memory Model

When we access the elements of a one-dimensional array in our programs, we should think of them as depicted in Figures 6.1: a column of variables each with its own index. Knowledge of their more complicated representation in memory, their *memory model* shown in Figure 6.3, is often necessary to understand array concepts beyond simply accessing the array's elements. For example, in Section 6.6.1 we used the one-dimensional array memory model to gain an understanding of how two methods could share the same array.

Similarly, to access the elements of multi-dimensional arrays we should think of them as depicted in Figures 6.29 through 6.32. However, an understanding of their representation in memory is necessary to understand the full power of this programming construct. Generally speaking, Java represents a multi-dimensional array as a grouping of one-dimensional arrays.

Consider the code segment below that declares a two-dimensional array `named prices`, containing two rows and three columns.

```
double[][] prices = { {12.4, 2.6, 3.2},
                      {11.6, 5.2, 9.8} };
```

The memory model Java uses to store these values is the grouping of one-dimensional arrays shown in Figure 6.33. The variable `prices` references a one-dimensional array of reference variables that stores the address of two additional one-dimensional arrays in the grouping. Each of these additional arrays stores the values of one row of the array in *row-major order*, which means that all of the elements of one row of the array (in this case whose type is `double`) are stored in contiguous memory cells.

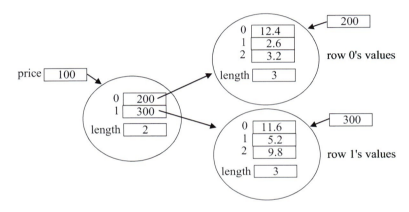

**Figure 6.33**
The memory model of a 2 row x 3 column two-dimensional array

Generally speaking, for a two-dimensional array, the first element of the reference variable array always refers to the array that stores the values in row 0 of the array; the second element locates the array that stores the values in row 1 of the array, and so on. Each of the arrays referred to by the reference variable array are of the type mentioned in the array's declaration. For an array with 4 rows and 6 columns, there would be one 4-element reference variable array and four 6-element arrays containing the values stored in the rows of the array.

Examining the representation of the two-dimensional array shown in Figure 6.33, we can deduce that the number of rows in the array can be fetched by coding `prices.length`, and the number of columns in the first and second rows of the array can be fetched by coding `prices[0].length` and `prices[1].length` respectively.

For the array `ages` shown in Figure 6.32, the following code would produce the output: 3 5 2.

```
System.out.println(ages[0].length + " " + ages[1].length + " " +
                   ages[2].length);
```

An understanding of the two-dimensional memory model is essential to understanding that the array `ages` shown in Figure 6.32 could be created with the following code segment, which produces the three lines of output shown below it.

```java
int[] row0 = {10, 11, 12};
int[] row1 = {20, 21, 22, 23, 24};
int[] row2 = {30, 31};

int[][] ages = new int[3][]; // the number of columns
                             // need not be specified

ages[0] = row0;
ages[1] = row1;
ages[2] = row2;

for(int row = 0; row < ages.length; row++)
{
    for(int col = 0; col < ages[row].length; col++)
    {
        System.out.print(ages[row][col] + " ");
    }
    System.out.println();
}

10 11 12
21 22 23 24 25
30 31
```

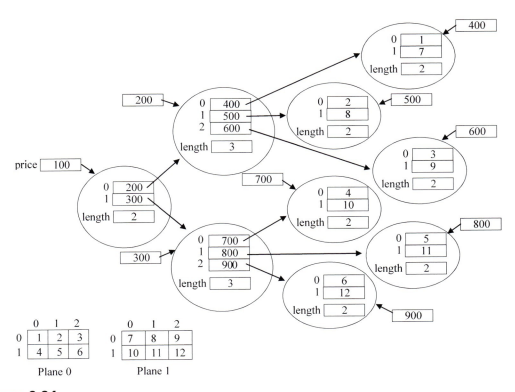

**Figure 6.34**
Memory model of a 2 row x 3 column x 2 plane three dimensional array

The memory model of a 2 row x 3 column x 2 plane three-dimensional array is shown in Figure 6.34., assuming the values stored in the two planes of the array are shown at the bottom of the figure.

## 6.11 ADDITIONAL SEARCHING AND SORTING ALGORITHMS

Not all searching and sorting algorithims are equivalent from a speed of execution viewpoint, which is referred to as an algorithm's *speed complexity*. The two algorithms previously discussed in this chapter, the Sequential Search and the Selection Sort, are on the slower end of the spectrum. Two of the three algorithms discussed in this section, the Binary Search and the Merge Sort are considerable faster, and this speed difference becomes significant when the number of items to be searched through, or sorted, is large. All three of the algorithms are more easily understood by visualizing the array of values horizontally, with element zero on the left side.

### 6.11.1 The Binary Search Algorithm

A precondition of the Binary Search algorithm is that the n element array being searched is *sorted* in *ascending* order. Consider the sorted array shown below. Its left and right boundaries are elements zero and 17 respectively.

The first item examined by the Binary Search algorithm would be the middle element of array whose index is the average of the left and right boundary element numbers: 8. If this is the item being searched for, the algorithm ends and returns the index of the middle element. If the item being searched for is smaller than the middle element, then the item must be to the left of it because the array is sorted in ascending order. Therefore, the right boundary of the array being searched is moved left to the index of the middle element minus 1. Otherwise, the item being search for must be larger than the middle element, so the left boundary of the array to be searched is moved right to the index of the middle element plus 1.

This process continues until the item is found, or the left boundary of the array being searched becomes greater than the right boundary. In the later case, the item being search for is not in the array, and the algorithm returns -1.

Figure 6.35 illustrates three iterations of the algorithm's search process used to locate the value 27 stored in an n = 18 element sorted array. In the 1st iteration the index of the left boundary of the array to be searched (designated **L1** in the figure) is set to zero, and the right boundary (**R1**) is set to n -1 , which in this case is 17. The middle element (**M1**) is set to (**L1** + **R1**) / 2 = 8. Since element 8 stores the value 39 which is larger than 27, the right boundary of the array to be searched (**R2**) is set to element **M1** – 1 = 7.

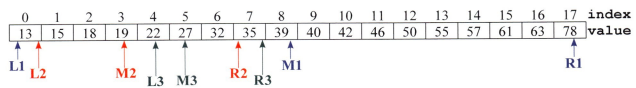

Li is the left boundary, **Ri** is the right boundary, and **Mi** is the middle element for iteration **i**

**Figure 6.35**
Progression of the Binary Search for the value 27

The second iteration sets the middle element (M2) to (L2 + R2) / 2 = 3. Since element 3 stores the value 19 which is smaller than 27, the left boundary of the array to be searched (L3) is set to element M2 + 1 = 4. The third iteration sets the middle element (M3) to (L3 + R3) / 2 = 5. Since element 5 stores the value being searched for, 27, the algorithm returns the index of M3:= 5.

Because the Binary Search algorithm eliminates half of the remaining array from the search by moving the left or right array boundaries during each iteration of its search process, its average speed is proportional to $\log_2(n)$, where n is the number of items to be searched. This is denoted as $O(\log_2(n))$, which is called the algorithm's Big-O value. In contrast, the average speed of the Sequential Search is proportional to n, denoted as O(n). For small values of n, their speed difference is negligible. However, when n is one million, the Binary Search algorithm is approximately 50,000 times faster than the Sequential Search algorithm.

The method `binarySearch`, shown in Figure 6.36, is an implementation of the Binary Search algorithm. It searches the array passed to its first parameter, `sortedArray`, for the value passed to its second parameter, `target`. Line 20 returns the index of the array that contains the target value. If the value is not in the array, line 23 returns -1.

Lines 3 and 4 initialize the left and right boundaries of the array to the lowest and highest element numbers in the array. The while loop (lines 7 – 22) ends when the array's left boundary index becomes greater than its right boundary index. Each iteration of the loop, these indexes are used on line 9 to compute the middle element number. This element of the array is part of the Boolean conditions on lines 10 and 14 that determines if the right (`target` value smaller than the middle element), or left (`target` value larger than the middle element) array boundary should be changed. If neither boundary should be changed, the target value must equal the middle element, and line 20 returns its index. Otherwise, the next iteration of the loop begins with line 9 recalculating the middle index between the repositioned right and left boundaries.

## 6.11.2 The Insertion Sort Algorithm

Consider the array depicted in Figure 6.37a, in which all of its elements are in ascending order except the right most element, element 7. We can use a three-step process to sort the array. It begins, by copying element 7's value into the variable `temp`, shown at the top left side of the figure. Then all of the elements left of element 7 that are greater than temp (elements 6 through 3), are moved right one position in the array, as shown in Figure 6.37b. Finally `temp` is copied into the last

```
1   public int binarySearch(int[] sortedArray, int target)
2   {
3     int leftBoundary = 0;
4     int rightBoundary = sortedArray.length - 1;
5     int middleIndex;
6
7     while (leftBoundary <= rightBoundary)
8     {
9       middleIndex = (leftBoundary + rightBoundary) / 2;
10      if(target < sortedArray[middleIndex])
11      {
12        rightBoundary = middleIndex - 1;
13      }
14      else if(target > sortedArray[middleIndex])
15      {
16        leftBoundary = middleIndex + 1;
17      }
17      else
19      {
20        return middleIndex;
21      }
22    }
23    return -1;
24  }
```

**Figure 6.36**
The method binarySearch

element of the array moved right (element 3), as shown in Figure 6.37c. This set of three sorting operation steps, which assumes that the only element out of ascending order in an array to be sorted is its *right most* element, forms the basis of the Insertion Sort.

To comply with the assumption of the operation set, the Insertion Sort begins on the left side of the array and uses the operations to sort elements 0 and 1. This subset of the array is sorted first, because within it only the right most element (element 1) could be out of order. Having sorted this

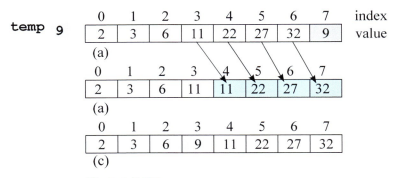

**Figure 6.37**
A sorting process used by the Insertion Sort

two-element subset, the set of operations is then used to sort element 0, 1, and 2. Within this subset of the array, since elements 0 and 1 have already been sorted, only the right most element (element 2) could be out of order. This process of expanding the sub-array to be sorted by one element per iteration of the operation set continues until the array is sorted.

The four tables presented in Figure 6.38 show the changes to an array whose elements are: 6, 3, 5, 1, 4, 7, and 2, during the first four iterations of the operation set. Starting with the first iteration (a sub-array size of two elements) at the top of the figure, the three rows of each table shows the changes made by the three steps of the sorting operation during one of the four iterations.

**Figure 6.38**
The first four iterations of the Insertion Sort

The method insertionSort shown in Figure 6.39, is an implementation of the Insertion Sort algorithm. Generally speaking, this algorithm is not any faster than the Selection Sort. The Big-O value of both of these algorithms is O($n^2$).

Each iteration of the for loop, that begins on line 3, corresponds to one of the three row tables shown in Figure 6.38. Beginning with element 1, during each iteration another element of the array is placed in its proper position within the sorted array to its left. Lines 5 and 6 place the element's value and current index into the variables temp (first row of the tables) and tempsIndex respectively. The while loop that begins on Line 7 determines the sorted position of the element by decrementing tempsIndex by 1 (line 10), whenever the right term in its Boolean condition determines that the element just to the left of tempsIndex is greater than the value stored in temp. When this is the case, line 9 also copies the larger value into the element one position to its right (arrows in Figure 6.38).

When the while loop ends, the array is as depicted in the second row of the tables shown in Figure 6.38, and tempsIndex stores the index of the sorted position of the ith element of the original array. Line 12 sets that element's value into element tempsIndex, and the array is as depicted

```
1    public static void insertionSort(int[] anArray)
2    {
3      for(int i = 1; i < anArray.length; i++)
4      {
5        int temp = anArray[i];
6        int tempsIndex = i;
7        while(tempsIndex > 0 && anArray[tempsIndex - 1] > temp)
8        {
9          anArray[tempsIndex] = anArray[tempsIndex - 1];
10         tempsIndex--;
11       }
12       anArray[tempsIndex] = temp;
13     }
14   }
```

**Figure 6.39**
The method insertionSort

in the third row of the tables shown in Figure 6.39

### 6.11.3 The Merge Sort Algorithm

The Merge Sort algorithm is one of the fasted sorting algorithms. Its average speed to sort n items is proportional to $n\log_2(n)$. The Big-O value of Selection Sort and Insertion Sort is $O(n^2)$, which makes them 50,000 times slower than the Merge Sort when the number of items to be sorted, n, is one million. It is also an example of a divide-and-conquer algorithm because it divides the array into a left and right sub-array, and applies the merge process to each of these two sub-arrays.

**The Merge Process**

Consider the two sorted arrays, left and right, shown in the lower portion of Figure 6.40. They can be *merged* into one sorted array named temp, shown at the top of the figure, using a process that begins by comparing the values in the first two elements of the arrays (1 and 2), and then copies the smaller of the two values into element zero of the array temp. For the arrays shown in the figure, left[0] would be compared to right[0], and left[0] would be copied into temp[0].

Then the value in the next element of the array that had the smaller element in the previous comparison is used in the next comparison, and the smaller value is copied into element 1 of the array temp. For the arrays shown in the figure, left[1] would be compared to right[0], and right[0] would be copied into temp[1].

This process is repeated in subsequent comparisons, until all of the elements of one array have been copied to the array temp. For the arrays shown in the figure, this would occur after the values 1 to 6 have been copied into the array temp. Then, all of the remaining elements of the other array (the values 7 and 8) are copied into temp. The values of the array elements used in

Figure 6.40 were chosen to be representative of the order in which the merge process copies them into the array `temp`.

The merge process forms the basis of the Merge Sort algorithm that accepts *one* unsorted array, and sorts it into ascending order. Since the merge sort process sorts *two* arrays that are already *sorted*, the question arises: how can we use it to sort one unsorted array?

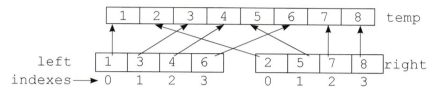

**Figure 6.40**
The merge process

To answer this question, consider the case when the values in the left half of the array are already sorted, and the values in the right half of the array are also already sorted. This would be the case if the array to be sorted was a concatenation of the arrays `left` and `right` shown in Figure 6.40. Then the Merge Sort algorithm could divide the array into a left and right sub-array, and apply the merge process to these two sub-arrays. It would complete the sort by copying the contents of the array `temp` back into the array to be sorted. The signature of a method that implements this merge process could be:

```java
public static void merge(int[] anArray, int[] temp)
```

But once we realize that the merge process could be used to sort any portion of an array that could be divided into two adjacent already sorted parts that were not necessarily of equal length, we could increase the usability of the method by adding three parameters to the method. These parameters would define the left index of the left sorted part named `from`, the right index of the adjacent right sorted part named `to`, and the ending index of the left sorted part named `mid`. (The implied starting index of the right adjacent part would be `mid +1`.)

For example, if we concatenate the arrays left and right in Figure 6.40 to form one eight-element array: `from` would be 0, `mid` would be 3, and `right` would be 7. The expanded signature of the method is given below.

```java
public static void merge(int[] anArray, int from, int mid, int to,
                         int[] temp)
```

The application MergeApp shown in Figure 6.41 contains an implementation of the merge method on lines 20–62 that uses this signature. The application invokes it on lines 12 and 16 to merge sorted portions of the arrays `arrayA` and `arrayB`, defined on lines 7 and 8. The output produced by lines 11, 13, 15, and 17 is shown in Figure 6.42. The blue and yellow highlighting in this figure indicates the left and right sub-arrays to be merged. The line below each of the highlighted lines shows the contents of the arrays after the merge method has sorted the highlighted portions of the arrays.

Lines 23 and 24 set the integer variables `leftIndex` and `rightIndex` to the index of the first element in the left sub-array and the index of the first element of the right sub-array respectively. Line 25 initializes `tempIndex`, the index of the element in the `temp` array to be written to, to the index of the first element in the left array. The while loop that begins on line 28, continues until all of the elements of the left or right sub-arrays have been written to the array `temp`.

During each iteration of the loop, a value from the left (line 32) or the right (line 37) sub-array is copied into the array `temp`, depending on which one is smaller, as determined by the `if-else` statement that begins on line 30. Before the next loop iteration begins, either line 33 or line 38 moves either the left or right sub-array index to the right one element, and line 40 moves `tempIndex` right one element.

After all of the elements of the left or right sub-arrays have been written to the array `temp`, lines 44–55 writes the uncopied elements of the other array to the array `temp`. Then lines 58–61 writes the now sorted values from the array `temp` back into the left and right sub-arrays.

```
1    import java.util.Arrays;
2
3    public class MergeApp
4    {
5      public static void main(String[] args)
6      {
7        int[] arrayA = {1, 3, 4, 6, 2, 5, 7, 8};
8        int[] arrayB = {1, 3, 4, 6, 2, 5, 7, 8};
9        int[] temp = new int[8];
10
11       System.out.println(Arrays.toString(arrayA));
12       merge(arrayA, 0, 3, 7, temp);
13       System.out.println(Arrays.toString(arrayA));
14
15       System.out.println("\n" + Arrays.toString(arrayB));
16       merge(arrayB, 2, 3, 4, temp);
17       System.out.println(Arrays.toString(arrayB));
18     }
19
20     public static void merge(int[] anArray, int from, int mid,
21                              int to, int[] temp)
22     {
23       int leftIndex = from;
24       int rightIndex = mid + 1;
25       int tempIndex = from;
26
27       //copy smaller of left and right sub-arrays to temp
28       while(leftIndex <= mid && rightIndex <= to)//not at rt. side
29       {
30         if(anArray[leftIndex] < anArray[rightIndex])
31         {
32           temp[tempIndex] = anArray[leftIndex];
```

```
33            leftIndex++;
34          }
35        else
36        {
37          temp[tempIndex] = anArray[rightIndex];
38          rightIndex++;
39        }
40        tempIndex++;
41      }
42
43      //reached rt. side of one sub-array; copy other into temp
44      while(leftIndex <= mid)
45      {
46        temp[tempIndex] = anArray[leftIndex];
47        tempIndex++;
48        leftIndex++;
49      }
50      while(rightIndex <= to)
51      {
52        temp[tempIndex] = anArray[rightIndex];
53        tempIndex++;
54        rightIndex++;
55      }
56
57      // copy sorted subset from temp to anArray
58      for(tempIndex = from; tempIndex <= to; tempIndex++)
58      {
60        anArray [tempIndex] = temp[tempIndex];
61      }
62    }
63  }
```

**Figure 6.41**
The application **mergeApp**

```
[1, 3, 4, 6, 2, 5, 7, 8]
[1, 2, 3, 4, 5, 6, 7, 8]

[1, 3, 4, 6, 2, 5, 7, 8]
[1, 3, 2, 4, 6, 5, 7, 8]
```

**Figure 6.42**
The output produced by the application **mergeApp**

## The Merge Sort Process

The one remaining question is: how will the Merge Sort algorithm use the merge method to sort an array of n elements that does not consist of two adjacent sorted n/2 arrays? The answer to this question is that it recursively divides the array into two unsorted sub-arrays until the size of each sub-array is one. This is called the recursion's base case. Nothing further needs to be done to sort these one-element sub-arrays; each one is already sorted. Now the `merge` method can be used to merge adjacent one-element sub-arrays into two-element sorted sub-arrays; then adjacent two element sub-arrays can be merged into sorted four-element sub-arrays, with the process continuing until each sorted sub-array contains n/2 elements. This merge sort process ends with one final invocation of the `merge` method to merge the two sorted n/2 sub-arrays into a sorted array.

As an illustration of this merge sort process, consider the case of an unsorted eight-element array, n = 8, that has been divided into left and right unsorted four-element sub-arrays. Before the merge method is invoked to sort these sub-arrays, each is divided into two-element sub-arrays, and then each of these is divided into one-element sub-arrays. Since each of these one-element sub-arrays can be considered sorted, the merge process can begin.

The bottom row of Figure 6.43, row 1, depicts these left and right one-element sub-arrays. The left side of row 2 shows a red one-element sub-array and its adjacent blue one-element sub-array, being merged (by the `merge` method) into the red two-element sub-array shown on the left side of row 3. Similarly, rows 4 and 5 show two adjacent one-element sub-arrays being merged into the blue two-element sub-array on row 5. Then these adjacent two-element sorted sub-arrays are merged into the red sub-array shown on row 6.

After a similar process is performed on the four one-element sub-arrays on the right side of row 1, the `merge` method is invoked one more time to sort the two sorted four–element sub-arrays (one of which is shown on the left side of row 6 of Figure 6.43).

The static method `mergeSortProcess`, shown in Figure 6.44, is a *recursive* implementation of the merge sort process described above. (We will learn more about coding recursive methods in Chapter 9.) Assuming the following code segment was used to invoke the method:

```java
int[] arrayA = {5, 3, 6, 2, 1, 8, 7, 4};
int[] temp = new int[arrayA.length]
mergeSortProcess(arrayA, 0, arrayA.length-1, temp)
```

the array `arrayA` would be sorted by the method.

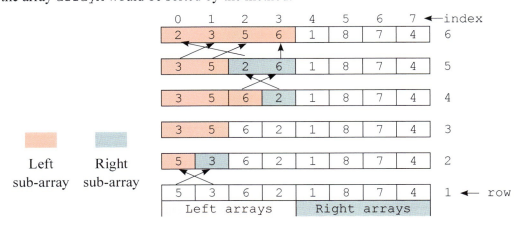

**Figure 6.43**
The sorting of the left four-element sub-array using the merge process

Line 9 is the first of a set of seven recursive invocations that sorts the left half of the array, anArray. The second and fifth of these invocations divides the left half of the array into the set of four one-element sub-arrays depicted on the left side of row 1 of Figure 6.43. The second invocation merges elements 0 and 1 (rows 2 and 3 of the figure), and the fifth invocation merges elements 2 and 3 (rows 4 and 5 of the figure). Line 11 recursively sorts the right side of the array in a similar manner. Finally, line 13 invokes the merge method to combine the left and right sub-arrays into one sorted array. It is important to realize that each recursive invocation of the method could reenter the if statement that begins on line 4, before its execution ends.

```
1    public static void mergeSortProcess(int[] anArray, int from,
2                                        int to, int[] temp)
3    {
4      if(from < to) //one or more elements to sort
5      {
6        int middle = (from + to) / 2;
7
8        //sort the left sub-array
9        mergeSortProcess(anArray, from, middle, temp);
10       //sort the right sub-array
11       mergeSortProcess(anArray, middle + 1, to, temp);
12       //merge the left and right sorted sub-arrays
13       merge(anArray, from, middle, to, temp);
14     }
15   }
```

**Figure 6.44**
The recursive method mergeSortProcess

## 6.12 DELETING, MODIFYING, AND ADDING DISK FILE ITEMS

In Section 4.8.5, it was mentioned that Java, like most programming languages, does not contain a method to delete or modify a file data item or to add a data item anywhere in the file except at its end. These operations can be performed by algorithms that *combine* the disk I/O methods discussed in Chapter 4 with the use of arrays and loops. An array is used because *all* of the data must be read into RAM memory to delete or modify a data item or to add an item to an arbitrary position in a data file. Because disk data files normally contain large data sets, this can easily be accomplished by reading each item into an element of the array and placing the read statement inside a loop.

In the remainder of this chapter, we will discuss these algorithms and their processing of a file of primitive data items that are all of the same type. The use of algorithms to process a file that contains the data members of several objects, with the data members possibly being different types, will be discussed in Chapter 7.

### Deleting an Item From a Disk File

The algorithm to delete a data item from a file would be:

1.  Open the file, read the number of items contained in the file, and allocate an array of that size

2. Inside a `for` loop, read all of the file's data items into the array

3. Close the file

4. Delete and recreate the file and write the new number of items to the file

5. Inside a `for` loop, write the elements of the array, *except* the item to be deleted, to the file

6. Close the file

When the algorithm ends, there would be one less item in the file, the deleted item, and the remaining data would be in their original order.

The item to be deleted can be specified by its position in the file, e.g., "delete item number 25," or by specifying the data value to be deleted, e.g., "delete the deposit 34.56." When the position in the file is specified, Step 5's loop variable is used to decide if the next element of the array should be written to the file. Assuming Step 1 of the algorithm stored the number of items read from the file in the variable `count`, and Step 2 reads the data into the array `data`, the following code fragment illustrates Step 5's process when deleting item 25 from the file:

```java
//delete item 25
for(int i = 0; i < count; i++)
{
    if(i != 25 - 1)
    {
        //write the item, data[i], to the file
    }
}
```

When the value of the data item to be deleted is specified, the decision to write the next element of the array back into the file is based on the contents of the array element. Assuming Step 1 of the algorithm stored the number of items read from the file in the variable `count` and then read the data into the array `data`, the following code fragment illustrates Step 5's process when deleting all of the occurrences of 35.56 from the file:

```java
//delete 35.56 from the file
for(int i = 0; i < count; i++)
{
    if(data[i] != 35.56)
    {
        //write the item, data[i], to the file
    }
}
```

The application `DeleteFileItem` shown in Figure 6.45 deletes a game score input by the program's user from the disk text file `scores.txt`. It uses the six-step algorithm discussed in this section and the file input and output methods discussed in Chapter 4. The number of items in the file is read from the file on line 16 and then used to size the array on line 17. It is also used on line 31 to write the new number of file items into the file after it is deleted and recreated by lines 29 and 30. The value to be deleted from the file is parsed into the variable `deletedItem` on line 35 and then used in the Boolean condition on line 38 to prevent the deleted item from being rewritten to the file.

```
1    import java.util.Scanner;
2    import java.io.*;
3    import javax.swing.*;
4
5    public class DeleteFileItem
6    {
7      public static void main(String[] args) throws IOException
8      {
9        double[] data;
10       double deletedItem;
11       int count = 0;
12
13       //Step 1: Open the file, read the number of items, allocate the array
14       File fileObject = new File("score.txt");
15       Scanner fileIn = new Scanner(fileObject);
16       count = fileIn.nextInt();
17       data = new double[count];
18
19       //Step 2: Read all of the file's data items into the array
20       for(int i = 0; i < count; i++)
21       {
22         data[i] = fileIn.nextDouble();
23       }
24
25       //Step 3: Close the file
26       fileIn.close();
27
28       //Step 4: Delete and recreate the file
29       FileWriter fileWriterObject = new FileWriter("data.txt");
30       PrintWriter fileOut = new PrintWriter(fileWriterObject, false);
31       fileOut.println(count - 1);
32
33       //Step 5: write the elements of the array without the deleted item
34       String s = JOptionPane.showInputDialog("enter score to delete");
35       deletedItem = Double.parseDouble(s);
36       for(int i = 0; i < count; i++)
37       {
38         if(data[i] != deletedItem)
39         {
40           fileOut.println(data[i]);
41         }
42       }
43
44       //Step 6: Close the file
45       fileOut.close();
46     }
47   }
```

**Figure 6.45**
The application **DeleteFileItem**.

### Detecting an End of a File

If the number of items in the file was not stored in the file, then line 16 of Figure 6.33 would be replaced with the following code fragment that counts the number of items in the file before the array is declared and then closes and reopens the file. In addition, line 31 would be removed from the program.

```java
while(fileIn.hasNext()) //count the data items
{
  count++;
  fileIn.nextDouble();
}
fileIn.close();
fileObject = new File("data.txt");
fileIn = new Scanner(fileObject);
```

### Modifying an Item Stored in a Disk File

The algorithm to modify an item in a disk file would be the same as the deletion algorithm except that an `else` clause would be added to Step 5's `if` statement (line 38 of Figure 6.33). Assuming the new value of the data item was stored in the variable `newValue`, the `else` clause would be coded as:

```java
else
{
   //write the new value to the file
}
```

Because the number of data items in the file would remain the same, Step 4 (line 31 of Figure 6.33) would write the original number of data items back into the file.

### Inserting a New Item into a File

To insert a new item into a file, its position in the file and its value must be known. The algorithm, shown below, is the same as the deletion algorithm except for Step 5, and the number of items in the file written to the file in Step 4 would be increased by one:

1. Open the file, read the number of items contained in the file, and allocate an array of that size
2. Inside a `for` loop, read all of the file's data items into the array
3. Close the file
4. Delete and recreate the file and write the new number of items to the file
5. Inside a `for` loop, write the elements of the array, *and the new item* to the file
6. Close the file

Assuming the following: the new item's position in the file is stored in the variable `itemNumber`; the new value is stored in the variable `newValue`; and position numbers in the file begin at zero, then the Step 5 `for` loop becomes:

```
//add newValue to the file at position itemNumber
for(int i = 0; i < count; i++)
{
  if(i == itemNumber)
  {
    //write the newValue to the file
  }
  //write the item, data[i], to the file
}
```

In addition to modifying text files and data files, these file operations will also enable us to record players' scores and update the high scores of a game.

## 6.13 CHAPTER SUMMARY

The concept of an array presented in this chapter provides us with a powerful tool for storing, retrieving, and processing data, especially large data sets. Unlike primitive variables, which contain only a single value, an array contains multiple data elements that are all of the same type. When an array is created, its data items are all initialized to their default values. The index of an array always begins at zero and extends to n-1, where n is the number of elements in the array (the *size* of the array). To distinguish one element from another, we use an index after the array name, as in an element's name, grade[4], which is the name of the fifth element of the array.

In Java, all arrays are stored inside an object. This object is declared using a syntax similar to that used to declare non-array objects. A set of brackets is added to the declaration after the object's type, and a second set of brackets containing the size of the array is written after the keyword new. Every array has a public data member named length, which stores the size of a one-dimensional array or the number rows in a two-dimensional array. Two-dimensional arrays also contain an array of public data members named length whose elements store the number of elements in each row of the array.

Loops are often used to efficiently input, output, and process the data in an array using the loop variable as an index into the array. Array elements can be used in any Java statement where a variable can be used; they can receive input and be output, used in mathematical expressions, assigned values, passed as an argument into a method, and returned from a method. In addition, like any object, the location of an array object can be passed to a method and returned from it. The concept of parallel arrays is implemented using either multiple one-dimensional arrays or using multidimensional arrays. In either case, we can use this concept to organize related information such as student ID numbers and GPAs and quickly and efficiently access it.

Sorting arrays and searching them for particular values, including minimum and maximum values, are very common programming operations. Three commonly used sorting algorithms are the Selection Sort, the Insertion Sort, and the Merge Sort. Two commonly used search algorithms are the Sequential Search and the Binary Search. The Merge Sort and the Binary Search algorithms are more complex than the other three algorithms, and the Binary Search requires that the elements of the array being searched be sorted in ascending order. However, these two algorithms offer an increasingly large speed advantage over the other three algorithms as the number of items to be sorted, n, increases.

An array's elements can be either primitive or reference variables. An array of objects can be simulated by creating an array in which each element is a reference variable. For example, we can create an array of snowmen, or more correctly, an array of reference variables that refer to Snowman objects. The position or speed of all these Snowmen objects can easily be changed within a loop to create a parade of Snowmen objects that appear to be marching around the game board screen.

The System class method arraycopy is used to copy a sequential set of elements from one array into another array. Other API methods include toString, sort, and fill, which converts all of an array's elements to a single string, efficiently sorts the elements into ascending order, or sets an array's elements to a given value, respectively.

Finally, arrays are used in the implementation of algorithms that insert new items into a text file and that delete or update existing items. These algorithms use the disk I/O methods discussed in Chapter 4 to read an existing data set from a disk file into an array. Then, the file is deleted and recreated, and the data set is written back to the file with new items inserted into it, or existing items deleted or updated.

## Knowledge Exercises

1. True or false:
   a) An array is a technique for naming groups of memory cells.
   b) All the elements of an array need *not* be of the same data type.
   c) The size of an array can be dynamically allocated.
   d) Once an array is created, its size cannot be changed.
   e) The largest index of an array is its length - 1.
   f) An array cannot be passed into a method.
   g) Arrays can only be one or two dimensional.
   h) Arrays can be initialized when they are created.
   i) An efficient way to perform an operation on an entire array is to process it in a loop.
   j) In Java, the first index or subscript always begins with 1.
   k) An enhanced for loop (aka a for-each loop) can be used to sum all of the elements of an array of integers to 23.
   l) An enhanced for loop (aka a for-each loop) can be used to set all of the elements of an array of integers to 23.
   m) The Insertion Sort algorithm is faster than the Merge Sort Algorithm.
   n) The Sequential Search algorithm is slower than the Binary Search algorithm

2. Give two features of an array that makes it more powerful than a set of non-array variables.

3. Mention at least two differences between an array element and a non-array variable.

**4.** Explain the difference between an array and an array object.

**5.** Assume that the array `gameScores` has been created using the following declaration:

```
int[] gameScores = new int[100];
```

Answer the following questions with respect to this array:

True or false:

**a)** The size of this array is 100.

**b)** The first element in this array is `gameScores[1]`

**c)** The last element in this array is `gameScores[100]`

**d)** This is a valid assignment to this array: `gameScores[5] = 93.2;`

**e)** When invoked, `gameScores.length` would return the value 99.

**f)** Give the Java statement to store the value 12 the second element of the array.

**g)** Give the statement to output the last element of the array to the system console.

**h)** Give the Java statements to output all of the elements of the array to the system console.

**i)** Give the Java statements to output the average of all of the elements of the array.

**j)** Draw a picture of the memory allocated by the declaration.

**6.** Find at least two errors in the following code and explain what should be done to fix them:

```
//prices start at $0 (not available) and increase from $5, to $10, $15....
    int size = 25;
    double[] ticketPrice = new double [size];
    for (int i = 1; i <= 25; i++)
    {
       ticketPrice[i] = i * 5;
    }
    System.out.println ("The price of a tier " + " i " + " ticket is:   " +
                        ticketPrice[i]);
```

**7.** Assume that you have been given these declarations below, answer the questions that follow them.

```
        final int MAX = 45;
        int[] x = new int[MAX];
        double[] y = {22.54, 3.6, 54.76, 10.8, 5.62};
        double z;
```

**a)** How many elements does the array x contain?

**b)** What is the subscript or index of the last element of array x?

**c)** What is the largest valid subscript of array y?

**d)** Write the statements to multiply the very first element of the array by 7.

**e)** Write the statements that increase the last element of array y by 20.5.

**f)** Write a statement that assigns the sum of the first 3 elements of array y to z.

**8.** Give a statement to allocate an array that can store:

**a)** Three thousand characters using the one-line declaration syntax

**b)** Two hundred strings using the two-line declaration syntax

   c) Five thousand `Snowmen` objects using the one-line declaration syntax

   d) Five quiz scores for 100 students

9. Give the statement(s) to:

   a) Declare three parallel arrays that can store the names, weights, and target weights for 50 people in a weight loss clinic

   b) Output all of the information stored in the arrays declared in part a to the system console, one person per line

   c) Output Joe Smith's weight and target weight to the system console

   d) Output all of the names to the system console in alphabetical order

10. Write a method that is passed two arrays of doubles, each of the same size, and returns an array whose ith element is the sum up to the ith elements of the two arrays passed to it.

11. Which arrays shown in Figure 6.34 would change, and how would they change, if the number of planes in the array grew from 2 to 10?

12. What changes would have to be made to the merge method shown in Figure 6.41 to merge two portions of an array that are sorted in descending order?

## Programming Exercises

1. Refer to the program in Figure 6.24. Modify the code in the `keyStruck` method to include the instructions to move the third parent snowman and its child 20 pixels to the right each time the "M" key is struck.

2. As part of a research project, you have collected the following data and have initialized and stored it in an initialized array using the declaration:

```java
int[ ] ages = {21, 32, 45, 23, 19, 41, 27, 20 , 21, 43,
               39, 24, 25, 22, 44};
```

   Write a program to do each of the following tasks (with all output going to the system console):

   a) Search for a value input by the user and report if it is found or not

   b) Search for and output the minimum and maximum ages in the data set

   c) Calculate and output the average age

   d) Copy the ages to a new array called `sortedAges`, sort this array in ascending order, and then output both arrays

3. Write a program to accept a given number of names, input by the program user, and write the names in sorted order to a disk file named Students.txt. Then, ask the user which name should be eliminated from the file and eliminate that name from the file. Finally, read all of the names from the modified file and output them in reverse alphabetical order.

4. Write a graphical application that includes a class that defines a solid disk object whose diameter, color, and location are specified when an object is constructed. When the program is launched, the user should be asked how many disks to display on the game board, then asked the size, color, and location of each disk. The disks should then be displayed on the game board at their specified locations.

5. Modify the program described in Programming Exercise 4 so only disks whose diameters are 50 pixels or smaller are displayed when the down-arrow key is struck and only those disks that are larger than 50 pixels are displayed when the up-arrow key is struck.

6. Write a graphical application that includes a class that defines a flower with a red center whose petal color and location is specified when a `Flower` object is constructed. When launched, the program should display a garden of 100 flowers at random locations on the lower portion of the game board. The (x, y) locations of the flowers will be randomly generated and be in the range ($7 \leq x \leq 500 - w$) and ($300 \leq y \leq 500 - h$), where w and h are the width and height of the flower.

7. Modify the program described in Programming Exercise 6 so every time the down-arrow game board button is clicked, 20 of the remaining flowers disappear from the garden.

8. Write a graphical application that includes a class that defines a light-gray colored raindrop whose height is 6 pixels and whose width is 4 pixels. When the application is launched, 300 raindrops should appear on the game board at random locations. The (x, y) locations of the raindrops will be in the range ($7 \leq x \leq 496$) and ($30 \leq y \leq 494$).

9. Modify the program described in Programming Exercise 8 so when the Start button on the game board is clicked, the raindrops move downward two pixels every 40 milliseconds, giving the appearance that it is raining. When a raindrop reaches the bottom of the game board (the y coordinate of its location is greater than 500), reset its y coordinate to 30.

10. Add the garden described in Programming Exercise 6 to Programming Exercise 8.

11. Add the garden described in Programming Exercise 6 to Programming Exercise 9.

12. Using the skills developed in this chapter, continue the implementation of the parts of your game that require multiple instances of one of your game pieces. To facilitate the processing of these objects, they should be part of an array of objects.

## Enrichment

Investigate the Quick Sort and Heap Sort algorithms and discuss their advantages and disadvantages over the Selection Sort algorithm.

Investigate why the Binary Search algorithm is faster than the Sequential Search algorithm.

## References

Knuth, Donald, *The Art of Computer Programming, Volume 3: Sorting and Searching,* 2nd ed. New York: Addison-Wesley, 1998.

Levitin, Analy. *Introduction to the Design and Analysis of Algorithms*, 3rd ed. New York: Addison-Wesley Longman, 2011.

McAllister, William. *Data Structures and Algorithms.* Sudbury, MA: Jones and Bartlett Publishers, 2009.

# METHODS, CLASSES, AND OBJECTS: A SECOND LOOK

## In this chapter

In this chapter, we will extend our knowledge of the features that can be incorporated into the classes we write, our knowledge of the String and the wrapper classes, and explore two other often-used classes defined in the Java Application Programming Interface (API). We will learn the techniques and motivation for writing classes whose objects share a data member and whose methods invoke each other, as well as the techniques and motivation for defining classes whose data members are objects. In addition, we will discuss what it means to compare, copy, and clone objects and how to write methods that perform these operations. An understanding of the topics in this chapter will enable us to more efficiently write complex programs, increase the reusability of the classes we write, and process numeric values that are beyond the size and precision of the primitive numeric types.

After successfully completing this chapter, you should:

- Understand static data members and their ability to share storage among all instances of a class within an application
- Become more familiar with the distinction between public and private methods
- Understand the fundamental differences between deep and shallow comparisons and copies
- Be able to compare two instances of a class
- Be able to use the deep copy technique to copy data members and clone objects

- Know how to create strings from primitive values, convert strings to characters, tokenize a string, and utilize other common string-processing methods
- Be able to create and use a wrapper class object and its autoboxing feature
- Understand how to aggregate an object into a class and the advantages of doing so
- Comprehend the relationship between, and implementation of, inner and outer classes
- Be able to use the `BigInteger` and `BigDecimal` classes for processing large numbers of arbitrary precision

## 7.1 STATIC DATA MEMBERS

Consider a worker class named `Student` that contains two data members named `idNumber` and `gpa` and a two-parameter constructor. The following code fragment would produce the `Student` objects `ryan` and `mary` depicted in Figure 7.1, assuming the first and second arguments passed to the constructor are used to initialize data members `idNumber` and `gpa`, respectively. As discussed in Chapter 3, each instance contains storage for its two data members.

```
Student ryan = new Student(1567, 3.26);
Student mary = new Student(2373, 2.87);
```

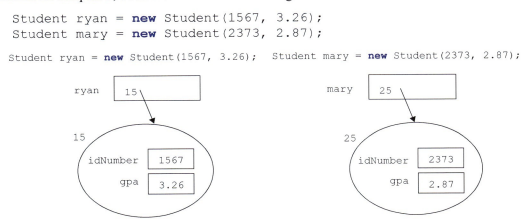

**Figure 7.1**
Two **Student** objects and the data members allocated to them.

Like methods, data members of a worker class can be declared to be static data members by including the keyword **static** in the data member's declaration statement. For example:

```
private static int studentCount = 0;
```

When a data member of a class is declared to be static, each instance of the class declared within an application does not contain storage for the data member. Rather, *one* storage cell is *shared* among all objects declared within an application. For example, if an additional static data member named `studentCount` were added to the class `Student`, the memory allocated to the two `Student` instances `ryan` and `mary` shown in Figure 7.1 would be expanded by one shared integer variable shown at the bottom of Figure 7.2.

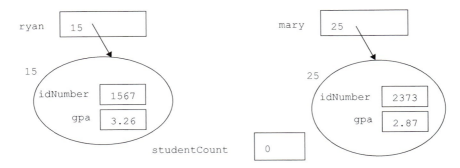

**Figure 7.2**
Two **Student** objects and the shared static data member **studentCount**.

A very common use of static data members is to keep track of the number of instances of a class (objects) that have been declared within an application. To accomplish this, a line of code to increment the static data member is included in each of the class's constructors. Below is an implementation of the Student class's two-parameter constructor that uses the class's static data member studentCount to keep track of the number of objects declared in the class:

```
public Student(int idNumber, double gpa)
{
    studentCount++; //counts the number of Student objects declared
    this.idNumber = idNumber;
    this.gpa = gpa;
}
```

Figure 7.3 shows the changes to the data member studentCount after two Student objects have been constructed with this version of the constructor. Normally, static data members in a class are declared with *private* access, and a get method is coded in the class to fetch the value of the data member. When the data member is being used to count the instances of a class, a set method is not coded to generally limit the data member's write access to the class's methods (and specifically, to the class's constructors).

**Figure 7.3**
The changes to the static data member **studentCount** after two objects are created

It is good coding style to declare the get method to be a static method. This forces the invoker (as shown below) to code the name of the class in the invocation statement rather than the name of an object, which implies to its reader that the value being fetched does not belong to a particular object. For example:

```java
int numberOfStudents = Student.getStudentCount();
```

Figure 7.4 uses the concepts discussed in this section to keep track of the number of instances of the class Student that are declared within in a program. Line 2 declares the static data member studentCount and initializes it to zero. This variable is incremented within the class's two-parameter constructor on line 8 every time the constructor is invoked to create an object. The class's toString method (lines 13–18) does not return the value of the static variable because normally the string it returns includes only the values of a particular object's data members. The number of Student instances declared in a program can be fetched by invoking the class's getStudent-Count method (lines 20–23). As previously discussed, this is a static method, and the class does not contain a setStudentCount method to restrict applications' write access to the static variable.

```java
1   public class Student
2   { private static int studentCount = 0;
3     private int idNumber;
4     private double gpa;
5
6     public Student(int idNumber, double gpa)
7     {
8       studentCount++; //counts the number of Student objects declared
9       this.idNumber = idNumber;
10      this.gpa = gpa;
11    }
12
13    public String toString()
14    {
15      String s = "id is " + idNumber +
16                  "\ngpa is "  + gpa;
17      return s;
18    }
19
20    public static int getStudentCount()
21    {
22      return studentCount;
23    }
24  }
```

**Figure 7.4**
The worker class **Student**.

Another common use of static data members in a class is to define final constants, because to have every instance of the class store the same constant is not an efficient use of main memory. For example:

```java
private static final int DEGREES_PER_CIRCLE = 360;
```

This data member could not be assigned a new value, and could be used in the code of any method in its class by simply coding the name of the variable. If the data member is declared with `public` access, then methods that are not part of the class could also use the variable by preceding the method invocation with the name of the class in which the constant is defined followed by a dot. For example:

```
Math.PI; //PI is a data member of the Math class defined
         // as a public, static, final constant
```

and the statement `Math.PI = 10.2;` would result in a translation error caused by the by the attempted assignment of a new value.

## 7.2  METHODS INVOKING METHODS WITHIN THEIR CLASS

A method in a worker class can invoke another method in its class. This is a common coding technique and, if used properly, can reduce the time required to develop a class and make our programs easier to read and understand.

Suppose that the UML diagram that specified the class `Student` shown in Figure 7.4 also required a method named `show` to be part of the class that outputs the annotated values of the data members of an object to the system console. One way to code the method would be:

```
public void show()
{
   String s = "id is " + idNumber +
              "\ngpa is "  + gpa;
   System.out.println(s);
}
```

However, a better way to code this method would be to take advantage of the fact that the UML diagram also specified that a `toString` method would be part of the class, and a method in a class can invoke other methods in its class. Knowing this, the `show` method would be coded after the `toString` method was completed and verified (taken for a test drive), so it could be invoked to perform some work for the `show` method. This approach reduces the code of the `show` method to one executable statement, as shown below:

```
public void show()
{
   System.out.println(toString()); //toString does all the work
}
```

Figure 7.5 is an expanded version of the class `Student` shown in Figure 7.4 with this coding of the `show` method added to it (lines 25–28).

Normally, when a nonstatic worker method is invoked within client code, its name is preceded by the name of an object followed by a dot. It would be impossible to use this syntax to invoke the `toString` method on line 27 of Figure 7.5 because objects (instances of worker classes) are declared in client code. Because line 27 is syntactically correct, the question of which object's data members will be output to the console by the invocation of toString on line 27 arises. The answer is: the object the client code used to invoke the show method. When a nonstatic method of a class is invoked by another method in the class, the method operates on the same object upon which the method invoking it is operating.

For example, the toString method invoked on line 27 of Figure 7.5 would return a string containing Ryan's student information when the following client-code fragment was executed:

```
StudentV2 ryan = new StudentV2(1567, 3.26);
ryan.show();
```

_____
**NOTE**    *When a method in a class invokes another method in its class, the invocation statement is not preceded by the name of an object followed by a dot, and both methods operate on the same object.*

```
1    public class StudentV2
2    { private static int studentCount = 0;
3      private int idNumber;
4      private double gpa;
5
6      public StudentV2(int idNumber, double gpa)
7      {
8        studentCount++; //counts the number of Student objects declared
9        this.idNumber = idNumber;
10       this.gpa = gpa;
11     }
12
13     public String toString()
14     {
15       String s = "id is " + idNumber +
16                  "\ngpa is "  + gpa;
17       return s;
18     }
19
20     public static int getStudentCount()
21     {
22       return studentCount;
23     }
24
25     public void show()
26     {
27       System.out.println(toString());
28     }
29   }
```

**Figure 7.5**
The class **StudentV2**.

## Private Class Methods

Another example of a worker class method invoking a method in its class evolves from the design process discussed in Section 1.7. When a UML diagram of a class specifies that a complicated method is to be included in the class, it is good programming practice to divide it into several simpler methods that are added to the complicated method's class. This is consistent with the divide and conquer problem-solving technique. Once each of the simpler methods have been coded and tested, often in parallel by several different programmers, the complicated method is written as a series of invocations of the simpler methods that are part of its class.

Because the only reason the simple methods were written was to perform the work of a more complex method in their class, the simpler methods are normally declared to be *private* methods. Private methods can only be invoked by the code of other methods within their class, and their signature begins with the keyword **private** rather than with the keyword **public**. When this is done, we say that the method has private access, and an attempt to invoke a private method from within a method that is not a member of its class results in a translation error. Often, methods are declared private to prevent methods that are not part of their class from invoking them. We will discuss this further in Section 7.4.

## 7.3 COMPARING OBJECTS

In Section 6.8, we discussed algorithms for searching, finding minimums and maximums, and sorting an array of objects. Fundamental to all of these algorithms is the ability to compare two objects. Generally speaking, the phrase "compare two objects" is ambiguous. It could mean that we want to compare the contents of a particular data member of two objects or the contents of two or more data members of two objects, or it could mean that we want to compare the contents of the reference variables that refer to the objects. Therefore, before we write a method that compares two objects for a particular application, we have to define what it means to "compare two objects" in the context of that application.

The simplest case is when the objects being compared are strings, but even then we would have to decide whether to simply compare the length of the strings or compare the strings for equality or lexicographical order and decide if these comparisons should be case sensitive. Once we define what it means to compare two string objects for a particular application, then in most cases, either the `String` class's length method or its `equals` or `compareTo` method (or its case-insensitive versions of these methods) can be used to compare the strings. The use of these methods to compare string objects was discussed in Section 4.2.3, and the use of these methods to compare data members of objects that are strings was discussed in Section 6.8.

When the objects being compared are not strings, we normally add a method to the object's class to perform the comparison after defining what it means to compare two objects. It is good coding style to name these methods `equals` or `compareTo`, or to at least use these words in a longer method title.

A fish tank analogy is useful in gaining an understanding of how to write and use these methods as well as the methods that will be discussed in the next section of this chapter. Figure 7.6

depicts two snowman objects: `sm1` and `sm2` in a fish tank. In this analogy, reference variables float at the top of the tank because they are light (They only contain one address). Objects are depicted at the deeper levels of the tank because they contain multiple data members, which make them heavy. Our snowmen contain three data members: each snowman's (x, y) location and a reference variable name.

A *shallow* comparison is performed at the surface of the tank. It compares the contents of the two reference variables that float on the surface of the tank (e.g., `sm1` and `sm2` in Figure 7.6). A *deep* comparison is performed at the bottom of the tank. A deep comparison compares the contents of two objects. The methods that perform shallow and deep comparisons are fundamentally different and will be discussed separately.

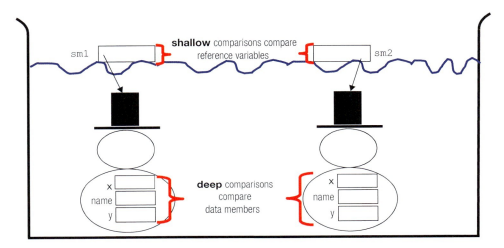

**Figure 7.6**
A fish tank analogy of shallow and deep comparisons.

### 7.3.1 Shallow Comparisons

In Chapter 4, we used the relational operators to compare two primitive values. For example, to determine if the values stored in the integer variables `age1` and `age2` are equal, we used the equality operator (==):

```
if(age1 == age2)
```

This comparison is a *shallow comparison* because primitive variables contain one value, so they would float on the top of a fish tank. Because reference variables also float, the same syntax used to perform a shallow comparison of two primitive values can be used to perform a shallow comparison of two objects. In effect, a shallow comparison of two objects determines if two reference variables refer to the same object.

Normally, a method named `equals`, such as the method `equals` in the `String` class, performs a *deep* comparison of two objects. It compares information contained inside the objects. For this reason, when coding a shallow `equals` method in the class of the objects being compared it is good coding practice to name the method `shallowEquals`. This name clearly indicates that the method is making a shallow comparison. The following method, which would be coded inside the class `ParentSnowman` (Figure 6.18), performs a shallow comparison of the `ParentSnowman` object that invoked it and the object passed to its parameter. It uses the equality relational operator to perform the comparison.

```java
public boolean shallowEquals(ParentSnowman ps) //a shallow comparison
{
    if(this == ps) //this contains the address of the invoking object
    {
     return true; //the invoking object and ps refer to the same object
    }
    else
    {
      return false; //ps does not reference the invoking object
    }
}
```

An exception to this comparison-method naming convention is the method `equals` in the API class `Object`. It performs a shallow comparison of two objects. The following code fragment illustrates the use of this shallow comparison method. It outputs the Boolean value `true` and then `false` because the variables `ps1` and `ps2` contain the same address and `ps1` and `ps3` do not.

```java
ParentSnowman ps1 = new ParentSnowman();
ParentSnowman ps2 = ps1; //ps2 is initialized to the address in ps1
ParentSnowman ps3 = new ParentSnowman();
boolean sameAddresses;

sameAddresses = ps1.equals(ps2); //shallow comparison, returns true
System.out.println(sameAddresses);
sameAddresses = ps1.equals(ps3); //shallow comparison, returns false
System.out.println(sameAddresses);
```

## 7.3.2 Deep Comparisons

Deep comparisons compare the contents of two objects' data members. As previously mentioned, before we write a method that performs a deep comparison for a particular application, we have to determine which of the objects' data members to compare for that application. For example, if we decide that two snowmen are equal if they are at the same game board position, then the x and y data member of the two objects would be compared. Once this decision is made, the class's `get` methods are used to fetch the data members, and they are compared using the relational operators if they are primitive variables. If they are reference variables that refer to other objects, they are compared using the deep comparison method in the objects' class.

The method shown in Figure 7.7, which would be coded in the class `ParentSnowman`, performs a deep comparison of two `ParentSnowman` objects: the object that invokes it and the object passed to its parameter. As depicted in Figure 7.6, each `ParentSnowman` object contains its (x, y) location and a reference to its family name (a string). The method returns `true` when the two objects are at the same game board (x, y) location *and* the objects' family name, referenced by string data member `name`, are the same.

```
1   public boolean equals(ParentSnowman ps) //a deep comparison
2   {
3     if(x == ps.getX() && y == ps.getY() &&
4         name.equals(ps.getName()))
5     {
6       return true; //same location and family name
7     }
8     else
9     {
10      return false; //different location and/or family name
11    }
12  }
```

**Figure 7.7**
A deep comparison method named **equals** that would be part of the **ParentSnowman** class.

It should be noted that the invocation of the `equals` method on line 4 of Figure 7.7 is an invocation of the `String` class's `equals` method. This method is invoked because `name` is a string variable and the argument that follows its name on line 4, `ps.getName()`, returns a reference to a `String` object.

There are four common errors made when coding the third term of the Boolean condition on lines 3 and 4 of Figure 7.7:

```
1. name == ps.getName()
2. this.getName() == ps.getName()
3. name.equals(ps)
4. this.equals(ps)
```

When either of the first two errors is made, a shallow comparison of the `name` data members is performed, and the Boolean condition evaluates to `false` even when the strings are the same. The two addresses, not the strings, are being compared. When the third error is made, a string is being compared to a `ParentSnowman` object, and the `Object` class's `equals` method is invoked, which also makes a shallow comparison.

When the fourth error is made, the program ends in a runtime *StackOverflow* error. Two `ParentSnowman` objects are being compared causing line 4 to repeatedly invoke the same method of which it is a part. This is a concept called recursion. It is not considered a syntax error because when recursion is properly used, it can facilitate the coding of many algorithms. We will learn more about the proper use of this coding technique in Chapter 9.

Deep comparisons are also performed to compare the relative order of two objects. A method that compares two objects to determine their relative order is normally named `compareTo`, and it returns an integer. The string class contains a method named `compareTo` that determines the lexicographical order of two `String` objects. Aside from changing the name of the method presented in Figure 7.7 and the returned type and value, `compareTo` methods would use the less than (<) or the greater than (>) operator to compare primitive data members and use previously coded `compareTo` methods to compare data members that are objects.

## 7.4 COPYING AND CLONING OBJECTS

The deep and shallow fish tank analogy also helps us to understand the techniques used to copy and clone objects. We can make both shallow and deep copies of objects, and clones of objects can easily be created from deep copies of objects. Figure 7.8 illustrates the difference between a shallow and a deep copy. Shallow copies copy the contents of one object's reference variable into another object's reference variable. Deep copies copy all of the values of one object's data members into the data members of another object. We will begin with a discussion of shallow copies.

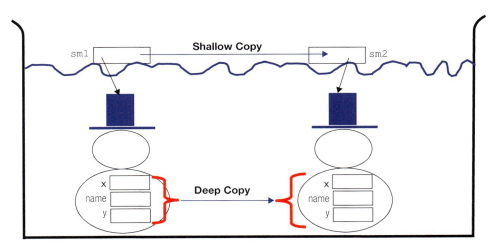

**Figure 7.8**
A fish tank analogy of shallow and deep copies.

### 7.4.1 Shallow Copies

In Chapter 2, we used the assignment operator to copy the contents of one primitive variable into another. For example, the following line of code copies the value stored in the integer variable `age1` into the variable `age2`:

```
age2 = age1;
```

This statement actually performs a shallow copy between two primitive variables because primitive variables contain only one value, so they would float on the top of a fish tank. Because reference variables also float (contain one value, an address) and the assignment operator can be used to assign reference variables, the same syntax is used to make a shallow copy of an object. The following line of code makes a shallow copy of object `sm1` into object `sm2`:

```
sm2 = sm1; //a shallow copy of object sm1 into object sm2
```

Although we say we are making a shallow copy of an object, we are actually copying the contents of one object's reference variable into the other object's reference variable, as shown at the top of Figure 7.8. It is important that we understand the consequences of this.

Referring to Figure 7.8, after the shallow copy of object `sm1` into `sm2` is complete, the address of the snowman object on the right side of the fish tank that was stored in the reference variable `sm2` has been overwritten with the address of the snowman object on the left side of the fish tank. Now both reference variables, `sm1` and `sm2`, refer to the *same* object. As a result, the snowman on the left now has two names. In addition, the snowman on the right side of Figure 7.8 is no longer part of the program (unless another variable in the program also stored its address) because the address of the object is no longer known to the program. When an object's address is not stored in a program reference variable, the Java memory manager reclaims its storage.

> **NOTE** *A shallow copy gives one object two names, and it may eliminate an object from the program.*

The following code fragment makes a shallow copy of object `ps1` into `ps2`, and as a result outputs the data members of the object declared on line 1 twice:

```
1   ParentSnowman ps1 = new ParentSnowman(250, 250, "A");
2   ParentSnowman ps2 = new ParentSnowman(10, 20, "X");
3
4   ps2 = ps1; // makes a shallow copy of object sm1 into object ps2
5   System.out.println(ps1.show());
6   System.out.println(ps2.show());
```

### 7.4.2 Deep Copies and Clones

As shown in the bottom of Figure 7.8, when we make a deep copy of an object, the values of its data members are copied into the data members of another object. Unlike performing a shallow copy, when a deep copy is complete both objects *still exist*, and the values stored in their data members are identical. The method `arraycopy` discussed in Section 6.9.1 can be used to deep copy one array object into another.

Generally speaking, a method has to be added to a class to be able to make deep copies of instances of the class. A deep copy method uses the class's `set` methods to copy the data members of the object that invoked it into the data members of the object sent to its parameter.

The method shown in Figure 7.9 is a deep copy method, which would be coded in the class `ParentSnowman`. As depicted in Figure 7.8, each `ParentSnowman` object contains its (x, y) location and the object's family name, referenced by the string data member `name`:

```
1   public void deepCopy(ParentSnowman ps) //a deep copy into ps method
2   {
3       ps.setX(x);
4       ps.setY(y);
5       ps.setName(name);
6   }
```

**Figure 7.9**
A **deepCopy** method that would be part of the **ParentSnowman** class.

In some cases, it is desirable to deep copy a subset of one object's data members into another object. When this is the case, it is good programming practice to name the method copy, rather than deepCopy, to alert the reader of the method's signature to the fact that not all of an object's data members are being copied.

## Cloning Objects

When an object is cloned, a new instance of the object's class is *created*, and the values of all of an existing object's data members are copied into the corresponding data members of the new object. If one object existed before the clone was created, *two* objects exist after it is created. To create a clone of an object, a method (usually named clone) is coded in the object's class. The method is a nonvoid method that returns the address of the newly created clone object.

Figures 7.10 and 7.11 show two alternate codings of a clone method, which would be coded in the class ParentSnowman. Both methods return the address of a newly created clone of the object that invoked them. The version shown in Figure 7.10 invokes the class's deepCopy method on line 4 to copy the values of the data members of the object that invoked the method into the clone object created on line 3. This version of the method assumes that the class contains a deep copy method and a no-parameter constructor. The new object is identical to (an exact copy of) an existing object.

```
1   public ParentSnowman clone() //a deep copy
2   {
3      ParentSnowman theClone = new ParentSnowman();
4      this.deepCopy(theClone);
5      return theClone;
6   }
```

**Figure 7.10**
A clone method using a **deepCopy** method that would be part of the class **ParentSnowman**.

The alternate coding of the clone method presented in Figure 7.11 uses the class's three-parameter constructor on line 3 to copy the values of the data members into the clone when it is constructed. If each object only contains three data members, then the newly created object is identical to (an exact copy of) an existing object. Generally speaking, to produce an exact copy of an object with n data members, this version of the clone method would have to invoke an n-parameter constructor on line 3 of Figure 7.11.

```
1   public ParentSnowman clone() //a deep copy
2   {
3      ParentSnowman theClone = new ParentSnowman(x, y, name);
4      return theClone;
5   }
```

**Figure 7.11**
An alternate clone method that would be part of the class **ParentSnowman**.

If it is appropriate to a particular application for the clone method to copy only a subset of an object's data members into the newly created object, then line 4 of Figure 7.10 would be changed to an invocation of the class's copy method, and the clone method would be renamed partialClone to indicate that invocations of this method do not make an identical copy of the object that invoked it.

Figure 7.12 is the code of a class named ParentSnowmanV2 that is an expanded version of the ParentSnowman class shown in Figure 6.18. The expanded version adds the following methods to the class:

- a copy method (lines 29–35) that copies four of an object's data members into another object
- a partial-clone method (lines 36–41) that invokes the copy method
- a shallow comparison method (lines 42–52)
- a deep comparison method (lines 53–63) that compares the hatColor data members of two objects
- a method that detects collisions (lines 64–75) between two snowmen

In addition, three static data members (lines 5–7) and a get method (lines 93–96) to fetch one of these data members have also been added to the class.

As discussed in Section 7.1, the three static data members declared on lines 5, 6, and 7 of Figure 7.12 are shared by all instances of this class. The first of these, snowmanCount initialized to zero, will be used to count the number of snowmen constructed. It is incremented inside the no-parameter constructor (line 18) and the four-parameter constructor (line 27) every time these constructors execute. The client can fetch the value of the variable snowmanCount using the get method coded on lines 93–96.

The other two static variables, w and h, store the width (40) and height (77) of a snowman, as depicted in Figure 4.9. Because the class's show method draws all snowmen with the same width and height, it is appropriate that these two variables be shared by all instances of the class. The variables are used in the Boolean condition coded within the collidedWith method (lines 64–75) that detects a collision between the snowman that invoked it and the snowman passed to its parameter ps. The values of the variables x and y used on lines 66 and 67, and within other methods of the class, are the values of the x and y data members of the snowman that invoked the method. Alternately, we could code these data members as this.x or this.y.

The class's copy method (lines 29–35) copies four of a snowman's seven nonstatic data members (lines 31–34). When the method completes its execution, the snowman passed to its parameter will have the same name, hat color, and location as the snowman that invoked the method. To prevent methods that are not part of the ParentSnowmanV2 class from erroneously invoking this method to make a deep copy of *all* of an object's data members, it is declared as a private method on line 29.

The copy method is invoked on line 39 by the class's partialClone method, which means that clones will have only the same name, hat color, and location as the snowman from which they were cloned. Their xSpeed, ySpeed, and visible data members will retain their default values (set on lines 12–14). As previously discussed in Section 7.2, the fact that the copy method is a private method does not prevent the class's clone method from invoking it.

The deep comparison performed on line 55 of the `equals` method determines if two snowmen have the same hat color by invoking the API `Color` class's `equals` method. If they do, the method returns the value `true`.

```java
1    import java.awt.*;
2
3    public class ParentSnowmanV2
4    {
5      private static int snowmanCount = 0;
6      private static int w = 40;
7      private static int h = 77;
8      private int x = 8;
9      private int y = 30;
10     private String name;
11     private Color hatColor= Color.BLACK;
12     private int xSpeed = 2;
13     private int ySpeed = 2;
14     private boolean visible = true;
15
16     public ParentSnowmanV2()
17     {
18        snowmanCount++;
19     }
20     public ParentSnowmanV2(int intialX, int intialY, String name,
21                            Color hatColor)
22     {
23        x = intialX;
24        y = intialY;
25        this.name = name;
26        this.hatColor = hatColor;
27        snowmanCount++;
28     }
29     private void copy(ParentSnowmanV2 ps) //copies 4 data members
30     {
31        ps.setX(x);
32        ps.setY(y);
33        ps.setName(name);
34        ps.setHatColor(hatColor);
35     }
36     public ParentSnowmanV2 partialClone()
37     {
38        ParentSnowmanV2 theClone = new ParentSnowmanV2();
39        this.copy(theClone);
40        return theClone;
41     }
42     public boolean shallowEquals(ParentSnowmanV2 ps)
43     {
44        if(this == ps)
45        {
```

```java
46         return true;
47       }
48     else
49     {
50         return false;
51     }
52   }
53   public boolean equals(ParentSnowmanV2 ps)
54   {
55     if(hatColor.equals(ps.getHatColor())) //same hat color
56     {
57         return true;
58     }
59     else
60     {
61         return false;
62     }
63   }
64   public boolean collidedWith(ParentSnowmanV2 ps)
65   {
66     if( !(x > ps.getX( ) + w || x + w < ps.getX( ) ||
67           y > ps.getY( ) + h || y + h < ps.getY( )))
68     {
69      return true;
70     }
71     else
72     {
73      return false;
74     }
75   }
76   public void show(Graphics g) // g is the game board object
77   {
78     int[] xPoly = {x + 20, x + 15, x + 25};
79     int[] yPoly = {y + 25, y + 30, y + 30};
80
81     g.setColor(hatColor);
82     g.fillRect(x + 15, y, 10, 15);  // hat
83     g.fillRect(x + 10, y + 15, 20, 2);  // brim
84     g.setColor(Color.WHITE);
85     g.fillOval(x + 10, y + 17, 20, 20); // head
86     g.fillOval(x, y + 37, 40, 40);  // body
87     g.setColor(Color.RED);
88     g.fillPolygon(xPoly, yPoly, 3); // nose
89     g.setColor(Color.BLACK);
90     g.setFont(new Font("Arial", Font.BOLD, 16));
91     g.drawString(name, x + 16, y + 62); // name
92   }
93   public static int getSnowmanCount()
94   {
```

```
95      return snowmanCount;
96    }
97    public int getXSpeed()
98    {
99      return xSpeed;
100   }
101   public void setXSpeed(int newXSpeed)
102   {
103     xSpeed = newXSpeed;
104   }
105   public int getYSpeed()
106   {
107     return ySpeed;
108   }
109   public void setYSpeed(int newYSpeed)
110   {
111     ySpeed = newYSpeed;
112   }
113   public void setHatColor(Color newHatColor)
114   {
115     hatColor = newHatColor;
116   }
117   public Color getHatColor()
118   {
119     return hatColor;
120   }
121   public int getX()
122   {
123     return x;
124   }
125   public void setX(int newX)
126   {
127     x = newX;
128   }
129   public int getY()
130   {
131     return y;
132   }
133   public void setY(int newY)
134   {
135     y = newY;
136   }
137   public String getName()
138   {
139     return name;
140   }
141   public void setName(String newName)
142   {
143     name = newName;
```

```
144    }
145    public boolean getVisible()
146    {
147       return visible;
148    }
149 }
```

**Figure 7.12**
The class **ParentSnowmanV2**.

The application shown in Figure 7.13 uses most of the concepts discussed up to this point in this chapter. When the game board's Start button is clicked, a snowman guard, whose family name is "G" patrols his game board garden looking for three green-hat snowmen who have wandered into the garden (Figure 7.14a). When he finds (collides with) one, he positions the green-hat snowman behind himself and continues his search (Figure 7.14b). Each time he reaches the border of his garden, he clones himself and posts the clone at the garden's edge (Figure 7.14c) to guard the garden from wandering snowmen. After the guard has found the three green-hat snowmen and posted six clones at the garden's boundaries, the animation ends (Figure 7.14d).

```
1    import edu.sjcny.gpv1.*;
2    import java.awt.*;
3
4    public class DeepAndShallow extends DrawableAdapter
5    {  static DeepAndShallow ge = new DeepAndShallow ();
6       static GameBoard gb = new GameBoard(ge, "Deep and Shallow");
7       static ParentSnowmanV2[] ps;
8       static boolean gameOver = false;
9
10      public static void main(String[] args)
11      {  ps = new ParentSnowmanV2[10];
12         ps[0] = new ParentSnowmanV2(100, 200, "G", Color.BLUE);
13         ps[1] = new ParentSnowmanV2(300, 275, "1", Color.GREEN);
14         ps[2] = new ParentSnowmanV2(300, 400, "2", Color.GREEN);
15         ps[3] = new ParentSnowmanV2(100, 100, "3", Color.GREEN);
16
17         gb.setTimerInterval(3, 20);
18         showGameBoard(gb);
19      }
20
21      public void draw(Graphics g)
22      {
23         for(int i = 1; i < ps.length; i++)
25         {
26            if(ps[i] != null) //the snowman exists
27            {
28               ps[i].show(g);
29            }
30         }
31         ps[0].show(g); //the patrolling guard
```

```
32      }
33
34      public void timer3()
35      { int x, speed, y;
36        if(ParentSnowmanV2.getSnowmanCount()== 10)
37        {
38          gb.stopTimer(3);
39          gameOver = true;
40        }
41        //move the guard
42        x = ps[0].getX();
43        x = x + ps[0].getXSpeed();
44        ps[0].setX(x);
45        y = ps[0].getY();
46        y = y + ps[0].getYSpeed();
47        ps[0].setY(y);
48
49        //is ps[0] at a border?
50        if(ps[0].getX() >= 460 || ps[0].getX() <= 6)
51        {
52          speed = ps[0].getXSpeed();
53          speed = -speed;
54          ps[0].setXSpeed(speed);
55          ps[ParentSnowmanV2.getSnowmanCount()] = ps[0].partialClone();
56        }
57        if(ps[0].getY() >= 423 || ps[0].getY() <= 30)
58        {
59          speed = ps[0].getYSpeed();
60          speed = -speed;
61          ps[0].setYSpeed(speed);
62          ps[ParentSnowmanV2.getSnowmanCount()] = ps[0].partialClone();
63        }
64
65        // has ps[0] found a green-hat wandering snowman?
66        for(int i = 1; i <= ps.length; i++)
67        {
68          if(ps[i] != null && ps[0].collidedWith(ps[i]) &&
69             !ps[0].equals(ps[i]))
70          {
71            ps[i].setX(ps[0].getX()); //position wanderer behind ps[0]
72            ps[i].setY(ps[0].getY());
73          }
74        }
75      }
76
77      public void leftButton()
78      {
79        if(gameOver == true)
80        { for(int i=0; i<=3; i++) //move the three intruders left
```

```
81          {
82            ps[i].setX(ps[i].getX() - (i * 3));
83          }
84          ps[0].setX(ps[0].getX() - 1); // move the guard
85        }
86      }
87    }
```

**Figure 7.13**
The application **DeepAndShallow**.

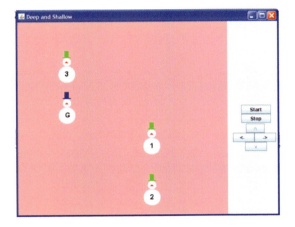

(a) Game board when the program is launched

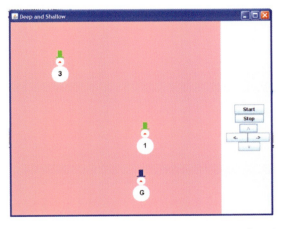

(b) Game board after green-hat snowman 2 is found and placed behind the guard

(c) Game board after three clones are posted and green-hat snowman 3 is about to be found

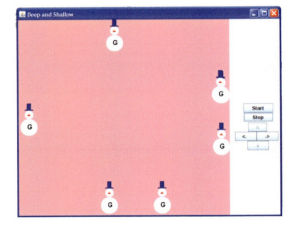

(d) Game board after six clones have been posted and all the wonderers have been found

**Figure 7.14**
Graphical output produced by the application **DeepAndShallow**.

This animation uses an array of ten `ParentSnowmanV2` snowmen objects, whose class is shown in Figure 7.12; the array, `ps`, is declared on line 11 of Figure 7.13. The patrolling snowman guard and the three green-hat snowmen, declared on lines 12–15, are referenced by indices 0 and 1–3, respectively. The remaining six elements of the array will be used to reference the clone snowmen.

The patrolling of the guard and the game termination are dependent on `timer3`. Line 17 of the main method sets `timer3`'s increment to 20 milliseconds, which means that the `timer3` call back method (lines 34–75) executes every 20 milliseconds. Its code determines if the patrol is over (lines 36–40), moves the patrolling guard (lines 42–56), posts clone guards (lines 50–63) and gathers up the intruders (lines 66–74). Line 36 determines if ten snowmen have been constructed, which would mean that all six guards have been posted. If so, the patrol is ended by line 38, which stops `timer3`. While the timer is ticking, lines 42–47 use the `Snowman` class's `set` and `get` methods to fetch, change, and overwrite the current values of the patrolling guard's (x, y) location every 20 milliseconds. This keeps the snowman on patrol.

Lines 50 and 57 determine if the guard has reached a vertical (line 50) or horizontal (line 57) edge of the garden. If it has, lines 52–54 and lines 59–61 reflect the guard off the edge by changing the sign of the x and/or y speed data member. Then, lines 55 and 62 invoke the `partialClone` method to create the clone snowman and store its returned address in the next available element of the array `ps`. The index of this element is the static value returned from the `getSnowmanCount` method, which is invoked on the left side of these lines. Because the `partialClone` method in the `ParentSnowmanV2` class (Figure 7.12) copies the current (x, y) position of the patrolling snowman into the clone, the clone is positioned at an edge of the garden.

Just before the `timer3` method ends, the `for` loop that begins on line 66 indexes through the last nine elements of the array. For each of these elements, the `if` statement's Boolean condition on lines 68 and 69 determines if:

- the element of the array references a snowman (is not `null`)
- the referenced snowman has collided with the patrolling guard (`ps[0]`) as determined by the `collidedWith` method
- the referenced snowman is an intruder as determined by the `equals` method (Its hat color is not equal to the guard's hat color.)

When this is the case, the (x, y) position of the green-hat wandering snowman is set to the (x, y) position of the patrolling guard (lines 71–72). On the next tick of `timer3`, the patrolling guard is only moved two pixels, so the guard and the snowman remain in a collided state, and the wandering snowman's position is reset by lines 71–72 to the patrolling guard's new position. The resulting effect is that the wandering snowman goes on patrol with the guard. It cannot be seen on patrol because line 31 of the `draw` method draws the patrolling guard, `ps[0]`, last (i.e., on top of the green-hat snowmen that have joined the patrol).

After the game ends, a series of left button clicks will separate the patrolling guard from the green-hat guards that have joined the patrol as shown in the center portion of Figure 7.15. This is accomplished by decrementing the x coordinates of each green-hat patrolling snowman (line 82) and the guard (line 84) by a different amount on each button click. Until the game ends, the left button is inactive because the body of the `if` statement on line 79 that separates the snowmen is only executed when the Boolean variable `gameOver` is set to `true` on line 39 of the `timer3` call back method.

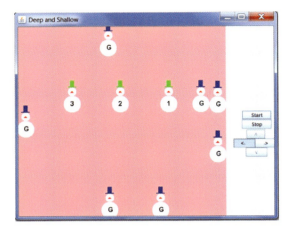

**Figure 7.15**
Graphical output produced by the application **DeepAndShallow**
after the animation ends and several left button clicks have been performed.

## 7.5 THE STRING CLASS: A SECOND LOOK

In Section 2.5, we discussed the creation of String objects, and in Section 4.2.3, we discussed the String class's methods equals and compareTo, which are used to compare two strings. In addition to these methods, the class contains a rich collection of methods used to create strings, to convert strings to characters, and to process string data.

### 7.5.1 Creating Strings from Primitive Values

Aside from the one-parameter constructor discussed in Chapter 2 that is passed a string literal or a string object such as

```
String name1 = new String("Robert");
String name2 = new String(name1);
```

the String class also contains several overloaded constructors. Each of these creates a new string object and returns its address. Two of the most frequently used constructors have a character array passed to them. The following code fragment uses the one-parameter version of these two methods to create the string name1 initialized to *Joanne Jones* and the three-parameter version to create the string name2 initialized to *anne Jo*. (The second argument sent to the three-parameter version of the constructor would be *zero* to include the first character of the array in the string object.)

```
char[] c = {'J', 'o', 'a', 'n', 'n', 'e', ' ', 'J', 'o', 'n', 'e', 's'};
String name1 = new String(c); //all characters used
String name2 = new String(c, 2, 7); //7 characters used, starts @ index 2
```

The static method valueOf in the String class also can be used to create and return the address of a string object initialized to the argument passed to it. Overloaded versions of this method use a `char`, `int`, `long`, `float`, or `double` parameter. Integer type `byte` and `short` arguments can be passed to the `int` parameter version of this method. In addition, there is a version of the method that accepts a character array passed to it. The following code fragment demonstrates the use of this overloaded method, to output the string: *x102030405.556.66yz*.

```java
char c = 'x';
byte b = 10;
short s = 20;
int i = 30;
long l = 40;
float f = 5.55f;
double d = 6.66;
char[] cArray = {'y', 'z'}

String s2 = String.valueOf(c) + String.valueOf(b) + String.valueOf(s) +
            String.valueOf(i) + String.valueOf(f) + String.valueOf(l) +
            String.valueOf(d) + String.valueOf(cArray);

System.out.println(s2);
```

### 7.5.2 Converting Strings to Characters

The `String` class method `charAt` can be used to convert a particular character contained in the string object that invoked it to type `char`, and it returns the character. The following code fragment stores the character `'S'` in the variable `c`.

```java
String aString = "Joe Smith";
char c = aString.charAt(4);   //character numbers begin at zero
```

The method `toCharArray` converts a string object that invokes it to an array of characters and returns the address of the array. After the following code fragment executes, the character arrays `c1` and `c2` contain the same character sequence:

```java
char[] c1 = {'J', 'o', 'a', 'n', 'n', 'e', ' ', 'R', 'a', 'y'};
char[] c2;
String aString = "Joanne Ray";
c2 = aString.toCharArray();
```

### 7.5.3 Processing Strings

The `String` class contains several methods to process string data. Two of these methods, `compareTo` and `equals` (and their related methods `compareToIgnoreCase` and `equalsIgnoreCase`) were discussed in Section 4.2.3. Table 7.1 describes other `String` class methods often used to process strings.

All of these methods are nonstatic methods. They can be used to determine the existence or location of a given substring in a string, fetch a substring from a specified position in the string, produce an uppercase or lowercase version of a string, replace the first or all occurrences of a substring with a given string, and tokenize a string to determine if a string begins or ends with a specified string.

**Table 7.1**

String Processing Methods in the **String** Class

| Function | Method and Parameter Type | Example and Description |
|---|---|---|
| Locate a given substring in a string | indexOf | `int i = s1.indexOf(target);` |
| | | Returns the index of the *first* occurrence of substring `target` in the string `s1` |
| | Parameter(s): String *or* | `int i = s1.indexof(target, start);` |
| | String, int | Returns the index of the first occurrence of substring `target` that begins at or after the index `start` in the string `s1` |
| Fetch a substring from a string | substring | `String s2 = s1.substring(start);` |
| | | Returns the substring of `s1` from index `start` to the end of `s1` |
| | Parameter(s): | `String s2 = substring(start, end);` |
| | **int** *or* | Returns the substring of `s1` from index `start` to |
| | **int, int** | index end −1 |
| Convert a string to upper or lower case characters | toUpperCase | `String s2 = s1.toUpperCase();` |
| | | Creates a clone of string `s1` consisting of all uppercase characters |
| | toLowerCase | `String s2 = s1.toLowerCase()` |
| | | Creates a clone of string `s1` consisting of all lowercase characters |
| Replace a given substring in a string with a given substring | replaceFirst | `String s2 = s1.replaceFirst(target, new);` |
| | Parameter(s): String, String | Returns a string with the first occurrence of the substring `target` in `s1` replaced with the string `new` |
| | replaceAll | `String s2 = s1.replaceAll(target, new);` |
| | Parameter(s): String, String | Returns a string with all occurrences of the substring `target` in `s1` replaced with the string `new` |
| Determine if a string begins or ends with a given string | startsWith | `boolean b = s1.startsWith(s2);` |
| | Parameter: String | Returns *true* if the string `s1` begins with the string `s2` |
| | endsWith | `boolean b = s1.endsWith(s2);` |
| | Parameter: String | Returns *true* if the string `s1` ends with the string `s2` |
| Tokenize a string | split | `String[] s1 = s1.split(" +");` |
| | | Returns a string array whose elements are the substrings of `s1` that are separated by one or more spaces |
| | Parameter(s): String *or* | `String[] s1 = s1.split(" +" , n);` |
| | String, int | Returns a string array whose elements are the substrings of `s1` that are separated by one or more spaces; there will be `n` or fewer elements in the returned array |

The application `StringProcessing` presented in Figure 7.16 uses some of the methods described in Table 7.1 to process a sentence input by the user. If the word *Hello* appears at the beginning of the sentence it is eliminated, and if the word *Tom* is in the sentence it is changed to *XXX*. A typical input and corresponding output are given in the left and right sides of Figure 7.17, respectively.

Line 16 uses the `String` class method `split` to create a new `String` array and place each word of the sentence input on line 11 into its elements. Then, it stores the address of the array returned from `split` in the variable `sArray` that is declared on line 8. The string consisting of a space followed by a plus sign passed to `split` on line 16 instructs the method to consider one or more spaces as tokens, in this case, word delimiters in the sentence. Line 19 clones the string input on line 11 and stores its address in the variable `s2`.

Lines 20–23 remove the word *Hello* from the beginning the cloned string s2. The `indexOf` method is used in the `if` statement's Boolean condition on line 20 to determine if the substring "*Hello*" begins at the index zero of the string s2. If it does, the `substring` method is used on line 22 to return the substring of s2 that begins at index 6 (after the word *Hello* and the space that follows it). The address of this new string object is stored in (shallow copied into) s2. Line 20 could have been coded as shown below:

```
if(s2.startsWith("Hello"))
```

The `replaceAll` method is invoked on line 24. It effectively creates a clone of the string object s2 and replaces all occurrences of the word *Tom* with the string literal "XXX." The returned address of the modified clone is then assigned to (shallow copied into) the variable s2.

```
1    import javax.swing.*;
2
3    public class StringProcessing
4    {
5      public static void main(String[] args)
6      {
7        String s1, s2;
8        String[] sArray;
9        int nWords;
10
11       s1 = JOptionPane.showInputDialog("Enter a sentence, Please\n" +
12                                        "Don't begin it with Hello,\n" +
13                                        "don't include the word Tom.\n" +
14                                        "Hello will be removed, and \n" +
15                                        "Tom replaced with XXX.");
16       sArray = s1.split(" +"); //stores each word in separate elements
17       nWords = sArray.length; //the number of words
18
19       s2 = new String(s1);
20       if(s2.indexOf("Hello") == 0)
21       {
```

```
22          s2 = s2.substring(6); // equivalent to s2 = s2.substring(0, 6)
23      }
24      s2 = s2.replaceAll("Tom", "XXX");
25
26      JOptionPane.showMessageDialog(null, "There are " + nWords +
27                                    " words in your sentence:\n" +
28                                    s1 + "\nThe revised sentence is:\n" +
29                                    s2);
30   }
31 }
```

**Figure 7.16**
The application **StringProcessing**.

(a) Input                                                    (b) Output

**Figure 7.17**
Input to the application **StringProcessing** and the corresponding output.

## 7.6 THE WRAPPER CLASSES: A SECOND LOOK

As discussed in Section 2.7.3, the six numeric wrapper classes (e.g., Integer, Double, etc.) contain methods that parse a string into integer or real values that can then be stored in primitive variables. In addition to these methods, all of the wrapper classes contain constructors to create a wrapper class object and also contain a collection of useful constants. A seventh wrapper class, the class Character, contains methods to perform common operations on characters. In this section, we will discuss these additional features of the wrapper classes and a related topic called autoboxing.

### 7.6.1 Wrapper Class Objects

A wrapper class's one-parameter constructor can be used to create a wrapper object. Wrapper class objects contain a single private primitive data member whose type is consistent with the class's name. For example, an object in the class Double contains a double primitive data member, and an instance of an Integer contains an int data member. The argument passed to the one-parameter constructor is stored in the object's data member. Envisioning the primitive value being wrapped in the object is the basis of the phrase *wrapper classes*.

The wrapper classes contain methods that return the value stored in an object's data member. These methods perform the function of `get` methods, but their names begin with the primitive type they return followed by the word *Value*. For example, the `Integer` class contains a method named `intValue` that returns the value of the class's integer data member, and the `Character` class contains the method `charValue` that returns the value of the class's character data member.

The `Integer` and `Double` classes also contains the methods `byteValue`, `shortValue`, `longValue`, `floatValue`, and `doubleValue` that cast the returned value of the data member into the other numeric primitive types. The other numeric wrapper classes contain five similarly named methods used to cast the data member they return into different numeric types. The following code segment wraps the value 20 in an `Integer` object and outputs the value as an integer and a double (e.g., 20 followed by 20.0):

```
Integer n = new Integer(20);
System.out.println(n.intValue() + " " +
                  n.doubleValue()); //outputs: 20 20.0
```

Each of the wrapper classes contains an `equals` and a `compareTo` method to perform a deep comparison of the data wrapped in the object that invoked them and the object sent to their parameter. The `equals` method returns the Boolean value `true` when the two objects are equal, otherwise it returns `false`. The equality operator (==) can be used to perform a shallow comparison to determine if two wrapper class reference variables refer to the same object.

The `compareTo` method returns an integer, which is negative, zero, or positive when the invoking object is less than, equal to, or greater than the object sent to its parameter, respectively. This version of the method coded in the numeric wrapper classes always returns -1, 0, or 1. The integer returned from the `Character` class's version of the method also gives an indication of the lexicographic separation of the characters contained in the objects being compared.

The following code fragment outputs the value -25. The value is negative because the character 'a' appears before 'z' in the Unicode table, and its absolute value is 25 because 'a' is 25 characters before 'z'.

```
Character c1 = new Character('a');
Character c2 = new Character('z');
System.out.println(c1.compareTo(c2));  //outputs: -25
```

The wrapper classes do not contain set methods to change the value of the data member wrapped in the object. This is because wrapper class objects, like `String` objects, are *immutable*. Once a value has been stored in a wrapper class's data member or inside a `String` object, the value cannot be changed. As is the case with `String` objects, the assignment operator can be used to reassign the address stored in the object's reference variable to a newly created object that contains the assigned (different) value. Although this gives the appearance that the value stored in the object has changed, in reality, the new value has been stored in a different object.

The assignment operator can also be used to shallow copy (the address of) two wrapper class objects. The following code fragment outputs the value 12.5 twice. Although it initially creates two instances of a `Double`, d1 and d2, after the third line executes, these variables reference the same object. The object containing the value *54.6* is reclaimed by the Java memory manager. The coding of the variables d1 and d2 in the argument sent to the `println` method are two implicit invocations of the `Double` class's `toString` method.

```
Double d1 = new Double(12.5);
Double d2 = new Double(54.6);
d2 = d1; //d1 and d2 reference the same object which contains 12.5;
System.out.println(d1 + " " +  d2); //outputs: 12.5 12.5
```

## 7.6.2 Autoboxing and Unboxing

The autoboxing feature of wrapper classes makes it easier to use wrapper class objects in our programs. This feature automatically "wraps" primitive values into wrapper objects. For example, wrapper class objects can be declared using the abbreviated syntax used to declare `String` objects, as discussed in Section 2.5. The following line of code wraps, or boxes, the integer 20 in an `Integer` object and writes its address in the variable n1:

```
Integer n1 = 20; //autoboxing of the value 20 in an object declaration
```

When this statement executes, the autoboxing feature creates an `Integer` wrapper object, stores (boxes) 20 in its data member, and returns the object's address. The statement is equivalent to the following statement:

```
Integer n1 = new Integer(20);
```

Autoboxing can also be used to effectively reassign or set the primitive value stored in a wrapper class object. The following code fragment outputs the value 3.6. The right side of line 2 uses autoboxing to create a new `Integer` wrapper object, stores 3.6 in its data member, and returns its address. The returned address is then stored in the variable n1. The wrapper object containing the value 2.5 is reclaimed by the Java memory manager.

```
1    Double n1 = 2.5;
2    n1 = 3.6; //Autoboxing of the value 3.6 in an assignment statement
3    System.out.println(n1);
```

It should be noted that if the value to be boxed in a wrapper class object (e.g., n2) is already stored in another wrapper class object (e.g., n1) of the same type, then a new object is not created. Rather, n2 is set to refer to n1's object. The only exception to this is if the long form of the object-declaration grammar is used to declare and initialize the new object. This caveat also applies to `String` objects. The code fragment shown in Figure 7.19 demonstrates these concepts, as well as the use of the equality operator and the wrapper class's `equals` method. The output it produces is shown at the bottom of the figure.

Lines 2, 7, and 11 do not create a new object but simply assign n2 the object's address that is stored in n1. Line 16 creates a new object even though the object n1 created on line 15 stores the same value because the long form of the object-declaration syntax (which includes the keyword **new**) is used to create it.

```
1    Integer n1 = 20;
2    Integer n2 = 20; //a new object is not created, n2 is assigned n1
3    if(n1 == n2) System.out.println("n1 and n2 refer to the same object");
4    if(n1.equals(n2)) System.out.println("n1 & n2 contain the same value");
5
6    n1 = 30;
7    n2 = 30; //a new object is not created, n2 is assigned n1
8    if(n1 == n2) System.out.println("n1 & n2 refer to the same object");
9    if(n1.equals(n2)) System.out.println("n1 & n2 contain the same value");
10
11   n2 = n1; //a new object is not created, n2 is assigned n1
12   if(n1 == n2) System.out.println("n1 & n2 refer to the same object");;
13   if(n1.equals(n2)) System.out.println("n1 & n2 contain the same value");
14
15   n1 = 40;
16   n2 = new Integer(40); //a new object is created
17   if(n1 == n2) System.out.println("n1 & n2 refer to the same object");
18   if(n1.equals(n2)) System.out.println("n1 & n2 contain the same value");
```

**Output produced:**

n1 & n2 refer to the same object
n1 & n2 contain the same value
n1 & n2 refer to the same object
n1 & n2 contain the same value
n1 & n2 refer to the same object
n1 & n2 contain the same value
n1 & n2 contain the same value

**Figure 7.18**
Examples of when autoboxing creates new objects.

The *unboxing* feature of wrapper classes allows us to use the name of a numeric wrapper class object in arithmetic expressions. The following code fragment outputs the values *7* and *16*. The value stored in the object n2 is unboxed from it on lines 2, 3, and 4. The unboxing fetches the value 7 from the object on lines 2 and 3, and the value 8 on line 4.

```
1    Integer n2 = 7;
2    int n3 = n2; //auto Unboxing of n2
3    n2++; //auto Unboxing of n2, incrementing, and Autoboxing the new value
4    n2 = n2 * 2; //auto Unboxing, multiplying, and Autoboxing the new value
5    System.out.println(n3 + " " + n2);
```

The location of wrapper class objects can be passed to and returned from a method using the same syntax used to pass any object's location to or from a method. The most common use of wrapper class objects is to pass a primitive value to a generic method that is expecting an object or to store a group of primitive values in a Java collection object. Generic methods and collections, and the role wrapper objects play in their use, will be discussed in Chapter 10.

### 7.6.3 Wrapper Class Constants

The six numeric wrapper classes all contain static data members named MAX_VALUE, MIN_VALUE, and SIZE. The values of a class's MAX_VALUE and MIN_VALUE constants are the maximum and minimum values that can be stored in the primitive numeric data member of an instance of that class. These are the same maximum and minimum values, shown in Table 2.1, that can be stored in primitive numeric *variables*. The value of the constant SIZE is the number of bits that make up the primitive data member's storage cell, which is also *shown in Table 2.1.*

The following code fragment produces the output 127 -128 8, which are the maximum and minimum values that can be wrapped in a Byte object, and the size of the object's data member (8 bits). These are the same values presented on the first row of Table 2.1, which specified the range and size of the primitive numeric types.

```
System.out.println(Byte.MAX_VALUE, + " " + Byte.MIN_VALUE, +
                   " " + Byte.SIZE);
```

### 7.6.4 The Character Wrapper Class

The wrapper class Character contains all of the methods, constants, and the autoboxing features of the numeric wrapper classes discussed previously in Section 7.6. Its value method, named charValue, returns the character stored inside the Character instance that invokes it. Naturally, the Character class's constants such as MAX_VALUE, MIN_VALUE, and SIZE store values relevant to primitive char values, and the class's methods operate on Character objects and are passed char parameters.

In addition to the analogous numeric wrapper class methods, the Character class contains two static methods named toUpperCase and toLowerCase that change the case of a character primitive passed to their char type parameter. The Character class also contains seven other static methods described in Table 7.2 that return a Boolean value. These methods can be used to determine if the character passed to it is a digit or a letter, an uppercase or lowercase letter, or is Java whitespace. The methods are very useful in programs that process text information.

Figure 7.19 contains a program ParseSentence that demonstrates the use of four of the methods shown in Table 7.2 to determine the number of upper and lowercase letters, digits, and whitespace in an input sentence. A typical input sentence and the corresponding output the program produces is shown in Figures 7.20a and 7.20b, respectively.

The code inside the for loop that begins on line 14 of Figure 7.19 counts the number of occurrences of the four different types of characters contained in the sentence input on line 13. The String class's length method is invoked on line 14 to determine the number of characters in the sentence.

Each time through the loop, the loop variable is passed to the String class's charAt method to fetch the ith character from the sentence. Lines 17, 21, 25, and 29 use four of the character-testing methods presented in Table 7.2 to determine if the character returned from the charAt method is an upper or lowercase letter, digit, or whitespace.

**Table 7.2**

The Character-Testing Methods in the Class **Character**

| Method Name and Parameter List | Returns **true** if the Character Passed to its Parameter is: | Code Example |
|---|---|---|
| isDigit(char c) | a digit in the range 0 to 9 | `Character.isDigit('4');` returns `true` |
| isLetter(char c) | an upper or lower case letter of the alphabet | `Character.isDigit('C');` returns `true` |
| isLetterOrDigit(char c) | an upper- or lowercase letter or digit (0-9) | `Character.isLetterOrDigit('C');` returns `true` `Character.isLetterOrDigit('6');` returns `true` |
| isLowerCase(char c) | a lowercase letter of the alphabet | `Character.isDigit('c');` returns `true` |
| isSpaceChar(char c) | a space character | `Character.isSpaceChar(' ');` returns `true` |
| isUpperCase(char c) | an uppercase letter of the alphabet | `Character.isUpperCase('B');` returns `true` |
| isWhiteSpace(char c) | Java defined white space (e.g., space, tab, or a new line character) | `Character.isWhiteSpace(' ');` returns `true` |

```
1    import javax.swing.*;
2
3    public class ParseSentence
4    {
5      public static void main(String[] args)
6      {
7        int upperCase = 0;
8        int lowerCase = 0;
9        int numeric = 0;
10       int whitespace = 0;
11       char c;
12
13       String sentence = JOptionPane.showInputDialog("Enter a sentence");
14       for(int i = 0; i < sentence.length(); i++)
15       {
16         c = sentence.charAt(i);
17         if(Character.isUpperCase(c))
```

```
18           {
19              upperCase++;
20           }
21           else if(Character.isLowerCase(c))
22           {
23              lowerCase++;
24           }
25           else if(Character.isDigit(c))
26           {
27              numeric++;
28           }
29           else if(Character.isWhitespace(c))
30           {
31              whitespace++;
32           }
33        }
34        JOptionPane.showMessageDialog(null, "The sentence contains:\n" +
35                                    upperCase + " Upper case letters,\n" +
36                                    owerCase + " Lower case letters,\n" +
37                                    numeric + " Digits and\n" +
38                                    whitespace + " Whitespace characters");
39     }
40  }
```

**Figure 7.19**
The application **ParseSentence.**

(a) Input                                     (b) Output

**Figure 7.20**
An input to the application **ParseSentence** and the resulting output.

## 7.7 AGGREGATION

Just as a group of primitive variables can be collected into an object by declaring them as data members in the object's class, instances of other types of objects can also be collected, or aggregated, into an object. We have already utilized this concept many times in this textbook. For example, lines 10 and 11 of Figure 7.12 indicate that a String and a Color object will be part of a `ParentSnowmanV2` object. As a result, the `ParentSnowmanV2` class would be considered an **aggregated** *class*.

| Definition |
| --- |
| An **aggregated** class is a class that includes in its data members instances of other classes. |

Aggregating an object into a class is a simple task. As shown in Figure 7.21, which contains lines 10–11 and lines 20–28 of Figure 7.12, we simply declare a data member that can reference the object (lines 10 and 11) and assign the reference variable the address of an object (lines 11, 25, and 26).

```
10      private String name;
11      private Color hatColor= Color.BLACK;
  :
20      public ParentSnowmanV2(int intialX, int intialY, String name,
21                              Color hatColor)
22      {
23        x = intialX;
24        y = intialY;
25        this.name = name;
26        this.hatColor = hatColor;
27        snowmanCount++;
28      }
```

**Figure 7.21**
A code fragment from an aggregated class.

The difficult part of the aggregation shown in Figure 7.21 falls on the authors of the `String` and `Color` classes. They had to anticipate the operations that would be performed on aggregated strings or `Color` objects and provide methods to perform these operations. In the case of the `String` class, this includes operations such as comparing two strings, outputting a string to the console, and all of the other operations that were discussed in Section 7. 5. These methods are invoked by the code of the aggregated class to operate on the objects.

Properly anticipating the operations that will be performed on an aggregated object is a key component of the concept of aggregation. In addition, where possible, the signatures of these methods are standardized, as is the case for the `equals` method in the `String` and `Color` classes. Providing commonly used methods whose signatures are standardized facilitates the use of aggregation in our programs.

Instances of a class that we write can also be aggregated into other classes using the same syntax discussed above. (In this case, the burden of identifying the operations that will be performed on the aggregated objects and writing the classes falls on us.) This use of aggregation gives us the ability to extend the design concept of divide and conquer, used to divide complicated methods into smaller methods, to classes we write. The component objects of a large class (e.g., a `ParentSnowman` class) can be identified (e.g., a `Hat` object and a `Nose` object), and then the component classes can be written. Once written, instances of these classes can be aggregated into the larger class. In addition, instances of component classes can be aggregated into the classes of other programs just as instances of API classes are used in most Java programs.

The concept of aggregation gives us the ability to:

- use instances of existing objects in classes we write
- extend the design concept of divide and conquer to classes we write
- define a complicated object as an aggregation of component objects defined in other classes
- easily operate on aggregated component objects as separate entities

Figure 7.22 shows the UML representation of a class named SnowmanV8 that aggregates a Hat and String object into it. The symbol for aggregation in a UML diagram is the diamond shown below the SnowmanV8 class. The lines that connect it to the Hat and String classes indicate that the SnowmanV8 class aggregates at least one Hat and one String object into it. The last two data members of the SnowmanV8 class specify that one of each of these objects is aggregated into the class. For this reason aggregation is said to be a HAS-A relationship, e.g. a SnowmanV8 object *has a* Hat.

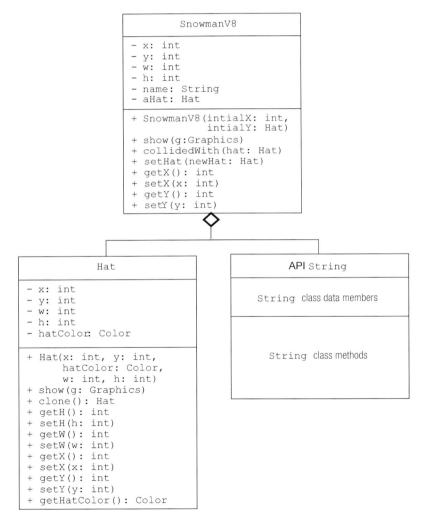

**Figure 7.22**
UML diagram of the **SnowmanV8** and the **Hat** classes.

During the design of the `Hat` class, it was anticipated that classes that aggregate hats will want to include hats of different colors and sizes. The last three parameters of the class's constructor were included in its parameter list to allow for this, as were its last three data members. The `Hat` class's `show` method will use these data members to draw a properly sized and colored hat. In addition, it has been anticipated that classes that aggregate `Hat` objects will want to clone them, so the class includes a clone method. Finally, it was assumed that once created, a hat's color would not be changed, so a `setHatColor` data member was not included in the `Hat` class.

Figure 7.23 shows the code of the class `Hat` that is specified in Figure 7.22. Lines 22 and 23 of the `show` method scale the hat top and its brim using the hat's specified width (w) and height (h). This unburdens the authors of all classes that aggregate hats from knowing how to scale a `Hat` object. That task is left to the hat specialist, which illustrates another advantage of aggregation. In addition, they do not have to include the `Hat` class's data members and method in their class, making the aggregated easier to code and understand. The clone method, lines 25–29, invokes the class's constructor in line 27 to create a clone of the `Hat` object that invokes it and returns the address of the newly created clone on line 28.

```
1    import java.awt.*;
2
3    public class Hat
4    {
5      private int x;
6      private int y;
7      private int w = 20;
8      private int h = 17;
9      private Color hatColor;
10
11     public Hat(int x, int y, Color hatColor, int w, int h)
12     {
13       this.x = x;
14       this.y = y;
15       this.hatColor = hatColor;
16       this.w = w;
17       this.h = h;
18     }
19     public void show(Graphics g)
20     {
21       g.setColor(hatColor);
22       g.fillRect(x + w/4, y, w/2, (int)(h*0.9));   // hat top
23       g.fillRect(x, y + (int)(h*0.9), w, (int)(h*0.2));   // brim
24     }
25     public Hat clone()
26     {
27       Hat theClone = new Hat(x, y, hatColor, w, h);
28       return theClone;
29     }
30     public int getW()
```

```
31    {
32        return w;
33    }
34    public int getH()
35    {
36        return h;
37    }
38    public int getX()
39    {
40        return x;
41    }
42    public void setX(int newX)
43    {
44        x = newX;
45    }
46    public int getY()
47    {
48        return y;
49    }
50    public void setY(int newY)
51    {
52        y = newY;
53    }
54    public Color getHatColor()
55    {
56        return hatColor;
57    }
58 }
```

**Figure 7.23**
The class **Hat**.

Figure 7.24 shows the code of the class SnowmanV8 that is specified in Figure 7.22. This class begins the aggregation of a String and a Hat object with the declaration of its last two data members on lines 9 and 10. Line 16 of the constructor completes the aggregation of the String object by creating a string and setting its address into the data member name.

The aggregation of the Hat object is completed on line 52 of the setHat method that assigns the address of a Hat object passed to its parameter on line 50 to the data member aHat declared on line 10. This means that until the setHat method is invoked, a SnowmanV8 object should be drawn without a hat on his head. This is easily accomplished by including an if statement (line 22) in the class's show method that only invokes the Hat class's show method (line 26) when the data member aHat does contain its default value, null. This demonstrates another advantage of aggregation: aggregated objects can easily be treated as separate entities in a program. The snowman can be drawn with or without a hat.

Before the hat is drawn, it must be positioned on the snowman's head. This is accomplished by lines 24 and 25, which use the Hat class's setX and setY methods to set the (x, y) position of the hat above the snowman's head. The argument sent to these methods uses the Hat class's setW and `setH` methods to fetch the height and width of the hat, which are used to center the hat on the snowman's head.

Lines 38–49 of Figure 7.24 contain the code of the `SnowmanV8` class's `collidedWith` method specified in Figure 7.22. It detects a collision between the snowman that invokes it and the `Hat` object passed to its parameter. It uses the `Hat` class's `get` methods in the Boolean expression on lines 40 and 41 to decide if a collision has occurred.

```
1    import java.awt.*;
2
3    public class SnowmanV8
4    {
5      private static int w = 40;
6      private static int h = 77;
7      private int x;
8      private int y;
9      private String name; //data members for aggregated objects
10     private Hat aHat;
11
12     public SnowmanV8(int intialX, int intialY)
13     {
14       x = intialX;
15       y = intialY;
16       name = "sm"; //aggregates a String object into this class
17     }
18     public void show(Graphics g)
19     { int[] xPoly = {x + 20, x + 15, x + 25};
20       int[] yPoly = {y + 8, y + 13, y + 13};
21
22       if(aHat != null) //snowman has a hat
23       {
24         aHat.setX(x + w/2 - aHat.getW()/2); //locate the hat on head
25         aHat.setY(y - aHat.getH());
26         aHat.show(g); //draw the hat
27       }
28       g.setColor(Color.WHITE);
29       g.fillOval(x + 10, y, 20, 20); // head
30       g.fillOval(x, y + 20, 40, 40); // body
31       g.setColor(Color.RED);
32       g.fillPolygon(xPoly, yPoly, 3); // nose
33       g.setColor(Color.BLACK);
34       g.setFont(new Font("Arial", Font.BOLD, 16));
35       g.drawString(name, x + 10, y + 45); // name
36     }
37
38     public boolean collidedWith(Hat hat)
39     {
40       if( !(x > hat.getX( ) + hat.getW() || x + w < hat.getX( ) ||
```

```
41                    y > hat.getY( ) + hat.getH() || y + h < hat.getY( )))
42          {
43            return true;
44          }
45          else
46          {
47            return false;
48          }
49        }
50        public void setHat(Hat newHat)
51        {
52          aHat = newHat; //aggregates a Hat object into this class
53        }
54        public int getX()
55        {
56          return x;
57        }
58        public void setX(int newX)
59        {
60          x = newX;
61        }
62        public int getY()
63        {
64          return y;
65        }
66        public void setY(int newY)
67        {
68          y = newY;
69        }
70      }
```

**Figure 7.24**
The class **SnowmanV8**.

Figure 7.25 presents the application `Aggregation`. When launched, it displays a hatless snowman and a hat rack containing six different hats, as shown in Figure 7.26a. The keyboard cursor-control keys are used to move the snowman to the hat he wishes to wear, perhaps the blue hat as shown in the upper right side of the figure (7.26b). The chosen hat is cloned and positioned on his head (Figure 7.26c), and follows him around the game board as shown on the lower right side of the figure (7.26d).

The application's `draw` method (lines 23–32) draws the hat rack on lines 25 and 26, and then its `for` loop invokes the hat class's `show` method to draw the six hats created on lines 12 to 17. The parameters sent to the `Hat` class's five-parameter constructor specify different locations, colors, and sizes for each hat.

Line 31 of the `draw` method invokes the `SnowmanV8` class's `show` method to draw the snowman that was created on line 8 on the game board. When the application is launched, the snowman's data member, `aHat`, declared on line 10 of the Figure 7.24, still contains its `null` default value. This causes the snowman to be drawn without a hat, as shown in Figure 7.26a, because the Boolean condition on line 22 of Figure 7.24 is false.

Every time a cursor key is struck, the code of the switch statement (Figure 7.25, lines 37–62) inside the keyStruck call back method moves the snowman two pixels left, right, up, or down. Then, the if statement (lines 66–69) uses the loop variable of the for loop to check each hat in the array hats to determine if the snowman has chosen (collided with) any of the hats on the hat rack.

When a hat is chosen it is cloned, and the clone is aggregated into the snowman object by invoking the hat class's setHat method and passing it the address of the cloned hat (line 68). The aggregation is accomplished by line 52 of Figure 7.24, which assigns the cloned hat's address (passed to the setHat method) the snowman's data member aHat. Because the data member is no longer null, lines 24–25 of Figure 7.24 position the aggregated hat centered and on top of the snowman's head at its current position, and line 26 draws the hat at that position.

```
1    import edu.sjcny.gpv1.*;
2    import java.awt.*;
3
4    public class Aggregation extends DrawableAdapter
5    { static Aggregation ge = new Aggregation();
6      static GameBoard gb = new GameBoard(ge, "Aggregation");
7      static Hat[] hats = new Hat[6];
8      static SnowmanV8 sm;
9
10     public static void main(String[] args)
11     {
12       hats[0] = new Hat(40, 100, Color.RED, 20, 17);
13       hats[1] = new Hat(120, 100, Color.ORANGE, 25, 21);
14       hats[2] = new Hat(200, 100, Color.YELLOW, 20, 17);
15       hats[3] = new Hat(280, 100, Color.GREEN, 40, 34);
16       hats[4] = new Hat(360, 100, Color.BLUE, 30, 25);
17       hats[5] = new Hat(440, 100, Color.MAGENTA, 35, 29);
18       sm = new SnowmanV8(250, 250);
19
20       showGameBoard(gb);
21     }
22
23     public void draw(Graphics g)
24     {
25       g.setColor(Color.BLACK); //the hat rack
26       g.fillRect(20, 95, 460, 5);
27       for(int i=0; i<hats.length; i++)
28       {
29         hats[i].show(g);
30       }
31       sm.show(g);
32     }
```

```
33    public void keyStruck(char key) //call back method
34    {
35      int newX, newY;
36
37      switch (key) //to move the snowman
38      {
39        case 'L':
40        {
41          newX = sm.getX() - 2;
42          sm.setX(newX);
43          break;
44        }
45        case 'R':
46        {
47          newX = sm.getX() + 2;
48          sm.setX(newX);
49          break;
50        }
51        case 'U':
52        {
53          newY = sm.getY() - 2;
54          sm.setY(newY);
55          break;
56        }
57        case 'D':
58        {
59          newY = sm.getY() + 2;
60          sm.setY(newY);
61        }
62      }
63      //acquiring a new Hat
64      for(int i = 0; i<hats.length; i++)
65      {
66        if(sm.collidedWith(hats[i])) //a hat is chosen
67        {
68          sm.setHat(hats[i].clone()); //clone the hat and add it to sm
69        }
70      }
71    }
72 }
```

**Figure 7.25**
The application **Aggregation**.

**Figure 7.26**
Output generated by the application **Aggregation**.

## 7.8 INNER CLASSES

An *inner class* is a class defined inside another class. Just as classes can contain data members and methods, they can contain other classes. The class that contains the inner class is called the *outer* class. Normally, a class is defined as an inner class only if the outer class will aggregate instances of the inner class. Consider the Hat class (Figure 7.23) discussed in the previous section. Because both the class SnowmanV8 and the application Aggregation declared Hat objects, the Hat class was not coded inside the SnowmanV8 class. Inner classes are most often used in Java programs that use a Graphical User Interface (GUI), also called a point-and-click interface. In this section, we will become familiar with the syntax of inner classes and the ability of the inner and outer classes to access each other's data members and methods.

Figure 7.27 presents the class PhoneBook that contains an inner class PhoneNumbers, which begins on line 28 and ends on line 48. Instances of the inner class contain a person's office, cell, and home phone numbers. These three strings are declared as aggregated data members of the inner class on lines 30–32, and the class's constructor assigns them input values (lines 36–40) when a PhoneNumbers object is created. The class's show method (lines 43–47) outputs the three phone numbers to the system console.

```java
1    import javax.swing.*;
2
3    public class PhoneBook
4    {
5      private String[] name;
6      private PhoneNumbers[] numbers;
7
8      public PhoneBook() //a phone book has three listings
9      {
10       name = new String[3];
11       numbers = new PhoneNumbers[3];
12
13       for(int i = 0; i < name.length; i++)
14       {
15         name[i] = JOptionPane.showInputDialog("enter your name");
16         numbers[i] = new PhoneNumbers(i);
17       }
18     }
19     public void showAll()
20     {
21       for(int i = 0; i < name.length; i++)
22       {
23         System.out.println("\nName: " + name[i]);
24         numbers[i].show();
25       }
26     }
27
28     private class PhoneNumbers //an inner class
29     {
30       private String home;
31       private String cell;
32       private String office;
33
34       public PhoneNumbers(int i)
35       {
36         home = JOptionPane.showInputDialog("enter " + name[i] +
37                                     "'s HOME number");
38         cell = JOptionPane.showInputDialog("enter " + name[i] +
39                                     "'s CELL number");
40         office = JOptionPane.showInputDialog("enter " + name[i] +
41                                     "'s OFFICE number");
```

```
42        }
43      public void show()
44      {
45         System.out.println("PhoneNumbers: home:" + home +
46                            " cell:" + cell +  " office:" + office);
47      }
48    } //end of the inner class Phonenumbers
49  }
```

**Figure 7.27**
The class **PhoneBook** and its inner class **PhoneNumbers**.

The outer class PhoneBook declares two parallel arrays each containing three elements on lines 10 and 11 and assigns their addresses to the variables name and numbers, declared on lines 5 and 6. After creating the arrays, the for loop (lines 13–17) in the outer class's constructor completes the aggregation of the String and PhoneNumbers objects into the outer class by creating new instances of these classes and assigning their addresses to the elements of the parallel arrays name and numbers (lines 15 and 16).

> **NOTE**   *The code of an outer class can invoke a constructor in an inner class.*

Each time the inner class's constructor is invoked on line 16, it not only creates a new object, but it also accepts input into the data members of the newly created object on lines 36–41. The argument passed to this one-parameter constructor on line 16 is the loop variable declared on line 13. Lines 36, 38, and 40 of the constructor use this value to index into the outer class's name array, which causes the person's name that was just input on line 10 to become part of the prompts output by lines 36–41.

> **NOTE**   *The code of an inner class can access the data members of its outer class.*

The outer class's showAll method (lines 19–26) outputs all of the names and numbers in the two parallel arrays to the system console. Inside its for loop, line 23 outputs a person's name, and then line 24 invokes the inner class's show method to output that person's phone numbers.

> **NOTE**   *The code of an outer class can invoke the methods in an inner class.*

In general:

- the code of an inner and outer class can access each other's members (both data members and methods)
- an inner class is not visible outside of the outer class

The application InnerClass, shown in Figure 7.28, declares a PhoneBook object to store the names and phone numbers of a person's three best friends. Then, it invokes the class's showAll method to output the names and numbers input by the program user. Figure 7.29 shows two typical first inputs and a typical console output produced by the program.

```
1    public class InnerClass
2    {
3      public static void main(String[] args)
4      {
5        PhoneBook bestFriends = new PhoneBook();
6        bestFriends.showAll();
7      }
8    }
```

**Figure 7.28**
The application **InnerClass**.

(a)                                                        (b)

**Console Output:**
Name: Alice
PhoneNumbers: home:657-2342 cell:574-8976 office:345-6589

Name: Tom
PhoneNumbers: home:367-4367 cell:754-3564 office:386-1212

Name: Annie
PhoneNumbers: home:456-4698 cell:765-8294 office:839-5623

**Figure 7.29**
Two typical inputs to the application **InnerClass** and a typical set of outputs.

## 7.9 PROCESSING LARGE NUMBERS

Occasionally, there is a need to process an integer that is larger or smaller than the maximum or minimum values that can be stored in the primitive type long. For example, the encryption used on the Internet involves processing prime numbers that contain 309 digits, which far exceeds the 19-digit maximum value that can be stored in the primitive type long. Similarly, we might need to process a real number that is larger or smaller than the maximum or minimum values of the primitive type double or require more than the 15 digits of precision the type double provides.

The Java API contains two classes that can be used to process numbers that are too large or too small to be stored in primitive types or that require more than 15 digits of precision; they are the BigInteger and BigDecimal classes. As their names imply, they can be used to process numbers beyond the range of the primitive integer and real types, and the `BigDecimal` can also provide a specified number of digits of precision. Objects in these classes, like `String` and wrapper class objects, are immutable.

Processing of objects in these classes is performed by using the methods that are part of these classes. For example, addition is performed by the method `add`, which adds the object that invoked it to the object passed to its parameter and returns a reference to an object that contains their sum. There are methods to perform all of the operations normally performed on primitive numeric types, including modulo arithmetic, methods that are analogous to the `Math` class's methods, and methods to perform other common operations on numbers such as finding the greatest common denominator, generating a prime number, and determining if a number is prime.

## The `BigInteger` Class

Consider a program to generate a specified term of the Fibonacci sequence. The first two terms of this sequence, f1 and f2, are both defined as 1. Any other term in the series is defined as the sum of the two previous terms: fn = fn-2 + fn-1. From term 93 (f93) on, the values of the terms exceed the size of the primitive type `long`.

The application `FibonacciTerm`, shown in Figure 7.30, demonstrates the use of some of the constants and methods in the class `BigInteger`. The program calculates and outputs a specified term (greater than 2) of the sequence and identifies those terms that are larger than the maximum value of the primitive type `long`. A set of program inputs and corresponding outputs are shown in Figure 7.31.

Line 1 of Figure 7.31 imports the class `BigInteger` into the program, and lines 10–12 create three instances of the class. The first two are assigned the address of the class's static object that stores the value 1. There are two other static objects defined in the class, `TEN` and `ZERO`, which store the values 10 and 0, respectively. Line 12 uses the class's `valueOf` method that returns the address of a `BigInteger` object set to the value passed to its parameter. In this case, the maximum value of the primitive type `long` is passed to the method, which is a static constant in the wrapper class `Long`.

The `for` loop that begins on line 16 computes the terms of the sequence from 3 to the number input on line 14. Each time through the loop, the `add` method is used on line 19 to calculate the next term of the sequence and the address of the object containing the value returned from the method is assigned to the variable `fn`. Line 20 sets `fnMinus1` to the previous value of `fn`.

When the loop ends, line 22 uses the class's `toString` method to convert the calculated value stored in the object `fn` to a string before it is output. The conversion could have been coded as an implicit invocation of the `toString` method:

```
System.out.println("f" + n + " = " + fn);
```

Finally, the `BigInteger` class's `compareTo` method is used in the Boolean condition on line 23 to determine if the calculated term of the sequence is larger than the maximum value of a `long` type primitive. The integer value the method returns is interpreted in the same way as the integer value retuned from the `String` class's `compareTo` method.

```
1    import java.math.BigInteger;
2    import javax.swing.*;
3
4    public class FibonacciTerm
5    {
6      public static void main(String[] args)
7      {
8        int n;
9        BigInteger temp;
10       BigInteger fnMinus1 = BigInteger.ONE;
11       BigInteger fn = BigInteger.ONE;
12       BigInteger longMaxValue = BigInteger.valueOf(Long.MAX_VALUE);
13
14       String s = JOptionPane.showInputDialog("enter the term number");
15       n = Integer.parseInt(s);
16       for(int i = 3; i <= n; i++)
17       {
18         temp = fn;
19         fn = fnMinus1.add(fn);
20         fnMinus1 = temp;
21       }
22       System.out.println("f" + n + " = " + fn.toString());
23       if(fn.compareTo(longMaxValue) > 0)
24       {
25         System.out.println("Which EXCEEDS the maximum value of " +
26                            "type long");
27       }
28       else
29       {
30         System.out.println("Which does NOT exceed the maximum value of " +
31                            "type long");
32       }
33     }
34   }
```

**Figure 7.30**
The application **FibonacciTerm**.

| Inputs to Three Executions of the Program: |
|---|
| 92 |
| 93 |
| 300 |
| **Corresponding Outputs:** |
| f92 = 7540113804746346429 |
| Which does NOT exceed the maximum value of type long |

f93 = 12200160415121876738
Which EXCEEDS the maximum value of type `long`

f300 = 222232244629420445529739893461909967206666939096499764990979600
Which EXCEEDS the maximum value of type `long`

**Figure 7.31**
Sample inputs to the application **FibonacciTerm** and the corresponding outputs they produce.

## The `BigDecimal` Class

As previously mentioned, the `BigDecimal` class can be used to represent real values to a specified precision. The code fragment shown in Figure 7.32 computes and rounds up the number 176 divided by 7 to a precision of 19, 18, 17, and 16 digits. The resulting `BigDecimal` object, returned from the three-parameter version of the class's `divide` method, is output at the bottom of the figure using an implicit invocation of the `BigInteger` class's `toString` method. The `divide` method divides the object that invoked it by the first argument sent to it.

The second argument sent to the `divide` method specifies the precision of the computed value. The third argument specifies the rounding mode used to determine the rightmost digit of precision. This can either be an integer or a constant defined in the class `RoundingMode`. The class's constant HALF_UP, used in Figure 7.32, is used to perform the conventional upward rounding.

```
    BigDecimal one76 = BigDecimal.valueOf(176);
    BigDecimal seven = BigDecimal.valueOf(7);

    System.out.println(one76.divide(seven, 19, RoundingMode.HALF_UP));
    System.out.println(one76.divide(seven, 18, RoundingMode.HALF_UP));
    System.out.println(one76.divide(seven, 17, RoundingMode.HALF_UP));
    System.out.println(one76.divide(seven, 16, RoundingMode.HALF_UP));
```

**Output:**

25.1428571428571428571
25.142857142857142857
25.14285714285714286
25.1428571428571429

**Figure 7.32**
Use of the **BigDecimal** class's divide method.

## 7.10 ENUMERATED TYPES

Enumeration is the process of defining a new type and specifying, or enumerating, a finite set of values that instances of the type can assume. The use of enumeration can make our programs more readable. Java supports enumerated types. The following enumeration statement defines the enumerated type `Team` and specifies that there are three values in its set of values: `Yankees`, `Braves`, and `Giants`.

```
// Declaration of an enumerated type
   enum Team {Yankees, Braves, Giants}
```

An enumeration statement is coded at the class level; it cannot be coded inside (local to) a method. The values that appear in the statement can be any valid identifier, which implies that they cannot be strings or primitive literals. The following declarations are invalid:

```
// Invalid enumeration statements: values not identifier names
enum Team {"Yankees", "Braves", "Giants"} //can't contain quotes
enum ID {NY Yankees, Atlanta Braves, SF Giants} //spaces not allowed
```

An enumeration statement can also be written in a separate Java file whose name is the same as the statement's enumerated type name; e.g., `Team`.

At an abstract level, the identifiers can be thought of as static constants in a class whose name is the enumerated type name (e.g., `Team`) and whose values are the identifier names. In this abstract view, the enumerated values are analogous to the static `double` constant `PI` in the `Math` class whose value is the double 3.141592653589793. The following code fragment outputs *3.141592653589793 Yankees* to the system console:

```
// Accessing the values of enumerated types
enum Team {Yankees, Braves, Giants}

System.out.println(Math.PI + " " + Team.Yankees);
```

Continuing the analogy, just as the numeric constant `Math.PI` can be assigned to a variable of its type (i.e., `double`), an enumerated constant can be assigned to a variable of its type (e.g. `Team`). The following code fragment also outputs *3.141592653589793 Yankees* to the system console:

```
// Assigning an enumerated type value
enum Team {Yankees, Braves, Giants}

Team myTeam = Team.Yankees;
double valueOfPi = Math.PI;
System.out.println(valueOfPi + " " + myTeam);
```

For the most part, considering the identifiers in an enumeration statement to be analogous to static constants is consistent with the Java syntax of enumerations. An exception to this is when an enumerated type variable is used in a switch statement after the keyword **switch**. In this context, the enumerated type name is not used to qualify the identifier coded as the choice value after the keyword **case**. In the code fragment shown in Figure 7.33, when an enumerated value such as Yankees is used within the switch statement, the type name `Team` is not used to qualify the identifier, as shown on line 6. When the identifier is used in other statements (e.g., line 7 of Figure 7.33), the type qualifier is used.

```
     // Using enumerated types in switch statements
1    enum Team {Yankees, Braves, Giants}
2
3    Team myTeam = Team.Yankees;
4    switch (myTeam)
5    {
6      case Yankees: // no type name qualifier used here
7      System.out.println(myTeam + " " + Team.Yankees);
8    }
```

**Figure 7.33**
Syntax of enumerated types in a **switch** statement.

The API interface Enum defines a set of methods that implement operations commonly per-formed on enumerated types. When discussing them, it useful to move away from the abstract view of an enumeration's identifiers being static constants to a more concrete view of them. While it is true that the enumerated type is a class, it is a special kind of class. In addition, the identifiers are not static constants in the class, but rather each identifier is a static reference variable that refers to an instance of the class.

As such, like static constants, we access the contents of these reference variables by the name of the identifier proceed by the name of the class followed by a dot (just as we have been doing). Figure 7.34 shows the three objects created by the enumeration shown below, the variables that reference them, and the contents of the variable myTeam after the assignment statement is executed:

**Figure 7.34**
Three objects of the enumeration **Team**.

As shown in Figure 7.34, each object has an ordinal value associated with it, which always begins with zero. The values are assigned sequentially to the identifiers in the order (left to right) in which they appear in the enumeration statement. The Enum class's method ordinal returns the ordinal value assigned to the object that invoked it. The code fragment below outputs 1 to the system console.

```
// Invocations of the Team class' ordinal method
enum Team {Yankees, Braves, Giants}

Team myTeam = Team.Braves
System.out.println(myTeam.ordinal());
```

The `ordinal` method can also be used with an enumerated type object in the same way any other method is used with an instance of its class. For example, the statement

```
System.out.println ( "The ordinal value of " + Team.Giants +
                    " is " + Team.Giants.ordinal() );
```

results in the console output *The ordinal value of Giants is 2.*

---

**NOTE**    *The ordinal values of an enumerated type always begin with zero.*

The methods in the class `Enum`, four of which are shown in Table 7.3, operate on an enumerated type's objects. The class's `toString` method returns the name of the object's identifier converted to a string. The code fragment below outputs *Yankees Yankees* using an explicit and implicit invocation of the method:

```
// Invocations of the Enum class's toString method
enum Team {Yankees, Braves, Giants}

Team myTeam = Team.Yankees
System.out.println(Team.Yankees.toString() + " " + myTeam.Yankees);
```

The `Enum` class's `compareTo` method is an implementation of the method defined in the interface `Comparable`. The comparison it makes is based on the ordinal values associated with the object that invoked the method and the argument passed to it. The following code fragment outputs -2 because the identifier `Yankees`' ordinal value (0) is two less than the identifier `Giants`' value (2).

**Table 7.3**
Commonly Used Methods in the Class Enum

| Method Name and Parameter List | Returned Type | Description |
|---|---|---|
| compareTo(EnumType enum2) | int | diff = enum1.compareTo(enum2)<br>Returns the difference between the ordinal values of enum1 and enum2, positive for<br> emum1 > enum2 |
| equals(EnumType enum2) | boolean | equal = enum1.equals(enum2)<br>Returns true when the ordinal values of enum1 and enum2 are equal, otherwise false |
| ordinal() | int | value = enum1.ordinal()<br>Returns the ordinal values of enum1 |
| toString() | String | value = enum1.toString()<br>Returns the value of enum1 |

```
// Invocations of the Team class' compareTo method
enum Team {Yankees, Braves, Giants}

Team myTeam = Team.Yankees
System.out.println(myTeam.compareTo(Team.Giants));
```

The `Enum` class's method `equals` returns `true` when the object that invoked it has the same ordinal value as the object passed to its parameter.

## 7.11 CHAPTER SUMMARY

Java classes consist of data members and methods that operate on the data, and an object is an instance of a class. When a data member is declared to be static, all instances of the class share the variable. Often, a static variable is incremented inside a class's constructor to keep track of the number of objects that have been created.

It is good programming practice to write a complicated method as several simpler methods that it can invoke. Usually, the simpler methods are given private access to prevent methods that are not part of the class from invoking them. Methods can invoke private methods that are part of their class by simply coding the method's name and an argument list.

The object addresses stored in two reference variables can be compared using the relational operators, and they can be copied using the assignment operator. These are referred to as a shallow comparison and a shallow copy, respectively. After a shallow copy, two reference variables refer to the same object. To compare or copy objects, we first need to define which of their data members will be compared or which will be copied. Comparing and copying the data members of two objects is referred to as deep comparisons and deep copies. In both cases, a method has to be written to perform these operations.

Deep comparison methods return a Boolean value, and it is good programming practice for the methods to be named `compareTo`, as defined in the API interface `Comparable`, or named `equals` when the comparison is performed to determine equality. The `String` class contains deep comparison methods with these names. Deep copy methods either copy all of the data members from one object to another or copy all of the data members into a newly created object called a clone and return the address of the clone object. The names of deep copy methods ordinarily contain the word "copy," such as the `arraycopy` method in the `System` class, and clone methods are usually named `clone`.

In addition to deep comparison methods, the `String` class contains methods to perform common operations on `String` objects. These include locating and fetching substrings (the methods `indexOf` and `substring`), changing the case of a string (`toUpperCase` and `toLowerCase`), replacing a part of a string with another string (`replaceFirst` and `replaceAll`), and determining if a string begins or ends with a particular string (`startsWith` and `endsWith`). In addition, its `split` method can be used to place substrings of a string separated by a designated delimiter, usually white space, into the elements of the array it creates and returns. The substrings are called tokens, and the process is called tokenizing the string.

Autoboxing is the automatic construction of a wrapper class object without having to explicitly invoke the class' constructor, and auto-unboxing is the process of fetching the primitive value stored in a wrapper class object without having to invoke a `get` method. This feature can be used to pass a primitive value to a wrapper-class parameter or to assign a retuned wrapper class object to a primitive variable. The `Character` wrapper class contains a variety of methods used to process characters such as determining if a character is a letter or a digit, if it is lower or upper case, or if it is white space. The numeric wrapper classes contain static constants whose values are the maximum and minimum numeric values that they can wrap. The methods in the classes `BigInteger` and `BigDecimal` give us the ability to process numbers whose absolute value is too large to be stored in primitive types or that require more than 15 digits of precision. Objects in these classes, like `String` and wrapper class objects, are immutable.

Aggregation is the process of declaring a data member of a class to be a reference to an object. This permits us to define a complex object as an aggregate of simpler component objects, extending the concepts of reusable code and divide and conquer to the design of classes. A class, called an inner class, can also be defined within another class called an outer class. The inner class can access the data members defined in the outer class and vice versa. The outer class can create instances of the inner class and invoke its methods. Enumeration is the process of defining a type and specifying, or enumerating, the values that instances of the type can assume. The use of enumeration can make our programs more readable.

## Knowledge Exercises

1. True or false:
   **a)** Static data members allow one storage cell to be shared among all instances of their class.
   **b)** A method cannot invoke another method in its class.
   **c)** Methods that are declared `private` can be invoked by other methods within their own class.
   **d)** A deep comparison determines if two reference variables refer to the same object.
   **e)** To make a clone of an object, we make a shallow copy of it.
   **f)** The variables `s1` and `s2` refer to two different objects. After I make a shallow copy of `s2` into `s1`, I have two identical objects.
   **g)** Autoboxing constructs a wrapper class object without explicitly invoking the class's constructor.
   **h)** An outer class can invoke the methods of its inner class.

2. Consider the class `Student` shown in Figure 7.4.
   **a)** Why is its data member `studentCount` declared to be static?
   **b)** Why is the class's `get` method declared to be a static method?
   **c)** Write the statement to output the variable `studentCount` to the system console.
   **d)** Why does the class not contain a public method named `setStudentCount`?

3. Explain the difference between a deep and a shallow comparison.

4. Explain the difference between a deep and a shallow copy.

5. Explain the difference between a deep copy and a clone.

6. How does the method `equals` in the API `Object` class differ from the `equals` method in the `String` class?

7. Write a code fragment to output *Two Objects* to the system console if the variable s1 and s2 refer to two different objects.

8. Write a method that could be added to the class `Student`, shown in Figure 7.5, which would clone the `Student` object that invoked it.

9. What is output by these statements, assuming the following declarations have been made:

```
String s1 = "Computers rock"; String s2 = "Hello world";
```
a) `System.out.println(s2.indexOf("world"));`
b) `System.out.println(s1.substring(10));`
c) `System.out.println(s2.replaceFirst("world", "everyone"));`
d) `System.out.println(s2.starts("world"));`
e) `String[] s = s2.split();`
   `System.out.println(s[1]);`
f) `if`(s1.equalsIgnoreCase("Computers Rock")
   ```
   {
   System.out.print("True - these are the same.");
   }
   ```
   **else**
   ```
   {
   System.out.print("False - they are not the same.");
   }
   ```
g) `System.out.println(s2.substring(3, 7);`

10. Give the code to:
   a) create an instance of the wrapper class `Integer` that contains the value 20 without explicitly invoking the class's constructor
   b) set the integer variable `age` to the value stored in the `Integer` instance `number`
   c) output the maximum and minimum values that can be stored in a primitive variable declared to be type `long` to the system console
   d) output `true` to the system console if the character contained in the variable `aCharacter` is white space or a digit
   e) Declare a public class data member that stores the number of centimeters in a meter.
   f) Output the maximum integer that can be stored in the primitive type `short`.

11. Define aggregation in the context of a Java class.

12. Give three advantages of using aggregation in the classes we design.

13. How would you represent an integer in your program that was larger than the maximum value of the primitive type `long`?

14. How would you input an integer to your program that was larger than the maximum value of the primitive type `long`?

15. How would you double the integer discussed in Exercise 13?

16. Give the code to define two `BigInteger` objects initialized to 1,234,567,890,123,456 and 9,876,543,210,654,321, multiply the numbers, and output the result.

17. Assume an enumerated type `CarColor` has been declared as:

    enum `CarColor` {RED, WHITE, SILVER, BLACK, BLUE}

    a) What is the ordinal value of SILVER?

    b) Write a statement to create a variable, `favoriteColor`, of type `CarColor` and set it to BLUE.

    c) Write a statement to output the `favoriteColor` and its ordinal value to the system console.

## Programming Exercises

1. Add a deep comparison method and a clone method to the class shown in Figure 7.4. The deep comparison method should return 0 when two instances of the class are equal (i.e., both objects' id numbers and GPA are equal). Then write an application that declares an instance of the class named s1 and two other instances named s2 and s3. The object s2 should have the same id as s1, and s3 should have the same GPA as s1. Output the three objects to the system console followed by *s1 equals s2* or *s1 equals s3*, as determined by two invocations of the deep comparison method. Then clone s1, store the returned address in s2, and repeat all of the output.

2. Write a program that accepts an arithmetic expression that does not contain parentheses and verifies that is correctly written. It is correctly written if each of the operators in the expression is between two operands preceded and followed by a space: for example 2 * 3 + 5. Output a correct expression to the system console. Otherwise, output the expression up to the point were the first error was detected, then a caret (Shift 6 key stroke), and then the remainder of the math expression. The second line of output, in both cases, should be the number of tokens (operators and operands) that were in the original expression. (Use the `split` method in the `String` class.)

3. Modify the class `PhoneBook` shown in Figure 7.27 so each of the three listings in a `PhoneBook` instance will also have an address consisting of a street, city, state, and zip code. To accomplish this, add another inner class named `Address` to the class `Phonebook`. The new information should be input in a similar way to that of the phone numbers. To verify your modifications to the class, write an application that declares an instance of a `PhoneBook`, accepts user inputs, then outputs the entire phonebook.

4. Write a program that calculates and outputs the sum of the integers from 1 to 10,000,000,000. Hint: the sum is (10,000,000,000 * 10,000,000,001)/2, which is not equal to 3,883,139,820,726,120,960.

5. Write a program to multiply two real numbers of any size and precision input via a dialog box and output their product with seven digits of precision, rounded up.

# Enrichment

1. Investigate and learn who was the first to discover that the sum of the integers from 1 to n is (n * (n +1)) /2 and the circumstances under which he discovered it.

2. Explore the Fibonacci sequence to discover its presence in art, architecture, music, and nature and investigate the relationship of the Fibonacci sequence to the Golden ratio.

3. Research the Fibonacci searching algorithm.

# INHERITANCE

## In this chapter

In this chapter, we expand our knowledge of object oriented programming into the advanced topics of inheritance, polymorphism, interfaces and adapter classes, and the serialization of objects. These OOP concepts can significantly reduce the time and effort required to design and develop a software product.

We will learn that Java supports two forms of inheritance, chain inheritance and multiple child inheritance. Both of these allow us to rapidly create a class from a similar existing class and to easily expand and/or modify the new class to adapt it to the requirements of a particular project. When used as a design tool, inheritance not only reduces the cost of a software product under development, but it also reduces the cost of future products by increasing the reusability of the classes we write. Using inheritance, application-dependent parts of a method can be written in a way that they can invoke methods that implement the yet-to-be-determined requirements of future products.

Polymorphism is another fundamental characteristic of OOP, which allows things to exist in many ("poly") different forms ("morph"), such as when one array references many different types of objects or when one invocation morphs itself into an invocation of a method appropriate to a particular launch of a program. Polymorphism also allows us to pass different types of objects to one type of parameter.

Interfaces allow us to define the signature and functionality of related methods without having to implement them, and adaptor classes facilitate the use of interfaces. Using object serialization, we can easily save a collection of objects to a disk file and reuse the objects in a future launch of the same or different program.

After successfully completing this chapter you should:

- Understand the advantages, terminology, syntax, and importance of using inheritance
- Know how to implement a child class that inherits data members and methods from an existing parent class using the `extends` clause
- Be able to invoke and modify an inherited method and expand inherited methods and data members
- Be able to distinguish between overriding and overloading methods
- Know how to use inheritance as part of the design process
- Understand the processes that Java uses to locate a method at translation and run time
- Be able to comprehend and use polymorphism and polymorphic arrays
- Understand abstract classes, interfaces, and adapter classes and how to implement and use them
- Write and read a group of objects to and from a disk file

## 8.1 THE CONCEPT OF INHERITANCE

| Definition |
| --- |
| **Inheritance** is an OPP programming concept in which new classes that contain all of the data members and methods of an existing class can be efficiently created and then expanded and/or modified. The concept of inheritance implies that two classes have a relationship with each other in which one class, called a *child* class, inherits attributes from the other class, called the *parent* class. |

The concept of **inheritance** is fundamental to object oriented programming. If properly used, it can greatly reduce the time and effort required to develop a software product. For example, suppose that one of the classes specified during the design of a new program is similar to an existing class in that the existing class contains many of the data members and methods listed in the new class's UML diagram. The best way to develop the new class would be to simply add the existing class to the program and modify and/or add to it. One approach to this would be to copy the source code of the existing class, paste the code into a new class, and then modify the copied code. A better approach would be to use the concept of inheritance.

Although we may have been importing the existing class into our programs for many years, we may not have its source code. For example, the Java API does not contain the source code of any of the classes included in it. Rather, it contains the classes' translated byte codes. This fact would eliminate the copy and paste alternative but not the inheritance alternative. To use the concept of inheritance, we only need the bytecodes of the existing class. In addition, software engineering studies reveal that copying, pasting, and modifying code that we did not write can be more time consuming than a completely independent development of a new class. Inheritance allows us to modify an existing class that was added to a new program in a way that does not introduce the errors that are associated with the copy-paste-modify alternative.

Even if there are no existing classes that contain many of the data members and methods of the classes specified for a new program, the time and cost to develop the program can still be reduced using the concept of inheritance during the design process. Finally, the use of inheritance in the design of our programs also makes them easier to read and intuitively easier to understand because the classes we write better model the real world. Because we know that children inherit attributes from their parents, it is intuitive that a game's new `ChildSuperHero` class would inherit attributes from an existing game's `ParentSuperHero` class. The attributes inherited by the `ChildSuper-Hero` class would be the data members and the methods of the `ParentSuperHero` class, which could then be efficiently expanded or modified to model the child super hero.

In summary:

- Inheritance reduces the cost and time to develop a software product
- Inheritance is the best way to incorporate and then morph an existing class into a new class
- We do not need the source code of the existing class, only its byte code translation, to utilize the concepts of inheritance
- Inheritance is used in the OOP program-design process even when there are no existing classes to be morphed and incorporated into the program

## 8.2 THE UML DIAGRAMS AND LANGUAGE OF INHERITANCE

Inheritance introduces a new feature into UML diagrams and has a set of terms associated with it. An early understanding of this feature and the jargon of inheritance is fundamental to the remainder of the material in this chapter.

### Inheritance UML Diagrams

Figure 8.1 shows the UML diagram of the classes `RowBoat` and `SailBoat`. The `RowBoat` class's UML diagram contains five data members and twelve methods, and the UML diagram of the `SailBoat` contains no data members and one constructor method. Instances of the class `SailBoat` will actually contain more data members and methods than those listed in the class's UML diagram because the upward-pointing arrow in the center of the figure indicates that the `SailBoat` class *inherits from* the `RowBoat` class. As noted next to the arrow in the figure, the Java keyword used to establish this relationship is **extends.**

### The Parent-Child Relationship

The concept of inheritance implies that two classes have a relationship with each other in which one class, called a *child* class, inherits attributes from the other class, called the *parent* class. The attributes inherited are all of the data members and all of the methods of the parent class *except* for the parent class's constructors. The child is its parent, and the relationship between a child and its parent is referred to as an *IS-A* relationship.

As indicated on the left side of Figure 8.1, there are two other pairs of terms that are used in the literature to refer to the parent and *child* class. The parent class is sometimes called the *super class*,

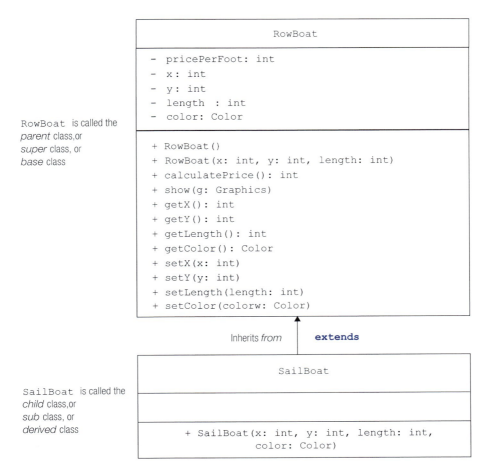

RowBoat is called the *parent* class, or *super* class, or *base* class

SailBoat is called the *child* class, or *sub* class, or *derived* class

**Figure 8.1**
The class **RowBoat** and the class **SailBoat**.

and then the child class is called the *subclass*. Alternately, the term *base class* can be substituted for parent class, in which case the child class is referred to as a *derived class*. These three pairs of terms: *parent* class-*child* class, *super* class-*sub* class, and *base* class-*derived* class should not be unpaired and intermixed.

Because a child class inherits all of the data members and methods of the parent class and contains all of the data members and methods specified in its own UML diagram, a child class's data members and methods add to, or *extend*, a parent class. As specified in Figure 8.1, all instances of the classes SailBoat and RowBoat will have five data members, but the SailBoat class extends the complement of methods that can operate on a SailBoat object from 12 to 13.

**NOTE** *Inheritance does not work in reverse. Parents do not inherit the data members and methods added to the child class.*

### Establishing the Parent-Child Relationship

When a child class is implemented, the parent-child relationship is established by the inclusion of an `extends` *clause* on the right side of the class's heading. This clause begins with the keyword `extends` followed by the name of the parent class. For example:

```
public class SailBoat extends RowBoat
```

**NOTE**
*To establish an inheritance relationship, an* `extends` *clause is included at the end of the class statement of the child class:*
```
public class ChildClassName extends ParentClassName
```

### Forms of Inheritance

A class can only extend or inherit from *one* class. In *chain inheritance* a child class can be the parent of another class. This is supported in Java, as is the ability for several child classes to inherit from the same parent class. These two forms of inheritance are illustrated in the upper-left and upper-right portions of Figure 8.2, respectively.

*Multiple inheritance*, the concept that a child class can inherit attributes from *more than one* parent, is not supported in Java. Multiple inheritance is depicted in the lower-right portion of Figure 8.2.

We say that class B on the top left side of Figure 8.2 *directly* inherits from class A, as do classes B, C, and D at the top right side of the figure. A class that directly inherits from another class extends it by including an `extends` clause in its heading. We say that classes C and D on the top left side of Figure 8.2 *indirectly* inherit from class A because they either inherit from a class that directly inherits from class A (in C's case) or directly inherit from a class that indirectly inherit from class A (in D's case).

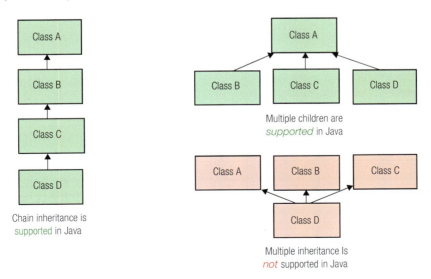

**Figure 8.2**
Various forms of inheritance.

## 8.3 IMPLEMENTING INHERITANCE

In addition to the keyword **extends**, which is used to indicate that a child class inherits from a parent class, there are other keywords and concepts that are associated with inheritance. Most of these are used in the implementation of a child class, but an understanding of some of these keywords, such as **final** and **abstract**, and the concepts associated with them, apply to the implementation of a parent class. In the remainder of this section, we will discuss the keywords and concepts of inheritance that apply to the implementation of a child class; we will discuss the relevant parent class issues in Section 8.4.

Figure 8.3 presents the code of the class RowBoat specified in the top portion of Figure 8.1. The class does not utilize any of the concepts of inheritance presented in this chapter. Nevertheless, it can become a parent class if another class extends it. This class will be the parent of child classes used in parts of this chapter to demonstrate the basic of concepts inheritance and the use of the keywords associated with these concepts.

```java
1    import java.awt.*;
2    public class RowBoat
3    {
4      private static int PRICE_PER_FOOT = 10;
5      private int x, y, length;
6      private Color color = Color.GREEN;
7
8      public RowBoat()
9      {
10
11     }
12     public RowBoat(int x, int y, int length)
13     {
14       this.x = x;
15       this.y = y;
16       this.length = length;
17     }
18     public int calculatePrice()
19     {
20       return length * PRICE_PER_FOOT;
21     }
22     public void show(Graphics g)
23     {
24       int[] xBoat = {x , x + length, x + 6 * length/7,  x + length/14};
25       int[] yBoat = {y,  y, y + length / 7, y + length / 7};
26       int price = calculatePrice();
27       g.setColor(color); //draw the Boat
28       g.fillPolygon(xBoat, yBoat, xBoat.length);
29       g.setColor(Color.BLACK); //draw the boat's price in black

30       g.setFont(new Font("Arial", Font.BOLD, 16));
31       g.drawString("$" + String.valueOf(price), x + 10, y + 16);
```

```
32      }
33      public int getX()
34      {
35         return x;
36      }
37      public int getY()
38      {
39         return y;
40      }
41      public int getLength()
42      {
43         return length;
44      }
45      public Color getColor()
46      {
47         return color;
48      }
49      public void setX(int x)
50      {
51         this.x = x;
52      }
53      public void setY(int y)
54      {
55         this.y = y;
56      }
57      public void setLength(int length)
58      {
59         this.length = length;
60      }
61         public void setColor(Color color)
62      {
63         this.color = color;
64      }
65   }
```

**Figure 8.3**
The class **RowBoat**.

The RowBoat class's three-parameter constructor (lines 12–17 of Figure 8.3) can be used to create and position a rowboat on the game board at the (x, y) location passed to its first two parameters. The value passed to the constructor's third parameter is the size (length) of the rowboat. The x, y, and length data members of a rowboat created with the class's default constructor (lines 8–11) would retain the default value of the type int: 0. Because the constructor does not include a parameter to specify the color of the boat, it would default to green (line 6).

The show method (lines 22–32) draws a rowboat on the game board at its current (x, y) location and then draws the price of the boat on it (lines 29–31). The price is returned from the invocation of the class's calculatePrice method on line 26. Line 20 of this method multiplies the length of the boat by the static variable PRICE _ PER _ FOOT to determine the price of the boat.

The application ShowTwoRowBoats shown in Figure 8.4 creates two rowboats of lengths 200 and 150 feet (lines 7-8) and displays them on the game board (lines 16-17) as shown in Figure 8.5.

```
1    import edu.sjcny.gpv1.*;
2    import java.awt.*;
3
4    public class ShowTwoRowBoats extends DrawableAdapter
5    { static ShowTwoRowBoats ge = new ShowTwoRowBoats();
6      static GameBoard gb = new GameBoard(ge, "Show Two Row Boats");
7      static RowBoat rb1 = new RowBoat(30, 150, 200);
8      static RowBoat rb2 = new RowBoat(30, 250, 150);
9
10     public static void main(String[] args)
11     {
12        showGameBoard(gb);
13     }
14     public void draw(Graphics g)
15     {
16        rb1.show(g);
17        rb2.show(g);
18     }
19   }
```

**Figure 8.4**
The application **ShowTwoRowBoats**.

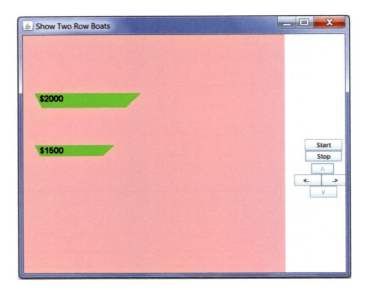

**Figure 8.5**
The output produced by the application **ShowTwoRowBoats**.

### 8.3.1 Constructors and Inherited Method Invocations

The class SailBoat is specified in the bottom portion of Figure 8.1. Sailboats use rowboats for their hull and are delivered without a mast and sail. As delivered, they actually are rowboats, except for the fact that the purchaser can specify the color of the boat. Because they are so similar to rowboats, we can utilize the concept of inheritance to rapidly develop their class.

To begin with, they will inherit all of a rowboat's attributes as indicated by the arrow that connects them to the class `RowBoat` in Figure 8.1. This will save the time and cost associated with declaring a sailboat's five data members, writing and verifying the associated `set` and `get` methods, and writing and verifying the methods to draw them and to calculate their price.

To implement the expanding capability into the `SailBoat` class, the ability to specify the color of the boat when it is purchased, a four-parameter constructor is included in the `SailBoat` class. When a sailboat is constructed, the color of the new boat will be passed to the constructor's fourth parameter.

Figure 8.6 presents the code for the class `SailBoat`. Because we are using inheritance by including the `extends` clause at the end of its heading (line 3), the class consists of only ten lines of code. A sailboat's location, price per foot, length, and color can be stored in its inherited data members. In addition, the values stored in the data members can be fetched and set, the sailboat's price can be calculated, and the boat can be drawn on the game board using the methods inherited from the `RowBoat` class.

### Invoking A Parent Class Constructor

Parent class constructors are *not* inherited, but they can be invoked within the code of a child class's constructor. The `SailBoat` class's constructor (lines 5–9 of Figure 8.6) invokes the parent class's constructor on line 7 and passes it the (x, y) location of the sailboat and its length. The invocation begins with the keyword **super,** rather than the name of the parent (also known as super) class, followed by an argument list. This is the syntax a child class uses to invoke a parent class constructor. Lines 14–16 of Figure 8.3 then execute and place the values passed to it into the `SailBoat` object's inherited data members `x`, `y`, and `length`.

---

**NOTE** *When a child class constructor invokes a parent class constructor, the invocation statement must be coded as the first line of the child class constructor.*

Every time a child class constructor is executed, a parent constructor must be executed before the remainder of the child class's constructor is executed. If an explicit invocation, such as the one on line 7 of Figure 8.6, is not included as the first line of a child class constructor, the parent's no-parameter constructor is automatically executed. In this case, the parent class must:

1. contain the code of a no-parameter constructor, or
2. contain no constructors at all, in which case the Java default constructor will be executed

If one of these two conditions is not met, and the first line of the child class is not an explicit invocation of a parent constructor, the child class will not translate.

### Invoking a Parent Class Method

A child class method can invoke any parent method whose access is designated public or whose access is designated protected. We will discuss protected access, its use, and its implications later in this chapter.

Because the `RowBoat` class does not contain a four-parameter constructor, line 8 of Figure 8.6 invokes the method `setColor` to store the color of the new sailboat that was passed to the constructor on line 3. If the `SailBoat` class contained a `setColor` method, it would have executed. Because it does not, we move up the inheritance chain to the parent class. The parent class does contain a public `setColor` method (lines 61–64 of Figure 8.3), and the invocation on line 8 causes it to execute.

```
1    import java.awt.*;
2
3    public class SailBoat extends RowBoat
4    {
5      public SailBoat(int x, int y, int length, Color color)
6      {
7        super(x, y, length); //invoke parent constructor
8        setColor(color);   //access parent's protected data method
9      }
10   }
```

**Figure 8.6**
The class **SailBoat**.

An alternate and equivalent coding for line 8 of Figure 8.6 would be:

```
this.setColor(color);
```

Because all of the `RowBoat` class's `set` methods are public, line 7 of Figure 8.6 could have been coded as the following three lines. The one-line alternative shown in the figure is preferred.

```
setX(x); //or this.setX(x);
setY(y); //or this.setY(y);
setLength(length); //or this.setLength(length);
```

**NOTE** *The syntax used to invoke a parent method from within a child method is the same syntax (that was discussed in Chapter 7) used to invoke another method in its class.*

The application `InheritanceBasics` presented in Figure 8.7 creates two rowboats and a cyan-colored sailboat and then displays them on the left and right sides of the game board, respectively. The program's output is shown in Figure 8.8

The `show` method is invoked on line 20 of Figure 8.7 to display the sailboat whose location, size, and color is specified on line 9. Because a `SailBoat` object (sb1) invoked the method, the search for the method begins in the `SailBoat` class just as it does for classes that do not extend other classes. If the `SailBoat` class contained a `show` method with a graphics parameter, it would have been executed. Because it does not, we move up the inheritance chain to the parent class `RowBoat`. It contains a public `show` method with a graphics parameter (line 22 of Figure 8.3), and the invocation on line 20 causes it to execute. The inherited `show` method draws the sailboat object sb1.

Line 26 of the inherited `show` method invokes the method `calculatePrice`. The search for this method also begins in the `SailBoat` class because the `show` method that issued the invocation is operating on an instance of this class, sb1. Because the SailBoat class does not contain a cal-culatePrice method, the search continues up the inheritance chain, and RowBoat class's version of the method executes.

```
1    import edu.sjcny.gpv1.*;
2    import java.awt.*;
3
4    public class InheritanceBasics extends DrawableAdapter
5    {  static InheritanceBasics ge = new InheritanceBasics();
6       static GameBoard gb = new GameBoard(ge, "Inheritance Basics");
7       static RowBoat rb1 = new RowBoat(30, 150, 200);
8       static RowBoat rb2 = new RowBoat(30, 250, 150);
9       static SailBoat sb1 = new SailBoat(260, 150, 200, Color.CYAN);
10
11      public static void main(String[] args)
12      {
13         showGameBoard(gb);
14      }
15
16      public void draw(Graphics g)
17      {
18         rb1.show(g);
19         rb2.show(g);
20         sb1.show(g);
21      }
22   }
```

**Figure 8.7**
The application **InheritanceBasics**.

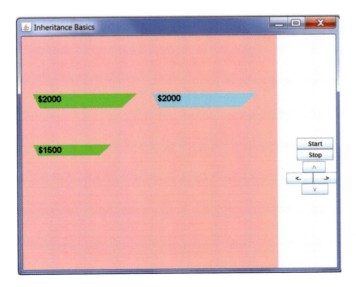

**Figure 8.8**
The output produced by the application **InheritanceBasics**.

### 8.3.2 Overriding Methods

Consistent with the concept of inheritance, the SailBoat class's four-parameter constructor added to the attributes inherited from its parent class. As previously mentioned, child classes can also modify the inherited attributes. The mechanism for modifying an inherited method is called *overriding* a method, which allows a child class to contain a method whose signature is exactly the *same* (same returned type, name, and parameter list) as the parent's method it is modifying.

Suppose that a second version of a sailboat, named SailBoatV2, was being offered for sale. This type of sailboat is not only delivered in a specified color, but it also has a mast installed on it. In order to properly display the new type of sailboat (with a mast), the RowBoat's show method would be overridden. The modified version of the method, coded in the new SailboatV2 class, would incorporate the drawing of the mast into its version of the method.

Because the UML diagram of the RowBoat shown in Figure 8.1 contains many more data members and methods than the UML diagram of the SailBoat class, we may be tempted to make the new class a child of the RowBoat class. If we do this, in addition to overriding the inherited show method, we would also have to rewrite the code of the SailBoat class's four-parameter constructor when the new class is coded. A better approach would be to take advantage of the fact that Java supports chain inheritance, which is depicted on the left side of Figure 8.2, and make the new class a child of the SailBoat class. The new class would then inherit all of the attributes (data members and methods) of both the RowBoat and the SailBoat classes, which gives it the ability to invoke the SailBoat class's four-parameter constructor. This approach to the design of the new class is depicted in Figure 8.9.

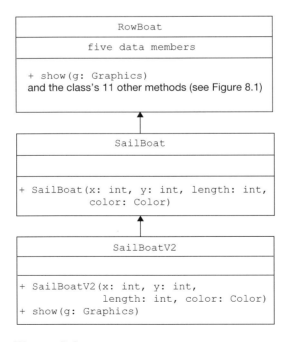

**Figure 8.9**
The inheritance chain of the class **SailBoatV2**.

The implementation of the class `SailBoatV2` is shown in Figure 8.10. As specified in Figure 8.9, it extends the class `SailBoat` (line 3). Its four-parameter constructor (lines 5–8) simply invokes its parent's four-parameter constructor on line 7, passing it the (x, y) location, length, and color of the new sailboat that was passed to it. It also overwrites the `show` method it inherits from the `RowBoat` class (lines 11–17).

```
1    import java.awt.*;
2
3    public class SailBoatV2 extends SailBoat //overriding a parent method
4    {
5      public SailBoatV2(int x, int y, int length, Color color)
6      {
7        super(x, y, length, color); //invoke the parent's constructor
8      }
9
10     @Override //translator verified an inherited method has this signature
11     public void show(Graphics g) // overwrites the parent's method
12     {
13       super.show(g); //invoke the parent's method to draw the boat
14       g.setColor(Color.BLACK); //draw the mast
15       g.fillRect(getX() + getLength()/2, getY() - getLength()/2,
16                  3, getLength()/2);
17     }
18   }
```

**Figure 8.10**
The class **SailBoatV2**.

## Invoking a Parent's Version of an Overwritten Method

The overridden version of the `show` method coded in the `SailBoatV2` class begins by invoking its inherited `show` method (line 13 of Figure 8.10) to draw the hull of the sailboat. As when invoking an inherited constructor, the keyword **super** is used in the invocation. When invoking a nonconstructor inherited method, the keyword **super** is followed by a dot.

The `SailBoatV2` class's inheritance chain is used to locate the invoked method. The syntax `super.` that proceeds the name and argument list of the invocation on line 13 tells the translator that we do not want the search to begin for the invoked method in the `SailBoatV2` class but rather to begin the search in its parent class. Otherwise, the `SailBoatV2` class's `show` method would invoke itself.

Because the `RowBoat` does contain a `show` method whose parameter is a `Graphics` object (line 22 of Figure 8.3), this method executes and draws the hull of the boat. Then, lines 14–16 of Figure 8.10 incorporate the modification to this method by drawing the sailboat's mast. If the search up the inheritance chain did not locate a `show` method whose parameter was a `Graphics` object, the translation of the `SailBoatV2` class would have ended in a translation error.

### The @Override directive

The @Override directive that appears on line 10 of Figure 8.10 instructs the translator to search up the SailBoatV2 class's inheritance chain for a method with the same signature that is coded on the line that follows it. If it cannot find a method with that signature, the translation ends in an error.

It is good programming practice to include this translation directive before the signature of a method that is meant to override an inherited method. Suppose the method name or parameter list typed on line 11 was syntactically correct but did not match the parameter list of the method it was overriding. For example, suppose the signature with the method's name was misspelled as shown below:

```
11   public void shown(Graphics g) //does NOT override inherited show method
```

Without the directive on line 10, the class would translate, but the inherited show method would not have been overridden. The client invocation on line 20 of Figure 8.11 would then cause the inherited method to execute, and the sailboat would be drawn without a mast.

Figure 8.11 presents the application OverRidingMethods, which is the same application presented in Figure 8.7, except the sailboat it creates on line 9 is now a SailBoatV2 object. As a result, the SailBoatV2 class's overridden show method is invoked on line 20, and the sailboat is drawn with a mast. The output it produces is shown in Figure 8.12.

```
1    import edu.sjcny.gpv1.*;
2    import java.awt.*;
3
4    public class OverRidingMethods extends DrawableAdapter
5    { static OverRidingMethods ge = new OverRidingMethods();
6      static GameBoard gb = new GameBoard(ge, "OVERRIDING METHODS");
7      static RowBoat rb1 = new RowBoat(30, 150, 200);
8      static RowBoat rb2 = new RowBoat(30, 250, 150);
9      static SailBoatV2 sb1 = new SailBoatV2(260, 150, 200, Color.CYAN);
10
11     public static void main(String[] args)
12     {
13       showGameBoard(gb);
14     }
15
16     public void draw(Graphics g)
17     {
18       rb1.show(g);
19       rb2.show(g);
20       sb1.show(g);
21     }
22   }
```

**Figure 8.11**
The application **OverRidingMethods**.

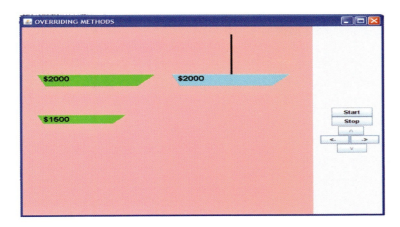

**Figure 8.12**
The output produced by the application **OverRidingMethods**.

## Final Methods

A method can be declared to be a `final` method by coding the keyword **final** in its signature immediately after the method's access modifier. When a method is declared to be final, it cannot be overridden by a child class. An attempt to do so results in a translation error. For example, if the signature of the `show` method on line 22 of the `RowBoat` class (Figure 8.3) was coded as shown below, the `SailBoatV2` class shown in Figure 8.10 could not override it.

```
22      public final void show(Graphics g)
```

Methods that enforce security on systems are usually declared to be final to prevent them from being overridden.

## Overriding versus Overloading Methods

The concepts of overriding and overloading methods are often confused because both concepts can be used to code a new method that has the same name as an existing method. In addition, the two topics are often considered to be more restrictive than they actually are. Before concluding our discussion of overriding methods, we will discuss the differences between, and commonalities shared by, these concepts.

One difference between the concepts of overriding and overloading methods also allows us to identify which concept is being used. When two methods in an inheritance chain have the same name and the same parameter list, the concept of *overriding* methods is being used. When two methods in an inheritance chain, or within the same class, have the same name and different parameter lists (i.e., either the number and/or type of the parameters are different), the concept of *overloading* methods is being used.

A second difference is that the concept of overriding a method cannot be used to modify the functionality of a method coded in its class because two methods with the same name and parameter list cannot be coded in the same class. The code of an overridden method and the code of the method that overrides it must appear in two different classes in an inheritance chain. The concept of overloading a method is less restrictive. The code of an overloaded method and that of the method it overloads can appear in the same class or in different classes within an inheritance chain.

The concepts of overriding and overloading methods have many things in common:

- both concepts are used to modify or expand the functionality of an existing method
- both concepts can be used to produce a new method that has the same name as an existing method
- both static and nonstatic methods can be overridden and overloaded
- a child class can overload and override any of its inherited methods
- the translator always uses the same technique to locate and identify a method that is being invoked regardless of the whether the method has been overridden or overloaded

This section will conclude with a summary of the search path the translator uses to locate an invoked overridden or overloaded method, and a summary of the syntax used to invoke inherited methods.

## Summary of the Method Search Path

When an overloaded or overridden method is invoked, the translator uses the same search process to locate the method that it uses to locate all invoked methods. The class of the object's reference variable, or the class of an invoked static method, is searched for a method whose name and parameter list matches the name and argument list in the invocation statement. If a match is *not* found in that class, the search continues up the class's inheritance chain.

## Summary of the Inherited Method Invocation Syntax

As we have learned, a child class method can invoke a method inherited from its parent. If the method is not overridden in the child class, the method is invoked by coding the name of the method followed by an argument list. When the method is a static method, this syntax is preceded by the name of the parent class followed by a dot. If the parent method is overridden and is not a static method, the invocation is preceded by the keyword **super** followed by a dot.

## 8.3.3 Extending Inherited Data Members

A child class's ability to extend the attributes it inherits is not limited to overriding and overloading inherited methods or including new methods in its class. It can also extend the data members it inherits by declaring additional data members inside its class definition. Figure 8.13 presents the inheritance chain of a class named `SailBoatV3`, which is a sailboat delivered with a mast and a sail. To facilitate the implementation of the new class, it extends the `SailboatV2` class because, in all other aspects, this new type of sailboat is a `SailBoatV2` object.

As shown in its UML diagram, the `SailBoatV3` class will override its inherited `calculatePrice` method. The new version of this method will use the class's new data members `sailArea` and `pricePerSquareFoot` to calculate and include the cost of the sail in the boat's price. The boat's `sailArea` will be specified using the last parameter of the class's five-parameter constructor. In addition, the inherited `show` method will be overwritten. This version of the method will be used to draw the sail on the boat's mast.

NOTE *The name of a data member added to a child class can be the same as the name of an inherited data member, but it is good programming practice to avoid duplicating inherited data member names.*

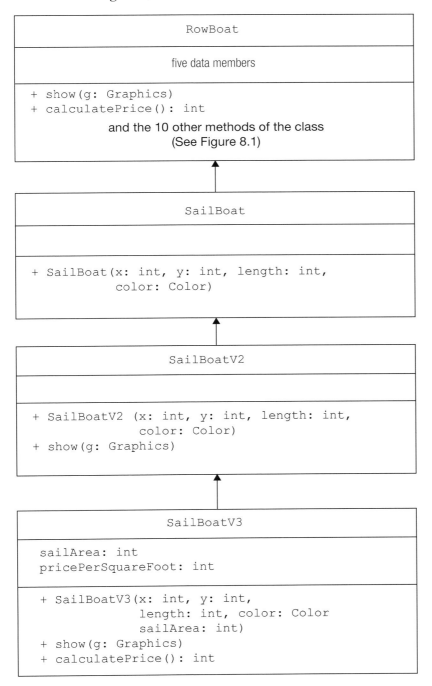

**Figure 8.13**
The inheritance chain of the class **SailBoatV3**.

Figure 8.14 shows the implementation of the SailBoatV3 class that extends the class Sail-BoatV2 (line 3). Its two additional data members, pricePerSquareFoot and sailArea, are declared on lines 5 and 6. Line 12 of the class's constructor stores the sail area passed to its last parameter in the data member sailArea. Line 19 of the expanded calculatePrice method multiplies these data members to determine the sail's price and then adds this product to the price returned from line 18's invocation of RowBoat's version of the method.

Lines 25–31 implement additional functionality of the overridden show method by defining the (x, y) coordinates of the triangular sail's vertices and then drawing the sail. Line 32 invokes the class's inherited show method to draw the boat's hull and mast.

Figure 8.15 presents the application ExtendingDataMembers, which is the same application presented in Figure 8.11, except it creates a yellow instance (sb2) of the class SailBoatV3 on line

```
1    import java.awt.*;
2
3    public class SailBoatV3 extends SailBoatV2
4    {
5      private static int pricePerSquareFoot = 2;
6      private int sailArea; // additional data members
7
8      public SailBoatV3(int x, int y, int length,
9                        Color color, int sailArea)
10     {
11       super(x, y, length, color);
12       this.sailArea = sailArea;
13     }
14
15     @Override
16     public int calculatePrice() //invokes the method it overrides
17     {
18       int hullPrice = super.calculatePrice(); //invokes RowBoat's method
19       return hullPrice + sailArea * pricePerSquareFoot;
20     }
21
22     @Override
23     public void show(Graphics g)
24     {
25       int[] xSail = {getX() + getLength()/2, getX(),
26                      getX() + getLength()/2,};
27       int[] ySail = {getY() - getLength()/2, getY() - getLength()/8,
28                      getY() - getLength()/8};
29
30       g.setColor(Color.WHITE); //draw the sail
31       g.fillPolygon(xSail, ySail, xSail.length);
32       super.show(g);
33     }
34  }
```

**Figure 8.14**
The class **SailBoatV3**.

10. As a result, the `SailBoatV3` class's version of the `show` method is invoked on line 22, and the yellow sailboat is drawn with a sail as shown in the bottom right portion of Figure 8.12. Although the lengths of the two sailboats declared in the application (lines 9–10) are both 200, the cost of the second boat (sb2) is higher because of the $600 additional cost of the boat's 300-square-foot sail (at $2 per square foot as per line 5 of Figure 8.14).

```
1    import edu.sjcny.gpv1.*;
2    import java.awt.*;
3
4    public class ExtendingDataMembers extends DrawableAdapter
5    { static ExtendingDataMembers ge = new ExtendingDataMembers ();
6      static GameBoard gb = new GameBoard(ge, "EXTENDING DATA MEMBERS");
7      static RowBoat rb1 = new RowBoat(30, 150, 200);
8      static RowBoat rb2 = new RowBoat(30, 250, 150);
9      static SailBoatV2 sb1 = new SailBoatV2(260, 150, 200, Color.CYAN);
10     static SailBoatV3 sb2 = new SailBoatV3(260, 300, 200, Color.YELLOW, 300);
11
12     public static void main(String[] args)
13     {
14       showGameBoard(gb);
15     }
16
17     public void draw(Graphics g)
18     {
19       rb1.show(g);
20       rb2.show(g);
21       sb1.show(g);
22       sb2.show(g);
23     }
24   }
```

**Figure 8.15**
The application **ExtendingDataMembers**.

**Figure 8.16**
The output produced by the application **ExtendingDataMembers**.

**Parent Class Methods Invoking Child Class Methods**

As previously discussed at the end of Section 8.3.1, when the `RowBoat` class's `show` method invokes the method `calculatePrice` (line 26 of Figure 8.3), the search for the method begins in the class of the object that invoked the `show` method. When line 22 of Figure 8.15 executes, the search for the `calculatePrice` method begins in sb2's class, `SailBoatV3`. Because this class overrides the inherited version of the `calculatePrice` method, sb2's price is calculated by its version of the method coded on lines 16–20 of Figure 8.14. This is precisely what should happen because otherwise the cost of the sail would not be included in the price of the sailboat sb2. The Java process used to locate invoked methods, which is summarized at the end of Section 8.3.2, causes the `RowBoat` class's `show` method to invoke the `SailBoatV3` class's `calculatePrice` method to determine the price of a `SailBoatV3` sailboat instance.

## 8.4 USING INHERITANCE IN THE DESIGN PROCESS

The time and effort required to create a new class can be greatly reduced if we can extend the attributes of an existing class using the basic techniques of inheritance discussed in the previous section. These techniques include inheriting methods and data members into the new class, overriding and overloading these methods to change and extend their functionality, and adding new methods and data members to the new class. But even if there are no existing classes that provide some of the functionality of the classes specified for a new program, the time and cost to develop the program can still be reduced using the concept of inheritance during the design process.

Suppose your Uncle Ed asked you to develop a Java program to "keep track of the inventory" of a boat store he was about to open that will carry rowboats, sailboats, and powerboats. After several follow-up conversations with him, you have determined that "keeping track of the inventory" means knowing the location of each boat on his storage lot, knowing each boat's price and size, and other details that are particular to the type of the boat such as the number of oars, the sail area, and the horsepower of a powerboat. Translating all of this into an OPP design, you concluded there will be three worker classes in the program and produced the UML diagrams shown in Figure 8.17.

Before proceeding to the coding phase of Uncle Ed's (or any other) program, we should apply the basic concepts of inheritance previously discussed in this chapter and the other more advanced inheritance concepts, such as *abstract classes*, to the design process.

### 8.4.1 Abstract Classes

After the UML diagrams that describe the objects that will be part of the program are prepared, their data members and methods should be compared to determine their commonalities. An examination of the data members of the classes specified in Figure 8.17 reveals that the first five data members in all three classes are the same. In addition, the signatures of all of their methods, except for their constructors, are the same. If we were to give these UML diagrams to three programmers to implement, each programmer would have to code the same five data members into their class and write the same six `set` and `get` methods to change and fetch the values of the data members. In addition, the code of their `calculatePrice`, `show`, and `toString` methods would share some similar code.

```
┌─────────────────────────────────────┐   ┌─────────────────────────────────────┐
│            RowBoatV2                 │   │            SailBoatV4                │
├─────────────────────────────────────┤   ├─────────────────────────────────────┤
│ - pricePerFoot: int                 │   │ - pricePerFoot: int                 │
│ - x: int                            │   │ - x: int                            │
│ - y: int                            │   │ - y: int                            │
│ - length : int                      │   │ - length : int                      │
│ - color: Color                      │   │ - color: Color                      │
│ - oars : int                        │   │ - sailArea: int                     │
├─────────────────────────────────────┤   ├─────────────────────────────────────┤
│ + RowBoatV2 (x: int , y: int,       │   │ + SailBoatV2 (x: int , y: int,      │
│            length: int, c: Color,   │   │            length: int, c: Color,   │
│            oars: int)               │   │            sailArea : int)          │
│ + calculatePrice(): int             │   │ + calculatePrice(): int             │
│ + show(g: Graphics)                 │   │ + show(g: Graphics)                 │
│ + toString(): String                │   │ + toString(): String                │
│ + getX(): int                       │   │ + getX(): int                       │
│ + getY(): int                       │   │ + getY(): int                       │
│ + getLength(): int                  │   │ + getLength(): int                  │
│ + getColor(): Color                 │   │ + getColor(): Color                 │
│ + setX(x: int)                      │   │ + setX(x: int)                      │
│ + setY(y: int)                      │   │ + setY(y: int)                      │
└─────────────────────────────────────┘   └─────────────────────────────────────┘
```

```
┌─────────────────────────────────────┐
│            PowerBoat                 │
├─────────────────────────────────────┤
│ - pricePerFoot: int                 │
│ - x: int                            │
│ - y: int                            │
│ - length : int                      │
│ - color: Color                      │
│ - horsePower: int                   │
├─────────────────────────────────────┤
│ + PowerBoat (x: int , y: int,       │
│            length: int, c: Color,   │
│            horsepower: int)         │
│ + calculatePrice(): int             │
│ + show(g: Graphics)                 │
│ + toString(): String                │
│ + getX(): int                       │
│ + getY(): int                       │
│ + getLength(): int                  │
│ + getColor(): Color                 │
│ + setX(x: int)                      │
│ + setY(y: int)                      │
└─────────────────────────────────────┘
```

**Figure 8.17**
The class design of a boat store's inventory application.

To avoid this duplication among the three classes, a forth class named `Boat` is added to the design as shown at the top of Figure 8.18. This class will be an *abstract class*. A class is designated to be abstract by including the keyword **abstract** in its heading. For example:

```
public abstract class Boat //an abstract class
```

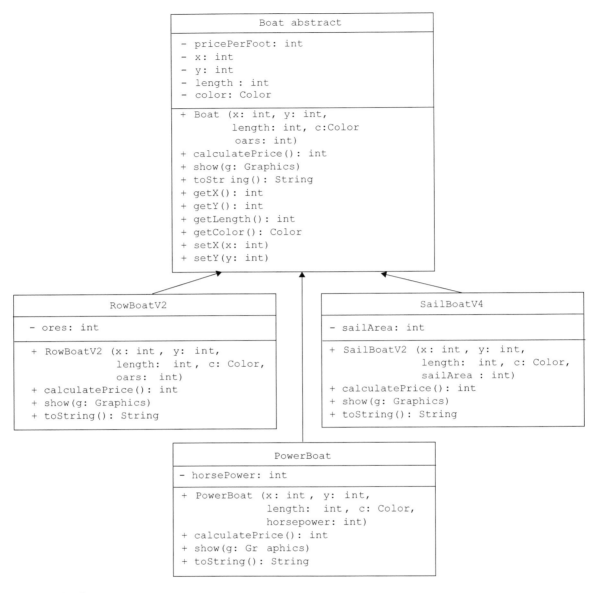

**Figure 8.18**
The use of inheritance in the design of a boat store's inventory application.

An abstract class is used to collect data members and methods that are common to several classes into one class. It is not meant to be the class of one of the types of objects that will make up a program. For example, you cannot purchase an instance of a `Boat` object from Uncle Ed. He only sells rowboats, sailboats, and powerboats. Consistent with this use of abstract classes, an attempt to declare an object in an abstract class results in a translation error.

As shown in the bottom portion of Figure 8.17, after the abstract `Boat` class is added to the design of Uncle Ed's program, the duplicated five data members and the `set` and `get` methods are eliminated from the original three classes and moved into the UML diagram of the `Boat` class.

Then, as indicated by the arrows in the figure, the original three classes become subclasses of the Boat class. By simply including the keyword **extends** in the heading of the classes they code, the authors of the original three classes no longer have to code five of their class's six data members or the six set and get methods. But the reduction in effort does not end here.

Each of the original classes also contained methods to draw the boat it defines and calculate its price as well as a toString method. The signatures of these methods are the same in all three classes, and your conversations with Uncle Ed revealed that they share some common functionality. He has told you that the base price of each type of boat is calculated in the same way because they share a common hull. In reflecting on what he said, you realize that this introduces some common functionality into the show methods because each boat's hull will look the same. It also introduces some common functionality into the calculatePrice method because each boat's hull will be priced in the same way. Because each of the toString methods will return the annotated values of the classes' first five data members, these methods also share some common functionality.

Methods in the child classes that have the same signature and share some common functionality also become part of the parent class's UML diagram, as shown in the UML diagram of the Boat class, which now includes a calculatePrice, a show, and a toString method. Unlike the set and get methods that were eliminated from the child classes, some trace of these relocated methods are retained in the UML diagrams of the child classes to provide the functionality that is not common to each child class.

For example, the functionality of calculating the additional cost of a powerboat's motor would have to be retained in the PowerBoatV2 class, and the cost of a rowboat's oars would be calculated in the RowBoat class. In the design presented in Figure 8.18, the child classes provide additional functionality by overriding the Boat class's calculatePrice, show, and toString methods. The code of these methods would invoke Boat's version of the method to calculate and return the price of the boat's hull, draw the boat's hull, and to build and return a string containing the annotated versions of Boat's five data members.

Comparing the UML diagrams in Figures 8.17 and 8.18, we can see that the use of inheritance in the design presented in Figure 8.18 has significantly reduced the effort required to produce Uncle Ed's program. The number of data members to be coded by the programmers has been reduced from 18 to 8, and the number of methods has been reduced from 30 to 22. In addition, the constructor in the Boat class will implement the commonality within the constructors in the other three classes, which will reduce the effort required to produce the constructors in the other three classes.

Figures 8.19–8.22 present the implementation of the design depicted in Figure 8.18. The Boat class is declared abstract on line 4 of Figure 8.19. Consistent with our design philosophy, it includes all of the data members common to the other three classes, and its methods provide the functionality shared by the other three classes. Those classes extend the Boat class (line 3 of Figures 8.20–8.22). They each include a data member particular to their type of boat (e.g., line 5 of Figure 8.20), and their methods invoke Boat's methods (e.g., lines 9, 15, 21, and 31 of Figure 8.20) before adding the functionality particular to their type of boat. For example, line 16 of Figure 8.20 computes the cost of the oars, lines 22-26 draw the oars, and line 31 adds the number of oars to toStrings returned strings. The implements clause in the heading of the class Boat (line 4 of Figure 8.19) will be discussed in Section 8.7.

The application `DesignTechniques` shown in Figure 8.23 uses the new design to add a rowboat with four oars (line 8), a sailboat with a 200-square-foot sail (line 9), and a powerboat with a 400-horsepower motor (line 10) to Uncle Ed's inventory. The boats are then displayed on his lot (Figure 8.24).

```java
1    import java.awt.*;
2    import java.io.Serializable;
3
4    public abstract class Boat implements Serializable //contains attributes
5    {                                                  //common to all boats
6      private static int PRICE_PER_FOOT = 10;
7      private int x, y, length; //data members common to all types of boats
8      private Color color;
9
10     public Boat(int x, int y, int length, Color color)
11     {
12       this.x = x;
13       this.y = y;
14       this.length = length;
15       this.color = color;
16     }
17     public int calculatePrice() //will be overridden
18     {
19       return length * PRICE_PER_FOOT;
20     }
21     public void show(Graphics g)  //will be overridden
22     {
23       int[] xBoat = {getX() , getX() + length, getX() + 6*length/7,
24                     getX() + length/14};
25       int[] yBoat = {getY(), getY(), getY() + length/7,
26                     getY() + length/7};
27       int price = calculatePrice();
28       g.setColor(color);
29       g.fillPolygon(xBoat, yBoat, xBoat.length);
30       g.setColor(Color.BLACK);
31       g.setFont(new Font("Arial", Font.BOLD, 16));
32       g.drawString("$" + String.valueOf(price), x + 10, y + 16);
33     }
34     public String toString() //will be overridden
35     {
36       return "Location: (" + x + ", " + y +"), length: " + length +
37                     ",Color: " + color;
38     }
39     public int getX() //get & set methods common to all types of boats
40     {
41       return x;
```

```
42      }
43      public int getY()
44      {
45        return y;
46      }
47      public int getLength()
48      {
49        return length;
50      }
51      public Color getColor()
52      {
53        return color;
54      }
55      public void setX(int x)
56      {
57        this.x = x;
58      }
59      public void setY(int y)
60      {
61        this.y = y;
62      }
63    }
```

**Figure 8.19**
The abstract class **Boat**.

```
1     import java.awt.*;
2
3     public class RowBoatV2 extends Boat
4     {
5       private int oars; //extended (additional) data member
6
7       public RowBoatV2(int x, int y, int length, Color c, int oars)
8       {
9         super(x, y, length, c);
10        this.oars = oars;
11      }
12      @Override
13      public int calculatePrice() //overrides parent method
14      {
15        int hullPrice = super.calculatePrice();
16        return hullPrice + oars * 10;
17      }
18      @Override
19      public void show(Graphics g) //overrides parent method
20      {
21        super.show(g);
```

```
22      g.setColor(Color.BLACK);
23      for(int i = 1; i <= oars; i++) //each ore
24      {
25        g.fillRect(getX() + i*10, getY() - 20, 2, 20); //handle
26        g.fillOval(getX() + i*10-2, getY() - 30, 6, 10); //paddle
27      }
28    }
29    public String toString() //overrides parent method
30    {
31      return super.toString() + ", Oars: " + oars;
32    }
33  }
```

**Figure 8.20**
The child class **RowBoatV2**.

```
1    import java.awt.*;
2
3    public class SailBoatV4 extends Boat
4    {
5      private int sailArea; //extended (additional) data member
6
7      public SailBoatV4(int x, int y, int length,
8                        Color color, int sailArea)
9      {
10       super(x, y, length, color);
11       this.sailArea = sailArea;
12     }
13     @Override
14     public int calculatePrice() //overrides parent method
15     {
16       int hullPrice = super.calculatePrice();
17       return hullPrice + sailArea * 2;
18     }
19     @Override
20     public void show(Graphics g) //overrides parent method
21     {
22       int[] xSail = {getX() + getLength()/2, getX(),
23                      getX() + getLength()/2};
24       int[] ySail = {getY() - getLength()/2, getY() - getLength()/8,
25                      getY() - getLength()/8};
26
27       super.show(g);
28       g.setColor(Color.BLACK); //draw the mast
29       g.fillRect(getX() + getLength()/2, getY() - getLength()/2, 3,
30                  getLength()/2);
31       g.setColor(Color.WHITE); //draw the sail
32       g.fillPolygon(xSail, ySail, xSail.length);
33     }
```

```
34      public String toString()  //overrides parent method
35      {
36        return super.toString() + ", Sail Area: " + sailArea;
37      }
38    }
```

**Figure 8.21**
The child class **SailBoatV4**.

```
1     import java.awt.*;
2
3     public class PowerBoat extends Boat
4     {
5       private int horsePower;  //extended (additional) data member
6
7       public PowerBoat(int x, int y, int length,
8                        Color color, int horsePower)
9       {
10        super(x, y, length, color);
11        this.horsePower = horsePower;
12      }
13      @Override
14      public int calculatePrice()  //overrides parent method
15      {
16        int hullPrice = super.calculatePrice();
17        return hullPrice + horsePower * 3;
18      }
19      @Override
20      public void show(Graphics g)  //overrides parent method
21      {
22        int[] xSail = {getX() + getLength()/2, getX(),
23                       getX() + getLength()/2,};
24        int[] ySail = {getY() - getLength()/2, getY() - getLength()/8,
25                       getY() - getLength()/8};
26
27        super.show(g);
28        g.setColor(Color.BLACK);  //draw the shaft
29        g.fillOval(getX() - 13, getY() + getLength()/7 , 30, 4);
30        g.setColor(Color.GRAY);  //draw the propeller
31        g.fillOval(getX() - 20, getY() + getLength()/7, 20, 6);
32        g.fillOval(getX() - 13, getY() + getLength()/7 - 7, 6, 20);
33      }
34      public String toString()  //overrides parent method
35      {
36        return super.toString() + ", Horsepower: " + horsePower;
37      }
38    }
```

**Figure 8.22**
The child class **PowerBoat**.

```
1    import edu.sjcny.gpv1.*;
2    import java.awt.*;
3
4    public class DesignTechniques extends DrawableAdapter
5    {
6      static DesignTechniques ge = new DesignTechniques();
7      static GameBoard gb = new GameBoard(ge, "Design Techniques");
8      static RowBoatV2 rb1 = new RowBoatV2(50, 200, 120, Color.YELLOW, 4);
9      static SailBoatV4 sb1 = new SailBoatV4(220, 200, 200, Color.GREEN, 200);
10     static PowerBoat pb1 = new PowerBoat(50, 300, 200, Color.MAGENTA, 400);
11
12     public static void main(String[] args)
13     {
14       showGameBoard(gb);
15     }
16
17     public void draw(Graphics g)
18     {
19       rb1.show(g);
20       sb1.show(g);
21       pb1.show(g);
22     }
23   }
```

**Figure 8.23**
The application **DesignTechniques**.

**Figure 8.24**
The output produced by the application **DesignTechniques**.

## 8.4.2 Designing Parent Methods to Invoke Child Methods

In addition to creating an abstract class to collect the common attributes shared by the various objects that will be part of a program, there are other inheritance concepts that should be considered when designing and coding the methods in an abstract or nonabstract parent class. One of them is the ability of a parent method to invoke a child class's method.

As discussed at the end of Section 8.3.3, the code of a method in a super class that is operating on an instance of a direct or indirect subclass can invoke a method coded in the subclass. The syntax used is the familiar syntax of coding the method's name followed by the appropriate argument list. For example, if a nonstatic method named `extras` is added to the child class `RowBoatV2`, shown in Figure 8.20, then it could be invoked inside any of the methods of its parent class `Boat`, shown in Figure 8.19, by coding: `extras();`

This presents an alternate approach to adding functionality to an inherited method during the design phase. Instead of child classes overriding an inherited method, they simply include a method that implements their version of the added functionality, and the code of the parent's inherited method includes an invocation of this method. The signature of the method added to the child classes must be the same in all of the child classes that intend to add functionality to the inherited method.

If this design approach was taken to calculate the price of a rowboat, sailboat, and powerboat, the `Boat` class's `calculatePrice` method, lines 17–20 of Figure 8.19, would be changed to the version of the method at the top Figure 8.25. This version of the method invokes the method `extras` to calculate an additional cost to be added to the price of the hull for oars, a sail, or a motor. The empty version of the method extras shown at the bottom of the figure has to be added to the `Boat` class or it will not compile. The child classes' `calculatePrice` methods in Figures 8.20, 8.21, and 8.22 would be replaced with the code of the `extras` method shown in the upper, middle, and lower portions of Figure 8.26, respectively.

```
public int calculatePrice()
{
    return length * PRICE_PER_FOOT + extras();
}

public int extras()
{

}
```

**Figure 8.25**
A parent method that invokes the child's method **extras** and the empty implementation of the **extras** method coded in the parent class.

```
public int extras() //RowBoatV2's version of the method extras
{
    return oars * 10;
}

public int extras() //SailBoatV4's version of the method extras
{
    return sailArea * 2;
}

public int extras() //PowerBoat's version of the method extras
{
    return horsePower * 3;
}
```

**Figure 8.26**
Three child class implementations of the method **extras**

### 8.4.3 Abstract Parent Methods

An alternative to including the empty version of the method extras shown at the bottom of Figure 8.25 is to code it as an abstract method in the parent class, in this case, the class Boat (Figure 8.19). Abstract methods include the keyword **abstract** in their signature before their returned type. In addition, their signature ends with a semicolon. As shown below, they do not contain an open and close brace or any code.

```
public abstract int extra();
```

When this approach is used, the parent class must be declared abstract because the parent class no longer contains an implementation of a method it invokes. In addition, the translator will verify that each nonabstract class that inherits directly or indirectly from the abstract class implements a method whose signature matches the signature of the abstract method. If it does not, the child class will not translate. In effect, the inclusion of an abstract method in a parent class is a promissory note, enforced by the translator, that child classes will implement (override) the abstract method.

The use of abstract methods in a super class is considered to be good programming practice when:

- The super class will not be instantiated. Its sole purpose is to collect the common data members and functionality shared by its direct and indirect subclasses.
- Most of its direct and indirect subclasses will add functionally to the super class method that invokes the abstract method.

In the event that a subclass does not need to add functionality to the super class method that invokes an abstract method, the subclass would implement the abstract method with an empty code block.

### 8.4.4 Final Classes

A class can be declared to be a `final` class by coding the keyword **final** in its heading immediately after the class's access modifier. When a class is declared `final`, it cannot be extended. An attempt to do so results in a translation error. For example, if the heading of the `PowerBoat` class (line 3 of Figure 8.22) was coded as shown below, then it could not be a parent class.

```
3    public final class PowerBoat extends Boat
```

Classes that contain methods that enforce security on systems are usually declared to be `final` to prevent their methods from being overridden.

A class cannot be declared `abstract` and `final` because it would be rendered useless. If it were abstract, instances of the class could not be created; if it were also final, it could not be extended. In short, nothing could be done with it.

### 8.4.5 Protected Data Members

When a method or a data member in a class is designated to have private access, the method can only be invoked and the data member can only be directly accessed by the methods defined inside the class. A private method cannot be invoked by methods defined outside of its class. A private data member can be indirectly accessed by a method defined in another class by invoking its `set` and `get` methods. When a method or a data member is designated to have public access the method can be invoked, and the data member can be directly accessed, by methods defined outside of its class.

A class's methods and data members can also be declared to have protected access by beginning their declaration with the keyword **protected**.

```
    protected int count;
```

The access modifier `protected` is less restrictive than `private` access and more restrictive than `public` access. Restrictions imposed by protected access are package dependent.

When a method or a data member is designated to have `protected` access, the method can be invoked, and the data member can be directly accessed, by methods defined inside its class *and* its direct and indirect subclasses. As illustrated in the bottom and top left portions of Figure 8.27, the access is permitted whether or not the parent's protected data members/methods and the child classes are defined in the same package.

Methods in nonchild classes can only access another class's protected methods, and directly access its protected data members, if the nonchild class is defined in the same package as the protected methods and data. This restriction is illustrated in the top right and bottom portions of Figure 8.27.

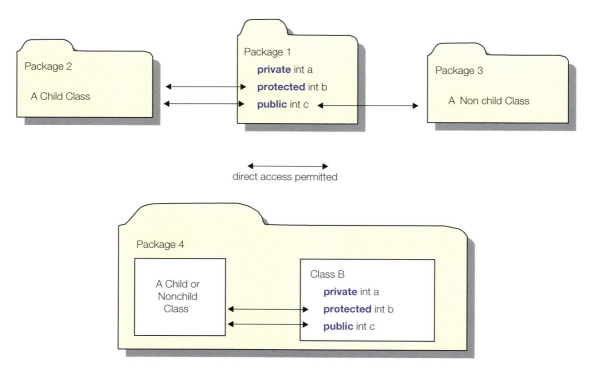

**Figure 8.27**
Restrictions imposed by **`private, protected`**, and **`public access`**.

**NOTE** *Protected methods and data members are hidden from nonchild classes defined in separate packages.*

### 8.4.6 Making a Class Inheritance Ready: Best Practices

When designing a class, we should always consider the possibility that other classes may extend it. If for some reason we want to prevent the class from being extended, the class is declared `final`. If a nonfinal class contains a constructor, it should also contain a no-parameter constructor even if its code block is empty, otherwise the child class's constructors will always have to explicitly invoke a parent constructor. A parent class that was created to collect the methods and data members common to other classes should be declared abstract.

Each method in a nonfinal class should be examined to decide if its functionality could be compromised if it were overridden in a subclass. When that is the case, the method should be declared `final`. To permit restricted modifications to a `final` method, the method should invoke an abstract method whose signature is defined within the `final` method's class, then subclasses can add functionality to a `final` method by implementing the abstract method. This abstract method approach should also be used when the algorithm of a parent class method requires that child classes add functionality particular to them because the translator will verify that the child classes implement the abstract method. This approach should also be considered when it is anticipated that a child class is likely to override a parent method.

A parent data member that stores a constant should always be declared as `final` to prevent it from being changed. Generally speaking, it is good programming practice to declare all nonfinal data members in a parent class to be private rather than protected and, where appropriate, include `set` and `get` methods to permit access to them. This maintains the encapsulation of the data members, which eliminates the possibility that a method in a child class could unintentionally access the data members by using a variable with the same name that it neglected to declare.

## 8.5. POLYMORPHISM

Polymorphism is the idea that something can exist in several different forms. We have already discussed several uses of polymorphism in computer science. One use of polymorphism we discussed is overloading methods. A method can be overloaded or morphed into a new form, with the new form having a different parameter list. These different forms of the method can be coded inside the same class, such as constructors with several different parameter lists, or one form of a method's parameter list can be coded in a super class, and another form could be coded in its subclass.

Other uses of polymorphism occur within the concept of inheritance. Two of these uses were already discussed. The first is the inheritance concept of overriding methods. In this use of polymorphism, one form of a method exists in the super class, and another form of the method, with the exact same signature, exists in the subclass. The second involves the invocation of a method by a parent method. Due to the search path used to locate the invoked method at run time, this invocation could take on the form of an invocation of a parent class method or a child class method with the same signature.

Polymorphism is also used to indicate that a child can take on the form of a parent because a child is also a parent. This should not be surprising because we have already learned that a child class inherits everything from a parent: all of its data members and all of its methods (except for its constructors). This polymorphic inheritance concept opens up a set of programming practices that makes our programs easier to write and easier to understand. In the remainder of this section, we will discuss these programming practices and the syntax used to incorporate them into the programs we write.

### 8.5.1 Parent and Child References

Because a child object is also considered to be a parent object, a parent reference variable can store the address of, or point to, a child object. This is a form of polymorphism because it permits a parent reference variable to assume many different forms. It can be a reference to a parent object, or it can be a reference to an instance of any class that inherits directly or indirectly from it.

Line 4 of the following code fragment illustrates the use of this form of polymorphism. Line 1 declares the variable `aBoat` to be a `Boat` class reference variable. Because the class `PowerBoat` (Figure 8.22) extends the class `Boat` (Figure 8.19), the variable can be morphed into a reference to a `PowerBoat` object. This is accomplished using the assignment statement on line 4. After line 4 executes, the variable aBoat stores the address of a PowerBoat object, the same object referenced by pb1.

```
//A super class reference variable can reference a subclass object
1   Boat aBoat; //declares a reference variable in the super class Boat
2   PowerBoat pb1 = new PowerBoat(50, 300, 200, Color.MAGENTA, 400);
3
4   aBoat = pb1; //aBoat and pb1 now reference the same powerboat
```

Consistent with this form of polymorphism, a super class reference variable that refers to one type of subclass object can be reassigned to reference an instance of another one of its subclasses. After the following code sequence executes, the variables aBoat and sb1 both reference the same SailBoatV4 object, whose class (Figure 8.21) also extends Boat.

```
//A super class reference variable can reference any subclass object
1   Boat aBoat; //declares a reference variable in the super class Boat
2   PowerBoat pb1 = new PowerBoat(50, 300, 200, Color.MAGENTA, 400);
3   SailBoatV4 sb1 = new SailBoatV4(220, 200, 200, Color.GREEN, 200);
4
5   aBoat = pb1; //aBoat references a powerboat
6   aBoat = sb1; //aBoat now references a sailboat
```

**NOTE** *A super class reference variable can refer to any instance of a class that directly, or indirectly, inherits from it.*

Using the syntax of coercion, the address of a child class object stored in a parent reference variable can be coerced into a child reference variable. After line 6 of the following code fragment executes, the child reference variable pb2 stores the address of a powerboat. If pb2 were declared to be a reference to a subclass of Boat other than the PowerBoat class, line 6 would result in a translation error.

```
//A subclass reference can be coerced into a child reference variable
1   Boat aBoat; //declares a reference variable in the super class Boat
2   PowerBoat pb1 = new PowerBoat(50, 300, 200, Color.MAGENTA, 400);
3   PowerBoat pb2;
4
5   aBoat = pb1; //aBoat now references the same PowerBoat child
6   pb2 = (PowerBoat) aBoat; //valid when aBoat references a PowerBoat
```

There is one restriction on the use of assignment statements that mixes child and parent reference variables. A child class reference variable cannot be assigned the address of a parent class object because a parent object is not a child object. An attempt to do so results in a translation error. A good way to remember this restriction comes from the old family adage: Parents can point to their children when they correct them, but it is rude for children to point to their parents.

The following code fragment uses the nonabstract parent class RowBoat defined in Figure 8.3 and the SailBoat class that extends it (Figure 8.6). Assigning the location of the parent class object declared on line 1 to the child class reference variable, sb1, on line 4 produces a translation error, as does line 5, which attempts to coerce the address of the parent RowBoat object into the child class reference variable.

```
   //A subclass reference variable can NOT reference a superclass object
1  RowBoat rb1 = new RowBoat(30, 150, 200);
2  SailBoat sb1;
3
4  sb1 = rb1; //syntax error: child reference assigned a parent object
5  sb1 = (SailBoat) rb1; //coercion does not remedy the problem
```

**NOTE**   *The addresses of parent objects cannot be assigned to child reference variables.*

### 8.5.2 Polymorphic Invocations

**Definition**

A **polymorphic invocation** is the act of invoking a method using a parent reference variable that refers to a child object.

When a method is invoked using a parent reference variable that refers to a child object, it is referred to as a **polymorphic invocation**. Consider the client code fragment shown in Figure 8.28 that uses the super class `Boat` (Figure 8.19) and its subclass `PowerBoat` (Figure 8.22). Although the variable `aBoat` declared on line 1 is of type `Boat`, it has been assigned the address of a child `PowerBoat` object. This is valid because parents can point to children. The `show` method is invoked on line 5 using this parent reference variable, which makes line 5 a polymorphic invocation of the `show` method.

```
1     static Boat aBoat = new PowerBoat(50, 300, 200, Color.MAGENTA, 400);
2
3     public void draw(Graphics g)
4     {
5        aBoat.show(g);
6     }
```

**Figure 8.28**
Polymorphic invocation of the method **show** by the object referenced by **aBoat**.

The translator always looks into the class of the reference variable that invoked a nonstatic method to verify the signature of the method, for both polymorphic and nonpolymorphic invocations. As a result, line 5 begins its search in the class `Boat` for a method named `show` whose parameter list is a `Graphics` object. Because the `Boat` class contains a method with that signature (line 21 of Figure 8.19), line 5 is valid syntax. The parent class `Boat` need not implement the method `show`; it can simply define the method's name and its signature as an abstract method.

If the class `Boat` did not contain a `show` method whose parameter list matched line 5's argument list, the translator's search would progress *up* through the classes in `Boat`'s inheritance chain. Because the class `Boat` does not explicitly extend a class, the search would end unsuccessfully in the class `Object`, and line 5 of Figure 8.28 would produce a translation error.

| | |
|---|---|
| NOTE | *The class of the parent reference variable used in a polymorphic method invocation must include, or have inherited, an implementation or an abstract version of the invoked method.* |

At runtime, the Java Runtime Environment uses a different starting point in its search to locate the method named in a polymorphic invocation. Unlike the translator that begins its search in the class of the parent reference variable coded in the invocation statement, the runtime environment begins its search in the class of the object referenced by the variable. For example, the search for the show method invoked on line 5 of Figure 8.28 would begin in the PowerBoat class because the variable aBoat references the PowerBoat object assigned to it on line 1. In effect, the invocation is morphed at runtime into an invocation of the show method that correctly draws a powerboat.

The programming language concept use to implement this form of polymorphism is called *dynamic binding*. The invocation is attached, or bound to, the method to be executed during runtime. Line 5 of Figure 8.29 is not a polymorphic invocation because line 1 declares pb1 to be a PowerBoat reference variable and assigns it the location of a PowerBoat object. For nonpolymorphic invocations, the method located by the translator's search to verify the existence of a method with the appropriate signature is the method executed at runtime.

```
1    static PowerBoat pb1 = new PowerBoat(50, 300, 200, Color.MAGENTA, 400);
2
3    public void draw(Graphics g)
4    {
5      pb1.show(g);
6    }
```

**Figure 8.29**
Nonpolymorphic invocation of the method **show** by the object referenced by **pb1**.

The application PolymorphicInvocations shown in Figure 8.30 is a modification of the application DesignTechniques presented in Figure 8.23. This version of the application uses polymorphic invocations inside its draw call back method to produce the output shown in Figure 8.31, which is the same output produced by the original version (Figure 8.24).

Line 11 of Figure 8.30 creates three Boat reference variables, which are then assigned (lines 15–17) the location of the three objects created on lines 8, 9, and 10. This is valid syntax because all three of these objects' classes (Figures 8.20–8.22) extend the class Boat (Figure 8.19).

Because the variables boat1, boat2, and boat3 now reference child objects, the invocations on lines 23–25 are polymorphic invocations. The appearance of a properly drawn rowboat, sailboat, and powerboat on the game board shown in Figure 8.31 confirms that the search path used by the Java runtime environment to locate the show method it executed began in the classes of the objects rather than the class of the three reference variables (i.e., Boat). If the search had begun in the Boat class, its show method would have drawn three hulls without oars, or a sail, or a propeller (lines 23-32 of Figure 8.19).

```
1    import edu.sjcny.gpv1.*;
2    import java.awt.*;
3
4    public class PolymorphicInvocations extends DrawableAdapter
5    {
6      static PolymorphicInvocations ge = new PolymorphicInvocations();
7      static GameBoard gb = new GameBoard(ge, "Design Techniques");
8      static RowBoatV2 rb1 = new RowBoatV2(50, 200, 120, Color.YELLOW, 4);
9      static SailBoatV4 sb1 = new SailBoatV4(220, 200, 200, Color.GREEN, 200);
10     static PowerBoat pb1 = new PowerBoat(50, 300, 200, Color.MAGENTA, 400);
11     static Boat boat1, boat2, boat3;
12
13     public static void main(String[] args)
14     {
15       boat1 = rb1;
16       boat2 = sb1;
17       boat3 = pb1;
18       showGameBoard(gb);
19     }
20
21     public void draw(Graphics g)
22     {
23       boat1.show(g);
24       boat2.show(g);
25       boat3.show(g);
26     }
27   }
```

**Figure 8.30**
The application **PolymorphicInvocations**.

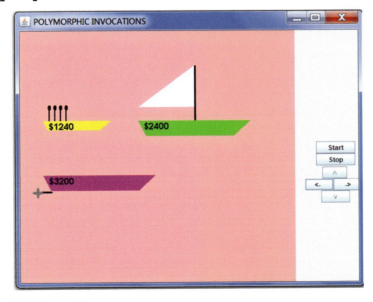

**Figure 8.31**
The output produced by the application **PolymorphicInvocations**.

### 8.5.3 Polymorphic Arrays

> **Definition**
>
> A **polymorphic array** is an array of parent reference variables that are used to store references to child objects.

**Polymorphic arrays** are declared using the syntax discussed in Section 6.5, which is used to declare any array of reference variables. For example, the array `inventory` declared below has the potential to become a polymorphic array because the class `Boat` defined in Figure 8.19 is the super class of the subclasses defined in Figures 8.20–8.22:

```
Boat[] inventory = new Boat[9];
```

If and when an element of the array `inventory` is assigned the address of a subclass object, it is then being used as a polymorphic array. Arrays of abstract class reference variables can only be used as polymorphic arrays because we cannot create an instance of an abstract class.

Each element of a polymorphic array could be assigned the address of the *same* type of subclass instance, in which case the array would be called a *homogeneous* polymorphic array. When at least two *different* subclass objects are referenced from within the array, the array is being used as a *nonhomogeneous* polymorphic array. Nonhomogeneous polymorphic arrays bring the power of arrays into the concept of inheritance and further reduce the number of lines of code required to produce an application.

The application `PolymorphicArrays` shown in Figure 8.32 is a modification of the application `PolymorphicInvocations` presented in Figure 8.30. It uses a polymorphic array to store a nine-boat inventory of Uncle Ed's boat store. The output it produces is shown in Figure 8.33.

Line 11 of Figure 8.32 creates a polymorphic array named `inventory` whose elements are reference variables in the abstract class `Boat` (Figure 8.19). Each time the loop that begins on line 15 executes, lines 17–21 create three new boats whose classes are shown in Figures 8.20–8.22. Then, lines 22–24 add them to Uncle Ed's inventory by storing them in the polymorphic array. The loop variable, `i`, is used on lines 17–20 to change the (x, y) location, number of oars, sail area, and size of the boats. It is also used on lines 22–24 to change the elements of the array that store the boats' addresses.

The `for` loop that begins on line 32 uses polymorphic invocations of the `show` method to draw each boat on the game board, which represents Uncle Ed's boat storage lot.

```
1    import edu.sjcny.gpv1.*;
2    import java.awt.*;
3
4    public class PolymorphicArrays extends DrawableAdapter
5    {
6      static PolymorphicArrays ge = new PolymorphicArrays();
7      static GameBoard gb = new GameBoard(ge, "POLYMORPHIC ARRAYS");
8      static RowBoatV2 rb;
9      static SailBoatV4 sb;
```

```
10      static PowerBoat pb;
11      static Boat[] inventory = new Boat[9];
12
13      public static void main(String[] args)
14      {
15        for(int i = 0; i < 3; i++)
16        {
17          rb = new RowBoatV2(10 + i * 130, 75, 120, Color.YELLOW, i * 2 + 2);
18          sb = new SailBoatV4(10 + i * 170, 250, 110 + i * 15, Color.GREEN,
19                              200 + i * 20);
20          pb = new PowerBoat(20 + i * 160, 350, 120 + i * 15, Color.MAGENTA,
21                             400);
22          inventory[i * 3] = rb;
23          inventory[i * 3 + 1] = sb;
24          inventory[i * 3 + 2] = pb;
25        }
26
27        showGameBoard(gb);
28      }
29
30      public void draw(Graphics g)
31      {
32        for(int i = 0; i < 9; i++)
33        {
34          inventory[i].show(g);
35        }
36      }
37  }
```

**Figure 8.32**
The application **PolymorphicArrays**.

**Figure 8.33**
The output produced by the application **PolymorphicArrays**.

## Advantages of Polymorphic Arrays

The addresses of the new boats created on lines 17–21 of Figure 8.32 could have been assigned directly into the array elements on these lines, in which case, lines 8–10 and 22–24 would be eliminated from the program. This approach would have reduced the program to 31 lines with much of the programs brevity coming from the use of a polymorphic array.

An alternative approach to this program would have been to declare three nonpolymorphic arrays, one for each type of boat, as shown below:

```
RowBoatV2[3]  rb = new RowBoatV2[3];
SailBoatV4[3]  sb = new SailBoatV4[3];
PowerBoat[3]  pb = new PowerBoat[3];
```

The addition of these three lines and the additions to the body of the output loop (line 34), which now requires an output of three arrays rather than one, would expanded the 31-line version of the program to a 36-line program. Reductions in coding effort are typically realized when polymorphic arrays are used.

In addition, if the details of the nine boats in Uncle Ed's inventory, including their type, were to be input by the program user instead of being hard coded (as on lines 17–21), the polymorphic approach would reduce the storage requirements of the program. Any mix of nine rowboats, sailboats, and powerboats could be saved in the nine-element polymorphic array, but the three-nonpolymorphic-array approach would require that all three arrays be expanded to nine elements to accommodate the case when all of the boats are of one type (e.g., all sailboats).

### 8.5.4 Polymorphism's Role in Parameter Passing

Because a super class can point to (i.e., store the address of) an instance of any of its subclasses, a parameter whose type is the super class can be passed an argument whose type is any of its subclasses. Taking this concept to its extreme, because all classes inherit directly or indirectly from the class `Object`, any object's address can be passed to a parameter whose type is `Object`.

Suppose we wanted to code a method that determined if two of Uncle Ed's boats occupied the same (x, y) location. We would code the method in the super class `Boat` (Figure 8.19) to enable any instance of its subclasses (a rowboat, a sailboat, or a powerboat) to invoke it. The method would compare that object's x and y data members to those of the objects passed to its parameter. To ensure that any of these three types of boats could be passed to the method, the parameter's type would be the super class `Boat`. The code for the method is given below:

```
1    public boolean samePosition(Boat aBoat) //code in the superclass Boat
2      {
3        if(x == aBoat.x && y == aBoat.y)
4          {
5            return true;
6          }
7        else
```

```
8        {
9            return false;
10       }
11   }
```

If the method was to determine if any of Uncle Ed's boats occupied the same (x, y) location, the static method shown below could be coded in the super class `Boat`. The method signature contains one parameter, a reference variable that can store the address of an array of instances of the class `Boat` or instances of `Boat`'s subclasses. When the method is invoked, it is passed the polymorphic array that contains Uncle Ed's boat inventory. It returns `true` if two or more boats are at the same (x, y) location.

```
1    public static boolean samePositionV2(Boat[] boats) //coded in the
2    {                                                  //superclass Boat
3      for(int i = 0; i< boats.length; i++)
4      {
5        for(int j = i + 1; j< boats.length; j++)
6        {
7          if(boats[i].x == boats[j].x && boats[i].y == boats[j].y)
8          {
9            return true;
10         }
11       }
12     }
13     return false;
14   }
```

### 8.5.5 The methods `getClass` and `getName` and the `instanceof` operator.

Suppose your Uncle Ed expanded the requirements of his inventory program to include outputting the inventory of a specified type of boat. For example, print the details of all of the sailboats in the inventory. Then when a customer expressed an interest in a sailboat, Uncle Ed could give the customer a list of the sailboats currently in his inventory.

If the three nonpolymorphic arrays were used in the program, the type of the boat the customer was interested in could be used in the Boolean conditions of nested `if-else` statements to decide which of the three arrays to output. The following pseudocode fragment uses this approach to output the type of boat stored in the input string `typeSpecified`:

```
if(typeSpecfied.equalsIgnoreCase("rowboat")
{
    //a for loop to output the contents of the rowboat array
}
else if(typeSpecified.equalsIgnoreCase("sailboat")
{
    //a for loop to output the contents of the sailboat array
}
else
{
```

```
        //a for loop to output the contents of the powerboat array
  }
```

Although this implementation of the new requirement is rather straight forward, as discussed at the end of the previous section, this three-nonpolymorphic-array approach increases the program's size and its storage requirements. A more efficient single-polymorphic-array implementation of the new requirement could be used if there was some way of identifying the type each object referenced in the polymorphic array. The following pseudocode fragment could then be used to output only the type of boat stored in the input string `typeSpecified`:

```
for(int i=0; i < inventory.length; i++)//inventory is a polymorphic array
{
    if( //inventory[i] is of the typeSpedified )
    {
        System.out.println(inventory[i].toString());
    }
}
```

Fortunately, the API classes `Object` and `Class` provide the ability to identify the type, (i.e., the class) of any object.

## The `getClass` Method in the Class Object

All classes inherit from the class `Object`. It is a super class of all classes contained in the API and the implied super class of every programmer defined class. The class `Object` is at the top of every class's inheritance chain. We have already taken advantage of this fact in Chapter 3 when we used the `toString` method inherited from the class `Object` to output the location of an object.

One of the other methods inherited from the class `Object` is its `getClass` method. This method has an empty parameter list and returns the location of an instance of a `Class` object.

## The getName Method in the Class `Class`

When an object is constructed information about the object, such as its class name and the name of the class it extends, is recorded in an instance of a `Class` object that is created by the Java Virtual Machine and associated with the constructed object. The location of the associated `Class` object can be fetched by invoking `Object`'s `getClass` method on the constructed object, which can then be used to invoke any of the methods in the class `Class`.

One of these methods, `getName`, can be used to determine the name of any object's class. The method has an empty parameter list and returns a string containing the class's name. The following code fragment uses the five-parameter constructor of the class `PowerBoat` (Figure 8.22) to construct the object pb and uses the `getClass` and `getName` methods to output the name of pb's class, `PowerBoat`:

```
1    PowerBoat pb = new PowerBoat(160, 350, 120, Color.MAGENTA, 400);
2    Class c = pb.getClass();
3    System.out.println(c.getName());
```

Often lines 2 and 3 are combined into one line:

```
System.out.println(pb.getClass.getName());
```

This abbreviated code version is used in the following code fragment to output only the Power-Boat objects stored in the polymorphic array inventory:

```
for(int i=0; i < inventory.length; i++)
{
  if(inventory[i].getClass().getName().equalsIgnoreCase("PowerBoat"))
  {
     System.out.println(inventory[i].toString());
  }
}
```

The application ObjectAndClass shown in Figure 8.34 is a modification of the application PolymorphicArrays presented in Figure 8.32. When launched, it asks the user what type of boat the customer is interested in and then uses the getClass and getName methods to identify that subset of Uncle Ed's inventory and outputs a description of these boats to the system console. The graphical and console output produced by the application is shown in Figure 8.35.

Line 8 of Figure 8.34 and the body of the loop that begins on line 15 create a polymorphic array named inventory whose elements are reference variables in the abstract class Boat defined in Figure 8.19. Each time the loop executes, lines 17–21 create three new boats whose classes are shown in Figures 8.20–8.22. The addresses of these objects are placed directly into the elements of the polymorphic array on lines 17, 19, and 21.

The Boolean condition of the *if* statement coded on line 29 uses the methods getClass and getName to determine if the class name of the object referenced by the ith element of the array inventory is the same as the string s input on line 25. If it is, the object is output to the console on line 31 using a polymorphic invocation of the toString method. The console output is shown in the bottom portion of Figure 8.35. Figure 8.35a shows the dialog box displayed by line 25 containing the user input *SAILBOATV4*, which resulted in the console output shown at the bottom of Figure 8.35. Figure 8.35b shows the graphical output produced by the polymorphic invocations of the show method (line 41 of Figure 8.34).

```
1    import edu.sjcny.gpv1.*;
2    import java.awt.*;
3    import javax.swing.*;
4
5    public class ObjectAndClass extends DrawableAdapter
6    {  static ObjectAndClass ge = new ObjectAndClass();
7       static GameBoard gb = new GameBoard(ge, "getClass and getName Methods");
8       static Boat[] inventory = new Boat[9];
9
10      public static void main(String[] args)
11      {
12          String s;
13
```

```
14        // Use of a polymorphic array
15        for(int i = 0; i < 3; i++)
16        {
17          inventory[i*3] = new RowBoatV2(10 + i*130, 75, 120,
18                                Color.YELLOW, i*2 + 2);
19          inventory[i*3 + 1] = new SailBoatV4(10 + i*170, 250 , 110+ i *15,
20                                Color.GREEN, 200 + i*20);
21          inventory[i*3 + 2] = new PowerBoat(20 + i*160, 350 , 120+ i *15,
22                                Color.MAGENTA, 400);
23        }
24
25        s = JOptionPane.showInputDialog("Interested in, a rowboatV2," +
26                                "\na sailboatV4, or a powerboat?");
27        for(int i = 0; i < inventory.length; i++)
28        {
29            if(inventory[i].getClass().getName().equalsIgnoreCase(s))
30            {
31              System.out.println(inventory[i].toString());
32            }
33        }
34        showGameBoard(gb);
35    }
36
37    public void draw(Graphics g)
38    {
39      for(int i = 0; i < 9; i++)
40      {
41        inventory[i].show(g);
42      }
43    }
44  }
```

**Figure 8.34**
The application **ObjectAndClass**.

## The instanceof Operator

Java provides a more succinct syntax than that used on line 29 of Figure 8.34 for determining the class of an object: its relational operator `instanceof`. This is a binary operator that can be used in a Boolean expression. Its first operand must be a reference variable, and its second operator must be a case-sensitive class name. The operator returns the value `true` when the class name is the class of the object referenced by the first operand. The Boolean condition on the last line of this code fragment evaluates to `true`.

```
Boat[] inventory = new Boat[2];
inventory[0] = new PowerBoat(50, 100, 200, Color.MAGENTA, 400);

if(inventory[0] instanceof PowerBoat)
```

(a)                                        (b)

**System Console Output:**

Location: (10, 250), length: 110, Color: java.awt.Color[r=0,g=255,b=0], Sail Area: 200
Location: (180, 250), length: 125, Color: java.awt.Color[r=0,g=255,b=0], Sail Area: 220
Location: (350, 250), length: 140, Color: java.awt.Color[r=0,g=255,b=0], Sail Area: 240

**Figure 8.35**
The output produced by the application **ObjectAndClass**.

Because a string variable cannot be used as one of the arguments, it cannot be used in the Boolean condition on line 29 of Figure 8.34 to determine if an element of the array `inventory` is an instance of the class whose name is stored in the string `s`.

The two most common uses of the `instanceof` operator are to:

1. Ensure that the casting of a polymorphic reference to an object does not result in a syntax error

2. Eliminate the need to include an implementation or an abstract version of a method in a parent class when the method is invoked polymorphically

The code fragment below demonstrates both of these uses. The `instanceof` operator is used on line 8 to prevent the translation error associated with an attempt to cast the `RowBoatV2` object declared in line 3 into a `PowerBoat` reference on line 10. In addition, because the casting permits a nonpolymorphic invocation of the `show` method on line 11, the translator looks into the `Power-Boat` class, rather than the `Boat` class, to verify the method's signature. The `Boat` class would not have to include a `show` method with the same signature as the `PowerBoat` class.

```
1    Boat[] inventory = new Boat[2]; //used as a polymorphic array
2    inventory[0] = new PowerBoat(50, 100, 200, Color.MAGENTA, 400);
3    inventory[1] = new RowBoatV2(50, 300, 75, Color.YELLOW, 2);
4    PowerBoat pb1;
5
6    for(int i = 0; i < inventory.length; i++)
7    {
8        if(inventory[i] instanceof PowerBoat) //show the powerboat(s)
```

```
 9      {
10        pb1 = (PowerBoat) inventory[i];
11        pb1.show()
12      }
13   }
```

> NOTE
>
> *When using a preexisting super class to implement a polymorphic array, the use of the* `instanceof` *operator and casting eliminates the syntax error associated with using the elements of the array to polymorphically invoke a child class method whose signature is not defined in the parent class. It also eliminates the need to include a version of the method in the super classes that we write.*

## 8.6 INTERFACES

An **interface** is very similar to an abstract super class that contains only abstract methods and/or static final constant definitions. They are most easily understood by comparing them to this type of super class. Like a class, the source code of an interface is saved in a file with a `.java` extension, and its translation is sorted in a file with a `.class` extension. In addition, it is good programming practice to begin the name of an interface with a capital letter.

| Definition |
| --- |
| An **interface** is a specification of the signatures of related methods that are implicitly abstract and/or a declaration of public constants that are implicitly static and final. |

Figure 8.36 compares the syntax and keywords associated with an abstract super class and an interface. At the bottom of the figure, it also compares the syntax of heading of a class that *extends* an abstract super class and a class that *implements* an interface. As shown on the top right side of the figure, the heading of an interface substitutes the keyword **interface** for the two keywords **abstract** and **class** used in the definition of an abstract super class. In addition, the interface definition eliminates the keyword **abstract** used in the method signatures defined in an abstract class. Because the constant definitions included in an interface are implicitly `static` and `final`, these keywords are not used and the constants should be initialized. Interface methods and constant definitions are always implicitly `public`. They cannot be declared to be `private` or `protected`.

As shown in the bottom right side of Figure 8.36, a class that implements an interface uses the keyword **implements** in its heading rather than the keyword **extends**. Consistent with the use of these keywords, we say that a class implements an interface rather than extends it.

A syntactical difference not shown in Figure 8.36 is that while a class's heading can state that it extends one (and only one) super class, it can state that it implements more that one interface. When this is the case, the names of the interfaces in the class's `implements` clause are separated by commas. For example:

```
public class Class1 implements Interface1, Interface2, Interface3
```

| Abstract Super Class | Interface |
|---|---|
| Definition of the super class `Parent` | Definition of the interface `AnInterface` |

```
public abstract class Parent
{ public static final int a = 10;
  // other constants can
  // be included

  public abstract int extra();
  //other abstract methods
  //can be included
}
```

```
public interface AnInterface
{ public int a = 10;
  // other constants can
  // be included

  public int extra();
  //other signatures
  //can be included
}
```

| Heading of a class that extends the super class Parent | Heading of a class that implements the interface AnInterface |
|---|---|

```
public class Child extends Parent
```

```
public class AClass implements  AnInterface
```

**Figure 8.36**
A comparison of abstract super class and interface syntax.

When a class implements one or more interfaces and also extends a class, the `extends` clause is coded in its heading before the `implements` clause. For example:

```
public class Class2 extends Parent implements Interface1, Interface2
```

A class that includes an `implements` clause in its heading must implement all of the methods whose signatures are included in the interface. There are only two exceptions to this. The first exception is when the class is an abstract class, in which case it cannot implement any of the methods, and its subclasses must include implementations of all of the interface methods. The second exception is when the class inherits implementations of the methods. These inherited implementations are treated like any other inherited methods. For example, the same search techniques are used to locate them at translation and runtime, and subclasses can override the inherited implementations. In addition, the inherited version of the overridden method can be invoked by preceding the method name with the keyword **super** followed by a dot.

As is the case with abstract classes, we cannot declare an instance of an interface, but the type of a reference variable can be the name of an interface. A very important use of interface reference variables and interfaces in general is will be discussed in Chapter 10.

In summary, an interface can be considered to be an abstract super class that contains only public abstract methods and public static final constant definitions, with the following idiosyncrasies:

- a class can implement several interfaces
- interfaces and abstract classes have syntactical differences (shown in Figure 8.36)
- interfaces cannot contain method implementations
- interfaces are used in the coding of generic classes

## When to Define and Use an Interface

The similarities of an interface and an abstract class can be a source of confusion when trying to decide which construct to use for a particular programming application. An interface is preferred when we want to standardize the signatures and functionality of methods that implement a commonly performed task on objects that may not be related. By "may not be related," we mean that with the exception of the class `Object`, the classes that perform these common tasks may not share a common ancestor.

For example, the need to compare two objects was anticipated to be such a common task that an interface named `Comparable` is included in the Java API. It defines the signature of a method named `compareTo`, and the interface's documentation describes the functionality of the method. Many nonrelated classes included in the API, such as the `String` class and the `BigInteger` class, implement this interface, and they all implement the functionality described in the interface's documentation. They all compare two objects and return a zero, a negative or a positive value, that reflects the equality or ordering of the two objects being compared. This use of interfaces facilitates the use of any class's `compareTo` method if we know that the class has implemented the interface `Comparable`. In general:

- an *interface* is defined to standardize the signatures and functionality of methods that implement a commonly performed task on objects that may not share a common ancestor other than the class `Object`
- interfaces facilitate the use of methods by standardizing both their signature and their functionality, as described in their documentation

The code of the interface `Drawable` is shown in Figure 8.37. It defines the signatures of two methods commonly used in game applications. As is typically the case, the description of the interface, which is given in Table 8.1, contains the signatures of the methods and describes the functionality of the two methods. It is considered good programming practice that all implementations of an interface's methods conform to the functionality described in the interface's documentation.

```java
1    import java.awt.*;
2
3    public interface Drawable
4    {
5      boolean canDraw(int drawableWidth, int drawableHeight);
6      void show(Graphics g);
7    }
```

**Figure 8.37**
The interface **Drawable**.

**Table 8.1**
The Documentation of the Interface Drawable

| The Interface `Drawable` | |
| --- | --- |
| Methods | |
| **Returned Type** | **Signature and Functionality Description** |
| **boolean** | `canDraw(`**int** `width, `**int** `height)`<br><br>Returns `true` if the object that invokes it can be drawn on a `Graphics` area whose lower right corner is at location (`width, height`) |
| **void** | `show(Graphics g)`<br><br>Draws the game piece that invoked it on the graphic object `g` at its current (x, y) location |

To close out our discussion of interfaces, consider the following scenario. The author of the game application `InterfaceUse`, shown in Figure 8.38, purchased a package containing the translated versions (bytecodes) of several game piece class implementations. The documentation of the package, which included a copy of Table 8.1, stated that all of the game-piece classes implemented the interface `Drawable` described in that table.

Six instances of two of these classes, `TopHat` and `SnowmanV9`, are declared on lines 11–16 of the application. Knowing that both of these classes implement the interface `Drawable`, the application programmer realized that the addresses of the six objects could be efficiently stored in a polymorphic array of type `Drawable` (which is declared on line 7 and assigned on lines 11–16 of Figure 8.38), and that the objects could then be efficiently drawn/not drawn using invocation of the two methods defined in the interface (lines 22–27 of Figure 8.38).

The output of the program is given in Figure 8.39, which reflects the fact that top hats can only be drawn if they are completely on the game board, and snowmen cannot be drawn if they are completely off the game board. The source code of the two game-piece classes and the class `GamePiece` that they extend (which in this hypothetical scenario, the application programmer never saw) are given in Figures 8.40, 8.41, and 8.42, respectively.

```
1    import edu.sjcny.gpv1.*;
2    import java.awt.*;
3
4    public class InterfaceUse extends DrawableAdapter
5    { static InterfaceUse ge = new InterfaceUse();
6      static GameBoard gb = new GameBoard(ge, "INTERFACES", 700, 700);
7      static Drawable[] items = new Drawable[6];
8
9      public static void main(String[] args)
10      {
```

```
11        items[0] = new TopHat(-10, 30, Color.BLUE, 51, 60); //part off
12        items[1] = new TopHat(350, 360, Color.BLACK, 51, 60);
13        items[2] = new TopHat(600, 640, Color.GREEN, 51, 60); //part off
14        items[3] = new SnowmanV9(-10, 120, Color.BLUE, 80, 152); //part off
15        items[4] = new SnowmanV9(200, 360, Color.BLACK, 80, 152);
16        items[5] = new SnowmanV9(400, 640, Color.GREEN, 80, 152); //part off
17        showGameBoard(gb);
18      }
19
20    public void draw(Graphics g)
21    {
22      for(int i = 0; i < items.length; i++)
23      {
24        if(items[i].canDraw(700, 700))
25        {
26          items[i].show(g);
27        }
28      }
29    }
30  }
```

**Figure 8.38**
The application **InterfaceUse**.

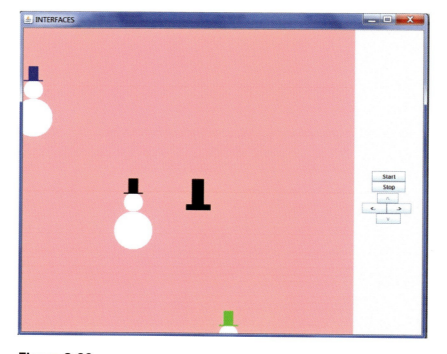

**Figure 8.39**
The output produced by the application **InterfaceUse**.

```
1    import java.awt.*;
2
3    public class TopHat extends GamePiece implements Drawable
4    {
5
6      public TopHat(int x, int y, Color hatColor, int w, int h)
7      {
8        this.x = x;
9        this.y = y;
10       this.hatColor = hatColor;
11       this.w = w;
12       this.h = h;
13     }
14     public void show(Graphics g)
15     {
16       g.setColor(hatColor);
17       g.fillRect(x + w/4, y, w/2, (int)(h*0.9));   // hat top
18       g.fillRect(x, y + (int)(h*0.9), w, (int)(h*0.2));   // brim
19     }
20     public boolean canDraw(int gbWidth, int gbHeight) //Completely on the
21     {                                                 //game board
22       if(x >= 6 && x + w <= gbWidth
23          &&
24          y >= 30 && y + (int)(h * 1.1) <= gbHeight)
25       {
26         return true;
27       }
28       else
29       {
30         return false;
31       }
32     }
33   }
```

**Figure 8.40**
The class **TopHat**.

```
1    import java.awt.*;
2    import javax.swing.*;
3
4    public class SnowmanV9 extends GamePiece implements Drawable
5    {
6      public SnowmanV9(int x, int y, Color hatColor, int w, int h)
7      {
8        this.x = x;
9        this.y = y;
10       this.hatColor = hatColor;
```

```
11        this.w = w;
12        this.h = h;
13      }
14      public void show(Graphics g)
15      {
16        g.setColor(Color.WHITE);
17        g.fillOval(x + 20, y + 30, 40, 40); //head
18        g.fillOval(x, y + 70, 80, 80); //body
19        g.setColor(hatColor);
20        g.fillRect(x + 30, y, 20, 30); //hat
21        g.fillRect(x + 20, y + 30, 40, 2); //brim
22      }
23      public boolean canDraw(int gbWidth, int gbHeight) //Not completely off
24      {                                                 //the game board
25        if(x + w >= 6 && x <= gbWidth
26            &&
27            y + h > 30 && y <= gbHeight)
28        {
29          return true;
30        }
31        else
32        {
33          return false;
34        }
35      }
36    }
```

**Figure 8.41**
The class **SnowmanV9**.

```
1     import java.awt.*;
2
3     public abstract class GamePiece
4     {
5         protected int x;
6         protected int y;
7         protected int w;
8         protected int h;
9         protected Color hatColor;
10
11    }
```

**Figure 8.42**
The abstract class **GamePiece**.

As shown in Figures 8.40 and 8.41, the TopHat and SnowmanV9 classes implement the interface Drawable and include an implementation of the functionality of the two Drawable methods particular to them. The implementer of the TopHat class decided that a top hat can only be drawn if it is completely on the game board, so the version of the method coded in Figure 8.40 returns true when this is the case. Snowmen will eventually be made to enter the game board from its edges, so they can be drawn if any part of them is on the game board. The code of the SnowmanV9's canDraw method coded in Figure 8.41 returns true when this is the case.

The output of the program shown in Figure 8.39 contains one top hat and three snowmen. This confirms the fact that the polymorphic invocations of the canDraw and show methods on lines 24 and 26 of Figure 8.38 are locating the correct subclass methods. As noted by the comments at the end of lines 11 and 13 of Figure 8.38, the blue and green top hats are partially off the game board, in which case their canDraw method returns false, and they are not drawn. All three snowmen are either partially or completely on the game board, in which case their canDraw method returns true, and they are all drawn.

The data members common to the classes TopHat and SnowmanV9 are collected in the abstract class GamePiece (Figure 8.42), which they extend. They are declared in this super class with protected access (lines 5–9 of Figure 8.42). As indicated in the top half of Figure 8.27, this gives the subclasses' methods the ability to access them directly without using set and get methods (e.g., lines 17 and 18 of Figure 8.40). In our hypothetical scenario, the application would be coded in a separate package, so it would not be able to access these data members.

### 8.6.1 Adapter Classes

When an interface contains a significant number of methods, it is good programming practice to provide an adapter class for the interface. The term adapter class is a generic term for a class that implements an interface with methods that contain empty code blocks. It is also good programming practice to assign the name of the adapter class the name of the interface class it implements, concatenated with the word "Adapter." For example, the name of the adapter class for the interface Drawable shown in Figure 8.37 would be DrawableAdapter. The code of this class is given in Figure 8.43.

```java
public class DrawableAdapter implements Drawable
{
    boolean canDraw(int drawableWidth, int drawableHeight)
    {

    }
    void show(Graphics g);
    {

    }
}
```

**Figure 8.43**
The adapter class **DrawableAdapter**.

The adapter class is provided to permit a new class to implement only the methods defined in the interface that are relevant. When this is the case, the new class extends the adapter class and then overrides the empty methods with its implementation. For example, if the specification of the class `RocketShip` only required that it implement the `show` method in the `Drawable` interface, then, assuming the `DrawableAdapter` class shown in Figure 8.43 exists, the code of the `Rocket-Ship` class would be written as follows:

```java
public class RocketShip extends DrawableAdapter
{
    // the data members of the class RocketShip

    @Override
    public show (Graphics g)
    {
        //the code to draw a RocketShip object
    }

    //the remainder of the methods of the class RocketShip
}
```

The game programming environment contains an interface named `Drawable` that defines the signatures of all of the `draw` call back methods described in Appendix A. The game environment also contains the adapter class `DrawableAdapter`, so a game program's class does not have to implement all of the call back methods if it extends `DrawAbleAdapter`, as does line 4 of Figure 8.37.

It should be noted that when a new class is a child class the use of an adapter class is not an alternative, because a class can only extend one class. The new class's heading would have to contain an `implements` clause, and all of the interface methods would have to be implemented. The interface methods not used by the class would simply contain an empty code block.

## 8.7 SERIALIZING OBJECTS

**Definition**

**Object serialization** is the act of disassembling objects before writing them to a disk file.

**Object deserialization** is the act of reassembling objects after they are read from a disk file.

In Section 4.8, we discussed techniques used to transfer information to and from a disk file. As part of these techniques, information is written to the disk using the methods in the `Print-Writer` class (e.g., `println` and `print`). These methods write a string to the file, which means that the information in the file is represented as ASCII characters. Any piece of information written to the file that is not a string must be converted to a string before it is written.

This means that when the contents of the variables `houseNumber` and `quantity` defined in the code fragment below are written to the disk, they produce the same output to the disk: the three characters *175*.

```java
String houseNumber = "175"
```

```
int quantity = 175;
```

Because the type of the information written to the file (e.g., `String` and `int`)is not represented in the file, a written description of the information in the file must be provided with the file to properly read and process the data in the file. When a reference to an object is included in the parameter passed to the `PrintWriter`'s output methods, the object's `toString` method is implicitly invoked, and the returned string is written to the file. In this case, the file description should include not only the types of the data members written to the file, but also the order in which they were written and the objects' classes, so the object written to the file can be properly reconstructed by the program that reads the information from the file.

The `writeObject` method in the class `ObjectOutputStream` presents a better alternative for writing the data members of an object to a disk file. When this method is used to write an object to a file, all of the information required to reconstruct the object when it is read from the file (the data members' types, the order in which they were written, and the class of the objects) is written to the file by the method. This information can then be used by the `readObject` method contained in the `ObjectInputStream` class to reconstruct the object when the method is used to read the object from the file. The gleaning of all of this additional information from objects when they are written to a file is called **object serialization**, and the use of this information to efficiently recreate objects when they are read from a file is called **object deserialization**.

Object serialization allows us to write all of an object's data members to a disk file as a single entity by simply invoking the `ObjectOutputStream` class's `writeObject` method and passing the object to the method's parameter. Object deserialization allows us to read all of an object's data members from a disk file by simply invoking the `ObjectInputStream` class's `readObject` method. This method recreates a serialized object and returns the address of the recreated object. Because the class of each object is written to the file, the file can contain different types of objects. When these objects are related as subclasses of the same super class, the file can be written to and read from polymorphically.

The application `SerializingObjects` presented in Figure 8.44 demonstrates the serialized writing and reading of objects to/from a disk file. It is a modification of the application `PolymorphicArrays` shown in Figure 8.32. This version of the application outputs the nine-boat inventory of Uncle Ed's boat yard, stored in a polymorphic array, to a serialized disk file using the `writeObject` method and reads the objects back into the array using the `readObject` method. Sample outputs produced at various points in the program's execution are given in Figure 8.45.

Line 12 of Figure 8.44 creates a polymorphic array named `inventory` whose elements are reference variables in the abstract class `Boat` (Figure 8.19). Each time the loop that begins on line 16 executes, lines 18–22 create three new boats whose classes are shown in Figures 8.20–8.22. Then, lines 23–25 add them to Uncle Ed's inventory by storing them in the polymorphic array. When the program in Figure 8.44 is launched, line 37 of the `draw` method displays the boats on the game board because each element of the array `inventory` contains a non-null reference (line 35). The initial output of the program is shown in Figure 8.45a.

When the game board's right arrow button is clicked, line 59 of the button's call back method writes the serialized version of all of the boat objects to a disk file named "Inventory." The file is created and attached to the `ObjectOutputStream` object `outFile` on lines 52 and 53; this is the object used on line 59 to invoke the `writeObject` method.

After subsequent clicks of the game board's up arrow button, line 46 of the button's call back method deletes the boats from the polymorphic array by setting all of its elements to `null`. When the call back method ends, the game environment invokes the `draw` call back method. This method then displays an empty game board (Figure 8.45b) because line 35 prevents the `show` method from executing. If it had executed, the program would have been terminated by a `NullPointerException` because all of the elements of the array `inventory` are `null`.

To restore and redisplay Uncle Ed's inventory, line 77 of the left button call back method reads the serialized boat objects from the disk file "Inventory" and places their addresses into the polymorphic array. The file is opened and attached to the `ObjectInputStream` object `inFile` on lines 72 and 73; this is the object used on line 77 to invoke the `readObject` method. After the left button call back methods ends, the `draw` call back method executes and line 37 of the `draw` call back method displays the restored nine-boat inventory on the game board (left side of Figure 8.42) via polymorphic invocations to the boats' `show` methods. The redisplay of the inventory verifies that line 59 correctly wrote the serialized objects to the disk file, and line 77 correctly read them back into the polymorphic array.

The coercion used in Figure 8.44 on line 77 is necessary because the `readObject` method, invoked on that line, returns a reference whose type is `Object`. When writing and reading serialized objects, the exceptions coded on lines 64, 81, and 84 must be caught (as shown) inside the methods that perform the disk I/O. Alternately, a `throws` clause can be included in the methods' headings. If the methods override a method, the overridden method must contain the same `throws` clause, or the `throws` clause alternative cannot be used. Because the call back methods override the methods in the `DrawableAdapter` class, the `catch` clause alternative was used in this program.

```
1    import edu.sjcny.gpv1.*;
2    import java.awt.*;
3    import java.io.*;
4
5    public class SerializingObjects extends DrawableAdapter
6    {
7       static SerializingObjects ge = new SerializingObjects();
8       static GameBoard gb = new GameBoard(ge, "SERIALIZING OBJECTS");
9       static RowBoatV2 rb;
10      static SailBoatV4 sb;
11      static PowerBoat pb;
```

```java
12      static Boat[] inventory = new Boat[9];
13
14      public static void main(String[] args)
15      {
16        for(int i = 0; i < 3; i++)
17        {
18          rb = new RowBoatV2(10 + i * 130, 75, 120, Color.YELLOW, i * 2 + 2);
19          sb = new SailBoatV4(10 + i * 170, 250, 110 + i * 15, Color.GREEN,
20                              200 + i * 20);
21          pb = new PowerBoat(20 + i * 160, 350, 120 + i * 15, Color.MAGENTA,
22                             400);
23          inventory[i * 3] = rb;
24          inventory[i * 3 + 1] = sb;
25          inventory[i * 3 + 2] = pb;
26        }
27
28        showGameBoard(gb);
29      }
30
31      public void draw(Graphics g)
32      {
33        for(int i = 0; i < 9; i++)
34        {
35          if(inventory[i] != null)
36          {
37            inventory[i].show(g);
38          }
39        }
40      }
41
42      public void upButton() //delete the RAM based inventory
43      {
44        for(int i = 0; i < 9; i++)
45          {
46            inventory[i] = null;
47          }
48      }
49      public void rightButton() //output inventory to the file
50      {
51        try
52        { FileOutputStream fos = new FileOutputStream("Inventory");
53          ObjectOutputStream outFile = new ObjectOutputStream(fos);
54
55          for(int i = 0; i < 9; i++)
56          {
57            if(inventory[i] != null)
58            {
59              outFile.writeObject(inventory[i]);
60            }
```

```
61              }
62          outFile.close();
63        }
64      catch(IOException e)
65        {
66        }
67      }
68
69    public void leftButton() //input inventory from the file
70      {
71      try
72      { FileInputStream fis = new FileInputStream("Inventory");
73        ObjectInputStream inFile = new ObjectInputStream(fis);
74
75        for(int i = 0; i < 9; i++)
76          {
77            inventory[i] = (Boat) inFile.readObject();
78          }
79        inFile.close();
80      }
81      catch(IOException e)
82        {
83        }
84      catch(ClassNotFoundException e)
85        {
86        }
87      }
88    }
```

**Figure 8.44**
The application **SerializingObjects**.

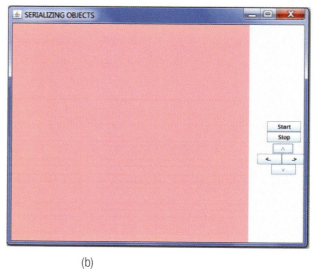

(a)                                    (b)

**Figure 8.45**
Outputs produced by the application **SerializingObjects**.

In order for an object to be serialized, its data members must be serializable. Primitive variables and strings are serializable, as are primitive arrays. The API documentation indicates that if a class implements the interface `Serializable`, then instances of the class are serializable; in addition, objects whose data members reference these serializable objects are serializable. The documentation of the API classes state which interfaces they implement. The API `Color` class, the `BigDecimal` and `BigInteger` classes, and many other API classes implement the interface `Serializable`.

The heading of the class whose objects are permitted to be serialized should indicate that it implements the interface `Serializable`, and all of its data members should be serializable. If any of the class's data members are not serializable, they should be declared `transient`.

The `Serializable` interface is imported from the API `java.io` package (line 3 of Figure 8.44), and it does not contain any method signatures to implement. Because all of the objects being serialized in the application `SerializingObjects` extend the class `Boat`, the `implements` clause was added to that class's heading (line 4 of Figure 8.19).

## 8.8 ■ CHAPTER SUMMARY

Inheritance establishes a parent-child relationship between two classes in which all of the methods and data members of the parent class become part of the child class. Including the keyword **extends** in the class's heading of any Java class designates it as a child class, and the class name that follows it designates its parent class. A Java class can have one parent, and it can have multiple children unless the class is declared to be `final`. A child class also inherits the data members and methods of its parent's class's parent recursively. When a method is invoked on an object, the runtime environment begins its search for the method in the object's class and continues the search up the class's inheritance chain.

Functionality is added to an inherited class by coding additional data members and methods in the child class and by overriding an inherited method: that is, including a method in a child class that has the same signature as an inherited method. The translator will verify the signature of an overridden method if the child class includes the `@Override` directive before the signature of its version of the method. This is considered to be good programming practice. Inherited methods can be overloaded in the child class by changing the type or number of parameters in their parameter list.

To prevent a method from being overridden, the keyword **final** is used in its signature. When a class is declared to be `final`, it cannot be extended. Methods that enforce security on systems are usually declared to be `final` to prevent them from being overridden. An abstract class is used to collect data members and methods that are common to several classes into one parent class, which is considered to be good design practice. A class is designated to be abstract by including the keyword **abstract** in its heading before the keyword **class**. An abstract class cannot be instantiated.

Parent class constructors are not inherited, but they can be invoked as the first line of a child class constructor by coding the keyword **super** followed by an argument list. If the child does not explicitly invoke a parent constructor, the parent's default constructor is implicitly invoked. The child can also invoke inherited `public` or `protected` methods, including parent methods that were overridden, by beginning the invocation with the keyword **super** followed by a dot. This is often done in overridden methods to include the functionality of the parent method in the child's version of the method. Methods and data members whose access is designated `protected` are hidden from non-child classes contained in a separate package. Protected methods and data members of a class can be accessed by members in the same package as the class as well as by members in its subclass.

Polymorphism is a powerful feature of inheritance that is based on the fact that parent reference variables can store the address of a child class object. This permits us to store references to any type of child object in one array of parent reference variables, and to execute each child's version of a method by invoking it on each element of the polymorphic array. It also permits a child class instance to be passed to, and processed by, a method whose parameter type is that of the parent class. The method can perform child class specific processing by using the `getClass` and `getName` methods and the `instanceof` operator to determine the name and class of the object passed to the method. Alternately, polymorphism also permits a parent method to invoke a child class method to perform child class specific processing. The parent class usually includes an abstract version of the method to impose a translator enforced requirement that its children provide an implementation of the method.

`Interfaces` are similar to `abstract classes` that only contain abstract methods and static final constants. Interfaces are used to share constants and to standardize the signatures and functionality of methods that perform common tasks on objects that may not share a common ancestor. When a class includes an `implements` clause in its heading, it must provide an implementation for every method defined in the interface. Alternately, it could extend a class (referred to as an `adapter class`) that provides empty implementations of the interface's methods and override one or more of the methods. A class can implement multiple interfaces, and interfaces play an important role in the implementation of generic methods and classes.

Objects can be transferred to and from disk files using the techniques called serializing and deserializing, respectively. Object serialization is the act of disassembling objects before writing them to a disk file, and object deserialization reassembles them after they are read from the disk file.

## Knowledge Exercises

1. True or false:
    a) Parent class is to child class as base class is to super class.
    b) A parent class can inherit data members and methods from to a child class.
    c) A Java parent class can have multiple child classes that inherit its data members and methods.
    d) A parent class includes an `extends` clause in its heading to specify its child class.
    e) A child class inherits all the methods of its parent class including the parent's constructors.
    f) In Java, a child class may only extend (inherit from) one class.

**g)** Several child classes can inherit from the same parent.

**h)** Parent class constructors are not inherited, but they can be invoked from within the child class.

**i)** When two methods in an inheritance chain have the same name but different parameter lists, we say they are overridden.

**j)** An inherited method can be invoked by a method within a child class.

**k)** The keyword `final` is used to prevent a method from accidentally being overridden.

**l)** A class can implement more than one interface.

**m)** To extend a class, we must have the source code of the class.

**n)** By default, a parent's no-parameter construct is always invoked when a child class constructor begins execution.

2. Explain the difference between chain inheritance and multiple inheritance. Which one does Java support?

3. What are two advantages of using inheritance in the software design and implementation processes?

4. Give the statement used in a child class method to invoke an inherited two-parameter constructor.

5. Explain the restrictions imposed by these three types of access: public, private, and protected.

6. Give the statement used in a child class method to invoke an inherited method named `output` that has no parameters and is not overridden.

7. Give the statement used in a child class method to invoke an inherited method named `input` that has no parameters and is overridden.

8. Why should the `@Override` directive be used, and where is it coded?

9. How can we prevent a method from being overridden by a child class?

10. Give two reasons for overriding an inherited method.

11. Explain when you would overload a method instead of overriding it.

12. How can we prevent a class from being extended? Give an example of when we would want to impose this restriction.

13. Explain how an abstract class is used during the design process.

14. True or false:

**a)** A parent reference variable can store the address of a child object.

**b)** A child reference variable can store the address of a parent object.

**c)** The address of a child object stored in a parent reference variable can be assigned to a child reference variable.

**d)** When a method is invoked on a parent reference variable, the version of the method in the parent's class always executes.

**e)** Child references variables can be passed to parent type parameters.

15. Give the declaration of a 200-element polymorphic array that can store instances of the child classes `Train` and `Airplane` that extend the class `Transporter`.

16. What are the differences between using `extends` and `implements` in a class's heading?

17. What can be included in an interface, and what is an advantage interfaces have over abstract classes?

18. What is an adapter class, and what is the advantage of extending an adapter class?

19. Explain what you would do to implement an adapter class for the interface `ManyMethods` that defines 20 method signatures.

## Programming Exercises

1. Develop a UML diagram for a class named `Vehicle` that has three private data members: `price`, `color`, and `model`. Its methods will include a no parameter constructor and a three-parameter constructor, a `toString` method, `set` and `get` methods, and a method to input all of the values of its data members. Assume the class `Vehicle` extends the class `Transporter`.

2. Implement the class described in Exercise 1 and write an application that verifies your implementation. You can assume the `Transporter` class has no data members or methods.

3. Cars and trucks have a price, color, and model. Cars also have a radio type, and trucks have a maximum tonnage that they can haul. Develop the UML diagrams for a car and a truck class using the concepts of inheritance to reduce the time and effort required to develop the classes. All of the data members should be private, and each class should have a four-parameter constructor, a `toSting` method, `set` and `get` methods, and a method to input all of the values of its data members.

4. Implement the classes described in Exercise 3 and write an application that verifies your implementation. Then, change the application so it can be used to input a mix of 10 cars and trucks and output them to the system console.

5. Modify Exercise 4 to include the use of a polymorphic array.

6. Write an application that asks the user how many two-dimensional shapes (squares, rectangles, circles and ellipses) to draw on the game board, as well as the type, location, and color of each shape. Any of the circles or squares can be drawn filled or unfilled. After all inputs have been performed, the shapes will appear on the game board. The name of each shape will be displayed just above it, as will the formula to compute the shapes' area if the shape is a circle or a rectangle. When user strikes the S, R, C, or E key, all of the squares, rectangles, circles, or ellipses will alternately appear or disappear respectively. Your design should utilize the techniques of inheritance and polymorphism to minimize the effort required to produce the program.

7. Supermarkets carry three categories of items in their inventory: canned goods, flowers, and produce. Every item in the store has a name, a unit price, and a quantity in stock. In addition, produce items have an expiration date and a weight (because they are sold by the pound), and flower items have a color and a variety (i.e., house plant, garden plant, arrangement).

Develop UML diagrams for each of the three categories of items, canned goods, produce, and flowers, utilizing the techniques of inheritance and polymorphism to minimize the effort required to implement the classes, then implement the classes and verify their implementation. All of the data members should be private, and each class should have a constructor that can be passed the values of all of its data members, a `toString` method, `set` and `get` methods, a method to input all of the values of its data members, and a method to compute an item's price.

The price of an item is its base price plus a 15% profit margin. The base price of a canned-good item is just its unit price. The base price of a produce item is its unit price times its weight, and the base price a flower item is its unit price, except for arrangements which have a $5.00 preparation fee.

8. Design and implement a class called `SuperStore` that clients can use to declare a store that sells the canned goods, produce, and flowers described in Exercise 7. When an instance of this class is created, its constructor will be passed the number of items (canned goods plus produce plus flower items) that the store will carry, and the city location of the store (a string). The class will contain:

   a) a method (named `Superstore(maxNumOfItems, city)` )
      to create an instance of a super store and specify its location and the maximum number of items the store will carry;

   b) a method (named `addItem(anItem)`) to add a new canned good, produce, or flower item to the store's inventory (one method);

   c) a method (named `outputInventory()`) to output all the information for the entire inventory (all canned goods, produce, and flowers) to the system console preceded by the store's name and location,

   d) a method (named `outputGenericGroup(integerCategoryID)`) to output all the information for the entire inventory of either canned goods, produce, or flowers to the console, preceded by the store's location. Your design should include a polymorphic array to store the Superstore's inventory.

   **Note:** Whenever an item is output, the output should include all of an item's input information, preceded by the item's generic category (e.g., *This item is a Canned Good*) and the item's calculated selling price.

9. Write an application that creates an instance of the superstore described in Exercise 8, allows the user to enter the initial inventory (items a–d below), and then repeatedly outputs the inventory (item e below).

   a) What is the maximum number of items that will be in the new store's inventory?

   b) What is the location of the store?

   c) How many items will be in the initial inventory?

   d) Repeatedly present a menu to allow the user to select the generic category of an item (an integer) and then request the information for that item until all items have been entered.

   e) Repeatedly present the user with the following menu until a "3" is entered:

      Enter 1 to output all the information for all of the items in the inventory

      Enter 2 to output all the information for all of the items in a particular generic category

      Enter 3 to quit the program.

## Enrichment

1. Why does Java not allow multiple inheritance? How is the diamond problem a consequence of multiple inheritance?

2. How can most of the features of multiple inheritance be simulated in Java?

# CHAPTER 9

# RECURSION

## In this chapter

In this chapter we introduce recursion, a very powerful tool used in problem solving in which a problem's solution is expressed in terms of a simpler version of itself. The implementation of the recursive solution results in a method that invokes itself. We will examine the execution path of a recursive method, explore a methodology for discovering and implementing recursive algorithms, and practice this methodology on a set of progressively more difficult problems.

Although recursion can provide succinct and eloquent solutions to many problems, such as the Towers of Hanoi problem, the drawing of fractals, and the solution to many puzzles, the implementation of some recursive solutions can produce runtime problems. They can require large amounts of RAM memory and can result in unacceptably long execution times. We will identify the characteristics of recursion that cause these problems and learn a technique called dynamic programming used to solve one cause of unacceptably long execution times.

After successfully completing this chapter you should:

- Understand recursion and a recursive method's execution path
- Be able to design and implement a recursive solution to a problem by discovering its base case, a reduced solution, and a general solution
- Understand why recursive solutions require more time and storage than their iterative counterparts
- Know when to use a recursive solution and when an iterative solution would be more practical or efficient
- Understand how dynamic programming techniques can improve the efficiency of a recursive algorithm

## 9.1 WHAT IS RECURSION?

In general, recursion is defining something in simpler terms of itself, a property often referred to as self-similarity. In computer science, recursion is a technique used in the coding of methods and formulating algorithms. Usually, these methods or algorithms refer back to or are applied to themselves. When this technique is used to code a method, we say that the method is *recursive*. Before the execution of a recursive method ends, it either invokes itself or another method whose execution eventually leads to an invocation of the recursive method. Figure 9.1 illustrates both of these forms of recursion.

```java
public int aRecusiveMethod(int p)
{
    //code of the beginning
    //of the method

    int value = aRecusiveMethod(21)

    //remaining code of the method
}
```

**A Method Reinvoked by Itself**

```java
public void methodA()

  //beginning code
  //of the methodA

    methodB();

  //remaining code
  //of the method
}
```

```java
public void methodB()

  //beginning code
  //of the methodB

    methodC();

  //remaining code
  //of the method
}
```

```java
public void methodC()
{
  //beginning code
  //of the methodC

    methodA();

  //remaining code
  //of the method
}
```

A Method Eventually Reinvoked by
Another Method

A Reinvocation of methodA

**Figure 9.1**
The two forms of recursive methods.

In mathematics, recursion is often used to define functions and series that can also be defined without using recursion. For example, a non-recursive definition of ten factorial (10!) is:

$$10! = 10 * 9 * 8 * 7 * 6 * 5 * 4 * 3 * 2 * 1$$

This non-recursive definition of 10! can be generalized to a non-recursive definition of **n!** for any positive value of n.

| Definition |
| --- |
| The non-recursive definition of **n!** for values of n ≥ 0 |
| **n!** ≡ n * (n - 1) * (n - 2) * (n − 3) * (n − 4)* ....* 3 * 2 * 1 *and* 0! ≡ 1 |

Alternately, the definition of 10! can be more succinctly stated recursively as

$$10! \equiv 10 * (10 - 1)! \ and \ 0! \equiv 1$$

This recursive definition can be generalized to a recursive definition of **n!** for any positive value of n.

---

**Definition**

The recursive definition of **n!**

$$n! \equiv n * (n - 1)! \ and \ 0! \equiv 1$$

---

The equivalence of the recursive and non-recursive definitions can be easily understood by examining the non-recursive definition of 10! and 9!

$$10! = 10 * \underbrace{9 * 8 * 7 * 6 * 5 * 4 * 3 * 2 * 1}_{(10 - 1)! = 9!} \qquad 9! = 9 * \underbrace{8 * 7 * 6 * 5 * 4 * 3 * 2 * 1}_{(9 - 1)!}$$

The last nine terms in the equation for 10! are contained in the right side of the equation for 9!, so 10! can certainly be expressed as 10 * 9!, which is the recursive definition of 10!. Having been shown this example, most of us would accept the fact that 9! can be used to calculate 10!, that is:

$$10! = 10 * 9!$$

This is the recursive way of calculating 10! which we now understand because we have realized that 9! = 9* 8 * 7 * 6 * 5 * 4 * 3 * 2 * 1. In effect, we have used the non-recursive definition of 9! to understand the recursive definition of 10!.

A recursive definition typically appears to define an entity in simpler terms of itself. The two uses of the factorial operator in the recursive definition of n! could be considered an example of this because the definition states that for positive values of n,

"n *factorial* is equal to n times n minus one *factorial*."

What makes this part of the recursive definition acceptable is that, although the word "factorial" is used in two phrases that make up the sentence ("n *factorial*" and "n minus 1 *factorial*"), the two phrases are different. In addition, the recursive definition of n! contains another crucial part: zero factorial is defined as one (0! ≡ 1).

The reason this second part of the definition is crucial to the validity of a recursive definition is that the recursive definition relies on being able to calculate (n − 1)! in order to calculate n!. Knowing that the value of zero factorial is defined as one gives us the ability to calculate (n − 1)!. This fact may come as a surprise, but it becomes more obvious after a close examination of Figure 9.2, in which the recursive definition of n! is used in a progressive way to calculate (4)!. The right side of line 6 completes the calculation by substituting the value one (1), which is defined to be the value of zero factorial (0!)

The recursive definition of n factorial: n! ≡ n * (n − 1)! *and* 0! ≡ 1.

```
1   4! = 4 * (4 - 1)!
2      = 4 * 3!
3      = 4 * (3 * 2!)
4      = 4 * (3 * (2 * 1!))
5      = 4 * (3 * (2 * (1 * 0!)))
6      = 4 * (3 * (2 * (1 * 1)))
7      = 24
```

**Figure 9.2**
Calculating 4! using the recursive definition of n factorial.

The progression from lines 2 to 5 of Figure 9.2 is analogous to the progression of four phone calls shown at the top of Figure 9.3 initiated by you after your friend Evie asks you the value of four factorial. Remembering the recursive definition of n factorial, you know 4! is 4 * 3!. Because you don't know the value of 3!, you call your friend Logan and ask him the value of 3!. He realizes it is 3 * 2! and calls his friend Skyler to ask her the value of 2!, who calls Ryan to ask him the value of 1!. Finally, Ryan calls Breanne to ask her the value of 0!,

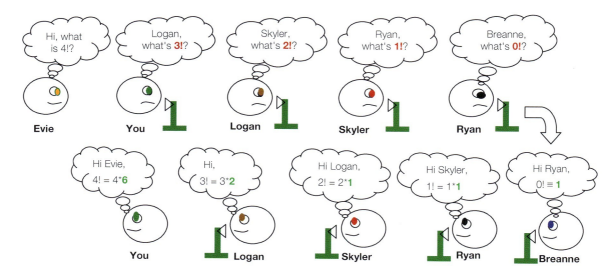

**Figure 9.3**
A progression of five phone calls to determine the value of four factorial.

This leads to the end of the sequence of four phone calls as depicted at the bottom-right of Figure 9.3. In response to Ryan's call, Breanne examines the definition of 0! and tells Ryan the value of 0! is *defined* as 1 and hangs up. Ryan multiplies 1 by the value of 0! that Breanne told him, 1, tells Skyler the value of 1! is 1, and hangs up his phone. This scenario continues with Skyler telling Logan the value of 2! is 2, and Logan telling you the value of 3! is 6. Finally, you multiply 4 by the value of 3! that Logan told you, 6, and you tell Evie the value of 4! is 24.

Recursion is not only used to more succinctly define formulas and series in mathematics, but it is also used to more succinctly define algorithms in computer science. It is for this reason that programming languages permit the two types of recursive invocations illustrated in Figure 9.1. If we were going to write a method that calculated n!, and the recursive definition of n! was used as the method's algorithm, then, when it was used to calculate 4!, the sequence of four phone calls illustrated in Figure 9.3 would be the method invoking itself four times. Evie asking you the value of 4! would be the initial invocation of the method.

Not all algorithms can be expressed recursively, but the effort expended in implementing those that can be is significantly less than implementing a non-recursive version of the algorithm. For this reason, an understanding of how recursive methods execute, how to formulate and implement a recursive algorithm, and some problems associated with the use of recursion is an essential tool to have in our programming toolbox.

## 9.2 UNDERSTANDING A RECURSIVE METHOD'S EXECUTION PATH

A recursive method is invoked, like any other method, by coding its name followed by an argument list used to pass values to the method's parameters. If the method returns a value, the value is either assigned to a variable for use in subsequent statements or used in the statement that contains the invocation of the method. Looking at the invocation statement, there is no way to determine if the method being invoked is recursive or not. Below is an invocation of a recursive method named `fact` that returns 4!, which could also be the invocation of a method with the same signature that is non-recursive:

```
long fourFactorial = fact(4);
```

The recursive version of this factorial method would differ from the non-recursive version within the implementation of the method. The recursive version implements the recursive definition of n factorial using the coding model shown at the top of Figure 9.1. Figure 9.4 shows the code of the method `fact` that calculates the value of n! recursively.

```
1    public long fact(int n)
2    {
3      long nMinus1Factorial, nFact;
4      if(n == 0) //return the definition of 0!
5      {
6        return 1;
7      }
8      else //calculate (n-1)! and then n!
9      {
10       nMinus1Factorial = fact(n-1); //fact invokes itself here
11       nFact = n * nMinus1Factorial;
12       return nFact;
13     }
14   }
```

**Figure 9.4**
A recursive method that calculates n!.

If the Boolean condition on line 4 of Figure 9.4 is `true`, line 6 returns 1, the value of 0! specified in the definition of n!. Otherwise, line 10 of the method invokes itself. Consistent with the first part of recursive definition of n!, it passes `fact` the value of n-1, and the method calculates and returns the value of (n-1)!. Then line 11 uses the returned value to calculate n factorial, which is returned on line 12.

Although the calculations performed by lines 10 and 11 are coded sequentially, they do not execute sequentially because line 10 of the initial invocation of the method initiates the first of the progression of four phone calls depicted at the top of Figure 9.3. When calculating 4!, the first of these phone calls (or, more accurately, recursive *invocation*s) is passed the value 3 (i.e., 4 - 1).

The three subsequent recursive invocations of the method by line 10 pass the values 2, 1, and finally 0 to the method. The line-by-line execution sequence of the method to reach this point, beginning with the initial invocation of the method, is given below and is represented by the red arrows in Figure 9.5.

Lines 1, 2, 3, 4, 8, 9, 10 //which passes the *first* recursive invocation the value 3
Lines 1, 2, 3, 4, 8, 9, 10 //which passes the *second* recursive invocation the value 2
Lines 1, 2, 3, 4, 8, 9, 10 //which passes the *third* recursive invocation the value 1
Lines 1, 2, 3, 4, 8, 9, 10 //which passes the *fourth* recursive invocation the value 0

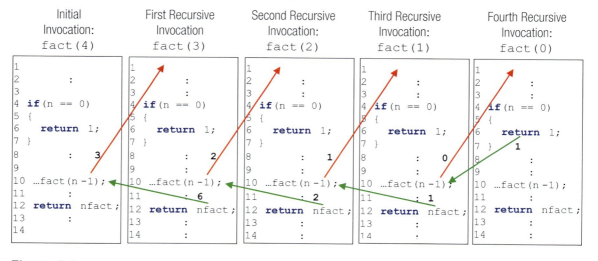

**Figure 9.5**
The execution sequence of the invocations of the method **fact** to calculate 4!

Because the fourth recursive invocation of the method is passed the value zero, its execution sequence is lines 1, 2, 3, 4, 5, and 6 because the Boolean condition on line 4 for this execution of the method evaluates to `true`. As a result, line 6 returns the value 1 (0!) to line 10 of the third recursive invocation (as indicated by the green arrow on the right side of Figure 9.5). Then lines 11 and 12 of the third, second, and first recursive invocations execute, returning the values 1, 2, and 6 (as indicated by the other three green arrows in Figure 9.5). Finally, lines 11 and 12 of the initial invocation of the method execute and return 24 = 4 * 6.

Two important observations to make from an examination of Figure 9.5 are that:

1. because of the recursive invocations spawned by line 10 of the initial invocation of the method, a considerable amount of time is required to complete the execution of this line of code

2. the recursive invocations of the method would have continued had it not been for the fact that the fourth recursive invocation was passed the value zero

Armed with an understanding of the execution path of recursive methods, we will discuss the techniques used to discover recursive algorithms and the nuances of implementing them.

## 9.3 FORMULATING AND IMPLEMENTING RECURSIVE ALGORITHMS

Most people do not possess an innate ability to think recursively. When shown the non-recursive and recursive definitions of n factorial, most of us would say that we are able to understand the non-recursive definition, but we are confused by its recursive counterpart. Therefore, it should come as no surprise that most of us have trouble recognizing that there is a recursive solution to a problem and have even more trouble trying to discover the algorithm even after we are told that one does exist.

Fortunately, we can learn to think recursively because the discovery of recursive algorithms can be methodized, and once discovered, many recursive algorithms are implemented in a very similar way. After gaining a basic understanding of the methodized process, lots of practice facilitates the learning curve.

### 9.3.1 The Base Case, Reduced Problem, and General Solution

The recursive-algorithm discovery process is broken into four discovery steps:

1. identify the *base case* or cases
2. identify the *reduced problem* or problems
3. identify the *general solution*
4. combine the base case, reduced problem, and general solution into a recursive algorithm

We have already used a base case, reduced problem, and general solution in the program presented in Figure 9.4 without identifying them by name. The base case, reduced problem, and general solution of the recursive algorithm for n factorial implemented in Figure 9.4 are identified in Table 9.1.

Prior to coding the method shown in Figure 9.4, we did not discover these three parts of the recursive algorithm for n!. They were discovered by the person that originally formulated the recursive definition of n!, who was probably born with the ability to think recursively. We simply discussed a method that implemented this definition of n! to gain insights into the execution path of a recursive method. This was a useful exercise because an understanding of the method's execution path, and an awareness of these three parts of the recursive definition of n!, do facilitate an understanding of the discovery process.

**Table 9.1**
The Base Case, Reduced Problem, and General Solution for n!

| Base Case | Reduced Problem | General Solution |
|-----------|-----------------|------------------|
| $0! \equiv 1$ | $(n-1)!$ | $n * (n-1)!$ |

## Discovering the Base Case

The recursive-algorithm discovery process begins with the identification of the problem's base case. To discover the base case, we search for a particular instance of the problem whose solution is known. For example if we were trying to discover the recursive algorithm for n factorial, we would ask ourselves if there is a particular value of n: 0, or 1, or 2, or 3, or 4, etc., whose factorial value is known. Most people know that 0! is defined as 1, which is the base case for n factorial. The base case for another problem, $x^n$, is also a definition: $x^0$, which is also defined as 1. For some problems, the base case is not a definition but a trivial case of the problem that most of us know, such as $1 * 1 = 1$. Another example of a trivial base case is associated with the problem of outputting a string of n characters in reverse order. In this case, when n is one, we simply output the string.

When the problem involves an integer n, often (as we have seen) the base case is the solution to the problem when $n = 0$ or, for some problems, when $n = 1$. The determination of the base case is a crucial first step in the discovery process because it is used to discover the reduced problem, which is then used to discover the general solution. In addition, when we implement the algorithm, as shown on line 4 of Figure 9.4 and on the far right side of Figure 9.5, it is the base case that halts the progression of recursive invocations and is sometimes referred to as the *stopping condition*. Some problems, as we will see, contain multiple base cases.

## Discovering the Reduced Problem

Identifying the reduced problem is often the most difficult part of the four-step discovery process. Usually, it can be identified by considering the following three criteria. The reduced problem:

1. is a problem similar to the original problem
2. is usually between the original problem and the base case and is usually closer to the original problem than it is to the base case
3. becomes the base case for all versions of the original problem when *progressively reduced*

For example, the reduced problem for n! is $(n-1)!$. Clearly, this is similar to the original problem in that it also involves n and uses the factorial operator. It is between the original problem and the base case (0!), and for most values of n ($n > 2$), it is closer to the original problem than it is to the base case. This would be an acceptable reduced problem if progressive reductions caused it to become the base case for all values of n.

By progressive reductions, we mean that we repeatedly apply the relationship between the candidate reduced problem and the original problem to the reduced problem to produce new versions of the problem. For n!, the relationship is that the number used in the reduced problem (n − 1) is one less than the number used in the original problem (n). Applying this relationship to the reduced problem (n − 1)!, the new version of the problem becomes ((n − 1) − 1)! = (n − 2)! on the first reduction. Subsequent new versions of the problem are ((n − 2) − 1)! = (n − 3)!, (n − 4)!, (n − 5)!, etc. Because this progressive reduction of (n − 1)! for any positive value of n will eventually become the base case, (n − 1)! is an acceptable reduced problem for n!.

An example of an unacceptable reduced problem for n! is (n − 2)!, although it satisfies most of our criteria. It is a problem similar to the original problem, it is between the base case (0!) and the original problem, and it is also closer to the original problem than it is to the base case. What makes it unacceptable is that progressive reductions, for *odd* values of n, do not result in the base case. For example, for n = 7 the reduced problem would be (7 − 2)! = 5!, and its progressive reductions would be:

$$(5 − 2)! = 3!, \quad (3 − 2)! = 1!, \quad (1 − 2)! = -1!.$$

The reductions skip over the base case, zero factorial. They never become the base case for odd values of n. Another unacceptable candidate reduced problem is (n + 1)!. For n = 7, the reduced problem would be (7 + 1)! = 8!, and its progressive reductions would be 8!, 9!, 10!, 11!, etc. The result would be an infinite series that never becomes the base case.

Some problems, as we will see, contain multiple reduced problems.

### Discovering the General Solution

The general solution is the solution to the original problem. To discover the general solution, we think of a way to solve the original problem assuming that we have already found a valid reduced problem. That is, we think of a way of use the solution to the reduced problem in the solution of the original problem.

In the case of n!, this translates into the question of how (n − 1)! can be used to calculate n factorial. The answer is multiplying (n − 1)! by n, so the general solution for n! is n × (n − 1)!

The first three steps of the recursive-algorithm discovery process are summarized in Table 9.2.

### 9.3.2 Implementing Recursive Algorithms

Once we have discovered the base case, reduced problem, and general solution for a particular problem, they are combined into a recursive algorithm. Finding the correct combination usually involves some creativity, which comes naturally to some people while the rest of us have to develop this creative ability through practice.

For many problems, the base case, reduced problem, and general solution are combined in a similar way. For a subset of these problems, they are combined in an identical way, which is depicted in the flow chart shown in Figure 9.6. By working with this subset of problems, we will begin to develop the ability to think recursively. Continued practice with the super set of problems will further develop our skills.

The algorithm shown in Figure 9.6 is most easily understood by comparing it to a particular implementation of it: the code of the method to recursively compute n! presented in Figure 9.4. The

**Table 9.2**

The recursive algorithm discovery process

| Step | Process | Comments |
|------|---------|----------|
| 1:<br>Base Case Discovery | Search for a particular instance of the problem whose solution is known, because it is a defined solution or it is a trivial solution that is known to most people. | The base case for n! is $0! \equiv 1$<br><br>If the problem involves an integer n, the base is often when $n = 0$ or $n = 1$. |
| 2:<br>Reduced Problem Discovery | Search for a version of the problem that:<br>• is similar to the original problem<br><br>• usually is between the original problem and the base case *and* closer to the original problem<br>• when progressively reduced becomes the base case for *all versions* of the original problem | The reduced problem for n! is $(n - 1)!$<br>$n! \leq (n - 1)! \leq 0!$<br><br><br>The progressive reductions of $(n - 1)!$ are:<br>$(n - 1)!, (n - 2)!, (n - 3)!$, etc., which becomes the base case, 0!, for all values of n. |
| 3:<br>General Solution Discovery | Think of a way to solve the original problem, assuming that we have already found a solution to the reduced problem. | The reduced problem is used in the general solution, e.g.,<br>$n! = n * (n - 1)!$ |

problem of calculating n! is one of the problems in the subset of problems whose three components (base case, reduced problem, and general solution) can be combined exactly as shown in Figure 9.6.

Figure 9.7 represents the code of this method with comments added to it to aid in an understanding of the manner in which the algorithm combines its three components. These comments refer to the blue-font numbers shown on the left side of each of the flow-chart symbols shown in Figure 9.6.

The `if` statement coded on line 4 of Figure 9.7 represents the question in symbol 2 of the flowchart, which is used to decide if the problem to be solved is the base case. The `return` statement (line 6) inside the `if` statement's code block represents flowchart symbols 3 and 4 that terminate the algorithm after returning the base case solution.

Symbol 5 of the flowchart is typically the most confusing part of the algorithm because it is the most confusing part of recursion. It calculates the solution to the reduced problem using this same algorithm. It is the recursive part of the algorithm. The right side of line 10 implements symbol 5 by re-invoking the method and passing it the reduced problem. As we have learned, this symbol of the flowchart can occupy a significant portion of the algorithm's execution time. Every time it is entered, it spawns another execution of the algorithm, beginning at symbol 1, to calculate the solution to a new (reduced) factorial problem.

After flowchart symbol 5 calculates the solution to the reduced problem, symbol 6 uses it to calculate the general solution to the original problem. Line 11 of Figure 9.7 implements flowchart symbol 6. After symbol 7 returns the problem's solution (line 12 of Figure 9.7), symbol 8 ends the algorithm.

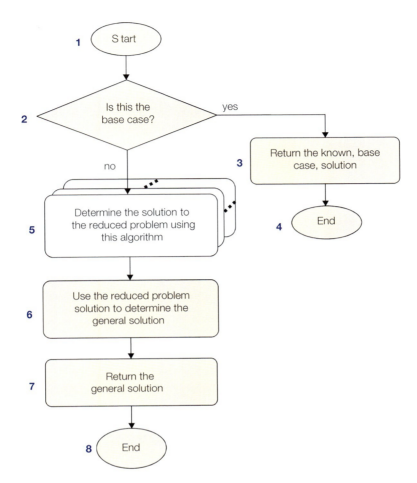

**Figure 9.6**
A template for some recursive algorithms.

```
1    public long fact(int n)
2    {
3      long nMinus1Factorial
4      if(n == 0) //Flow chart symbol 2
5      {
6        return 1; //Flow chart symbols 3 and 4
7      }
8      else
9      {
10       nMinus1Factorial = fact(n-1); //Flow chart symbol 5
11       nFact = n * nMinus1Factorial; //Flow chart symbol 6
12       return nFact; //Flow chart symbols 7 and 8
13     }
14   }
```

**Figure 9.7**
A recursive method that calculates n! commented to correlate to the algorithm presented in Figure 9.6.

### 9.3.3 Practice Problems

Now that we have acquired a basic understanding of recursion, the best way to extend our ability to think recursively is to apply our newly acquired skills to a set of problems that can be solved recursively. The problems presented in Table 9.3 are tabulated in an order intended to extend these skills in an incremental manner. As we move from the problems at the top of the table to those at the bottom of the table, their recursive solutions become increasingly dissimilar to the recursive solution of n!. For this reason, which is consistent with the adage that "practice makes perfect," it is best to work our way through all of the problems in the order in which they are tabulated. Table 9.4 (included in the Chapter Summary) presents the base case, reduced problem, and general solution for each of the problems presented in Table 9.3

**Table 9.3**

Several Problems That Have Recursive Solutions in Difficulty Order

| Problem | Base Case | Reduced Problem | General Solution |
|---|---|---|---|
| Factorial of a positive integer, n! | $0! \equiv 1$ | $(n-1)!$ | $n * (n-1)!$ |
| A number x raised to a positive integer, $x^n$ | | | |
| Sum of the integers from 1 to n | | | |
| Product of two positive integers, $m \times n$ | | | |
| Output an n character string, s, in reverse order | | | |
| **Problems with Multiple Base Cases and Reduced Problems** | | | |
| Generate the $n^{th}$ term of the Fibonacci Sequence, fn | | | |
| Find the greatest common divisor of two positive integers m and n, GCD(m, n), for m > n | | | |
| **A Problem with Multiple Base Cases** | | | |
| Search a sorted list of items for the item I | | | |
| **A Problem that Uses the Reduced Problem Twice** | | | |
| Towers of Hanoi: Move n rings from tower A to tower B using tower C | | | |

As noted in the table, some problems have multiple base cases and reduced problems, and one problem uses its reduced problem twice in its general solution. As we have learned, the starting point is the determination of a problem's base case, then its reduced problem, and then its general solution. They should be entered into a copy of the last three columns of the table below the column entries for n!, and in most cases, they can be combined into a recursive solution using the algorithm depicted in Figure 9.6.

The correctness of the discovered base case, reduced problem, and general solutions should be verified by comparing them to the entries in Table 9.4 in the Chapter Summary. Implementing each problem's recursive solution before moving on to the next problem is highly recommended because it augments the learning process.

It is not unusual in the beginning, or at some other point in this learning process, not to be able to discover one or more of the three components of the recursive solution (i.e., its base case, reduced problem, or general solution). When this is the case, it is still useful to implement the recursive algorithm using the component(s) presented in Table 9.4. Consistent with this idea, many students begin by skipping the discovery process and simply implement a recursive method to calculate $x^n$ using the components given in the second row of Table 9.4 and the flow chart presented in Figure 9.6.

A description of the last problem in Table 9.3, The Towers of Hanoi, is given in the beginning of the next section.

## 9.4 A RECURSION CASE STUDY: THE TOWERS OF HANOI

The recursive solution to the Towers of Hanoi problem is a good example of the simplicity and power of recursive algorithms. Its recursive solution can be implemented as seven lines of code. Applying the techniques we have learned to produce a recursive solution, this problem will serve as a good capstone to our discussion of how to formulate and implement recursive algorithms. Not only will this reinforce our knowledge of the discovery process, but the implementation of the problem's recursive algorithm will introduce an often-used nuance into the parameter list of a recursive method that is not used in the solutions of the other problems presented in Tables 9.3 and 9.4.

### Statement of the Problem

The problem was conceived by the French mathematician Eduardo Lucas in 1883. It involves three towers and a set of n disks or rings, each with different diameters. The original legend claimed that the Brahmins of an ancient Indian temple were charged with moving 64 golden disks, and when the last one was in its final place, the world would come to an end.[1] As we will see, there is no need to worry about this because the disks had to be moved in a specified order, and if one disk were move per second it would take 585 billion years ($2^{64}$ - 1 seconds) to relocate the disks.

The left side and right sides of Figure 9.8 illustrate the problem's starting and ending points for four rings (n = 4). The rings are initially stacked in decreasing order by size on one of the towers, which we will refer to as the starting tower. The left side of Figure 9.8 shows four rings stacked on a starting tower named A. The right side of the figure shows the four rings relocated to the tower named B, which we will refer to as the destination tower. We will refer to the third tower shown in the figure, whose name is C, as the extra tower.

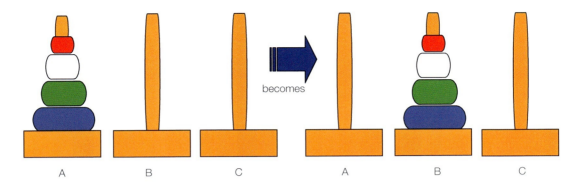

**Figure 9.8**
The Towers of Hanoi problem's starting and ending points using four rings.

The solution to the problem is a specification of the order in which to move the rings that will relocate all of them from a designated starting tower (tower A) to a designated destination tower (tower B) without violating the following two conditions:

1.  Only one ring (a top ring) can be moved at a time, and it must be placed on a tower before another ring is moved.
2.  A larger ring cannot be placed on top of a smaller ring.

These conditions imply that when the problem is solved, the rings will be stacked on the designated destination tower in decreasing size order, as shown on the right side of Figure 9.8. The problem solutions (i.e., the order in which the rings are moved to relocate them from tower A to tower B) for two, three, and four rings are given in Figure 9.9. Figure 9.10 depicts the three-ring solution.

Notice that there is a pattern to predicting the number of moves that will be needed for n rings. For two rings, there are three moves, for three rings, there are seven moves, and for four rings, there are fifteen moves. In general, the minimum number of moves for n rings will be $2^n -1$. This is why moving the legendary 64 golden disks would require $2^{64} -1$ moves and extraordinarily long time.

## The Base Case

We have learned that the formulation of a recursive solution to a problem begins with a search for its base case: a known, defined, or trivial solution to the problem. We have also learned that when the problem involves n items, a good place to begin the search is when n = 0 or n = 1. This problem involves n rings, so we will begin by considering the case when there are zero rings. This is a legitimate base case for this problem because the trivial solution would be to do nothing. An alternate base case is when n = 1 because if we were asked to move one ring from tower A to tower B, we would simply state "move the top ring on tower A to tower B." Both of these are trivial solutions because most people would know them, and they do not require a consideration of the two conditions of the Towers of Hanoi problem. Either of these base cases can be used in the recursive solution to the problem. The n = 1 base case is the one that appears in Table 9.4.

| Two-Ring Solution | Four-Ring Solution |
|---|---|
| 1- move one ring from tower A to tower C | 1- move one ring from tower A to tower C |
| 2- move one ring from tower A to tower B | 2- move one ring from tower A to tower B |
| 3- move one ring from tower C to tower B | 3- move one ring from tower C to tower B |
|  | 4- move one ring from tower A to tower C |
| **Three-Ring Solution** | 5- move one ring from tower B to tower A |
| 1- move one ring from tower A to tower B | 6- move one ring from tower B to tower C |
| 2- move one ring from tower A to tower C | 7- move one ring from tower A to tower C |
| 3- move one ring from tower B to tower C | 8- move one ring from tower A to tower B |
| 4- move one ring from tower A to tower B | 9- move one ring from tower C to tower B |
| 5- move one ring from tower C to tower A | 10- move one ring from tower C to tower A |
| 6- move one ring from tower C to tower B | 11- move one ring from tower B to tower A |
| 7- move one ring from tower A to tower B | 12- move one ring from tower C to tower B |
|  | 13- move one ring from tower A to tower C |
|  | 14- move one ring from tower A to tower B |
|  | 15- move one ring from tower C to tower B |

**Figure 9.9**
Three Towers of Hanoi problem solutions.

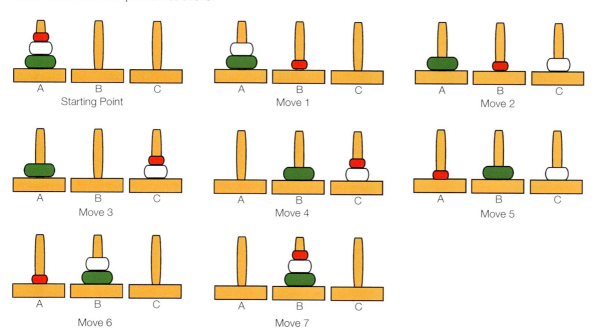

**Figure 9.10**
The solution to the three-ring Towers of Hanoi problem.

**NOTE** *Towers of Hanoi base case:*
*n = 1: Move 1 ring from one tower to another tower*

## Reduced Problem

To discover the reduced problem, we can use a new tool often employed when the problem involves n items. We try to solve very simple versions of the problem, not quite as trivial as the base case, but close to it. Then, we examine the solutions looking for similarities and try to generalize the similarities into a reduced problem. For example, suppose we were able to produce the two- and three-ring solutions shown in Figure 9.9, which many non-recursive thinking people could probably do. If we are visual learners, it helps to sketch out each step of the solutions, as has been done in Figure 9.10 for the three-ring solution.

Examining Figure 9.10 and the two-ring solution in Figure 9.9, we notice that just before the half-way point of both solutions (move 4 of Figure 9.10 and move 2 of the two-ring solution), all of the rings except for one have been moved to tower C. Examining the moves made after the mid-point of both solutions (moves 5–7 in Figure 9.10 and move 3 of the two-ring solution in Figure 9.9), we realize that these also move all of the rings except for one.

Because the ability to move all but one ring from one tower to another tower is common to both the two- and three-ring solutions, perhaps this could be the reduced problem. When generalized, it becomes: move n-1 rings from one tower to another tower. This generalization does satisfy the three criteria for a reduced problem restated below and is the one that appears in Table 9.4:

1.  It is similar to the original problem: move n rings from one tower to another tower.
2.  It is closer to the original problem than either of the problem's base cases (n = 0 and n = 1), and it is between the original problem and these base cases.
3.  When progressively reduced, it does eventually become one of the base cases: move one or move zero rings.

Another way of discovering this reduced solution would be to compare the illustration of the starting point in Figure 9.10 to the illustration of move 3 in that figure and to compare the illustrations of move 4 to move 7. From these comparisons, we would be likely to observe that the problem could be solved if we knew how to move n-1 rings, and then conclude that we need to make a call to a friend who knows how to move n-1 rings from one tower to another tower.

**NOTE**    *Towers of Hanoi reduced problem:*
*Move n-1 rings from one tower to another tower.*

## The General Solution

To discover the general solution, we ask ourselves how we can use the reduced problem to solve the original problem. In the case of the Towers of Hanoi, this question becomes: "how can we use the ability to move *n-1* rings to solve the problem of moving n rings from one tower to another tower?" The answer can often be found by examining the solutions developed to the very simple versions of the problem previously used to determine the reduced problem.

The three move sequences on both sides of move 4 in Figure 9.10, which shows the n = 3 solution, represent a movement of 3-1 rings from one tower to another. This means that if move 4 of Figure 9.10 was preceded and followed with a version of the reduced problem, it would be the general solution of the n = 3 ring problem:

1.  use the reduced problem to move 2 rings from tower A to C (moves 1–3)
2.  move 4 (move 1 ring from tower A to tower B)
3.  use the reduced problem to move 2 rings from tower C to B (moves 5–7)

Once we have found a way to use the reduced problem to solve one of the simpler problems used in the discovery of the reduced problem (e.g., the 3 ring problem), its use is extrapolated to the n ring general solution. This is the general solution presented in Table 9.4.

**NOTE**

*Towers of Hanoi general solution:*
*1. use the reduced problem to move n-1 rings from tower A to C*
*2. move 1 ring from tower A to tower B*
*3. use the reduced problem to move n-1 rings from tower C to B*

## Implementation

The base case, reduced problem, and general solution of this problem can be combined into a recursive algorithm using the flow chart shown in Figure 9.6. The application presented in Figure 9.11 implements this algorithm in a method named `hanoi` (lines 8–24). The signature of the method contains four parameters: the number of rings to be moved, followed by the name of the starting tower, the name of the destination tower, and the name of the third tower. It is invoked on line 5 to output the moves required to transfer four rings from tower A to tower B. The output produced by the program is shown in Figure 9.12.

As the names of the last three parameters in the signatures of the `hanoi` method on lines 8 and 9 indicate, the method uses the tower name passed to its parameter (`fromTower`) as the starting tower, and the tower names passed to the method's second and third parameters (`toTower` and `thirdTower`) are used as the destination tower and the extra tower, respectively. As a result, when the method is invoked recursively on line 20 of the general solution to move all but the bottom ring from the starting tower to the extra tower, the second argument used in the invocation is the parameter `thirdTower`, and the last argument is the parameter `toTower`. This effectively swaps roles of the extra tower and the destination tower during this invocation of the method, and n-1 rings are relocated to the extra tower.

Similarly, when the method is invoked on line 23 of the general solution to move the n-1 rings placed on the extra tower from the extra tower to the destination tower, the first argument used in the invocation is the method's parameter `thirdTower`, and the last argument is the method's parameter `fromTower`. This effectively swaps roles of the extra tower and the starting tower during this invocation of the method.

When the method `hanoi` is invoked, and line 12 detects the base case (the value passed to `nRings` is 1), the output produced by lines 14–15 includes the names of the towers passed to the method's first and second parameters `fromTower` and `toTower`. This ensures that when the invocations on lines 20 and 23 degenerate to the base case, the values of the first and second arguments passed to the method will be included in the base case's output (lines 14–15).

```
1   public class TowersOfHanoi
2   {
3     public static void main(String[] args)
4     {
5       hanoi(4, "A", "B", "C"); //output the solution for four rings
6     }
7
8     public static void hanoi(int nRings, String fromTower,
9                              String toTower, String thirdTower);
10    {
11
12      if(nRings == 1) //base case
13      {
14        System.out.println("move one ring from tower " + fromTower +
15                           " to tower " + toTower);
16        return;
17      }
18
19      //general solution
20      hanoi(nRings-1, fromTower, thirdTower, toTower); //reduced problem
21      System.out.println("move one ring from tower " + fromTower +
22                         " to tower " + toTower);
23      hanoi(nRings-1, thirdTower, toTower, fromTower); //reduced problem
24    }
25  }
```

**Figure 9.11**
The application **TowersOfHanoi**.

```
move one ring from tower A to tower C
move one ring from tower A to tower B
move one ring from tower C to tower B
move one ring from tower A to tower C
move one ring from tower B to tower A
move one ring from tower B to tower C
move one ring from tower A to tower C
move one ring from tower A to tower B
move one ring from tower C to tower B
move one ring from tower C to tower A
move one ring from tower B to tower A
move one ring from tower C to tower B
move one ring from tower A to tower C
move one ring from tower A to tower B
move one ring from tower C to tower B
```

**Figure 9.12**
The output produced by the application **TowersOfHanoi**.

## 9.5 PROBLEMS WITH RECURSION

Because only a small percentage of the population has an innate ability to think recursively, most of us need to be trained in how to discover and implement recursive algorithms. To a certain extent, the discovery and implementation process can be methodized, but a good deal of effort is necessary to become a good recursive programmer.

Another problem with recursion is that applications that use recursive algorithms tend to run more slowly. If two versions of the same application were developed, one that used a recursive algorithm and one that used a non-recursive algorithm, the non-recursive version would typically run faster. The difference in speed is due to the manner in which modern computer systems transfer execution to, and return from, an invoked method and the larger number of method invocations that recursive algorithms typically perform by repeatedly invoking themselves.

Every time a method is invoked, whether or not it is recursive, the runtime environment has to suspend the execution of the program to perform tasks associated with the invocation. Typically, these tasks include allocating the memory for the invoked method's parameters and local variables and transferring the value of the arguments into these parameters. Not only does this take time, but each method invocation requires additional RAM memory for the storage of the method's parameters and local variables.

Storage must also be allocated to save the contents of the CPU registers and the invoking method's return address to complete the invoking method's execution. Java stores this information in an area of storage called the *run-time stack*. After each invocation completes its execution, the invoking method cannot continue its execution until the information is retrieved from the run-time stack and stored in the CPU's registers.

As shown in Figure 9.5, the recursive method to calculate n! invokes itself four times to calculate 4!; to compute 40! requires 40 invocations, and n! requires n invocations. A non-recursive, or *iterative*, version of the method is given in Figure 9.13. It does not issue any method invocations during its execution regardless of the value of n. Its speed advantage over the recursive version increases with increasing values of n. In addition, it does not require storage allocated for the parameters, local variables, CPU register values and return addresses associated with the additional invocations of the recursive version of the method.

```java
1   public static long factIterative(int n)
2   {
3     long nFact = 1;
4     for(int i = n; i >= 1; i--)
5     {
6       nFact = nFact * i;
7     }
8     return nFact;
9   }
```

**Figure 9.13**
An iterative method that calculates n!.

The number of invocations issued by some recursive algorithms can make the recursive solution incalculable from a time viewpoint. The implementation of the recursive definition of the **Fibonacci sequence** is one such example.

---

**Definition**

The recursive definition of the terms of the **Fibonacci sequence**:

$f_1 \equiv 1$ and $f_2 \equiv 1$;

for $n \geq 2$: $f_n = f_{n-1} + f_{n-2}$

---

Consistent with this definition, the first eight terms of the sequence are 1, 1, 2, 3, 5, 8, 13, and 21. This recursive definition has two base cases, $f_1 \equiv 1$ and $f_2 \equiv 1$, two reduced problems, $f_{n-1}$ and $f_{n-2}$, and its general solution is $f_n = f_{n-1} + f_{n-2}$. While this may look innocent, when these base cases, reduced problems, and the general solution are combined as shown in Figure 9.6 and implemented into a recursive method, the number of recursive invocations made to calculate the 40th term in the sequence, f40, is 204,668,309. The reason there are this many invocations is illustrated in Figure 9.14, where the arrows in the figure should be interpreted as the method invoking itself to calculate a term of the series. Referring to the top of the figure, to calculate f40, the method is invoked to calculate f39 and f38. To calculate f39, the method is invoked to calculate f38 and f37. As shown in the remainder of the figure, during the recursive definition of f40, f39 is calculated once, but f38 is calculated twice, f37 three times, f36 five times, f35 eight times, etc.

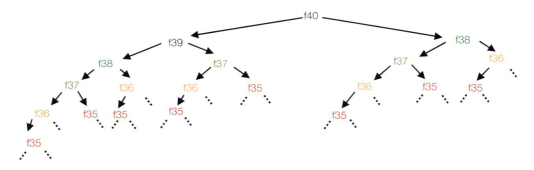

**Figure 9.14**
Some of the 204,668,309 invocations required to calculate the 40th term of the Fibonacci sequence.

Another problem with recursion is that during a recursive method's execution, if the recursive chain of invocations gets too long, the storage required for the return addresses and CPU register contents can exceed the capacity of the run-time stack. When this happens, the method's execution will produce a runtime `StackOverflowException` error, and unless the exception is caught, the application will be terminated. Below is a summary of the problems with recursion that were discussed in this section:

1. Most programmers need to be trained in how to discover and implement recursive algorithms.

2. The number of recursive invocations issued by a recursive method can make it significantly slower than its iterative counterpart.

3. Methods that implement recursive algorithms can require prohibitively large amounts of RAM storage.

4. Recursive methods are prone to terminating in a `StackOverflowException` error.

One solution to the last three problems will be discussed in Section 9.5.2.

### 9.5.1 When to Use Recursion

In light of the problems associated with recursion, and considering the fact that recursive algorithms have an iterative counterpart, the question of when we should use recursion in our programs arises. The short answer is when the recursive algorithm significantly reduces the algorithm-discovery and implementation time, and the additional storage requirements and execution time associated with a recursive method are acceptable.

This is not the case for most of the problems presented in Table 9.3. Certainly, the first five problems presented in the table would normally not be coded using recursion because their non-recursive (iterative) solution is easy to discover and simple to code. They were included in the table to facilitate the learning process. On the other end of the spectrum, recursion is usually used to find a greatest common divisor and in the solution to the Towers of Hanoi problem. The following three-line general solution of the Towers of Hanoi is much simpler than a non-recursive solution to the problem:

1. move n-1 rings from tower A to tower C

2. move one ring from tower A to tower B

3. move n-1 rings from tower C to tower B

Other common uses of recursion include the solution of puzzles, such as mazes, the Sudoku puzzle, the Eight Queens problem, the Knight's Tour, the searching and sorting of lists of data, and the drawing of fractals.

### Fractals and the Sierpinski Triangle

Fractals are mathematical or geometric objects that have the property of self-similarity, that is, each part of the object is a smaller or reduced copy of itself. Geometric fractals are implicitly recursive because they begin by drawing a shape and then extend the drawing by repeatedly redrawing the shape at smaller and smaller scales. Generally speaking, the repetitions are infinite, although the drawing process is normally terminated when the shapes become too small to see.

Given an equilateral triangle, the Sierpinski fractal is produced by creating three equilateral triangles whose vertices are the three original vertices and the midpoints of the sides adjacent to these vertices. This process is then repeated recursively for the three resulting equilateral triangles. The first three steps in this process are shown in Figure 9.15.

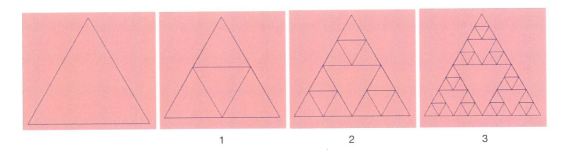

**Figure 9.15**
The first three steps in the creation of a Sierpinski Triangle.

The fractal shown in Figures 9.16 is a Sierpinski Triangle on which the process has been repeated seven times. It was created by the application `RecursiveFractal` shown in Figure 9.17. Line 20 of the application invokes the recursive method `drawSierpinski` (lines 31–47) to draw the fractal. The invocation passes the method the number of times to repeat the Sierpinski process (plus one for the drawing of the original triangle), the vertices of the original triangle (declared as `Point` objects on lines 8, 9, and 10), and the graphics object `g` because the method draws the triangles (lines 39–41). The vertex at the top of Figure 9.16 is `p1`, the lower left vertex is `p2`, and the lower right vertex is `p3` (lines 8-10).

**Figure 9.16**
A six-iteration Sierpinski fractal.

Line 34 tests for the base case, which is when the number of invocations of the method has been decremented to zero by line 42. The general solution is in lines 44–46, which recursively invokes the method to draw three triangles. The vertices of these triangles are one of the vertices passed to the method and the midpoints of the lines joining the other two vertices. Each of these three invocations spawns 363 additional invocations of the `drawSierpinski` method for the fractal drawn by the application. The locations of the midpoints of the sides of the triangle passed as the third and fourth arguments on lines 44–46 are calculated by the `midPoint` method (lines 23–29). The two integer data members of the API `Point` class (x, y) are public data members, which eliminates the need to invoke `set` and `get` methods on lines 26 and 27.

The recursive execution sequence of the lines 44–46 draws all of the blue lines that make up the mostly blue large upper triangle shown in Figure 9.16, before the mostly blue large lower left triangle is drawn, which is drawn before the mostly blue large lower right triangle is drawn.

```
1    import edu.sjcny.gpv1.*;
2    import java.awt.*;
3
4    public class RecursiveFractal extends DrawableAdapter
5    {
6      static RecursiveFractal ge = new RecursiveFractal();
7      static GameBoard gb = new GameBoard(ge, "RECURSIVE FRACTAL");
8      static Point p1 = new Point(250, 70); //vertices of the 1st triangle
9      static Point p2 = new Point(25, 460);
10     static Point p3 = new Point(475, 460);
11
12     public static void main(String args[])
13     {
14       showGameBoard(gb);
15     }
16
17     public void draw(Graphics g)
18     {
19       g.setColor(Color.BLUE);
20       drawSierpinski(8, p1, p2, p3, g);
21     }
22
23     public static Point midPoint(Point p1, Point p2)
24     {
25       Point midPoint = new Point();
26       midPoint.y = p1.y + (p2.y - p1.y)/2;
27       midPoint.x = p1.x + (p2.x - p1.x)/2;
28       return midPoint;
29     }
30
31     public static void drawSierpinski(int iterations, Point p1, Point p2,
32                                       Point p3, Graphics g)
33     {
34       if(iterations == 0) //base case
35       {
36         return;
37       }
38       //general solution
39       g.drawLine(p1.x, p1.y, p2.x, p2.y); //draw a triangle
40       g.drawLine(p2.x, p2.y, p3.x, p3.y);
```

```
41      g.drawLine(p3.x, p3.y, p1.x, p1.y);
42      iterations--;
43    //reduced problems to draw top, left & right side triangles recursively
44      drawSierpinski(iterations, p1, midPoint(p1,p2), midPoint(p1,p3), g);
45      drawSierpinski(iterations, p2, midPoint(p2,p1), midPoint(p2,p3), g);
46      drawSierpinski(iterations, p3, midPoint(p3,p1), midPoint(p3,p2), g);
47    }
48  }
```

**Figure 9.17**
The application **RecursiveFractal**.

### 9.5.2 Dynamic Programming

Dynamic programming is a technique that can sometimes be used to solve three of the problems associated with recursion: unacceptably long execution times, excessive memory requirements, and a StackOverflowException error. It does this by reducing the number of recursive invocations. The basis of this technique is the idea that once a value is computed recursively, it should not be computed again.

For example, Figure 9.18 shows the 25 invocations required to compute the seventh term of the Fibonacci series recursively. During this computation, once the first invocation to compute f3, shown on the lower left side of the figure, completes its execution, the other four invocations to compute f3 shown in the figure could be eliminated because the value of f3 is already known. Once computed, if that value was stored in a static class-level variable, the other four invocations of f3 could be replaced with a new base case that simply returned the value stored in the variable. A similar approach would eliminate four of the five invocations to compute f1, seven of the eight to compute f2, two of the three to compute f4, and one of the invocations to compute f5. The result would be that only seven invocations would be required to compute f7 recursively: one invocation to compute f7, and six more recursive invocations to compute f6, f5, f4, f3, f2, and f1 (see highlights in Figure 9.19).

Figure 9.19 illustrates this improved process of computing f7 = 13 using dynamic programming in the implementation of its recursive algorithm. The invocation of the method to compute f7 still spawns the recursive invocations shown on the far left side of Figure 9.18 to compute f6 though

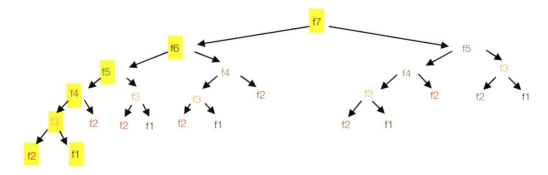

**Figure 9.18**
The 25 invocations required to compute the seventh term of the Fibonacci sequence recursively.

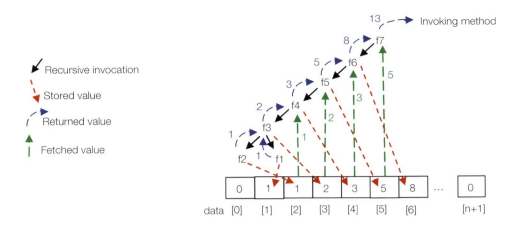

**Figure 9.19**
The seven invocations required to compute the seventh term of the Fibonacci sequence recursively using dynamic programming.

f1 (black arrows in Figure 9.19). Now, however, after these terms are computed and before they are returned (blue arrows in Figure 9.19), the computed values are stored in an array (red arrows) named `data` in Figure 9.19. In addition, before a recursive invocation is made to compute the value of fi, the $i^{th}$ element of the array is examined to see if it is nonzero. If it is, the value has already been computed, in which case the value is fetched from the array (green arrows in Figure 9.19), and the recursive invocation is not issued.

Referring to the left side of Figure 9.18, this eliminates the need to recalculate f2 when calculating f4, to recalculate f3 when calculating f5, to recalculate f4 when calculating f6, and to recalculate f5 when calculating f7. When dynamic programming is applied to the calculation of the $40^{th}$ term of the Fibonacci series, the number of invocations of the recursive method is reduced from 204,668,309 invocations to 40 invocations.

The application `FibonacciDynamic` shown in Figure 9.20 contains two implementations of the recursive algorithm to calculate the $n^{th}$ term of the Fibonacci series. One of these implementations incorporates dynamic programming into the algorithm. After the user is asked to enter the number of the term to be calculated, the application invokes both methods and then outputs the calculated values and the number of invocations required to perform the calculations. A typical input and the resulting outputs produced by the application are shown in Figure 9.21.

The output statement that begins on line 18 invokes the non-dynamic implementation, `fib`, and produces the first two lines of output shown in Figure 9.21. It is passed the number of the term to be calculated, which was input and parsed on lines 13–16. The method `fib` (lines 28–42) counts the number of times it is invoked by incrementing the counter variable `invocations` on line 31. The variable is defined as a class-level variable on line 6, so all of the recursive invocations share it.

Line 33 of the method identifies the two defined base cases and returns the base case value, one, on line 35. Lines 38 and 39 invoke the method recursively to compute the two reduced problems, and their resulting sum is returned on line 40. A typical set of recursive invocations generated by this method when it is passed n = 40 and n = 7 are shown in Figures 9.14 and 9.18, respectively.

The output statement that begins on line 23 invokes the dynamic implementation, fibDynamic, and produces the last two lines of output shown in Figure 9.21. Before the dynamic version of the method is invoked on line 23, line 21 sets the invocation counter back to zero. Like its non-dynamic counterpart, fib, this method (lines 44–75) is passed the number of the term to be calculated (line 44), counts the number of times it is invoked (line 48), and identifies the two defined base cases on line 51. Unlike its dynamic counterpart, line 53 stores the value of these base cases (one) in the array data before returning the value. The array data is defined as a static class-level array on line 7, and its $i^{th}$ element is used to store the ith term of the sequence after it is calculated.

Lines 56–59 check for an additional base case, the value in the $n^{th}$ element of the array data is non-zero, in which case it returns the value. This prevents the recursive invocations to calculate fn-1 and fn-2 when the $n^{th}$ term of the sequence has already been calculated and stored in the array.

Line 62 checks the value data[n-1] to determine if the value of fn-1, the first reduced problem, has not been calculated. When that is the case, line 64 issues a recursive invocation to calculate it and stores the returned value in element n-1 of the array. Line 64 then sets the variable rp1 to the calculated value. Lines 67–71 perform the analogous operations for the second reduced problem, fn-2. The general solution, the value of fn, is calculated and returned on lines 72 and 73.

```
1    import javax.swing.*;
2    import java.text.DecimalFormat;
3
4    public class FibonacciDynamic
5    {
6       static long invocations = 0;
7       static long[] data = new long[101];
8
9       public static void main(String[] args)
10      {
11         DecimalFormat f = new DecimalFormat("#,###");
12
13         String s = JOptionPane.showInputDialog("Enter the term number," +
14                                 " n, to be evaluated:" +
15                                 " 1<= n <=100");
16         int n = Integer.parseInt(s);
17
18         System.out.println("fn = " + f.format(fib(n)) +
19                            "\ncalculated making " + f.format(invocations) +
20                            " invocations");
21         invocations = 0;
22         System.out.println();
23         System.out.println("fn = " + f.format(fibDynamic(n)) +
24                            "\ncalculated making " + f.format(invocations) +
25                            " invocations");
26      }
27
28      public static long fib(int n)
29      {
```

```
30        long rp1, rp2;
31        invocations++;
32
33        if(n == 1 || n == 2) //defined base cases
34        {
35          return 1;
36        }
37        else //general solution
38        { rp1 = fib(n-1); //calculate first reduced problem
39          rp2 = fib(n-2); //calculate second reduced problem
40          return rp1 + rp2;
41        }
42     }
43
44     public static long fibDynamic(int n)
45     {
46        long rp1 = 0;
47        long rp2, gs;
48        invocations++;
49
50        //three base cases
51        if(n == 1 || n == 2) //defined base cases
52        {
53          data[n] = 1;
54          return 1;
55        }
56        else if(data[n] != 0) //dynamic programming base case
57        {
58          return data[n];
59        }
60        else //general solution
61        {
62          if(data[n-1] == 0) //calculate first reduced problem
63          {
64            data[n-1] = fibDynamic(n-1);
65          }
66          rp1 = data[n-1];
67          if(data[n-2] == 0) //calculate second reduced problem
68          {
69            data[n-2] = fibDynamic(n-2);
70          }
71          rp2 = data[n-2];
72          gs = rp1 + rp2;
73          return gs;
74        }
75     }
76  }
```

**Figure 9.20**
The application **FibonacciDynamic**.

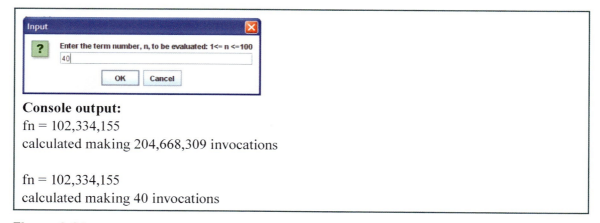

**Figure 9.21**
An input to the application **FibonacciDynamic** and the resulting outputs

## 9.6 CHAPTER SUMMARY

Recursion is a problem solving tool that can provide a more succinct, elegant solution to a problem than solutions based on other problem solving techniques. Recursive algorithms are implemented within a recursive method, which is a method that repeatedly invokes itself either directly or indirectly until a condition, called a base case, is reached and terminates the sequence of invocations. If the base case is not reached, the method terminates in a stack overflow runtime error because the RAM memory, dedicated to saving the information required to complete each invocation, has been exceeded. While most people don't naturally possess the innate ability to think recursively, they can learn how to do so via a divide-and-conquer methodology reinforced with lots of recursive problem solving practice.

The methodology consists of discovering a problem's base case, reduced problem, and general solution and combining these components into a recursive solution to the problem. The base case is a known, defined, or trivial solution to a similar but usually simpler problem. If the problem involves an integer, n, the base case is usually a version of the problem when n is zero or one. For example, the base case for $x^n$ could be the definition, $x^0 = 1$, or the trivial case $x^1 = x$.

The reduced problem is a simpler version of the problem that satisfies this condition: when the relationship between the problem and reduced problem is repeatedly applied to the reduced problem, it becomes the base case. For example, the relationship between $x^n$ and the candidate reduced problem $x^{n-1}$ is the reduction of the exponent by one. When this is repeatedly applied to the reduced problem $x^{n-1}$, it becomes $x^{n-2}$, which becomes $x^{n-3}$, which eventually becomes both base cases: first $x^1$ and then $x^0$. The discovery of the reduced problem is normally the most difficult part of the methodology.

The general solution is the recursive solution to the original problem under the assumption that the solution to the reduced problem is known. For example, if we know how to calculate $x^{n-1}$, then $x^n$ can be calculated by multiplying $x^{n-1}$ by x. Once a valid base case, reduced problem, and general solution have been discovered, the last step of the methodology is to combine them as shown in Figure 9.6. While the methodology cannot be used to formulate all recursive algorithms, by practicing with problems within its domain, we will develop the skills necessary to extrapolate the methodology to the recursive solution of problems beyond its domain.

It is important to understand not only how to use recursion, but when to use it or not use it as well. It should be used when the recursive algorithm significantly reduces the algorithm-discovery and implementation time and when the additional storage requirements and execution time are acceptable. Appropriate problems for recursive solutions are those whose structures are inherently recursive, such as trees, mazes, nested lists, and fractals.

Solutions for some of the common recursive problems are presented in Table 9.4.

**Table 9.4**
Base Cases, Reduced Problems, and General Solutions for Several Problems With Recursive Solutions

| Problem | Base Case | Reduced Problem | General Solution |
|---|---|---|---|
| Factorial of a positive integer, n! | $0! = 1$ | $(n-1)!$ | $n * (n-1)!$ |
| A number x raised to a positive integer, $x^n$ | $x^0 = 1$ | $x^{(n-1)}$ | $x * x^{(n-1)}$ |
| Sum of the integers from 1 to n | sum = 1 for n = 1 | Sum of the integers from 1 to $(n-1)$ | n + sum of the integers from 1 to $(n-1)$ |
| Product of two positive integers, $m \times n$ | $m * 1 = m$ | $m * (n-1)$ | $m + m * (n-1)$ |
| Output an n character string s in reverse order | $n == 1$ output s | Output the last $n-1$ characters of string s in reverse order | Output the last $n-1$ characters of string s in reverse order. Then output the first character of s |
| **Problems with Multiple Base Cases and Reduced Problems** | | | |
| Generate the $n^{th}$ term of the Fibonacci Sequence, fn | $f_1 = 1$ and $f_2 = 1$ | $f_{n-1}$ and $f_{n-2}$ | $f_{n-1} + f_{n-2}$ |
| Find the greatest common divisor of two positive integers m and n, GCD(m, n), for m > n | if m = n, GCD = m | GCD(m − n, n) and GCD(m, n − m) | if(m > n)<br>    GCD(m − n, n)<br>else<br>    GCD(m, n − m) |

*(Contd.)*

| Problem | Base Case | Reduced Problem | General Solution |
|---|---|---|---|
| **A Problem with Multiple Base Cases** | | | |
| Search a sorted list of items for the item I | If the list is empty, return not found <br><br> If the middle item is I, return found | Search a designated sorted sub list for I | if I > middle item, sub list is the items after it, <br><br> else sub list is items before it. <br><br> Search the sub list for I |
| **A Problem that Uses the Reduced Problem Twice** | | | |
| Towers of Hanoi <br> Move n rings from tower A to tower B using tower C | n = 1: Move 1 ring from one tower to another tower | Move n–1 rings from one tower to another tower | Move n–1 rings from A to C <br><br> Move 1 ring from A to B <br><br> Move n–1 rings from C to A |

## Knowledge Exercises

1. True or false:

   a) A method that invokes itself directly or indirectly is said to be recursive.

   b) By definition, zero factorial is equal to one.

   c) Finding the base case is the most difficult part of discovering a recursive algorithm.

   d) Every problem has a recursive solution.

   e) Implementations of recursive solutions can result in a `StackOverFlow` error.

   f) Recursion is useful in drawing fractals.

   g) Implementations of recursive solutions always execute quickly.

2. Which invocation of a recursive method takes the longest time to complete: the first invocation or the last?

3. Which of the flow-chart symbols in Figure 9.6 makes the algorithm it depicts recursive?

4. Calculate the value of 8! using both iterative and recursive techniques.

5. Calculate the value of the sixth term of the Fibonacci sequence using both iterative and recursive techniques.

6. How many terms of the Fibonacci sequence are calculated when the recursive technique (Figure 9.7) is used to calculate the sixth term of the sequence?

7. What is the name of the technique used to reduce the calculations performed in Exercise 6?

8. How many terms of the Fibonacci sequence are calculated when the technique of Exercise 7 is applied to Exercise 6?

9. Give the base case, reduced problem, and general solution used in the recursive solution of the calculation of the sum of the even integers from n up to m, where both n and m are even.

10. Explain why (n-2)! is not a valid reduced problem for n!.

11. Why is it important in the calculation of a factorial that zero factorial be defined as 1? (0! = 1)

12. Use a recursive algorithm for the greatest common divisor to compute the greatest common divisor of 15 and 255.

13. What is the last step in the recursive solution-discovery methodology discussed in this chapter?

14. How many moves would be required in the Towers of Hanoi problem to move six rings? How many for ten rings? How many for n rings?

## Programming Exercises

1. Write a recursive method that is passed two integers, x and y, and returns the value of x raised to the power y. Include the method in an application that verifies its functionality.

2. Write a recursive binary search method that is passed an array of integers and an integer value and returns the index of the array that contains the integer passed to it. If the integer is not found, the method returns -1. Include the method in an application that verifies its functionality.

3. Write a recursive method that calculates the sum of the elements of an integer array passed to it. Include the method in an application that verifies its functionality.

4. Write both a recursive and an iterative method to find and return the greatest common divisor of two integer arguments, x and y, passed to it. Include the methods in an application that verifies their functionality.

5. Write a recursive method that returns `true` when the string passed to it is a palindrome. A palindrome is a string that reads the same backwards and forwards. For example, "MADAMIMADAM," "TOOT," and "WOW." Include the method in an application that verifies its functionality.

6. Write a recursive method that outputs the string passed to it in reverse. Include the method in an application that verifies its functionality.

7. Write a graphical application that moves one of the Towers of Hanoi rings from one tower to another every time the up button of the game board is clicked. The program should begin by asking the user to input the number of rings to be relocated, and show the entire solution.

## Enrichment

1. Binary trees are recursive structures. Find out how binary tree traversals are performed and explain the recursive algorithms for in-order, pre-order and post-order tree traversals. Why is recursion a suitable approach to tree traversals?

2. How can a recursive algorithm be used to count the nodes in a binary tree?

3. Fractals have the property of self-similarity, and they are often implemented recursively. Research the characteristics of some well-known fractals, such as the Koch snowflake, the Cantor Set, and the Mandelbrot and Julia sets. Explore their algorithms and implementations.

4. Investigate the Heap Sort and Quick Sort recursive algorithms to discover why they are so efficient. Explain briefly how the algorithms work.

5. The Eight Queens and the Knight's Tour problems both have recursive solutions. Investigate these problems and the recursive algorithms used to solve them.

6. Recursion is used in solving mazes. Research a recursive algorithm for traversing a maze and explain the base case, the reduced problem, and the general solution.

## References

Barnsley, Michael. *Fractals Everywhere*. San Diego, CA: Academic Press, Inc., 1988.

Mandelbrot, Benoit. *The Fractal Geometry of Nature*. NewYok: W.H. Freeman and Co., 1977.

Peitgen, Heinz-Otto, et al. *Fractals for the Classroom, Strategic Activities*, Part One. New York: Springer-Verlag, 1991.

Peitgen, Heinz-Otto, et al. *Fractals for the Classroom, Complex Systems and Mandelbrot Set*, Vol. 2. New York: Springer-Verlag, 1992.

Roberts, Eric. *Thinking Recursively*. NewYork: John Wiley and Sons, 1986.

Roberts, Eric. *Thinking Recursively with Java*, 20th Anniversary Ed. NewYork: John Wiley and Sons, 2005.

## Endnotes

[1] Epp, Suzanna, *Discrete Mathematics with Applications*, 4th Ed., Brooks Cole, 2011, pp. 290 and 328.

# THE API COLLECTIONS FRAMEWORK

### In this chapter

In this chapter, we will learn how to use a set of classes that are part of the Java's API to efficiently store and process large data sets, and become familiar with a set of associated interfaces that defines the methods that are part of these classes. Each of these API classes uses a different one of the classic storage schemes that facilitates common operations performed on the data they store, and implement methods that are particular to the schemes they use. The classes are written in a generic way, which enables them to store and process data sets comprised of instances of any class. After successfully completing this chapter, you should:

- Understand the power of a generic class and a generic method
- Be familiar with the composition of the API Collections Framework
- Understand the generic interface hierarchy defined in the Collections Framework
- Understand the difference between a value parameter list and a type parameter list
- Be familiar with the API interface `List`
- Know how to declare instances of generic classes, and apply the principle of polymorphism to these declarations
- Understand the storage scheme implemented in the generic class `ArrayList`, and be able to create applications that use it to efficiently store and process data sets
- Be able to use the methods defined in the `Collections` class to process data sets

## 10.1 OVERVIEW

Programs often store and process information comprised of a group, or *collection*, of instances of one class. For example, one program processes a collection of maintenance work orders, another a collection of student transcript objects, and another a collection of personnel records. Although the objects these programs store and process are instances of different classes, programs of this type share a common set of operations that are usually performed on the objects. For example, each of these programs has to *add* objects to their collection, as well as *retrieve* them from their collection. Two other common operations on collections of objects are *removing* an object from the collection, and *modifying* an object in the collection.

To facilitate the storage and processing of information groups such as these (i.e., work orders, transcripts, and personnel records), the Java API provides a group of *collection classes*. Unlike the classes we have encountered thus far in this textbook, these classes are coded in a generic way. A single instance of one of these classes, a *collection object*, can be declared to store an information group consisting of instances of any class. In addition, each collection class implements one of the classic storage schemes that facilitate the common operations performed on groups of objects.

The collection classes are part of the API *Collections Framework*. The framework also includes:

- A set of interfaces that define the generic signatures and general functionality of methods common to the collection classes, such as the methods `add` and `remove` that place an item into and eliminate an item from a collection
- A class named `Collections` that implements algorithms that efficiently perform common operations on collections of objects such as `sort`, `binarySearch`, `min`, and `max` whose names imply their functionality

## 10.2 THE FRAMEWORK INTERFACES

Eight of the framework's core collection interfaces are shown in blue in Figure 10.1. They are divided into two groups: those that extend the interface `Map` and those that extend the interface `Collection`. The core interface `Map` is not a sub-interface; it does not extend another interface.

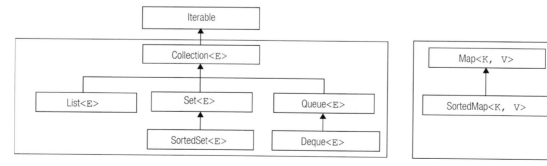

**Figure 10.1**
The core interfaces of the Java collections framework (shown in blue).

The other seven core interfaces are sub-interfaces; they directly extend another interface. The Framework's collection classes implement one, or more, of these interfaces.

The significance of the inheritance chains shown in the figure is that a class that implements one of the core interfaces must implement all of the methods whose signatures are contained in it *and* in its parent interfaces. In addition, any method that can operate on an instance of a class that implements a parent interface can also operate on an instance of a class that implements one of the parent's child interfaces.

> **NOTE**    *Classes that implement the core framework interfaces are called collection classes*

All of the core interfaces are generic. This means that at least one of the methods whose signature and functionality they define can be passed instances of any class, and they can return an instance of that class. Figure 10.1 uses the Java syntax of a generic *type parameter list*, e.g. `<E>`, coded after the name of the interface to indicate that the interface is generic. For example, methods defined in the interface `Collection`, and all of its sub-interfaces can be passed one object of any type, and so the type parameter list that follows its name contains one generic parameter, `E`. An object stored in the API collection classes that implements these interfaces is called an *element*.

Methods defined in the interface `Map` and its sub-interface can be passed objects of two different types, so their names are followed by a type parameter list that contains two generic parameters, `K` and `V`, separated by a comma. Classes that implement these interfaces store collections of a *key* object and its associated *value* object, and the key object is used to specify which value object is to be operated on. For example, a key could be a string object containing the string "Tom", and its associated value could be an object containing Tom's address and phone number.

Java uses the generic type parameter list notation in its API documentation of interfaces to identify the interface as a generic interface. For example, its description of the interface `List` begins with:

```
java.util

Interface List <E>

Type Parameters:
    E - the type of the elements of this list
```

## 10.2.1 The API `List` Interface

As shown in Figure 10.1, the interface `List` is one of the Framework interfaces that extend the interface `Collection`. It refines the functional description of some of the methods whose signatures and general functionality are defined in the interface `Collection`, and also defines the signature and functionality of additional methods. The refinement of the functionality of the methods described in the interface `List` is consistent with the concept of an ordered collection, or sequence, of objects. The object to be operated on by the method is referred to by its position (*index*) in the sequence.

**Table 10.1**
Methods defined in the List interface

| Method Signature | Example and Description |
|---|---|
| `int size()` | `int numOfElements = c1.size();`<br>Returns the number of elements in the list `c1` |
| `boolean isEmpty()` | `boolean empty = c1.isEmpty();`<br>Returns `true` if the list `c1` is empty |
| `boolean add(E obj)` | `boolean done = c1.add(anOrder);`<br>Returns `true` if the object `anOrder` was added the *end* of the list `c1` |
| `void add(int index, E obj)` | `c1.add(3, anOrder);`<br>adds `anOrder` as the new 4th element in the list `c1`. The indexes of the old 4th element and the elements after it are increased by 1, (0 ≤ index ≤ size) |
| `E get(int index)` | `E address = c1.get(3);`<br>Returns a reference to the 4th element in the list `c1`, `null` if the element does not exist, (0 ≤ index < size) |
| `E remove(int index)` | `E address = c1.remove(3);`<br>Returns a reference to the 4th element in the list `c1`, (`null` if the element does not exist), and removes it from the list. The indexes of the elements above it are decreased by 1, (0 ≤ index < size) |
| `E set(int index, E object)` | `E address = c1.set(3, anOrder);`<br>Returns a reference to the 4th element in the list `c1`, (`null` if the element does not exist), and then replaces it with anOrder, (0 ≤ index < size) |

Table 10.1 describes several of the more commonly used methods specified in the `List` interface used to add, remove, retrieve (get), and modify (set) elements stored within collection classes that implement this interface. The type `E` used as the returned type and/or parameter type in some of the method signatures in left column of the table, implies that the method can return and/or be passed an object of any type. For this reason, these methods are called generic methods. The add, get, set, and remove methods throw an `ArrayIndexOutOfBoundsException` if the index passed to them is not within the range specified in the right column of the table.

## 10.3 THE FRAMEWORK'S COLLECTION CLASSES

Classes that implement the framework interfaces must provide implementations of all of the methods defined in the interface they implement, and all of the methods defined in that interface's inheritance chain. In addition, the algorithms they use in these implementations should be consistent with the description of the methods' general functionality contained in the documentation of the interface.

The collection classes that are part of the API Collections Framework, such as the Array-List, LinkedList, PriorityQueue, HashMap, and TreeMap to name a few, provide these implementations. ArrayList and LinkedList implement the interface List, PriorityQueue implements Queue, HashMap implements Map, and TreeMap implements the interface Sorted-Map. Since these interfaces contain generic methods, as shown in Table 10.1 for the interface List, they are called *generic* classes and the elements they operate on can be instances of any class.

**NOTE**

*Generic classes cannot store collections of primitive values. However, they can store instances of the primitive wrapper classes (e.g.,* Integer, Double, *and* Character*).*

## 10.3.1 Declaring a Generic Object

Normally, the objects stored in a particular instance of an API collection class are all instances of the same class, and that class is specified when the collection object is declared. The following statement declares an instance of the generic class ArrayList named tasks, that will be used to store a collection of WorkOrder objects.

```
ArrayList<WorkOrder> tasks = new ArrayList<>();
```

The left side of the statement uses a Java type *argument* list, <WorkOrder>, to specify the class of the objects that will be stored in the collection. When the collection class instance is going to be used to store objects of one type, as in this case only store instances of the class WorkOrder, a type argument list should always be included in the declaration immediately after the name of the class on the left side of the statement. Including it provides Java type checking, and is considered good programming practice. In this case, an attempt to add an object to the collection tasks that is not an instance of the class WorkOrder will result in a translation error.

The right side of the declaration includes an empty type *argument* list coded as <>, which is called the *diamond* operator. Prior to Java SE 7, this type argument list would have also included the name of the class of the objects stored in the collection coded as: <WorkOrder>. This is no longer necessary and its use is considered redundant, because the class in this type argument list can be inferred from the argument list on the left side of the declaration. That being said, the following two statements are equivalent, although the first version is preferred, and will be used in the remainder of this chapter.

```
ArrayList<WorkOrder> tasks = new ArrayList<>(); //preferred syntax
ArrayList<WorkOrder> tasks = new ArrayList<WorkOrder>();
```

Another level of type checking is associated with both of the above declarations. The variable tasks can only be assigned the address of an ArrayList object that is a collection of WorkOrder objects. In the following code segment, the third line results in a translation error. Although student-Records is an instance of an ArrayList, it is a collection of Transcript objects.

```
ArrayList<WorkOrder> tasks = new ArrayList<>();
ArrayList<Transcript> studentRecords = new ArrayList<>();
```

```
tasks = studentRecords; //translation error; srudentRecords is
                        //not a WorkOrder object collection
```

As is the case with non-generic classes, the declaration of an instance of a generic class can be coded on two lines, as shown below.

```
ArrayList<WorkOrder> tasks;
tasks = new ArrayList<>(); //diamond operator could be coded as
                           //<WorkOrder>
```

The following statement outputs all of the elements in an `ArrayList` object named `tasks` to the system console via an implied polymorphic invocation of the `toString` method in the `<WorkOrder>` class on all of the elements in the collection.

```
System.out.println(tasks);
```

### 10.3.2 Polymorphism

Recall from Chapter 8 that polymorphism is the idea that something can exist in several different forms. Consistent with the concept of polymorphism, an instance of any class that implements the interface `List` (e.g., the `ArrayList` or `LinkedList` classes) could be referred to by the reference variable `aList` declared in the below statement, as long as the collection consisted of `WordOrder` objects.

```
List<WorkOrder> aList;
```

The assignment of the collection object's address to the reference variable `aList` could be made by via a completion of the two-line object declaration syntax:

```
List<WorkOrder> aList;
aList = new ArrayList<>();
```

or the one-line syntax could be used to declare the collection object:

```
List<WorkOrder> aList = new ArrayList<>();
```

One restriction on the use of the polymorphic syntax is that the signature of the method being invoked (e.g., `add`) must be able to be located within the inheritance chain of the type of the reference variable used in the method invocation (e.g., `aList`). Since `aList` in the above example is of type `List`, the search will begin in the interface `List`. The signature of the method `add` is defined in that interface, so the third line in following code segment does *not* produce a translation error.

```
List<WorkOrder> aList = new ArrayList<>();
WorkOrderV2 aWorkOrder = new WorkOrderV2("8A", "Clean windows");
aList.add(aWorkOrder);
```

However, the `ArrayList` class contains the code of a method named `trimToSize()`, whose signature is not defined within the inheritance chain of the interface `List`. Therefore, the second line of the following code segment produces a translation error that indicates the translator cannot find the `trimToSize` method.

```
List<WorkOrder> aList = new ArrayList<> ();
aList.trimToSize(); // translation error
```

The remedy would be to return to the non-polymorphic declaration of the collection `aList`.

```
ArrayList<WorkOrder> aList = new ArrayList<>();
aList.trimToSize();
```

It is not uncommon to use the polymorphic declaration statement in descriptive text such as: *Assuming we have declared* `List<WorkOrder> aList`, *the statement to add the* `WorkOrder` *instance* `ploishDoorKnobs` *to the collection is:* **boolean** `success = aList.add(polishDoorKnobs)`;

### 10.3.3 The `ArrayList` Collection Class

As previously mentioned, the class `ArrayList`, is one of the API FrameWork collection classes that implements the interface `List`. As such, it provides implementations of all of the methods defined in that interface, some of which are described in Table 10.1. The class also contains three constructors, and two methods not defined in the `List` interface: `trimToSize` and `removeRange`.

The storage scheme implemented in this collection class should be thought of as a *variable* length array of objects. Like an array, each of the objects (called elements) stored in it are referred to using an index whose minimum value is zero. The initial *capacity* of the list can be specified when it is created, which is analogous to specifying the length of an array in its declaration. The below line of code creates a list whose initial capacity is 200.

```
ArrayList<WorkOrder> aList = new ArrayList<>(200);
```

If not specified, the capacity is set to a default value. The number of objects currently in the list is called its *size*, which can be fetched via an invocation of the method `size`, as shown in Table 10.1. This would only be analogous to an array's length when the list is full to its current capacity.

**NOTE** *An* `ArrayList's` *size is the number of elements (objects) currently in the collection. Its capacity is the number of elements that can be added to the collection before it has to expand. Its capacity is always greater than, or equal to, its size.*

Unlike an array, the maximum value of the index used to refer to the list's elements, is one less than the number of objects currently in the list (i.e., size - 1 ). In addition, a new element can be added as a new first element, between two existing elements, or after the last element. These additions cause the list's size to increase by one, and may cause the capacity to increase. Similarly, an element can be removed from the list, which causes the list's size to decrease by one.

For all but the most time critical applications, it is good practice to accept the default `Array-List` capacity by declaring an `ArrayList` collection using the class' no parameter constructor.

```
ArrayList<WorkOrder> aList = new ArrayList<>();
```

From a memory consumption viewpoint, it is good practice to invoke the method `trimToSize` after removing a significant number of elements from a large collection. This method reduces the capacity of the list to its current size.

The application `LinkedListApp`, shown in Figure 10.2, demonstrates the use of two `Array-List` collection objects. Work orders of an apartment building are added to, retrieved, modified, and removed from the collections. The work orders are instances of the class `WorkOrder` shown in Figure 10.3. Each work order contains two data members: `apartmentNumber` and `description` declared on Lines 3 and 4 of that figure. Figure 10.4 shows the output produced by the program.

```java
1 import java.util.ArrayList;
2 import java.util.List;
3
4 public class ArrayListApp
5 {
6   public static void main(String[] args)
7   {
8     WorkOrder taskInProgress;
9
10    ArrayList <WorkOrder> tasks = new ArrayList();
11    List<WorkOrder> completedTasks = new ArrayList<>();
12
13    WorkOrder taskA = new WorkOrder("1C", "Polish doorknob");
14    WorkOrder taskB = new WorkOrder("8A", "Rats in kitchen");
15    WorkOrder taskC = new WorkOrder("8A", "Replace bulb");
16    WorkOrder taskD = new WorkOrder("12B", "Toilet backing up");
17    WorkOrder taskCCorrected = new WorkOrder("4A", "Replace bulb");
18
19    tasks.add(taskA); //add elements to the end of the collection
20    tasks.add(taskB);
21    tasks.add(taskC);
22    tasks.add(taskD);
23
24    System.out.println("The initial tasks collection");
25    for(int i = 0;  i < tasks.size(); i++) //all elements in collection
26    {
27      System.out.println(tasks.get(i));
28    }
29
30    tasks.set(2, taskCCorrected);
31    System.out.println("\nThe tasks collection, element 2 corrected");
32    for(int i = 0;  i < tasks.size(); i++)
33    {
34      System.out.println(tasks.get(i));
35    }
36
37    taskInProgress = tasks.remove(1); // second element
38    System.out.println("\nWorking on " + taskInProgress);
39    System.out.println("The tasks collection after completing " +
40                       taskInProgress);
```

```
41    for(int i = 0;  i < tasks.size(); i++)
42    {
43      System.out.println(tasks.get(i));
44    }
45    completedTasks.add(0, taskInProgress);
46
47    taskInProgress = tasks.remove(2); // section element
48    System.out.println("\nWorking on " + taskInProgress);
49    System.out.println("The tasks collection after completing: " +
50                       taskInProgress);
51    for(int i = 0;  i < tasks.size(); i++)
52    {
53      System.out.println(tasks.get(i));
54    }
55    completedTasks.add(0, taskInProgress);
56
57    System.out.println("\nEnd of workday. Work completed:");
58    System.out.println(completedTasks); //outputs all elements
59
60    tasks.trimToSize();
61  }
62 }
```

**Figure 10.2**
The application **ArrayListApp**

```
1    public class WorkOrder
2    {
3      String apartmentNumber;
4      String description;
5
6      public WorkOrder(String location, String description)
7      {
8        apartmentNumber = location;
9        this.description = description;
10     }
11
12     public String toString()
13     {
14       return "Apartment " + apartmentNumber + ", " + description;
15     }
16   }
```

**Figure 10.3**
The class **WorkOrder**

```
The initial tasks collection
Apartment 1C, Polish doorknob
Apartment 8A, Rats in kitchen
Apartment 8A, Replace bulb
Apartment 12B, Toilet backing up

The tasks collection, element 2 corrected
Apartment 1C, Polish doorknob
Apartment 8A, Rats in kitchen
Apartment 4A, Replace bulb
Apartment 12B, Toilet backing up

Working on Apartment 8A, Rats in kitchen
The tasks collection after completing: Apartment 8A, Rats in kitchen
Apartment 1C, Polish doorknob
Apartment 4A, Replace bulb
Apartment 12B, Toilet backing up

Working on Apartment 12B, Toilet backing up
The tasks collection after completing: Apartment 12B, Toilet backing up
Apartment 1C, Polish doorknob
Apartment 4A, Replace bulb

End of workday. Work completed:
[Apartment 12B, Toilet backing up, Apartment 8A, Rats in kitchen]
```

**Figure 10.4**
The output produced by the program **ArrayListApp**

Line 10 of the application shown in Figure 10.2 is a type-safe declaration of a `ArrayList` collection object named `tasks`, that can store a collection of `WorkOrder` objects. An attempt to add anything other than a `WorkOrder` instance to this collection would produce a translation error. The four work orders declared on lines 13–16 are added to the end of the collection using the `ArrayList` class's `add` method on lines 19–22

Lines 24-28 produces the first group of outputs shown in Figure 10.4. The `for` loop that begins on line 25 outputs all of the objects in the collection `tasks`. It uses the `ArrayList` class's `size` method to determine when to terminate the loop. Inside the loop, line 27 retrieves each object in the collection by invoking the `ArrayList` class's `get` method. The method is passed the loop variable, `i`, as the location of the element to be retrieved and output.

Line 30 uses the `ArrayList` class's `set` method to replace the erroneous third element of the collection with the corrected version declared on line 17. Then lines 31-35 produces the second group of outputs shown in Figure 10.4. Its `for` loop outputs the corrected list of work orders.

Line 37 uses the `ArrayList` class's `remove` method to remove and return the most urgent work order, `taskB` stored in element 1, from the `tasks` collection. The method is passed the element number to be operated on. Lines 38-44 produces the third group of outputs. Line 38 outputs the work order returned by the `remove` method, and then the current contents of the `tasks` collection is output inside the loop that begins on line 41. Line 45 uses the *two* parameter version of the `ArrayList` class's `add` method to add the work order removed from the `tasks` collection to the beginning of the `completedTasks` collection declared on line 11.

In a similar manner, Lines 47-55 processes the next most urgent work order contained in the `tasks` collection, element 2, and produces the fourth group of outputs shown in Figure 10.4. Line 55 adds the work order to the *beginning* of the `completedTasks` collection.

Lines 57-58 produces the last group of outputs: the current contents of the `completedTasks` collection. The coding of the reference variable `completedTasks` on line 58 is actually an implied invocation of the `toString` method in the class `AbstractCollection`. This class is part of the `ArrayList` class's inheritance chain, and the method issues a polymorphic invocation of the `WorkOrder` class's `toString` method to build the string it returns. Line 60 uses the `ArrayList` class's `trimToSize` method to reduce the capacity of the `tasks` collection to its current size: two elements.

The variable `completedTasks` is defined on line 11 as a reference to a `List` that stores the address of an `ArrayList` collection object. This polymorphic reference can be used, because the `ArrayList` class implements the `List` interface, and within the program only methods that are defined in that interface (the `add` and `get` methods) are used to operate on the `completedTasks` collection. The method `trimToSize` could not be used to reduce the capacity of the `completedTasks` collection, because the method is not defined in the `List` interface. The address of the `tasks` `ArrayList` collection could be assigned to the variable `completedTasks`, because they are both collections of `WorkOrder` objects and `ArrayList` implements the `List` interface.

### 10.3.4 Passing Generic Collection Objects to a Method

A generic collection object is passed to a method using the same syntax used to pass non-generic objects to a method. We simply code the name of the variable that references the collection as an argument in the invocation statement. For example, if the variable `tasks` was declared an `ArrayList` instance that stores `WorkOrder` objects, then the collection of work orders could be passed the method `processTasks` using the following invocation statement.

```
processTasks(tasks) ;
```

There are two syntax options for the method's parameter list. A generic type parameter list, e.g., `<WorkOrder>`, could be included within the definition of the parameter being passed the generic collection object, or the generic type parameter list could be left out. The first option is used in the signature of the `processTasks` method shown below.

```
public static void processTasks(ArrayList<WorkOrder> theTasks)
                               // type-safe parameter definition
```

When this syntax is used, the translator verifies that the collection being passed to the method is a collection of `WorkOrder` objects. Since most collections are *homogeneous*, that is they are collections of one type of object, this signature syntax is most often used. The alternative parameter list syntax would be:

```java
public static void processTasks(ArrayList theTasks) // non type-safe
                                                    // parameter definition
```

The parameter's type could be the name of an interface. For example, the type of the parameter in the below signature is `List`.

```java
public static void processTasks(List<WorkOrder> theTasks) // polymorphic
                                                          // type-safe parameter definition
```

Consistent with the principal of polymorphism, this method could be passed any collection instance whose class implements the interface `List`, and since the parameter in the above signature is type-safe the collection passed to it could only contain `WorkOrder` objects.

Within the method, any of the methods defined in the class or interface used in the parameter's definition, can be invoked on the collection passed to the method. For example, the following method adds three work orders to the collection passed to it, and then fetches and outputs the new size of the collection. It could be passed any collection instance whose class implements the interface `List`.

```java
public static void processTasks(List<WorkOrder> theTasks) // polymorphic
                                                          // type-safe parameter definition
{
    WorkOrder taskX = new WorkOrder("3B", "Vacuum Rugs""");
    WorkOrder taskY = new WorkOrder("1A", "Install screens");
    WorkOrder taskC = new WorkOrder("7C", "Paint kitchen");

    theTasks.add(taskX);
    theTasks.add(taskY);
    theTasks.add(taskZ);

    System.out.println("The number of work orders is " +
                        theTasks.size());
}
```

### 10.3.5 Using Generic Collection Objects as Data Members

A data member of a class can be a reference to a generic collection object, using the same syntax used to define a generic collection parameter. For example, the class `Apartment` shown below contains a polymorphic data member named `tasks` that can reference a generic `List` collection of `WorkOrders`. The class's constructor assigns the data member the address of the collection of work orders passed to it when an instance of the class is created. Consistent with the concepts of polymorphism, the class of the object passed to the constructor would have to implement the interface `List`.

```java
public class Apartment
{
```

```
    private List<WorkOrder> tasks;

    public Apartment(List<WorkOrder> theTasks)
    {
        tasks = theTasks;
    }

    // other methods

}
```

Any of the methods defined in the class `Apartment` can invoke the methods defined in the class or interface coded in data members definition (in this case defined the interface `List`) on the object the data member references. For example, a method defined in the class `Apartment` could include the following invocation to retrieve the second work order in the collection `tasks`.

```
    WorkOrder aWorkorder = tasks.get(1);
```

In addition, after retrieving the work order from the collection, the method could invoke any method in the `WorkOrder` class on it. For example, it could invoke the `WorkOrder` class's `toString` method as shown below.

```
    String aptAndDescription = aWorkOrder.toString();
```

## 10.4 THE FRAMEWORK'S COLLECTIONS CLASS

The `Collections` class implements *algorithms* that efficiently perform common operations on the objects contained in a collection. The class contains 52 static methods, most of which are passed an instance of a class that implements a specific framework core interface, or an extension of one of these interfaces. Table 10.2 shows some of the frequently used methods.

The six methods in the top portion of the table can only be invoked on objects whose class implements the interface `List`. The five methods in the bottom portion of the table can be invoked

**Table 10.2**
Collections Class Methods

| Method | Description |
|---|---|
| **Operate on collection objects whose class implements `List`** | |
| binarySearch | Returns the index of a specified element using the elements' `compareTo` method; The collection must be sorted |
| copy | Copies one list's elements into another |
| indexOfSubList | Returns the index of the first occurrence of a specified sublist of elements |
| replaceAll | Replaces all occurrences of a specified element with a specified element |
| sort | Sorts the list's elements using their overridden `compareTo` method |
| swap | Swaps the position of two elements whose indices are specified |

*(Contd.)*

| Method | Description |
|---|---|
| **Operate on a collection object whose class implements `Collection`** | |
| `addAll` | Adds all specified elements, or all elements of an array, to a collection |
| `disjoint` | Determines if two collections have no elements in common |
| `frequency` | Determines the number of occurrences of a specified element |
| `max` | Returns the largest of the elements using their overridden `compareTo` method |
| `min` | Returns the smallest of the elements using their overridden `compareTo` method |

on objects whose class implements the interface `Collection`. The `Collections` class's `binarySearch`, `sort`, `max`, and `min` methods require that the class of the objects stored in the collection implement the `compareTo` method defined in the interface `Comparable`. It would be up to the implementer to decide when two objects are equal, or one is less than or greater than the other. The `binarySearch` method assumes that the objects in the collection are sorted.

The application `CollectionsClassApp`, shown in Figure 10.5, demonstrates the use several of the `Collections` class's methods to operate on an `ArrayList` collection of `WorkOrderV2` objects. The code of `WorkOrderV2` class, shown in Figure 10.6, adds an implementation of the `compareTo` method (lines 20-23) to the code of the WorkOrder class shown in Figure 10.3. Line 22 of the method invokes the `String` class's `compareTo` method to compare the *apartment number* of two work orders. Figure 10.7 shows the output of the program.

Lines 17-20 of the application (Figure 10.5) adds the four work orders defined on lines 12-15 to the `ArrayList` object `tasks` defined on line 10, then lines 22-26 output the collection. Lines 28-31 use the Collections class's `max` and `min` methods to retrieve the work orders whose apartment numbers are the highest and lowest in the collection. The output they produce is the second group of outputs in Figure 10.7

Line 33 uses the Collections class's `sort` method to sort the elements of the collection in apartment number order. The method invokes the `compareTo` method in the `WorkOrder2` class to determine the sorted ordering of the elements. Lines 34-38 output the sorted collection, as the third group of outputs. Line 41 uses the `binarySearch` method to determine the element number of work order `taskB`, defined on line 13, which is the last output of the program.

```
1    import java.util.ArrayList;
2    import java.util.Collections;
3
4    public class CollectionsClassApp
5    {
6      public static void main(String[] args)
7      {
8        WorkOrderV2 taskInProgress;
```

```
9
10      ArrayList <WorkOrderV2> tasks = new ArrayList();
11
12      WorkOrderV2 taskA = new WorkOrderV2("18A", "Rats in kitchen");
13      WorkOrderV2 taskB = new WorkOrderV2("43C", "Polish doorknob");
14      WorkOrderV2 taskC = new WorkOrderV2("24A", "Replace bulb");
15      WorkOrderV2 taskD = new WorkOrderV2("12B", "Toilet backing up");
16
17      tasks.add(taskA); //add elements to the end of the collection
18      tasks.add(taskB);
19      tasks.add(taskC);
20      tasks.add(taskD);
21
22      System.out.println("The initial tasks collection");
23      for(int i = 0;  i < tasks.size(); i++) //all elements
24      {
25        System.out.println(tasks.get(i));
26      }
27
28      System.out.println("\nThe work order on the highest floor is " +
29                    Collections.max(tasks));
30      System.out.println("The work order on the lowest floor is " +
31                    Collections.min(tasks));
32
33      Collections.sort(tasks);
34      System.out.println("\nThe tasks sorted in floor number order");
35      for(int i = 0;  i < tasks.size(); i++)
36      {
37        System.out.println(tasks.get(i));
38      }
39
40      System.out.println("\n" + taskB + " is now element number " +
41                    Collections.binarySearch(tasks, taskB));
42    }
43  }
```

**Figure 10.5**
The application **CollectionsClassApp**

```
1    public class WorkOrderV2 implements Comparable <WorkOrderV2>
2    {
3      String apartmentNumber;
4      String description;
5
6      public WorkOrderV2(String location, String description)
7      {
8        apartmentNumber = location;
9        this.description = description;
```

```
10    }
11
12      @Override
13      public String toString()
14      {
15        return "Apartment " + apartmentNumber +
16                ", " + description;
17      }
18
19      @Override
20      public  int compareTo(WorkOrderV2 aWorkOrder)
21      {
22        return apartmentNumber.compareTo(aWorkOrder.apartmentNumber);
23      }
24  }
```

**Figure 10.6**
The class **WorkOrderV2**

The initial tasks collection
Apartment 18A, Rats in kitchen
Apartment 43C, Polish doorknob
Apartment 24A, Replace bulb
Apartment 12B, Toilet backing up

The work order on the highest floor is Apartment 43C, Polish doorknob
The work order on the lowest floor is Apartment 12B, Toilet backing up

The tasks sorted in floor number order
Apartment 12B, Toilet backing up
Apartment 18A, Rats in kitchen
Apartment 24A, Replace bulb
Apartment 43C, Polish doorknob

Apartment 43C, Polish doorknob is now element number 3

**Figure 10.7**
The output produced by the program **CollectionsClassApp**

## 10.5 CHAPTER SUMMARY

The API collections framework contains a group of generic classes, called collection classes, that implement many of the classic schemes used to efficiently store and process large data sets. These implementations include the classes ArrayList, LinkedList, and PriorityQueue, whose data element objects are sequentially accessed. Also included are the classes HashMap, and TreeMap whose data value objects are accessed by specifying a key, that is associated with a data value object when it is added to the data set.

The collection classes are generic in the sense that the data that they store and process can be instances of any class. This greatly extends the range of the applications they can be used in, thereby reducing the time and cost required to develop a software product. Most often, the data objects stored in an instance of a collection class will all be instances of one class. The syntax used to declare these homogeneous collection class instances includes the name of the data objects' class. An attempt to store any other type of data instance in the collection results in a translation error.

The Collections Framework also includes a hierarchy of interfaces that define the signatures and functionality of methods that perform common operations on large data sets such as adding, retrieving, removing, and replacing data objects. Each collection class implements these interfaces in a manner that is consistent with their scheme for storing the data objects. Consistent with the concept of polymorphism, an instance of any collection can be referenced by a variable whose type is the name of one of the interfaces its class implements.

Also included in the Framework is class named `Collections`. This class contains static methods whose algorithms efficiently perform common operations on data objects stored in collection classes that implement the interfaces `Collection` or `List`. Some of the more frequently used methods are `sort`, `binarySearch`, `min`, and `max`, whose names imply their functionality.

## Knowledge Exercises

1. Give the interfaces in the inheritance chain of the interface `List`.

2. Is the size or the capacity of an `ArrayList` analogous to an array's length?

3. What happens when an element is added to an `ArrayList` object whose size is equal to its capacity?

4. Is the declaration `ArrayList myList = new ArrayList();` type-safe?

5. Give the type parameter list of the interface `List`.

6. Give a *one* line type-safe declaration of an instance of the class `ArrayList` that will be used to store 200 `String` objects before it expands.

7. Give a *two* line type-safe declaration of an instance of the class `ArrayList` that will be used to store 200 `String` objects before it expands.

8. Give a type-safe declaration of a reference variable named `employeeRecords` that can reference the object declared in Exercise 7.

9. Give a type-safe *polymorphic* declaration of a reference variable named `employeeRecords` that can reference the object declared in Exercise 7.

10. What is the name of the Java operator `<>` ?

11. What is wrong with the following declaration used to store a list of `Listing` objects?

```
List<Listing>  myList = new List<>();
```

12. Give the signature of a method that could be passed an instance of an `ArrayList` that must be a collection of `Book` objects.

13. Modify you answer to Knowledge Exercise 12 so that the method could be passed an instance of any collections class that implemented the interface `List`.

14. Give the definition of a class level data member named `books` that could store a `List` collection of `Book` objects.

15. Give the code to invoke the `Book` class's `toString` method on the third book stored in collection `books` defined in Knowledge Exercise 14.

16. True or False:
    a) The collections framework is part of the API.
    b) The collections framework contains many generic classes that implement storage schemes commonly used to efficiently store large data sets.
    c) The elements stored in an instance of the framework class `ArrayList` can be associated with a key.
    d) The `sort` method in the `Collections` class can be used to sort the values of an instance of the framework class `HashMap`.

17. In order to use four of the methods in the `Collections` class, the class of the elements stored in the collection must implement a method defined in an API interface. What are the four methods? What method must be implemented, and what is the name of the interface that defines its signature?

18. Given the declaration: `ArrayList<Book> myBooks = new ArrayList<>();` give *one* line of code to
    a) Output the number of elements in the collection.
    b) Replace the second element in the collection with the first element in the collection.
    c) Output the second element in the collection.
    d) Output all of the elements in the collection.
    e) Sort all of the elements in the collection.
    f) Reduce the capacity of the collection to its size.

## Programming Exercises

1. Write a program that adds the three strings "Tom", "Dorothy", and "Harriet" to an `ArrayList` collection. Then output the entire collection to the system console using one line of code, followed by the size of the collection.

2. Complete Programming Exercise 1, and after it performs its output add the ability for the user to replace one of the elements, then output the collection again. The element number to be replaced, and the new element, should be input by the user using input dialog boxes.

3. Write a program that uses a type-safe instance of an `ArrayList` to store a collection of strings. When launched it will display the below menu in an input dialog box, process the

users selection, and then redisplay the menu. Use input dialog boxes for input, and the System console for output.

```
Enter 1 to add a new element to the collection
      2 to fetch and output an element from the collection
      3 to delete an element from the collection
      4 to replace an element in the collection
      5 to sort the collection
      6 to output the entire collection
      7 to terminate the program
```

4. Add a new menu item to Programming Exercise 3 that asks the user to input a string to be located in the collection. Use the Collections class's `binarySearch` method to determine the element number of the string and then output its index. If the string is not in the collection, output "That sting is not in the collection".

5. Code the following modification to Programming Exercise 4: if the list was *not* sorted before the selection of the new menu item, menu selection 6 still shows the collection in *un*sorted order.

6. Modify Programming Exercise 3 so that it stores a collection of `Book` objects. Each book has an integer ISBN number and a string title. The class `Book` should contain appropriate constructors. Menu selection 5 should sort the collection by title.

7. Modify Programming Exercise 5 so that it stores a collection of `Book` objects. Each book has an integer ISBN number and a string title. The class `Book` should contain appropriate constructors. Menu selection 5 should sort the collection by ISBN number.

8. Code a class named `Library`. Each instance of the class will contain a data member that is a type-safe `ArrayList` collection of `Book` objects whose class is defined in Programming Exercise 7. The `Library` class will also contain methods that perform the functions available on the menu described in Programming Exercise 3. Code an application that declares an instance of a `Library`, display the menu, and then invoke the methods of the `Library` class to service the user menu selections.

## Enrichment

1. Investigate the differences between a queue and a priority queue.

2. Investigate the collections class `HashMap`.

3. Investigate the techniques used to write generic Java classes, like the API `ArrayList` class, that can store a collection objects of *any* class and contains methods to perform operations on the objects.

4. Complete Programming Exercise 6, modified to store the collection of books in a type-safe `HashMap` collection whose keys are isbn number. Make the relevant changes to the menu text to reflect access into the collection via a given ISBN number.

## References

Horstmann, Cay. *Java SE 8 for the Really Impatient*. Upper Saddle River, NJ: Pearson, 2014.

Mcallister, William, and Fritz, S. Jane. *Programming Fundamentals Using Java, A Game Programming Approach*. Dulles, VA: Mercury Learning and Information, 2015.

# DESCRIPTION OF THE
# GAME ENVIRONMENT

## A.1 OVERVIEW OF THE GAME ENVIRONMENT

The game environment is comprised of the interface `Drawable` and the two classes `DrawableAdapter` and `GameBoard`. To use the game environment in an application, the interface and these two classes must be included as part of the application (see Appendix B).

Figure A.1 shows a Java application that displays the game environment's window shown in Figure A.2. It assumes the game environment package `edu.sjcny.gpv1` has been added to the system's CLASSPATH variable. If the alternate approach described in Appendix B and in the *IDE Specific Tools* subfolder contained on the book's DVD, which does not require a change in the system's CLASSPATH variable, was used to incorporate the game environment into the application's project, the import statement may not be necessary.

```
1   import edu.sjcny.gpv1.*; //May not be necessary
2   public class GameWindowDemo extends DrawableAdapter
3   {
4      static GameWindowDemo ga = new GameWindowDemo();
5      static GameBoard gb = new GameBoard(ga, "The Game's Title");
6
7      public static void main(String[] args)
8      {
9         showGameBoard(gb);
10     }
11  }
```

**Figure A.1**
The application **GameWindowDemo** that displays the game environment window.

As shown on line 2 of Figure A.1, game programs that use the game environment must extend the class `DrawableAdapter` and declare a static class level instance of the application's class using the default (no-parameter) constructor, as shown on line 4. Then, an instance of the class `GameBoard` is declared, passing the constructor the class level instance of the application's class and the title of the game (line 5). Finally, the `showGameBoard` method in the `DrawableAdapter` class is invoked from within the `main` method (line 9) and passed the `GameBoard` object declared on line 5. This method displays the application's window shown in Figure A.2.

**Figure A.2**
A game application's window.

### The Game Window

As shown in Figure A.2, a game application's window contains six buttons on its right side. The large pink panel to the left of the buttons is called the game board. Game piece objects are displayed on the game board. The color of the game board can be changed by invoking the API `Component` class's `setBackground` method on the `GameBoard` object (declared on line 5 of Figure A.1) and passing it the new board color (an instance of an API `Color` class object).

### Timers and Timer Methods

In addition to the six buttons, a `GameBoard` object has three timers associated with it. These begin ticking when the game's player clicks the game window's Start button, and they stop ticking when the game window's Stop button is clicked. The `GameBoard` class contains methods (subprograms) that the programmer can invoke to stop and start a timer, and a method to change the rate at which a timer ticks. These methods are invoked on the `GameBoard` object declared on line 5 of Figure A.1. Section A.2.1 gives the signatures and a description of each of these methods. By default, the tick rates of the timers (named 1, 2, and 3) are once every second, once every half second, and once every quarter second, respectively.

Each timer has a call back method, or subprogram, associated with it, which the game environment invokes every time the timer ticks. The names of the methods, which are described in Section A.2.3, are `timer1`, `timer2`, and `timer3`. The class `DrawableAdapter` contains empty implementations of the methods. If the programmer includes (overrides) these methods in a game program, the game environment will invoke (or "call back") the programmer's versions of the methods after every tick of the timers. Java code placed inside of these methods can be used to keep track of a game's time and to animate objects on the game board.

### Game Player Action Methods

There are eight other call back methods in the game environment, which are described in Section A.2.3. Seven of these are invoked by the game environment when the game player performs input actions common to most games. Four of these are associated with the game window's left, right, up, and down buttons, one is associated with the keyboard, and two are associated with the mouse. Empty implementations of the methods are coded in the class `DrawableAdapter`. If the programmer includes (overrides) these methods in a game program, the game environment invokes (calls back) the programmer's overridden version of the methods every time the game player clicks a directional button, presses a keyboard key, or drags or clicks the mouse on the game board.

The eighth call back method in this group of methods is associated with redrawing the game window. It is called by the game environment every time the game window needs to be redrawn (e.g., is minimized and then restored) and every time the seven game player input action call back methods or the three timer call back methods complete their execution. An empty implementation of this method is also included in `DrawableAdapter` class.

### Game Window Coordinate System

The game window has a Cartesian coordinate system associated with it as shown in Figure A.3. The coordinate system's origin is in the upper left corner of the game window, with the positive x direction to the right and the positive y direction downward. The height and width of the top and left borders of the window place the upper left corner of the game board at (5, 30). The game window can be sized by using the last two parameters of the game board's four-parameter constructor to specify the coordinates of the lower right corner of the game board, which defaults to (500, 500).

**Figure A.3**
The game environment coordinate system.

## A.2 DESCRIPTION OF THE GAME ENVIRONMENT'S CLASSES AND INTERFACE

The game environment is comprised of two classes, named GameBoard and DrawableAdapter, and one interface named Drawable.

### A.2.1 The GameBoard Class

The class GameBoard contains two constructors. One creates a default-sized game board with a programmer specified title, and the other adds the ability to specify the game board's size. A game application must construct a static GameBoard object and pass it a static instance of the application's class (see lines 4 and 5 of Figure A.1). Assuming the static instance of the application class was named ga, the following line of code creates the GameBoard instance gb with a default game board size, 500 x 500 pixels:

```
static GameBoard gb = new GameBoard(ga, "The Game's Title");
```

The GameBoard object can be used within the game application class to invoke the class's other three methods that are used to set the time increment of any of the GameBoard object's three timers and to start and stop these timers. The following invocation stops timer 2:

```
gb.stopTimer(2);
```

## Constructors

**public** GameBoard(Object app, String windowTitle)

This method constructs a GameBoard object, defaulting to the coordinates of the lower right corner of the game board to (500, 500).

*Parameters:*

> app is an instance of the application's class.
> windowTitle will be displayed as the title of the application's window in its title bar.

**public** GameBoard(Object app, String windowTitle,
               **int** xMaxValue, **int** yMaxValue)

This method constructs a GameBoard object whose lower-right corner is specified by the last two arguments passed to it.

*Parameters:*

> app is an instance of the application's class.
> windowTitle will be displayed as the title of the application's window in its title bar.
> xMaxValue is the x-pixel coordinate of the lower-right corner of the game board.
> yMaxValue is the y-pixel coordinate of the lower-right corner of the game board.

## Methods

**public void** setTimerInterval(**int** timerNumber, **int** interval)

This method sets the interval of one of the game environment's three timers. The default increments for the timers are 1000ms (1 second) for timer 1, 500ms (1/2 second) for timer 2, and 250 ms (1/4 second) for timer 3.

*Parameters:*

> timerNumber is the number of the timer (1, 2, or 3) whose interval is being set.
> interval is the time between ticks of the timer in milliseconds (e.g., 1000 = 1 second).

**public void** startTimer(**int** timerNumber)

This method starts the timer whose number (1, 2, or 3) is passed to it. While the timer is ticking, the timer's call back method (timer1, timer2, or timer3) will be executed on each subsequent tick of the timer. Ticking is stopped when the game player clicks the game board's Pause button or when the GameBoard class's stopTimer method is invoked. Ticking is restarted when the Start button is clicked or this method is reinvoked.

*Parameters:*

timerNumber designates the timer to be started: 1, 2, or 3.

**public void** stopTimer(**int** timerNumber)

This method stops the timer whose number (1, 2, or 3) is passed to it. After this method is invoked, clicking the game board's Start button will *not* restart the timer. The timer's call back method (timer1, timer2, or timer3) will not be executed until the timer is started again via an invocation of the startTimer method, which will also reactivate the game board's Start button.

*Parameters:*

timerNumber designates the timer to be stopped: 1, 2, or 3.

### A.2.2 The DrawableAdaper Class

A game program's class must extend the class DrawableAdaper (as on line 2 of Figure A.1). It provides empty implementations of the eleven call back methods defined in the game package interface Drawable. A description of these eleven methods is given in Section A.2.3. In addition, it provides a method that displays an instance of a GameBoard object passed to it (line 9 of Figure A.1).

### Methods of the Class DrawableAdapter

**public static void** showGameBoard(GameBoard gb)

This method displays the game program's window. Normally, it is invoked as the last statement in the game program's main method.

*Parameters:*

gb is the application's GameBoard object.

### A.2.3 The Interface Drawable

The interface Drawable defines eleven call back methods invoked by the game environment. They are coded (as required) in the game application's class (the class that contains the method main). They are used to service various actions by the game's player (e.g., a mouse click or drag, a keystroke, or a button click), and to perform processing such as animation every time a game environment's timer ticks.

The call back method draw is invoked by the game environment when the game window has to be redrawn (e.g., it is dragged to a new location) and after any of the other ten call back methods complete their execution.

## Call Back Methods

**public void** draw(Graphics g)

This method is invoked when the game application window is initially displayed or needs to be redisplayed and each time one of the other ten call back methods complete their execution.

*Parameters:*

g is an instance of the API class Graphics attached to the game board, which is passed into this method when it is invoked by the game environment. It can be used to draw two-dimensional shapes on the game board by invoking the methods in the Graphics class.

**public void** timer1()

This method is invoked every time timer 1 ticks. The timer ticking can be started or stopped by invoking the GameBoard class's startTimer and stopTimer methods, respectively. If the timer is ticking, it is stopped whenever the Stop button in the game's window is clicked and restarted whenever the Start button in the game's window is clicked.

**public void** timer2()

This method is invoked every time timer 2 ticks. The timer ticking can be started or stopped by invoking the GameBoard class's startTimer and stopTimer methods, respectively. If the timer is ticking, it is stopped whenever the Stop button in the game's window is clicked and restarted whenever the Start button in the game's window is clicked.

**public void** timer3()

This method is invoked every time timer 3 ticks. The timer ticking can be started or stopped by invoking the GameBoard class's startTimer and stopTimer methods, respectively. If the timer is ticking, it is stopped whenever the Stop button in the game's window is clicked and restarted whenever the Start button in the game's window is clicked.

**public void** leftButton()

This method is invoked whenever the Left button in the game's window is clicked.

**public void** rightButton()

This method is invoked whenever the Right button in the game's window is clicked.

**public void** upButton()

This method is invoked whenever the Up button in the game's window is clicked.

**public void** downButton()

This method is invoked whenever the Down button in the game's window is clicked.

**public void** keyStruck(**char** key)

This method is invoked whenever a key on the keyboard is struck. If the key is held down, the method is continually invoked until the key is released.

*Parameters:*

key contains the upper case version of the character that was struck. The cursor control keys return 'L', 'R', 'U' or 'D' when the left, right, up, or down arrows are struck.

**public void** mouseClicked(**int** x, **int** y, **int** buttonPressed)

This method is invoked whenever a mouse button is clicked.

*Parameters:*

x and y are the game board coordinates of the mouse cursor location at the time the mouse was clicked.

buttonPressed contains a 1 if the left mouse button was clicked or a 3 if the right mouse button was clicked.

**public void** mouseDragged(**int** x, **int** y)

This method is continually invoked while the mouse is being dragged.

*Parameters*

x and y are the game board coordinates of the mouse cursor location at the time the method is invoked.

# USING THE GAME
# ENVIRONMENT PACKAGE

The game environment can be easily used within the Eclipse, NetBeans, and JCreator IDEs without changing the operating system's CLASSPATH variable by following the IDE-specific directions listed below. Alternately, the package `edu.sjcny.gbv1`, which is in the `Package` subfolder of the `Game Environment\Class, Package and JAR file` folder on the DVD that accompanies this text can be stored on your system and added to its CLASSPATH variable. Then, the following import statement can be used to incorporate the game environment into a game application:

```
import edu.sjcny.gpv1.*;
```

## NON-CLASSPATH ALTERING IDE-SPECIFIC INSTRUCTIONS

### Eclipse IDE
Method 1: Import the Eclipse project template

1. Create a folder and bring up Eclipse into that folder.
2. Import the project `EclipseGameTemplate7` into the folder.
   - Click File - Import – General - Existing Projects into Workspace – Next
   - Browse to the DVD folder:
     `Game Environment\IDE Specific Tools\Eclipse\Workspace`
     and click the `EclipseGameTemplate7` template folder, then click OK
   - Check the box next to *Copy Projects Into Workspace*, then click Finish
3. Open the project `EclipseGameTemplate7` and add the program-specific code to it.

Method 2: Add the game environment JAR file or its classes to a new Eclipse project

Either the JAR file `gameEnvironment.jar` contained in the folder `GameJAR` or the classes contained in the `GameClasses` folder can be added to any existing Eclipse project and its build path. Both of these folders are in the `Game Environment\IDE Specific Tools\Eclipse` subfolder on the DVD that accompanies this textbook. To add them to an existing Eclipse project's build path:

1. Launch Eclipse in the existing project's workspace
2. Locate and copy the folder `GameJAR` or `GameClasses`
3. Right click the project node in Eclipse's Package Explorer view pane, then click Paste
4. Right click the project node in the Package Explorer view pane, then click Properties - Java Build Path - Libraries
   (a) To add the `gameEnvironment.jar` file, click "Add JAR's…" and locate and check the `gameEnvironment.jar` JAR file, click OK, click OK

(b) To add the `GameClasses` folder, click "Add Class Folder" and locate and check the `GameClasses` folder, click OK, click OK

**NetBeans IDE**

1. Create a folder with a name relevant to the program being developed
2. Copy the NetBeans project `NBGameTemplate7` located in the `Game Environment\IDE Specific Tools\NetBeans` subfolder on the DVD that accompanies this textbook and paste it into the folder created in Step 1
3. Open the project `NBGameTemplate7` and add the program-specific code to it

**JCreator IDE**

Method 1

1. Create a folder with a name relevant to the program being developed
2. Copy the JCreator project `JCGameTemplate7` located in the `Game Environment\IDE Tools\JCreator` subfolder on the DVD that accompanies this textbook and paste it into the folder created in Step 1
3. Open the project `JCGameTemplate7` and add the program-specific code to it

Method 2

1. Create a JCreator project
2. Copy and paste the folder `edu` (i.e., the package `edu.sjcny.gpv1`, contained in the `Game Environment\IDE Tools\JCreator` subfolder on the DVD that accompanies this book, into the project's class folder
3. Include the following import statement in the application:

```
import edu.sjcny.gpv1.*;
```

# ASCII TABLE

| Decimal | Octal | Hex | Binary | Char | Description |
|---------|-------|-----|--------|------|-------------|
| 000 | 000 | 000 | 00000000 | NUL | (null) |
| 001 | 001 | 001s | 00000001 | SOH | (start of Heading) |
| 002 | 002 | 002 | 00000010 | STX | (start of text) |
| 003 | 003 | 003 | 00000011 | ETX | (end of text) |
| 004 | 004 | 004 | 00000100 | EOT | (end of transmission) |
| 005 | 005 | 005 | 00000101 | ENQ | (enquiry) |
| 006 | 006 | 006 | 00000110 | ACK | (acknowledge) |
| 007 | 007 | 007 | 00000111 | BEL | (audible bell) |
| 008 | 010 | 008 | 00001000 | BS | (backspace) |
| 009 | 011 | 009 | 00001001 | HT | (horizontal tab) |
| 010 | 012 | 00A | 00001010 | LF | (line feed, new line) |
| 011 | 013 | 00B | 00001011 | VT | (vertical tab) |
| 012 | 014 | 00C | 00001100 | FF | (form feed) |
| 013 | 015 | 00D | 00001101 | CR | (carriage return) |
| 014 | 016 | 00E | 00001110 | SO | (shift out) |
| 015 | 017 | 00F | 00001111 | SI | (shift in) |
| 016 | 020 | 010 | 00010000 | DLE | (data link escape) |
| 017 | 021 | 011 | 00010001 | DC1 | (device control 1) |
| 018 | 022 | 012 | 00010010 | DC2 | (device control 2) |
| 019 | 023 | 013 | 00010011 | DC3 | (device control 3) |
| 020 | 024 | 014 | 00010100 | DC4 | (device control 4) |
| 021 | 025 | 015 | 00010101 | NAK | (negative acknowledge) |
| 022 | 026 | 016 | 00010110 | SYN | (synchronous idle) |
| 023 | 027 | 017 | 00010111 | ETB | (end of trans. block) |
| 024 | 030 | 018 | 00011000 | CAN | (cancel) |
| 025 | 031 | 019 | 00011001 | EM | (end of medium) |
| 026 | 032 | 01A | 00011010 | SUB | (substitute) |
| 027 | 033 | 01B | 00011011 | ESC | (escape) |
| 028 | 034 | 01C | 00011100 | FS | (file separator) |
| 029 | 035 | 01D | 00011101 | GS | (group separator) |
| 030 | 036 | 01E | 00011110 | RS | (record separator) |
| 031 | 037 | 01F | 00011111 | US | (unit separator) |
| 032 | 040 | 020 | 00100000 | SP | (space) |
| 033 | 041 | 021 | 00100001 | ! | |

*(Contd.)*

| Decimal | Octal | Hex | Binary | Char | Description |
|---------|-------|-----|--------|------|-------------|
| 034 | 042 | 022 | 00100010 | " | |
| 035 | 043 | 023 | 00100011 | # | |
| 036 | 044 | 024 | 00100100 | $ | |
| 037 | 045 | 025 | 00100101 | % | |
| 038 | 046 | 026 | 00100110 | & | |
| 039 | 047 | 027 | 00100111 | ` | |
| 040 | 050 | 028 | 00101000 | ( | |
| 041 | 051 | 029 | 00101001 | ) | |
| 042 | 052 | 02A | 00101010 | * | |
| 043 | 053 | 02B | 00101011 | + | |
| 044 | 054 | 02C | 00101100 | , | |
| 045 | 055 | 02D | 00101101 | – | |
| 046 | 056 | 02E | 00101110 | . | |
| 047 | 057 | 02F | 00101111 | / | |
| 048 | 060 | 030 | 00110000 | 0 | |
| 049 | 061 | 031 | 00110001 | 1 | |
| 050 | 062 | 032 | 00110010 | 2 | |
| 051 | 063 | 033 | 00110011 | 3 | |
| 052 | 064 | 034 | 00110100 | 4 | |
| 053 | 065 | 035 | 00110101 | 5 | |
| 054 | 066 | 036 | 00110110 | 6 | |
| 055 | 067 | 037 | 00110111 | 7 | |
| 056 | 070 | 038 | 00111000 | 8 | |
| 057 | 071 | 039 | 00111001 | 9 | |
| 058 | 072 | 03A | 00111010 | : | |
| 059 | 073 | 03B | 00111011 | ; | |
| 060 | 074 | 03C | 00111100 | < | |
| 061 | 075 | 03D | 00111101 | = | |
| 062 | 076 | 03E | 00111110 | > | |
| 063 | 077 | 03F | 00111111 | ? | |
| 064 | 100 | 040 | 01000000 | @ | |
| 065 | 101 | 041 | 01000001 | A | |
| 066 | 102 | 042 | 01000010 | B | |
| 067 | 103 | 043 | 01000011 | C | |
| 068 | 104 | 044 | 01000100 | D | |
| 069 | 105 | 045 | 01000101 | E | |
| 070 | 106 | 046 | 01000110 | F | |
| 071 | 107 | 047 | 01000111 | G | |
| 072 | 110 | 048 | 01001000 | H | |
| 073 | 111 | 049 | 01001001 | I | |
| 074 | 112 | 04A | 01001010 | J | |

| Decimal | Octal | Hex | Binary | Char | Description |
|---------|-------|-----|--------|------|-------------|
| 075 | 113 | 04B | 01001011 | K | |
| 076 | 114 | 04C | 01001100 | L | |
| 077 | 115 | 04D | 01001101 | M | |
| 078 | 116 | 04E | 01001110 | N | |
| 079 | 117 | 04F | 01001111 | O | |
| 080 | 120 | 050 | 01010000 | P | |
| 081 | 121 | 051 | 01010001 | Q | |
| 082 | 122 | 052 | 01010010 | R | |
| 083 | 123 | 053 | 01010011 | S | |
| 084 | 124 | 054 | 01010100 | T | |
| 085 | 125 | 055 | 01010101 | U | |
| 086 | 126 | 056 | 01010110 | V | |
| 087 | 127 | 057 | 01010111 | W | |
| 088 | 130 | 058 | 01011000 | X | |
| 089 | 131 | 059 | 01011001 | Y | |
| 090 | 132 | 05A | 01011010 | Z | |
| 091 | 133 | 05B | 01011011 | [ | |
| 092 | 134 | 05C | 01011100 | \ | |
| 093 | 135 | 05D | 01011101 | ] | |
| 094 | 136 | 05E | 01011110 | ^ | (caret) |
| 095 | 137 | 05F | 01011111 | _ | (underscore) |
| 096 | 140 | 060 | 01100000 | ` | |
| 097 | 141 | 061 | 01100001 | a | |
| 098 | 142 | 062 | 01100010 | b | |
| 099 | 143 | 063 | 01100011 | c | |
| 100 | 144 | 064 | 01100100 | d | |
| 101 | 145 | 065 | 01100101 | e | |
| 102 | 146 | 066 | 01100110 | f | |
| 103 | 147 | 067 | 01100111 | g | |
| 104 | 150 | 068 | 01101000 | h | |
| 105 | 151 | 069 | 01101001 | i | |
| 106 | 152 | 06A | 01101010 | j | |
| 107 | 153 | 06B | 01101011 | k | |
| 108 | 154 | 06C | 01101100 | l | |
| 109 | 155 | 06D | 01101101 | m | |
| 110 | 156 | 06E | 01101110 | n | |
| 111 | 157 | 06F | 01101111 | o | |
| 112 | 160 | 070 | 01110000 | p | |
| 113 | 161 | 071 | 01110001 | q | |
| 114 | 162 | 072 | 01110010 | r | |
| 115 | 163 | 073 | 01110011 | s | |

*(Contd.)*

| Decimal | Octal | Hex | Binary | Char | Description |
|---------|-------|-----|--------|------|-------------|
| 116 | 164 | 074 | 01110100 | t | |
| 117 | 165 | 075 | 01110101 | u | |
| 118 | 166 | 076 | 01110110 | v | |
| 119 | 167 | 077 | 01110111 | w | |
| 120 | 170 | 078 | 01111000 | x | |
| 121 | 171 | 079 | 01111001 | y | |
| 122 | 172 | 07A | 01111010 | z | |
| 123 | 173 | 07B | 01111011 | { | |
| 124 | 174 | 07C | 01111100 | \| | (vertical bar) |
| 125 | 175 | 07D | 01111101 | } | |
| 126 | 176 | 07E | 01111110 | ~ | (tilde) |
| 127 | 177 | 07F | 01111111 | DEL | (delete) |

# JAVA KEYWORDS

## Java Keywords

| | | | | |
|---|---|---|---|---|
| abstract | default | if | private | this |
| assert[2] | do | implements | protected | throw |
| boolean | double | import | public | throws |
| break | else | instanceof | return | transient |
| byte | enum[3] | int | short | try |
| case | extends | interface | static | void |
| catch | final | long | strictfp[1] | volatile |
| char | finally | native | super | while |
| class | float | new | switch | |
| continue | for | package | synchronized | |

1: added in version 1.2
2: added in version 1.4
3: added in version 5.0

# JAVA OPERATORS AND THEIR RELATIVE PRECEDENCE

1 is highest precedence

| Operator | Description | Precedence | Operator | Description | Precedence |
|---|---|---|---|---|---|
| *postfix operators* | | 1 | *equality operators* | | 7 |
| ++ | postfix increment | | == | is equal to | |
| -- | postfix decrement | | != | is not equal to | |
| *unary operators* | | 2 | *bitwise* AND | | 8 |
| ++ | prefix increment | | & | bitwise AND | |
| -- | prefix decrement | | *bitwise exclusive* OR | | 9 |
| + | leading plus | | ^ | exclusive OR | |
| - | leading minus | | *bitwise inclusive* OR | | 10 |
| ! | logical not | | | | inclusive OR | |
| ~ | Bitwise complement | | *logical* AND | | 11 |
| *multiplicative operators* | | 3 | && | conditional AND | |
| * | multiplication | | *logical* OR | | 12 |
| / | division | | || | conditional OR | |
| % | remainder | | *ternary* | | 13 |
| *additive operators* | | 4 | ?: | conditional | |
| + | addition | | *assignment* | | 14 |
| - | subtraction | | = | assignment | |
| *shift operators* | | 5 | += | addition assignment | |
| << | shift left | | -= | subtraction assignment | |
| >> | shift right | | *= | multiplication assignment | |
| >>> | unsigned shift right | | /= | division assignment | |
| *relational operators* | | 6 | %= | remainder assignment | |
| < | less than | | &= | bitwise AND assignment | |
| <= | less than or equal to | | ^= | bitwise exclusive OR assignment | |
| > | greater than | | |= | bitwise inclusive OR assignment | |
| >= | greater than or equal to | | <<= | bitwise left shift assignment | |
| instanceof | class comparator | | >>= | bitwise right shift assignment | |
| | | | >>>= | bitwise unsigned right shift assign | |

# GLOSSARY OF PROGRAMMING TERMS

**Abstract class**  A class that includes the keyword abstract in its signature and cannot be instantiated; it is used during the design process to collect data members and methods common to several classes

**Aggregated class**  A class that contains at least one data member that references an object

**Aggregation**  The concept of referencing objects from a class's data members

**Algorithm**  A step-by-step solution to solving a problem or task that a computer system can execute

**Applet**  A Java program that runs from within another program, which is typically a Web browser; it has restrictions placed on its instruction set consistent with this execution mode's need for enforced security

**Applet container program**  The program, typically a Web browser, within which an applet runs; the container invokes the methods that are part of the applet's lifecycle

**Applet lifecycle**  The period of time that begins when an applet's execution is initiated and ends when it is terminated; during this time period, the applet's container program invokes the applet methods `init`, `start`, `paint`, `stop`, and `destroy` to manage its execution

**Application Programming Interface (API)**  A collection of packages containing interfaces and implementations of classes and data structures that can easily be incorporated into a Java program

**Application software**  All non-operating system software, typically for use by human users

**Argument**  A value passed to a method when it is invoked

**Argument list**  A sequence of argument names separated by commas enclosed in a set of parentheses

**Array**  An ordered collection of primitive or reference variables stored inside an object, which are sequentially associated with an integer beginning with zero; arrays are an implementation of the mathematical concept of subscripted variables

**Array of objects**  An array of reference variables that contains the addresses of a set of instances of the same class

**ASCII Table**  A specific tabulation of characters and control characters and the bit patterns used to represent them

**Assignment**  The act of changing the contents of a variable

**Atomic components**  Graphical user interface (GUI) components that cannot contain other components, such as text fields and buttons; most of the program user's interactions are with these components

**Autoboxing**  A context-sensitive feature of Java in which primitive literals or variables are replaced with instances of wrapper classes that contain their values

**Base case**  Part of the methodology of formulating recursive algorithms, which is a known or trivial solution to the problem

**Base class**  A class that is inherited from, also known as a parent or super class

**Binary numbers**  A number system based on two, as opposed to the decimal system, which is based on ten

**Bit**  A single unit of storage that can assume two states, which are referred to as off and on, or zero and one or false and true

**Boolean expression**  An expression involving relational and logic operators that evaluates to true or false

**Buffer**  Memory used to temporarily store data during program execution

**Byte**  A set of eight contiguous (adjacent) bits, often used to represent a single character in the Modern Latin (English) alphabet

**Byte codes**  The translation of a program produced by the Java language translator into intermediate code

**Central processing unit (CPU)**  Electronic circuitry that interprets and executes instructions; the CPU can perform arithmetic and logic operations, has the ability to skip or re-execute instructions based on the truth value of a logic operation, and contains a limited amount of storage called registers

**Chain inheritance**  When the parent class of a class extends another class

**Child class**  A class that inherits from (extends) another class; also known as a sub or derived class

**Class**  A collection of variables and methods; a blueprint for an object

**Class-level variable**  A variable defined within a class but outside of a method's code block

**Cloning an object**  Creating a new instance of a class and (deep) copying the values of all of the data members of an existing instance of the class into the new instance

**Code block**  A set of instructions enclosed with a set of open and close braces, { }

**Collection**  A data structure that is accessed without specifying a key

**Collections Framework of the API**  Part of the API that contains generically implemented data structures, methods that perform common operations on data elements, and a set of associated interfaces

**Computer system**  A set of electronic circuits, mechanical devices and enclosures, and instructions that these devices execute to perform a task

**Concatenation**  The act of appending one string to another

**Concurrency**  Executing several programs, or several parts of a program, at the same time

**Constructor**  A method in a class that is used to create an instance of a class and return its address; its name is the same as the class's name

**Consumer**  A process that expends data

**Content pane**  The portion of a widow or other top-level container that holds the visible components added to the container

**Control of flow statement**  A statement that overrides the default sequential execution path of a program, such as a decision statement, a repetition (loop) statement, or a subprogram invocation

**Counting algorithm**  An algorithm that counts by adding an increment to, or subtracting a counting increment from, the current value of a counter

**Data members**  The variables defined within a class, class level variables

**Data structure**  An organization of data within memory to facilitate its processing from a speed and memory requirements viewpoint

**Deep comparison of two objects**  Comparing the values of one or more of the data members of an object to the corresponding data members of another instance of the class

**Deep copy of an object** Copying the values of one or more of the data members of an instance of a class into the corresponding data members of another instance of the class

**Derived class** A class that inherits from (extends) another class; also known as a child or subclass.

**Deserializing objects** The act of reassembling objects after they are read from a disk file

**Dialog box** A predefined pop-up graphical interface used to pause a program's execution until the program user acknowledges a message or performs an input

**Divide and conquer** Expressing or defining a complicated entity as a set of less complicated entities; for example, expressing the solution to a complex problem as the solutions to a set of simpler problems, or defining the data members of a complex class to be instances of less complicated classes

**Dynamic binding** Delaying the process of locating an invoked method until runtime

**Dynamic programming** A programming technique aimed at reducing execution time, which avoids repetitive processing by saving and then reusing prior processing results

**Element** One of the variables contained in an array or one object contained in a data structure

**Enumerated type** A user defined type created within a Java program by specifying its type name and allowable values within an `enum` statement

**Event** An asynchronous occurrence during a program's execution that can be used to redirect the execution path of a program

**Event handler** A method that is executed when an event occurs

**Exception class** The API class `Throwable` or a descendent of that class

**Exception error message** A string contained within an exception object that normally contains descriptive error information

**Exception object** An instance of the API class `Throwable`, or one of its decedents, which can be passed to a `catch` clause when an error is detected during the execution of a method

**Exceptions** A programming construct that promotes the reusability of methods by deferring the decision as to what action to take when an error condition is detected to the invoker of the method

**Final class** A class that cannot be a parent class; it cannot be extended

**Flow chart** A graphical representation of an algorithm

**Fractal** A mathematical or geometric object that has the property of self-similarity; that is, each part of the object is a smaller or reduced copy of itself

**General solution** Part of the methodology of formulating recursive algorithms; it is a solution to the original problem that uses the portion of the methodology known as the reduced problem

**Generic class** A class that contains generic methods and is coded in a way as to permit the type of its data members to be specified when an instance of the class is created

**Generic method** A method that can perform its algorithm on any type of objects passed to it

**Generic parameter** A parameter that can be passed an object of any type and whose type is specified using a type placeholder

**Generic parameter list** A list of the type placeholders, coded within a method's signature, that are used in the method's parameter list

**Generics** A programming concept that promotes reusability by permitting the type of a method's parameters and returned value to be specified by the method's invoker and permitting the type of a class's data members to be specified when an instance of the class is created

**Get method** A method used to fetch the values of a class's private data members

**Graphical User Interface (GUI)** A means of interacting with the program user via a point-and-click mode, as opposed to a text-based mode, aimed at facilitating the I/O process

**Hypertext Markup Language (HTML)** A scripting language for writing instructions to be downloaded and executed by a Web browser to build and display a Web page; the script can contain instructions to download and execute a Java applet

**Index** The integer associated with a variable in an array

**Inheritance** A programming concept in which a new class can contain all of the data members and methods of an existing class by simply including an `extends` clause in its heading

**Inner class** A class that is defined within another class

**Input method** A method normally named `input` that ordinarily permits the program user to input the values of all of an object's data members

**Instance of a class** A specific object in the class

**Integrated Development Environment (IDE)** A program used by a programmer to develop a software product; it contains a collection of tools (e.g., a syntax checker, translator, editor, file-management system) that facilitate the development process

**Interface** A Java construct used to specify the signatures of related methods that are implicitly abstract and/or a declaration of public constants that are implicitly static and final

**Iterator** An object that can be used to perform time-efficient processing on all of the data elements contained in any data structure that imposes an ordering on its data elements

**Java Development Kit (JDK)** A set of tools used to develop Java programs; these tools include the API classes, a debugger, a compiler, an interpreter, an applet viewer, a documentation generator, a disassembler, various linking, loading, and binding tools, and a runtime environment

**Java Virtual Machine** A virtual computer system whose programming language is Java byte codes

**Key** A value associated with a data element that can be used to refer to the element

**Layout manager** A predefined protocol for the sizing and positioning of components added to a GUI container

**Listener list** An association of events and their event-handler methods that is part of a GUI component object

**Local variable** A variable defined within a code block whose scope is limited to the instructions within the code block

**Loop** A sequence of instruction that is repeated a specified number of times or until a Boolean value becomes true or false

**Map** A set of data structures that associate a key with each data element stored in the structure; the key can be used to specify the data element on which to operate

**Menu mnemonic** A menu shortcut key (hot key) associated with a terminal menu item

**Methods** The subprograms defined within a class, a sequence of instructions that perform a particular task

**Multidimensional array** An array in which each variable of the array is associated with 2, 3, … indices, for example an array of rows and columns

**Multiple inheritance** When a class inherits from more than one class; this is not supported in Java

**Multitasking** Executing several threads of an application at the same time or giving the impression that they are executing at the same time

**Nested loops** Coding loops inside of loops

**Nested statements** Statements that are contained within another statement or another statement's statement block

**Non-void method** A method that returns a value, whose type is specified in the method's signature

**Object** A particular occurrence of a class that contains all of the class's non-static data members

**Object oriented programming (OOP)** An approach to programming (a programming paradigm) aimed at facilitating the development of programs that deal with objects, such as starships, people, or Web pages

**One-dimensional array** An array in which each variable of the array is associated with one index

**Operating system software** A program to manage the resources of a computer system and to permit a user of the system to interact with it, usually via a point-and-click interface

**Overloading methods** The act of writing two or more methods in the same class that have the same name but different parameter lists

**Overriding a method** Rewriting an inherited method using the exact same signature of the inherited method

**Parallel arrays** A use of multiple one-dimensional arrays in which the ith element of each array is associated with the same entity; for example, if Mary's age was stored in the second element of one array, then the rest of Mary's information would be stored in the second element of the other arrays

**Parameter** A variable that can receive a value (an argument) passed to a method when it is invoked

**Parameter list** A sequence of parameter names, each proceeded by its type, separated by commas, and enclosed in a set of parentheses

**Parent class** A class that is inherited from, also known as a super or base class

**Parsing** The act of changing a string into a numeric; also the act of separating a string into its component parts that are separated by a specified delimiter

**Platform** A particular CPU model and operating system

**Platform independence** The concept that the programmer's translation of a program can be transmitted to, and then run on, any computer system

**Polymorphism** The ability of one invocation to morph itself into an invocation of a parent's version of a method or any of its children's versions of the method; rooted in the fact that a parent reference variable can refer to an instance of a child class

**Pop-up menu** A space-saving alternative to a menu-bar-based drop-down menu that remains invisible until the user performs a platform-dependent mouse or keyboard action on a GUI component

**Precedence rules** A specification of the order in which to perform a set of operations

**Primitive variable** A variable that can store a numeric value, a Boolean value, or one character; the type used in its declaration is one of the primitive types

**Primitive type** The Java types `byte`, `short int`, `long`, `float`, `double`, `char`, and `boolean`

**Priority queue** A queue that associates a priority with each of its data elements; the elements assigned the highest priority are fetched and deleted (on a first-in-first-out basis) before those of lower priority

**Private data member** A data member of a class that cannot be directly accessed by methods that are not part of the class; `get` and `set` methods are used to fetch and change their values

**Producer** A process that generates data

**Pseudorandom numbers** Apparent, but not truly, random numbers

**Public data members** Data members of a class that can be directly accessed by methods that are not part of the class; they are accessed by coding their name preceded by either the name of an instance of the class or the class name, followed by a dot

**Queue** A data structure in which the data elements are fetched and deleted on a first-in-first-out basis

**Random access memory (RAM)** High-speed, high-cost storage physically located in close proximity to the central processing unit

**Recursion** The act of defining something in terms of itself

**Recursive method** A method that invokes itself or initiates a sequence of method invocations that eventually leads to an invocation of itself

**Reduced problem** Part of the methodology of formulating recursive algorithms, it is a problem similar to the original problem, usually between the original problem and the base case, usually closer to the original problem, and (when progressively reduced) becomes the base case for all versions of the original problem

**Reference variable** A variable that can store a memory address; the type used in its declaration is the name of a class

**Registering an event handler** The act of associating an event-handler method with a particular event that could be performed on a GUI component

**Runtime** the time during which the program is in execution

**Scope of a variable or a method** The range of a program's instructions within which a variable can be used or a method can be invoked

**Sentinel loop** A loop that ends on a particular value of the data it is processing or on a particular user input; for example, a negative deposit

**Serializing objects** The act of disassembling objects before writing them to a disk file so they can be recreated when they are read from the disk

**Set methods** Methods used to change the values of a class's private data members

**Shallow comparison** Comparing the contents of one variable to the contents of another variable using the equality (==) operator

**Shallow copy** Copying the contents of one variable into another using the assignment (=) operator

**Shared buffer** Memory used to temporarily share a data item among one or more threads

**Show method** A method named `show` that ordinarily outputs all of the data members of an object or draws the object

**Signature of a method** The first line of a method's code

**Software engineer** A computer professional that produces programs that are error free, within budget, on schedule, and satisfy the customers' current and future needs

**States of a thread** The six statuses a thread can assume from the time it is created to the time it is terminated

**Static data member** A class's data member that is designated to be shared by all instances of the class by including the keyword `static` in its declaration

**Static method**  A method that is designated to be invoked by preceding the method name by the method's class name followed by a dot; they are intended to be methods that do not operate on instances of the class

**String**  A finite sequence of characters

**Subclass**  A class that inherits from (extends) another class, also known as a derived or child class

**Super class**  A class that is inherited from, also known as a base and parent class

**Swapping algorithm**  An algorithm that swaps the values contained in two variables

**Synchronized buffer**  A buffer whose access is managed in a way that imposes protocols of proper access to the data on the threads that share the buffer

**Syntax**  The rules for forming properly constructed program instructions; the grammar of a programming language

**Text file**  A file whose information is intended to be characters and is therefore interpreted using the ASCII or Unicode tables; ordinarily the file extension .txt is appended to the file's name

**Thread**  An independent execution path through a program

**Token**  A component part of a string that is terminated by a specified delimiter, for example, a space

**Tokenizing a string**  Extracting all of the tokens from a string

**Top-level container**  The basic building block component of a graphical interface, which contains the other GUI components that make up the interface

**toString method**  A method named toString whose task is to return the string representation of an object; ordinarily, the string contains the annotated values of all of an object's data members

**Totaling or summation algorithm**  An algorithm that computes the sum of a set of numeric values by repeatedly adding each value to the subtotal of the values in the set that preceded it

**Type placeholder**  Any valid identifier that is not the name of a class used within the application of which it is a part; a placeholder is used as a type of a generic parameter and can be used as a returned type

**Unboxing**  A context-sensitive feature of Java in which an instance of a wrapper class object is replaced with the primitive value it contains

**Unicode**  An expanded tabulation of characters and control characters and the bit patterns used to represent them

**Universal modeling language (UML) diagram**  A graphical representation of a class that specifies the class's name, data members, and the signatures of its methods; it is used to design a class

**Variable**  A named memory cell that can store a specific type of data item

**Void method**  A method that does not return a value

**Worker method**  A method that is invoked by another method to perform a specific task (work) for it; for example, fetching the value of one of an object's data members or drawing the object

**Wrapper class**  An API class that contains non-static primitive data members of a particular type

# USING THE ONLINE API DOCUMENTATION

The documentation of the Application Programing Interface (API) is available online. To access it, you can Google: *Java API documentation* and click the link that begins with `docs.oracle.com/javase`, such as the one shown below:

http://docs.oracle.com/javase/7/docs/api/

To quickly locate the documentation on a particular class, you can Google the class's name and then click the link to the class's documentation. The following link was displayed after Googling *Java Math class*:

http://docs.oracle.com/javase/7/docs/api/java/lang/Math.html

Clicking this link displays the information shown in Figure G.1, which is typical of the format of the documentation for any class. As shown in the figure, the class name is at the top of the documentation. Below it is the package that is imported into a class to gain access to the API class and its methods. This package name can be copied from the documentation and pasted into the class's file just before its class heading. It is preceded by the keyword **import** and followed by a semicolon.

Below the package name is the specification of the class's access and inheritance details. In the case of the `Math` class, this information indicates that the class's access is public, the class is final (which means it cannot be extended as a parent class), and its parent class is the class `Object`. Below that is a general description of the class.

Below the general descriptive information is a *Field Summary* (Figure G.2), which is a tabulation of the name and description of all of the data members contained in the class. This is followed by a *Method Summary*, which is a tabulation of the names of each method in the class and their parameter list followed a brief description of the method's functionality.

To the left of each data member's name in the Field Summary is its type, which may be preceded by the keyword **static**. Static data members are accessed by preceding their name with the name of the class followed by a dot. To the left of each method's name in the Method Summary is the method's returned type, which may be preceded by the keyword **static**. Static methods are invoked by preceding their name with the name of the class followed by a dot. Non-static methods are invoked by preceding their name with the name of an instance of the class followed by a dot.

More detained documentation on a data member or a method can be displayed by clicking the name of the data member in the Field Summary or the name of the method in the Method Summary. Figure G.3 was displayed when the method name `acos`, shown at the bottom of Figure G.2, was clicked.

**Figure G.1**
The top portion of the online documentation of the **Math** class.

**Figure G.2**
The partial Field Summary and Method Summary of the API Math class.

---

### acos

```
public static double acos(double a)
```

Returns the arc cosine of a value; the returned angle is in the range 0.0 through *pi*. Special case:
  • If the argument is NaN or its absolute value is greater than 1, then the result is NaN.

The computed result must be within 1 ulp of the exact result. Results must be semi-monotonic.

**Parameters:**

  a - the value whose arc cosine is to be returned.

**Returns:**

  the arc cosine of the argument.

---

**Figure G.3**
Detailed documentation of the Math class's **acos** method.

# COLLEGE BOARD AP COMPUTER SCIENCE TOPIC CORRELATION

| Topics Tested in the AP CS A Exam[1] | Sections | Topics Not Tested in the AP CS A Exam, But Potentially Relevant/ Useful | Sections |
|---|---|---|---|
| **Comments** | | | |
| Java code: /* */, | 3.2.5 | | |
| // | 2.4.3 | | |
| Javadoc: @parm and @return | 3.2.5 | Javadoc tool | 3.2.5 |
| /** */ | 3.2.5 | | |
| **Primitive Types** | | | |
| int, double, boolean | 2.3 | char, byte, short, long, float | 2.3 |
| **Operators** | | | |
| Arithmetic: +, -, /, *, % | 2.6.1 | | |
| Increment & Decrement ++, -- | 5.2.1 | | |
| Assignment: =, +=, -=, *=, | 2.6.2 | | |
| /=, %= | 2.6.2 | | |
| Relational: ==, !=, <, <=, >, >= | 4.2.1 | | |
| Logical: !, &&, ‖ | 4.2.2 | | |
| Numeric casts: (int), (double) | 2.6.3 | | |
| String Concatenation + | 2.4.2 | | |
| **Object Comparison** | | | |
| Object identity: (==, !=) vs. | 7.3.1 | implementation of equals | 7.3.2 |
| object equality: (equals), | 7.3.1, 7.3.2 | Comparable | 7.10, 8.6, |
| String compareTo | 4.2.3 | | 10.4 |
| **Escape Sequences:** | | | |
| \", \\, \n, inside strings | 2.4.3 | \', \t, | 2.4.3 |
| **Input/Output** | | | |
| System.out.println | 2.4 | Scanner, System.in, | 4.7, 4.7 |
| System.out.print | 2.4 | Stream input/output | 4.8.1, 8.7 |
| | | GUI input/output | 2.7 |
| | | Parsing input: Integer.parseInt, | 2.7.3 |
| | | Double.parseDouble | 2.7.3 |

*(Contd.)*

| Topics Tested in the AP CS A Exam[1] | Sections | Topics Not Tested in the AP CS A Exam, But Potentially Relevant/ Useful | Sections |
|---|---|---|---|
| **Exceptions** | | | |
| ArithmeticException | **2.6.1** | try/catch | **4.9** |
| NullPointerException | **8.7** | throws | **4.8.3, 4.9** |
| IndexOutOfBoundsException | **6.3, 6.9.1** | | |
| ArrayIndexOutOfBoundsException | | | |
| IllegalArgumentException | **3.2.1** | | |
| **Arrays** | | | |
| 1-dimensional arrays | **6.1-6.3** | | |
| 2-dimensional rectangular arrays, | **6.10.1** | ragged arrays (non-rectangular) | **6.10.1** |
| intializer list: { ... } | **6.7** | arrays with 3 or more dimensions | **6.10.2** |
| row major order of 2-dimensional array elements | **6.10.2** | | |
| **Control Statements** | | | |
| if, if-else | **4.3, 4.4** | switch | **4.6** |
| while, for | **5.5, 5.2** | break, continue | **5.7, 4.6** |
| enhanced for, (for-each) | **6.4.1** | do-while | **5.6** |
| return | **3.2.3** | | |
| **Variables** | | | |
| parameter variables, | **3.2** | | |
| local variables | **3.2.4** | | |
| private instance variables: | **3.6.3** | final instance variables, | **6.3** |
| visibility (private) | **3.6.3, 8.4.5** | | |
| static (class) variables | **7.1** | | |
| visibility (public, private) | **7.1** | | |
| final | **6.3, 6.10.1** | | |
| **Methods** | | | |
| visibility (public, private), | **3.6.3, 7.2** | visibility (protected) | **8.3.1, 8.4.5** |
| static, non-static | **2.7.1, 2.8.1** | | |
| method signatures | **3.1** | public static void main(String[] args) | **2.1, 2.8.2** |
| overloading, overriding | **3.7, 8.3.2** | | |
| parameter passing | **3.2, 3.8** | | |
| Constructors | | | |
| super(), super(args) | **8.3.1** | default initialization of instance variables | **3.5.3** |

| Topics Tested in the AP CS A Exam[1] | Sections | Topics Not Tested in the AP CS A Exam, But Potentially Relevant/ Useful | Sections |
|---|---|---|---|
| **Classes** | | | |
| new, | 3.5.3 | | |
| visibility: public, private | 3.5.2, 7.8 | final, | 8.4.4 |
| accessor methods: get, show, | 3.6.3, 3.6.1 | visibility (private, protected) | 8.4.5 |
| toString | 3.6.4 | inner classes (nested classes) | 7.8 |
| modifier (mutator) methods: | 3.6.3, 3.6.4 | enumerations | 7.10 |
| set, input | | | |
| Design/create/modify a class. | 3.5, 8.4 | | |
| Create subclasses of a super | 8.1 - 8.3 | | |
| class: (abstract, non-abstract). | 8.4.1, 8.3 | | |
| Create class that implements an interface. | 8.6 | | |
| **Interfaces** | | | |
| Design/create/modify an interface. | 8.6 , 8.6.1 | | |
| **Inheritance** | | | |
| Understanding interface hierarchies. | 10.2 | | |
| Design/create/modify subclasses. | 8.4 | | |
| Design/create/modify classes that implement interfaces. | 8.6, 10.4 | | |
| **Packages** | | | |
| import *packageName.classname* | 2.7.3 | import *packageName..** | 1.8.4 |
| | | static import | 3.1.1 |
| **Miscellaneous OOP** | | | |
| "is-a" and "has-a" relationships | 8.2, 7.7 | instanceof, *(class)* cast | 8.5.5 |
| null, | 2.7.1, 2.7.2 | this.var | 3.6.2 |
| | 3.5.3, 4.2.1 | this.method(args) | 7.3.2, 7.4.2 |
| this, | 3.6.2 | | 8.3.1 |
| super.*method(args)* | 8.3.2 | | |
| **Standard Java Library** | | | |
| Object, | 7.3.1, 8.5.2 | clone | 7.4, 7.4.2 |
| | 8.5.4, 8.5.5 | autoboxing, auto-unboxing | 7.6.2 |
| Integer, Double | 2.7.3 | | |
| String, | 3.6.3, 4.2.3 | | |
| | 7.5 | | |
| Math, | 2.6.4 | Collection<E> | 10.2 |
| List<E>, | 10.2.1 | Arrays class | 6.9.2 |
| ArrayList<E> | 10.3.3 | Collections class | 10.4 |

# ACM/IEEE TOPICS AND MINIMAL INSTRUCTION TIME GUIDELINES

The ACM/IEEE Computer Science Curriculum 2013[2,3] presents guidelines which organize the typical computing Body of Knowledge into a set of Knowledge Areas (KA). Some of the Knowledge Areas presented in this book include, but are not limited to:

**AL - Algorithms and Complexity**

**PL -  Programming Languages**

**SDF- Software Development Fundamentals**

**SP - Social Issues and Professional Practice**

These topics are described in terms of "Lecture hours", representing the minimal time to present the material but it does not include time for self-study, assessment, lab activities, etc.

| KA | Knowledge Unit | Topics covered | Hours |
|----|----------------|----------------|-------|
| SP | History | History of computer hardware, software, Internet, WWW | 1 |
| PL | Language Translation | Interpretation, translation pipeline | 1 |
| PL | Basic Type Systems | Primitive types, type safety and errors | 1 |
| PL | OOP | Object oriented-design: classes and objects, methods, fields | 8 |
| SDF | Fundamental Programming Concepts | Syntax, semantics, variables, primitive data types, expressions and assignments, simple I/O, conditionals, iteration, recursion, functions, parameters | 8 |
| AL | Fundamental Data Structures and Algorithms | Simple numerical algorithms, sequential and binary search, insertion, selection and merge sort, simple string processing | 8 |
| SDF | Algorithms and Design | Concept and properties of algorithms, role of algorithms and problem solving, problem solving strategies (iteration, divide and conquer, backtracking), algorithm implementation, design concepts and principles (abstraction, decomposition) | 8 |
| SDF | Development Methods | Intro to program correctness (testing, pre/post conditions), debugging strategies, documentation and programming style | 4 |
| SDF | Fundamental Data Structures | Arrays, ArrayList Class, Strings | 6 |

## Endnotes

[1] *Computer Science A Course Description*, College Board AP, Fall 2014, https://secure-media.collegeboard.org/digitalServices/pdf/ap/ap-computer-science-a-course-description.pdf

[2] *Computer Science Curriculum 2013*, Curriculum Guidelines for Undergraduate Degree Programs in Computer Science, ACM/IEEE Joint Task Force Report, December 20, 2013.

[3] *http://cs2013.org*

# SOLUTIONS TO SELECTED ODD NUMBERED KNOWLEDGE EXERCISES

## CHAPTER 1

**1. b)** The number of computers grew from 200 to 800 – a factor of 4

**3.** Operating systems (such as: Windows. Linux or Apple OS X) are the instructions used by the computer system to schedule tasks, to allocate memory and other system resources, to detect errors and to perform other computer system functions. Application software is commonly used by the human user, while system software is used by the computer system. Examples of application software include word processors, spreadsheets, mail readers, Web browsers, and game programs.

**5.** Both a and c are characteristics of secondary storage which is nonvolatile, has a very large capacity and is slower and cheaper than RAM.

**7. a)** A device that is only used for output is a printer or a speaker.

**c)** Devices used for both input and output include touch screens, flash drives, floppy disks, and writable CDs, DVDs.

**9.** The computer as we know it today was the work of many people over hundreds of years, beginning with the development of early calculating machines: the abacus, the slide rule, Napier's bones and the Pascaline. The modern computer was based on the designs of Babbage, von Neumann, Mauchly, and Eckert. Lady Ada Lovelace and Grace Hopper were pioneers in the field of programming languages. Metcalfe and Boggs, Cerf and Kahn and Berners-Lee connected computers together into networks, the Internet and the World Wide Web, respectively.

**11. b)** loses its contents if power is interrupted.

**13. c)** chips, replacing the larger transistor circuits.

**15. a)** First programmer - Lady Ada Augusta Byron, the Countess of Lovelace
**b)** Inventor of the Java programming language – James Gosling

**17.** Platform independence is the ability of software to run on any computer system or platform. Every manufacturer's chipset has its own unique machine language and therefore usually requires its own translating program to translate from source code instructions to its machine language. Java achieves platform independence by compiling the source code instructions into byte code, which is later translated on the end user's computer into its own specific machine code.

**19.** A class is a group of related data members and member methods. It is the template used to create an object. An object is a particular instance of a class. From one class we can create an unlimited number of objects or instances of the class, just as with a blueprint we can create many houses, or with a cookie cutter, we can create many batches of cookies.

**21. a)** CPU – central processing unit    **c)** I/O – input/output

**e)** JVM – Java virtual machine    **g)** GUI- graphical user interface

**23. d)** (5, 30) since it is 5 pixels to the left of the left boundary and 30 pixels below the top.

**25. (1)** character data, **(2)** translated instructions, and **(3)** numeric data.

**27. a)** 01010011 = 83 in decimal    **b)** 00101111 = 47 in decimal

## CHAPTER 2

**1. a)** False, the contents of the variable may change but the data type does not
**c)** False    **e)** False

**3.** A variable is a named memory cell that stores one data item that can change during program execution. Primitive variables can store a single numeric data value, one character, or one Boolean truth value. Reference variables store (RAM) memory addresses.

**5. a)** `boolean false`                    **c)** `double` 0.0

**7.** Numeric literals, containing decimals such as 19.5, are assumed to be type double. If a numeric literal is to be assigned to a `float` variable, the letter `f` for float, must be appended to the literal to inform the translator that a loss of precision is acceptable, otherwise an error results. (This is a correct declaration `float` weight = 19.5f;)

**9. a)**
```
System.out.println("Sara Larson");
System.out.println("Smalltown, USA");
```

**b)**  `System.out.println("Sara Larson" + "\n"Smalltown, USA");`

**11.**

The `String` object at
memory address 1024
`int` distance = 675; `String` myName = "Jane";

**13. a)**    17 - 5 * 2 + 12 = 19                    **c)**    (48 + 12) / 12 + 18 * 2 = 41
**d)**    21 - 9 + 18 + 4 * 3.7 = 44.8

**15.** `double` average = `((double)`(55 + 57 + 60)) / 3;

**17. a)**    True                              **b)**    False, it is used for output
**c)**    True                              **d)**    False, it would return the empty string ("")
**e)**    True

**19.** sBalance = JOptionPane.showInputDialog("Type your current " + "checking account balance");

**21.** `double`  deposit;
deposit = Double.parseDouble(sDeposit);

**23.** `final int` NUMBER _ OF _ DAYS = 7;      or      `public static final int` NUMBER _ OF _ DAYS = 7;

# CHAPTER 3

**1. a)**    True                              **b)**    False, it is the method signature
**c)**    False                             **d)**    False, this method returns a value

**3. a)**    The signature of a method that does not operate on an object must contain the keyword `static`.
**c)**    When we invoke a static method, we begin the invocation statement with the name of the class followed by a dot.

**5. a)**    True
**c)**    False, the client method sends an argument into the worker method's parameter
**e)**    False, a method can only return a single value
**g)**    False
**h)**    False, value parameters

**7.** The statement following the statement that invoked the method executes next.

**9.** `static double` checkAmount;

**11. a)**    drawRect                         **c)** drawOval
**e)**    fillOval, using the same value for the height and width

**13. a)**    House is to object as blueprint is to class.
**c)**    The name of the graphic used to specify a class is a UML diagram.
**e)**    Member methods of a class are usually designated to have private access.

**15. a)** The address of the object `joe`

**(c)**

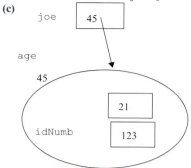

```
Person joe = new Person();
```

**17. a)**
```
public CoffeeCup(int size, double price)
{  this.size = size;
   this.price = price;
}
```

**b)** `CoffeeCup cup1 = new CoffeeCup(8, 3.85);`
**c)** `System.out.println(cup1);`
**d)** `System.out.println(cup1.tostring());`
**e)** CoffeeCup@456af2 (the address, 456af2, will probably be different)
**f)** `g.drawString(cup1.toString(), 200, 250);`

**19.**
```
public void show(Graphics g)
{
    g.drawString("size is: " + size, 250, 250);
    g.drawString("price is: " + price, 250, 280;
}
```

**20.**

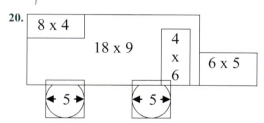

**21.** This might be a typical response based on the model given in Exercise 20

| Component | Shape | Shape's X or Line's $X_1$ coordinate | Shape's Y Line's $Y_1$ coordinate | Width Line's $X_2$ coordinate | Height Line's $Y_2$ coordinate |
|---|---|---|---|---|---|
| window | rectangle | x | y | 8 | 4 |
| body | rectangle | x | y | 18 | 9 |
| door | rectangle | x + 14 | y + 2 | 4 | 6 |
| cab | rectangle | x + 18 | y + 4 | 6 | 5 |
| rear tire | circle | x + 3 | y + 8 | 5 | 5 |
| front tire | circle | x + 11 | y + 8 | 5 | 5 |

**23. a)** `this.total = total * 2;`

**c)**
```
public void setTotal(int total)
{
   this.total = total;
}
```

**e)**  `int currentTotal = myAccount.getTotal();`
   `myAccount.setTotal(currentTotal * 2);`

**g)**  `public void toString()`
   `{`
      `System.out.println("The total is: " + total );`
   `}`

**i)**  `private`

**25. a)**  `static Starship largest(Starship ship1, Starship ship2);`

**b)**  `ship1 = largest(ship1, ship2);`

**c)**  The new color.

**d)**  `public boolean sameModel(Starship ship1, Starship ship2);`

**e)**  `isSame = sameModel(ship1, ship2);`

# CHAPTER 4

**1. a)**  True    **c)**  False    **e)**  True

**3.** Method invocations and control-of-flow (or control) statements, such as decision and loops, alter the execution path.

**5.** `if (myBalance ==10.0)`
   `{`
      `System.out.println(myBalance);`
   `}`
    `else`
   `{`
      `System.out.println("my balance is not 10.0");`
   `}`

**7. a)**  True

**c)**  True, although it can be empty

**e)**  True

**g)**  True

**9. a)**  False, but it is good programming style to include a default statement

**c)**  True

**e)**  True

**g)**  False, it can only be written as a switch statement if the selection statements are of the appropriate type

**11.** `if(item.equals("Hamburger"))`
   `{`
      `System.out.println("You ordered a Hamburger.");`
   `}`
   `else if(item.equals("Taco"))`
   `{`
      `System.out.println("You ordered a Taco.");`
   `}`
   `else if(item.equals("BLT"))`
   `{`
      `System.out.println("You ordered a BLT sandwich.");`
   `}`
   `else`
   `{`
      `System.out.println("You did not place a valid order.");`
   `}`

**13. a)**
```
Scanner consoleIn = new Scanner(System.in);
System.out.println("Type the year of your birth: ");
int birthYear;
birthYear = consoleIn.nextInt();
```
**b)**
```
Scanner consoleIn = new Scanner(System.in);
String name;
System.out.print("Enter your name: ");
name = consoleIn.nextLine();
```

**15. a)**  True    **b)**  False    **c)**  True

**17. a)**
```
File fileObject = new File("e:/Dates.txt");
Scanner fileIn = new Scanner(fileObject);
int year;
year = fileIn.nextInt();
```
**b)**
```
File fileObject = new File("e:/Names.txt");
Scanner fileIn = new Scanner(fileObject);
String name;
int age;
age = fileIn.nextInt();
fileIn.nextLine();  // to flush the buffer
name = fileIn.nextLine();
```

**19.**
```
import java.io.*;
public class DiskIO
{
    public static void main(String[] args) throws IOException
    {
        double myBalance =2567.00;
        double yourBalance = 3876.25;
        new // if file exists it will be deleted
        FileWriter fileWriterObject = new FileWriter("c:/Balances.txt");
        PrintWriter fileOut = new PrintWriter(fileWriterObject, false);

        fileOut.println(myBalance + " " + yourBalance);
        fileOut.close();
    }
}
```

**21.** `inputfile.close();`


# CHAPTER 5

**1. a)**  False, it is possible for a while loop body not to execute at all
  **c)**  True                        **e)**  False, it is a pretest loop
  **g)**  True                        **i)**  True
  **k)**  False, when the Boolean condition becomes false.
  **m)**  True, since the loop is never entered the loop control variable is not changed
  **o)**  True

**3.**
```
int n;
int count =1;
int sum =0;
String instring;
instring = JOptionPane.showInputDialog("Type a number: " );
```

```
    n = Integer.ParseInt(instr);
    while(count <= n)
    {
        if (count % 2 ==0)      //number is even
        {
            sum = sum + count;
        }
        count++;
    }   //end while
    JoptionPane.showMessageDialog(null, "The sum of even integers " +
                                  "from 1 to " + n + " is " + sum);
```

**5. a)** The value of i is never equal to 20, so the loop never terminates.

**b)** Because the loop does not terminate the output statement after the loop is never reached and is not executed.

**7. a)** Output: 8, 5, 2, -1

**b)**
```
    for (int x = 8; x >= -1; x = x - 3)
    {
        System.out.println(x);
    }
```

**9.**
```
int trys = 0;
int input;
String sInput;
do
{
    trys++;
    sInput = JOptionPane.showInputDialog("Enter a number from 0 to 5");
    input = Integer.parseInt(sInput);
    if(input >= 0 && input <= 5)
    {
        JOptionPane.showInputDialog("Thanks for the valid input");
        break;
    }
    else
    {
        JOptionPane.showInputDialog("invalid input");
    }
} while(trys < 3);
```

**11. a)**
```
    int randomNumber;
    Random randomObject = new Random(); // uses time of day
    for(int i=1; i<=20;, i++)
    {
        randomNumber = randomObject.nextInt(501));

        System.out.print(randomNumber);
    }
```

**c)**
```
    int randomNumber;
    int min =7;
    int max =500;
    Random randomObject = new Random(2468); // uses seed
    for(int i=1; i<=20;, i++)
```

```
    {
        randomNumber = min + randomObject.nextInt(500 - min + 1);
        System.out.print(randomNumber);
    }
```

# CHAPTER 6

1. a) True
   e) True
   i) True
   m) False

   c) True
   g) False, arrays can be multi-dimensional
   k) True

3. An array element is a reference variable, while a non-array element may be a primitive or a reference variable. An array variable is able to store many elements, while a primitive variable only stores one. An array variable uses square brackets ([ ]) and an index to indicate the position of an element in the array, while a non-array variable does not.

5. a) True
   e) False, 100

   c) False, `gameScores[99]`
   g) `System.out.println(gameScores[99]);`

   i)
   ```
   int total = 0;
   for(int i = 0; i <  gameScores.length; i++)
   {
       total = total + gameScores[i];
   }
   System.out.println(total / gameScores.length);
   ```

7. a) 45
   e) y[4] = y[4] + 20.5;

   c) 4
   f) z = y[0] + y[1] +y[2];

9. a)
   ```
   String[] names = new String[50];
   double[] weights = new double[50];
   double[] targetWeights = new double[50];
   ```

   c)
   ```
   for(int i = 0; i < names.length; i++)
   {
       if(names[i].equalsIgnoreCase("joe smith")
       {
           System.out.println(weight[i] + " " + targetWeight[i]);
       }
   }
   ```

11. The size arrays on the right side of Figure 6.35, stored at locations 400 through 900, would increase from 2 to 10 elements.

# CHAPTER 7

1. a) True
   e) False, a deep copy

   c) True
   g) True

3. A shallow comparison compares reference variables or the addresses of two objects to determine if they refer to the same object or two different objects. A deep comparison compares the contents of the data members of two objects to determine if they are the same.

5. Explain the difference between a deep copy and a clone. A deep copy copies the values of the data members of one object into the data members of another object, using the set method. When an object is cloned, a new instance of the object's class is created, and the values of all of an existing object's data members are copied into the corresponding data members of the new object. There are now two objects instead of one.

7. `if(s1 != s2)`

```
{
    System.out.println(" Two objects");
}
```

**9. a)** *6*　　　　　　　　　　　　　　　**c)** *Hello everyone*

**e)** *Hello*　　　　　　　　　　　　　　**g)** lo w

**11.** Aggregation is combining objects so that the instance of one class is a field in another class. It establishes a "has a" relationship.

**13.** Use the API BigInteger class to create a BigInteger object.
```
BigInteger num1 = new BigInteger ("123456789101112133456789");
```

**15.** Invoke the BigInteger multiply method on the BigInteger object. For example,
```
BigInteger num1 = new BigInteger ("123456789101112133456789");
BigInteger num2 = new BigInteger.valueOf(2);
BigInteger largenum = num1.multiply(num2);
```

**17. a)** 2

　　**b)** `CarColor favoriteColor = CarColor.BLUE;`

　　**c)** `System.out.println(CarColor.BLUE + " " + favoriteColor.ordinal());`

# CHAPTER 8

**1. a)** False　　　　　　　　　　　　　　　**c)** True
　　**e)** False, constructors are not inherited　**g)** True
　　**i)** False, they are overloaded　　　　　　**k)** True
　　**m)** False, all we need are the class's byte codes

**3.** Reduced coding time: a parent class can collect functionality and data members common to several classes into one class so they need only be coded once in the parent class.

Code reusability: A child can inherit all of the data members and methods of a previously developed class not coded as part of its program, and then add methods and data members or overwrite methods that are not suited for its applications.

**5.** Public: Child classes and client code have direct access. Protected: Child classes have direct access but not client code in a separate package. Private: Neither child classes nor client code have direct access.

**7.** `super.input();`

**9.** Declare the method to be final.

**11.** When you wanted to expand its parameter list.

**13.** An abstract class is used to collect all of the data members and methods that are common to two or more classes that will make up a program. The classes simply extend it, and then add the data members and methods specific to them to it.

**15.** `Transporter[] vehicles = new Transporter[200];`

**17.** An interface can contain the signatures of related methods that are implicitly abstract and/or declarations of public constants that are implicitly static and final. An advantage of an interface is that any class that implements the interface must implement all of the methods defined in the interface.

**19.** Include the `implements ManyMethods` clause in the adapter class's signature, and implement all 20 of the methods defined in the interface with empty code blocks.

# CHAPTER 9

**1. a)** True

　　**c)** False, usually the most difficult part is the discovery of the reduced problem

**e)**  True, if the base case is not realized

**g)**  False; typically they are slower than their loop base (iterative) counterparts because of the time required to transfer execution to the recursive invocations they make

3. The symbol with the number 5 to its left

5. Iterative: $f1 = 1$; $f2 = 1$; $f3 = 1 + 1 = 2$; $f4 = 1 + 2 = 3$; $f5 = 2 + 3 = 5$; $f6 = 3 + 5 = 8$;

       $f7 = 5 + 8 = 13$; $f8 = 8 + 13 = 21$;

   Non-iterative: $f8 = f7 + f6 = (f6 + f5) + (f5 + f4) =$

           $(f5 + f4) + (f4 + f3) + (f4 + f3) + (f3 + 1) =$

           $(f4 + f3) + (f3 + 1) + (f3 + 1) + (1 + 1) + (f3 + 1) + (1 + 1)(1 + 1) + 1 =$

           $(f3 + 1) + (1 + 1) + (1 + 1) + 1 + (1 + 1) + 1 + (1 + 1) + (1 + 1) + 1 +$

           $(1 + 1)(1 + 1) + 1 =$

           $(1 + 1) + 1 + (1 + 1) + (1 + 1) + 1 + (1 + 1) + 1 + (1 + 1) + (1 + 1) + 1 +$

           $(1 + 1)(1 + 1) + 1 =$

           21

7. Dynamic programming

9. Base case: `if`(m == n) `return` n;

   Reduced problem: sum of the even integers from m-2 to n

   General Solution: m + the reduced problem

11. Because that is the base case, which halts the recursive invocations.

13. Combine the base case, reduced problem and general solution into a recursive algorithm, using a flow chart similar to the one shown in Figure 9.6

15. To move six rings:  $2^6 - 1$   For ten rings: $2^{10} - 1$   For n rings: $2^n - 1$

# CHAPTER 10

1. Iterable, Collection, List

3. It expands to a larger capacity, and then the element is added to the `ArrayList` object.

5. Interface List <E>

   Type parameters:

   E – the type of the elements of this list

7. `ArrayList <String> s1;`

   `s1 = new ArrayList <String> (200);`   or   `s1 = new ArrayList < > (200);`

9. `List <String> employeeRecords;`

11. List is an interface, therefore it can't be instantiated (coded after the keyword **new**). Only class names can be coded there.

13. `public void aMethod(List <Book> theBooks)`

15. `String s = books.get(2).toString();`

17. The four methods in the `Collections` class are `binarySearch`, `sort`, `min`, and `max`. The name of the method that must be implemented is `compareTo`, which is defined in the interface `Comparable`.

# INDEX